F1412 LYN

Caudillos in Spanish America
1800–1850

CAUDILLOS IN SPANISH AMERICA 1800–1850

JOHN LYNCH

CLARENDON PRESS · OXFORD

This book has been printed digitally and produced in a standard specification in order to ensure its continuing availability

OXFORD
UNIVERSITY PRESS

Great Clarendon Street, Oxford OX2 6DP

Oxford University Press is a department of the University of Oxford.
It furthers the University's objective of excellence in research, scholarship,
and education by publishing worldwide in

Oxford New York

Auckland Bangkok Buenos Aires Cape Town Chennai
Dar es Salaam Delhi Hong Kong Istanbul Karachi Kolkata
Kuala Lumpur Madrid Melbourne Mexico City Mumbai Nairobi
São Paulo Shanghai Singapore Taipei Tokyo Toronto

with an associated company in Berlin

Oxford is a registered trade mark of Oxford University Press
in the UK and in certain other countries

Published in the United States
by Oxford University Press Inc., New York

ISBN 0-19-821135-X

PREFACE

Caudillos and dictators have tended to occupy centre stage of Spanish American history, frequent actors in government, recurring heroes of society. One of the most insistent questions put to the historian of Spanish America is, Why do constitutions fail? How can we explain the prevalence of caudillism? What were its origins, its nature, its meaning? Scholars have not evaded the subject. The caudillo, regional chieftain turned national ruler, is recognized in profile by historians and social scientists, though some of his features remain obscure, and existing interpretations tend to lack the realism of chronology and of case studies. The present enquiry is an attempt to supply these needs, and proceeds on the assumption that it was a combination of conditions and events that produced the caudillo, and that he is to be explained not in terms of cultural values or Hispanic tradition or national character but as part of a historical process in which personalist leaders accumulated functions and added to their power in response to specific interests and to some extent in successive stages.

The method of the book is first to seek origins, establish character, and define roles, moving in a chronological framework from early to mid-nineteenth century, then to show particular caudillos in action, testing the leadership of each by reference to that of the others. Selection has been dictated by practical as well as theoretical considerations, by an awareness of the historian's finite condition as well as a search for a comparative typology. Moreover, a sharp focus on a limited number of caudillos avoids the risk of losing sight of the theme and writing only a general history of Spanish America. Evidence for the structural aspects of the subject comes mainly from Argentina, Venezuela, and Mexico, though in studying some topics, such as bandits and guerrillas, I have found it useful to range beyond these countries. In the case studies I have added the career of Rafael Carrera of Guatemala to those of his contemporaries in Argentina, Venezuela, and Mexico, in order to provide contrast as well as comparison.

The idea of writing a comparative history of caudillism came to me in the wake of studying the Argentine dictator Juan Manuel de Rosas, and my principal case of comparison was Venezuela in the age of José Antonio Páez, with the addition perhaps of examples from Mexico and Central America. At that point I received, out of the blue, a reassuring suggestion from the Mexican historian Moisés González Navarro, who with the Rosas model in mind recommended that I turn my attention to Antonio López de Santa Anna. I must confess that without the personal encouragement and bibliographical advice of my distinguished colleague, for which I am grateful, I would have hesitated to rush into this particular period of Mexican history or to add Santa Anna to my gallery of caudillos, though his absence would have diminished the subject. I also owe deep debts of gratitude to other colleagues and collaborators, to Peter Blanchard, Malcolm Hoodless, and especially Andrew Barnard, whose research assistance eased the task of studying country after country, caudillo after caudillo, and of turning raw material into the semblance of a story. I am also grateful to the students of my postgraduate seminar for their patience in listening to this subject over the years and for the ideas and references they have supplied, particularly Guadalupe Jiménez, Leonardo León, and Rafael Varón. Parts of three chapters in more primitive form have been tried out in congresses in recent years and these papers are cited in the bibliography. I am pleased to record my thanks to all the archives listed in the sources, especially to the Archivo General de la Nación, Buenos Aires, the Archivo General de la Nación, Caracas, and the Public Record Office, London. Special thanks are also due to the British Library, the Library of University College London, the University of London, and the Institute of Latin American Studies. Finally I thank my daughter Caroline for her great help in preparing the manuscript for publication.

J.L.

CONTENTS

LIST OF MAPS

ABBREVIATIONS

AGI	Archivo General de Indias, Seville
AGN	Archivo General de la Nación, Buenos Aires; Archivo General de la Nación, Caracas
BAE	Biblioteca de Autores Españoles
BAGN	*Boletín del Archivo General de la Nación*, Caracas
BANH	Biblioteca de la Academia Nacional de la Historia, Venezuela
BHN	Biblioteca de Historia Nacional, Colombia
BL	British Library, London
BLAR	*Bulletin of Latin American Research*
BN	Biblioteca Nacional, Madrid
CDIP	Colección documental de la independencia del Perú
FHRV	Fuentes para la historia republicana de Venezuela
HAHR	*Hispanic American Historical Review*
HMC	Historical Manuscripts Commission, London
JLAS	*Journal of Latin American Studies*
LARR	*Latin American Research Review*
PRO	Public Record Office, London
RIIHJMR	*Revista del Instituto de Investigaciones Históricas Juan Manuel de Rosas*

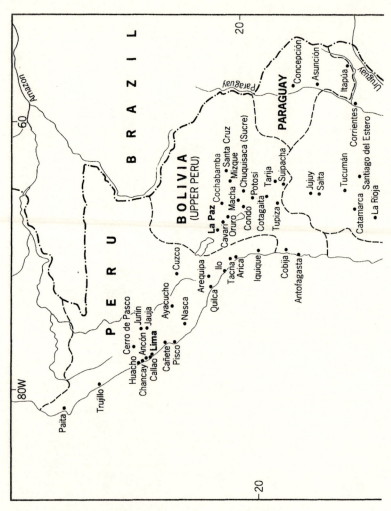

Map 1. Southern South America and Peru 1800–1850

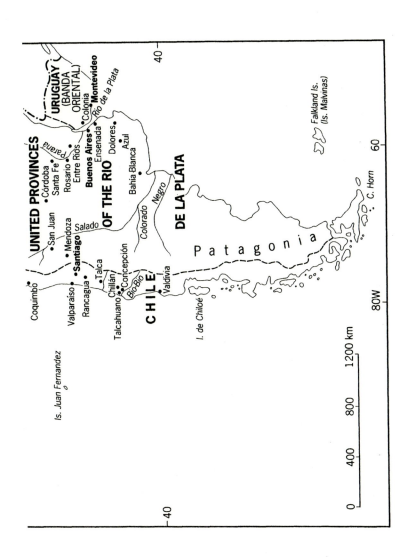

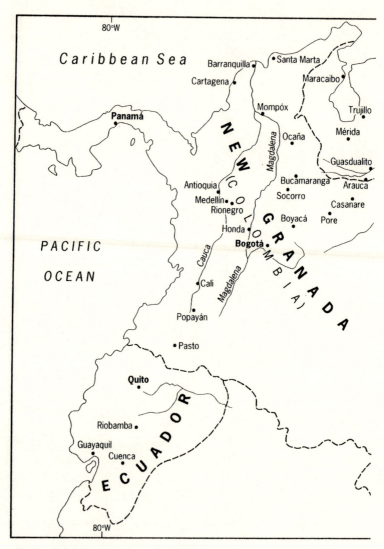

Map 2. Northern South America 1800–1850

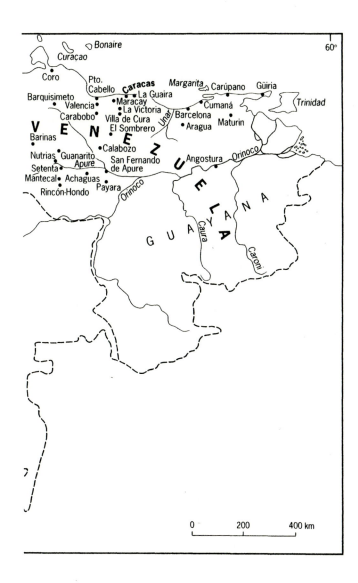

xvi

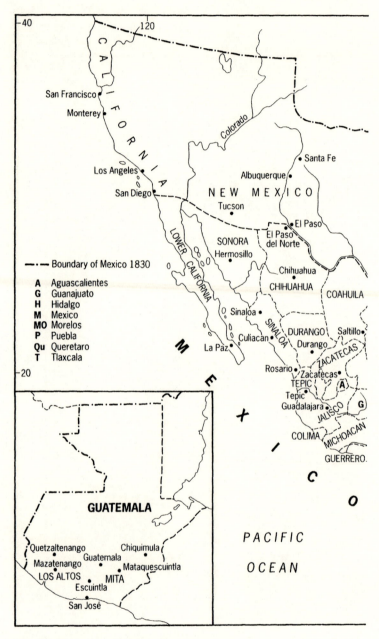

Map 3. Mexico and Central America 1830

100°W

80 Philadelphia

Washington

UNITED   STATES

Missouri

Mississippi

ATLANTIC

OCEAN

TEXAS

New Orleans

FLORIDA

San Antonio

Bahama Is.

Rio Grande

Corpus Christi

Camargo

NUEVO LEÓN

Matamoros

Gulf of Mexico

CUBA

Monterrey

TAMAULIPAS

Victoria

20

SAN LUIS POTOS

San Luis Potos

Tampico

Mérida

YUCATAN

Jamaica

Qu

H

VERA

Campeche

Caribbean Sea

Mexico

Jalapa

CAMPECHE

M

MO

T

P

Vera Cruz

Puebla

CRUZ

TABASCO

BR. HONDURAS

Chilpancingo

Oaxaca

San Christóbal

Acapulco

Ayutla

OAXACA

CHIAPAS

GUATEMALA

EL SALVADOR

NICARAGUA

Managua

L. Nicaragua

COSTA RICA

San José

PANAMA

0   200   400   600   800 km

100°W

80

I
Caudillo Structures

I
PRECURSORS AND PREMONITIONS

1. *Terms of Power*

The cult of the caudillo was a republican cult, created in war and revolution. In 1835 a group of military malcontents in Venezuela denounced José Antonio Páez, formerly president and now presidential protector: 'Venezuela can never enjoy peace as long as General Páez is there, for if he is in power he converts the country into his own plaything, and if he is out of power he makes the government his tool and constantly conspires to return. The result is that there is no possibility of a stable and secure system.'[1] A partisan document, written by rebels recently crushed by Páez. But it was the work of experts and identified some of the essential marks of the caudillo. He exercised a power which was independent of any office and free of any constraint; and in seeking to perpetuate himself he tended to destabilize government. The definition was not complete in itself or valid for all time, but it called attention to political trends and contemporary perceptions.

The term 'caudillo' hardly entered the political consciousness of colonial Spanish America. In the beginning it conveyed little more than its basic meaning, a leader; royal officials sometimes used the word to describe a rebel leader, but not a political type. The word acquired more general currency in the war of independence, when it gained a military dimension without however signifying a special title or function. Gradually it became more sharply defined, with a sense more specific than 'leader', less exact than 'president'. The term lay midway between a description of leadership and a reference to office, and its meaning was understood by contemporaries. A caudillo could rule with or without an office of state; he could exercise power with or without a constitution; his authority and legitimacy were personal and did not depend on formal institutions. Spanish Americans recog-

[1] Presidencia de la República, *Pensamiento político venezolano del siglo XIX: Textos para su estudio* (15 vols.; Caracas, 1960–2), xii. 200.

nized a caudillo when they saw one and they believed that his actions were peculiar to his type, not simply those of a president or general in disguise.

The caudillo had three basic qualifications: an economic base, a social constituency, and a political project. He first emerged as a local hero, the strong man of his region, whose authority derived from ownership of land, access to men and resources, and achievements that impressed for their value or their valour.[2] A caudillo would ride out from his hacienda at the head of an armed band, his followers bound to him by personal ties of dominance and submission and by a common desire to obtain power and wealth by force of arms.[3] His progress then depended on the strength of the state. In societies where succession to office was not yet formalized, caudillism filled the gap; political competition was expressed in armed conflict and the successful competitor ruled by violence, not by right of inheritance or election. Such rule would be subject to further competition and could rarely guarantee its own permanence; caudillo politics—survival of the strongest—supplanted peaceful negotiation. Caudillos were thus likely to emerge when the state was in disarray, the political process disrupted, and society in turmoil; personalism and violence took the place of law and institutions, and the rule of the powerful was preferred to representative government. While military men could become caudillos, and caudillos could receive military titles, the two things were not synonymous. Military intervention in politics, favoured treatment in the budget, and domination of the state by the army could exist under various forms of government and were not the preserve of caudillism.[4]

Driven by natural qualities of leadership, supported by an extended family, and progressing by personal influence and timely intimidation, the caudillo then established a *clientela*, which would take him to power and keep him there. The core of the *clientela* was an armed band and beyond that a network of dependants and supporters active in various roles and in different degrees. The whole team was held

---

[2] Eric R. Wolf and Edward C. Hansen, '*Caudillo* Politics: A Structural Analysis', *Comparative Studies in Society and History*, 9 (1966–7), 168–79.

[3] Raymond T. J. Buve, 'Peasant Movements, Caudillos and Land Reform during the Revolution (1910–1917) in Tlaxcala, Mexico', *Boletín de Estudios Latinoamericanos y del Caribe*, 18 (1975), 118–19.

[4] Robert L. Gilmore, *Caudillism and Militarism in Venezuela, 1810–1910* (Athens, Oh., 1964), 5–6, 47.

together by the bond of patron and client, the essential mechanism of the caudillo system. The patron–client relationship may be defined as an informal and personal exchange of resources, economic or political, between parties of unequal status. Each party sought to advance his interests by offering assets which he controlled—offices, land, favours—in exchange for those beyond his control—manpower, arms, supplies. Personal loyalty and, where it existed, spiritual kinship helped to seal the bond, which was a purely informal understanding, not a contract in law and indeed often an invitation to break the law. Yet an element of permanent obligation was built into the arrangement, and it was not easily revoked, even when it clashed with other loyalties. These relations established a vertical linkage and served to undermine horizontal group or class affiliations, especially those of clients. Patron–client relations were also based on manifest inequalities of wealth and power: the patrons usually monopolized certain assets that were of vital importance to the clients.[5] For all its imbalance, the system had a coherence of its own. Individual alliances grew into a pyramid as patrons in turn become clients to more powerful men in order to gain access to resources they did not directly control, until they all became subject to the superpatron.

The prototype was the landlord–peasant relationship. The landlord wanted labour and with it obedience, loyalty, and deference. The peasant sought a minimum of social and physical security: land, credit, subsistence, and protection. How could these needs be satisfied on a stable basis? The preferred means was a relationship of dominance and dependence, of patrón and peon, as on a hacienda. Dependence could take various forms: peons could be wage labourers, seasonal labourers, forced labourers, or labourers who owed service in return for land or grazing rights, when they were variously called *aparceros, colonos, conuqueros, medieros,* and *yanaconas.* A landlord with a *clientela* had a basic qualification for the caudillo system and could move on to political action, either as a contender for power or as a client of a supercaudillo. Caudillo competition and rule thus drew peasants into political struggles as fighters or producers, often against their will. As caudillos usually sided with local hacendados against the claims of their workers, they might have to use force on peasants or

[5] S. N. Eisenstadt and Luis Roniger, 'The Study of Patron–Client Relations and Recent Developments in Sociological Theory', in S. N. Eisenstadt and Rene Lemarchand (eds.), *Political Clientelism, Patronage and Development* (London, 1981), 276–7.

else mobilize them by promises and incorporate them into a system of mass clientage.[6]

Leader and landlord, godfather and patron, the caudillo could now make a bid for political power. First he built a local or regional power base; then as his domain grew from local to national dimensions he might win supreme authority in the state and rule his country from the presidential palace, though even then his power remained personal, not institutional. The local and national caudillo differed from each other in degree of power rather than in role or character. Some historians, it is true, distinguish between caudillo types and call the local caudillo a cacique. 'Cacique' was an Arawak work meaning 'chief'; the Spaniards introduced it into Mexico and Peru and used it to designate a hereditary Indian chief incorporated into the Spanish system of authority. In republican Mexico, without losing its colonial meaning, the term was applied to local *jefes* and became part of received usage. According to this formula caudillos have an urban mentality, a national vision and policy; they strive for social change, defend a programme and a constitution, and represent a transitional stage towards constitutional government. Caciques, on the other hand, have a rural mentality and regional objectives; they defend the status quo, lead peasant protests, and retain traditional forms of domination.[7] The distinctions are not entirely consistent with history or logic, and in themselves hardly justify a difference of nomenclature between a national and a local caudillo. True, the emergence of a national state in Mexico was seriously retarded by a series of provincial power bases, where landowners dominated political life, monopolized economic wealth, and controlled the population, supported to a greater or lesser degree by military and clerical allies. Regional power was expressed by the regional caudillo, or cacique, who assembled and managed a coalition of local forces to consolidate his position against the central government. In this sense the cacique was a regional caudillo. But other countries had similar, if not identical, regional structures to those of Mexico without finding it necessary to invoke the concept of *caciquismo*. Whether the historian uses the term caudillo or cacique to describe the regional leader is a matter of common usage rather than a semantic imperative.

The caudillo, it could be said, possessed dictatorial powers. The

[6] Buve, 'Peasant movements, Caudillos and Land Reform', 119–21.

[7] Fernando Díaz Díaz, *Caudillos y caciques: Antonio López de Santa Anna y Juan Alvarez* (Mexico, 1972), 3–5.

concept of dictatorship had a long history. It was known to the ancient Greeks as an elective form of tyranny, and to the Romans as a variation of republican government, whereby the ruler was allowed an extraordinary power though one limited in time. Dictatorship approached its modern form in the French Revolution, when its ideological base and mass support marked it out from the traditions of absolute monarchy, and when theoreticians came to regard it as a positive ideal rather than a necessary evil. Revolutionary dictatorship aimed to establish democracy by means of a strong and irresistible authority. A popular dictatorship? The French Revolution introduced a new concept, the dictatorship of the enlightened vanguard, which would express what the the people ought to think and give them what they ought to have.[8] Edmund Burke regarded this as pure despotism, exercised by a minority who had betrayed their trust in order to obtain power, and enforced by military violence.[9] For John Stuart Mill 'the assumption of absolute power in the form of a temporary dictatorship' was something that might be tolerated in exceptional circumstances, but normally dictatorship, like the patronage politics which it practised, was the opposite of freedom and representation.[10]

In Spanish America dictatorship became a familiar term to observers of independence and a form of government practised by more than one of the liberators. For Bolívar, the supreme constitutionalist, dictatorship was a desperate cure for desperate ills, not an option allowed by his political thought. On various occasions in Venezuela, Peru, and Colombia he became 'dictator and supreme chief of the republic', the possessor of extraordinary powers, justified in his own mind by the need to save the revolution and by the support he received from popular opinion.[11] This was a pragmatic view of dictatorship, one which saw the dictator as a protector of the people from anarchy and oppression. Hispanic tradition was familiar with the concept of a 'protector' of special groups in society. The Spanish crown had early sought to counteract the human calamity of colonization by establishing the office of *protector de indios*, and subsequently experimented with other forms of special jurisdiction for Indians,

---

[8] J. L. Talmon, *The Origins of Totalitarian Democracy* (London, 1970), 209–11.

[9] Edmund Burke, *Reflections on the Revolution in France* (London, 1986), 141–2, 344–5.

[10] John Stuart Mill, *Representative Government* (London, 1926), 207, 226–7.

[11] Speech to the Caracas Assembly, 2 Jan. 1814, in Simón Bolívar, *Escritos del Libertador* (Caracas, 1964–), vi. 8–9; Bolívar to Diego Ibarra, Bogotá, 28 June 1828, in *Memorias del General O'Leary* (34 vols.; Caracas, 1981), xxxi. 146–7.

notably the General Indian Court.[12] The Enlightenment and its early liberal disciples in Spanish America were hostile to the concept of special protection for vulnerable groups and sought to integrate all in a national society. But dictators were aware of the political advantage of appealing to popular sectors and of the legitimacy they could earn from the protection and benefit accorded to the silent masses. So the dictator became a protector – protector of laws, protector of groups, protector of pueblos – and rulers like Juan Manuel de Rosas and Antonio López de Santa Anna became skilful manipulators, adept at giving people an illusion of protection and participation while confining them to the status quo. The dictator as protector was not an objective usage but one which served the purpose of propaganda. And it did not deceive everyone. In Argentina contemporary critics of Rosas, such as Domingo Faustino Sarmiento and Juan Bautista Alberdi, called him a dictator in a pejorative sense, meaning a ruler with absolute power unrestrained by a constitution and responsible to no one. W. H. Hudson spoke of 'the Caudillos and Dictators... who have climbed into power in this continent of republics and revolutions'.[13]

In certain circumstances, and in a nineteenth-century context, the terms 'caudillo' and 'dictator' are interchangeable and mean an absolute ruler exercising personal power. In other cases the terms are different, though the difference is one of degree rather than kind, with a suggestion that the dictator's power is slightly more institutionalized than that of the caudillo. In yet other contexts the terms convey a significant contrast of image and are not synonymous. First, in most of Spanish America the term 'caudillo' could be applied to a regional as well as a national leader, whereas the dictator was unmistakably national in his domain. Second, 'caudillo' carries an indication of the leader's route to the top, from a local to a central power base. The term 'dictator' is not a career description but simply a designation of power and its plenitude in the national state. Finally there is a chronological progression from caudillo to dictator. The caudillo held sway in an economic, social, and political framework whose structures were simple, not to say primitive, in form. The dictator presided over a more developed economy, a more complex alliance of interest groups, and a government which possessed greater

[12] Woodrow Borah, *Justice by Insurance: The General Indian Court of Colonial Mexico and the Legal Aides of the Half-Real* (Berkeley and Los Angeles, 1983), 64–5, 409–10.
[13] W. H. Hudson, *Far Away and Long Ago* (London, 1967), 91.

resources. Caudillism was the first stage of dictatorship, and the dividing line was about 1870. The division was not absolute. The term 'dictator' was used before this date, usually by bureaucrats and theorists rather than in general speech, and it conveyed a similar pejorative sense. The designation 'caudillo' lasted beyond its normal limits, because remnants of caudillism survived into otherwise modernized or modernizing societies.[14] There were no unchanging rules. These usages arise from the perceptions and language of contemporaries and from the habits of later historians, and may be said to have been prescribed by practice.

As the caudillo emerged from local life into national history, changed the poncho for the uniform and the ranch for the palace, he could be seen to be autonomous and absolute. Autonomous in that he owed obedience to no one beyond him. Absolute in that he shared his power with no other person or institution. Ideally he was also permanent, seeking power for life, with the right to nominate his successor. The claim was normally challenged and fighting broke out. Born of a weak state, the caudillo further destabilized the state when he made his bid for power, or rebelled against those who possessed power, or provoked rivals when he obtained power. By definition a caudillo was incompatible with the existence of an imperial state headed by a monarch, ruled by the monarch's laws, and administered by the monarch's officials. So the caudillo was not to be found in colonial Spanish America. Nevertheless, even before 1810, there were premonitions and precursors.

2. *Estancias,* Hatos, *and Haciendas*

In colonial Spanish America personal, as distinct from official, authority usually derived either from ownership of property or from repudiation of its owners. The great estate generated a dual leadership: the leadership of the proprietor and the leadership of the dispossessed. The logic of lawlessness in the eighteenth century often began on the land. The extension of private property, the formation of estates, the marginalization of the rural population created conditions in which poor and landless people might seek leaders and join bands in search of subsistence and booty. And in response proprie-

---

[14] Inés Quintero, *El ocaso de una estirpe* (Caracas, 1989), 19–23, 44–50.

tors would lead out hacienda forces to crush the dissidents. The process was not inevitable, or universal, but it was common enough to form a pattern throughout Spanish America with variations according to region.

The classic account of lawlessness in Argentina was written in 1801 by Félix de Azara, Spanish scientist and man of enlightenment, who thought one *jornalero* in Spain was worth three in the Río de la Plata, and who divided the denizens of the pampas into gauchos and farmers, or into 'thieves, drunkards, and gamblers' on the one hand and those who were 'economically motivated, educated, and industrious' on the other, the difference lying in the degree of material progress, concentration in rural communities, and presence of civilizing institutions such as churches, schools, and private property.[15] Modern research tends to show that the Río de la Plata was by no means one great cattle ranch encircled by roaming gauchos. In spite of the growth of ranches and the expansion of cattle production and hide exports, arable agriculture remained a vital economic activity; in the course of the later eighteenth century grain production, mainly wheat, was kept alive by poor tenant farmers, whose output overtook livestock, and compared favourably with the great wheat-growing areas of Spanish America, central Chile, and the Bajío of Mexico.[16] Cereal production displayed greater productivity for less land occupation and its existence indicated, at least until 1815, that there were more options for labour than the life of a ranch peon.[17] If the labour force of cattle estancias was subject to frequent rotation, its mobility was due less to the restlessness of the gaucho than to the existence of alternatives which gave the *campesinos* opportunities to leave the estancia seasonally to work on grain-producing farms, or in their own cultivation or cattle rearing.[18] Outside the sector of working peasants, unlikely recruits for outlaw bands, there was another rural type, those who did not seek work but lived by choice on the

---

[15] Félix de Azara, *Memoria sobre el estado rural del Río de la Plata y otros informes* (Buenos Aires, 1943), 5–6, 8–9.

[16]. Juan Carlos Garavaglia, 'Economic Growth and Regional Differentiations; The River Plate Region at the End of the Eighteenth Century', *HAHR* 65, 1 (1985), 51–89.

[17] Juan Carlos Garavaglia and Jorge Gelman, *El mundo rural rioplatense a fines de la época colonial: Estudios sobre producción y mano de obra* (Buenos Aires, 1989), 37–8.

[18] Jorge Gelman, 'New Perspectives on an Old Problem and the Same Source; The Gaucho and the Rural History of the Colonial Río de la Plata', *HAHR* 69, 4 (1989), 715–31; Garavaglia and Gelman, *El mundo rural rioplatense*, 82–3.

margin of society, hunting or exploring and coming in seasonally. The gaucho was essentially a creature of the nineteenth century, when occupation of the land by estancias and conscription for the regular army gave free horsemen few reasons to settle and many to escape. But estancia expansion had already begun in the eighteenth century and it was then that the origins of rural alienation were to be found. Meanwhile beyond the countryside of Buenos Aires, in remoter 'frontier' districts where the rural population was more scattered and agricultural activities were less intense, opportunities abounded for enterprising outlaws and contrabandists.

Alongside arable agriculture, cattle farming entered a period of growth in the late eighteenth century and estancias began to occupy new land in response to new opportunities. The greater export outlets opened by *comercio libre* from 1778 stimulated the production of hides for markets in Europe and of salt meat for the slave consumers of the Americas; land values appreciated; a new generation of immigrants arrived to create wealth in commerce and invest it in land and livestock. Hide exports, population increase, and growth of the urban market were indicators of a new period in the expansion of estancias and help to explain their attraction as an investment. Only those with capital had a chance of becoming landowners, for only they could withstand the lengthy bureaucratic process of land acquisition, and pay the high legal fees and development costs of a new estancia. According to a Spanish official reporting to the viceroy of the Río de la Plata in 1795, 'only the wealthy succeed in establishing estancias and in subjugating the poor and forcing them into service through a wretched labour contract; or more likely these take to robbery and contraband in which they find a more secure means of subsistence'.[19] Powerful estancieros were already appropriating available land on both banks of the River Plate, forming estancias, according to another report to the viceroy, 'which occupy more land than a European kingdom', appropriating livestock previously the common property of the poor, and paying low wages to their ranch peons. Land concentration by wealthy estancieros, therefore, appropriated land and cattle previously used by rural people, forcing 'numerous poor farmers to become nomads and vagrants'.[20] Peons were at the mercy of seasonal factors, and to keep them in dependence during non-working months

---

[19] Quoted by Ricardo E. Rodríguez Molas, *Historia social del gaucho*, 2nd edn. (Buenos Aires, 1982), 79.
[20] Quoted ibid. 80, 82.

proprietors might allow them to squat on the estancia or steal a few cattle, but as a privilege not a right.[21] The majority of the rural poor accepted their fate, clinging to a corner of an estancia for subsistence agriculture and livestock farming, but persecuted by the new proprietors as landless and workless. Ill fortune seldom came alone. Those who decided to seek a life beyond the law were pursued with new vigour. The formation of large estates gave landlords the opportunity to organize their own bands, authorized by the viceroy, in order to defend cattle from rustlers and from free slaughter for hides, thus legitimizing the private armies of the estancias and their *jefes*.[22] It was a short step from this to sealing off their entire estancias not only to private encroachers but also to government inspectors, the better to kill off thousands of cattle for their hides without any public control: 'the hacendado guards his estancia like an enclosed reserve and permits no one to enter his vast estate'.[23]

The gauchos, the mounted nomads of the pampas, included various rural types from part-time ranch peons to rebels against society. Spaniards saw a stereotype, an outlaw and rustler, living on estancia hospitality or, in its absence, on robbery: 'His favourite passions are gambling of any kind, horse racing, games, and women'.[24] Government officials of the late colonial period did not distinguish between good and bad gauchos but considered all of them vagrants and thieves, while the gauchos themselves held a different perception and believed in freedom of movement and communal ownership of livestock. Most of the intendants were convinced that Americans had a passion for liberty and for life beyond institutions. The intendant of Córdoba, the marquis of Sobremonte, believed that the preference of rural people to live dispersed outside urban jurisdiction derived from 'their natural love of liberty, placing themselves out of sight of magistrates and priests, who would harrass them for their frequent excesses and robberies of cattle'.[25] If this were true of Córdoba, a tiny oasis of

---

[21] Samuel Amaral, 'Rural Production and Labour in Late Colonial Buenos Aires', *JLAS* 19, 2 (1987), 235–78.

[22] Memoria de Cevallos, Buenos Aires, 12 June 1778, in Sigfrido A. Radaelli (ed.), *Memorias de los virreyes del Río de la Plata* (Buenos Aires, 1945), 12–13.

[23] Manuel Cipriano de Melo to viceroy, 1 Sept. 1791, BL, Add. MS 32,604, fo. 232.

[24] Description of Peru, Chile, and Buenos Aires compiled by members of an expedition fitted out in 1783–4 by the Spanish government, BL, Add. MS 17,592, fo. 467. This Spanish report used the term 'Guazo ú hombre de campo'.

[25] Sobremonte to Gálvez, 6 Nov. 1785, BL, Egerton MS 1815; Sobremonte to Viceroy Loreto, 6 Nov. 1785, in José Torre Revello, *El marqués de Sobre Monte* (Buenos Aires, 1946), pp. c–ci.

civilization, how much more true of La Rioja, a semi-desert on the outer fringe of empire, the future base of Facundo Quiroga, which Sobremonte found a joyless place, 'poor' and 'miserable', with few institutions, an unarmed militia, virtually no commerce, and all the signs of natural barbarism. As for San Juan, a province otherwise productive in maize, fruits, and wines, its llanos were the home of scattered families of mestizos and Indians living completely beyond the reach of officials and priests, paying no taxes, surviving on unproductive farms by robbing the cattle of nearby estancias, and resisting all efforts to bring them into villages because 'they abhor society'.

Intendants such as Sobremonte believed that to bring people within the bounds of law and civilization two things were necessary, the establishment of urban institutions and the extension of private estates.[26] Others such as Francisco de Paula Sanz were more specific: he advocated sale of crown land in units of reasonable size, better management of estancias to preserve resources, and a campaign to clear the territory of contrabandists, thieves, vagrants, and outlaws by improved law enforcement agencies modelled on the *Acordada* in Mexico.[27] Azara advocated the allocation of land in moderate lots to Indians and others who would actually work their estates, and not in vast estancias to absentee landlords.[28] But the landed élite, backed by most officials, strove to accumulate land for the benefits of size, to appropiate cattle into estancias, and to limit the traditional prerogatives of gauchos. The clash of interests was inevitable. The gauchos looked back to ancient customs. The government viewed the gauchos as potential rebels. And the estancieros wanted land and labour at all costs. The result was the development of harsh social laws and anti-vagrancy campaigns, passport requirements, and forced military service, a rural code which continued almost without interruption from colony to republic. Hounded by state and society, many rural people took flight beyond the frontier or found refuge in outlaw bands. The interior would soon become the home of caudillos and their *montoneros*, a terrifying threat not only to Buenos Aires but to the landed élite in general. The slightest loss of control by Buenos Aires invited insubordination. The British invasions of 1806–7 provided such an occasion, when the flight of the viceroy increased contempt for authority among gauchos and militia alike. At Fort Melincué news of

---

[26] Report of 6 Nov. 1785, in Torre Revello, *El marqués de Sobre Monte*, pp. xci–cviii.
[27] Informe sobre la Banda Oriental, Sanz to Viceroy Loreto, 4 Aug. 1785, BL, Add. MS 32,604, fos. 143–95.
[28] Azara. *Memoria sobre el estado rural del Río de la Plata*, 18–19.

the British success arrived on 9 July 1806. The militiamen were heard to cry 'that now there was no king or authorities. These people became so insolent that no one would obey the commandant. . . . There is no limit to their arrogance and boldness.'[29]

In Venezuela the occupation of the llanos followed a different route, though it reached a similar destination. Commercialized agriculture such as cacao and hides had little sale within the colony and depended wholly on export outlets, many of them in the hands of foreigners and beyond the control of the colonial oligarchy. In the 1790s cacao exports plunged owing to the fall in Mexican demand and Spain's inability to absorb the surplus. So the Caracas planters began to substitute coffee for cacao, and, more pointedly, to turn to the llanos as an alternative enterprise and a source of additional property, in order to commercialize cattle and expand salt beef exports to the Caribbean.[30] The shift to the llanos had social consequences. In the plains the new landlords, or more often their overseers, confronted the wild llaneros, a mixed race of Indians, blacks, and zambos, semi-nomadic hunters in a land which impressed Alexander von Humboldt for its monotonous landscape, its human emptiness, its burning sky, an atmosphere darkened by dust, where only an occasional palm tree relieved the featureless horizon.[31] The original population of this fearsome country was augmented by migrants and fugitives from the creole-dominated coast, some in search of land and opportunities, some seeking escape from the law. But for whites the llanos became a kind of outback, where they would find no food, water, society, or security.

The push into the plains at the end of the eighteenth century simply quickened a process that had already begun.[32] From about

---

[29] Luis de la Cruz, 'Viaje desde el fuerte de Ballenar hasta la ciudad de Buenos Aires', in Pedro de Angelis, *Colección de obras y documentos relativos a la historia antigua y moderna de las provincias del Río de la Plata*, 2nd edn. (5 vols.; Buenos Aires, 1910), i. 25.

[30] Miguel Izard, 'Sin domicilio fijo, senda segura, ni destino conocido; los llaneros del Apure a finales del período colonial', *Boletín Americanista*, 33 (1983), 14–21; 'Sin el menor arraigo ni responsabilidad; llaneros y ganadería a principios del siglo XIX', *Boletín Americanista*, 37 (1987), 128–39; 'Venezuela: Tráfico mercantil, secesionismo político e insurgencias populares', in Reinhard Liehr (ed.), *América Latina en la época de Simón Bolívar* (Berlin, 1989), 207–25.

[31] Alexander von Humboldt, *Personal Narrative of Travels to the Equinoctial Regions of the New Continent during the Years 1799–1804* (6 vols.; London, 1814–29), iv. 302.

[32] Adelina C. Rodríguez Mirabal, *La formación del latifundio ganadero en los llanos de Apure: 1750–1800* (Caracas, 1987), 179–84, 209–21, 229–38.

1760 the 'conquest of the llanos' saw the formation, by grant or purchase, of extensive cattle estates, followed by the establishment of new townships; the owners were a relatively small group of families, some from the plantation aristocracy of Caracas, others from previously settled parts of the llanos. The formation of vast *hatos* tended to marginalize the llaneros and to define private property over the open range and wild cattle. The llaneros were accustomed to various traditional usages. Some possessed cattle which they pastured on *ejidos*, or communal land; others enjoyed customary, but not proprietory, rights which gave access to cattle without known owners; and others, living near *hatos* and working for them as *peones* llaneros, received plots and pasture in return for labour and were described by Humboldt as 'partly freed men and partly slaves'.[33] The commercialization of land use affected all llaneros, but especially those who had lived by hunting wild cattle; this came to be defined as rustling and punished as delinquency, as the ranching élites invoked the law and looked for the protection of the colonial government. In self-defence many llaneros assembled into bands to raid estates and procure a subsistence; from this they could become a permanent threat to persons and property, and a constant danger to law and order. Even granted that llanero culture regarded rustling as a custom not a crime, there were still many outlaws in the llanos, so many indeed that they reduced some areas to a state of virtual rebellion. Their chiefs were effectively leaders of criminal gangs, whose activities became inherent in the life of the plains. Already there was a progression from llanero to rustler, to bandit, a sequence which would eventually lead to guerrilla fighter.

The native llaneros were joined by other groups in the late eighteenth century. Among these were fugitive and rebel Indians, some from the north, some from the other side of the Apure, some fleeing colonial jurisdiction, and all seeking to avoid exploitation by officials or hacendados. The Spanish authorities themselves admitted that 'all the corregidores have more or less become accomplices in the maltreatment of the Indians in their charge'.[34] Displaced Indians and other groups of *gente baja* (low-class people) were often given shelter by hacendados in need of labour, who were then denounced by officials for encouraging disorder and enabling Indians to escape

---

[33] Humboldt, *Personal Narrative*, iv. 320; Miguel Izard, *Orejanos, cimarrones y arrochelados* (Barcelona, 1988), 60–1.
[34] Governor of Cumaná to Crown, 13 Dec. 1767, AGI, Caracas 201.

tribute. Other rebel Indians formed *rochelas*, or bands under 'captains', sometimes eighty strong and including blacks and *zambos*; they lived by plunder, attacking *hatos* and hunting cattle.[35] The marginal population was further increased by the constant arrival of slaves, fugitives from northern plantations or cattle ranches, some living as lone hunters, others joining bands to survive outside the law. *Pardos* too made their way to the llanos, fleeing from racial discrimination and lack of opportunities in the centre-north in search of new horizons; these were people whom the white élites, seconded by *cabildos* and *audiencias*, regarded as *mulatos notorios* and disqualified for office and advancement. In addition to fugitive Indians, slaves, and *pardos*, many others living on the margin of society and the law were comprehensively categorized by the ruling groups as *vagos y mal entretenidos*, and were pursued simply for not having an occupation, as *arrochelados*, troublemakers, or dissidents of one kind or another. From Barquisimeto it was reported that 'the utter poverty of these districts has increased the number of vagrants and thieves, whose outrages have aroused the complaints of hacendados'.[36]

Outlaws, rustlers and robbers were not isolated criminals operating as solitary raiders but were organized in bands under leaders who could impose their authority. The band of Indians marauding out of Nuestra Señora de Los Angeles near Calabozo in 1786 acted under a 'principal caudillo' named Estevan, who resisted arrest and was shot by a patrol. According to Juan José Blanco y Plazos, the municipal procurator of Caracas, new arrivals in the llanos were immediately corrupted by local delinquents and recruited into bands, living by plunder, attacking ranchers and officials, and so destroying security 'that roads can be used only at the greatest risk of life and property'.[37] In the Spanish view fugitives and vagrants banded together with a specific object—to live as rebels against white society. According to Humboldt, 'the *llanos* were then [around 1800] infested by an immense number of robbers, who assassinated the whites that fell into their hands with an atrocious refinement of cruelty. . . . The

---

[35] Josef Gabaldón to Governor, Calabozo, 28 July 1779, AGN Caracas, Gobernación y Capitanía General, vol. xxii, 1779, fos. 94–7, 217.
[36] Audiencia de Caracas, Cartas y expedientes, 1789–96, AGI, Caracas 167; Francisco Navarro to Governor, Barquisimeto, 22 Oct. 1779, AGN, Caracas Gobernación y Capitanía General, vol. xxii, 1779, fos. 288–9.
[37] Magistrate of Calabozo to Governor, 15 March 1786, AGN Caracas, Gobernación y Capitanía General, vol. xxxiii, 1786, fo. 22. Blanco y Plazos quoted by Izard, *Orejanos, cimarrones y arrochelados*, 42.

llanos were even then the refuge of malefactors, who had committed crimes in the missions of the Oroonoko, or who had escaped from prisons on the coast'.[38] In the 1790s ranchers were complaining that bands of *cuatreros* or rustlers now had 'formal establishments and settlements in the mountains and other inaccessible places'.[39]

Bandit chiefs were beginning to assert their leadership, to acquire fame as well as fortune, and to emulate the deeds of 'Guardajumo' ('Smokescreen'), an Indian who robbed ranches and itinerant merchants in the region between Barcelona and Calabozo until he was caught in 1802.[40] As rustlers became more aggressive and the authorities still failed to respond, the victims began to take the law into their own hands; the élite too formed bands, landlords divided along clan and family lines, ranchers fought ranchers as well as rustlers. In 1796 the hacendado Tomas Paz del Castillo reported to the captain general on violence and disorder in the llanos; he singled out the activities of a group of bandidos, rapists, killers, and robbers, led by Ermenegildo de la Caridad López, *el Xerezano*, and his brother-in-law Pedro Peña, both free *zambos* who lived openly in the village of Cachipo, near Barcelona, with the complicity of most of the inhabitants. Corpses of travellers, mutilated, beheaded, and hanging from trees were a common sight in the llanos of Calabozo. By 1800 the failure of the judicial and police authorities in the llanos allowed the bandoleros to expand their operations and not only to rob cattle but also 'to carry off women, burn houses, kill the owners, and plunder travellers'. In September 1801 it was reported from San Carlos that there were four or five bands of outlaws with at least fifteen men each, equipped with firearms, and engaged on a campaign of rape, assault, plunder, and robbery.[41]

By the end of the eighteenth century the greater opportunities to commercialize cattle production for markets in the Caribbean caused both sides to press harder on resources, ranchers for cattle, land, and labour, rustlers for a share in the profits of trade. The authorities and the *hateros* replied with greater repression, lashings, executions, and a renewed campaign against *vagos*. Violence and harrassment were counter-productive, converting rustlers into bandits, and instigating a

---

[38] Humboldt, *Personal Narrative*, vi. 56–7.

[39] Quoted by Izard, *Orejanos, cimarrones y arrochelados*, 72.

[40] Manuel Landaeta Rosales, *Gran recopilación geográfica, estadística, e histórica de Venezuela* (2 vols.; Caracas, 1889), ii. 235.

[41] Izard, *Orejanos, cimarrones y arrochelados*, 74; 'Sin domicilio fijo', 49–52.

spiral of terror which reached a peak on the eve of independence. Between the magistrate and the bandit life was a lottery for the llaneros. At the end of the colonial period those opting for freedom and independence in the llanos were branded as rogues and vagabonds, and driven into banditry under chieftains who would lead them to subsistence, rustling, and contraband; they were joined by criminal outlaws, less tolerated but no less elusive.[42] Socio-racial lines were drawn and renewed confrontation was evident between the creole élite on the one hand and Indians, slaves, mestizos, and *pardos* on the other. It is not to be supposed that life outside the llanos was more civilized. Spanish settlements in the jurisdiction of Cumaná, though governed by local officials and paying tithes, all qualified for Sarmiento's description of barbarism, the breeding ground of banditry, 'lacking gaol, church, school, charitable and public institutions', while their melancholy inhabitants lived in adobe houses completely without furniture and containing 'not even a bed'.[43]

Mexico, at least in its central regions, was stronger in officials and institutions than Argentina and Venezuela, and the colonial state normally functioned as a powerful deterrent to lawlessness. But even in Mexico large areas were beyond effective control; there was no professional rural police and the only law-enforcement agency in the highways and byways of the colony was the Tribunal of the *Acordada* which in the eighteenth century fought a losing battle against crime. In remoter regions, where viceregal authority was lost amidst desert and distance, powerful individuals and interest groups often managed to entrench themselves and create private fiefdoms beyond the reach, if not the jurisdiction, of public officials.[44] In rural Mexico the population was thin on the ground, with a density of only seven per square mile; where it was difficult to concentrate this in official settlements the great estate filled the vacuum.[45] The lords of the land—local caciques in effect—thus became brokers mediating between the government and the rural communities they controlled.

---

[42] Miguel Izard and Richard W. Slatta, 'Banditry and Social Conflict on the Venezuelan Llanos', in Richard W. Slatta (ed.), *Bandidos: The Varieties of Latin American Banditry* (Westport, Conn., 1987), 39–40.

[43] Governor of Cumaná to Crown, 9 Dec. 1761, AGI, Caracas 201.

[44] Brian R. Hamnett, *Roots of Insurgency: Mexican Regions, 1750–1824* (Cambridge, 1986), 55.

[45] François Chevalier, *Land and Society in Colonial Mexico: The Great Hacienda* (Berkeley, Calif., 1963), 294–6; Eric Van Young, 'Mexican Rural History since Chevalier: The Historiography of the Colonial Hacienda', *LARR* 18, 3 (1983), 5–61.

Colonial officials tended to deal not with the mass of the people but with their caciques, whom they troubled for taxes but otherwise left alone in their domains. As long as the king reigned and the viceroy ruled, mediation of this kind was mostly peaceful, but it only needed an insurrection to transform local *jefes* into rebel leaders.

Hacienda owners were often allowed by the colonial state to dispense a kind of private justice to their work force, to peons as well as to slaves, and the hacienda gaol, as well as the hacienda chapel, became part of the rural landscape. The viceregal authorities sometimes gave landowners a kind of commission in the rural security forces, which they then exercised not only to maintain law and order but also to coerce their own peons. In remote areas informal hacienda armies hunted bandits and kept the peace. Inside the estate, workers were made aware of the sanctions behind hacienda authority. But it was the sheer size of the hacienda and its community rather than any commission from the state that gave the landowner his power and his following. Inside its gates workers could find security and subsistence, as well as a taskmaster. The Mexican hacienda became the home of a patriarchal society, a powerful centre of patron–client relations, organized along hierarchical and paternalistic lines. Many haciendas had large resident populations, 200, 500, or even 1,000 people. They acted as a magnet to draw Indians away from their pueblos, constituting in effect alternative communities bound together by informal ties of loyalty and solidarity. The patrón became a cacique and exercised a mediating role between his domain and the outside world.[46] Landowners, of course, were not always powerful and successful. In northern Peru, clientelism was a sign of weakness rather than of strength: landowners used patriarchal and political leverage to compensate for economic failure and Indian resistance, and to preserve their authority over subordinate social and racial groups.[47] In Mexico, in contrast, the proprietor was father to the patrón.

To what extent was rural Mexico disturbed by social conflict, criminality, and banditry? If the hacienda had its chieftain, did hacienda expansion provoke the emergence of alternative chieftains? Mexico, unlike the Argentine pampas and the Venezuelan llanos, was not a frontier of new settlement. Yet the eighteenth century saw great

[46] Eric Van Young, *Hacienda and Market in Eighteenth-Century Mexico: The Rural Economy of the Guadalajara Region, 1675–1820* (Berkeley, Calif., 1981), 264–7.

[47] Susan E. Ramírez, *Provincial Patriarchs: Land Tenure and the Economics of Power in Colonial Peru* (Albuquerque, NM, 1986).

competition for land and renewed growth of large estates in central
Mexico and Oaxaca; these trends were exacerbated by population
increase, which stimulated growth but also increased the pressure on
land, and by the new economic opportunities in the regional, viceregal, and world markets during a time of mining boom and freer trade.
Competition did not necessarily make estates out of villages and
peons out of peasants. In the Bajío, Michoacán, and Oaxaca small-
holdings survived on the margins of the large haciendas, while rental
and sharecropping arrangements were common thoughout central
Mexico. Exploitation of rural resources could proceed without reducing Indian and peasant communities to landlessness and peonage. It
could be done by leaving the targets in place, mobilizing the productive capacity of existing villages through taxation and coerced labour,
and enabling viable peasant communities to survive with their land
and traditional way of life more or less intact.[48]

Nevertheless, while peasants across central and southern Mexico
were generally neither victims nor enemies of Spanish rule, there
were regions where oppression prevailed, where social crisis could
simmer and mass outrage erupt, waiting only for mobilization by a
strong leader. This happened in the Bajío.[49] What had been a stable
agrarian society became a breeding ground for bandits and insurgents.
The creoles had the best lands in the Bajío, and the majority of the
rural population lived as dependants—tenants or peons—on great
estates. They were not rebellious as long as their standards of living
were tolerable. But after 1750 security and subsistence degenerated
into a precarious struggle for survival, and the Bajío experienced an
agrarian crisis which made it ready for revolution. At a time of
population growth, mining boom, and profitable estate cultivation, it
was the élites who advanced, while the poor suffered. The expansion
of haciendas, financed from mining profits, took place at the expense
of modest rancheros.[50] A growing number of families were reduced
to living as poor tenants and squatters.[51] Meanwhile the shift from
maize production to wheat for the benefit of the creole market was
another blow to the poor. As maize was squeezed out to marginal

[48] D. A. Brading, *Haciendas and Ranchos in the Mexican Bajío: León 1700–1860*
(Cambridge, 1978), 150–8; William B. Taylor, *Drinking, Homicide and Rebellion in
Colonial Mexican Villages* (Stanford, Calif., 1979), 160–1.
[49] John Tutino, *From Insurrection to Revolution in Mexico: Social Bases of Agrarian
Violence 1750–1940* (Princeton, NJ, 1986), 46–7.
[50] Brading, *Haciendas and Ranchos in the Mexican Bajío*, 159–62.
[51] Tutino, *From Insurrection to Revolution in Mexico*, 73.

lands, prices rose, shortages appeared, and soon, in 1785–6, many parts of Mexico suffered a crisis of subsistence. Price rises led to rent rises and evictions for those tenants unable to pay. In Mexico, no less than in Argentina and Venezuela, agrarian change turned peons into rebels. Indians and *campesinos* were not docile. Protest was endemic in colonial Mexico, taking the form of spontaneous and often leaderless local outbursts in reaction to threats to community interests from outside. But these spasms were usually short-lived and exhausted themselves without spreading or provoking massive retaliation. If there were killings, villagers might flee to the hills, though not to remain there as bandits; they usually preferred to negotiate a return.[52] The Spanish colonial system was built to absorb protest, and it normally provided prospects of legal redress. So rural and peasant grievances were not always expressed in violence or outlawry; some were simply endured, some were peacefully resolved, and some were subject to different degrees of violence. Élite intransigence, encroaching haciendas, landless villages, dearth, and recession did not necessarily constitute causes that would arouse rebels and attract leadership.[53] The permanent structures of rural Mexico were more or less accepted; it was the extraordinary grievances or exceptional maladies that produced dissent and banditry. The source of protest can be classified in four types of conflict:[54] (1) administrative abuses and fiscal pressures involving confrontation between subjects and officials; (2) conditions on the land, usually landlords demanding more work for less pay, leading to disputes with day labourers, resident workers, and tenants; (3) changes in customary rights, often between haciendas and villages, or concerning mining practices; and (4) pressure on food supplies following harvest failure. When these conditions were present bandit chieftains could look for new recruits, and peasants who were more peacefully disposed would fear the worst.

Argentina, Venezuela, and Mexico each had its own agrarian history in the eighteenth century, but each experienced a common trend: the strengthening of the great estate—the estancia, the *hato*, and the hacienda—accompanied by renewed exploitation of resources and unwonted attacks upon tradition. Pressure and response

[52] Taylor, *Drinking, Homicide and Rebellion*, 115–16, 120.
[53] Hamnett, *Roots of Insurgency*, 44–6.
[54] These have been identified by Hamnett, ibid. 74–5, 77.

produced new types of informal leadership, the leadership of the hacendado and the leadership of the bandit. Clientelism could work both ways, not only for the landlord but also for the labourer. *Patrón*–peon became a sign of division as well as of unity, and the bond of kinship was available to the bandit as well as to the hacendado.

3. *Bandits and Guerrillas in the Hispanic World*

Few parts of the Hispanic world were free from banditry. It depended on rural conditions, police presence, and opportunities for gain. In the late eighteenth century opportunity was a strong seducer, as greater wealth and more crowded trade routes provided new attractions for criminals. A common pattern can be seen in both Spain and Spanish America, not only in the incidence of banditry but also in the transition from bandits to guerrillas, a transition marked by the outbreak of war or revolution, when rural leaders might acquire ideology, military command, and political ambitions.

In Spain bandoleros were the offspring of rural impoverishment, unpopular laws, and personal delinquency. Bands of robbers and criminals, virtually immune in the absence of a police force in the countryside, made many parts of southern Spain dangerous territory. Criminality was compounded by the activities of contrabandists, especially in the area of Cádiz, Málaga, the frontier with Gibraltar, and the inland mountain route of Antequera, Estepa, and Ecija. Large profits were to be made on goods subject to heavy duties, such as tobacco. A high tobacco tax and underpaid customs officials were a fatal combination, an open incitement to contraband; in the sierras armed bands of two to three hundred men operated with impunity, the military often looking the other way. In the region of Ecija well-armed smuggling bands about one hundred strong were capable of defeating military units and occupying towns while they sold their goods; these groups seldom robbed on the highway unless they needed horses and arms but in their chosen territory they were ruthless.[55] The growth of rural delinquency was closely related to worsening conditions of life for the Andalucian peasant and the contrasting affluence of the upper sectors, especially in the fertile

---

[55] Joseph Townsend, *A Journey through Spain in the Years 1786 and 1787*, 2nd edn. (3 vols.; London, 1792), ii. 305–7; iii. 47–8, 52.

valley of the Guadalquivir, where concentration of property continued to enrich the few and marginalize the many. Criminality was deeply rooted in Andalucía, and in Seville, Cádiz, and Málaga mugging, robbery, and attacks on persons and property were daily occurrences.[56] A typical profile of an Andalucian bandit chief was that of Diego Corrientes, a native of Utrera, a *jornalero* who came into conflict with the law and preferred to flee from justice to take his chance in the hills as a *capitán de bandidos*. Corrientes specialized in stealing horses from farms and haciendas and taking them to sell in Portugal, and for three years he operated successfully, gaining a popular reputation for dash and daring and generosity to the poor, until he was taken and executed in Seville in 1781 at the age of twenty-four.[57] The helplessness of the authorities was reflected in the fury of the retribution. The leaders of the *Tenazas* band, taken near Seville in 1794, were hanged and quartered, and their heads were displayed on the public highways.[58]

Spain was slightly ahead of Spanish America in making guerrillas out of bandits, but the two processes can be observed not so much in sequence as in parallel. During the war with France in 1793–5 Spanish irregular units included not only the traditional *miqueletes* and *somatenes* but even bands of contrabandists from the Sierra Morena. The smugglers were formed into an independent 'free corps', though not always with great success. One such unit, commanded by the later 'dictator' of Córdoba, Colonel Pedro Agustín Echávarri, was so undisciplined that it proved more dangerous to the civilian population than to the enemy.[59] But the day of the guerrillas finally arrived in the next war with the French, the war of independence.

Numerous guerrilla bands sprang up in Spain in 1809. Service with the bands offered 'more freedom and less discipline' than the regular army; men could fight without leaving their home front; and above all they could expect better material benefits, the Junta Central having decreed that all money seized from the French was the legitimate property of the guerrillas. So they became corsairs by land,

---

[56] Ibid. iii. 18.
[57] Constancio Bernaldo de Quirós and Luis Ardila, *El bandolerismo andaluz* (Madrid, 1973), 38–42
[58] Ibid. 54–6.
[59] Charles J. Esdaile, *The Spanish Army in the Peninsular War* (Manchester, 1988), 37, 91, 98.

and many guerrillas doubled as bandits, or vice versa, their activity giving rise to a popular slogan, '¡Viva Fernando y vamos robando!'[60] A number of contrabandists became guerrillas, but without abandoning their first career; indeed in the absence of authority this was now more lucrative. Contraband thus accompanied robbery and plunder as another way of waging war and rewarding followers. For all these reasons many recruits preferred to join the guerrillas rather than the regular army and, with the encouragement of the chieftains, many deserters from the army joined the guerrillas. The guerrillas attained their maximum importance in 1812 and by the end of that year they numbered over 38,000 organized into twenty-two different bands. Their main contribution to the war effort was to keep resistance alive in areas still awaiting Wellington's army, and to force the French to commit more troops to Spain than they had intended.[61]

Soon a number of caudillos emerged, leaders of bands and powers in their own lands. In the north the forces of Francisco Longa cleared the Basque coast with the help of a British naval squadron and captured Santander, while in Aragon the *partidas* of José Joaquín Durán and Ramón Gayán effectively harrassed the enemy. But the greatest victories were won by Francisco Espoz y Mina who built up a force nearly 10,000 strong in Navarre and pinned down the French in Pamplona.[62] Mina was a complete caudillo in the sense that he went beyond military action to assume a political role. He established an effective provincial administration, complete with its own hospitals, arms workshops, and retail outlets for sale of goods imported from France to help the patriot cause. Mina invented a simple system of raising funds for his guerrillas: he established a chain of customs posts which charged all traders, legitimate or not, a duty on their goods in exchange for protection. And Navarre became known to merchants for the law and order that prevailed, in contrast to the bandit-infested Andalucía. The very success of Mina led to ruthless power struggles with rival caudillos and at the same time forced the French to strike back; they inflicted severe reverses on the caudillo forces in Navarre, though at the cost of their own strength in front

---

[60] Ibid. 139, 141; Jean-René Aymes, *La Guerre d'Indépendence espagnole (1808–1814)* (Paris, 1973), 50–6.

[61] Gabriel H. Lovett, *Napoleon and the Birth of Modern Spain* (2 vols.; New York, 1965), ii. 666–709; Esdaile, *The Spanish Army in the Peninsular War*, 161, 163–4.

[62] Francisco Espoz y Mina, *Memorias*, ed. M. Artola (BAE 146–7; Madrid, 1961–2); José María Iribárren, *Espoz y Mina, el guerrillero* (Madrid, 1965), 121–5; Lovett, *Napoleon and the Birth of Modern Spain*, ii. 709–19.

of Wellington and without preventing the guerrillas from making a come-back in Aragon.

Guerrillas had built-in weaknesses. The first was lack of co-ordination. Many chieftains were as intent on establishing themselves as caudillos in their own localities as they were on fighting the French: they suppressed any rival bands who intruded to challenge them and refused to accept the authority of the military commanders. Moreover, their recruiting campaigns weakened the Spanish regular forces by drawing off valuable manpower.[63] These features anticipated uncannily the personal and policy problems which Bolívar would face from the caudillos in Venezuela. There were further points of resemblance. Large numbers of the Spanish *partidas* remained little more than bandits who preyed on their countrymen as much as they did on the enemy, exactly as their contemporaries were doing in Venezuela and Mexico. And in the ultimate analysis guerrillas could only win permanent victories when integrated into larger units and supported by regular armies. These features too were reproduced in Spanish America.

The bands reflected social structure and were not necessarily heroes to the people among whom they had to live and whom they often failed to protect. The Spanish caudillos were not popular leaders, sons of the people, or fighters for justice. They were rarely ordinary peasants, for the patriarchal nature of Spanish society ensured that they generally had to be men of some substance in the local community for their leadership to be accepted. Many of the guerrilla leaders were actually regular officers wedded to military privilege and firm for the *fuero*.[64] After the war they wanted their reward. Mina, however, was denied the viceroyalty of Navarre and publicly repudiated by Ferdinand VII; he returned to Pamplona and made a vain attempt to raise the garrison in a caudillo-type revolt before fleeing to France.

The Spanish model of bandit and guerrilla is relevant to the study of Spanish American caudillism, not as a direct influence, much less a causal factor, for which there is no evidence and little probability. Rather it was a parallel development arising out of similar conditions and supported by social and economic structures common to the whole Hispanic world. Pressure on land, power to the landlords,

---

[63] Esdaile, *The Spanish Army in the Peninsular War*, 161.
[64] Ibid. 178, 197.

ejection of the peasants, gaps in government authority, these tended
to destabilize rural areas and encourage the formation of bands
organized for subsistence and plunder under natural leaders who
assembled a client network and proved themselves by their success.
Bandits were incipient guerrillas, their leaders caudillos in miniature.
According to Jorge Escobedo, senior Spanish official and expert
on colonial affairs, there was an inherent public-order problem in
America, for its people were naturally insubordinate, and 'the intendants could not even move a paving stone in the street without being
resisted'; so America needed strong government, which it did not
always receive, and private power seeped into the gaps.[65] Responding
to similar conditions and challenges, rural groups and their leaders
bred similar types, and bandits and guerrillas made their appearance
on both sides of the Atlantic. In Spain the guerrilla chiefs and local
caudillos made no claims to popular status but regarded themselves
as part of the élites. In Spanish America, on the other hand, some
chieftains nurtured popular pretensions and others have had these
qualities attributed to them by later historians.

Spanish American bandits are sometimes measured against the
model of the social bandit, that pre-political rebel born of social
division, deprivation, and injustice, regarded as a criminal by lords
and governments, but protected as a hero and fighter for justice by
peasant communities. Social banditry had no ideology and looked
back to a traditional social order, not forward to a revolutionary
one.[66] Spanish American bandits had some affinity with this social
type but parted company at key points.

In the Río de la Plata the gauchos bore some of the marks of the
social bandit. They were victims of social conflict and outcasts in
their own land, as the authorities enforced the interests of powerful
ranchers and left the deprived with few alternatives outside the
montoneros. The gauchos looked backwards to traditional customs, not
forward to revolutionary claims. And many turned to the life of the
outlaw because of a particular incident of injustice or oppression at
the hands of the military or civil authorities. But the gauchos were
not social bandits or heroes of rural communities. They followed a
lone existence, practising gratuitous violence and living by the knife

---

[65] Jorge Escobedo, 'Manifiesto', Madrid, 2 Aug. 1802, BN, MS 3073, fos. 25–6.
[66] Eric J. Hobsbawm, *Primitive Rebels: Studies in Archaic Forms of Social Movement in
the Nineteenth and Twentieth Centuries* (Manchester, 1959), 13–29; and the same
author's *Bandits* (New York, 1981), 151–2.

and the lance; they were part of a marginal frontier society, without the link of the bandit to the peasant and without a base among the rural masses; and their purpose gave no hint of popular distribution of gains.[67] In contrast Peruvian bandits in the environs of Lima came unmistakably from the popular sectors, in particular from the mixed races, within the heart of colonial society, operating between the coastal valleys and the viceregal capital.[68] Yet these too lacked class motivation and were just as capable of terrorizing their own people as they were of attacking the rich; and in the absence of any political allies they remained addicted to plunder rather than protest.

In the Venezuelan llanos cattle rustling, robbery, and other forms of conflict were a way of life for the llanero in a frontier society where violence ruled and anarchy prevailed. Unlike social bandits, llaneros were not the protegés of peasant society but an independent people. Although they were classified as criminals by colonial authorities, they were creatures of the frontier wedded to custom and tradition rather than social bandits defying oppression. But further subdivisions are required; just as there were *gauchos malos*, so there were delinquent llaneros. In fact the historian can distinguish between three types. Some remained and took their punishment or endured their misery, though their docility was lack of power to protest rather than happiness with their life. Others joined a band and sought a livelihood outside the law. And yet others, having committed a crime within civil society, fled to the mountains and joined a *partida*. Such was the band operating along the Apure river in 1789, 'a strong *partida* of robbers numbering about sixty and including whites, mulattos, and Indians', and too elusive to be taken by ill-armed security forces. In the region of Pao bandits enjoyed the protection and succour of strong family networks, which made them difficult to capture and to hold.[69] Any of these could graduate from bandit to guerrilla, given the opportunity of war and revolution.

---

[67] Richard W. Slatta, *Gauchos and the Vanishing Frontier* (Lincoln, Nebr., 1983), 118–25, and *Bandidos*, 49, 65, 191–8.

[68] Alberto Flores Galindo, *Aristocracia y plebe: Lima 1760–1830* (Lima, 1984), 139–48, 235; Carmen Vivanco Lara, 'Bandolerismo colonial peruano: 1760–1810', in Carlos Aguirre and Charles Walker (eds.), *Bandoleros, abigeos y montoneros: Criminalidad y violencia en el Perú, siglos XVIII–XX* (Lima, 1990), 25–56.

[69] Draft Circular to magistrate of Calabozo, Caracas, 14 April 1789, AGN Caracas, Gobernación y Capitanía General, vol. xli, 1789, fo. 257; magistrate of Pao to Governor, 13 June 1789, ibid. fos. 30, 95. See also Izard and Slatta, 'Banditry and Social Conflict', in Slatta (ed.), *Bandidos*, 33–47.

The interior zones of Argentina and Venezuela were classic frontiers of settlement, where in the course of the eighteenth century land and cattle were commercialized, communal usages eroded, and the people of the plains pushed into poverty and peonage. Government agencies were thin on the ground and officials fleeting figures. There was space for domination and for resistance. Local heroes of the élites and of the people could raise their heads, mobilize their bands, and go into action without colliding at every turn with intendants and institutions. These were the proto-sites of bandits, guerrillas, and eventually caudillos.

Mexico was different. What in Venezuela was a loss of peasant prerogatives, in Mexico was a crisis of subsistence. But here too the rural masses used banditry more for economic survival than prepolitical protest. The advance of the hacienda and the retreat of the peasant were real enough, but crime was a way of escape and an expression of personal opportunism, not necessarily a blow for peasant interests. Bandits appeared when there were gaps in royal administration and, after independence, weakness in the central government, rather than as a form of social protest.[70] And unemployment in itself did not create criminals. Banditry could be a by-product of economic growth. When deprivation for some coincided with prosperity for others, then conditions were ripe for delinquency, and day labourers, dispossessed peasants, and unemployed artisans became ready recruits into outlaw bands.

The later Bourbon period was a time of increased trade, greater movement of goods on the highways, and more opportunities and temptations for bandits to gain instant wealth and cash. This was the background to the upsurge of banditry in New Galicia, especially around Guadalajara, in the last decades of the colony.[71] The bandido was not the same as the *vago*, who was usually the victim of economic stagnation and recession. Vagrants were at the margin of society but still within it. Beyond were the bandits, no doubt recruiting greater numbers, including vagrants, when recession followed growth, and opportunity for lawful occupation diminished; this would account for the increased incidents of banditry which occurred in the unstable

---

[70] Paul J. Vanderwood, 'Nineteenth-Century Mexico's Profiteering Bandits', in Slatta (ed.), *Bandidos*, 11–31.
[71] William B. Taylor, 'Bandit Gangs in Late Colonial Times: Rural Jalisco, Mexico, 1794–1821', in Paul J. Vanderwood (ed.), 'Social Banditry and Spanish American Independence', *Biblioteca Americana*, 1, 2 (1982), 37–56.

conditions of the 1790s and 1800s. Banditry was not a class movement. Landlords sometimes struck deals with bandit chiefs, buying
protection, or receiving stolen goods, or collaborating in contraband.[72]
Bandits attacked villages as well as haciendas; and villagers might
prefer to hunt bandits for a reward rather than pay them protection
money. This indicates that much banditry was pure criminality, and
few regions of Mexico were without criminals. Zacatecas and the
Bajío had their share of bandit groups and highway robbers. In
Guadalajara and Valladolid brigands raided royal tax offices and
robbed travellers.[73] Viceroy Branciforte (1794–7) made efforts to
extirpate banditry, fearing that it might prove to be the prelude to a
general insurrection; this was alarmist, and many of the bandits
captured turned out to be army deserters. As a form of defiance
banditry, like rebellion, was a local not a general phenonemon. To
acquire a political role and a caudillo's status a bandit
chief would need to expand his horizons.

4. *Absolute Monarchy: The Sole Arbitrator*

In Spain the caudillo, as a type who graduated from informal leadership to a military role, and added political pretensions to his military
success, did not exist under the old regime. The sovereignty of the
king, the authority of his ministers, and the omnipresence of the
bureaucracy left few gaps for the insertion of private power or the
exercise of personal authority. No doubt the combination of a large
estate and seigneurial jurisdiction gave a great lord considerable
power over peasants, villages, and even towns, but by the eighteenth
century this was essentially an economic power and in the ultimate
analysis even the highest aristocrat was subject to the sovereign and
his law courts. It needed the war of independence from 1808, the
deposition of the legitimate monarch, the collapse of his government,
and the spread of public anarchy, to convert the bandit into a guerrilla
and to raise the guerrilla chief to the status of caudillo.

The same was true of Spanish America. The Laws of the Indies
were the king's laws and they were obeyed for that reason. The great

---

[72] Hamnett, *Roots of Insurgency*, 64–5.
[73] Christon I. Archer, *The Army in Bourbon Mexico, 1760–1810* (Albuquerque, NM, 1977), 91–2.

divisions of empire were headed by viceroys, who had under them presidents, governors, captains-general, *audiencias, corregidores, alcaldes mayores*, and latterly intendants. Between these officials and the minor bureaucrats assisting them there was little room for personal political domains and no justification for the cult of caudillism. The colonial state became more absolutist in the years after 1760, when Charles III and his ministers pressed harder on the colonies for revenue and resources. The Bourbon vision of empire allowed no political space between the imperial state and its American subjects. Viceroys, who had previously acted as informal brokers between the claims of the crown and the interests of local oligarchies, now issued non-negotiable demands. But the king's government remained a civilian government which derived its legitimacy from historic authority and habits of obedience rather than from military force. Force existed and could be summoned if needed, though Spain did not have the resources to maintain large garrisons of regular troops in America.

From 1760 a new militia was developed, and to encourage recruits members were admitted to the *fuero militar*, giving them the same protection of military law as that enjoyed by the regular army, and creating the possibility of military dominance at the expense of civil jurisdiction. Imperial defence and internal security were increasingly committed to creole officers and troops of mixed race, a weapon which might ultimately be turned against Spain. The imperial government was aware of these dangers, which were never as great as they appeared, and sought to ensure that military privilege was not dispensed indiscriminately to Americans, and that the preference in favour of Spaniards for civil office was also applied to higher military commands. In these circumstances there was little possibility of the emergence of an autonomous creole military.[74]

But there is a further question. Was the Bourbon state in America a militarized state? If Spaniards were preferred for high military rank, were the Spanish military also preferred for senior civil offices? Out of twenty-six intendants in the Río de la Plata between 1782 and 1810, seventeen had been army officers, three naval officers, three

---

[74] Ibid. 28–31, 191–222; Allan J. Kuethe, *Military Reform and Society in New Granada, 1773–1808* (Gainesville, Fla., 1978), 5–6, 185–7. Gary M. Miller, 'Status and Loyalty of Regular Army Officers in Late Colonial Venezuela', *HAHR* 66, 4 (1986), 667–96, argues that in Venezuela Spanish army officers suffered from declining financial rewards and in 1808 were ready to exchange royal patronage for that of the local élites.

lawyers, and three professional bureaucrats.[75] In Peru some 40 per cent of the intendants had a military background.[76] A number of viceroys in Mexico, Peru, and the Río de la Plata also had military credentials and were capable of acting as professional soldiers. Yet what does this mean? A new trend in royal government? A militarization of the colonial bureaucracy? The aristocracy in Spain dominated the higher military. As the aristocracy were also the first choice for viceroyalties, it would not be surprising if the status of soldier and aristocrat sometimes coincided in appointments. At the next social level, the best graduates, lawyers, and bureaucrats sought jobs in the peninsula not in the colonies; outside of this élite a military career was one of the few on which a Spaniard could base a good curriculum vitae if he were reconciled to a career in America. The vital test was the action of officials, not their provenance. Viceroys and intendants applied royal laws and civil policies, all of them endlessly debated by bureaucrats in Madrid. American offices remained civil offices, subject to civil jurisdiction. And the *audiencias*, dominated by university-trained lawyers, remained powerful constraints on executive officials. There was, in short, no serious evidence of a militarization of American government and society under the Bourbons. In any case, as has been seen, militarism—the intervention of the military in politics and the dominance of the military in the state—is not the same as caudillism. The historian looks in vain for a glimpse of a caudillo in the colonial bureaucracy or the colonial army.

This leaves the private sector. It has been suggested that there were two types of caudillos in colonial Spanish America: leaders of popular rebellions and oligarchic leaders who exerted economic, social, and political control over the men and resources of great estates.[77] Powerful persons of course existed and flourished, especially among the owners of haciendas remote from centres of bureaucracy. But unlike their counterparts in Spain, hacendados in America did not possess seigneurial jurisdiction. And in spite of their economic resources, they did not attempt to appoint officials, appropriate taxes,

---

[75] John Lynch, *Spanish Colonial Administration, 1782–1810: The Intendant System in the Viceroyalty of the Río de la Plata* (London, 1958), 73–4.

[76] John Fisher, *Government and Society in Colonial Peru: The Intendant System 1784–1814* (London, 1970), 239–50.

[77] Migual Izard, 'Tanto pelear para terminar conversando: El caudillismo en Venezuela', *Nova Americana*, 2 (1979), 46–7.

create policy, destabilize the imperial bureaucracy, or challenge the legitimate authorities. They had too much to lose to risk all in insubordination, preferring to operate as manipulators rather than caudillos.

Sometimes authority was challenged from below and the challenge grew into violent protest. Spanish officials referred to rebel leaders as 'capitanes', sometimes as 'caudillos', and more often without any particular designation. The leaders of the *comuneros* in New Granada and Venezuela called themselves 'capitanes' and gave their subordinates lesser military ranks. In Peru Tupac Amaru already held office as a cacique and appeared to claim a greater title than this. In 1781, among the shock waves of the rebellion of Tupac Amaru, the intendant of Salta, Andrés Mestre, reported that creole leadership was behind a minor movement in Jujuy:

A creole traitor of Santiago called Josef Quiroga seduced the greater part of the common people and managed to induce 200 Christian creoles to leave their work and join the Indians in the reduction of Tovas, whose simple minds he persuaded that the time had come to throw off the yoke and domination of the Spaniards and it would be easy to destroy these and take possession of their families and possessions. To accomplish this arduous object, the Caudillo advised the Tovas to seek the support and friendship of the Mataca people.[78]

Mestre took prompt and ruthless action and executed seventeen rebels, but failed to take Quiroga 'the principal caudillo of the movement'.[79]

Urban uprisings and rural rebellions were inherent in the history of eighteenth-century Spanish America, part of the expectations of colonial government, and part of the experience of most social sectors, creoles, *campesinos*, ethnic groups, and slaves.[80] Most of these rebellions had individual leaders: Juan Francisco de León in Venezuela in 1749; Tupac Amaru in Peru in 1780; Juan Francisco Berbeo and José Antonio Galán in New Granada in 1781. Some of the leaders, notably Tupac Amaru, drew on kinship and client networks for their core support and sought to extend their base by

---

[78] Andrés Mestre to Gálvez, Jujuy, 24 Apr. 1781, AGI, Buenos Aires 143.

[79] Mestre to Viceroy Vertiz, Jujuy, 24 Apr. 1781, in Manuel de Odriozola (ed.), *Documentos históricos del Perú* (10 vols.; Lima, 1863–79), i. 357.

[80] Anthony McFarlane, 'Civil Disorders and Popular Protests in Late Colonial New Granada', *HAHR* 64, 1 (1984), 22–7, and 'The "Rebellion of the Barrios": Urban Insurrection in Bourbon Quito' *HAHR* 69, 2 (1989), 328–30.

promises and policies to particular interest groups such as muleteers, small farmers, miners, and artisans.[81] They employed violence to secure their objectives, and in the case of Tupac Amaru seemed to have a political as well as a social goal. At this point resemblance to the caudillo ceases. Colonial rebellions tended to be coalitions of disparate forces rather than closely linked networks of faithful followers; the bond of clientage was less secure than it was in caudillism. The authority of the rebel leaders was not the absolute power of the caudillo over his band but one diluted by the great variety of aims, responses, and solidarity within the rebel ranks. Even the position of Tupac Amaru was ambiguous and his perception of himself unclear. Was he an agent of the king of Spain, or an Inca with his own royal power? In either case, he had a bias towards legitimate rather than personalist authority, and he did not resemble a caudillo. The programmes of most of the rebel leaders were not designed to seize power from the existing government and retain it by force. Rather they were statements of protest against abuse of authority by the colonial state, against tax collectors, officials, administrative and fiscal innovations, and they sought to persuade the colonial government to return to more traditional practices and policies, not to step down and make way for a new regime. As for results, these were leaders of temporary movements, not the authors of an alternative government. Any sighting of the caudillo in the colonial period, therefore, is a mirage.

Colonial government and society were scenes of intense competition. Rivalries between jealous officials, disputes between landowners and merchants, tension between proprietors and peons and between whites and castes, and contention between regions for priority in the imperial order, these were the routines of colonial life, and the occasion of a ceaseless flow of documents between America and Spain. Agitation and protest encouraged the growth of interest groups, any of which, individually or in alliance, could conceivably generate leaders to resolve differences by persuasion or force. But the role was pre-empted. There was already a sovereign arbitrator, the king, whose authority was universally accepted, whose legitimacy was not disputed, and whose mediation between conflicting claims was a traditional function of monarchy. As long as the monarch was

---

[81] Scarlett O'Phelan Godoy, *Rebellions and Revolts in Eighteenth Century Peru and Upper Peru* (Cologne, 1985), 218–19, 228–43, 260–1.

in his palace, his officials at their desks, and his military at their posts, there was no room for the caudillo. The fall of the Bourbons in 1808, however, left America a desert empty of traditional laws and institutions. Now there were wide political spaces to be filled, and the essential conditions for informal leadership were at last in place. Once caudillos became possible, they soon became inevitable, and the age of absolutism gave way to the age of caudillism.

2
INDEPENDENCE: NURSERY
OF CAUDILLOS

The caudillo was a child of war and a product of independence. When, in 1808, the French invasion of Spain severed the metropolis from its colonies and created a crisis of authority among its subjects, the political landscape was transformed and familiar signposts disappeared. Viceroys were deposed, *audiencias* dispersed, intendants killed. In capital and country colonial institutions were demolished, to be replaced at first by nothing then by makeshift substitutes. In highland Peru, as he moved his army in search of the Spanish enemy after the battle of Junín, General Sucre reported to Bolívar: 'I have just arrived here to find not a single magistrate nor any authority to deal with, because they have all fled; so I am unable to give you precise news of the resources available in this province, only what the inhabitants have told me'.[1] As the colonial state collapsed and institutions perished, social groups competed to fill the vacuum.[2] The wars of independence incorporated two processes, the constitutionalism of the politicians and the personal power of the caudillos, and they were fought with two arms, regular forces and local guerrillas. These movements were part allies, part rivals. To compete and rule in such circumstances a soldier had to be a politician, and politicians had to control the soldiers. The wars were a struggle for power as well as for independence.

The armies of liberation were not professional armies but informal systems of obedience in which various interest groups were brought together by military chieftains. There was now a progression from plainsman, to vagrant, to bandit, to guerrilla fighter, as local proprietors or new leaders sought to recruit followers. While such bands might enlist under one political cause or another, the underlying factors were still rural conditions and personal leadership. The logic and chronology of these processes varied throughout Spanish

---

[1] Sucre to secretary general of Bolívar, Challuanca, 24 Sept. 1824, in O'Leary, *Memorias*, xxii. 498.
[2] Gilmore, *Caudillism and Militarism in Venezuela*, 47, 69–70, 107.

America. In some regions liberators arrived who could recruit bands
into battalions. In others extraordinary leaders arose who dictated
events and moulded local interests to their policies. In the Río de la
Plata, on the other hand, caudillos emerged in two stages, first as
delegates of the centre in the war effort against Spain, then as leaders
of the regions in conflict with the centre.

1. *Río de la Plata: Delegates and Dissenters*

The revolution of May 1810 in Buenos Aires was a civilian movement with a military power base. The leadership quickly moved to
sever relations with Spain and, in the capital at least, to dismantle the
colonial state. The viceroy was replaced by a junta, the *audiencia* by
a republican tribunal, the Spanish bureaucracy by local appointees.
In the following years the executive changed form—and changed
hands—many times, but it did not lose its revolutionary credentials
or abandon its twin objectives, a liberal system in a unitary state.[3]
The new leaders were professional revolutionaries, men who saw
independence as a career as well as a policy and who promoted
individual as well as collective interests. They needed allies, in particular a militia to protect the revolution at home and an army to carry
it abroad. In creating these things they enhanced the importance of
the armed forces and increased the prestige, and the budget, of the
military; for these too the revolution became a business.[4] In the
hands of professional politicians like Bernardino Rivadavia and career
officers like José de San Martín the May Revolution was a respectable revolution. The idea of taking orders from wild men on horseback or of sharing power with gaucho caudillos would have seemed
preposterous.

The first wave of revolutionary expansion followed the same model
and was accomplished through political and military action rather
than the agency of caudillos. It soon became obvious, however, that
the May Revolution was not immediately popular among regional
élites, whose political, social, and economic interests were often

---

[3] David Bushnell, *Reform and Reaction in the Platine Provinces 1810–1852* (Gainesville,
Fla., 1983), 8–19.
[4] Tulio Halperín Donghi, *Politics, Economics and Society in Argentina in the Revolutionary Period* (Cambridge, 1975), 191, 200.

different from those of the capital. Buenos Aires dispatched expeditionary forces to Upper Peru, Paraguay, and the Banda Oriental. In Upper Peru the *porteño* armies were received with suspicion by the creoles and violence by the royalists; the defeat of General Belgrano in 1813 with the loss of 3,000 men and desertion of many others severely curtailed the prospects of the revolution in the north-west. To its own interior provinces Buenos Aires sent emissaries not armies. In Tucumán and Cuyo its political agents were forced to delegate power to local oligarchies and to leave the revolution in the hands of conservative interests and their dependent militias.

The combination of royalist pressure and regional resistance forced Buenos Aires to rethink its political strategy and to inaugurate a new phase of revolutionary expansion in the years 1815–20. It could not win the war in the north-west without the collaboration of the interior and without the men and supplies which only the interior could supply. To secure these it had to delegate authority to local officials and militias who made the war effort their own but who identified with the province rather than the capital. Thus the central government itself encouraged the growth of regional autonomy and initiative; the demands of war and the need for men and supplies forced it to grant exceptional freedom to its local agents, whom it had to recruit among those who already possessed adequate power and prestige in their own districts.[5] These were the seeds of regional caudillism.

The interaction of frontier warfare and local conditions was first seen in Salta where the central government resigned itself to fighting a defensive war and elected to do so with local resources. To achieve this it co-opted a regional caudillo who would collaborate at least in defence of the revolution and who had the status to mobilize his province and tap its reserves of men, agriculture, and livestock. Martín Güemes, a creole officer and landowner in Salta, came from a family whose background in land and office was typical of the Argentine caudillos. Success on the frontier earned him military promotion by the central government and approval from the local *cabildo*, which asserted its own identity in appointing him governor of Salta. His political legitimacy strengthened his personal position as landowner and patrón and enabled him to attract a military force from the whole province. For over five years, from 1815, Güemes governed Salta

[5] Ibid. 262–3.

with a large measure of autonomy from Buenos Aires and the support of the popular sectors as well as of his élite allies. As the region continued to be a theatre of war against royalist forces in Upper Peru, part of the gaucho population was permanently mobilized into rural militias. These preyed upon local estancias and rich merchants, seizing crops, cattle, and other property, while Güemes himself issued decrees requisitioning cattle, confiscating goods, and levying compulsory donations to the war effort.

How did this system of government manage to survive? In the first place it had the support of the central government. Once the campaign against Upper Peru was abandoned as unfeasible, Güemes undertook the defence of the frontier at minimum expense by making the Salta aristocracy pay for it. The conservative governments in Buenos Aires, therefore, were prepared to tolerate his autonomist leanings and populist policies as a necessary defence of the revolution.[6] In the second place Güemes was the representative of a powerful group of Salta families related by kinship and interest.[7] These, of course, were exempt from his plunder, and ultimately participated in the actions of their caudillo until his death in action in 1821.

Meanwhile the Güemes system had been subverted from within. As the royalist danger receded, so the natural inclination of these ranching communities towards family feuds reasserted itself; the most powerful estancieros prevailed and sought to express themselves through new caudillos. But the Güemes experience illustrated a further truth. In addition to reflecting environment, conditions, and personal ambition, the caudillos also responded to shortage of funds. Regular armies had to be clothed, fed, and paid, in default of which desertion was automatic. Caudillos did not have to clothe their followers; they fed them off the land, and they promised them payment in loot. They too suffered losses, but not so much from desertion as from temporary absenteeism during harvest time. Caudillism was a cheaper form of waging war. The governments in Buenos Aires quickly learnt this lesson, but in applying it they fashioned a weapon that would subsequently be used against themselves. In the hands of some of the caudillos it was a fearsome weapon. Facundo Quiroga, the Tiger of the Pampas, became a tiger who could not be controlled,

---

[6] Ibid. 64–9.
[7] Roger M. Haigh, *Martín Güemes: Tyrant or Tool? A Study of the Sources of Power of an Argentine Caudillo* (Fort Worth, Tex., 1968), 51–2.

yet he too began his political life as the government's agent in La Rioja.

La Rioja was a primitive province, its capital squalid, its country-side a desert. But it had resources which could be turned to war and the government wanted them: livestock, mules, a transport sector, arable agriculture, and potential mineral wealth that might compensate for the loss of Potosí. The rural economy was dominated by powerful estancieros, fighting each other for finite resources and now resentful of the loss of traditional trading outlets in Chile and Upper Peru. Quiroga came from such a family, one which had frequently held municipal and military office during the colony and under the revolution.[8] He had the status and power, therefore, to command this reservoir of war supplies and mobilize it for the north-west frontier. He began modestly enough, succeeding his father in 1816 as captain of militia in San Antonio de los Llanos and becoming commandant of Malanzán in 1818. In both offices he needed an armed force around him to enable him to carry out his duties. These were to recruit troops and assemble cattle for the army of the north, tasks which gave him great initiative and power, either to collaborate with the government or remain aloof, to spare estancias or exploit them, to declare a man a worker or a vagrant, a peon or a soldier.[9] It was during these years of delegated authority in the service of the revolutionary government that men like Quiroga, already powerful landowners, acquired military and political credentials, and became *señores de horca y cuchillo*.[10] At this stage the caudillo arose not against the structure of power at the centre but within it.

Güemes and Quiroga, however, were not the only models of caudillos, nor the western provinces their only region. In the littoral, where the caudillo Artigas headed a loose federation of riverine neighbours resistant rather than responsive to Buenos Aires, a different process was at work, one more immediately linked to economic interests. If the provinces of the interior wanted protection for their economies, those of Sante Fe, Entre Ríos, and Corrientes, whose products were similar to the estancia resources of Buenos Aires, wanted freedom of trade and also demanded direct access to the sea

[8] *Archivo del brigadier general Juan Facundo Quiroga* (4 vols.; Buenos Aires, 1957–88), i. 36–8.
[9] Tulio Halperín Donghi, 'El surgimiento de los caudillos en el marco de la sociedad rioplatense postrevolucionaria', *Estudios de Historia Social*, 1 (1965), 121–49.
[10] David Peña, *Juan Facundo Quiroga*, 2nd edn. (Buenos Aires, 1971), 59–69.

by the rivers Uruguay and Paraná. They also resented handing over revenue and troops to Buenos Aires for a war not only against Spain but also against neighbouring Uruguay, many of whose political objectives they shared. They saw Buenos Aires as a new colonial power, monopolizing one port of entry and exit for the whole country. They remained aloof from the declaration of 'the independence of the United Provinces of South America' in 1816, and rejected the strongly centralized Constitution of 1819, which singularly favoured the city and province of Buenos Aires. Conditions were ripe for caudillism. There was no one to arbitrate: in the absence of a national state provincial autonomies proliferated and a number of small republics emerged, their governments sustained by dominant interest groups and led by a local chief.

The caudillo of Santa Fe, Estanislao López, owed his ascendancy less to his origins than to his personal qualities. He was a professional soldier, a leader who could resist pressure from Buenos Aires, contain the danger on the Indian frontier, and reassure estancieros on the maintenance of law and order in the countryside, in short a caudillo attentive to the major problems of his constituency. He declared in August 1819: 'We wish to form a small republic in the heart of our territory.'[11] He sought to secure free navigation of the rivers and to draw revenue from provincial-based customs duties. In fact López never established an independent republic and he gradually became reconciled to a larger national organization. But across the River Paraná, in Entre Ríos, Francisco Ramírez came nearer to success. Ramírez was the son of an estanciero of Arroyo Grande, whose family origin in land, trade, and royal service was the classical background of the caudillo, and enabled him to pass easily from service to the king to enrolment in the revolution.[12] Entre Ríos was a zone of new colonization, an expanding livestock area, with an estanciero class which controlled local office and the militia, while the commerce of the province was dominated by Buenos Aires. The conflict between Artigas and Buenos Aires brought war to Entre Ríos and made Ramírez a caudillo, representing the interests of the local ruling class. He came to define an independent position for Entre

---

[11] Emilio Ravignani, *Historia constitucional de la República Argentina*, 2nd edn. (3 vols.; Buenos Aires, 1930), ii. 819; see also Leoncio Gianello, *Estanislao López* (Santa Fe, NM, 1955).

[12] Halperín Donghi, *Politics, Economics and Society in Argentina*, 291–4, 308–30.

Ríos, free alike of the depredations of Buenos Aires and the populism of Artigas. His state was ruled by a *Jefe Supremo*, a kind of military dictatorship emanating from one man, who reassured conservative estancieros and protected them from outside pressures. In 1820 he founded the Republic of Entre Ríos with its own customs houses for direct trade with Europe. In the event, Ramírez did not have the political ability to rule an independent state; but if the experiment was short-lived the principles survived.

The caudillos of Argentina demanded autonomy rather than secession and preferred to detest Buenos Aires rather than desert it. In Uruguay the revolution took a different course. There the leading creoles sought freedom from Buenos Aires as well as from Spain, convinced that a new and more proximate dependence was at hand. These convictions were articulated by José Gervasio Artigas, a gaucho caudillo, whose career followed a familiar pattern. He was born to a landowning and military family in Montevideo, and started adult life as leader of a band of rustlers operating near the Brazilian frontier, from which he graduated to the rural police and the royal service.[13] By 1810 he was a man of some stature in the Banda Oriental and a recognized rural leader. In February 1811 he joined the independence movement in Buenos Aires, whose government gave him a small force to revolutionize the Banda Oriental. At this point, therefore, Buenos Aires treated Artigas, if not as an official delegate, at least as a revolutionary emissary. But soon he moved beyond this position. He came to command the vanguard of the patriot forces that defeated the Spaniards but then found that Buenos Aires and Portuguese Brazil had rival designs on their country, and that Buenos Aires was ready to make a deal with the Spaniards in order to keep out Portugal.

The power base of Artigas's movement was the estanciero class, whose opposition to imperial fiscal and land policy coincided with the interests of their province and the patriotism of their leader.[14] They trusted Artigas because of his own estanciero origins and because of his military success before 1811 in bringing law and order to the countryside. But Artigas also had a large popular following. He was proclaimed by his followers *Jefe de los Orientales* and, in the shadow of three enemies, they followed him across the River Uruguay to Entre

---

[13] *Archivo Artigas* (Montevideo, 1951), vol. ii, pt. 1.
[14] Halperín Donghi, *Politics, Economics and Society in Argentina*, 269–88; Eduardo Azcuy Ameghino, *Artigas en la historia argentina* (Buenos Aires, 1986), 31–55.

Ríos. It was a memorable withdrawal, a triumph in defeat. Artigas marched out of his homeland with 4,000 troops. He was followed in addition by 4,000 civilians, including landowners who abandoned their properties, fearful of Spanish reprisals and Portuguese brutality, people who sought independence in exile, leaving behind a scorched earth and an empty land.[15] This great Exodus of the Oriental People was a display of provincial (if not popular) sovereignty, an announcement in effect that the Banda Oriental preferred secession to subordination and would serve neither Spain nor Buenos Aires. Yet this act of defiance would have remained an empty gesture had it not been identified with a leader who had a purpose and a policy. Artigas claimed that he had already been chosen as leader by the people of Uruguay, who had appointed him 'as their general in chief', as indeed they had.[16] The Exodus confirmed his leadership and placed him at the head of an independent people. It also established his social credentials as a caudillo of the poor as well as of the rich, a protector of Indians as well as of creoles.

In the following years Artigas had three enemies, the Portuguese, the Spaniards, and the *porteños*. The Portuguese were forced to withdraw by British diplomacy. The Spaniards were defeated in Montevideo by Buenos Aires. And Buenos Aires was obliged to turn over Montevideo to Artigas, who now occupied the countryside. By 1815, therefore, resistance to old and new imperialists had transformed Artigas from a regional to a national caudillo. At last he ruled the Provincia Oriental, the *Patria Vieja*, as it came to be called.[17] He sought to disguise his absolutism and to establish, in appearance at least, a balance between personal power and élite participation. He did not place much confidence in the merchants and landowners of Montevideo, nor they in him. But he entrusted the government of Montevideo to its town council, the *cabildo*, and scrupulously respected its authority, while he personally concentrated on general policy, military organization, and rural development. It was an awesome task in a province ravaged by five years of war, its livestock reduced, its trade depressed. But Artigas sought to repair the destruction and to develop his country anew. He wanted to promote the economy of the whole of the Río de la Plata on the basis of freedom of trade for the

---

[15] John Street, *Artigas and the Emancipation of Uruguay* (Cambridge, 1959), 147–52.
[16] Eugenio Petit Muñoz, *Artigas: Federalismo y soberanía* (Montevideo, 1988), 68.
[17] Eduardo Acevedo, *José Artigas: Su obra cívica, Alegato histórico* (3 vols.; Montevideo, 1950), 465–553.

provinces in general and for Uruguay in particular, and with this in mind he encouraged an active British trade. But Artigas was interested in the distribution of wealth as well as its creation. The social policy of the regime was exceptionally radical for the Río de la Plata. Federalism in itself had social implications. Provincial resistance to centralism had to be paid for; the rich were pressed for donations, property and produce raided, peons recruited. The caudillos, like Buenos Aires itself, would try to attract slaves to their forces by offering emancipation in return for service. Artigas too appealed to the slaves, in southern Brazil as well as in his own province. This further alarmed people of property and caused a British observer to conclude that his 'popularity, although considerable, is entirely confined to the lower orders of the community'.[18] But what most alarmed the estancieros was the agrarian radicalism of Artigas and his determination not only to revive the rural economy but to grant land to his rural followers, a policy which caused Mitre to describe him 'the caudillo of vandalism and of semi-barbarous federation'.[19]

Artigas had a special skill in utilizing the marginal population as a political and military power base. There were no immediate political returns from his pro-Indian policy, but he recruited Indians to his cause from the earliest years of the revolution. He himself recorded that 'the infidel Indians abandoned their villages and swarmed into the countryside, volunteering their brave services to help build our great system.'[20] According to a Portuguese report, Artigas was identified as 'a true rebel who recruits all the gauchos of the countryside, and also Charrúas and Minuanos'.[21] To the alarm of many creoles, he even recruited Indians from Misiones. He attracted to his cause and protection the Guaraní Indian chief Andrés 'Andresito' Guacurarí and his followers, to whom he promised autonomy within his confederation; he received their deputies, interested himself in their production and trade, and received in return the enduring loyalty of their leadership.[22] The agrarian and Indian policies of Artigas alarmed

---

[18] Bowles to Croker, 21 Nov. 1816, Gerald S. Graham and R. A. Humphreys (eds.), *The Navy and South America 1807–1823: Correspondence of the Commanders-in-Chief on the South American Station* (London, 1962), 172–3.
[19] Bartolomé Mitre, *Historia de Belgrano y de la independencia argentina*, 6th edn. (4 vols.; Buenos Aires, 1927), i. 256.
[20] Artigas, 1811, Azcuy Ameghino, *Artigas en la historia argentina*, 225–6.
[21] Ibid. 228.
[22] Ibid. 236–46.

men of property not only in Montevideo and Buenos Aires but also in the neighbouring provinces of the littoral. There an uneasy balance was maintained between the demands of Buenos Aires and the influence of *artiguismo*, and the leading groups looked to their caudillos to protect them from both.

In Uruguay itself time was running out for Artigas. The Patria Vieja was brought to an abrupt end by a new wave of Portuguese invaders, the hostility of Buenos Aires, and desertion by the littoral caudillos. In September 1820 Artigas crossed the River Paraná into Paraguay in search of a temporary refuge. The xenophobic Dr Francia imposed instead a permanent asylum and Artigas never returned to the outside world. Uruguay had to wait until 1828 for its independence and domination by a new breed of caudillos, less revolutionary and more predatory than their predecessor. In Artigas caudillism effected a shift in political power from the city to the country, and within the country from those rich in land, livestock, and capital to those who could mobilize a numerous following of men. Artigas revealed the need for a constituency and showed the way to expand it beyond the caudillo's original base. He dealt in policy as well as patronage, in ideas as well as favours, and he seemed set to move the caudillo's horizon beyond the ambition to rule. Would Artigas have advanced from provincial caudillo to national leader, from personal to constitutional authority? The question is unanswerable, but the suspicion remains that Artigas was more than a caudillo and that for him the office was a stage to higher things.

In the Río de la Plata and its periphery caudillos emerged at the meeting place of central power and provincial response. If Güemes was a caudillo by co-optation, Ramírez a caudillo in defiance, and Artigas a caudillo in transit, there were others who were caudillos by default. These were to be found in Upper Peru.

2. *The Guerrillas of Upper Peru*

Upper Peru was a vital objective of the May Revolution. Economically it was a source of silver; strategically it was a springboard of counter-insurgency. Yet the region was not an easy target for liberation. The pretensions of Buenos Aires, the reluctance of creoles to subvert a society in which they were vastly outnumbered by Indians and mestizos, the military vigour of the viceroy in Lima, all made it difficult for the forces of liberation to secure a foothold in Upper Peru. But the revolutionary cause had one asset. This mountain corner of the Hispanic world was made by nature for irregular warfare. As the *porteño* armies fell back, caudillos took their place and became the only representatives of the revolution. Thus independence was first expressed in guerrilla resistance to royalist armies of occupation.

The guerrillas of Upper Peru, the *montoneros* of the peaks and plains, assembled spontaneously in bands of various sizes, and were held together less by military discipline than by personal allegiance to a successful caudillo.[23] Each valley, mountain, and village had its partisan group and its petty caudillo, who made their locality a miniature zone of insurrection, a *republiqueta*, where local patriotism burgeoned into local independence. There were six foci of resistance, each under the command of a senior guerrilla chief.[24] In the north, on the shores of Lake Titicaca, the priest Ildefonso de las Muñecas operated out of Ayata, and menaced the route from Lower Peru. In the central zone there were two extensive *republiquetas*. Juan Antonio Alvarez de Arenales commanded a band of some 500 men and an *indiada* based on Mizque and Vallegrande, harassing communications between Cochabamba, Chuquisaca, and Santa Cruz. The other, the *republiqueta* of Hayopaya hidden in the mountains and jungles between La Paz and Cochabamba, survived action against the enemy and bloody leadership disputes to emerge at independence still intact and unbowed. In the south, covering the route from Argentina over which the liberating armies passed, lay the *republiqueta* of José Vicente Carmago. The capital itself, Chuquisaca, was screened by another partisan group, that of Manuel Ascensio Padilla. And in the far east lay the extensive *republiqueta* of Ignacio Warnes, based on Santa Cruz de la Sierra and providing the ultimate refuge of all the guerrillas.

The most successful of the bands was that of Hayopaya, formed in 1814 by Eusebio Lira, a creole of Mohosa, son of a modest hacendado and militia captain and already a veteran of campaigns in Salta and Tucumán. Lira recruited a nucleus of creoles and Indians, all of whom had 'suffered persecution by the royalists', and soon led a

---

[23] René Danilo Arze Aguirre, *Participación popular en la independencia de Bolivia* (La Paz, 1979), 165–7, 197–203.

[24] Charles W. Arnade, *The Emergence of the Republic of Bolivia* (Gainesville, Fla., 1957), 32–56.

force of 300 guerrilleros. He had his work cut out controlling the *indiada* and punished an Indian captain with one hundred lashes for indiscriminate killing of royalists.[25] One of his most faithful followers was the young José Santos Vargas, a native of Oruro, a mestizo of humble origin and rudimentary education who was living the life of a vagrant and looking for better things when his brother, a priest, encouraged him to take up the cause of independence. He joined Lira's guerrilla in 1814 at the age of eighteen and was appointed *tambor*, or drummer boy, a post more hazardous than it appeared, always close to the chieftain and to the enemy. He spoke three languages, Spanish, Aymara, and Quechua, kept a cool head in times of stress, and in 1823 was promoted commandante. After a career of almost uninterrupted action Vargas survived independence to record his experiences in a vivid and picaresque chronicle of guerrilla warfare, full of spirit, humour, and sympathy for men 'who lived always on the edge of death'.[26]

The hero of Vargas's story was his first chief, Eusebio Lira, the model of all the caudillos, who joined the guerrillas after service in the army of Buenos Aires and fought also to avenge his father, killed by the royalists in 1815. A stout and overweight figure, incapable of beating a hasty retreat, Lira was not always a heroic or confident or predictable leader. But he had human qualities, understood his men, and allowed them to come and go, to run for cover, and to take leave during harvest time. He objected to unnecessary violence to creoles or to Indians. When his own mother and sister incited Indians to kill a creole cavalry sergeant on suspicion of spying, Lira was angry and told the women not to interfere.[27]

All the bands were plagued by leadership struggles, and Lira himself fell a victim to rivals rather than royalists. After an early challenge to his authority in 1815, he withdrew: 'He cut himself off from all his comrades, from all society, and even from the Indians, and hid himself in the mountains between Sihuas and Calahiri . . . sheltered by his *madama* Doña Manuelita Villanueva (niece of Father Vicente Montaño, an Augustinian friar).'[28] He even toyed with the idea of joining the royalists and sent the Spanish governor, Julian

---

[25] José Santos Vargas, *Diario de un comandante de la independencia americana 1814– 1825*, ed. Gunnar Mendoza L. (Mexico, 1982), 39–40, 46.
[26] 'Todo era andar tras de la muerte' (ibid. 12).
[27] Ibid. 91–2.
[28] Ibid. 62–3. The editor defines *madama* as 'amante de jerarquía superior'.

Oblitas, the head of an Indian to show his interest. Oblitas came to meet him in the mountains: 'he did not find Lira but met his girl friend, a beauty in those parts, and took advantage of his luck to spend the night with her; she was young and willing, and her charms caused Oblitas to forget his mission . . .'[29] The insult turned Lira back into a patriot, and he fought vigorously against the royalists in the following years, stoutly defending too his legitimacy against all challengers: 'I am the chief appointed by the junta of all the officers.'[30] Eventually, in 1817, Lira was cornered by his rivals, three officers Marquina, Morales, and Contreras, who were probably manipulated by Buenos Aires; they shot him in the back, surrounded by his own men. He died on 15 December with a priest on either side and a crucifix in his hand, crying 'I die a patriot, I die a Catholic Christian!'[31]

The assassination destabilized the guerrilla band and hampered its operations until the killers themselves were killed. At first Lira's enemies, some of them former royalists, took over the band and persecuted the *liristas*. This was one of its worst moments. Threatened by anarchy and liquidation, the other *liristas* came crying to Santos, 'Drum major, what shall we do, how can we escape?' And Santos, who always kept a cool head, replied 'We shall die if we are stupid enough.'[32] The *liristas*, who included 3,000 Indians, fought back and in due course, in March 1818, captured Marquina and Morales, who were sent to the chapel and shot. But vengeance was still incomplete: '"Marquina and Morales are dead," said the Indians, "that leaves Contreras"'.[33] Weakened by faction, the chieftains competed for the support of opportunist Indians. The new commandante José Manuel Chinchilla appealed to the *indiada* to name him as their chief: 'With one voice they all raised their cry in the square: Chinchilla is *jefe*, he is our chieftain, he is the one we choose.'[34] But another rival, one backed by Buenos Aires, appeared suddenly on the horizon. In February 1821 José Miguel Lanza, accompanied by four officers, arrived unannounced from Salta with a commission from Martín Güemes. He embraced Chinchilla like an old friend and comrade, a

---

[29] Ibid. 68.
[30] Ibid. 120.
[31] Ibid. 195–6.
[32] 'Moriremos si somos zonzos' (ibid. 219).
[33] Ibid. 223.
[34] Ibid. 225.

greeting sufficient to persuade Chinchilla promptly to resign his command and recognize Lanza as principal commandante. But retirement was not enough. A campaign of accusations was organized; on 20 March 1821 Lanza sent Chinchilla to the chapel and the next day had him shot in Cavari. On orders from the Río de la Plata Lanza undertook to federate the guerrillas, until he himself was captured by the Spaniards in June 1821. He survived the war of independence, reaching the rank of general and aspiring to greater things in the new administration. But he was qualified only to be a *montonero*. Sucre described him as 'more stupid than a mule . . . a beast . . . an animal on two feet', whose term as prefect of La Paz was a political and financial disaster, until Bolívar intervened to remove him.[35]

The anarchy of the guerrillas and the counter-offensive of the Spanish security forces destroyed the *republiquetas* in 1816, when their leaders were killed and their forces scattered. The Hayopaya band, exceptionally, regrouped and fought on until the end of the war. Otherwise the guerrillas were not a decisive force for independence, which was brought to Upper Peru in 1825 by the liberating army of Bolívar and Sucre. This was predictable, for the political motivation of the guerrillas had never been strong. To the Spaniards they were all 'caudillos insurgentes'.[36] But why did they rise? Material rewards, money, profit, and plunder were hardly their objects, for they earned barely sufficient to eat, clothe themselves, and survive, with an occasional peso or two thrown in. These meagre resources came from lands and haciendas within guerrilla areas of control, supplemented perhaps by contributions from wealthier guerrilleros or patriotic sympathizers and forced charges on Indian communities. Some fought in a spirit of sheer defiance, often seeking vengeance from royalists for a death or an injustice to their family, or in desperation following the sacking of their village. Political motivation was ambiguous. What distinguished a royalist from a patriot? Not place of birth, for Americans were to be found on both sides. 'There, among the enemy forces, was Pedro, brother of the dead corporal Igidio Garavito; brothers fought brothers, so it seemed'.[37] Men frequently passed from one side to the other. Treason was always a temptation in this long and obscure war. Lira often had to decide

---

[35] Sucre to Bolívar, 29 Feb. 1825, Bolívar to Sucre, 15 Mar. 1825, in O'Leary, *Memorias*, xxx. 61.

[36] Vargas, *Diario*, 362.

[37] Ibid. 171 (13 Sept. 1817).

quickly what to do with a suspect, pardon him or execute him before he could return to join the enemy. He was inclined to indulgence, for he himself was not above reproach.

The idea of *patria* did not convince everyone. If they fought for independence, this was not necessarily national independence; they fought for freedom from outside control, first Spanish then Argentine. Basically they fought for a simple cause, to be masters in their own house, followers of their own caudillo, even if this meant fighting men from their own country or allying with others from a foreign country. Isolated in their valleys and mountains and preoccupied with their local war, the guerrillas knew little of the continental revolution and it was 1819 before they had news from outside. 'On 28 March 1819 Captain Bustamante arrived at the village of Ichoca, the headquarters of the Division, and we all gathered round as the letters and papers were opened. It was then we discovered the situation in Lima, Chile and Colombia. For the first time we heard the name of Colombia and that of General Bolívar, and everything that had happened. Now we learnt it all.'[38] Meanwhile the guerrillas of Hayopaya had received some indoctrination. They were violent men, but not godless. Firmly Catholic, they went to Mass and confession, and allowed their enemies to confess before shooting them. Indeed it was almost a ritual: 'The condemned man was sent to the chapel and shot the following day'. And they listened to the priests.

The priest Oquendo rises the next morning, leaves his tent and shouts to the soldiers, 'Everybody out, to hear the word of God'. They gather in front of him and he says Mass. After the Gospel he begins to preach to the troops and to the whole congregation. Among other things he says: 'We are told that kings, intendants and other authorities are placed over us by God. True. But just as we get rid of certain forms of creation such as disease and illness and are expected to cure ourselves of these, so also we are obliged to throw off the yoke of tyranny, oppression, abuse and despotism, to seek our liberty, our independence, our happiness, our well-being, for now and for posterity. . . . These are the two destinies to which heaven has called us, my sons: to win or to die for our beloved Patria, for our independence and liberty. Do not fear for our cause: God protects us'.[39]

A typical guerrilla band would go into action with '168 armed infantry, 140 horsemen, and more than 800 Indians'.[40] Caudillos and officers were creoles of middle and lower rank, and their immediate

---

[38] Ibid. 242.
[39] Ibid. 171 (June 1817).

followers were mestizos. They regarded their *indiada* as allies, though not perhaps as equals, drawing on their services as auxiliaries, messengers, and spies, but rarely intregrating them into the guerrilla ranks. The Indians, unlike creoles and mestizos, took sides not for individual motives but in conformity with traditional allegiances. A cacique linked to a patriot chieftain would bring his community to the guerrilla; otherwise they would probably be *amedallados*, or royalists, paying tribute still to the Spanish authorities. Usually the Indians gave their allegiance to a particular guerrilla leader rather than an abstract cause. If that leader was eliminated, as was Lira, then they would demand vengeance on the rival caudillos, irrespective of their patriotism. Bound to a single guerrilla chief, the Indians participated in actions under their own captains. Some had lances and horses but most fought with slings and clubs.

Harrassed by royalist armies and guerrilla bands, the Indians had nothing to gain from the war and their preference was to withdraw and avoid commitments. While the royalists imposed tribute and labour services, the guerrillas had their own forms of exaction, and showed little respect for Indian lives and property. When an Indian peasant defended his livestock from arbitrary pillage by guerrilla soldiers, he was hauled before commandante Chinchilla and summarily shot, 'an innocent whom even the soldiers lamented as a victim of injustice'.[41] Lira, too, was subject to outbursts of cruelty. He sentenced two Indians brought before him on suspicion of spying to 200 lashes. One of them ran away protesting his innocence, only to be caught by Indians of Lira's band and clubbed and speared to death; thereupon Lira sentenced the other to die. The Indian went down on his knees sobbing and pleading with the caudillo:

'Señor, you see those birds in the trees there who know nothing of war and only want to eat and feed their young. We are the same. That man they have killed is my brother, and a poor man too. It is not true that we have done you any harm. Our country is kind like a true Patria, and it ought rather to protect and spare its people, especially innocents like us.' Hearing these pathetic pleas, Lieutenant Manuel Patiño and some other comrades were moved to intercede with the commandante and to free the wretched man, who was very grateful to his protectors.[42]

[40] Ibid. 226.
[41] Ibid. 239–40 (August 1818).
[42] Ibid. 119–20.

The war of guerrillas was long and cruel. By 1823, while the rest of Spanish America had something to show for its efforts, Upper Peru was still a scene of apparently aimless fighting in which captives passed quickly from chapel to execution squad to the grave. The few surviving guerrillas were fearful of massacre by royalist Indians in the event of a Spanish victory. Rival caudillos fought among themselves for control of men and resources. A corporal who had tried to stage a revolt within the patriotic ranks said that his life had been a miserable one anyway but his greatest regret was that he had not lived to see his ideas triumph and his country free. He requested a glass of *chicha* and permission to sing a few rebel songs, but the guerrillas would not allow it. He asked the priest to say a prayer and then blindfolded himself.[43]

The carnage in Upper Peru, 'the time of persecution' as it was called by the patriots, was brought to an end not by the efforts of the caudillos but by the entry of the liberators, who defeated the remnants of the royalists, ended Spanish rule, and endowed the new republic with a Bolivarian constitution and an enlightened president. But war had created caudillos and guerrillas, and war left a memory and a model of an alternative way to influence and power.

3. *The* Montoneros *of Central Peru*

San Martín bypassed Upper Peru and took the war of liberation directly to the Pacific. By July 1821 his Army of the Andes had liberated Chile and coastal Peru without the help of guerrillas and now he sought to win the war of ideas. In the interior of Peru, however, his writ did not run. There the Spaniards still held power, and there a number of guerrilla bands operated between 1821 and 1824.

The montoneros of central Peru represented a variety of interests. Popular causes? Up to a point. Indians? In some cases. Independence? Perhaps. Like guerrillas elsewhere in Spanish America, they appeared at the convergence of capital and province, and exemplified the interaction of rural conditions and personal leadership. Some of

---

[43] Ibid. 340–50 (21 Jan. 1824).

the leaders were creoles and mestizos of middle rank and modest fortune whose families and property had suffered at the hands of royalists and who now sought vengeance.[44] Others were genuinely populist, seeking advantage for their communities and their right to participate or not participate. Others were Indian *kurakas*, moved by a mixture of personal and communal motives, and not normally friendly towards whites of any political persuasion. The guerrilleros were joined inevitably by vagrants and delinquents, by bandit chiefs and their followers, such as those of the notorious Quirós, 'wearing long beards and dressed in the most grotesque manner', who used guerrilla operations as a means of personal plunder.[45] Guerrilla leaders sometimes practised forced conscription in the zones of their command, partly to overcome the reluctance of hacendados to release their workers, partly to forestall recruitment by royalists. To conscript was not to disavow their popular base but rather another sign that both sides competed keenly for popular and Indian support.

In spite of their disparate composition and motives, the *montoneros* played a special part in the patriot war effort, when they could be persuaded to collaborate. Until mid-1821 they attacked communications between the interior and the coast, cutting supply lines into the capital. During the retreat of the royalists from Lima in July 1821 the *montoneros* were well placed to harass the enemy and cut off stragglers. Operating in bands of fifty to a hundred each, most of them from a base at the town of Reyes, the *montoneros* maintained irregular warfare in the region between the central sierra and the coast, attacking and disappearing, preying on royalist routes, and keeping the Spanish army constantly on the alert. They were led by such men as Francisco Vidal, Ignacio Quispe Ninavilca, Gaspar Huavique, Francisco Herrera, and the Argentine officer Isidoro Villar, whom San Martín made commander-in-chief of the guerrillas of the sierra. But their contribution could not be decisive. Some communities in guerrilla territory, putting their agricultural interests first, refused to support the cause of independence, which appeared to them to serve foreign and élite priorities. The bands themselves lacked cohesion; interest and

---

[44] Raúl Rivera Serna, *Los guerrilleros del Centro en la emancipación peruana* (Lima, 1958), 20–1, 80–92, 108–13; the basic published documentation on the Peruvian guerrillas has been edited by Ella Dunbar Temple, *La acción patriótica del pueblo en la emancipación: Guerrillas y montoneras* (CDIP 5; 6 vols.; Lima, 1971).

[45] John Miller (ed.), *Memoirs of General Miller in the Service of the Republic of Peru*, 2nd ed. (2 vols.; London, 1829), i. 377–8, ii. 138–40.

motivation differed widely between men and between groups; and dissension between guerrilla chiefs, or between these and patriot officers, often arose out of regional, racial, or political rivalries. The fact remained that Indian suspicion of whites went too deep to transform popular guerrillas into instant patriots.[46]

The entry of the Colombian army from the north brought Bolívar and Sucre into contact with the *montoneros*. It was not a happy meeting. The Venezuelan generals had little more faith in the guerrillas than had San Martín, understanding rightly that they were Peruvians before all else. It was obvious that the caudillos of the sierra distrusted the Colombian army, and looked for direction to Peruvian leaders such as José de la Riva-Agüero and the marquis of Torre Tagle, both of whom were security risks, rather than to outsiders, however patriotic. The attempts of Bolívar and Sucre to bring them under the control of patriot officers were ineffective; in November 1823 guerrillas led by Ninavilca, Herrera, and other partisans of Riva-Agüero ambushed Colonel Villar, who was lucky to escape with his life.[47] Guerrilla anarchy apeared to be endemic:

The General in Chief of the army of Colombia [Sucre] and the Colonel of Batallion No. 1 of Peru have informed His Excellency the Liberator of the infamous behaviour of the montoneros, both in the face of the enemy and in the villages they occupy, pointing out that the outrages they commit arise from their total lack of discipline and the complete absence of good officers. General Sucre is finally convinced that if the government does not assign them tough officers, far from being any use to us the montoneros will exhaust all the resources of the country and leave nothing for the army.[48]

Bolívar, who had to contend with the Peruvian élite as well as with the Spanish army, regarded the guerrillas as part of the common enemy, and sought to destroy those who openly collaborated with royalists. Ninavilca, Mancebo, and Vidal in particular drew his anger as collaborators and as parasites on resources which his own army needed.[49] But Ninavilca had a power base. According to another

---

[46] Alberto Flores Galindo, *Buscando un Inca: Identidad y utopia en los Andes* (Lima, 1987), 220–1; Heraclio Bonilla, 'Bolívar y las guerrillas indígenas en el Perú', *Cultura, Revista del Banco Central del Ecuador*, 6, 16 (1983), 81–95; Charles Walker, 'Montoneros, bandoleros, malhechores: Criminalidad y política en las primeras décadas republicanas', *Pasado y Presente*, 2, 2–3 (1989), 119–37.

[47] Sucre to Valdés, 18 July 1823, in O'Leary, *Memorias*, xx. 204; Berindoaga to secretary general of Bolívar, 29 Nov. 1823 (ibid. xxi. 45–6).

[48] Espinar to Minister of War of Peru, 16 Jan. 1824 (ibid. xxi. 310).

[49] Bolívar to Heres, Cajamarca, 19 Nov. 1823 (ibid. xx. 601–2).

guerrilla leader, 'Ninavilca has a great ascendancy over the Indians, even though he is an absolute beast'.[50] The Indian caudillo professed himself a Peruvian patriot at war with the invading Colombians, whom he called 'a mob of thieves', despoilers of Peru, plunderers of its land, resources, money, and jobs, in alliance with the infamous Torre Tagle. 'Only Riva-Agüero can save us from the claws of these fiends: he alone is the true patriot'.[51] After three months in prison as a partisan of Riva-Agüero, Ninavilca escaped in November 1823 to form an alliance with three other guerrilla chiefs and raise the Huarochirí region on behalf of the Peruvian leader. But whom was he fighting for? He seems to have looked to Riva-Agüero for information and instructions: 'Above all I need Your Excellency to advise me of the present state of affairs with the Spaniards, whether I am to regard them as enemies and make war on them, or whether there is no reason to fear them and only Lima is the enemy'.[52]

The liberators, however, were desperate for support and supplies, and in preparing their army for the final push against the royalists they reluctantly sought the collaboration of the guerrillas in harassing, observing, and reporting on the enemy, in recruiting Indian ancillary troops, and in tracking down supplies for the army from the pueblos.[53] Sucre thought that, allocated firearms, 'they might recover their former enthusiasm', though the fact remained that many Peruvian landowners and creole patriots were reluctant to see Indian guerrillas armed, while Ninavilca himself would only commit himself to the patriot cause when he saw the Spaniards were doomed. Bolívar still had misgivings about the Indian chief, his independence, and his manipulation of the guerrilla leadership. While the united army was winning the battle of Ayacucho, Bolívar was ordering Ninavilca and his guerrillas to make their base in Chorrillos and cover the coast, keeping the area clear of the enemy.[54] But Bolívar had not heard the

[50] Francisco Herrera to Riva-Agüero, 17 Nov. 1823 (ibid. xxi. 47.)

[51] Ninavilca, Proclama, Canta, 16 Nov. 1823 (ibid. xxi. 48–9). On Ninavilca see Karen Spalding, *Huarochirí: An Andean Society under Inca and Spanish Rule* (Stanford, 1984), 230, 237, 292; Peter Guardino, 'Las guerrillas y la independencia peruana: Un ensayo de interpretación', *Pasado y Presente*, 2, 2–3 (1989), 101–17.

[52] Ninavilca to Riva-Agüero, Huaroquín, 17 Nov. 1823, in O'Leary, *Memorias*, xii. 50–1.

[53] Ezequiel Beltrán Gallardo, *Las guerrillas de Yauyos en la emancipación del Perú 1820–1824* (Lima, 1977), 117–27, 135–44.

[54] Santana to Sucre, Huarás, 9, 10 June 1824, in O'Leary, *Memorias*, xxii. 312–16; Sucre to Bolívar, 6 May 1824 (ibid. i. 162); Soler to Ninavilca, 11 Dec. 1824 (ibid. xxii. 575–6).

last of the Indian caudillo. In 1826 there was a conspiracy in Peru against the authority of the Liberator and against his life. Various suspects were arrested including Colonel Ninavilca, 'noble Indian who aspired to be Inca of Peru and who distinguished himself in the war against the Spaniards as commander of a band of montoneros'.[55] Nothing was actually proved against Ninavilca but he was detained, his war record still famous, his politics still obscure.

4. *Venezuela: Caudillo Prototypes*

The war in Venezuela was longer, harder, and bloodier than that in Argentina. The caudillos of the llanos were more closely engaged by the enemy, more directly involved in the fighting, and freer from the constraints of government than the caudillos of the pampas. At the same time they fought on a larger scale and with greater resources than those in Upper Peru and were an integral part of the war effort. They competed with and then yielded to Bolívar's military and political objectives, but in the end they preserved their power bases and survived to contest the peace.

In Venezuela colonial rural conditions were aggravated by revolution. As landowners struggled to protect and extend their estates, and the opposing armies to tax, plunder, and recruit, so the marginal population reacted and resisted.[56] The llanos became a refuge for vagrants, deserters, fugitive slaves, bandits, and the simply impoverished. War increased the motives and the opportunities for resistance. Men were forced into bands for subsistence and self-protection under a caudillo who could lead them to booty and save them from conscription. Thus banditry was a product of rural adversity and a cause of it, and for most of the bandidos survival was more important than ideology.

It is not uncommon to observe in these vast territories groups of bandits who, without any political motivation and with desire of pillage their only incentive, come together and follow the first caudillo who offers them booty taken from anyone with property. This is how Boves and other bandits of the same kind

---

[55] Apuntamientos del General Heres (ibid. v. 301).

[56] Miguel Izard, 'Sin el menor arraigo ni responsabilidad', 120–1; parts of this section have appeared in John Lynch, 'Bolívar and the Caudillos', *HAHR* 63, 1 (1983), 3–35.

have been able to recruit hordes of these people, who live by vagrancy, robbery and assassination.[57]

The transition from bandit to guerrilla to patriot was slow and obscure, and the styles were indistinguishable. Plunder was characteristic of the caudillo system, whether the caudillo operated in the private or the public sector, and pillage became a method of waging war used by all sides in default of regular revenue. There were variations of looting: confiscation of property, seizure of supplies, forced loans, donations, and fines.[58] The small bands of guerrillas who harassed the royalist lines of communication lived by looting. The seizure of booty was also authorized or tolerated by the major chieftains, and by Bolívar himself. At the first battle of Carabobo (1814), it was reported, 'the booty was immense', and soldiers held triumphantly in their hands not only articles of war, but money, equipment, and personal property of royalist officers.[59] Looting, therefore, while practised in a crude form by caudillos, was not exclusive to them. In a disguised, indirect, or even direct form, it was the only way of paying an army or of acquiring resources for the war effort. In effect, a revolutionary state without revenue had to impose an informal tax system. Exactions, forced loans, and fines were levied with a ruthlessness hardly different from that of the caudillos. And some of Bolívar's own caudillos used methods just as cruel as those of any royalist. Juan Bautista Arismendi offered Juan Andrés Marrero the chance to buy the lives of himself and his six sons; after taking the ransom, Arismendi had them all killed.[60]

Plunder and resources were not the only objectives of the guerrillas. Venezuela was torn by deep racial divisions and race was a prejudice exploited by both sides in the conflict. José Francisco Heredia, creole regent of the *audiencia* of Caracas, spoke of the 'mortal hatred' between whites and *pardos* in Valencia during the First Republic, and commented: 'The guerrilla band that later joined the king's side encouraged this rivalry, and it was commonly said by the European extremists that the pardos were loyalists and the white creoles were

---

[57] 'Reflexiones sobre el estado actual de los llanos', 6 Dec. 1813, cited in Germán Carrera Damas, *Boves: Aspectos socio-económicos de su acción histórica* (Caracas, 1968), 158.

[58] Ibid. 56, 73.

[59] *Gazeta de Caracas*, no. 73 (6 June 1814).

[60] Juan Vicente González, *La doctrina conservadora*, in Presidencia de la República, *El pensamiento político venezolano del siglo XIX*, i. 179.

revolutionaries whom it was necessary to destroy'. This was the policy, he added, of José Tomás Boves and other bandit chiefs, nominally royalists but in fact 'insurgents of another kind', who waged war on all white creoles: 'and so he became the idol of the pardos, who followed him in the hope of seeing the dominant caste destroyed'.[61] Boves promoted blacks and *pardos* in his band and promised them white property. When he occupied and plundered Valencia in June 1814 the Spanish authorities looked on helplessly; when he took Caracas he refused to recognize the captain general or to have his llanero forces incorporated into the royal army. His was a personal authority, expressing violence rather than legitimacy, and loyal to only a very distant king. Bolívar was convinced that royalist caudillos incited slaves and *pardos* to plunder in order to increase their commitment, morale, and group cohesion.[62]

But race vengeance also inspired the insurgents. In the struggle for Maturín in May 1815, the royalist commander Domingo Monteverde was defeated and his life was saved only by the cover given him by his *zambo* servant, 'for the insurgents would not fire on the *hombres de color*'.[63] The insurgent chieftain in this action was the *pardo* Manuel Piar, and Bolívar was to suffer from Piar an insubordination not dissimilar to that which the royalists experienced from Boves. Before that point was reached, however, the insurgents had to gain a foothold. After the collapse of the First Republic in July 1812 Venezuela underwent a royalist reaction. This was challenged in the course of 1813 by two movements, an invasion under Bolívar from the west and the onset of guerrilla operations in the east. Who were the guerrillas?

The first guerrilla thrust had a social and regional base but also a clear political objective; to resist the oppressive regime of Monteverde and fight for a free Venezuela. When, on 11 January 1813, Santiago Mariño headed a small expedition, the famous 'forty-five' from Trinidad to Güiria, he led forth his band from his hacienda like a true caudillo, to operate in territory where he had property, relations, slaves, and dependants. Mariño was no social bandit. Like Bolívar he came from the colonial élite of land and commerce; he had received

---

[61] José Francisco Heredia, *Memorias del Regente Heredia* (Madrid, n.d.), 41–51, 239.
[62] José de Austria, *Bosquejo de la historia militar de Venezuela* (2 vols.; Madrid, 1960), ii. 256; Bolívar to *Gaceta Real de Jamaica*, Sept. 1815, in Simón Bolívar, *Obras completas*, 2nd edn., ed. Vicente Lecuna and Esther Barret de Nazarís (3 vols.; Havana, 1950), i. 180.
[63] Heredia, *Memorias*, 172.

an education, and was described by some as 'the effeminate Mariño'.[64]
His aim was to mobilize social forces, not to change them. At first he
was a local rather than a regional caudillo, but he quickly increased
his stature through military success and reputation. Yet he never
projected a national, much less an American, vision of the revolution.
The strength of caudillos like Mariño lay in their tactical rather than
strategic sense. Without the guiding hand of Bolívar, the various
regional fronts could not have united in a national or continental
liberation movement.

Moreover this particular asset of the caudillos, a personal and
regional base for raising troops, was also a limitation. Such troops
were reluctant to leave their own province, and the caudillos were
unwilling or unable to compel them. At the beginning of 1818, troops
of Francisco Bermúdez refused to proceed to Guayana. In December
1818 even Mariño was powerless to persuade his men to follow him
out of the province, and he arrived at Pao not at the head of a
division, as Bolívar was expecting, but with an escort of thirty men.[65]
Insubordination was a further constraint. In 1819 Mariño was styled
General-in-Chief of the Army of the East, and 'responsible to the
Government for the conservation of all that part of the Republic', but
in fact he exercised no command at all over Bermúdez or other minor
caudillos. Insubordination began directly below Bolívar. In 1820
Mariño refused to obey Bolívar's summons to headquarters and, in a
gesture typical of the caudillo, retired in disgust to his hacienda in
Güiria, where he had resources, security, and a guard of loyal retainers, formerly his troops, now his peons.[66]

Yet the guerrillas kept resistance alive during the long years of
counter-revolution. In the course of 1814–16, a number of bands
emerged under leaders who were to become indispensable to the
patriot war effort: Pedro Zaraza in the upper llanos, José Antonio
Páez in the western llanos, Manuel Cedeño in Caicara, José Tadeo
Monagas in Cumaná, Jesús Berreto and Andrés Rojas in Maturín.
These groups rose from the ruins of the Second Republic. The
surviving patriots fled to the plains, jungles, and forests of the east to
escape royalist retribution. They then regrouped under a leader of

---

[64] José Domingo Díaz, *Recuerdos sobre la rebelión de Caracas* (Madrid, 1961), 262, a
scurrilous source; Caracciolo Parra-Pérez, *Mariño y la independencia de Venezuela* (5
vols.; Madrid, 1954–7), i. 134–8.
[65] Parra-Pérez, *Mariño y la independencia de Venezuela*, iii. 40.
[66] Ibid. iii. 242.

their choice, partly for self-preservation, partly for the revolutionary cause.[67] For a guerrilla to surrender or to be captured was to walk into execution. In this sense resistance was the only option left. Groups converged and coalesced, until they found a supercaudillo. Armed with *púas* (lances), and taking their horses and cattle from the llanos of Barcelona and Cumaná, the guerrillas fought successfully against regular forces, attacking communications, ambushing detachments, harassing towns, and then disappearing. They pinned down royalist forces in a number of different places and forced the Spaniards to maintain immobile garrisons.[68]

The guerrillas not only fought the royalists but also competed with each other. Leader rivalry, in Venezuela as in Upper Peru, obstructed operations, as caudillos struggled with each other for that supremacy which only military success and the ability to attract recruits could bring. No caudillo wanted to submit to another: each fought to remain independent, in a state of nature without a common power. Out of this internal war emerged the most powerful leaders: Monagas, Zaraza, Cedeño, Piar. This was in the east. Leadership in the western llanos demanded supreme physical talents, and it was this challenge which brought Páez to the fore:

To command these men and dominate the situation was needed a particular superiority and talent in using the lance with both hands, to fight on wild horses and to break them in during actual battle, to swim and to fight while swimming in swollen rivers, to lasso and kill wild beasts simply to get food, in short, to have the ability to dominate and overcome a thousand and more dangers which threaten in these conditions.[69]

Bolívar, too, possessed extraordinary natural talents, fortitude and endurance, and learned to compete with the caudillos on their own terms. His record of active service was in no way inferior to theirs. He conquered nature as well as men, overcoming the immense distances of America in marches which were as memorable as the battles. His severity was notorious, and no one doubted his implacability. Yet Bolívar was never a caudillo.[70] He always sought to institu-

[67] Daniel Florencio O'Leary, *Memorias del General Daniel Florencio O'Leary: Narración* (3 vols.; Caracas, 1952), i. 350.

[68] Fernando Rivas Vicuña, *Las guerras de Bolívar* (7 vols.; Bogotá, 1934–8, Santiago, 1940), ii. 85–95.

[69] Austria, *Historia militar de Venezuela*, ii. 454–6.

[70] For other interpretations see Gerhard Masur, *Simon Bolivar* (Albuquerque, NM, 1948), 253, and Jorge I. Domínguez, *Insurrection or Loyalty: The Breakdown of the Spanish American Empire* (Cambridge, Mass., 1980), 197–8, 226–7.

tionalize the revolution and to lead it to a political conclusion. The solution he favoured was a large nation-state with a strong central government, totally dissimilar to the federal form of government and the decentralization of power preferred by the caudillos. Bolívar never possessed a true regional power base. The east had its own oligarchy, its own caudillos, who regarded themselves as allies rather than subordinates. The Apure was dominated by a number of great proprietors and then by Páez. Bolívar felt most at home in Caracas and the centre-north. There he had friends, followers and officers who had fought under him in New Granada, in the *campaña admirable*, and in other actions in central Venezuela. Bolívar could give orders to Urdaneta, Ribas, and Campo as to trusted officers, assign them to one division or another, to this front or that. But from 1814 central Venezuela was occupied by the royal army, and Bolívar, who did not control the capital, had to assemble his power by a mixture of military and political success. As he himself said, he was forced to be a soldier and a statesman, 'simultaneously on the battlefield and at the head of government . . . both a chief of state and a general of the army'.

Bolívar was a dictator when he wrote these words. Bolivarian dictatorship, however, was not caudillism. It was less personal and more institutional; it dealt in policies as well as patronage. After the campaign of 1813 Bolívar entered Caracas in triumph on 6 August and established his first dictatorship, served by known supporters and backed by the army. His intention was to concentrate authority in order to defend and extend the revolution. There was some resentment, however, and he convoked an assembly on 2 January 1814, to which he explained his dictatorship: 'My desire to save you from anarchy and destroy our enemies and oppressors forced me to accept the sovereign power. . . . I have come to bring you the rule of law. Military despotism cannot ensure the happiness of a people. A victorious soldier acquires no right to rule his country'.[71] Subsequent Bolivarian dictatorships, in Peru and Colombia, embodied the same principles; they were a response to emergency, they represented policies not interests, and they restored law as well as order. Even at the height of his success and prestige, and in face of great provocation, he obeyed the law. In October 1824, some weeks after the battle

---

[71] Bolívar to Richard Wellesley, 14 Jan. 1814, in Simón Bolívar, *Escritos del Libertador*, vi. 63; speech to the Caracas assembly, 2 Jan. 1814 (ibid. v. 8–9).

of Junín, at a time when he was President of Colombia and Dictator of Peru, he received dispatches from the government in Bogotá which in effect revoked his extraordinary powers in Peru. There is no doubt that he could have led a revolt against this petty decision, inspired as it was by Santander; but he immediately delegated to Sucre command of the Colombian army. As O'Leary wrote, 'Bolívar thus gave an example of obedience to the law of his country, when a single word or sign on his part would have been sufficient to gain the wholehearted support of the army and the people of Colombia.'[72]

Bolívar was not alone in his dedication to constitutionalism. General Rafael Urdaneta, a Zulian, was a man of order and authority, but he never became a caudillo, never acquired *partidarios* or made *compromisos* binding him to a certain band. He was the complete professional soldier, later an official, executing always the orders of the central government.[73] But the supreme example of the non-caudillo was Antonio José de Sucre. As a young man, Sucre in 1813 accompanied the expedition of Mariño and fought in a number of important actions; but unlike his comrades Manuel Piar, José Francisco Bermúdez, and Manuel Valdés, he did not aspire to be an independent chieftain. He came from a wealthy Cumaná family and had received an education in Caracas. He was interested in the technology of warfare and became an expert in military engineering. 'He reduced everything to a method... he was the scourge of disorder', as Bolívar later wrote of him.[74] He served as an officer in the Army of the East for four years, and came under the influence of Bolívar in 1817, accepting appointment to his staff in preference to the factions of the east.

Decisions of this kind were a question of mentality and values. Sucre had a soldier's respect for obedience to authority. In placing his interests and career in Bolívar's hands, he added, 'I am resolved to obey you blindly and with pleasure'.[75] Sucre did not love fighting for fighting's sake, as did many caudillos. He preferred people to join the patriot cause out of conviction, and by October 1820 he was satisfied that western Venezuela was convinced: 'This triumph of

---

[72] O'Leary, *Narración*, ii. 282.

[73] See the correspondence of Urdaneta with Bolívar, in O'Leary, *Memorias*, vi. 7–272, and his 'Apuntamientos' (ibid. vi. 273–388).

[74] 'Resumen sucinto de la vida del General Sucre', 1825, *Archivo de Sucre* (Caracas, 1973–), vol. i, p. xli.

[75] Sucre to Bolívar, 17 Oct. 1817 (ibid. i. 12).

opinion is more brilliant than that of force'.[76] Sucre was aware of the alternatives: caudillism or professionalism. In 1817, commissioned by Bolívar to 'bring in' Mariño, he reported: 'I have no doubt that General Mariño will come to heel, as he has no alternative, except to be a guerrilla in the mountains of Güiria'.[77] His obedience to Bolívar never faltered. When Francisco Antonio Zea, vice-president of Venezuela, promoted him to the rank of brigadier general without Bolívar's cognizance, Sucre explained later 'that he had never intended to accept the promotion without General Bolívar's approval'.[78] In Peru he was 'the right arm of the Liberator and the mainstay of the army'.[79] Sucre and Urdaneta were the leading lights of the Bolivarians, an élite of professional officers devoted to the Liberator in war and to his government in peace.

Few of the caudillos followed this example. The years 1813–17 were a time of trial for the revolution, when the war on the enemy without was frustrated by the war of caudillos within. Yet the caudillos conformed to prevailing conditions more closely than did Bolívar, who lacked the resources they commanded. In the absence of a national army personal leadership was bound to be decisive, and without a national objective the structure of insurgency was inevitably informal.

Mariño was the first caudillo to confront Bolívar. In early 1813 he had under him Bermúdez, Piar, Valdés, and other minor chiefs who had recruited troops after landing at Güiria, forming a force of more than 1,500. After the occupation of Güiria, he captured Maturín and, later in the year, Cumaná and Barcelona. So Mariño grew into a supercaudillo through his style, his victories, and his violence. He repaid cruelty with cruelty. In Cumaná he had forty-seven Spaniards and creoles shot in reprisal; in Barcelona he executed sixty-nine conspirators, because 'the life of such men was incompatible with the existence of the State'.[80] Naming himself 'chief of the independent army', he established not only an autonomous military command in the east but a political entity separate from Caracas. Bolívar's position, weakened by a rival dictatorship in the east, was destroyed by the intervention of the royalist caudillo Boves and the triumph

---

[76] Sucre to Santander, 30 Oct. 1820 (ibid. i. 186).
[77] Sucre to Bolívar, 17 Oct. 1817 (ibid. i. 12).
[78] O'Leary, *Narración*, ii. 68.
[79] Ibid. ii. 252.
[80] Parra-Pérez, *Mariño y la independencia de Venezuela*, i. 245.

of the counter-revolution. Mariño eventually brought his forces to join those of Bolívar and fought alongside him in February and March 1814. The joint army regrouped at Valencia and Bolívar yielded the command to Mariño 'as a sign of his high opinion of his person and also to ensure the adhesion of the eastern officers to the common cause of Venezuela'.[81] Neither the eastern caudillos nor their forces distinguished themselves in these engagements. Bolívar and Mariño had to retreat from central Venezuela to the east, not to a safe base but to caudillo-inspired anarchy. There, in the port of Carúpano, they were repudiated and arrested by their own 'officers', Ribas, Piar, and Bermúdez, and escaped with the greatest difficulty.

Anarchic and divisive though they were, the caudillos maintained a revolutionary presence during Bolívar's absence. As José de Austria observed: 'While they did not advance, neither could they be totally destroyed.'[82] Guerrilla warfare was the appropriate method, given the resources available, the nature of the war, and the strength of the enemy. After the disasters of 1814 and the victory for royalism even in eastern Venezuela, the caudillos slipped away to recover and to fight another day, sure of finding followers, as Mariño did in 1816, from 'the slaves and bandits in the mountains of Güiria'.[83] They were joined by a few 'Carib tribes' from the banks of the Orinoco and later by some eighty men 'called the *Terecais*, because they went naked and all they used for a uniform was a *guayuco*'.[84] It was the counter-insurgency mounted by General Pablo Morillo that brought the caudillos out of their lairs, for it directly attacked the lives, property, and vital interests of themselves and other Venezuelan leaders, and made war the only hope of security, 'caught as they were in the desperate alternative of dying or fighting'.[85] And so the rural guerrillas were mobilized again, not as a social or political force, but as military units under strong leaders who offered them booty.

Meanwhile in Haiti, where he was planning a new invasion of Venezuela, Bolívar had to resolve the question of leadership. A group

[81] Austria, *Historia militar de Venezuela*, ii. 222, 226.

[82] Ibid. ii. 388.

[83] Moxó to Morillo, 10 Aug. 1816, in Parra-Pérez, *Mariño y la independencia de Venezuela*, ii. 70.

[84] Austria, *Historia militar de Venezuela*, ii. 321. In 1817 Piar recruited Indian volunteers in Guayana; see 'Diario de operaciones del General Piar', Feb. 1817, in O'Leary, *Memorias*, xv. 201.

[85] Austria, *Historia militar de Venezuela*, ii. 385.

of major caudillos was persuaded to recognize his authority for the expedition and until a congress could be held. The vote of the assembly was reinforced in the initial phase of the expedition at Margarita, whose caudillo, Arismendi, was a supporter of Bolívar's national authority. In a second assembly, held in the presence of Mariño, Piar, and other caudillos, the leadership of Bolívar was confirmed, and a unanimous vote was given against the division of Venezuela into east and west: 'that the Republic of Venezuela shall be one and indivisible, that His Excellency, President and Captain General Simón Bolívar is elected and recognized as its Supreme Head, and His Excellency General Santiago Mariño as his second-in-command.'[86] At the same time Bolívar agreed to legitimize the guerrilla chiefs by giving them titles and status in his army; the senior caudillos were made generals and colonels, and the others were given appropriate rank.

These rituals had only a limited significance. One of the reasons why Bolívar did not dominate the caudillos was that he did not dominate the battlefield. After the collapse of the first expedition from Haiti and the catastrophe of Ocumare, he was actually weaker than the caudillos, some of whom had at least secured a foothold in the east. Mariño and Bermúdez were now determined to deal with Bolívar, whom they called a deserter and traitor and regarded as inexpert in the art of war. A proclamation was published in Güiria (23 August 1816) deposing Bolívar and appointing Mariño as supreme chief, with Bermúdez as second-in-command. The army broke up, and civil war threatened the ranks of insurgency. The caudillos wanted to take Bolívar into custody, and he barely escaped with his life from Güiria to Haiti. The humiliation he suffered in 1816 owed something to his strategic errors. At this point in the revolution it was impossible to win on the northern coast of Venezuela, as it was too well defended. But he had still not learned this lesson or accepted the need for opening another front.

In the second invasion from Haiti Bolívar landed at Barcelona, and his initial plan was to assemble an army to attack, not Guayana, but the royalist forces blocking the way to Caracas. He thus made himself utterly dependent upon the caudillos, who were already operating separately in various parts of the east. He wrote to one caudillo after

---

[86] 'Acta de Reconocimiento de Bolívar como Jefe Supremo', 6 May 1816, *Escritos*, ix. 123–6.

another, calling on them to assemble around him in a great *proyecto de reunión*. He wrote to Piar, who had already marched on Guayana, instructing him to bring in his forces: 'Small divisions cannot achieve great objectives. The dispersion of our army, far from helping us, can destroy the Republic.'[87] He wrote to Mariño, Zaraza, Cedeño, and Monagas, ordering, requesting, appealing for unity and obedience. 'You know better than anyone that the basis of the army is subordination.'[88] But the caudillos did not suddenly change their ways; they stayed out, pursuing their separate objectives. The great army was an illusion, and Bolívar abandoned his hope of occupying Caracas; he could not even hold Barcelona. He had to make his way to Guayana, still without an army of his own, still without a caudillo power base, the victim not only of inexperience but of guerrilla anarchy.

The caudillos now went into virtual rebellion. First Bermúdez and Valdés revolted against Mariño, then Mariño against Bolívar, and Piar against all authority. Mariño convoked a minicongress at Cariaco to establish a provisional government and make himself legitimate. On 9 May 1817 he issued a proclamation to the peoples of Venezuela, a sign of his desire to be a national leader, not simply a regional caudillo. But a caudillo could not suddenly become a statesman. This was where Mariño lost his credibility. Bermúdez and Valdés had already left him for Bolívar. Now General Urdaneta, Colonel Sucre, and many other officers who had previously obeyed Mariño went to Guayana to place themelves under Bolívar's orders. The tide began to turn. Military success in Guayana and his own political sense enabled Bolívar to improve his prospects against the caudillos. It was now that Piar chose to rebel.

Piar was not a typical caudillo, for he did not possess an independent power base, regional or economic. He had to rely on his military abilities alone, rising—'by my sword and good luck'—to the rank of general in the forces of Mariño, a title he conferred upon himself.[89] He was a *pardo* from Curaçao and he made the *pardos* his constituency.[90] Bolívar, too, wanted to recruit blacks, to free the slaves and incorporate the *pardos*, in order to tilt the balance of military forces towards the republic, but he did not propose to mobilize them politically. Bolívar suffered much else from Piar, from his arrogance,

---

[87] Bolívar to Piar, 10 Jan. 1817 (ibid. x. 46).
[88] Bolívar to J. T. Monagas, 13 Jan. 1817, in O'Leary, *Memorias*, xv. 118.
[89] Parra-Pérez, *Mariño y la independencia de Venezuela*, ii. 368.
[90] Díaz, *Recuerdos sobre la rebelión de Caracas*, 336.

ambition, and insubordination. When in January 1817 a group of officers left Piar to join Bolívar, Piar demanded of his superior that he give them the severest punishment, the only lesson acknowledged by 'immoral, barbarous, and corrupt people like those. In such quarters clemency is seen as weakness; kindness is mistaken for lack of character and energy; all the virtues are reckoned for nothing. Your excellency ought to have known this.'[91] Bolívar endured these lessons in the law of the caudillo and tried to repay insults with reason, hinting that without political values the caudillos reverted to mere bandits: 'If we destroy ourselves through conflicts and anarchy, we will empty the republican ranks and they will rightly call us vagrants.'[92] But Piar was uncontrollable. He claimed the Orinoco campaign as his own theatre of war, Guayana and the Missions as his private domain. A contest for supremacy became outright rebellion. He appeared not to realize that the balance of power was turning against the caudillos, or perhaps this was the spur that drove him. The victory over the royalists at Angostura confirmed Bolívar's power and placed the initiative with him. He decided the moment had come to challenge factionalism and dissidence in the east, and in this mood he ordered Piar 'with the other caudillos and followers of his faction' to be hunted down.[93] Piar was captured, tried, and sentenced to death as a deserter, a rebel, and a traitor. Bolívar confirmed the sentence and had him publicly executed 'for proclaiming the odious principles of race war . . . for inciting civil war, and for encouraging anarchy'.[94] Piar represented regionalism, personalism, and Black revolution. Bolívar stood for centralism, constitutionalism, and race harmony. He later commented:

The death of General Piar was a political necessity which saved the country, for otherwise he would have started a war of pardos against whites, leading to the extermination of the latter and the triumph of the Spaniards. General Mariño also deserved to die because of his dissidence, but he was not so dangerous and therefore policy could yield to humanity and even to an old friendship . . . never was there a death more useful, more politic, and at the same time more deserved.[95]

The claim had a certain justification. Bolívar simultaneously warned and reassured the creole caudillos.

[91] Piar to Bolívar, 31 Jan. 1817, in O'Leary, *Memorias*, xv. 150–1.
[92] Bolívar to Piar, 19 June 1817, *Escritos*, x. 264.
[93] Bolívar to Cedeño, 24 Sept. 1817 (ibid. xi. 91).
[94] Bolívar, Manifesto to the peoples of Venezuela, 5 Aug. 1817 (ibid. x. 337).
[95] L. Peru de Lacroix, *Diario de Bucaramanga* (Caracas, 1976), 116–17.

The surest antidote to unrestrained caudillism was an effective army structure and a clear chain of command. With the authority and resources won from the victory in Guayana, Bolívar initiated a series of army reforms designed to create a professional army modelled on military institutions in Europe. The decree of 24 September 1817 marked the beginning of his campaign for professionalism and against personalism. This created the General Staff 'for the organisation and direction of the armies', a Staff for the whole army, and one for each division. The Staff was part of a career structure open to talent; it was also the source of command, instructions, and orders downwards to commanders, officers, and troops.[96] He established courts martial at all levels of the army. And in an attempt to move beyond plunder he created a *tribunal de secuestros* to administer the confiscation of royalist property for the benefit not of individual caudillo bands but of 'the national treasury'.[97] The caudillos became generals and regional commanders; their hordes became soldiers subject to military discipline defined at the centre. Reform extended to recruitment. Commanders were given quotas, and they were encouraged to seek troops outside their own territory and to stiffen discipline by distributing veteran troops among their various companies.

The caudillos did not abandon their regional power bases. But those who collaborated were employed in specific assignments. In the llanos of Barcelona and Caracas Monagas and Zaraza proved to be co-operative caudillos who concentrated on fighting, not factionalism, and even had the allegiance of local Indians and their chiefs such as Manaure and Tupepe. After the execution of Piar, Mariño was isolated and his government collapsed. Bolívar could afford to await his voluntary submission. He sent Colonel Sucre and General Cedeño on missions of pacification to persuade Mariño's allies and subordinates to acknowledge the authority of the supreme chief. His charges against Mariño were expressed in precise terms: while Piar was a 'rebel', Mariño was a 'dissident', a threat to authority and unity, and Bolívar made clear his determination 'to break up the faction of which you are caudillo'.[98] He believed that conditions were turning against eastern caudillism: 'Güiria can no longer provide support and resources for rebellious caudillos, who are isolated, harassed, and

[96] Decree, 24 Sept. 1817, *Escritos*, xi. 94–5.
[97] Regulation, 7 June 1817, Decree, 23 Sept. 1817, in O'Leary, *Memorias*, xv. 264–8, 305.
[98] Bolívar to Mariño, 17 Sept. 1817, in *Escritos*, xi. 27.

driven to despair by our troops as well as by those of the enemy.'[99] Bermúdez was appointed governor and military commandant of Cumaná, a province so impoverished by war that it was incapable of sustaining independent caudillism and had to be supplied from outside. But the tactic of using caudillos to control caudillos was not a complete success; it was impossible to subvert the system through the personnel and structure designed to protect it. Moreover, caudillos were conscious of hierarchy. While Bolívar regarded Bermúdez as an agent of unification, others knew him as a savage and vindictive rival, a medium of discord, not peace, the archcaudillo, who happened now to be on Bolívar's side. Mariño rejected the mission of Bermúdez and swore that 'no power on earth would remove him from his province.'[100] Conflict between the two caudillos simply held up the military effort in 1818 and enabled the royalists to dominate Cumaná. It was some time before Bolívar could pacify Mariño and persuade him to collaborate in an attack on the enemy; late in 1818 he appointed him general-in-chief of the Army of the East, with jurisdiction in the llanos of Barcelona, while other eastern districts were assigned to Bermúdez and Cedeño. But the struggle with caudillism was not over. Having reconciled the easterners, Bolívar had still to win over the strong man of the west, José Antonio Páez.

Páez was the perfect caudillo, the model against whom all others were measured. He was of, yet above, the llaneros; in, yet outside, the llanos. However modest his origins, he did not come from the margin of society. He was white, or could pass for white, son of a petty official, heir of the colonial bureaucracy; he had fled into the llanos after a private affray in Barinas, and was promoted a cavalry captain in the army of the First Republic. He underwent recognizable preparations for leadership, learning llanero life the hard way on a cattle estate, and becoming more successful than others in looting, fighting, and killing. His qualities of leadership attracted his first followers, and plunder retained them. Like most caudillos he specialized in guerrilla fighting rather than regular warfare, and he knew the plains and rivers of the south-west and the tactics suitable for that region. He was the prototype of the man on horseback, lance at the ready, leading his bands in cattle raiding, in fighting rivals, in defeating Spaniards. The ideological commitment of his followers was slight,

---

[99] Bolívar to Cedeño, 22 Sept. 1817, in O'Leary, *Memorias*, xv. 301–2; Bolívar to Zaraza, 3 Oct. 1817, in *Escritos*, xi. 157–8.
[100] Parra-Pérez, *Mariño y la independencia de Venezuela*, ii. 497–8.

and booty was a greater interest. His troops, or some of them, had previously fought for the enemy and were 'composed in large part of those ferocious and valiant zambos, mulattos, and blacks who had formed the army of Boves'.[101] But Páez had his own methods with the llaneros. Many of the Venezuelan officers he regarded as barbarians and assassins. Unlike them, he did not kill prisoners. Royalist llaneros received fair treatment. Those who were interested were welcomed into the patriot forces; the rest were sent home to spread his reputation for tolerance and gain more adherents. This was the force which he fashioned into an army of cavalry. This was the force Bolívar wanted for the army of independence.

Páez had already won a leadership struggle in 1816 before he faced Bolívar. Most Venezuelans regarded the phantom government of Dr Fernando Serrano at Trinidad de Arichuna as irrelevant, and they had little confidence in Colonel Francisco de Paula Santander, the New Granadan officer whom Serrano had appointed commander-in-chief of the Army of the West. This was a case, as José de Austria pointed out, where a formal 'constitutional' structure, isolated and powerless, had to yield to a more realistic authority, the caudillo; for the local military 'did not recognize any superior authority other than that gained by the valour and daring with which they fought. . . .' What the llanero soldiers wanted and the situation demanded was 'an absolute military chief' in command of operations, recruits, and resources. The so-called military revolt of Arichuna, therefore, was not a caudillo coup but a spontaneous movement among officers, llaneros, and priests to produce a leader who could deliver them from the enemy. 'The instinct of self-preservation was the principal incentive. Colonel Santander was not the leader needed for that war: in other campaigns, in other military and civil duties, his knowledge and intelligence could be useful; but for the difficulties then prevailing he lacked the essential qualities.'[102] According to Páez, he was 'elected' to replace Santander, for the troops wanted 'a supreme chief'.[103] There was a certain truth in the claim: this was how a caudillo was made, and these were his qualities, voted upon by a junta of senior military commanders in the Apure. It was a different route from that taken by Bolívar.

---

[101] Díaz, *Recuerdos sobre la rebelión de Caracas*, 324.

[102] Austria, *Historia militar de Venezuela*, ii. 454–5.

[103] José Antonio Páez, *Autobiografía del General José Antonio Páez* (2 vols.; Caracas, 1973), i. 83.

The guerrilla war which Páez then waged was a personal triumph; in the lands of the Arauca River and the plains of Apure he was supreme. But his force was not effectively linked to the independence movement, and while the Spaniards were harassed, they were not destroyed. Bolívar knew that he needed Páez and his army for the revolution. The two leaders came to terms.

Páez claimed that he commanded in the Apure 'with absolute independence and answerable to no human power'. Yet when Bolívar sent two officers from Guayana to ask that Páez recognize him as 'supreme head of the republic', the caudillo did not hesitate; he agreed without even consulting the officers who had elected him, and insisted to his reluctant troops that they do the same. So Páez submitted his authority to that of the Liberator, 'taking into account the military talents of Bolívar, the prestige of his name and his reputation abroad, and realizing above all the advantage to be derived from a supreme and central authority which would direct the different caudillos operating in various parts....'[104] When Páez first met Bolívar in the llanos at San Juan de Payara he was struck by the contrast between his civilized manner and the wild surroundings, between his refined appearance and the barbarism of the llaneros: 'There could be seen in one place the two indispensable elements to make war: the intellectual force which plans and organizes and the material force which brings them to effect, qualities which assist each other and which are ineffective without the other.'[105] The caudillo's stereotypes were false and he was wrong in assuming that Bolívar was an intellectual only. Moreover, he still played with the idea of an independent authority, and when a group of officers and llaneros at San Fernando de Apure attempted to install him as general-in-chief, he accepted, and it needed firm action by Bolívar to nip this movement in the bud. In his autobiography Páez tells the story as an innocent bystander, but this was not the impression of O'Leary.[106]

Incidents of this kind did not go unnoticed at the time. The caudillos were not helpless in the face of events; political and military options were open to them. This was why contemporary historians tended to criticize them for insubordination. Páez rejected the criticism:

[104] Ibid. i. 124.
[105] Ibid. i. 128.
[106] Ibid. i. 153–4; O'Leary, *Narración*, i. 489–91; *The 'Detached Recollections' of General D. F. O'Leary*, ed. R. A. Humphreys (London, 1969), 19–20.

Sr. Restrepo, speaking of the guerrilla chiefs who operated in various parts of Venezuela, says that they behaved like great lords of feudal times, with absolute independence, and that only slowly and reluctantly, especially the present writer, did they submit to the authority of the supreme chief. This historian forgets that at the time to which he refers there was no central government, and force of circumstances obliged the military chieftains to exercise an independent authority, as they did until Bolívar returned from abroad and requested us to recognise his authority as supreme chief.[107]

Páez omits to say that there were still many examples of insubordination. In February 1818 he refused to follow Bolívar's lead and take the offensive to the enemy, and instead continued to press the siege of San Fernando. There were good military reasons for his decision. San Fernando was important in itself and for an opening to New Granada, while to pursue Morillo northward into the mountains was to take the patriot cavalry into territory where the Spanish infantry was superior. The subsequent campaign was not to Bolívar's advantage. But there were also political elements in the caudillo's action, as O'Leary points out:

In this, too, Bolívar had to acquiesce, because the troops of the Apure were more like the contingent of a confederate state than a division of his army. They wanted to return to their homes. . . . Páez, accustomed to exercise a despotic will and the enemy of all subordination, could not reconcile himself to an authority which he had so recently recognized. And Bolívar, for his part, was too shrewd and tactful to exasperate the violent and impetuous Páez.[108]

Bolívar still understood the limits of his authority, his dependence on the resources of individual chieftains, the need for persuasion rather than compulsion. He tried to educate the caudillos into constitutional ways, patiently struggling to instil orderly behaviour into men who were anarchic by nature. He admonished Zaraza simply to obey orders: 'The Republic is on a straight and orderly course; there is no place for abuses, which now must give way to the law and the constitution.'[109] In preparing to invade New Granada, Bolívar was careful to avoid trouble from the caudillos, aware of the danger behind him as well as of the enemy ahead.

Bolívar led a trained army into New Granada, and the victory of

---

[107] Páez, *Autobiografía*, i. 155.
[108] O'Leary, *Narración*, i. 461.
[109] Bolívar to Zaraza, 13 Apr. 1819, in O'Leary, *Memorias*, xvi. 307.

Boyacá in August 1819 set the seal of success on his authority and his strategy. Meanwhile in Venezuela the caudillos were engaged in smaller operations, not always successfully and rarely in agreement among themselves. Páez ignored instructions from Bolívar to move towards Cúcuta and cut the enemy communications with Venezuela. He justified his action by claiming that he was more urgently required in Lower Apure, where anarchy had broken out for want of his authority, and where bandits, robbers, and rustlers had virtually taken over the province in place of recruits for the army: 'I am proud to tell you that my mere presence was enough to restore order; and that men hitherto running wild joined me in a flash and enabled me to form a division which is now the terror of western Caracas.'[110] Other caudillos had less success or fewer excuses. Mariño failed to link up with Bermúdez. Urdaneta was obliged to take Arismendi prisoner for insubordination. Bolívar needed the victory of Boyacá. He was now powerful enough to overlook the excesses of the caudillos and to post Arismendi and Bermúdez to military commands in the east.[111] His next task was to end the war in Venezuela.

The Carabobo campaign was important not only for the defeat of the Spaniards but also for the further integration of the caudillos into a national army. As divisional commanders, they led their troops out of their homelands to serve under a commander-in-chief whom they had so often repudiated in the past. To bring the republican army to its most effective position at the right time in the course of June 1821—this marked true progress in organization and discipline, the direct result of the military reforms of Bolívar. As the army advanced in search of its adversary, it consisted of three divisions: the first commanded by General Páez, the second under General Cedeño, and the third in reserve commanded by Colonel Plaza; General Mariño served on the General Staff of the Liberator himself. Bolívar described this army as 'the greatest and finest ever to bear arms in Colombia on any battlefield'.[112] The victory of 24 June crowned these great troop movements. Cedeño and Plaza fell in battle. Páez was promoted to general-in-chief on the field. And Mariño was left as commander-in-chief of the army, while Bolívar and Páez went on to enter Caracas.

[110] Páez to Bolívar, Achaguas, 2 Sept. 1819, in *Archivo del General José Antonio Páez* (2 vols.; Caracas, 1973), i. 142.
[111] Rivas Vicuña, *Las guerras de Bolívar*, iv. 152–5.
[112] O'Leary, *Narración*, ii. 90.

Carabobo, however, did not signify the death of the caudillos. While these warriors could be organized for war and marched into battle, peace would let them loose again. More turbulent than Güemes, less populist than Artigas, the Venezuelan caudillos were there to stay, guardians and scourges of governments.

5. Mexico: Clerical Caudillos

The Mexican countryside, like that of Venezuela, was a zone of estate power and bandit protest. The rural lawlessness surviving from the late colonial period, part social, part criminal in origin, quickly spread across central and southern Mexico as royal government collapsed and new opportunities opened for competing groups and leaders. Landless labourers, dispossessed peasants, contrabandists, the unemployed, all were likely recruits to brigandage, urged on by discontented elements higher up the social scale. The starting point was self-interest rather than social protest.[113] Royalist demands for men and resources might tempt villages to look to the local bandits for protection. But bandits could terrorize peasants as well as proprietors and in Mexico they did so. Royalists and rebels competed for plunder in a war which engaged interests as well as ideologies. After the capture of Oaxáca by the insurgents it was a free-for-all. According to a royalist spy, 'the looting was immense, and comprised a lot of money and cochineal, cotton and other products'.[114] Every side looted, royalists, revolutionaries, and independent guerrillas, and allegiance was determined not by conviction but by opportunity. Bandits might join the royal armies when these were winning, support the revolution when it came their way, and revert to banditry when neither offered a living. As the patriot and chronicler Carlos María Bustamante observed, many of the followers of guerrilla bands 'were people who attach themselves to the military units because they smell booty, and promptly disappear at the slightest change in the fortunes of war'.[115] Royalist generals were no less cruel and greedy

---

[113] Hamnett, *Roots of Insurgency*, 59, 64–5.

[114] Ernesto Lemoine Villicaña, *Morelos, su vida revolucionaria a través de sus escritos y de otros testimonios de la época* (Mexico, 1965), 263.

[115] Carlos María de Bustamante, *Cuadro histórico de la revolución mexicana* (3 vols.; Mexico, 1961), i. 321–2, 432.

than guerrilla chiefs. As in Venezuela, the transition from bandit to guerrilla was a painless process and the methods hardly differed. Merchants, miners, and landowners, anyone needing safe-conducts for their persons or property would have to negotiate with armed men straddling the routes, who might be royalists, rebels, or private operators.[116]

Rebel chieftains often came from the popular sectors and were mestizos, *mulatos*, or Indians. But the backgrounds and objectives of the rebel bands varied widely.[117] In the Bajío, where there was an element of social mobility, they were composed of small farmers, tenants, and similar groups, and were more likely to be mestizos than Indians. In the years around 1810 economic conditions and pressures on peasants rather than pure land hunger were the basic causes of rural distress and protest. Attacks on haciendas, therefore, did not signify social revolution but a search for subsistence. In Guadalajara, on the other hand, rebels took to arms with a different cry. Here the survival of village communities and competition for land rights set village against village, and communities against private estates, while there was also endemic conflict over customary usages. In the region of Guanajuato the majority of rebels were mestizos and poor whites, most of them agricultural workers or cow-hands born or resident on haciendas.[118] They became insurgents because they were overworked and underfed, and had too little land and too many debts; in these conditions a sudden dearth could make life precarious and drive peasants to strike at proprietors and creditors. At this level there were few explicitly political demands; peasants wanted to escape from debt and oppression and stirred themselves at the first sign of government vacillation and military weakness. More precise political aims were only articulated by the major caudillos. Many of these were priests and as such lacked some of the assets enjoyed by the Venezuelan *jefes*, but in other respects they showed unmistakable caudillo qualities.

Rebels in Mexico would have remained bandits had they not been mobilized by exceptional leaders who drew support not from personal domains but from bases of power to which they had access through their special status and prestige. Throughout Spanish America many

---

[116] Christon I. Archer, 'Banditry and Revolution in New Spain, 1790–1825', in Paul J. Vanderwood (ed.), 'Social Banditry and Spanish American Independence', *Biblioteca Americana*, 1, 2 (1982), 59–90.

[117] Hamnett, *Roots of Insurgency*, 197–8.

[118] Ibid. 188.

clerics joined the revolution, most as chaplains, some as fighting men, and others as a mixture of both. Mexico, however, produced two great priest-caudillos and a host of minor clerical warriors. Was this a legacy of a colonial Church dominated by Spaniards, of whom Hidalgo said 'they are not Catholics, except politically: their God is money'?[119] Was it a consequence of defeated ideals, the reaction of frustrated reformers? Was it a protest against the Bourbon attack on clerical privilege, an attack which culminated in the abolition of the *fuero* by Viceroy Venegas in 1812? Whatever the reason, priests led the way, responding in kind to the ferocity of royalist clergy, such as the Carmelite Fray Elias who strode through the war with a crucifix in one hand and a pistol in the other, and the Andalucian friar Antonio Martínez who would confess a rebel prisoner then shoot him.

Miguel Hidalgo, *cura* of Dolores, headed a parish, not a hacienda. But his parish was a source of friends, clients, and supporters. His concern for the people of Dolores was seen in the years before 1810 not only in his religious ministry but also in his efforts to improve their economic prospects and to promote useful agricultural and industrial projects. These seem to have been appreciated locally, and caused Bustamante to conclude that Hidalgo first won the hearts of his parishioners by offering them kindness and benefits.[120] But official obstruction turned him against Bourbon government, which stifled voices such as his and promised more than it fulfilled. His invocation of the Virgin of Guadalupe was a bid to anticipate criticism and to pre-empt ecclesiastical as well as political justification. Hidalgo therefore first acquired a personal following. He increased this by freeing prisoners from the local gaol. Then he summoned people to church, where his authority was legitimate, and where he announced that religion was in danger from the hated *gachupines* and their Spanish masters, that the time of freedom had come and unjust taxation was finished. In this way, combining the status of priest and rebel, representing social and racial resentments, and invoking religious justification, he acquired a reputation beyond Dolores. But this would not have been sufficient to make him a caudillo without a wider network of contacts. These he had already established with people who had links to the populace and could mobilize masses: *mayordomos*, village

---

[119] Quoted in Bustamante, *Cuadro histórico*, i. 331, ii. 512.
[120] Ibid. i. 201.

chiefs, innkeepers, muleteers, lower-rank militia officers, miners' spokesmen, parish priests in the various regions of Zacatecas, San Luis Potosí, and Guadalajara, a kind of underground network beneath the official regime and beyond Dolores.[121]

His followers came from the popular classes, their expectations raised by the promise of access to land and resources, an end to local grievances, corrupt officials, and unpopular taxes. The cavalry was led by *mayordomos* and recruited from *vaqueros* and other horsemen of the estates, 'almost all of them castes', and armed mainly with lances, machetes, and swords. The infantry were Indians from various pueblos under their chiefs, armed with slings, bows, clubs, and lances, 'and as many of them brought their women and children, the whole appeared more like a tribe of barbarians wandering from one place to another than an army on the march'.[122] These views of the conservative Alamán were confirmed by Bustamante: 'The army of Hidalgo, although divided into sections, marched without order, nor was it possible to integrate into it these great mobs of men, women and children.'[123] Hidalgo was not as successful as the Venezuelan caudillos in controlling his forces, 80,000 strong at their peak, and this was one of the reasons why he held back from attacking Mexico City, fearful of the destruction that his hordes would inflict or suffer. On the other hand he authorized the plunder of houses and haciendas belonging to Spaniards. 'Unlucky the estate of a European if Hidalgo's army passed by: with a tremendous cry of "Virgin of Guadalupe and death to the gachupines" they fell upon the maize fields and soon lifted the crop. At first the estates of Americans suffered less, but in the course of the war all came to be treated the same.'[124] And Hidalgo encouraged them: 'take it, my sons, it is all yours'. Rebuffed by the creoles, with whom he had much in common, Hidalgo had no alternative but to turn populist. This in turn alienated his first creole followers and reduced his support base.

Hidalgo entered Guadalajara as a victor and was greeted like a sovereign. Satisfied in the exercise of his own power, which was increasingly personal, he was not interested in the formation of a

[121] Christon I. Archer, 'Where Did All the Royalists Go? New Light on the Military Collapse of New Spain, 1810–1822', in Jaime E. Rodríguez O. (ed.), *The Mexican and Mexican American Experience in the 19th Century* (Tempe, Arizona, 1989), 25.
[122] Lucas Alamán, *Historia de Méjico* (5 vols.; Mexico, 1849–52), i. 580–1.
[123] Bustamante, *Cuadro histórico*, i. 65, 73.
[124] Alamán, *Historia de Méjico*, i. 381–2.

national government. He himself filled the vacuum of institutions and exercised a caudillo's patronage. According to Alamán, military promotions were there for the asking, and ministers were appointed without reference to any advice: 'the power that Hidalgo exercised was absolute.'[125] He converted the *audiencia* into a civil court, appointed magistrates from the insurgent side, and assumed the presidency himself. The new court wasted no time on war trials. He gave himself power of life and death, and for any Spaniards caught it was death, usually at night in batches of twenty or thirty, and often at the hands of the bandit chief Agustín Marroquin, whom Hidalgo freed from gaol and made his chief executioner.[126] Hidalgo seems to have had a cruel streak, as Bustamante noted, attributing it to the frustration of his development projects in Dolores and his subsequent bitterness against Spaniards. But his merciless decisions, an exercise in personal power without any institutional legitimacy, disgusted many of his fellow rebels and lost him any support he might have gained from the creoles. Bustamante looked for the best in his American hero: 'Hidalgo did much, but could have done more; if he had had the character of Morelos, who extracted gold from the same dirt, Mexico could have gained its independence in six months and with less bloodshed.'[127] It was to José María Morelos that the revolution now looked for policy, organization, and national vision.

Yet Morelos, like Hidalgo, lacked a material base. His influence, too, came first from his priesthood; this had raised him up from humble beginnings to the college of San Nicolás Obispo in Valladolid, and finally to the parish of Carácuaro, a respectable if not a comfortable living, and one which enabled him to trade in grain and consumer goods for the benefit of his parishioners. He was sponsored by Hidalgo, who had known him since his college days, recognized his exceptional qualities, and now commissioned him to extend the revolution to the Pacific. 'From the forests of Tierra Caliente went forth a tiger to tear apart the old lion of Iberia.'[128] He started out not from a hacienda but from a church, marching from his parish with his servants, a few old shotguns, and some lances to lead a major campaign.[129] He abandoned the identity of a pious priest to assume

[125] Ibid. i. 447, ii. 90; Hamnett, *Roots of Insurgency*, 134.
[126] Alamán, *Historia de Méjico*, ii. 103.
[127] Bustamante, *Cuadro histórico*, i. 202.
[128] Lemoine Villicaña, *Morelos*, 27–9, 31; Bustamante, *Cuadro histórico*, ii. 187.
[129] Lemoine Villicaña, *Morelos*, 167.

that of a military chieftain, helped too by his own dramatic personality. According to a royalist prisoner, 'the dress of the priest is white cotton trousers, shirt and jacket, a scarf around his waste, a silk band around his head, a pair of pistols in his belt, and a sword in his hand.'[130]

In the south, on the strength of his revolutionary credentials, Morelos received the support of several persons of substance such as the Bravo and Galeana families, who were part of an extended kinship network loyal to the revolution and to Morelos. With an independent command he was able to demonstrate his personal talents, intelligence, determination, and vision of independence. He was also able to develop new and better tactics, employing smaller, more disciplined, and more specialist units, and recruiting blacks and *mulatos* of the coast who knew how to use firearms. His Aguacatillo decree (17 November 1810) abolishing slavery and class distinctions had a political as well as a social object—to extend his support base. His success in the coastal region confirmed the commitment of the Bravo and Galeana families, whose resources in land, supplies, and manpower were indispensable to him, and whose extensive network of relations and dependants brought in new recruits to the movement. Thus this southern insurgent group, by its family ties, adhesion of numerous *clientela*, regional identity, and respect for the *cura* Morelos, was the Mexican model of insurgency. The supreme caudillo worked through the existing structure of power; he acquired not only a base but also a debt, which could be recognized in his pro-creole policy and his refusal to tolerate animosity towards whites. And the ultimate bond was that of personal ties and individual loyalty characteristic of the caudillo system. Hermenegildo Galeana, a faithful fighter for the revolution, 'loved Morelos to the point of idolatry, and respected him just as much, and always spoke to him with the utmost courtesy'.[131] Galeana in turn had a personal following among the Negroes of the southern zone, who called him 'Tata Gildo' and followed him blindly.

The execution of Hidalgo and his own early victories left Morelos as the recognized *primer jefe de la nación*, without equal or rival. His social policy in favour of the poor, Indians, and slaves was similar to that of Hidalgo but more precise, and calculated to strengthen his

---

[130] Bustamante, *Cuadro histórico*, i. 62.
[131] Ibid. ii. 62; Hamnett, *Roots of Insurgency*, 144–7.

power base. But caudillism was diluted by institutions. The Congress of Chilpancingo, a premature creation, weakened the caudillo's position, introducing politics, debate, and divisions within the insurgent ranks before a decisive military victory had even been won. The experience underlined the determination of Morelos, like Bolívar, to crown insurgency with a constitution; but it also demonstrated how risky it was for a caudillo to become the servant of a congress in the middle of a war. Morelos, moreover, underrated the enemy. He tried to fight the royalists on their own terms and tactics and to wage an open campaign for Puebla in 1811–13. This was not the role of a caudillo, and he found that he did not have a following among the popular classes in Puebla. He was defeated at Valladolid (23 December 1813) and Puruarán (5 January 1814), and while his prestige declined, so that of Agustín Iturbide rose on the royalist side. Congress became an incumbrance, the constitution a distraction. The Spaniards captured and killed his two closest comrades, Hermenegildo Galeana and the clerical caudillo Mariano Matamoros, and finally they closed in on Morelos himself. Populist caudillos, even one who reassured the whites, could not overcome their origins or secure a creole constituency without which independence was impossible.

After Hidalgo and Morelos, the remnants of insurgency survived as little more than a form of banditry. Indians who had gained land sought to defend it; mestizos formed bands to sack haciendas. All cried 'Viva la América y la Virgen de Guadalupe'. But they had no programme, no policy, only a determination to exploit the disarray at the top and the disorder in the countryside. Minor caudillos emerged such as Valerio Trujano, Albino García Ramos, Francisco Osorno, and Julián Villagrán. Trujano was 'a man born to be a general', a muleteer by origin who took advantage of the revolution to raise himself to the heights of insurgency, dominating the roads of the Mixteca to ambush Spanish detachments, supplies, and arms. 'He began to make his raids with a few people, but with such skill that his good name and fortune attracted many followers, and soon he was one of Morelos's most distinguished generals.'[132] Albino García was the scourge of the Bajío, 'the most active and terrible guerrilla chief produced by the insurrection'.[133] A mestizo—some said a pure Indian—from Salamanca, herdsman, contrabandist, hacienda over-

---

[132] Bustamante, *Cuadro histórico*, i. 288.
[133] Alamán, *Historia de Méjico*, ii. 249, 294, iii. 186, 189.

seer, he was a rebel by instinct, skilful on horse and in fights, an apprentice and then a master of insurgent leadership. He joined Hidalgo's movement but recognized no superior; as he boasted, only the mountains were above him. He was the prototype of the guerrilla chief, who adhered to the cause of independence without plan or policy, driven by an ambition to raid and rob, aims which were at the service of revolution in so far as he led the oppressed to plunder Spanish haciendas, but might equally be turned against others. 'The insolence of Albino', remarked Bustamante, 'was directed not only against Spaniards but also against Americans.'[134] He recruited into his band *vaqueros*, Indians, and people from villages in their hundreds. He imposed his dominance on other *partidas*, such as that of the caudillo Benito Loya, and he made himself feared in the province by attacking convoys and villages, patrols and travellers, Spaniards and Mexicans, in a relentless and indiscriminate guerrilla war.[135]

Albino García and his like were local caudillos, whose rebellion contained no possibility of growth or development. His war of independence was a regional war; he fought for his own space, to be lord of his own frontiers; national sentiment and organization were beyond his horizon. He sought to provoke a revolt of the *campesinos* and among them he had at least a safe area against capture: 'he can rely on the whole rabble in his favour, and it is impossible to catch him', reported a royalist commander. But he was eventually taken on 8 June 1812, shot and quartered.[136] Without a common plan, insurgency of this kind was open to the leadership of the strong, the daring, and the violent, many of whom were pathological killers. José Antonio Arroyo was a minor caudillo, a 'monster' whom Bustamante knew from personal experience:

He was a peasant, squat and with heavy shoulders, a mottled and spotty face, black and ferocious eyes, and a fierce and menacing appearance; he always wore his hat pulled well down, so that it was difficult to see his dark and ominous look; his voice was threatening, his speech short, his language coarse. He was a combination of ferocity and gross superstition; he affected much piety and deference to all the priests, and always kissed their hands respectfully. But he had no qualms in hitting a man on the head with an iron hammer and leaving him for dead.[137]

---

[134] Bustamante, *Cuadro histórico*, i. 292.
[135] Ibid. i. 320–2, 325; Fernando Osorno Castro, *El insurgente Albino García* (Mexico, 1982), 23–9, 39–50, 67–84; Hamnett, *Roots of Insurgency*, 180–2.
[136] Bustamante, *Cuadro histórico*, i. 437.
[137] Ibid. i. 431.

These were the rebels obedient only to themselves, used but not controlled by Hidalgo and Morelos, and bequeathed to Mexico as a new social type, a new military menace. Insurgency of this kind was contained by the security forces but never extinguished. Local caudillos like Mateo Colin, Pedro 'el Negro' Rojas, Gordiano Guzmán, Pedro Moreno, Manuel Muñiz, P. Luciano Navarrete, Miguel Borja, and P. Miguel Torres swarmed over the centre and the south, and if they did not desert the revolution they did not advance it.[138] They imposed themselves by personal power and intimidation, and as Bustamante pointed out, there was little to choose in character and style 'between these chiefs and those of the king'.[139] They also represented typical caudillo origins, being heads of kinship and clientage networks which prevailed regardless of political change. Royalist amnesty policy from 1816 encouraged the conversion of insurgent bands into government forces, patrons and clients moving effortlessly from one side to the other. The guerrillas did not cease to rob and raid, or abandon the life they had led as outlaws. If their new masters objected, they could always return to the old, though in Veracruz Guadalupe Victoria preferred to go underground rather than become a guerrilla opportunist. The security forces themselves and their officers began to take on some of the characteristics of caudillism, and regional commanders ruled their zones of operation like personal fiefdoms, happy in their distance from central control. This legacy of caudillism, handed down by both sides, survived into independence, to be alternatively a convenience and a menace to governments.

By 1821 the royalist government was forced to leave the entire southern zone of Michoacán and Guadalajara under the control of insurgent bands, the principal of which was led by Gordiano Guzmán, a *mulato* who received much of his support from coastal blacks and *mulatos*. Guzmán had links with other caudillos of the south, Vicente Guerrero and Juan Alvarez, who operated in the hinterland of Acapulco and kept alive a minimum commitment to the cause of independence. Alvarez, son of a Galician father in the southern countryside, had received a rudimentary education but was formed essentially by guerrilla war, first with Morelos then with Guerrero. His manifesto of 6 September 1820 exhorted the local population to

---

[138] Ibid. ii. 708–9; Hamnett, *Roots of Insurgency*, 178–9, 183–7, 194–6.
[139] Bustamante, *Cuadro histórico*, i. 432.

defend the rights of 'criollismo against rapacious gachupines' and to
fight for liberty. But Alvarez also fought for regional space, with some
success. The entire south-west remained outside effective government control, Spanish and republican alike. Independence in Mexico
was imposed not by the insurgent caudillos but by the formerly
royalist interest groups backed by the Spanish army. But the caudillos
were still there, secure in their regional retreats.

6. *The Legacy of War*

The wars of independence in Spanish America were won not by
caudillos and guerrilla bands but by regular armies; the army of the
Andes and that of Colombia taught the same lesson—caudillism
might be a cheaper way of waging war, but it was also less decisive,
unless incorporated into professional armies. Nevertheless war advanced the caudillo and outlined his profile more clearly. War legitimized the bandit chief and guerrilla leader and made him into a
military hero, increasing his opportunities and giving him a new
autonomy. He was now recognized as someone who had a role, a
following, a base of power. The wars of independence, therefore,
bequeathed to Spanish America caudillos in the making, and they
were there to stay and prosper. It was unlikely that they would
disappear with the end of the war and leave the field to new political
leaders. For these were special wars.

The wars of independence were not short, sharp conflicts, followed
by the departure of the soldiers and the entry of civilians. They were
long wars, involving five, ten, fifteen years of fighting. Institutions
were out of place. As Bustamante said, the insurgent congress in
Mexico was 'a monster without arms' which impeded Morelos rather
than helped him.[140] The revolution needed caudillos, men who already possessed local bases of power and prestige, and called on
them for lengthy service either in fighting or in raising supplies, but
in any case performing difficult and indispensable services for the
wartime state. At the same time the wars were fought over long
distances. Few caudillos operated under the immediate eye or close
presence of a central government or higher command; rather they
acted on their own initiative in remote provinces or distant fronts,

[140] Ibid. ii. 6.

where they made daily decisions without reference to higher authority. Duration and distance, these provided fertile ground for caudillism in most parts of Spanish America. Chile, by contrast, made a short, early bid for independence, followed by total counter-revolution and then a rapid liberation. Was this immunity from prolonged warfare one of the reasons why caudillism did not have the time or the opportunity to take firm root? Elsewhere the revolution discovered caudillos, endorsed them, promoted them, and made them a familiar part of the political landscape. War implanted caudillism and left it to grow.

3
THE NEW RULERS

1. *Caudillos and Constitutionalists in Argentina*

Peace perpetuated the structures of war and established in Spanish America a dual process, constitutionalism and caudillism. The two were not mutually exclusive. A caudillo could rule under a constitution, alongside a constitution, or without a constitution. But republican leaders tended to prefer one or the other, and caudillism was a matter of choice as well as of conditions. Statesmen such as Bolívar, Santander, San Martín, Rivadavia, were not caudillos but men seeking to place executive government within a framework of law and institutions. They did not have a personal economic base or social stronghold. They were professional politicians or soldiers, following the career track of revolution and its sequel. While they were far from being militarists, they preferred regular armies to irregular bands. Moreover they saw government primarily in terms of policies embodied in legislation, not patronage directed to interest groups. The caudillos, on the other hand, were bound by two constraints. A wide cultural gap divided them from the leaders of the first rank; they did not have a vision of political change and constitutional progress. And they were trapped by conditions, coming as they did from a family and regional base which defined the limits and objects of their power and policy. Regional power normally derived from ownership of land and control of labour, and was used to protect the region's resources, against the centre if necessary. A caudillo needed access to land and to patronage, the indispensable materials for building political power.

In Buenos Aires the war against Spain did not create caudillos. The war leaders were civilian politicians aided—or frustrated—by professional soldiers, and the war was fought on distant frontiers. In the process, they helped to produce caudillos in the interior, but not in Buenos Aires itself. There the transition from bureaucrats to caudillos took place after independence and arose out of a struggle for power within Buenos Aires and in response to threats from the

enemies outside. After a decade of conflict between capital and
provinces, between central government and regional rights, between
unitarians and federalists, the political framework of the Río de la
Plata collapsed. Independent republics proliferated, prepared to fight
for their existence and take the war to Buenos Aires itself. Provincial
caudillos—Estanislao López of Santa Fe, Francisco Ramírez of
Entre Ríos—led their gaucho hordes, the *montoneros*, against the
capital. On 1 February 1820 they defeated the forces of Buenos Aires
at the battle of Cepeda and proceeded to destroy the directorate, the
congress, and all traces of central authority. In the months which
followed Buenos Aires was submerged in almost total anarchy. The
unitarians were humiliated, while persons and property were at the
mercy of caudillos, gauchos, and Indians.

Buenos Aires looked to the south and asked the estancieros to lead
their rural militias to the rescue. They responded willingly, aware of
the danger to their own interests. Who could stand by while alien
caudillos threatened their government? Who wanted their well-stocked
estancias occupied or looted by *montoneros* fleeing from the poverty of
their own provinces? Juan Manuel de Rosas, leader of the southern
estancieros, was certainly ready to come. He later rationalized his
action as a defence of the common good: 'Rosas lived a contented
and anonymous existence. But from 1820 his troubles began, when
his fellow citizens took him away from his rural labours and obliged
him to help restore order.'[1] In the course of September 1820 Rosas
prepared his *peonaje*. When the governor of Buenos Aires urged him
to make haste, he replied drily, 'People of this class are not so
immediately aware of the approach of danger or the need for sacrifices.'[2] His basic recruiting ground was his own estancia: 'I spoke to
the hands on the estancia where I live on the frontier of the Monte;
they came forward to follow me, and with them and some cavalry
militia I marched to the assistance of our honourable capital which
was calling us to our duty with increasing insistence.'[3] So he led them
north from Los Cerrillos, dressed in red and well mounted. These
were the original Colorados del Monte, 500 men, and they joined the

---

[1] Rosas to Josefa Gómez, 25 July 1869, in *Cartas del exilio 1853–1875*, ed. José
Raed (Buenos Aires, 1974), 131.
[2] Rosas to Balcarce, 6 Sept. 1820, in Julio Irazusta, *Vida política de Juan Manuel de
Rosas, a través de su correspondencia* (8 vols.; Buenos Aires, 1970), i. 85.
[3] 'Manifiesto de Rosas', 10 Oct. 1820, in Juan A. Pradere and Fermín Chávez, *Juan
Manuel de Rosas* (2 vols.; Buenos Aires, 1970), i. 26–8.

army of Buenos Aires as the Fifth Regiment of Militia, the force of a caudillo to confront caudillos.

Rosas used his troops to fight and negotiate peace with the caudillos of the littoral and, in Buenos Aires itself, to defend the government of Martín Rodríguez. For the first time he deployed his *colorados* on the streets of the capital. If Colonel Aráoz de La Madrid is to be believed, the urban élite paid dearly for his intervention, for 'the bloodthirsty gaucho Rosas' used more force than was necessary and 'from that time he took pleasure in oppressing the enlightened classes with the men of the countryside'.[4] Thus the accusation was launched that Rosas used his gaucho hordes to intimidate the upper classes, and imposed rural barbarism on urban civilization. The year 1820 was important in the formation of Rosas. During it he acquired military power, a political reputation, and a reward for his services in the form of more land. He also acquired allies in the provinces. Acting on his own initiative, he made peace with Santa Fe (24 November 1820) by effectively buying off López with funds for his soldiers and cattle for his province, all charged to the Rodríguez government. Thus Rosas secured the friendship of a littoral caudillo, 'and made a point of cultivating him for such time as he would need his help'.[5]

The provincial caudillos did not have the means or the ambition to take over the central government. According to Manuel J. García, minister of finance, there was no possibility of the dismemberment of the state at their hands, 'because the rebel caudillos, the remnants of military anarchy in these provinces, do not possess the talents or the means to effect such a plan. . . . The purely personal authority of these chieftains is rapidly becoming a thing of the past'.[6] The caudillos of the littoral reached their peak in 1820 and then began to decline in disunity and disarray. Artigas was defeated by Ramírez, Ramírez was killed by López, and López was co-opted by Rosas. Ramírez was killed trying to rescue one of his women who had fallen into the hands of enemy troops, and López exhibited his head in a cage.[7] This was the way they lived. Caudillism was not finished in the littoral, but from now personalities counted less than interest groups.

---

[4] Gregorio Aráoz de La Madrid, *Memorias del general Gregorio Aráoz de La Madrid* (2 vols.; Buenos Aires, 1968), i. 197.
[5] Ibid. i. 188–9.
[6] García to Ponsonby, in Ponsonby to Canning, 5 Dec. 1826, PRO, FO 6/13.
[7] Aráoz de La Madrid, *Memorias*, i. 209.

The personalities were inferior and the interests weaker than those in Buenos Aires, and there was no one in the littoral, or in the rest of the country, to compare with Rosas, who was already in the forefront of estancia expansion and moving towards the centre of power in Buenos Aires and its province. For the moment central government remained in the hands of the professionals, Rodríguez and his ally Rivadavia, who was appointed president of the United Provinces of the Río de la Plata on 7 February 1826 with a unitary constitution and a modernizing programme.

Buenos Aires, which during the war had helped to create caudillos in the interior, now prepared the ground for caudillism in its own province. Post-war investment in land, cattle, and *saladeros* was aided by official agrarian policy. All governments in the Río de la Plata were concerned to increase land use and productivity. In Uruguay Artigas had sought to do this by incorporating deprived social sectors into the rural economy. In 1815 he issued a *Reglamento provisorio*, a plan to promote agricultural settlement through land grants to those who were willing to work them, with preference to blacks, *zambos*, Indians, and poor whites, all of whom could 'be granted estancia lots, if by their work and integrity they are ready to increase their own happiness and that of the province'. The source of the grants was to be vacant marginal land and land confiscated from *emigrados, malos europeos y peores americanos*, that is from royalists. There were urgent economic reasons for land development, and these can also be seen in Artigas's decrees forcing vagrants to work and urging estancias into production. But agrarian reform was also a social investment, the work of a populist caudillo concerned to mitigate the effects of estancia formation and to improve the prospects of the rural poor who could not afford to buy land. It was for these that Artigas legislated in 1815, and there is evidence that numerous grants of land and cattle were made.[8] But agrarian radicalism of this kind alarmed the estancieros and could be expected in time to alienate the very class on which any political movement depended. The project of Artigas was halted, therefore, not only by the onset of war with Portugal but also by the reversion of the revolution into conservative hands.

In Buenos Aires such a policy was not even contemplated, either

---

[8] Lucía Sala de Touron, Nelson de la Torre, and Julio C. Rodríguez, *Artigas y su revolución agraria 1811–1820* (Mexico, 1978), 267, 299–322; Halperín Donghi, *Politics, Economics and Society in Argentina*, 285–7.

by constitutionalists or caudillos. Powerful hacendados like Rosas directed expansion southwards against Indian territory. And government played its part when Manuel J. García introduced the system of emphyteusis—from 1822 in Buenos Aires province and in other provinces by the Constituent Congress of 1826—authorizing public land to be rented out for twenty years at fixed rentals.[9] This was not a policy of agrarian reform in the style of Artigas, but it made sense in other respects, for it simultaneously put land to productive use, including new land in the south and south-west of the province, and satisfied the land hunger of the dominant groups and the needs of foreign immigrants.[10] There was no limit to the area that an applicant might rent, and the land commissions which administered the scheme were dominated by landowners. From 1824 to 1827 a number of huge individual grants were made, 6.5 million acres to 112 people and companies, of whom ten received more than 130,000 each. By the 1830s some 21 million acres of public land had been transferred to 500 individuals. The agrarian regime of the Rivadavia period, like that of the colonial past, was based on the principle of renting land rather than owning it. But as the cattle industry grew in importance, as livestock property acquired a new value, so the estancieros began to desire freehold property without time limit, conditions, or rent. To get the terms right, to control the whole production process from the estancia to the port, to ensure supplies for export, the rural sector had to increase its political influence.

Juan Manuel de Rosas represented the rise of a new élite, the estancieros. The independence movement of 1810 had created a type of professional politician, bureaucrat, and soldier who made a career out of the revolution and out of the new state which the revolution founded.[11] They were allied to the urban merchants, though many of these had begun to move into land. By 1820 about half the *cabildo* members were merchants, half estancieros. The same proportion existed in the House of Represenatives. While the rural sector was increasing its political weight, so it was developing its military power, for the estancieros were authorized to maintain armed units for rural security and frontier defence. In the mid-1820s, therefore, two social

[9] John Lynch, *Argentine Dictator: Juan Manuel de Rosas 1829–1852* (Oxford, 1981), 21–2, 56–7.

[10] Jonathan C. Brown, *A Socioeconomic History of Argentina, 1776–1860* (Cambridge, 1979), 149–50.

[11] Halperín Donghi, *Politics, Economics and Society in Argentina*, 205.

groups could be identified, the career revolutionaries allied to the traditional merchant interest, and the new landed class, some of whom came from commerce and still maintained a foothold there. The first group looked abroad, for liberal ideas, foreign capital, and overseas trade. The second group turned inwards to develop land, cattle, and meat-salting plants, and to commercialize the livestock industry for export. They also sought political power corresponding to their economic strength, and served notice on the government of Rivadavia, which possessed political but not economic power, that the day of reckoning was near. The fall of Rivadavia signalled the arrival of the estancieros. Political control now coincided with economic power, and this was considerable. In 1830 the province of Buenos Aires had 5,516 square leagues of occupied land, and this was held by 980 people; of these, 60 people held almost 4,000 square leagues, or 76 per cent of the whole.[12] The rise to power of the merchant–estanciero group, their investment in land, their determination to control policy, these were the circumstances which created Rosas.

The same, of course, could be said of most of the Argentine caudillos, whose origins and careers conformed to classical proto-types. They were born to wealth and power, and came from families which had been owners of landed property and in many cases holders of military appointments since colonial times. They themselves pre-served this inheritance. Among the eighteen caudillos who ruled in the various provinces of Argentina between 1810 and 1870 thirteen were great landowners, one had a landed property of medium size, one was the owner of a shipyard, and some added entrepreneurial activities to those of the hacienda. They all held major military appointments, either in the army or in the militia; and of the twelve who had been old enough to fight in the wars of independence, nine had done so, while others had fought on the Indian frontier or in the civil wars. Wealth was an intrinsic qualification. Fifteen of the group were extremely wealthy, two were of medium wealth. Virtually all had some level of education, but political expectations were not good; nine died violently, three in exile. There was little evidence of social mobility in these careers. No doubt the revolution emancipated the creoles and gave them access to politics, the bureaucracy, and com-

---

[12] Andrés M. Carretero, 'Contribución al conocimiento de la propiedad rural en la provincia de Buenos Aires para 1830', *Boletín del Instituto de Historia Argentina 'Doctor Emilio Ravignani'*, 2nd ser. 13, 22–3 (1970), 246–92, see especially 251–2. (*Note:* 1 square league equalled 6,000 acres.)

merce; but social structure based upon land, wealth, prestige, and education remained essentially unchanged. According to the criterion of wealth, only two of the eighteen caudillos—Estanislao López and Félix Aldao—showed any signs of moving upwards, from medium to great wealth. The rest followed the tradition of their family in wealth and prestige, and simply added to their patrimony. The occupational route they followed had familiar signposts, from *estanciero*, via the military, to caudillo.[13]

Rosas, too, emerged from a landed and military background and he too was a creature of his class. 'In this sense', as his nephew Lucio V. Mansilla remarked, 'Rosas did not make himself, events made him, others made him, a number of extremely wealthy and self-interested people ... behind him these would be ruling.'[14] But Rosas was never a conformist, and there were elements of idiosyncrasy in his career. He was specifically qualified to lead the estancieros. He was never content to be an inheritor of wealth or to hang on the coat tails of his family. He set out to make his own way and to create his own fortune. As a pioneer estanciero he understood the rural economy from the inside; as lord of many peons he exemplified the social hegemony of the landowners; as frontiersman he knew how to deal with Indians. Moreover, in the recruitment of troops, the training and control of militia, and the deployment of units not only on the frontier but in urban operations, he had no equal. It was the military dimension of Rosas's early career which gave him the edge over his rivals. This culminated in his role during the guerrilla war of 1829 against the unitarian rebels, when he raised, controlled, and led the anarchic popular forces in the irregular army which defeated Lavalle's professionals. Rosas was a caudillo before he was elected governor. It did not matter that he was not the largest landowner in the province. In the group of about seventeen landowners with property over 50 square leagues (300,000 acres) Rosas occupied tenth place with 70 square leagues (400,000).[15] But his peons, his militia forces, his 'friendly' Indians were better armed and under firmer control than those of any rival.

Rosas was a source of patronage as well as focus of power. In the interests of the landed sector, he changed emphyteusis rentals into

---

[13] Rubén H. Zorrilla, *Extracción social de los caudillos 1810–1870* (Buenos Aires, 1972), 50–65, 129–30.

[14] Lucio V. Mansilla, *Rozas: Ensayo histórico-psicológico* (Paris, 1913), 145.

[15] Carretero, 'Propiedad rural', 273–92; his cousins, the Anchorena, were first with 134 square leagues.

freehold, and he lavished land upon his military and civilian sup-porters. The *boletos de premios en tierras*, or land certificates as rewards for military service, were one of the principal instruments of land distribution, and some 8,500 were issued in this period. One of the reasons for compensating loyal servants in this way was the lack of public revenue to cover salaries, grants, and pensions. There was obviously a political element at work, too, for land was the richest source of patronage available, a weapon for Rosas, a welfare system for his supporters. Rosas was the great *patrón* and the landowners were his *clientela*. In this sense *rosismo* was less an ideology than an interest, and one which grew with the province. There was no one outside the upper groups equipped to use these grants. The rural social structure was rigid, as the English observer William MacCann noted: 'There is as yet no middle class; the owners of land feeding immense flocks and herds form one class, their herdsmen and shep-herds form another.'[16] Certificates of less than one league were virtually useless in the hands of common soldiers or minor bureau-crats in a country where the existing agrarian structure averaged eight leagues each estate. But in the hands of people who already possessed estates or had the capital to buy them up cheaply, they were a powerful instrument for land accumulation. More than 90 per cent of land certificates granted to soldiers and civilians ended up in the hands of landowners or those who were buying their way into land.[17] Smaller people, who did not have capital for estancia development, sold their certificates to those who did. In other cases powerful men received the certificates of their clients and dependants, or collected them on behalf of their military followers. It all worked, with the help of a compliant administration, towards the extension of existing hold-ings. In the period 1830–52 the land area incorporated as a result of the Desert Campaign and the policy of improving relations with the Indians grew by 42 per cent. This land growth was greater than the growth in the number of estancias, 28 per cent, and in the number of proprietors, 17 per cent.[18] The trend of the Rosas regime was towards greater concentration of property in the hands of a small group.

The collaborators of the caudillo, then, enjoyed great security and

---

[16] William MacCann, *Two Thousand Miles' Ride through the Argentine Provinces* (2 vols.; London, 1853), i. 158; on the *boletos* see Lynch, *Argentine Dictator*, 62–3.

[17] Andrés M. Carretero, *La propiedad de la tierra en la época de Rosas* (Buenos Aires, 1972), 30.

[18] Ibid. 31.

privilege. In 1850, when total revenues reached 62 million pesos, principally from customs, the *contribución directa*, a tax on capital and property, provided only 3 per cent of the total, and even so most of this was paid by commerce rather than land.[19] The Anchorena were the most favoured clients. Rosas himself subsequently admitted that he had specifically exempted their estancias from state demands for peons and cattle, 'a distinction and a privilege which at that time was of supreme value to them and their estancias'.[20] Land opened many doors and these usually led back to more land. The administration was dominated by estancieros. The closest political adviser of Rosas, Nicolás Anchorena, was the greatest landowner of the province, owning some 306 square leagues. Juan N. Terrero, economic adviser of Rosas, had 42 square leagues and left a fortune of 53 million pesos. Angel Pacheco, Rosas's general, had 75 square leagues. Felipe Arana, minister of foreign affairs, had 42 square leagues. Even Vicente López, poet, deputy, and president of the high court, owned 12 square leagues.[21] Rosas was the centre of a large kinship group based on land. He was surrounded by a closely knit economic and political network, linking deputies, law officers, officials, military, all of whom were also landowners and related among themselves or with Rosas. The Anchorena were his cousins; the Ezcurra were close relatives; Felipe Arana was a distant relative; Lucio N. Mansilla was his brother-in-law; while Gervasio and Prudencio Rosas were his brothers. Rosas used his patronage to bind this group even closer.[22] In a letter, admittedly written in exile to make claims against the Anchorena, he pointed out that as governor, 'I served them with notorious favouritism in everything they asked and needed. Those lands they have, to a great extent they got them through me, buying them at very modest prices.'[23]

The polarization of society was not total. Between the patrón and the peon there existed a kind of rural middle sector, people who were engaged in market farming, transport, tenants, and retailers.[24] But

[19] Miron Burgin, *The Economic Aspects of Argentine Federalism 1820–1852* (Cambridge, Mass., 1946), 196.
[20] Rosas to Terrero, Southampton, 21 Nov. 1863, in Adolfo Saldías (ed.), *Papeles de Rozas* (2 vols.; La Plata, 1904–7), ii. 353–4.
[21] Carretero, *La propiedad de la tierra en la época de Rosas*, 38–9.
[22] Slatta, *Gauchos and the Vanishing Frontier*, 95–6.
[23] Rosas to Terrero, Southampton, 21 Nov. 1863, in Saldías (ed.), *Papeles de Rosas*, ii. 353–4.
[24] Brown, *A Socioeconomic History of Argentina*, 155–6, 159.

there was an important difference between the élite and the rest. While there was cohesion and solidarity among the landed class, the popular sectors were heterogeneous in composition and divided into disparate groups, peons on estancias, wage labourers, small farmers or tenants, marginal gauchos, and delinquents. Moreover the rural masses, whether free gauchos or working peons, enjoyed much less family stability and continuity. This was partly an urban–rural division between two cultures; but it was also a feature of the social structure. Whether it is interpreted in terms of town and country, civilization and barbarism, or landowner and labourer, this difference in the degree of family stability was a fundamental feature of Argentine society. Among the gauchos and peons relations between the sexes were merely temporary and the resulting families only loosely united. Marriage was the exception in the pampas, and the head of the rural family was the lone mother, the only permanent parent.[25] It was often the case that the father did not have the means to stay and sustain a family group: he had to sell his labour where he could, or he was recruited into the armies or *montoneros*. Many ranch jobs were short-term and there was a high turnover of peons.[26] The laws against vagrancy, pursuit of delinquents, and coercive controls over labour drove peons into the hands of proprietors, but as tied wage-earners and ranch-hands. This was alien to gaucho culture but it had some advantages and brought the peon into the network of patronage. The relation of patron and client was the essential bond, based upon a personal exchange of assets between these unequal partners. The landowner wanted labour, loyalty, and service in peace and war. The peon wanted subsistence and security.

Thus a *patrón* recruited a *peonada*, who would follow him blindly in ranching, politics, and war. The estanciero had to impose his authority not only by his wealth and status but also by his personal qualities in the rural environment. He had to be as resourceful a gaucho as his own peons. In an emergency he had to have enough skill and power to beat the Indians or resist the authorities. The estanciero was a protector, capable of defending his dependants against marauding bands, recruiting-sergeants, and rival hordes. He was also a provider, who developed and defended local resources, and could give employment, food, and shelter. In the process the

---

[25] Ibid. 157; Slatta, *Gauchos and the Vanishing Frontier*, 58–60.
[26] Slatta, *Gauchos and the Vanishing Frontier*, 32.

gaucho lost his freedom. He became virtually the property of the
patrón; if the estate was his sanctuary, it was also his prison. The
estancia was society in microcosm. Buenos Aires became a gaucho
state, its caudillo a great proprietor, its citizens a swarm of peons, for
these individual alliances multiplied, sought membership of a greater
group, and took protection from a higher chief. Patrons became
clients to more powerful men, and these swore loyalty to yet greater
leaders, until a peak of power was reached and they all became
clients of a superpatron. Rosas was the supreme caudillo, dispensing
patronage or punishment from the summit.

The first target of the rural alliance, as has been seen, was the
Rivadavia regime. Its liberal ideology, attempts to diversify the
economy, and encouragement of immigration, alerted the landed
interest, while the threat to 'nationalize' the revenues of Buenos Aires
and distribute them to other provinces in the interests of a greater
Argentina was regarded as the last straw, for it could only lead to
higher provincial taxation. The fall of Rivadavia and the advent of the
federalists brought a closer identity between 'the holders and the
administrators of power'.[27] In effect the Buenos Aires landowners
overthrew the existing ruling group, the politicians, bureaucrats, and
associated military, who were beginning to form an incipient oligarchy
of 'career revolutionaries', and took direct possession of the government of the province through their representative, Rosas, who, as
Sarmiento put it, 'applied the knife of the gaucho to the culture of
Buenos Aires'.[28] Rosas proceeded warily in taking power; there had
been a high turnover of governments in Buenos Aires. So each step
was measured. In 1827 he had accepted command of the militia of
the province, to the great chagrin of the older, regular army officers.[29]
In 1829 he fought a typical caudillo's campaign, a 'war of resources'
designed to achieve its objectives by waste and destruction of the
estancias of the unitarians, or as the British Consul described it, 'a
gaucho warfare against the properties in the country of all those who
were known to be parties to the revolution'. He sought to subvert the
regular army of General Lavalle, 'to harass and divide the regular
troops, to encourage them to desert, and to treat them well whenever

---

[27] Halperín Donghi, *Politics, Economics and Society in Argentina*, 211–15, 383.

[28] D. F. Sarmiento, *Facundo*, edición crítica y documentada, Prólogo de Alberto
Palcos (La Plata, 1938), 72; see also 132–5.

[29] Ponsonby to Canning, 20 July 1827, PRO, FO 6/18; Parish to Aberdeen, 12 Jan.
1829, PRO, FO 6/26.

they fall into his hands'.[30] Thus the defeat of Lavalle was the defeat of a professional army, a rival force, by the militia of Rosas and his estanciero allies.

Rosas was elected governor of Buenos Aires on 6 December 1829 and given absolute powers by a virtually unanimous vote of the House of Representatives, a body which was dominated by estancieros and linked to Rosas by many bonds of personal allegiance. Thus, as Sarmiento argued, 'the provinces had their revenge on Buenos Aires when they sent to her in Rosas the culmination of their own barbarism.'[31] But Rosas arrived with different thoughts. He was never a determinist. He firmly believed that threats to the stability of state and society originated not in economic and social conditions but in personal malice and inferior moral decisions, evils which could be eradicated from the body politic only by resolute government exacting obedience. He told the House of Representatives in 1832: 'There is no doubt that political upheavals in a state derive from the moral dispositions of its inhabitants, and that when the party of law and order arrives to repress outbreaks of anarchy, unless the original cause is removed, then the reaction is all the more violent.'[32] Once in office and endowed with extraordinary powers, Rosas still had to look over his shoulders for those who wanted to replace his brand of despotism by their own, and even against rival interests within the federalist movement, some of whom—he called them *anarquistas*— favoured constitutionalism. He also had to watch the regular army. The traditional military were still ready to strike at Rosas, as they did in the interior in 1831, a contest 'which although nominally carried on between the partisans of the Unitarian and Federalist factions, was in reality a struggle between the masses of the people against a military force . . . which aimed at nothing less than the establishment of its own despotic power throughout the whole country'.[33]

In 1832 there was opposition in the House of Representatives to the prolongation of his extraordinary powers, for fear of a permanent dictatorship. During the debates a distinction was made 'between powers conferred *ad hoc*, to meet the emergencies of the moment,

---

[30] Rosas to García, 29 Sept. 1830, in Juan Carlos Nicolau (ed.), *Correspondencia inédita entre Juan Manuel de Rosas y Manuel José García* (Instituto de Estudios Histórico-Sociales; Tandil, 1989), 44.

[31] Sarmiento, *Facundo*, 32.

[32] Rosas to House of Representatives, 1832, in Fox to Palmerston, 31 May 1832, PRO, FO 6/34.

[33] Parish to Palmerston, 20 July 1831, PRO, FO 6/32.

and the formal enactment of a fundamental law vesting, continuously, in one person, dictatorial powers, liable only to yearly revision of the legislature'.[34] At the end of the year he relinquished the extraordinary powers and completed his first term of office. An interregnum followed, during which Rosas won renown—and land—in war against the Indians, while his henchmen made life difficult for his successors. He rejected a call to return to power, not out of modesty but in order to raise his price, holding out for extraordinary powers. In fact he wanted to make extraordinary powers ordinary—a working definition of caudillism. As the British minister wrote:

To legalize, and *permanently* to vest in the Executive, powers tantamount to those now termed 'Extraordinary'; to engraft, in short, the 'Facultades Extraordinarias' upon the ordinary prerogatives of the Executive; or, in other words, to convert a Constitutional and Republican, into a virtually despotic system of Government, I take to be the object and aim of all Rosas's machinations.[35]

Eventually he accepted on condition that the legislature grant him the *suma del poder público*, to be exercised according to his own judgement. This it did on 7 March 1835, and Rosas began his long period of rule virtually on his own terms.

The provinces meanwhile were moved by conditions as well as by persons. Provincial autonomies were not merely subject to the centrifugal forces of the time; they responded to the absence of a national state and represented an attempt to create provincial institutions and a state apparatus where otherwise there was nothing. Some were more successful than others. All desperately needed institutions:

A Deputy declared—and he was confirmed in it by others—that in the whole of the four provinces of Santa Fe, Corrientes, Misiones and Entre Rios with a population of upwards of 80,000 souls there is but one legal Advocate, and that the administration of justice has been long in the hands of two ordinary Alcaldes who pronounce sentence even in criminal cases without hearing justification or appeal unless to a Priest who has been known to sign condemnations to death.[36]

Stability and security were rare conditions, to be found in the proximity of government rather than its distance. The provinces acted independently, therefore, first to guarantee social order under the

---

[34] Gore to Palmerston, 20 Nov. 1832, PRO, FO 6/34.
[35] Gore to Palmerston, 30 Aug. 1834, PRO, FO 6/40.
[36] Parish to Canning, 20 July 1826, PRO, FO 6/11.

dominance of local proprietors, and second to defend their interests against other provinces, especially Buenos Aires. In these circumstances, the caudillo history of each province was different. Santa Fe was governed by a typical caudillo, Estanislao López. Entre Ríos lost its caudillo Francisco Ramírez in 1821 and lapsed into leaderless anarchy, torn by what Governor Mansilla described in 1823 as 'caudillos del desorden'.[37] Corrientes did not have a caudillo.

Corrientes, a region of agriculture and industries as well as livestock, had a greater population and more diversified economy than Entre Ríos and Santa Fe, provinces possessed of little more than cattle and cowboys. The ruling groups in Corrientes agreed that internal order and independence from other provinces were best provided not by a military caudillo, who would make matters worse, but by solutions of a more constitutional kind. In contrast the civil and interprovincial wars in which Entre Ríos and Santa Fe had been embroiled had stirred up anarchic social forces easily exploitable by caudillos. In Santa Fe the search for internal and external security resulted in the triumph of a caudillo of military origin, Estanislao López, 'this imbecile gaucho' as General Paz described him, who won his laurels in war against Buenos Aires and defence against the Indians.[38] The 'constitutional statute' imposed by López on the province in 1819 actually defined the election of the governor as 'the appointment of its caudillo'.[39] He remained in power throughout the 1820s, even more securely after 1830, because constant pressure from Rosas convinced the local élite that López was the only possible guarantee of some kind of independent life for Sante Fe. Entre Ríos, starved of development and revenue, was too weak to resist Buenos Aires. Ramírez was succeeded by caudillos ready to compromise and collaborate with the enemy; its governor from 1821 to 1824, Lucio Mansilla, was no more than a servant of Buenos Aires.

One of the reasons for the weakness of Entre Ríos as a provincial state was its fiscal poverty. Corrientes, in contrast, had a greater income, enabling it to support a state apparatus, solid institutions,

---

[37] Cited by José Carlos Chiaramonte, 'Legalidad constitucional o caudillismo: El problema del orden social en el surgimiento de los estados autónomos del Litoral argentino en la primera mitad del siglo XIX', *Desarrollo Económico*, 26, 102 (1986), 178.

[38] José María Paz, *Memorias póstumas*, ed. Armando Braun Menéndez (Buenos Aires, 1945), 275.

[39] Cited by Chiaramonte, 'Legalidad constitucional o caudillismo', 181.

and political continuity, in the course of which power passed more or less peacefully from one government to another. In other words the military budget of a provincial state can be interpreted as expenditure on the preservation of social order and external security and not merely as the financing of military caudillos.[40] Corrientes was the model. Entre Ríos, on the other hand, deriving its military budget from declining resources, spent it on improvised reaction to social disorder and left it in the hands of governors who did not even fulfil the normal role of caudillos.

In these terms the provinces were involved not simply in personalism and caudillism but in state-making. Whether this interpretation can be applied to a caudillo such as Facundo Quiroga is less certain. His state 'revenue', especially extraordinary revenue, took the form of various kinds of looting. And for some provinces 'state-making' meant, for lack of alternatives, retaining institutions inherited from Spain and personnel who had previously served the crown.[41] Quiroga, whose career owed something to family influence as landowners and local officials, and then to delegated authority from the revolutionary government, finally became his own man and personally extended his power in the interior through a mixture of cruelty and cunning in his dealings with other caudillos rather than a process of state-building.

Thus Argentina came to be ruled by a cluster of caudillos, part civil, part military in character. Corrientes was an oasis of legality. In most provinces, anyone who tried to rule constitutionally was doomed by personalism, as Juan José Viamonte learnt to his cost in Buenos Aires in 1834: 'Against the paramount ascendancy which General Rosas has known to obtain for himself, and which he has thus thought fit to exercise... no administration such as General Viamonte's, who looked to legal and constitutional principles alone as the basis of their measures, could long hold out.'[42] That ascendancy prevailed, even in 1834 when he was not formally in office, through his personal influence or control over key ministers, such as General Mansilla, chief of police, Nicolas Anchorena, minister of finance, and Tomás Anchorena, minister of foreign relations. It was also exercised by widespread use of patronage; through his direct or indirect control of public finance, he was able to place a large number

---

[40] José Carlos Chiaramonte, 'Finanzas públicas de las provincias del Litoral, 1821–1841', *Anuario del IEHS*, 1 (Tandil, 1986), 159–98.
[41] Halperín Donghi, *Politics, Economics and Society in Argentina*, 79, 378–9, 394.
[42] Gore to Palmerston, 16 June 1834, PRO, FO 6/40.

of retainers and dependants on his payroll, especially in the army, which was expanded not only as an instrument of war and security but also as an object of patronage.[43] General Paz contrasted disciplined military authorities such as himself, who were sparing with promotions and decorations, and the caudillos who scandalously lavished rewards on their friends and followers: 'That is how the caudillos operate in all ages, and the tyrants in all countries.'[44] If personalism and patronage did not succeed, there was another weapon. The ultimate sanction of caudillo rule—of Rosas and the others—was violence; civilians were terrorized by the troops and the troops by the caudillos. Sarmiento pointed out, with some cynicism, that the armies of the caudillos were only held together by force and terror; deserters had their throats cut; the families of enemies were taken and put to forced labour or colonizing the desert.

These cruelties are the basis of the system; without them there would be no army, no mass uprising. Thus the system of the caudillos can be reduced to this simple definition: 'a bid for wealth and power, backed by the popular masses of the province they control and with the support of all the men, compelled by terror to act against their own interests; and the whole sustained by violation of all the laws of nature and economics accepted by societies everywhere.'[45]

2. *Venezuela: From War to Peace*

In the aftermath of the battle of Carabobo, Bolívar's satisfaction was tempered by his awareness of post-war political problems. He wanted the separation of military and political power but he could not obtain it. In 1821 under the Constitution of Cúcuta he was elected President and confirmed in his military power. In his case the danger was not abuse of absolute civil and military power but inability to attend to both. This allowed other generals to dominate and politicians to proliferate: 'Colombia, governed by the sword of its defenders, is a military camp rather than a body social.' He was convinced that

[43] Gore to Palmerston, 30 Aug. 1834, PRO, FO 6/40; Hamilton to Palmerston, 26 Jan. 1835, PRO, FO 6/46.

[44] Paz, *Memorias póstumas*, 324.

[45] Domingo Faustino Sarmiento, *Campaña en el ejército grande aliado de Sud América*, ed. Tulio Halperín Donghi (Mexico, Buenos Aires, 1958), 132.

'the command of the army and the direction of the Republic must be kept separate', and tendered his resignation as president, which was refused.[46] Meanwhile the caudillos were looking to him, as a patron and a problem.

If Venezuela were to organize itself peacefully, it was essential to satisfy and co-opt the caudillos. This he did in two ways: by giving them regional appointments and by granting them land. On 16 July 1821 Bolívar issued a decree which in effect institutionalized caudillism. In the west he established two politico-military regions, one for Páez, the other for Mariño. The eastern provinces he assigned to Bermúdez. Overtly all three were equal, and the country so divided into departments entered into the republic of Colombia on the same footing as other provinces. But from the start the government of Páez enjoyed hegemony, and from a regional caudillo Páez became a national hero, indisputable military and political leader of Venezuela. Established in the country's socio-economic centre around Caracas, commander of what remained of a disciplined army, the soldiers of the llanos of Apure, Páez was well placed to impose his authority over the other military caudillos, attentive to the oligarchy who surrounded him and the masses who idolized him. Mariño, rooted out from his homeland in the east and deserted by his own caudillos—Bermúdez, Monagas, Valdés—had lost his base, his clients, his patronage. General Páez was thus promoted to a position from which in one form or another he was to dominate Venezuela for the next twenty-five years.

But was there any alternative? While Bolívar was away in Colombia and Peru, he had to leave Páez in charge and the caudillos in their homelands, as this seemed the only realistic way to govern Venezuela, by a system of power applied from strong personal domains. The professional military he kept with him for his campaigns outside Venezuela, for they were more mobile than the caudillos, more useful as officers, and less motivated by political ambitions. But after the war their only base was the professional army, their career was the revolution, while the caudillo had come to represent basic economic and political interests that were virtually unchallengeable by the Bolivarians. Meanwhile, the civilian legislators had begun to resent the military, both caudillos and professionals, and to attack their claims upon resources. The House of Representatives in Bogotá sought to

---

[46] Bolívar to Antonio Nariño, 21 Apr. 1821, in *Selected Writings of Bolívar*, ed. Vicente Lecuna and Harold A. Bierck, Jr. (2 vols.; New York, 1951), i. 264–5.

remove the military *fuero* and abolish the right of soldiers to vote in
1825. O'Leary thought they were going too far and too fast, for the
soldiers had won the war and the republic still needed them. In
Colombia, he argued, men were everything, institutions nothing:

The government was still sustained through the influence and power of the
caudillos who had made independence. Institutions by themelves had no
force at all; the people were a machine which had ceased to function, being
too ignorant to take action; what is known as public spirit did not exist. It was
not politic, therefore, to provoke so powerful a class [the caudillos] in
society.[47]

If the war of independence was a struggle for power, it was also a
dispute over resources, and the caudillos fought for land as well as
for liberty. Bolívar was the first to acknowledge this and to provide
economic incentive as well as political access. His decree of 3
September 1817 ordered the confiscation by the state of all property
and land of the enemy, Americans as well as Spaniards, to be sold in
public auction to the highest bidder, or, failing that, to be rented out
on behalf of the national treasury.[48] The property was used not only
as an immediate income for the patriot government, but also as a
source of land grants to officers and soldiers of the republic according to their rank, promotion being regarded as a gauge of service.
The decree of 10 October 1817 ordered grants ranging in value from
25,000 pesos for a general-in-chief to 500 for an ordinary soldier.
The intention, as Bolívar put it, was 'to make of each soldier a
property-owning citizen'. It was also necessary to find a substitute
for a salary.

The caudillos were the first to benefit. One of the earliest grants,
by special request of Bolívar to the National Land Commission, was
that to General Cedeño, to enable him to establish a hacienda in the
sabanas of Palmar.[49] Even those out of favour were among the first
recipients. The Congress of Angostura in December 1819 confirmed
the award of cacao haciendas in Güiria and Yaguarapo to Mariño and
Arismendi. These were properties confiscated from Spaniards. The

[47] O'Leary, *Narración*, ii. 557.

[48] Decrees, 3 Sept., 10 Oct. 1817, in *Escritos*, xi. 75–7, 219–21; Universidad
Central de Venezuela, *Materiales para el estudio de la cuestión agraria en Venezuela
(1800–1830)*, vol. i (Caracas, 1964), 201–2, 204–5; Bolívar to Zaraza, 11 Oct. 1817,
in *Escritos*, xi. 227.

[49] Bolívar to Land Commission, 3 Dec. 1817, in *Materiales para el estudio de la
cuestión agraria*, i. 211; Parra-Pérez, *Mariño y la independencia de Venezuela*, iii. 225.

government also granted certain old properties belonging to Spaniards to Urdaneta, Bermúdez, and Soublette, most of whom had entered the war of independence without any kind of property. From 1821 the caudillos were pressing their claims for specific haciendas and lands directly on the executive, who usually preferred to pass the requests to the land tribunals. According to Carlos Soublette, Vice-President of Venezuela and not one to be duped by claimants, 'The military are among the strongest and most insistent claimants to confiscated property. They have fought successfully and undergone horrific deprivation . . . and it will be impossible to ignore them much longer'.[50] The most desirable properties were the commercial plantations in the north, many of whose owners had, if only nominally, supported the cause of independence and now fiercely resisted any attack on their property, even by the caudillos. But a hacienda was indispensable to a caudillo, great or small, not only as a source of independence but also as a base of retreat in times of emergency, where he could run for cover as his enemies closed in.

Páez was the most successful of all the caudillos. Yet Páez had used land as a medium of mobilization very early in his campaign.

When General Páez occupied Apure in 1816 he found himself alone in enemy territory, without help or prospects and without even the support of public opinion. He was therefore forced to offer his troops a free share in the properties belonging to the government of Apure. This was one of the most effective ways of retaining the support of the troops and attracting new recruits, as they all stood the same chance of gaining.[51]

This policy did not materialize, for Páez proved to be more interested in his own acquisitions than in those of his men.

Even before the end of the war in Venezuela, Páez was granted 'by the General Congress the right to redistribute national properties as President of the Republic', though it was confined to the army of Apure and the territory under his jurisdiction. These special prerogatives were delegated by Bolívar out of frustration over the failure of previous attempts to redistribute land among the military.[52] Before distribution, however, Páez acquired the best properties for himself. His holdings were not restricted to the llanos, but extended into the centre-north, the homeland of the traditional oligarchy. He began to

---

[50] Soublette to Minister of Finance, 5 Oct. 1821, in *Materiales para el estudio de la cuestión agraria*, i. 311.
[51] Briceño Méndez to Gual, 20 July 1821, in O'Leary, *Memorias*, xviii. 399.
[52] Decree, 18 Jan. 1821, in *Materiales para el estudio de la cuestión agraria*, i. 282–3.

appropriate land on a large scale in the valleys of Aragua in October 1821, when he applied for ownership of the Hacienda de la Trinidad, one of the largest in the area and previously the property of an *emigrado*, Antonio Fernández de León, whose family had founded the estate in the eighteenth century. He was awarded the property in November in exchange for the payment of wages in arrears. He also succeeded in his bid for the Yagua ranch.[53] A few years later, in 1825, he made an overtly generous offer to the Vice-President of Colombia to sell the government his own estates in Apure together with their cattle and horses so that the troops could be granted the land they had been promised in lieu of wages.[54] But this gesture was purely demagogic: it was designed to improve his reputation as a patrón and retain the loyalty of his troops, while reserving the right to buy back the debt vouchers, which were the first—and often the only—stage of a land grant.[55] The offer was rejected by Congress and Páez himself subject to much criticism for building a private fortune by 'scandalous speculation' in the land vouchers of his officers and men.[56] These were the tactics of many caudillos, who offered the troops sums of money (sometimes 50 or 60 pesos for vouchers worth 1,000) in exchange for these land certificates, a notorious abuse which extended throughout Venezuela and New Granada. The project had never been conceived as agrarian reform. But even as a means of paying wages it failed. According to Pedro Briceño Méndez, secretary of Bolívar and minister of war, 'none of those who have received their payments in the form of certificates actually possess them; all of these, or the greater part of them, have passed into other hands, the hands of profiteers who have paid the infamous price I have mentioned [5 per cent of true value).'[57]

Acquisition of land and the formation of estates helped to keep the caudillos in a state of contentment in the years immediately after independence and prevented them from turning their menacing gaze

---

[53] Soublette to Minister of Finance, 5 Oct. 1821, in *Materiales para el estudio de la cuestión agraria*, i. 311–12, 316–17; Manuel Pérez Vila, 'El gobierno deliberativo: Hacendados, comerciantes y artesanos frente a la crisis 1830–1848', in Fundación John Boulton, *Política y economía en Venezuela 1810–1976* (Caracas, 1976), 44–5.

[54] Páez to Santander, Feb.–Mar. 1825, in *Materiales para el estudio de la cuestión agraria*, i. 421–2; David Bushnell, *The Santander Regime in Gran Colombia* (Newark, Del., 1954), 281.

[55] Izard, *El miedo a la revolución*, 158–63.

[56] Antonio M. Briceño to Senate, Bogotá, 30 Mar. 1825, in Bushnell, *The Santander Regime*, 279.

[57] Briceño Méndez to Gual, 17 July 1821, in O'Leary, *Memorias*, xviii. 39.

upon the central oligarchy. A new élite of landowners, rewarded from
sequestered property or from public land, joined the colonial proprietors and in some cases replaced them. According to Santander, under
the law of 25 July 1823 some 4,800,000 acres had been distributed or
offered to claimants in settlement of military pay, and more land was
being sought by Congress for such purposes from the national total
of some 640,000,000 acres.[58] Meanwhile the military, who had not
received their due, complained bitterly about the operations of the
land commissions. Mothers, sons, and widows presented claims and
complaints against the land and property committees: 'More than a
third of the houses and estates of Venezuela have been confiscated,
but not to help those who most deserve it and who have the greatest
right to compensation.'[59] The troops and their dependants received
nothing; the caudillos everything.

First among the caudillos was Páez. He was shrewd enough to
realize that control of local resources, indispensable for a local caudillo, was insufficient for access to national power. The cattle ranches
of the llanos and the sugar estates of Cumaná could give leaders like
Páez and Mariño bases for regional action, but in the ultimate analysis these economies were dependent upon Caracas and subordinate
to its interests. This was the reason why Páez and other political
pretenders sought land in the centre-north and an alliance with the
established élite of that region. Páez was successful in acquiring a
new power base and in reassuring the landowners, merchants, and
officeholders of Caracas that he stood for order and stability; they in
turn tamed their chosen caudillo, dissuaded him from pursuing abolition of slavery, and converted him to new economic priorities. Thus
he came to identify with the agricultural and commercial interests of
Caracas; he turned his back on the llanos and the other regional
economies, and accepted the hegemony of the northern hacendados
and the exporting sector.

The land policy of independent Venezuela continued to favour the
powerful and influential. In the period of the conservative oligarchy,
1830–48, 96 per cent of public land granted in payment of military

[58] Santander to Briceño Méndez, 6 Jan. 1826, Santander to Montilla, 7 Jan. 1826,
in Roberto Cortázar (ed.), *Cartas y mensajes del General Francisco de Paula Santander,
1812–1840* (10 vols.; Bogotá, 1953–6), vi. 40–4; Páez, *Autobiografía*, ii. 297; Federico
Brito Figueroa, *Historia económica y social de Venezuela* (2 vols.; Caracas, 1966), i.
207–20.
[59] *El Venezolano* (Caracas, 2 Sept. 1822), in *Materiales para el estudio de la cuestión
agraria*, i. 327.

salaries was acquired in large units by twenty-five persons; the remainder went to thirty recipients; and all grants favoured high-ranking army officers.[60] While these national assets freed the government from the burden of military salaries, the rent or sale of national land, for whatever purpose, brought the treasury no significant income. Nor did the policy help to redistribute land, for it was biased towards higher military and civilian officials who invariably speculated in land certificates. In the following period, that of the liberal oligarchy of 1848–58, the process of land concentration was, if anything, accelerated. Now those interested in acquiring land had the benefit of the law of 10 April 1848 which expanded and facilitated the allocation of public land to private individuals. Again, without obvious benefit to the treasury, the policy favoured existing latifundists who were often already renting the land they bought, and new proprietors who had sufficient influence and money to purchase large units. Among the greatest beneficiaries were the family, friends, and clients of the two Monagas presidents, under whose patronage the scheme functioned vigorously. Vast expanses of national land were now alienated, especially in the provinces of Barcelona and Cumaná, the power base of the Monagas. Ten persons acquired 55 per cent of national land thus alienated, and the remainder was distributed among 136 recipients.[61]

This was in the future. Meanwhile, in the mid-1820s, Páez led the Venezuelan oligarchy in a separatist movement which would place their country under the control of the national élite, ruled from Caracas and not from Bogotá, and monopolizing its own resources. This was an alliance of landowners and military caudillos on behalf of a conservative and independent Venezuela. And it created a crisis for Colombia. Páez as a medium of authority was useful. Páez as a national leader was dangerous. Páez had few political ideas of his own and was prone to take advice; not, however, from Briceño Méndez or other Bolivarians, but from a faction in Caracas which Bolívar called 'the demagogues'. These encouraged him to believe that he had not received the power and recognition he deserved. His exasperation with legislators and politicians focused especially on those in Bogotá, civilians who reputedly filled their own pockets from development and welfare funds, and whom he regarded as oppressors

[60] *Materiales para el estudio de la cuestión agraria en Venezuela (1829–1860): Enajenación y arrendamiento de tierras baldías*, i (Caracas, 1971), p. xxxiii.
[61] Ibid. vol. i, pp. lx, lxv–lxviii.

of the 'poor military'.[62] In 1825 he urged Bolívar to take greater, even monarchical, powers and to make himself a Napoleon of South America. Bolívar rejected the idea, pointing out that Colombia was not France and he was not Napoleon.[63]

In April 1826 Páez was relieved of his command and summoned to Bogotá for impeachment by Congress on charges of illegal and arbitrary conduct in recruiting civilians for the militia in Caracas. The object, as Santander explained, was 'to make the first chiefs of the republic understand that their services and heroism are not a licence to abuse the citizens'.[64] But Páez resisted. Backed by the llaneros, and prompted perhaps by the Venezuelan military and the federalists around him, he raised the banner of revolt on 30 April, first in Valencia, then in the Department of Venezuela. Support for him was strong but not universal, for a sense of national identity was not sufficiently developed to appeal to everyone. His action was divisive. The other caudillos reacted variously. Mariño, Rojas, and Monagas aligned themselves with Páez; Bermúdez rejected him and offered to crush the rebellion.

Santander defined it precisely as a caudillo's rebellion: 'On 16 January Caracas was under the protection of the laws and recognized a legitimate and constitutional government; on 5 May Caracas found itself at the mercy of a chief whose authority came from rebellion and from force'.[65] But it was not merely a matter of legality, or personality. The fact was that the central government had committed a number of political errors and had misjudged the real independence of the military caudillos. Apart from the inherent merits of the case—the need to recruit militia in Caracas and the previous compliance of the government—Páez represented a military and to some extent a popular constituency in opposition to Intendant Juan de Escalona and his masters in Bogotá. It was unrealistic to appoint General Escalona, a known enemy of Páez, to administer Venezuela and then to replace Páez at the head of the army. A major caudillo could not be treated like this. Bolívar understood it, but Santander did not. Neither Páez nor his military colleagues would allow the army to pass into other

    [62] Sutherland to Canning, Maracaibo, 1 Sept. 1826, PRO, FO 18/33.
    [63] Bolívar to Páez, 6 Mar. 1826, in Simón Bolívar, *Cartas del Libertador*, ed. Vicente Lecuna (12 vols.; Caracas, 1929–59), v. 240.
    [64] Santander to Bolívar, 6 May 1826, in *Cartas y mensajes*, vi. 316.
    [65] Santander, Proclama, 6 July 1826, in Parra-Pérez, *Mariño y la independencia de Venezuela*, iv. 124.

hands. 'The chief now appointed to succeed him is General Escalona, a man hated by all the military of Venezuela, whom they see as a personal enemy of each of them by his negligent conduct towards the army during his administration.'[66]

The reaction of the Bolivarians was ambiguous. In Zulia General Urdaneta awaited orders from Bogotá and remained loyal to the Liberator. Like many of the military, however, he derived satisfaction from Páez's opposition to Congress, as it reinforced their pressure on Bolívar to establish a stronger government. Bolívar was now the focus of the personalism that he so abhorred. The British consul in Maracaibol reported, after an interview with Urdaneta, that the military 'remain constant in their attachment and obedience to their Chiefs, rather than to the Constitution and to Congress, and hope much from the return of the President... the civil power and republican principles have been making too rapid, or rather too rash, strides to destroy the military aristocracy....' According to the same source, the military were disillusioned with a government 'monopolized by General Santander and by a faction of shopkeepers in Bogotá.... My impression is that there are very few military men in the country that would not cheerfully cry out tomorrow, *Long live King Bolívar...*'.[67] Whatever the accuracy of this impression, it confirmed other indications that military opinion placed all its hopes in Bolívar.

The rebellion of Páez placed Bolívar in a dilemma. He did not approve of military rebellion against civil power. Yet in this particular case he had more sympathy with Páez than with Santander and the legislators, whom he saw as destroying their liberators and causing resentment among the military. He also knew that they were being unrealistic in trying to deprive a caudillo of his military command. In a mood of pessimism he identified military discontent, socio-racial violence, and caudillo affinity with both, to explain the phenomenon of caudillo rebellion. 'These two men [Páez and Padilla] have elements of power in their blood; therefore, it is useless for me to oppose them because my own blood means nothing to the people.'[68] It was in this mood, too, that he wrote his dramatic analysis of the racial origins and the moral history of Americans and expressed his preference for an 'able despotism'. Given the socio-racial formation

[66] Briceño Méndez to Bolívar, 26 Apr. 1826 (ibid. iv. 17–18).

[67] Sutherland to Canning, Maracaibo, 1 Sept. 1826, Sutherland to HM Chargé d'affaires, 2 Oct. 1826, PRO, FO 18/33.

[68] Bolívar to Santander, 7 and 8 June 1826, in *Selected Writings*, ii. 614.

of America, he asked, 'Can we place laws above heroes and principles above men?'[69] Bolívar here recognized the force of personalism and the power of the strong man, and gave it a structural explanation. It was in this context, too, that he wrote to Páez, admitting the danger of demoralizing the army and provoking provinces into taking power unto themselves. He denounced democrats and fanatics and asked, 'Who shall restrain the oppressed classes? Slavery will break its yoke, each shade of complexion will seek mastery.'[70] And the answer? In due course it was his Bolivian constitution with a life-term president empowered to appoint his successor. Meanwhile the government had to maintain law and order 'by means of the press, the pulpit, and the bayonet'.[71] So Bolívar stood for the continuation of Colombia under his dictatorship, exercised through extraordinary powers which the constitution allowed him, and the reconciliation of Venezuela through necessary reforms.

Bolívar moved into Venezuela in late 1826 to confront the rebellion of Páez. He warned the caudillo of his previous encounters with personalism.

General Castillo opposed me and lost; General Piar opposed me and lost; General Mariño opposed me and lost; General Riva-Agüero opposed me and lost; and General Torre Tagle opposed me and lost. It would seem that Providence condemns my personal enemies, whether American or Spanish, to perdition. But see how far Generals Sucre, Santander, and Santa Cruz have gone.[72]

He also made it clear that he went as president and not in a personal capacity, pointing out that his was the only legitimate sovereignty in Venezuela, whereas Páez's command came from the municipalities and was born in violence. Although he mobilized his forces, he did not want further violence. He had come to save Páez 'from the crime of civil war'.[73] Conciliation was also favoured by the majority opinion in both countries. There was little alternative. Bolívar was aware of the danger of trying to use force against Páez, 'since almost all the principal military commands throughout Colombia are filled by

---

[69] Bolívar to Santander, 8 July 1826, in *Cartas*, vi. 10–12.
[70] Bolívar to Páez, 4 Aug. 1826 (ibid. vi. 32).
[71] Bolívar to Páez, 8 Aug. 1826 (ibid. vi. 49–52).
[72] Bolívar to Páez, 11 Dec. 1826 (ibid. vi. 119–20).
[73] Bolívar to Páez, 23 Dec. 1826 (ibid. vi. 133–4).
[74] Watts (consul, Cartagena) to Bidwell, 5 Aug. 1826, PRO, FO 18/31.

natives of Caracas'.[74] So he compromised. On 1 January 1827 he received Páez's submission, but at a price, namely total amnesty for all the rebels, guarantees of security in their offices and property, and promises of constitutional reform.

Bolívar governed Venezuela in person from January to June 1827. He proceeded on the assumption that Venezuelans—Spanish Americans—were not fit for democracy. Abject, superstitious, and ignorant as they were, they did not understand the practice of good government. 'Instead of liberty, we find insubordination and licentiousness; under the name of patriotism, intrigue and teachery; venality in the place of public virtue, whilst personal revenge is covered by the cloak of justice.'[75] These faults, however, he attributed not to inherent inferiority but to Spanish oppression which had deprived Americans of training and experience in government. Therefore he found nothing iniquitous in a strong executive, if that was what Páez could provide. He confirmed the caudillo in his command with the title Superior Chief of Venezuela, a title which did not exist in the constitution and which Bolívar produced to recognize the facts of the case and legitimize a caudillo. Páez would never obey Bogotá, but he might obey Bolívar. Yet Páez's political role was determined not only by Bolívar. He was recognized as a valuable leader by the Caracas landowners, merchants, and others of the coalition that he kept together on a platform of peace and security and on the awareness of a mutual need. They recognized the need for a strong caudillo. In the east, where Mariño had been posted by Bolívar at the beginning of 1827, the caudillo of Cumaná found himself harassed by lesser caudillos as these fought over resources in a depressed region, while at the bottom social outcasts and underprivileged peasants took to arms in the plains and mountains of the interior until Monagas restored some semblance of law and order.[76]

Even so, with all his caudillo's cunning, Páez did not find it easy to govern Venezuela, and he confessed to Bolívar 'I have learnt how difficult is the art of governing, more so in times of danger such as we are now experiencing. Good intentions are not enough, nor vigilance, nor advice, to avoid discontent, intrigues, and one's own downfall.'[77] He had to fall back on the basic tool of the caudillo, patronage. In a sense he bought his support and co-opted troublemakers, though

[75] Ker Porter to Canning, Caracas, 24 Jan. 1827, PRO, FO 18/47.
[76] Parra-Pérez, *Mariño y la independencia de Venezuela*, iv. 389–411.
[77] Páez to Bolívar, 6 Sept. 1826, in O'Leary, *Memorias*, ii. 159.

in spite of his independence he always checked with the president before dispensing jobs:

Reasons of politics and convenience oblige me to speak to you about Colonel Escuté, at present in Valencia and working sincerely for our side, but frustrated by blows of poverty and misfortune. He is burdened with an enormous family and dependent entirely on the modest income his wife receives from the hacienda of Guataparo. His position, therefore, is highly unfavourable, and you must know that poverty often seizes a man and forces him to commit actions which are out of character and alien to his upbringing and principles.[78]

Páez proceeded to explain that while Escuté had performed useful services and edited a pro-government newspaper, his penury allied to a 'restless spirit' made him an agitator, especially among the bureaucracy. It would be useful to appoint him as an adjutant to Páez, which would keep him both quiet and under observation. 'One salary more or less will not ruin the state.' Bolívar agreed.

Government could be subverted not only by regional caudillos but also by weakness at the centre. When Bolívar left Venezuela to the rule of Páez, he returned to Bogotá in September to assume command of the administration. Amidst the growing anarchy of 1828, when the independence of the great magnates and the restlessness of the masses threatened to destroy the young republic, he spoke compulsively of the need for 'strong government'. 'I foresee the certain destruction of Colombia unless the government is given an enormous power, capable of stifling the anarchy which will raise a thousand seditious heads.'[79] He believed that the constitution did not conform to the social structure: 'We have made the executive subordinate to the legislative, which has been given a far greater share in administration than the nation's true interests require.'[80] He also believed that the legislative had excessive power over the military; it had given the civil courts absolute control in military cases, thus destroying discipline and undermining the confidence of the army. But he had little hope in the Congress of Ocaña and was strongly critical of its factionalism and hostility to Bolivarian policies. He was also outraged when the convention endorsed the rebellion of the *pardo* General José Padilla, who sought to rally Cartagena against Bolívar in favour of Santander and the Constitution of Cúcuta, a rebellion based on the

---

[78] Páez to Bolívar, Caracas, 21 Nov. 1828, 31 Feb. 1829 (ibid. ii. 178–9, 192).
[79] Bolívar to Páez, 29 Jan. 1828, in *Cartas*, vii. 138.
[80] Bolívar, message to Congress of Ocaña, 29 Feb. 1828, in *Obras completas*, iii. 789–96.

pardo population of the coast. His own view was that Padilla should be tried according to the law as an example to others, and in due course he was.[81]

The rebellion of Padilla had the 'effect of rallying all the people of property and influence round the person of General Bolívar, as the only one capable of now restoring tranquility in Colombia'.[82] As the Convention of Ocaña broke up in deadlock, Bolívar took the next logical step. He assumed dictatorship in June 1828, with apparently wide support; for he alone commanded respect, and Colombia needed what O'Leary called 'the magic of his prestige' to restore government and stability.[83] This was the opinion not only of the Bolivarians but also of outside observers, such as the British consul, Ker Porter, who believed that stability could not prevail 'unless the Liberator be invested with the fullest and most unlimited powers' in an outright dictatorship.[84] Yet even when he exercised absolute power in 1828–30 Bolívar did not rule like a caudillo or a despot; his dictatorship responded to no particular social or regional interest, and his respect for the rule of law did not desert him. It is true that he gave himself the right to issue decrees with the force of law and to name all state employees (27 May 1828); but his legislative programme, however controversial, responded to specific policy objectives in religion, education, and taxation, and was directed to interest groups only to protect regional agricultural and industrial production.[85] In 1829 he rejected a project to establish a monarchy in Colombia, presented to him without previous consultation.[86] He did not substantially extend his extraordinary powers. There was a decree on conspiracy (20 February 1828) already in existence, but it was not effectively applied, and he himself was the victim of an assassination attempt on 25 September 1828. This was not a caudillo-type conspiracy, much less a mass revolt, but an attempted coup designed to overthrow Bolívar. The moving spirit behind it was Santander, and the agents were Granadine army officers. Condemned to death by military tribunal, Santander was pardoned by Bolívar on the advice of his ministers,

---

[81] Bolívar to Páez, 12 Apr. 1828, in *Cartas*, vii. 215–17.

[82] Campbell to Dudley, Bogotá, 13 Apr. 1828, PRO, FO 18/53.

[83] O'Leary, *Narración*, ii. 601.

[84] Ker Porter to Canning, Caracas, 9 Apr. 1827, PRO, FO 18/47.

[85] David Bushnell, 'The Last Dictatorship: Betrayal or Consummation?', *HAHR* 63, 1 (1983), 65–105.

[86] Joaquín Posada Gutiérrez, *Memorias histórico-políticas* (BHN 41–4, 4 vols.; Bogotá, 1929), i. 283–4, 310–25.

advice he bitterly resented. Piar, Padilla, and others had died for the crime of rebellion, so why should Santander escape? Bolívar dreaded above all the resentment of the *pardos*, who saw their caudillos executed while whites escaped. 'Those of the same class as Piar and Padilla will say, and justifiably, that I have shown weakness only in favour of this infamous white, whose services do not compare with those of these famous patriots.'[87]

The dictatorship of Bolívar had support from the Bolivarians and the caudillos alike, and also from the bureaucracy and the clergy. In 1828 Sucre advised him that the people were disillusioned with written guarantees and theoretical liberty, and only wanted security of their persons and property, protected by a strong government. A year later Sucre added:

> I will always be sorry that in order to obtain this internal peace and stability you have not made use of your dictatorial power to give Colombia a constitution, which would have been sustained by the army, the cause of so many revolts against the laws. What the people want is peace and guarantees; as for the rest, I do not believe that they dispute for principles or political theories, which have caused so much damage to their right of property and security.[88]

Páez recognized the dictatorship promptly and considered it the best solution against the factionalism of the military and the mischief of the liberals. Dictator and caudillo both wanted the same thing, strong government and stability. Páez, it is true, also wanted the independence of Venezuela, but peacefully and without another revolution, because, as Soublette reported, 'he does not have the will to start another revolution, nor does he dare to break his often-repeated oaths of allegiance to you.'[89] But eastern Venezuela still bore the marks of caudillo rule, as Bolívar admitted to Sucre: 'I am sorry to tell you that in the east no one can achieve anything, thanks to its former caudillos. You, my dear General, are the only man with an unblemished record from that heroic but ill-starred country.'[90] And he refused to employ Mariño there, preferring a Bolivarian officer, General Salom, to bring it to peace and order. Bolívar seemed to accept that Venezuela, with its military fiefdoms, so unlike the rest of Colombia, might have to go its own way. He recognized that the

---

[87] Bolívar to Briceño Méndez, 16 Nov. 1828, in O'Leary, *Memorias*, xxxi. 239–40.
[88] Sucre to Bolívar, 7 Oct. 1829 (ibid. i. 557).
[89] Soublette to Bolívar, 28 Aug. 1828, 12 Jan. 1829, 21 Jan. 1829, in Parra-Pérez, *Mariño y la independencia de Venezuela*, iv. 474–5.
[90] Bolívar to Sucre, 28 Oct. 1828, in O'Leary, *Memorias*, xxxi. 232.

centre was too remote from the outlying districts, and government authority was dissipated by distance. 'There is no prefect, no governor, who does not invest himself with supreme authority, principally as a matter of absolute necessity. It might be said that each department has a government, distinct from the national, modified by local conditions or circumstances peculiar to the area, or even personal in nature.' These were conditions which bred caudillos. But what was their legitimacy?

> Are the military always to rule sword in hand? Will not the civilian population complain of the despotism of the army? I admit that the existing Republics cannot be governed except by the sword, and yet at the same time I cannot concede that the military spirit is incompatible with civilian rule.[91]

Bolívar now reached the peak of personal power. In spite of his preference for a political over a military solution, in spite of his long search for constitutional forms, he fell back in the end on personal authority, ruling through a dictatorship and co-opting the caudillos into a system which appealed to their own instincts on government. His dilemma remained unresolved. Every political measure—the Bolivian constitution, the life-term presidency, the liberal regime in Colombia—received only partial or temporary support, and that because of the prestige of the Liberator. Nothing else endured. Such social mobilization as had taken place during the war now ended. Even political participation by the creole élite was limited, except in so far as regional caudillos ruled in collaboration with local interests. The irreducible fact remained, that the source of the dictator's legitimacy was his own personal qualities. Bolívar ruled alone, the only stable thing in a world in turmoil.

At this moment, his judgement impaired perhaps by his very isolation, he presented the caudillos with a needless advantage. Unreconciled to a purely personalist solution, he decided to consult the people. On 16 October 1829, the Ministry of the Interior issued Bolívar's celebrated circular letter (31 August 1829) authorizing, indeed ordering, that public meetings be held where the citizens could give their opinions on a new form of government and the future organization of Colombia.[92] This was for Congress to determine, but the elected deputies were to attend Congress not as free

---

[91] Bolívar to O'Leary, 13 Sept. 1829, in *Selected Writings*, ii. 738–40; *Cartas*, ix. 125.

[92] José Gil Fortoul, *Historia constitucional de Venezuela*, 2nd edn. (3 vols.; Caracas, 1930), i. 650–63.

agents but as delegates mandated by written instructions. So Bolívar sought the will of the people and undertook to be bound by it for good or for ill.[93] But were the people free to express their will? Would not the caudillos control or intimidate the assemblies? Bolívar's closest friends and advisers had grave reservations about this procedure. Sucre advised him to reduce it to the simple right of petition; otherwise the right to give binding instructions 'will revive local pretensions'.[94]

Indeed the separatists immediately exploited these meetings to secure the opinions they wanted. Representation could not in itself frustrate caudillism. In Caracas the meeting of the people on 25 November 1829 was preceded on the night before by a meeting of 400 leading citizens in the house of the caudillo Arismendi, with other generals present, who pronounced for the independence of Venezuela and against Bolívar. Another example of pressure was given in a complaint from the town of Escuque to General Páez against the procedures adopted by the military commander of the district of Trujillo, Colonel Cegarra.

Even the popular assemblies have been the occasion of his insolence, since he has insisted that the citizens sign not what has been said and agreed in their meetings, but various papers which he himself has written in his own home, threatening with violence those who refused to obey. Is this freedom, Sir? Can a people speak freely when at the very time of their assembly they see a squadron of cavalry and a company of fusiliers forming up in the main square? If the papers which Sr. Cegarra wanted us to sign had contained fair and reasoned complaints, then our approval might have been sought at an opportune moment. But to require us to subscribe to a lot of insults, abuse, and insolence against General Bolívar does not seem proper, for we have always believed that we could reject his authority yet treat him with respect.[95]

Most of the towns and districts of Venezuela pronounced for independence from Colombia, and in favour of Páez against Bolívar, whom they called a tyrant and worse. The majority of the caudillos wanted independence. 'The untrammelled expression of popular desires' so ardently sought by Bolívar turned into a torrent of abuse and negation, and the Constitutional Congress of Colombia solved nothing.

[93] Bolívar to Páez, 25 Mar. 1829, in *Obras completas*, iii. 157–8.
[94] Sucre to Bolívar, 17 Sept. 1829, in O'Leary, *Memorias*, i. 552.
[95] Francisco A. Labastida to Páez, 23 Feb. 1830, in Secretaria del Interior y Justicia, vol. v, *Boletín del Archivo Nacional* (Caracas), 10, 37 (1929), 49–50.

In March 1830 Bolívar formally resigned his military and political offices, knowing that Venezuela and the caudillos had repudiated him. Bermúdez issued a strident proclamation calling Venezuelans to arms against the 'despot', the promoter of monarchy, the enemy of the republic. Mariño, who claimed to know 'the virtues, the views, the particular interests of every inhabitant of Cumaná', was outraged when Bolívar refused to employ him in the east.[96] Páez wanted an independent Venezuela, and independence meant opposing Bolívar. 'Venezuelans!' he proclaimed, 'We are completely united on two essential points: the conviction that the political life of Venezuela, its welfare and prosperity, depend upon secession, and that the influence of General Bolívar would be harmful for the new organization.'[97] The Constituent Congress of Venezuela assembled in Valencia on 6 May 1830. From his headquarters at San Carlos Páez sent a message. He protested his determination to relinquish power and to seek a well-earned rest as a private citizen. It was a familiar caudillo formula, used in all parts of Spanish America by dictators who had no intention of retiring. Páez also said: 'My sword, my lance and all my military triumphs are subject to the decisions of the law, in respect and obedience.'[98] It was a double-edged remark, reminding the legislators that, with his llaneros behind him and the oligarchy of wealth and office at his side, he was the supreme power in the land. This Congress founded the sovereign and independent republic of Venezuela, in which Páez retained the dual authority of president and army commander.

3. *Mexico: Caudillos in Search of Space*

The independence of Mexico was proclaimed not by a liberator, a republican, or a guerrilla leader, but by the royalist commander, Agustín de Iturbide, who in May 1822 persuaded the creole élite, the Church, and the military, to accept him as 'constitutional emperor'.

---

[96] Bermúdez, Proclamation, Cumaná, 16 Jan. 1830, in Parra-Pérez, *Mariño y la independencia de Venezuela*, v. 46; Mariño to Quintero, 2 Sept. 1829 (ibid. iv. 478).

[97] Páez, Proclama, 2 Mar. 1830, encl. in Lievesley to Aberdeen, La Guaira, 29 Mar. 1830, PRO, FO 18/78.

[98] Páez, Mensaje, Cuartel General de San Carlos, 30 Apr. 1830, encl. in Ker Porter to Aberdeen, Caracas, 12 June 1830, PRO, FO 18/78.

Iturbide had some of the characteristics of a caudillo: he was a landowner, soldier, personalist, and dealer in patronage. But Mexico was not Venezuela, and Iturbide was not Páez. The legitimacy he sought was on an altogether larger scale.

Mexico provided a less favourable environment for the caudillo than did other parts of Spanish America. The transition from colonial state, via independent empire, to federal republic took place without a revolutionary break with the past, and in the core provinces the institutional structure remained intact, offering few invitations to those seeking personal rule. Political life in Mexico was more crowded, debate more intense, and competition for power more severe than elsewhere. Here a caudillo could not find political space as easily as he could in Argentina and Venezuela, where the colonial state had been weaker, independence more destructive, and policy disputes left to career revolutionaries. Finally, the power base of the Mexican caudillo was less stable than that of his counterparts in Argentina and Venezuela. In these countries the caudillo's allies among the landed élite were able to provide him with political and military support—political support from their control of central institutions, military support from the manpower of their estates. Thus the caudillo's power base derived from a common source, the estancia, whose owners dominated the state. The military in these countries, moreover, were not completely dependent on army careers but often possessed or acquired their own estates as an alternative occupation. This was one of the reasons it was possible to integrate them into the rest of society. In Mexico, on the other hand, as in Peru, the army consisted of a professional military inherited from Spain. The officers were creole careerists, who had been recruited in the first place into the royal service and then, transferring their allegiance, had led the movement of independence, the army following behind intact and to some extent inert. From then onwards royalist generals were an integral part of Mexican political life and indeed became prime presidential material. This did not disqualify them from the status of caudillos, which depended on functions as well as origins. But it meant that they did not necessarily reproduce the typologies prevalent in Argentina and Venezuela.

Apart from a few favoured exceptions, men who were caudillo material from the beginning, the majority of the Mexican military were not a landed class or the recipients of any income independent of their military salaries. And Mexico did not possess an expanding frontier of settlement from which army officers could be rewarded with land. The type of estate expansion characteristic of post-colonial Argentina and Venezuela was not possible in Mexico, except perhaps in the far north. Most hacendados felt the effects of war and depression long after 1821. In the centre-north bankrupt landlords were forced to break up their estates, often selling the land to former tenants or neighbouring farmers. In the Bajío estates were partitioned among *rancheros* or sold to pay debts.[99] In the south commercially profitable land was already firmly occupied. There was no easy wealth in rural Mexico. This had a number of consequences. The Mexican military needed the army and depended on a military career, for they had no other; thus they identified with the military as a corporate group. This accounts for their fierce defence of the *fueros*. The army was not comparable to the other two major interest groups in Mexico: unlike the Church and the hacendados, it did not possess an independent source of wealth. It was therefore tempted to seek shortcuts to riches and power by periodically intervening in politics. The Mexican army could not remain independent of the state, for it relied upon impoverished and sometimes liberal governments for its income, and took an average of 80 per cent of the federal budget. While the army needed the state, so too the state depended on the army, if only to impose its rule in the regions. A civilian government was nothing without military backing, and political power at a provincial level was shared between the governor and the military comandante. But not in the whole province. In the backlands and mountains minor caudillos and bandit chieftains often held sway. And even in the heart of a province a military governor was sometimes indistinguishable from an independent caudillo. For all these reasons the caudillo in Mexico had to seek support among regular army units from a social sector which did not coincide with his political constituency among the major interest groups. He was also ready to accept recruits from marginal elements in the regions, from guerrillas and bandits, who would in effect sell their services to the highest bidder. The caudillo, therefore, responded to both political and social conditions in the decades after independence, conditions which were not exclusive to Mexico but took distinctively Mexican forms. To conquer the state, the caudillo first had to choose the best political moment; then to

---

[99] Jan Bazant, *Cinco haciendas mexicanas: Tres siglos de vida rural en San Luis Potosí 1600–1910* (Mexico, 1975), 35–47; Brading, *Haciendas and Ranchos in the Mexican Bajío*, 202–4.

mobilize his military and guerrilla support; and finally to move out of his base into political territory already occupied by rival claimants.

Caudillos and military were part of the great political divide which placed Mexicans in two different camps: centralists and federalists, conservatives and liberals. The centralist and conservative forces in Mexican society consisted of the higher ranks of the clergy, military, merchants, and landowners. Opposed to them were the federalists, liberals and provincials, standing for a mixture of ideology and interests, including regional industrial interests damaged by the economic policy of the central government. Liberal federalists wanted to reduce the power of Mexico City, substitute local militia for a standing army, restrain the sovereignty of central government by state rights, and free Mexico from colonial *fueros*. But liberalism operated within the existing framework of society. On many of the basic issues confronting Mexico—social structure, landed property—the distance between liberals and conservatives was not great. Indeed on economic development and industrialization there were no clear ideological divisions, though the Mexican most alive to entrepreneurial values was Lucas Alamán, a pure conservative. Caudillos used the two factions as political camouflage masking their personal ambition. No doubt their opportunism was an expression of character, but it was also a reflection of the consensus established by the early republican élites, which made it possible to change sides without total loss of credibility.

Regional caudillos in Mexico, in contrast to Argentina and Venezuela, found many obstacles on the road to power and were not at first strong enough to intervene decisively at the centre. The forces ousting Iturbide were a political miscellany consisting of republicans, royalists, and opportunists. They called a constituent assembly, which drew up a republican constitution (October 1824) representing the major interests. On the one hand it was federal: it created nineteen states and gave them substantial rights, opening a source of weakness and division not unlike the federalism bitterly criticized by Bolívar in Colombia ten years previously. While the constitution was federal, it was also conservative: it established Catholicism as the official religion and, in article 154, specifically retained the *fueros* of the Church and the army. As Juárez later commented, the Constitution of 1824 was 'a compromise between progress and reaction'.[100] General

---

[100] Josefina Zoraida Vázquez, 'Los primeros tropiezos', in El Colegio de México, *Historia general de México*, iii (Mexico, 1976), 9–34; Ciro Cardoso (ed.), *Mexico en el siglo XIX (1821–1910): Historia económica y de la estructura social* (Mexico, 1980).

Guadalupe Victoria, a respected symbol of resistance to the colonial order who had shed his guerrilla origins for a civilian role, was elected first constitutional president with the support of the liberals of the revolution. He in turn sought to establish a coalition government, including the conservative Lucas Alamán and the liberal federalist Miguel Ramos Arizpe. With the help of loans from the London money market, he provided a kind of stability until 1827.

Mexico was not ready for pure politics. Centralists fought federalists for power in a factional struggle which lacked a political framework. In the absence of parties the factions adapted the masonic movement to their activities and called themselves *escoceses* and *yorkinos*. As the British minister explained,

The 'Escoces' party is properly speaking composed of the aristocracy of the country, the great landed proprietors, who held titles of nobility under the Spanish government, but latterly all persons of property and respectability . . . have been called 'Escoces'. To the 'Yorkino' party generally belong the numerous restless spirits, the offspring of the revolutionary war . . . the middle and lower classes of the population in the large towns, half pay officers, persons without, and ambitious of obtaining, public employment and, in short, all that comprehensive description of persons who may gain something but have nothing to lose by any commotion taking place in the country.[101]

This intolerant conflict destabilized the government of President Victoria and prevented a ministerial consensus. The situation was worsened by fear of a Spanish restoration, which enabled the federalists to play the nationalist card against the more traditional centralists. In these circumstances the presidential succession in 1828 was settled not by elections but by a coup, which brought to power General Vicente Guerrero, a caudillo of the southern region, a hero of the war against Spain and a federalist backed by the liberal reformist from Mérida Lorenzo Zavala, who became his minister of finance. This radical regime was in turn ousted by a conservative *golpe* which placed Anastasio Bustamante in the presidency on 1 January 1830. Thus generals behaved like caudillos, and caudillos took lessons from generals.[102] The government headed by Bustamante was a pure conservative government, representing specific groups, landowners, clerics, and military, and following a political pattern prevalent throughout

66–76; Stanley C. Green, *The Mexican Republic: The First Decade 1823–1832* (Pittsburgh, 1987), 31–51, 68–85.

[101] Pakenham to Vaughan, 13 Jan. 1829, PRO, FO 50/53, fos. 56–63.
[102] Pakenham to Aberdeen, 30 Oct. 1829, PRO, FO 50/55, fos. 287–92.

Spanish America in the years around 1830. Opposition was not encouraged, either at the centre or in the provinces. Property rights were safeguarded, and corporate privileges defended, not least those of the Church. Anything approaching social subversion was immediately crushed.

The establishment of a conservative and centralist government in 1830 did not mean that a national state actually existed. The political map of Mexico consisted of a formal outline superimposed upon an intractable society. The country was divided into a series of regional power bases, where landowners dominated public life, monopolized economic wealth, and controlled the population. The other two interest groups, the army and the Church, had a national dimension, but were also allies of regional landowners. The triple alliance governed Mexico, and in the process became the source of further conflicts between national and local government. The military were usually willing to give centralism a chance in the hope of receiving more favourable budgetary treatment. 'They naturally suppose that, were the resources of the country concentrated, the Government would not be so constantly in a state of insolvency, and thus that they would receive their pay and appointments with greater regularity.'[103] But the central government was never able to prove this, for at the root of its problems was a fiscal failure. Direct taxes failed to produce large amounts of money because wealthy Mexicans and landowners in particular refused to pay them. The Mexican public would pay only sales taxes, *alcabala*, which fell hardest on the poor, and trade taxes, which hurt foreigners and merchants. Regionalism and geography worsened the situation: the states failed to pay their due 'contingencies' to the federal government, reducing it to further reliance on customs duties and other precarious revenues. Finally the public's refusal to grant the central government sufficient powers to impose new taxes was a fatal blow. Centralists, in other words, failed to establish their legitimacy and to get it accepted, and the field was left to the provinces.

Regional power was concentrated in the caudillos. In some cases, these held delegated powers from the central government as military or civil officials, in more or less the same way as their counterparts in Argentina. In other cases they were military who had become land-

---

[103] Pakenham to Aberdeen, 5 Mar. 1830, PRO, FO 50/60, fos. 189A–192; Cardoso, *México en el siglo XIX*, 59–60.

owners, and thus had a personal recruiting base as well as links to the army, links which gave them a political advantage over other land-owners of the region. Caudillos of this kind often used popular causes to consolidate their power against the central government. General Mariano Olarte, for example, so-called *padre del pueblo*, who led the peasant rebellion of Papontila in 1836, also exploited the movement to fight for a 'representative, popular, and federal regime'.[104]

These centrifugal forces also found expression in the persistence of banditry after independence. Guerrilla warfare changed imper-ceptibly into local brigandage as gangs lost their political patrons but retained their weapons, concentrating now mainly on crime. Some fought on out of habit. Others fought to protect the gains they had made during the war, especially if these involved land. Most took to banditry simply for loot and money. They were marginals who fought to join the mainstream, men in search of an alternative way to wealth and success; in the process they often graduated to a virtually entre-preneurial role in the local economy through deals with more legit-imate business partners.[105] The centre could only look on helplessly. In the years around 1830 bandit gangs plundered the rich sugar estates of the valley of Cuernavaca.[106] A band of sixty robbers at-tacked the mining town of Sombrerete in Zacatecas.[107] A convoy to the mines of Real del Monte was attacked and robbed, and two Britons were killed in the clash. Jalisco was infested by powerful robber bands, who controlled the principal communications and levied contributions on towns and villages close to the state capital.[108] In some cases, perhaps in response to foreign pressure, the government took vigorous action, but the deeper roots of disorder remained untouched.

Banditry, village uprisings, predatory armies, and caste wars, all were allowed to flourish in the vacuum of power left by the central government. The one institution capable of controlling banditry, the army, was itself a partner in this informal economy and often colluded with the enemies of the state, selling stolen goods for their mutual

---

[104] Quoted by Leticia Reina, *Las rebeliones campesinas en México, 1819–1906* (Mexico, 1980), 16–17.

[105] Vanderwood, 'Profiteering Bandits in Nineteenth-Century Mexico', 11–15.

[106] Pakenham to Aberdeen, 8 Jan. 1829, PRO, FO 50/53, fos. 33–9.

[107] Pakenham to Aberdeen, 31 Jan. 1829, PRO, FO 50/53, fos. 144–64.

[108] Pakenham to Aberdeen, 16 Jan. 1831, PRO, FO 50/65, fos. 106–9; Pakenham to Palmerston, 3 June 1831, FO 50/66, fos. 88–9.

profit. Hacendados, too, collaborated with bandits, making deals with their plunderers for fear of worse reprisals.[109] And caudillos recruited followers from the ranks of bandits in their conflicts with regional enemies or in their bids for power at the centre. The frequent *golpes* and attempted *golpes* allowed bandits to practise their trade under the pretence of politics, either to support or to oppose a government, according to the balance of power in their province: 'formidable bands, taking advantage of the prevailing confusion in 1829, and pretending to have armed themselves for political objects, commit with impunity their depredations upon private property.' Troops would then join in because they 'were ready to back any movement which offered the opportunity for riot and plunder'.[110] Thus bandits embraced with delight the chance to settle personal scores under political auspices and happily followed many routes to plunder and prestige, though not in accord with any ideology nor with the intention of redistributing land to peasants. In this they were not so different from the 'political' caudillos, though these had greater pretensions and a larger stage. In the decade following independence any regional caudillo with eyes to see could not but be impressed by the weakness of the state, the opportunism of the army, and the strength of interest groups. One who learnt these basic lessons early in his political life was Santa Anna.

Antonio López de Santa Anna was born in Jalapa in the province of Veracruz, where his father was subdelegate and his family—a creole family though one for which Santa Anna claimed *hidalguia*—had an extended network of friends and relations. In 1810 he opted for a career in the royal army and was soon active in the campaign of colonization in coastal Veracruz. As an officer responsible for distributing land and supplies he was able to extend his patronage and influence, and to improve his rank to lieutenant colonel. Santa Anna was not simply a royalist; he was a zealot whose ruthlessness in leading militia forces against rebel bands earned him a rebuke from his superiors.[111] But zealotry was not loyalty. He switched suddenly from royal to rebel officer in April 1821, when he came out in

---

[109] Vanderwood, 'Profiteering Bandits in Nineteenth-Century Mexico', 15–16.

[110] Pakenham to Aberdeen, 4 Mar. 1829, PRO, FO 50/53, fos. 267–71; Hamnett, *Roots of Insurgency*, 200.

[111] Archer, 'Where Did All the Royalists Go?', 39–40. On the early career of Santa Anna see José Fuentes Mares, *Santa Anna, el hombre*, 5th ed. (Mexico, 1984); Agustín Yáñez, *Santa Anna, espectro de una sociedad* (Mexico, 1982).

support of Iturbide's Plan of Iguala (24 February 1821), Mexico's formula of liberation, and joined the army of the three guarantees, 'union, religion, independence'. His motivation was hidden beneath layers of rhetoric, but was probably not unrelated to the conviction that the Spanish cause was finished and he could now become a full colonel.[112] This was the first step in his long odyssey of opportunism. It was also the first time he displayed one of his most distinctive talents, the ability to influence followers and recruit supporters. His action was thus decisive in bringing the province of Veracruz into the Plan of Iguala. Soon his followers were shouting 'Long live Santa Anna and kill the rest!'[113]

Santa Anna threw himself into his new role with dramatic gestures and extravagant proclamations, exploiting his territorial advantage to the utmost. He occupied a key theatre of war and the gateway to the Mexican economy. Jalapa fell to him on 29 May 1821. The assault on Veracruz failed but he personally earned further credit for bravery in front of the enemy, while the political and economic importance of Veracruz raised his profile still higher. But Spain was not his only target. He was reported to Iturbide as a 'conspirator and man of ambition', and it was clear that Santa Anna paraded his regional strength and local popularity in order to frighten his enemies in the government camp.

Iturbide had little reason to trust Santa Anna, for the caudillo was keeping his options open, jealous in particular of any encroachment on his position in Veracruz. He tried on his own initiative to subvert the royalist garrison holding out in San Juan de Ulúa; insubordination combined with failure drew an angry response from Iturbide who removed Santa Anna in November 1822 and ordered him to report to Mexico City. This was a familiar spectacle in Spanish America: the central government summons a recalcitrant caudillo to the capital; from a position of strength the caudillo resists; around him grows a rebellion. Santa Anna knew Iturbide was in serious trouble, cornered by politicians, starved of revenue, and helpless in a stagnant economy. So again Santa Anna seized the opportunity. He rose against Iturbide, in part incited by the merchants of Jalapa, in part driven by personal ambition, and overtly in outrage at the humiliating order which, he subsequently wrote, 'tore the bandage from my eyes. I

---

[112] Díaz Díaz, *Caudillos y caciques*, 52.
[113] Oakah L. Jones, *Santa Anna* (New York, 1968), 30.

beheld absolutism in all its power.'[114] With Guadalupe Victoria he devised the Plan of Veracruz (6 December 1822), which demanded the deposition of Iturbide, restoration of congress, and the three guarantees. Santa Anna did not rely on policy alone, but offered 'promotions, rewards and bonuses to the troops under his command'.[115] Deserted by his clients, rejected by the interest groups, and threatened by various 'Plans', Iturbide abdicated on 19 February 1823. Santa Anna later claimed that he had become 'arbiter of the destinies of my country'.[116] That is what he wanted to be. If it were not yet true, nevertheless at the age of twenty-nine many possibilities were opening up to him to become a national hero.

Like every caudillo, Santa Anna had a power base. His political lair was Veracruz, a land of promise only partly fulfilled. The commercial activity of the port contrasted sharply with the economic inertia of its hinterland. The war of independence damaged the commerce of Veracruz and Jalapa and left the economy of the region in ruins. There was potential wealth in cacao, tobacco, cotton, and sugar, but it was not fully developed and the region was underpopulated. In Jalapa on the eve of independence just over half the population were Spaniards, and over 40 per cent were mestizos and *pardos*, with more of the mixed races in the countryside. Nearer the coast, in Zempoala, mestizos and *pardos* formed together 73.9 per cent of the total population. This was the race mixture of the peons on the haciendas of Manga de Clavo and El Encero, many of whom became part of the regional *clientela* of Santa Anna. In the central plain of the province as far as the coastal zone a few powerful families owned vast estates, monopolizing land for cattle, exploiting their tenant farmers, and preventing the expansion of sugar and cotton plantations.[117] The result was depopulation, shortage of rural labour, and inflation of food prices. The landowners and merchants of Veracruz thus monopolized the wealth of the province, while the majority of Indians, blacks, and *mulatos* were marginalized. The late colonial trade of the port, however, primed by mining output and consumer imports, had been buoyant and profitable, and normally showed a substantial balance in

---

[114] W. S. Robertson, *Iturbide of Mexico* (Durham, N. C., 1952), 222.

[115] Díaz Díaz, *Caudillos y caciques*, 57.

[116] Antonio López de Santa Anna, *Mi historia militar y política, 1810–1874* (Mexico, 1905), 13.

[117] Alexander von Humboldt, *Ensayo político sobre el reino de la Nueva España*, 6th Spanish edn. (4 vols.; Mexico, 1941), ii. 301–6.

Mexico's favour. It was this wealth which helped to finance road development and improve communications between Veracruz and the interior of Mexico, thus bequeathing to the province a strategic importance and to Santa Anna a built-in advantage.

Santa Anna gained and exploited a great ascendancy in his own state, and when he came to make a push for power at the centre he had behind him the expectations of his paisanos. Merchants wanted a return of the commercial hegemony of Veracruz which they remembered from colonial times. Agriculturalists wanted the backing of their caudillo for favourable policies and protective tariffs; in 1841, for personal ends, he fulfilled some of these claims when he acted as spokesman of the *cosecheros* of cotton and tobacco. Those who gave him support in the province—local creoles, civil and military personnel, municipal authorities who could bring out the *jarochos*—hoped to secure his influence to promote their personal advancement, and some benefited from his patronage to obtain rewards either in a military career or in the bureaucracy. The Veracruz *clientela* of Santa Anna, therefore, was a source of support throughout his career and there was normally a coincidence between the personal objectives of the caudillo and the social aspirations of his paisanos.[118]

For the moment, however, Santa Anna was a caudillo waiting in the wings. He was sent to San Luis by the provisional government in 1823 to consolidate the revolution in the interior. There he proclaimed his Plan of San Luis calling for a federal republic, seen by some as a political bid and by others as a disposition to swim with the tide. He soon had an opportunity to demonstrate his federalism in action. He was appointed military governor of Yucatán where his independent style quickly alerted his superiors in Mexico City. Appreciating that Yucatán could not subsist without its traditional trade, he put aside a decree of the central government prohibiting trade with Spain and its colonies, and allowed trade with Cuba to continue without interruption.[119] He also planned an expedition to seize Cuba from Spain, but had to desist from this and depart from office, having probably identified too closely with federalist and even separatist interests.[120] Gómez Pedraza is supposed to have recommended the

[118] Díaz Díaz, *Caudillos y caciques*, 68.

[119] Morier to Canning, Jalapa, 19 Nov. 1824, PRO, FO 50/6, fos. 98–102.

[120] Morier to Canning, Mexico City, 28 Feb. 1825, PRO, FO 50/11, fos. 80–1; Alamán, *Historia de Méjico*, v. 840.

Cuban expedition, on the grounds that if it succeeded Mexico would gain glory, and if it failed the country would be rid of Santa Anna.

Santa Anna was an irritation to the central government, but obviously identified and exploited a number of trends in contemporary Mexico, the bias towards regional autonomy, the ability of local *jefes* to act independently, and the strength of personal networks. The size of the country, the underdevelopment of the economy, the weakness of infrastructure, all favoured the existence of regional caudillos, often acting in open defiance of the decrees of central government, if not in complete rebellion. Nevertheless, caudillism of this kind was not mere anarchy: through their influence, derived from military reputation and economic position, regional *jefes* became spokesmen of the rights of their paisanos and protectors of the municipalities; at the same time they channelled a modicum of government authority into their state, acting in effect as power brokers between the centre and the periphery. Referring to Santa Anna's administration in Yucatán, the Minister of Foreign Affairs Lucas Alamán wrote:

General Santa Anna acted without instructions or orders of any kind, but on his own authority alone; for this and other reasons he was relieved of his command in Yucatán. Nevertheless it would be useful not to give too much publicity to this, for it could affect the reputation of the government. The independence shown by the said general on this occasion could furnish our detractors with an argument to prove the lack of obedience on the part of those chiefs who are situated some distance from the centre of supreme authority.[121]

In 1825 Santa Anna left Yucatán and returned to his hacienda as a caudillo to his stronghold. So far his career had been a series of reactions to opportunities. A royalist officer to 1821; *trigarante* to 1822; collaborator with Iturbide's empire, then *golpista* against it; a republican in 1823 and a federalist in 1823–4; to Yucatán in 1825 with a plan to invade Cuba. He now had an unenviable reputation as 'a character who has successively served and betrayed every party that has figured in this country since the commencement of the revolutionary war'.[122] His actions were those of an adventurist, it is true, but they created enough publicity to focus attention on him and to attract a following at each stage; by 1825, therefore, although he had won few friends in the government, he had numerous followers among the military and the *jarochos*. He retired to Manga de Clavo,

---

[121] Alamán, 3 Aug. 1825, Díaz Díaz, *Caudillos y caciques*, 73.
[122] Pakenham to Aberdeen, 26 Sept. 1828, PRO, FO 50/45, fos. 136–42.

waiting and watching, preserving his options, committing himself to neither of the political factions, but remaining a focus for the interests of the merchants and agriculturalists of his region. While the factions fought it out in Veracruz state he adopted an olympian position, and was appointed officer commanding Veracruz and vice-governor of the state.

In the presidential election of 1828 Manuel Gómez Pedraza, war minister and former follower of Iturbide, ran against Guerrero, the caudillo from the south. The conservative and propertied elements rallied behind the moderate Gómez Pedraza, while Guerrero stood as the champion of the middle and lower classes and had too the support of Lorenzo Zavala, the radical journalist from Yucatán.[123] Gómez Pedraza was elected president by a small majority, but Guerrero refused to accept the result and on his behalf Zavala organized a rebellion and took over the capital in December 1828 with the help of the mob. In Veracruz Santa Anna, appreciating no doubt the popular appeal of Guerrero, led a revolutionary movement in his favour, allegedly in return for an offer of the ministry of war if he could persuade the congress of Veracruz to vote out Gómez Pedraza. Santa Anna could not deliver the vote; instead he raised his own forces and declared for Guerrero with a demagogic cry, 'Down with the Spaniards!'

Who were the followers of Santa Anna? As vice-governor of Veracruz he had access to the military garrison, from which he recruited 300 troops and took control of the castle of Perote commanding the main road from Jalapa to Veracruz. He was joined there by deserters from Puebla and by local peasantry, the *jarochos*. In addition he rounded up 200 convicts condemned to coastal works, making a total of 1,000 men.[124] For wages he managed to capture 15,000 pesos intended for the payment of government troops, while his men seized food and supplies from haciendas and villages. Among the leadership was Francisco Javier Gómez, an old friend of the insurgent Guadalupe Victoria and manager of his estates in Veracruz.[125] Santa Anna's efforts, however, did not raise the province and his forces were not sufficient to guarantee success. Pursued by government troops, he

---

[123] Pakenham to Vaughan, 13 Jan. 1829, PRO, FO 50/53, fos. 56–63.

[124] Pakenham to Aberdeen, 26 Sept., 2 Nov. 1828, PRO, FO 50/45, fos. 136–42, 228–33; Michael P. Costeloe, *La Primera República Federal de México (1824–1835)* (Mexico, 1975), 189–93; Green, *The Mexican Republic*, 158–9.

[125] O'Gorman to Bidwell, 26 Sept. 1828, PRO, FO 50/48, fos. 296–302.

took refuge in Oaxaca, and was only saved by the timely success of Zavala's rebellion in Mexico City. With the victory of the *golpistas* he returned to the government of Veracruz, professing loyalty to the new regime but viewed with suspicion even by Guerrero. Santa Anna brought his action to a close by intercepting a *conducta* (convoy of specie) from Mexico City to Veracruz and taking 25,000 dollars to pay his troops. He claimed that the sum constituted the export duties which the customs would levy at Veracruz; the government earned less credit for agreeing than did Santa Anna for paying his followers.[126]

In southern Mexico there was another power base. This was a region of contrasting zones, mountains, Tierra Caliente, and the Pacific coast, its agriculture productive in cotton, maize, beans, sugar cane, and tobacco, as well as in cattle. The population, too, was mixed: mestizo in Tierra Caliente, Indian and mestizo in the sierra, *mulato* and *zambo* on the coast. Great estates had already monopolized most of the fertile land of the south during the colonial period, though lack of population and communications prevented the growth of immense latifundia such as typified northern and central Mexico. Even so there was great inequality and a mass of miserable peons, suitable material for semi-forced recruitment into government or revolutionary forces. After independence two socio-economic zones can be identified: Tixtla and Chilapa; Tecpan and Acapulco. And two leading caudillos: the greater part of Tierra Caliente and Costa Grande was the power base of Juan Alvarez; most of the centre—Tixtla, Chilapa, and Chilpancingo—was that of Nicolás Bravo. The Alvarez zone contained various races, blacks, mestizos, Indians, and whites, and his *clientela* was predominantly mixed race; his principal hacienda was La Providencia near Acapulco. Bravo territory, on the other hand, had more parity between the various racial groups, Spaniards, mestizos, and *pardos*, and more conflict. The Alvarez population was of a low cultural level, generally violent, and containing enclaves of delinquents and outlaws, among whom drunkenness was the norm rather than an exception. Indian risings were not uncommon, usually in protest against racial and economic exploitation by the whites. For land concentration left resources in the hands of a few great proprietors, often at the expense of Indian land, while many of the Indians and blacks were landless.

---

[126] Pakenham to Aberdeen, 6 Apr. 1829, PRO, FO 50/53, fos. 321–5.

Property concentration, race mixture, and landless peasants made the south a region of *patrón*–peon, perfect for caudillos. The presence of rich, powerful proprietors such as the Galeana of Tecpan, the Bravo of Chilpancingo, the so-called *patriarcas del sur*, had made it easy for Morelos to secure the adhesion of their clients and dependants, their relatives, hacienda workers, and compadres, and following these, the Indians and blacks. It also raised the spectre of race war, which Morelos resisted through restoration of Indian community land. Vicente Guerrero inherited responsibility for this policy. He became the hero of the south, the defender of its interests, and the protector of its people. His victories in Tierra Caliente gave him a numerous following, and he found it easy to identify with the popular classes. Yet Guerrero—'a Mexican who owes nothing to art, everything to nature', as Zavala remarked—was incapable of taking up the social policy left by Morelos, and his political ambitions drew him to the centre.[127] There he became a national figure with a popular reputation, but he remained an uncultured provincial, probably manipulated by others and not equal to the challenge of rising from regional to national caudillo. The south was his base and the south was his retreat when he was ousted. The fall of Guerrero left a populist gap for others to fill. The zone of Zacatula, forgotten by the authorities, remote from government, and lacking in economic interest, was ideal territory for local bosses. Among these was Juan Alvarez. He made Guerrero his model and the federal constitution of 1824 his guide. His association with the legendary exploits of Morelos and Guerrero gave him a political status in the south which otherwise his birth and education did not warrant. From that time he became and remained the military chief of the Costa Grande, an official as well as a personal position. And unlike Santa Anna, he preferred the stability of his own domain to the lure of the centre.

4. *Caudillo Prospects*

Spanish America began its republican life with caudillos as well as constitutions, sometimes in concert with each other, sometimes in conflict. The caudillos augmented the position they had won in war.

---

[127] Quoted by Costeloe, *La Primera República Federal*, 217; on Alvarez see Díaz Díaz, *Caudillos y caciques*, 101–3.

To legitimacy they added land. To military prestige they added political authority. After two decades of independence the caudillo could be defined as an absolute ruler—of his locality, his region, or his country. He might have the assistance of ministers, the adornment of a legislature, the service of a bureaucracy; he might be called a governor, a supreme chief, or a president; he might be a soldier and he was often a general. But the ultimate criterion of his rule was personal authority, exercised according to his own judgement, and by virtue of his absolute power. If caudillism was a cheap way of fighting a war, it was not necessarily an economical way of governing a country. For it usually existed alongside a constitution, and constitutions created offices and filled them with officials. Caudillo patronage, too, expanded the public payroll. In most cases caudillos retained a full façade of institutions and actually used some of them. So the new states acquired the expense of constitutions without their benefits.

One of the most acute constitutional problems of the new republics, whose peoples had been accustomed only to hereditary monarchy, was the orderly replacement of one administration by another. Caudillism was particularly vulnerable to crises of succession, and usually resolved them by *golpes* or rebellions. The possibility of founding dynasties did not escape the caudillos. In Argentina Rosas seriously urged that, in the event of his death or assassination, he should be succeeded by his daughter Manuela. Paraguay took the first step towards hereditary succession when a compliant congress granted the dictator Carlos Antonio López the right to name a temporary successor; before he died, on 10 September 1862, he nominated his own son, already an heir apparent and now a far from transient ruler. Hereditary caudillism, this was a rare phenonemon, Paraguay's exhibit in the museum of politics. At the other end of the spectrum, the success of the Chilean political system and its exceptional immunity to caudillism was due in part to the skill of its constitution makers in designing a foolproof system of presidential succession. Orderly succession became virtually a test of non-caudillism.

In the post-war years caudillos took specific steps to increase their power. They established or expanded their haciendas, extended their *clientelas*, arranged their alliances, and decided their political priorities. In Argentina, Venezuela, and Mexico there was no basic difference in the ultimate power bases of the caudillos. The hacienda or estancia was the indispensable foundation, source of personal wealth, focus of manpower, place of retreat, and fortress in defeat. The networks of clients and alliances may have differed in detail but were the same in nature and function. Originating normally from a regional base, the caudillos of each country, once they struck out for hegemony, had to contend with regional resistance. The political framework differed from one country to another. The army and the Church were stronger in Mexico than they were in Argentina and Venezuela, the conflict of ideas was more intense, political space less open. With greater obstacles to overcome and harder deals to arrange, it was more difficult for the Mexican caudillo to make his way to power. More difficult, but not impossible.

Independence from colonial rule is normally followed by a process of state-building and nation-making, tasks for which few Spanish Americans were prepared. While the caudillos accumulated personal power, did they also increase the power of the state and defend the interests of the nation?

4
CAUDILLO STATE, NATION-STATE

1. *From Bourbon State to Caudillo State*

Nationalism came slowly to the Hispanic world, follower rather than creator of events. The colonial state was not succeeded immediately by nation-states. There was an interregnum during which liberating armies or caudillo bands first challenged the power of Spain and then destroyed it. In some regions the conflict was prolonged and from it emerged primitive wartime states, capable of mobilizing resources and recruiting troops. But these states were not yet nations. Even after independence had been won, the creation of new states preceded the birth of nations. For the growth of national consciousness was slow, its expression weak, and its diffusion imperfect.

Yet nations were already in process of formation. If the rhetoric of nationalism was subdued its character was gathering strength. It would be unrealistic to apply modern tests of nationality to the new republics of Spanish America and conclude that nations did not exist. Chronology counted: there were distinct stages of development, when nationality existed in embryo, then in incipient or partial form, and finally culminated in full nationhood. Creole nationality pre-dated independence and was to be found in a sense of loyalty to the *patria*, a growing consciousness of identity, a conviction that Americans were not Spaniards.[1] The individual began to identify himself with a group, and these groups possessed some of the qualifications of a nation: common descent, language, religion, territory, customs, and traditions, those signs which John Stuart Mill described as 'identity of political antecedents, the possession of a national history, and consequent community of recollection'.[2] The war of independence refined these sentiments and fashioned them into a more positive concept of nation. The revolution was a great cause. Spanish Americans now had their own heroes, their own victories, their own myths.

---

[1] Alexander von Humboldt, *Ensayo político sobre el reino de la Nueva España*, ii. 118.
[2] John Stuart Mill, *Representative Government*, 360.

Self-awareness became more than patriotism, more than love of native land; it became a shared experience, an assertion of nationality. At the same time as Americans began to disavow Spanish nationality, they were also aware of differences among themselves. Even in their pre-national state the various colonies rivalled each other in their assets and interests. Regional identity was nourished on regional resources, to be guarded and developed against the encroachments of others. America was too vast and diverse a continent to claim individual allegiance. Men were primarily Venezuelans, Mexicans, *porteños*, and it was in their own country, not America, that they found their national home, there developing a higher degree of communication among each other than with neighbours and outsiders. War itself nurtured nationality. The army of Colombia and the army of the Andes brought together men of different *patrias*, often in uneasy proximity, close observers of their differences and rivalries, and aware that many of their compatriots were fighting for Spain. National prejudices were born and stereotypes created. Argentines were 'gauchos', Peruvians 'indios', Venezuelans 'militares'. In defeating Spain they shattered America, reducing it to a series of nationalities divided from each other no longer by mutual ignorance but by knowledge and experience acquired in arms. To know a neighbour was to distrust him.

Nations could not be created in a day or in the lifetime of a single generation. During and after the wars of independence there were a number of forces hostile to the growth of strong nation-states. The hacienda was one of many bases of power and allegiance which challenged state institutions; peons were bound by duties to their *patrón*, whose authority was immediate and whose decision was final. Corporate privilege also diminished political sovereignty. The existence of military and ecclesiastical *fueros*, and the survival of Indian communities as corporate entities, gave legal structure to social enclaves and removed large sectors of the population from the direct jurisdiction of the state.[3] Regional secession or autonomy, often expressing extensive family networks and economic interests, these too were alternative sovereignties which correspondingly weakened national development. Finally, the caudillo, who usually emerged from a regional power base, was one of the strongest obstacles to the

[3] Richard N. Adams, *Nationalization* (Institute of Latin American Studies, University of Texas, Offprint Ser., 60; Austin, 1967), 469–89.

development of the nation-state. Personal sovereignty subverted constitutions. The caudillo became the state, and the state the property of the caudillo. Yet paradoxically caudillos could also act as defenders of national interests against territorial incursions, economic pressures, and other threats from outside, and so promote the independence and unity of their peoples and raise their national consciousness. Caudillos were the agents and the enemies of the nation-state.

National perceptions were confined to the creoles, for the *pardos* had only an obscure sense of nationality, and the Indians and blacks none at all.[4] Those Indians who joined patriot armies or guerrilla bands usually did so without ideological convictions, and they could change sides without compunction. They might act under duress, or from habit, or to acquire arms, but rarely on individual initiative. A guerrilla leader in Upper Peru admonished royalist Indians:

'The *patria* is the place where we live; the *patria* is the true cause which we ought to defend at all costs; for the *patria* we ought to sacrifice our interests and even our life.' Proclamations of this kind were issued on all sides, but for the moment we did not have a single Indian. We were speaking to thin air, as though it were a foreign country which we had to reconquer.[5]

The Indians of Upper Peru were more aware of traditional and communal allegiances, and the guerrillas could make no impression on those who had taken the king's medal, the *amedallados*:

They said it was for their king and lord that they were going to die, and not as rebels, nor for the *patria*; they did not know what this *patria* was, nor what it meant, nor what it looked like; they said that no one knew if the *patria* was a man or a woman. As for the king, they knew him, his government was well established, his laws were respected and duly observed. So they were put to death, all eleven of them.[6]

The caudillos and their mestizo followers in many cases had little more sense of nationality than the Indians. They were products of the environment in which they lived. In most rural societies of Spanish America a great gulf separated the landed proprietor from the landless peon. In New Granada the guerrilla band formed in 1817 by the Almeyda brothers, José Vicente and Ambrosio, who operated in and around the Valle de Tenza, north-east of Bogotá, was smaller than its Venezuelan counterparts and less successful in recruiting. The

[4] John Lynch, *The Spanish American Revolutions 1808–1826*, 2nd edn. (New York, 1986), 24–34.
[5] Vargas, *Diario*, June, 1816, 88.
[6] Ibid. 30 Dec. 1816, 118.

Almeydas proclaimed 'Salud y libertad', 'Viva la América libre'; they called upon the people to join them 'to rid us of shameful enslavement by the *godos*'; and they promised war against the enemies 'who have caused us such enormous damage'.[7] But the damage they had most in mind was that to their own property. The Almeydas were a wealthy creole family whose political activities had already brought them to the attention of the Spanish authorities; having escaped from prison in September 1817 they took to the mountains of Mochetá and from there sought to recover the extensive and well-stocked haciendas confiscated by the *junta de secuestros* in 1817.[8] Another guerrilla leader explained that 'Because of my love for the cause of America and my flight to join the movements to break from the Spanish chains in 1817, the agents of the Spanish government decreed the confiscation of my property.'[9] But the mass of the peasantry and the Indian communities remained indifferent to their pleas for recruits, and many fled to the mountains rather than enrol in an alien cause or, as the Almeydas put it, because 'they were not interested in the happiness of their country.'[10]

In Argentina and Venezuela, too, there was strong group cohesion among the élite of land, office, and trade, and little sign of solidarity among their subordinates. A caudillo was usually the centre of a vast kinship group based on land and linking legislators, bureaucrats, and military in a powerful political network. These had some idea of the nation and its assets, which they monopolized and used as patronage to bind their small oligarchy ever closer together. At the other end of society the popular sectors were illiterate; they had little access to education, only a minimal stake in society, and no incentive to develop an awareness of the nation. At the end of the colonial period the pampas and the llanos were inhabited by wild cattle and nomadic horsemen. By simple definition the gauchos and llaneros were free men on horseback. But the terms were used by contemporaries and by later historians in a wide sense to mean rural people in general. Greater precision would distinguish between the sedentary rural dwellers working on the land for themselves or for a patrón, and the pure gaucho and llanero, who was nomadic and independent, tied to no estate. And further refinement would identify others who lived by

---

[7] Oswaldo Díaz Díaz, *Los Almeydas* (*BHN* 99, Bogotá, 1962), 96–8.
[8] Manuel Caballero y Góngora, 22 Dec. 1817, Díaz Díaz, *Los Almeydas*, 34–5.
[9] Gregorio Prieto, quoted ibid. 119.
[10] Ibid. 112, 127, 145.

violence and near-delinquency and whom the state came to regard as criminal. The classical gaucho and llanero asserted his freedom from all formal institutions and embraced marginality as an ideal, not a flaw. He did not necessarily seek land; he lived by hunting, gambling, and fighting.[11] He was indifferent to government and its agents, and had no awareness of nationality.

In Argentina the term *patria* referred to a person's native province not to an Argentina nation. Esteban Echeverría, the young liberal and romantic, asked Argentines 'What does the *patria* mean for you?' His answer was a perfect description of 'Argentina' in the age of the caudillos: 'The fatherland for the *correntino* is Corrientes; for the *cordobés*, Córdoba; for the *tucumano*, Tucumán; for the *porteño*, Buenos Aires; for the gaucho, the *pago* where he was born.' Everyone fights for his own corner, and larger national interests are an 'incomprehensible abstraction'.[12] Nation or province, it was all the same to the gaucho. He felt no pull of patriotism, no sense of allegiance, no obligation to any state, central or local. As W. H. Hudson observed: 'The gaucho is, or was, absolutely devoid of any sentiment of patriotism and regarded all rulers, all in authority from the highest to the lowest, as his chief enemies, and the worse kind of robbers, since they robbed him not only of his goods but of his liberty.'[13] The llaneros of Venezuela, by compulsion and conviction, were equally marginalized from the nation. After the revolution Bolívar spoke of them as men who 'feel humiliated and frustrated, and they have lost hope of gathering the fruit of what they have won by their lances. They are resolute, ignorant llaneros, who have never regarded themselves the equals of other men with more knowledge and better appearance.'[14]

The ruling groups in the countryside imposed a system of coercion upon people whom they regarded as vagrants without employer or occupation. For the gaucho and the llanero the years after independence were even harsher than before.[15] Not for them involvement in nation building. Common usages and traditional practices observed during the colonial period gave way to republican laws which attacked

---

[11] Rodríguez Molas, *Historia social del gaucho*, 185–242; Germán Carrera Damas, *Boves*, 195–208.
[12] Esteban Echeverría, *Dogma Socialista* (La Plata, 1940), 112, 126–7.
[13] W. H. Hudson, *Tales of the Pampa* (London, 1916), 247.
[14] Bolívar to Gual, 24 May 1821, *Cartas*, ii. 348–9.
[15] Slatta, *Gauchos and the Vanishing Frontier*, 109–12.

vagrancy and organized the rural population for work. People were forced to carry identity cards, not as evidence of national identity but as certificates of residence and employment; a peon caught out of his hacienda without permission could be conscripted into the army or assigned to public works. Free access to cattle was now called rustling and punished with extreme severity.[16] Thus the gauchos and llaneros were converted from free nomads into hired ranch hands, *peones de hacienda*. The theory behind this legislation, common to both Argentina and Venezuela, was that idleness meant vagrancy, which equalled delinquency. The basic explanation, however, was that land concentration prevented the mass of the people from acquiring land, while hacienda expansion raised the demand for labour.

This primitive society was not qualified for constitutional government, political integration, or national participation. The state was distant, the nation vague. The hacienda dominated economic and social life and became the model of government. Hacendados ruled their domains by personal authority and demanded unqualified obedience. They were a powerful and cohesive class, unrivalled by any other. Argentina and Venezuela did not yet possess a substantial middle sector of commerce or industry, and there was no great concentration of peasants as in Mexico or Peru. The popular classes, superior in numbers, were heterogeneous in composition and divided into disparate groups, small farmers or tenants, peons on haciendas, wage labourers, gauchos, marginal llaneros, and delinquents. The subordinate condition of the lower sectors, their poor expectations, and their isolation in the immense plains combined to prevent the formation of an autonomous political movement from below. On the other hand they were ideal material for military mobilization and they were easily transformed into *guerrilleros*, bandoleros, or *montoneros*. The causes for which they fought were not national unity, defence of the state, or even class conflict. They were sectional struggles within the upper groups, disputes between landed proprietors or among leading families, attacks upon the existing government by its political opponents, or clashes between the dominant interests in neighbouring provinces. In a situation of equilibrium between factions, leaders would call on their dependants and round up their reserves, the

[16] *Materiales para el estudio de la cuestión agraria*, vol. i, pp. cii, cxvi, 83–4, 511–16; Benito Díaz, *Juzgados de paz de campaña de la provincia de Buenos Aires (1821–1854)* (La Plata, 1959), 202–18; Rodríguez Molas, *Historia social del gaucho*, 201.

better to tip the balance against their opponents. This was the caudillo state.

The constitutional contrast was stark. To leave the Bourbon state for a caudillo state was to move from a well-ordered household, fixed in its ways and ruled by the book, to a turbulent family, fearsome at the top and frayed at the edges, where authority was personal and obedience unpredictable.

2. *Wartime State*

The wartime state was rudimentary and the caudillos did not belong to it. The concept of the state, as a legal and political organization with the power to exact obedience and loyalty from its citizens, was a constant preoccupation of Bolívar's political thought; and the task of state-building was one which he began during the war of independence itself. He also had a high degree of national consciousness, however he might define the nation, and he believed that this was a prerequisite for a successful state: 'to establish a stable government a national spirit is needed.'[17] Ideas of this kind were not part of the caudillo mentality. Caudillos like Mariño never acquired the national, much less the American, vision of Bolívar. Mariño argued that it was necessary to conquer and hold the east as a precondition of liberating the west. Páez, on the other hand, maintained that the western front was the crucial battlefield: victory there would have enabled the royal army to defeat the eastern caudillos one by one, and thus 'the fate of the republic was at stake in the llanos of Apure.'[18] Without a central revolutionary leadership, the various regional fronts could never have joined into a national or continental liberation movement. Yet the caudillos often conformed to prevailing conditions more closely than Bolívar did. They provided the local leadership which alone could take the place of a national army, and they kept informal insurgency alive before national objectives had been defined.

Yet the caudillos were not devoid of national awareness and were capable of making basic distinctions. They followed the example of Bolívar in distinguishing between Spaniards and Americans. In the

[17] Angostura Address, 15 Feb. 1819, in Bolívar, *Obras completas*, iii. 691.
[18] Páez, *Autobiografía*, i. 109.

celebrated decree issued at Trujillo (15 June 1813) Bolívar made the position chillingly clear: 'Spaniards and Canarians, depend upon it, you will die, even if you are simply neutral, unless you actively espouse the liberation of America. Americans, you will be spared, even when you are guilty.'[19] The decree ruthlessly distinguished between Spaniards and Americans; it sought to cut through categories like royalism and republicanism and to make this a war between nations, between Spain and America. War to the death was an affirmation of Americanism, a clear signal that Americans had left their Spanish *nación*, that Venezuelans were aware of their identity. The caudillos willingly applied it. After the victory of San Félix (18 April 1817) Piar paraded his 200 royalist prisoners and separated the Americans and Spaniards: 'This morning all the Americans taken in yesterday's action were assigned to the Barlovento, Honor, and Conquista Battalions, and the Spaniards were kept in confinement.'[20] Not for long; Piar had them summarily shot.

Beyond these primitive instincts the wartime caudillos had only a faint idea of the nation. In 1813 Mariño named himself 'chief of the independent army', and he established not only an autonomous military command in the east but a political entity separate from Caracas and from the dictatorship of Bolívar. The Liberator, on the other hand, insisted on establishing a central authority for all Venezuela. While it made sense to have two military departments, it was essential to have one central government uniting east and west, Venezuela and New Granada:

If we establish two independent authorities, one in the east and the other in the west, we will create two different nations which, because of their inability to maintain themselves as such, or even more to take their place among other nations, will look ridiculous. Only a Venezuela united with New Granada could form a nation that would inspire in others the proper consideration due to her. How can we think of dividing her into two?[21]

Thus Bolívar's first projection of a greater Colombia, united for national strength and economic viability, was presented as an alternative to the anarchy of local guerrilla rule.

While the caudillos were an essential part of the war effort, they made little contribution to the wartime state. Bolívar had to impose a

---

[19] O'Leary, *Narración*, i. 158–60.
[20] Diario de Operaciones del General Piar, April 1817, in O'Leary, *Memorias*, xv. 241–2.
[21] Bolívar to Mariño, 16 Dec. 1813, *Cartas*, i. 88.

unified army structure on the caudillos, to institutionalize the army, and to establish a hierarchy of command.[22] One of the strengths of the caudillos, a regional base for raising troops, was also a weakness. These troops were unwilling to leave their own province, which for them was their whole world, and the caudillos were unable to compel them or to teach them national objectives. Bolívar fought against regionalism and immobility, and projected a Venezuelan army with a national identity:

The frequent desertion of soldiers from one division to another on the pretext of being natives of the province where their chosen division is operating, is a cause of disorder and insubordination in the army and encourages a spirit of provincialism which we have tried hard to overcome. All Venezuelans ought to have the same interest as their brothers in defending the territory of the Republic where they have been born, for Venezuela is essentially a single family composed of many individuals bound together by indissoluble ties and by identical interests.[23]

He urged the caudillos to help each other, ordering them to transfer men and supplies wherever necessary, 'according to the development of the war'. In the event they did not listen, and they remained local leaders rather than participants in a national effort. In the course of 1817–19 Bolívar organized three military groups, the Army of the East, the Army of the West, and the Army of the Centre under himself. Finally he created a Council of State as an interim measure until a constitution could be established after liberation. This consisted of the chief military and civil officers, and existed to deal with matters of state, defence, and justice. It was advisory only and depended on the supreme chief for its meeting.[24] Overtly the caudillos recognized the revolutionary state personified in Bolívar, but they did not change their ways. There were still occasions when they took regional viewpoints, and when they and their troops preferred to return to their homes in Cumaná, Barcelona, and Apure. Bolívar led a regular army into New Granada, while the caudillos remained in their homelands. As they did not take a 'national' view of the war, they were incapable of taking an 'American' view or of contributing to a continental liberation movement. The transnational

---

[22] See Chap. 2, sect. 4.
[23] Bolívar to Bermúdez, 7 Nov. 1817, in O'Leary, *Memorias*, xv. 449–50; Fernando Rivas Vicuña, *Las guerras de Bolívar*, ii. 85–95.
[24] Decree, 30 Oct. 1817, in *Escritos*, xi. 318–20.

transfer of resources in the interests of the revolution, something understood by the Bolivarian generals, was beyond the comprehension of the caudillos. When the war returned to Venezuela, so they returned to their duties. The Carabobo campaign briefly integrated the caudillos into a national army, and peace scattered them once again.

In Argentina the process and the chronology were different. The revolutionary government in Buenos Aires from the beginning was free to develop a political and legal organization, to recruit a central bureaucracy, and to mobilize military forces. These were first tested in expeditions to Paraguay and Upper Peru and then in action in the Littoral, and although they did not emerge with conspicuous success this was because they had to fight not only Spain but also the indifference or hostility of the regions. The army of Belgrano was a revolutionary force, not a caudillo horde. The army created by San Martín in Mendoza was a regular army and owed nothing to caudillism. But these armies were deployed on particular campaigns, mainly outside Argentina. Within the country the central authority of Buenos Aires was rejected by the regions, which possessed neither the advantages of national institutions nor a sense of national responsibility. In the absence of a national state the regions placed their interests in the hands of caudillos leading local forces of *montoneros*.

In Upper Peru, where liberation by the revolutionary regime in Buenos Aires was not acceptable to the local élite, the cause of independence was left to the guerrilla republics. The Indian sector had no sense of *patria*, as has been seen, nor had many of the mestizo guerrillas clear views of patriotic goals. They spoke of fighting for the *patria*, but this did not yet mean the nation. *Patria* in Upper Peru simply meant freedom and was accompanied by nominal acknowledgment of the new regime in the Río de la Plata, where freedom already existed. But allegiance of this kind did not survive the early years of the revolution, when it became clear that the armies of Buenos Aires aimed not only to liberate Upper Peru but to reduce it to a new dependency. When it also became clear that Buenos Aires did not have the means to do this, then the political orientation of Upper Peru would turn away from Buenos Aires towards self-determination. If we are to believe the guerrilla chronicler, José Santos Vargas, later recalling the times of his youth, this sentiment had always been present:

I had embraced the party of independence without knowing of any advantages it could bring, risking my youth and the best years of my life, living always on the edge of death, without any wage, for there was nothing and nobody to pay us; on Sundays we might have a small payment of two or four reales and on rare occasions two pesos, distributed without any class distinction between the first chief and the last soldier. But we were all supremely happy in the service of our liberty and our commitment to the cause. That was the joy we had, confident that the cause of our country's freedom would ultimately triumph; because the war was a national war and we knew well enough that a people in arms for its liberty and independence was rarely or ever forced into submission.[25]

3. *From Wartime State to Nation State*

Spanish America was at once receptive and indifferent to nationalist projects. Nationalism has two basic meanings. As a doctrine, it divides the world into nations, describes their character, interests, rights, and duties, and tests their existence in terms of language, race, culture, and religion.[26] As an organized political movement, nationalism is designed to further the aims and interests of a nation and ensure that the nation constitutes a sovereign state. In its more active sense it is frequently a response to foreign pressure, political, economic, or cultural, which is perceived as a threat to national identity and interests. In Spanish America the new nations found their identity first in reaction to the imperial pressure of the Bourbon state, then in the long war against Spain, and subsequently in conflicts with their neighbours and relations with foreign states. One of the first objectives of nationalism is independence, that is the creation of a sovereign state in which the nation is dominant. This was partially achieved in Spanish America in the years 1810–30. According to Bolívar, it was the revolution's only achievement: 'I am ashamed to admit it, but independence is the only benefit we have gained, at the cost of everything else.'[27] A second objective of nationalism is national unity, the incorporation within the frontiers of the new state of all groups

---

[25] Santos Vargas, Prefacio, *Diario*, 12.

[26] Elie Kedourie, *Nationalism*, 2nd edn. (London, 1961), 73; Ernest Gellner, *Nations and Nationalism* (Oxford, 1983), 3–7.

[27] Message to the Constituent Congress of Colombia, 20 Jan. 1830, in Simón Bolívar, *Proclamas y discursos del Libertador*, ed. Vicente Lecuna (Caracas, 1939), 398.

considered to belong to the nation. There is in some cases a third objective, to build a nation within an independent state, by extending down to the people as a whole the belief in the existence of the nation, hitherto held only by a minority.[28] In Spanish America the last two objectives were less clearly articulated than the first.

The post-war political settlement gave a new impetus to the nation-state, but also new challenges, from the regionalism of the caudillos and from the supranationalism of the Americanists. From the very beginning of the revolution Bolívar's thought transcended national restraints and expressed a wider Americanism. He had long desired the creation of the great state of Colombia, comprising Venezuela, New Granada, and Ecuador. He then sought to unite this with Peru and Bolivia in a Federation of the Andes. And he dreamed of the 'great day of America' when all the Spanish American peoples would come together in a league of nations or a federal union. These ideas, of course, operated at different levels of planning and possibility.[29] His idea of a greater Colombia, which existed for about a decade, was not a denial of national identity but an affirmation of it. He was seeking in effect one of the characteristic objectives of nationalism, namely national unity. He was trying to establish the appropriate size of a viable nation-state, seeking unity as a means to national strength and economic sufficiency. Unity would ensure peace and well-being as opposed to the anarchy of local caudillo rule, what he called 'mini-governments'. And unity would earn greater respect from other nations, from Britain and the United States. The Constitution of Cúcuta (12 July 1821) seemed to give him what he wanted. It created a strongly centralist state, a greater Colombia, comprising Venezuela, New Granada, and Quito, united under a single government with its capital in Bogotá, and subdivided not into three regions but into a number of departments.

Colombia, then, was Bolívar's nation-state, the embodiment of national unity. But he realized that if Venezuela were to organize itself peacefully, it was essential to satisfy and co-opt the caudillos. This he did, as has been seen, in two ways: by giving them regional appointments and by granting them land. From this settlement Páez emerged as a supercaudillo, progressing from the llanos to the centre-north, from *hatero* to hacendado, from hope of the underdogs to

---

[28] Hugh Seton-Watson, *Nations and States* (London, 1977), 1–9.

[29] Simon Collier, 'Nationality, Nationalism and Supranationalism in the Writings of Simón Bolívar', *HAHR* 63, 1 (1983), 37–64.

representative of the oligarchy, from regional to national leader. From 1826 Páez led the Venezuelan oligarchy in a separatist movement which would end by placing their country under the control of a national élite, ruled from Caracas and not from Bogotá, and monopolizing its own resources. This was an alliance of landowners and military caudillos on behalf of a conservative and independent Venezuela. While it was not expressed in terms of modern nationalism, it represented a search for the correct dimension of national unity, an alternative to the model designed by Bolívar.

These decisions did not necessarily make state-builders or nationalists out of the caudillos. For some in Venezuela Páez represented, not a man who had rescued their nation from the clutches of a superstate, but an intolerable centralist who trampled roughshod over the susceptibilities of Venezuela's own provinces and caudillos. In Argentina even louder voices were raised against the pretensions of a central government that made the demands appropriate to a state without offering the protection expected of a state. To defend their resources and fill the institutional gap, many provinces looked to the local strong man, who had often begun his public life as a delegate of the centre and now graduated to local leadership. Some provinces opted for informal autonomy, others declared their independence, and others prepared to join Artigas of Uruguay.

Uruguay itself developed a national position towards its neighbours soon after 1810. This was stimulated in part by the leadership of Artigas, in part by the action of interest groups. Uruguayan nationalism was a direct reaction to pressure from outside, not so much from Spain as from Argentina and Brazil, whose aims were seen as a threat to the political and economic interests of Uruguay. Artigas came to power, therefore, as a representative of the estancieros, who were ready to compete with similar economies in the Río de la Plata. He was also a champion of the rural poor capable, as few other caudillos were, of extending the nation to the mass of the people. Finally he was a military leader prepared to resist alien invaders. Uruguayan nationalism did not die with the departure of Artigas, but it was not strong enough in itself nor were its caudillos resolute enough on their own to carry it to victory. The giant neighbours fought each other to a standstill over Uruguay, but neither of them was powerful enough to defeat the other, and neither would allow the other to claim the prize. In these circumstances British diplomacy intervened to assist in the creation of a buffer state, which the caudillos inherited but did little to build. The other provinces of the former viceroyalty did not undergo precisely the same experience.

The provinces of the Littoral, caught between the pressure of Buenos Aires and what they regarded as the subversion of *artiguismo*, opted for various degrees of autonomous caudillism, as has been seen.[30] In the north-west separatism gave birth to the Federal Republic of Tucumán, created in 1819 by Bernabé Aráoz, governor of Tucumán. The new state comprised the provinces of Tucumán, Catamarca, and Santiago del Estero, and its constitution stated that Tucumán was 'a free and independent republic', with a president who had powers to nominate provincial governors. But the logic of separatism was not complete, for the other provinces did not want governors appointed by Tucumán. Caudillos existed by nature, not by nomination. Santiago del Estero resisted, asserted its own independence, and was immediately attacked by its new metropolis. Martín Güemes, caudillo of Salta, went to the assistance of Santiago, admonishing Aráoz, 'you have no right to attack this people, even on the pretext that it has proclaimed its independence, since it has the same right to do this as you have to make your province a republic'.[31] And his forces also went to liberate Catamarca from Tucumán's rule. Güemes, guardian of the northern frontier, was concerned chiefly with the effect of civil war on the war effort against Spain. Yet the proliferation of republics was not yet finished. On 17 January 1820 Córdoba declared its independence; on 30 January 1821 it adopted a constitution which vested executive power in a 'governor of the republic' and legislative power in a congress. On 1 March 1820, exercising what it regarded as 'the sovereignty of the people', La Rioja proclaimed its 'provisional independence' from Córdoba until a general congress of a federal kind should determine 'the form of government'.[32] Thus La Rioja became not so much an autonomous province as an independent fiefdom under a primitive caudillo, Facundo Quiroga, the Tiger of the Llanos.

Quiroga has retained a place in history largely through the publicity he received in Sarmiento's *Facundo*, a classic of Argentine literature. There he was not only dramatized as a monster of cruelty who raised terrorism to an art of government but was also promoted to a thesis— the conflict between civilization and barbarism—which became

---

[30] See Chap. 3, sect. 1.
[31] Güemes to Aráoz, 7 Feb. 1821, in *Archivo Quiroga*, i. 298–301.
[32] Circular de Francisco A. Ortiz de Ocampo, 1 Mar. 1820 (ibid. i. 131).

widely invoked to explain the state of Latin America.[33] Without Sarmiento, the memory of Quiroga would be as defunct as that of other minor caudillos of the time; instead, a life of crime and corruption has been elevated into national mythology. Yet Sarmiento never met Quiroga, never visited the llanos of La Rioja, and wrote his book from material supplied by fellow exiles in Chile. Juan Bautista Alberdi, who met Quiroga in Buenos Aires, showed a truer sense of proportion when he called him 'an obscure and useless guerrilla, chief of a miserable little place of 1,500 souls . . . a common killer'.[34]

The Quirogas preferred to rule in the wilderness than to serve in the capital, and it was in the western provinces that Facundo began and ended his political career, first as a delegate of central power, then as an agent of provincial government, fighting off enemies from outside and eliminating rivals within. Once he had won the struggle for power in La Rioja and become chief of its considerable militias, he began to extend his area of influence to neighbouring provinces, always at the request of their leaders, such as Salvador del Carril in San Juan, and Juan Bautista Bustos in Córdoba, and usually with advantage to himself. Quiroga became the archetype of the provincial caudillo; he stood for autonomy against the centre, though the only constructive claim he made—that the customs revenue of Buenos Aires be nationalized—was vitiated by his own impetuosity and the insolence of his challenge to Rosas.[35] Quiroga was an affront to Argentine identity, and the legends that grew around him were more potent and extravagant than those of any political cause. The peons of La Rioja attributed to him magical powers of success and survival. One of them told a sceptical General Paz: 'Sir, think what you like, but long experience tells us that Señor Quiroga is invincible in war, gambling, and love. So there is no battle that he has not won, no game of chance that he has lost, no woman whom he has failed to take if he wanted her.'[36] Quiroga's power was too personal to be a focus even of provincial patriotism. The cult of Quiroga subsumed all other loyalties. Pure personalism took over from institutions; those who had to deal with western Argentina dealt with Quiroga, not with a province, much less with a state. When General La Madrid became

[33] Sarmiento, *Facundo*, 109–20, 177–87, 189–223.

[34] Juan Bautista Alberdi, *Escritos póstumos* (16 vols.; Buenos Aires, 1895–1901), v. 183.

[35] David Peña, *Juan Facundo Quiroga*, 163–81.

[36] Paz, *Memorias póstumas*, 154.

governor of La Rioja in 1829 he found it difficult to attract a following

for no other reason than fear of Quiroga, for in reality this chieftain was not loved by his fellow countrymen, only feared, and to an extreme degree. Everyone in La Rioja said that Quiroga had great caches of treasure, derived from exactions which he had imposed on the people to pay his troops—a pretext, for they were never paid—as well as from the tithes and his monopoly of selling meat throughout the province.[37]

His cruelty was accompanied by arbitrary acts of generosity to individual paisanos, when the impulse took him. But his invincibility was not proof against ambush and assassination by political enemies in 1835.

The caudillos of Argentina demanded autonomy rather than secession. They were not all Quirogas, the epitome of personal power. Many responded to the needs of local economies, the claims of social groups, and the fiscal possibilities of the region. These interests could be articulated by provincial institutions, as in Corrientes, and owe little to caudillism. Other provinces preferred strong and personal leadership, men who had proved themselves capable of military resistance to outside pressure. This was the preference of Buenos Aires itself. Rivadavia had hoped to make Argentina a great nation-state through economic growth and new institutions. But his modernization programme was ahead of its time, and Buenos Aires had to abandon the pretence of leading a unitary state. The province was taken over by Rosas, leader of the agro-export interest, whose idea of nationality was confused. On the one hand, in a bizarre exercise in national unity, he sought to restore the boundaries of the former viceroyalty and to reclaim Uruguay, Bolivia, and even Paraguay. On the other hand within the core provinces he declined to sponsor a constitution or any project of national construction; rather than attempt to incorporate the other provinces he preferred to browbeat their caudillos. The caudillo of Buenos Aires was potentially a national caudillo, because he was stronger than the others and played a national role in foreign and commercial policy. As Alberdi said, 'Whoever has Buenos Aires as his capital, has the income and wealth of Argentina; for that reason, he who governs Buenos Aires is alone the national government.'[38] Rosas governed Buenos Aires and

---

[37] Aráoz de La Madrid, *Memorias*, i. 353.
[38] Alberdi, *Escritos póstumos*, vi. 259.

dominated the rest of the country. He reacted strongly to foreign blockade and intervention and rallied his countrymen in defence of the state. But this was not yet an Argentine state, nor did it have the attributes of a nation.

4. *Caudillo Nationalism*

While the caudillos were obstacles to the formation of nation states, not all of them were mere local chieftains. Some caudillos expressed a realistic sense of nationalism which defined the nation in terms of immediate interests. They responded effectively to external threat, either of neighbours or of foreign powers. And in defending the resources of their country against outsiders, they were forced to apply a distinction between natives and foreigners. In turn the growth of nationalism could enable a caudillo to strengthen his power base. This happened in Venezuela.

Towards the end of 1825, to organize defence against a supposed Negro conspiracy, Páez decided to call out the militia in Caracas. The methods allegedly employed to recruit reluctant citizens—the army was authorized to raid private houses and even open fire—led to his being reported to the central government in Bogotá, where his enemies and those hostile to the military-dominated Congress and were more than ready to make an issue of it.[39] Páez was relieved of his command by General Escalona and summoned to Bogotá for impeachment by Congress on charges of illegal and arbitrary conduct. There was a revolt in his favour in Valencia where the *cabildo* declared Páez fully reinstated in his command; and he asserted that he acted as the protector of the people 'in the exercise of their sovereignty, to provide for their own welfare and security'.[40] To some extent Páez was manipulated by a faction of liberal federalists; these made a pretence of consulting the people by working through the municipality of Caracas, which appointed Páez civil and military chief of Venezuela. The faction was headed by Mariño, a military caudillo in his own right with a record of unstable behaviour, Colonel Francisco Carabaño, a talented but turbulent republican, Dr Peña, former

[39] Bushnell, *Santander Regime*, 323–8.
[40] Proclamation, Valencia, 3 May 1826, encl. in Campbell to Canning, Bogotá, 9 June 1826, PRO, FO 18/27.

justice minister and now under impeachment for defrauding the treasury; associated with these were a number of merchants such as Tomás Lander, and Páez's new friends in the landed oligarchy.[41] But this was more than a conspiracy and a coup against the central government.

Caudillism and revolt were not synonymous. Venezuelan discontent had deeper causes, though not necessarily economic. Regional production received some protection from the government in Bogotá, which also allocated revenue and appointments even-handedly.[42] The root of the trouble was the factor of distance and time between Bogotá and Caracas, and from this the tendency towards inferior government, all of which strengthened a sense of Venezuelan identity and of threat from outside. Foreign observers were convinced that the vast state of Colombia would not work.

The idea of a country so extensive, so thinly inhabited and defective in its communications, united into a single Republic, the capital of which is at a greater distance from the exterior provinces, taking the embarrassments of travelling into consideration, than these are from Madrid is evidently replete with difficulties, the first and most obvious of which is the want of responsibility on the part of the various provincial magistrates.[43]

Páez certainly had support from the military, who suspected that Santander was undermining the *fuero militar* and victimizing the army. He also had support from his paisanos and comrades in arms:

The llaneros or plainsmen (who idolize him) have come foward strongly in the support of his cause, and would not hear of his resignation, or his being deprived of his military command. The troops it is thought throughout nearly the whole of the department will unanimously place themselves at his disposal—which together with the llanero horsemen will give him a force from twenty to thirty thousand men.[44]

But discontent was not confined to the military, nor support to the llaneros. Peasants too had grievances against the central government, which badly mismanaged the large sums allocated to those who had furnished the army with supplies during the war. These were paid by certificates which could only be redeemed by merchants who, in collusion with officials, paid peasants only a fraction of their value,

[41] Ker Porter to Canning, 26 July 1826, PRO, FO 18/35.

[42] Bushnell, *Santander Regime*, 287–90.

[43] Francis Hall, Report on Colombia, encl. in Sutherland to Canning, Maracaibo, 11 Mar. 1824, PRO, FO 18/8.

[44] Ker Porter to Canning, Caracas, 3 May 1826, PRO, FO 18/35.

the rest going to merchants and officials. As for redress of grievances, local justices were beyond the control of distant government.[45]

The reaction of the military, resentful of long arrears of pay, of llaneros, defrauded of their land grants, of peasants, cheated of their war credits, was in part a nationalist reaction against the dictates of Bogotá, which was seen as a neglectful and corrupt government, prejudicial to Venezuela's interests and an affront to Venezuela's identity. Thus, four years before independence was formally proclaimed, Páez took the powers of sovereignty which he wanted and needed: the regulation of militias, issue of money, distribution of offices and military appointments. He subsequently justified the process of secession which he thus began by appealing to obvious facts: 'Separation became a reality, because the Venezuelans did not want or respect laws which had so distant an origin. Order was maintained by men and not by public spirit or regard for institutions. A people with such a government cannot be content, and so Venezuela worked for its own happiness.'[46]

At first Bolívar did not accept this argument. He believed the conflict between centralism and federalism, and ultimately between unity and separatism, contained a racial problem. He was aware that there were strong objections to the choice of Bogotá as capital, not least the fact of its remoteness. But he argued that there was no alternative, 'for though Caracas appeared to be the more natural spot, from being more populous and influential, yet the province was chiefly composed of people of colour who were jealous of and opposed to the white inhabitants.' Thus it was necessary to diminish the influence of Caracas.[47] From the same facts the Venezuelan ruling class drew precisely the opposite conclusion. They wanted proximate power, even home rule, for Venezuela, 'a very energetic and concentrated system in consequence of its containing a great diversity of colour'.[48] Racial tension and *pardo* ambition required close supervision and control, and the élite could not but support Páez, because, like Rosas in Buenos Aires, he was virtually the only leader who

[45] Sutherland to Canning, Maracaibo, 1 Sept. 1826, PRO, FO 18/33.

[46] Gil Fortoul, *Historia constitucional de Venezuela*, i. 387–419; Bushnell, *Santander Regime*, 291–309.

[47] Ricketts to Canning, Lima, 18 Feb. 1826, C. K. Webster (ed.), *Britain and the Independence of Latin America, 1812–1830: Select Documents from the Foreign Office Archives* (2 vols.; London, 1938), i. 530.

[48] Ker Porter to Canning, Caracas, 9 Apr. 1827, PRO, FO 18/47.

could control the popular classes. Élite nationalism had a social dimension.

In time Bolívar too came to accept the situation and was prepared to let Venezuela go, if only because New Granadans would tire of their association with Venezuelan caudillos:

My opinion is that Congress ought to divide New Granada from Venezuela, for this is the strongest opinion and anything else an impossible dream. The more people think about it in New Granada, the less they will like the Venezuelan chieftains; and as the New Granadans have the capital of the republic here, they cannot imagine any other way out than obeying a government headed by a Venezuelan. This only revives the bitterest hostilities.[49]

Páez and his associates wanted an independent Venezuela. Páez spoke of sentiment and reminded Bolívar 'that Venezuelans deeply loathed the union with Bogotá and were resolved to make any sacrifice to obtain separation.'[50] But there was more to it than feeling. Caudillism now advanced because it coincided with Venezuelan nationalism, and this was an expression of interests as well as of identity. National identity, now sufficiently if narrowly rooted in Venezuela, was not at risk and in no danger of extinction. The real issue in Gran Colombia concerned political accountability by manageable units, or nations, as distinct from a superstate governed from distant Bogotá. From this arose a feeling that Venezuelans were disregarded and even repressed. In November 1829 and again in February 1830 there were public meetings in Caracas; these were crowded gatherings with heated discussion and a majority in favour of independence from Colombia.[51] Behind these the élite took control of events: 'Innumerable private meetings took place, till at length, one, consisting of 400 persons composed of the chief people of Caracas, estate holders and others, was held at the house of General Arismendi on the 24th November where it was voted unanimously that Venezuela ought to become a separate and independent state.'[52]

Páez assumed the *de facto* presidency of Venezuela on 13 January 1830. In May 1830 he was confirmed as provisional president by a constituent congress in Valencia; in October this sanctioned a new constitution, which in the event lasted until 1857. In March 1831

---

[49] Bolívar to Joaquín Mosquera, Guayaquil, 3 Sept. 1829, in O'Leary, *Memorias*, xxxi. 501.

[50] Páez to Bolívar, 1 Dec. 1829, in O'Leary, *Memorias*, ii. 224.

[51] Lievesley to Aberdeen, La Guaira, 27 Nov. 1829, PRO, FO 18/72.

[52] Ker Porter to Aberdeen, Private, Esher, 10 Feb. 1830, PRO, FO 18/78.

Páez was elected constitutional president and served until the completion of his term of office in February 1835. It was a civilian government, composed of ministers chosen by Páez—Santos Michelena, Andrés Narvarte, Diego Bautista Urbaneja—all men of talent and integrity. These events were a stage in Venezuelan nationalism, but, peaceful though they were, they did not signify the death of caudillism. On the contrary, it had acquired yet another function. Land and offices were regarded as Venezuelan assets which had to be defended against the encroachment of outsiders. The caudillos had begun as local leaders with access to limited resources. War gave them the opportunity to improve their personal fortunes and expand their bases of power. Peace brought them even greater rewards, and these they were determined to keep. The caudillos abandoned Colombia because they were Venezuelans and because they were determined to retain Venezuelan resources for themselves and their clients.

Caudillism and nationalism reinforced each other. The new constitution was acknowledged by all the cities, towns, and villages of Venezuela. In Caracas the only protest came from Archbishop Ramón Ignacio Méndez, who refused to take the prescribed oath and was promptly expelled by a special order of the executive without a murmur from public opinion.[53] But the logic of separatism did not stop at Páez. After secession the old caudillos and their llanero armies were reluctant to surrender to Páez and his merchant supporters the privilege and power which they had accumulated during the struggle for independence and the early years of the republic. Rather than challenge Páez directly for leadership of the country, they merely claimed the right to rule their own *patria chica* under a federalist system. But the government replied by drafting the centralist constitution of 1830 and eliminating military privileges.

The first reaction of the caudillos was rebellion and the first rebel was José Tadeo Monagas.[54] Asserting, rather belatedly, his loyalty to Bolívar and the nation of Colombia, gathering his large network of relations and clients, and claiming to represent the will of the people, the caudillo of the east took his stand early in 1831 in the heart of his regional power base. Monagas, perhaps with conscious irony, used more or less the same arguments against Caracas as Páez had used in seceding from Bogotá. He appealed to regionalist sentiment by

---

[53] Ker Porter to Aberdeen, 26 Nov. 1830, PRO, FO 18/78.
[54] Representation of officials and citizens of Aragua, 15 Jan. 1831, AGN, Caracas, Sec. Int. y Just., xxiv. fos. 300–1.

arguing that a Colombian federation would allow greater autonomy to the eastern provinces of Venezuela and end the monopoly of power claimed by Páez and his associates in the centre-north.[55] Páez responded by sending Mariño, another regional caudillo now masquerading as war minister, to deal with Monagas. The deal turned out to be a preposterous project for an independent state in the east, governed by Mariño with Monagas as second-in-command. Páez was horrified, dismissed Mariño, and went in person to see Monagas, whom he talked out of rebellion by conceding an amnesty.[56] In Páez's view the rebellion had received little popular support, for everyone agreed that 'Venezuela, through scarcity of resources, people, and wealth was in the business of simplifying the machinery of government, not complicating it', and that 'a federal government was incompatible with the special circumstances of the country.'[57] But there was a kind of understanding between the two caudillos. Monagas emerged unscathed and retained informal power in the east appropriate to a regional caudillo, while Páez continued to rule as constitutional president.

Access to public office and military appointments was an important ingredient of nationalism; national groups defined these as national assets and kept them as their preserve during war and peace. This was one of the reasons why the Venezuelan caudillos in 1820, when Bolívar was in New Granada, forced the vice-president of the government in Angostura, Francisco Antonio Zea, to resign. Zea was a civilian, a New Granadan, and a political weakling, qualities held in little respect by Venezuelan caudillos.[58] In his place Congress elected Arismendi, and he in turn appointed Mariño general-in-chief, based at Maturín. Thus the caudillos looked after their own. Exclusion of foreigners from office became one of the key issues in the allocation of resources after independence and one of the earliest manifestations of national susceptibilities. This explains why, after liberation, the Colombian army was unpopular in Peru and Bolivia. During the war the Peruvian guerrilla leader Ninavilca described the Colombians as 'a mob of thieves', despoilers of Peruvian resources.[59] To some extent Peruvian fears were justified, for Bolívar was not averse to

[55] Rafael Castillo Blomquist, *José Tadeo Monagas: Auge y consolidación de un caudillo* (Caracas, 1987), 27–9.
[56] Ker Porter to Palmerston, 28 June, 11 July 1831, PRO, FO 18/87.
[57] Páez, *Autobiografía*, ii. 144–5.
[58] Bolívar to Santander, 22 July 1820, *Obras completas*, i. 479.
[59] Ninavilca, Proclama, Canta, 16 Nov. 1823, in O'Leary, *Memorias*, xxi. 48–0.

shipping Venezuelan undesirables for service in Peru and moving his race conflicts elsewhere. 'The indications which have already appeared in the llanos of Venezuela of a hostility on the part of the coloureds against the whites' made it important to get these military units out of Venezuela and Colombia and into Peru, especially 'all the pardos who are known or suspected to have hostile intentions towards the white part of the population'.[60] Sentiments of nationality were for whites, not for blacks and *pardos*. In Bolivia Sucre found it impossible to overcome the resentment of Bolivians who regarded his forces as an army of occupation living off their country. Bolívar advised him: 'If I were you I would not remain in the south, because in the final analysis we suffer from the defect of being Venezuelans, just as we have been Colombians in Peru.'[61] In April 1828 Sucre was wounded by mutinous elements in Chuquisaca, while politicians 'sought to give the disturbance the appearance of a popular revolution'.[62] The government was forced to sign an agreement that all foreigners would be expelled.

The Americanists, on the other hand, regarded themselves as citizens of America, not of any particular region, and did not believe that country of origin was important for appointments. The Americanists tended to be civilian politicians, constitutionalists, diplomats, the antithesis of caudillos, and lacking a power base they had little defence against armed interest groups. In any case the trend of nationalism was against them in most parts of Spanish America. In 1824, when the Mexican government wished to appoint the Ecuadorian Vicente Rocafuerte secretary of its legation in London, nationalists in Congress refused to ratify the appointment on the grounds that he was not a Mexican citizen.[63]

The caudillos jealously guarded their national resources, land and offices, for these were their stock of patronage, the assets on which ultimately their power was based. Caudillos could attract a necessary clientage by promising their followers appointments and other rewards when they reached power. And clients would attach themselves to a promising patron in the expectation of preferment when he

[60] Report in Briceño Méndez to secretary of Bolívar, 21 June 1823, in O'Leary, *Memorias*, xx. 135–7.

[61] Sucre to Bolívar, 20 June 1827, in O'Leary, *Memorias*, i. 436; Bolívar to Sucre, 8 June 1827, in *Cartas*, vi. 305.

[62] Sucre to Bolívar, 27 Apr. 1828, in O'Leary, *Memorias*, i. 496.

[63] Jaime E. Rodríguez O., *The Emergence of Spanish America: Vicente Rocafuerte and Spanish Americanism 1808–1832* (Berkeley, Calif., 1975), 90.

reached the top. The system perpetuated personalism and retarded the process of state-building. For it was regarded as much safer to accept a personal promise from a caudillo than an anonymous undertaking from an institution, whether executive or legislative. The caudillo was real, the state a shadow. So the mutual needs of patron and client, founded on deeply rooted traditions of personal loyalty, were among the mainstays of caudillism in the new states as well as a source of social cohesion. They were also obstacles to political growth and allegiance to national institutions.

The history of nationalism provides examples of a further development, in addition to independence and unity. This is the process of nation-building, whereby nationalist movements seek to extend to the mass of the people a belief in the existence of the nation, hitherto held only by the élite, and to incorporate into the nation all sectors of the population. In Spanish America this objective was conspicuously absent from the policy of the caudillos and their post-war allies. The creole élite of landowners, merchants, and office-holders fought not only to take power from Spain but also to determine who should receive that power. The creation of nation-states was a slow and laborious process, during all stages of which the creoles retained control of the instruments of command and refused to share them with the popular sectors. The new rulers were a small but dominant minority, and for them the nation was simply the existing structure of power.[64] They defined the nation in an exclusive way in order to preserve the economic and social order which they had inherited from the colonial regime. Thus the nation was a creole nation, not a popular nation; its institutions were designed to safeguard the interests of the new ruling class, and these became identified with the constitutional republic. The constitution, of course, by means of literacy and property tests, disfranchised the majority of the people, and defence of the constitution became a process not of extending participation but of restricting it and preventing other social groups from joining the political nation.

In the aftermath of independence, around 1830, the population of Venezuela was about 900,000, half of whom were *pardos* and free blacks, over a quarter were whites, while slaves amounted to about 15 per cent. Among the whites some 10,000 people—landowners,

---

[64] Germán Carrera Damas, 'El nacionalismo latinoamericano en perspectiva histórica', *Revista Mexicana de Sociología*, 38, 4 (1976), 783–91, and *Venezuela: Proyecto nacional y poder social* (Barcelona, 1986), 73–110.

merchants, and their families and kinship groups—constituted the privileged élite, monopolizing power and institutions from the presidency down to the municipalities. Where they did not own land they controlled offices, and they prolonged the wartime establishments of higher military appointments which became mere sinecures, occupied by 'officers whose only obligation is to collect their salaries'.[65] The Constitution of 1830 reflected their power. To have the right to vote a man had to be twenty-one, literate, an owner of property yielding an annual income of 50 pesos, or to have a profession or office yielding 100 pesos a year.[66] Qualifications for electors and candidates were even higher. The literacy test was not immediately enforced; even so, the property tests alone disfranchised the majority of *pardos*. Subsequent constitutions in the nineteenth century nominally extended the franchise. The Constitution of 1857 proclaimed universal male suffrage; but it also provided for a more powerful president and was designed to prolong the rule of the Monagas family. The Constitutions of 1858 and 1864 also provided for universal male suffrage, but all these enactments were political façades, behind which real power was exercised by a succession of caudillos who continued to be the true representatives of the dominant interest groups.

The electoral system of the oligarchic republic was designed to give control of legislative institutions at municipal, provincial, and national level to the élite which dominated the economic and social life of Venezuela from 1830. Only 8 per cent of the population had the right to participate in the first stage of elections, but in practice only 4 per cent exercised this right. In the second and third stages the proportion of voting citizens was even less. In the elections of 1844 for vice-president and senators, in a population of some 1.1 million, 93,242 persons were registered to vote in the primary elections for electors, and 47,377 actually voted; 8,131 persons were registered as qualified to be chosen as electors, and of these 317 were named electors. Of the 93,242 persons with the right to vote, 22,200 were literate.[67] In the elections of 1846 for president, senators, and deputies, in a population of some 1.2 million, 128,785 persons were registered to vote in the primaries, and of these only 60,022 actually

---

[65] José Rafael Revenga, *La hacienda pública de Venezuela en 1828–1830*, ed. Pedro Grases and Manuel Pérez Vila (Caracas, 1953), 157 (27 June 1829).

[66] Constitution of 1830, V, 14, VII, 27, Luis Mariñas Otero (ed.), *Las constituciones de Venezuela* (Madrid, 1965), 225–7.

[67] Wilson to Aberdeen, 26 Feb. 1845, PRO, FO 80/32.

voted; 8,798 were registered as qualified to be chosen as electors, of whom 342 were named electors. Of the 128,785 persons with the right to vote, 39,022 were literate.[68] On the basis of these statistics it would take many generations to build a Venezuelan nation. Yet even the opposition groups accepted the system. In the elections of 1846 the liberals, including the radical Antonio Leocadio Guzmán, supported the continuation of the Constitution of 1830 and thereby the exclusion of the majority of Venezuelans from politics, seeking only 'new men and alternating government'. Ironically in 1846 Guzmán himself, a candidate for president, was excluded from the electoral register because he happened to owe legal fees to the law courts. Other forms of electoral manipulation and chicanery were practised as a matter of course.

In Argentina the revolutionary process from 1810 temporarily militarized the popular sectors and even gave them political pretensions.[69] These developments did not long survive the state of emergency. The electoral law of 1821 established universal male suffrage.[70] But under Rosas the law was a pretence behind which the caudillo ruled. Rosas had a state apparatus, based not on popular participation or consent but on personal control of the bureaucracy, the police, the paramilitary *mazorca*, and above all the regular army. Elections were open, closely controlled, mere instruments for producing majorities. There was no place for the gauchos or popular sectors in the Rosas state, no attempt to incorporate them into a nation. Even the army lacked national identity. A British observer noticed

the forced and unwilling service rendered by men often ill paid, fed and clothed, and severely treated; the absence of all national feeling or ardour, the greater part of the troops being either half Indians, drawn from a great distance, or foreigners, especially Spaniards, Basques, Italians, Brazilians, etc. serving unwillingly, on compulsion, most of them but recently and imperfectly trained as soldiers, anxious only to find an opportunity of desertion.[71]

Rosas himself had only a faint concept of nation, and seems to have regarded nationalism as a dangerous unitarian doctrine from which his countrymen should be protected. 'The government believes that

[68] Wilson to Palmerston, 26 Jan. 1847, PRO, FO 80/44; Gil Fortoul, *Historia constitucional de Venezuela*, ii. 7.

[69] Halperín Donghi, *Politics, Economics and Society in Argentina*, 166–8, 193.

[70] Bushnell, *Reform and Reaction in the Platine Provinces*, 22–3.

[71] Memorandum by Ouseley, August 1846, PRO, FO 6/123.

nothing will contribute more to creating a national spirit capable of overcoming feelings of petty localism than to provide each of the provinces of the Union with real advantages, hitherto unknown. Therefore it is urgently preparing for the National Congress the means to this end.'[72] This was the voice of Rivadavia, and he was speaking of his programme of modernization, a programme that envisaged national unity as well as independence. Rosas spoke in different terms.

The system of government which Rosas and his associates favoured was primitive in the extreme, utterly devoid of constitutional frame-work. They did not govern 'Argentina'. The thirteen provinces governed themselves, grouped only in a general Confederation of the United Provinces of the Río de la Plata. Even without formal union, however, the provinces were forced to delegate the management of certain common interests, mainly defence and foreign policy, to the government of Buenos Aires. And they could not ignore the demo-graphic imbalance in favour of Buenos Aires and its province (143,000 in a total population of 768,000 in the 1830s). Rosas, therefore, exercised some *de facto* control over the provinces, partly to prevent subversion and anarchy seeping into Buenos Aires, partly to have a secure base for economic and foreign policy, and partly to acquire a greater dimension for his regime. His policy was to wear down the provincial caudillos, to conquer them by patience. In interprovincial relations Rosas preferred informal power to a written constitution. He always argued that before national organization could take place the provinces must first organize themselves; the progress of the parts must precede that of the whole; and the first task was to defeat the unitarians, the people who really did wish to create a greater Argentina.[73] These were not the thoughts of an Argentine nationalist.

The regime which gave Rosas hegemony in Buenos Aires—the estancia, state patronage, and terrorism—could not be applied to the whole of Argentina. In the provinces of the west Rosas was seen as a caudillo who served the local interests of Buenos Aires; outside his own *patria* the loyalty of the hacendados and the service of their peons were not so easily procured. In the interior the federal party had weaker economic roots and a narrower social base; and in the remoter part of the confederation it could not automatically apply its

---

[72] *Mensaje del Gobierno a la Cuarta Legislatura*, Buenos Aires, 3 May 1824, encl. in Parish to Canning, 12 May 1824, PRO, FO 6/3.
[73] Lynch, *Argentine Dictator*, 110–12, 174–5.

control or regulate the use of terror. The pacification of the interior, therefore, meant the conquest of the interior by Buenos Aires. In so far as Rosas imposed unification, it was a victory not for Argentina but for Buenos Aires. This was a stage in the formation of the nation-state, but it was by no means the final one, and when Rosas fell the process of nation-building had hardly begun.

5. The Mexican Version

Mexican nationalism had strong roots in the colonial past, and it was from these that it derived some of its ambiguities. Was it Indian or was it Spanish? Creoles were torn between exaltation of Indian antiquity and pride in their conquistador descent.[74] Still Spaniards by nation, they were Mexicans by birth and culture, and saw around them the living proof of their identity, the resources, wealth, and human talents which made up their *patria* and prepared it for an autonomous existence. Creole patriotism first expressed a cultural rather than a political identity. But the war of independence took patriotism a stage further by repudiating the Spanish nation and, in spite of the efforts of creole royalists, sharpening divisions between Spaniards and Mexicans. Morelos had an instinctive belief in Mexican independence, but he also had to legitimize it. He distinguished clearly between *americanos* and *gachupines*. The revolution was justified, he argued, because the hated Spaniards were enemies of mankind, who for three centuries had enslaved the native population, stifled Mexico's development, and squandered its wealth and resources. And now, he declared, 'we have sworn to sacrifice our lives and property in defence of our holy religion and our *patria*.'[75]

Morelos's nationalism was confirmed by the armed struggle and formed in the harsh conditions of guerrilla warfare. He strove to evoke the spirit of a national army. On the grim march to Valladolid, before a battle which was to be disastrous, he issued a resonant manifesto to his troops:

[74] D. A. Brading, *The Origins of Mexican Nationalism* (Cambridge, 1985), 65; Anthony Pagden, *Spanish Imperialism and the Political Imagination: Studies in European and Spanish-American Social and Political Theory 1513–1830* (New Haven and London, 1990), 98, 101–2.

[75] Morelos, 23 Feb. 1812, in Lemoine Villicaña, *Morelos*, 195.

The *gachupines* have always sought to abase the Americans to the point of regarding us as brutes, incapable of initiative or even of the waters of baptism, and therefore useless to Church and state. But I see the opposite. Americans make first-class ecclesiastics, judges, lawyers, artisans, farmers, and, in the present case, soldiers. In the course of three and a half years I have learned, and everyone has seen, that the Americans are soldiers by nature.[76]

He spoke too of a 'Congreso Nacional' which would decide political and social policy, and of the 'Erario Nacional', which would reform taxation and revenue; as for the revolutionary leadership, he regarded himself as 'siervo de la nación'.[77] Finally, Morelos's nationalism had a profound religious content. In Mexico the Virgin of Guadalupe was a national as well as a religious symbol, an historic proof that God had shown a predilection for Mexico and conferred a distinct identity on its people. Morelos saw independence almost as a holy war in defence of religious orthodoxy against the secularist Bourbons and the idolatrous French. In Mexico, he asserted to the Bishop of Puebla, 'we are more religious than the Europeans', and he claimed to be fighting for 'la Religión y la Patria', and that this was 'nuestra santa revolución'.[78]

But Morelos made his greatest appeal to the common people, and his troops in the south were essentially popular forces. A royalist soldier, ex-prisoner of Morelos, reported on the insurgent army: 'None of them come from a decent family ... there are Indians, Negroes, *mulatos*, and delinquents, fugitives from their homelands. When anyone presents himself for service they ask him "que patria?", and he has to reply "la patria".'[79] The nationalism of Morelos had a social content which was rare at the time. In his proclamation issued at Aguacatillo in November 1810 he declared: 'People will no longer be designated as Indians, *mulatos*, or other castes, but, apart from Europeans, all will be known as *Americans*. ... No one will pay tribute, and there will be no slaves, and those who continue to hold them will be punished.'[80] This was the first attempt in Mexico to abolish caste distinctions and to make national identity the only test of social status. By the same argument race war was outlawed: 'There is no reason

[76] Morelos, 21 Nov. 1813 (ibid. 439–41).
[77] Ibid. 173.
[78] Morelos, 24 Nov. 1811, 8 Feb. 1812 (ibid. 184–5, 190).
[79] Ibid. 167–8.
[80] Bando de Morelos, 17 Nov. 1810 (ibid. 162).

why those who used to be called castes should want conflict between one group and another, whites against blacks, or blacks against natives, for that would be the greatest mistake of all'.[81]

The defeat of Morelos was also a defeat for his particular mixture of populism and nationalism. Political and military control of Mexico reverted to more conservative forces, and these manipulated the process towards independence to include the great interest groups— land, the army, the Church—which often integrated Spaniards and Mexicans. Did this mean, as has been argued, that Mexican national- ism now fell into abeyance?[82] Even during the war Iturbide played down the antagonism between creoles and *gachupines*, and pointed to the Americans on the royalist side. Equally, among the minor caudillos it would be difficult to find an outright nationalist, as Lucas Alamán was happy to point out: 'Albino García, reducing his policy to mere plunder, without the slightest political aim and without distinguishing between the place of birth of the owners of the properties which he invaded, forced everyone with anything to lose to defend themselves.'[83]

Mexico began its independence with two characteristics marking it off from Argentina and Venezuela. In the first place, by virtue of its great wealth, Mexico had been one of the most endowed and devel- oped of the Spanish colonies, and for the same reason one of the most 'colonial' and exploited. Mexico entered independent nation- hood with many of its colonial structures intact, and with worrying doubts concerning its new identity. In the second place, Mexico's new leaders had recently been royalists and their adhesion to Spain had been among the most resolute in Spanish America. The Mexican élite at independence was a political hybrid, born of diverse circum- stances, divided by many interests, and split by numerous loyalties. The instrument of independence, the Plan of Iguala (24 February 1821), called for a Catholic, united nation, in which Spaniards and Mexicans would be equal, caste distinctions abolished, and offices open to everyone: 'All inhabitants of New Spain, without any distinc- tion between Europeans, Africans and Indians, are citizens of this monarchy, with access to all positions according to their merits and virtues.'[84] The new regime, however, was intended for acceptance by the masses, not for their benefit. The Plan guaranteed the existing

---

[81] Bando de Morelos, Tecpan, 13 Oct. 1811 (ibid. 182).
[82] Brading, *The Origins of Mexican Nationalism*, 66.
[83] Alamán, *Historia de Méjico*, iii. 189.
[84] Plan de Iguala, 24 Feb. 1821, in Alamán, *Historia de Méjico*, v. 740.

social structure. The form of government would be constitutional
monarchy. Church property, privileges, and doctrines were preserved. Property rights and offices were assured to all those who held
them, with the exception of opponents of independence. In common
with Venezuela, the new nation was a creole nation not a popular
nation.

The political strategy of the Plan of Iguala, the formula 'union,
religion, independence', was to incorporate all parties, hitherto diver-
gent, into the new Mexico. At first many Spaniards, especially those
with kinship ties with Mexicans, remained in place and were to be
found in the bureaucracy, the army, and especially in land and law.[85]
But they were at risk. Mexicans had demanded for too long the right
to control jobs and opportunities in their own country to be frustrated
now. They were not prepared to tolerate Spaniards, who found that
once they had severed connections with the metropolis they could not
count on Iturbide or his successors. So Spaniards became the first
victims of Mexican nationalism and were hounded out of office, while
creoles assumed absolute control of government and resources.[86] As
Mexico searched for its political identity in the years ahead, the
caudillos could not make exclusive claims to nationalist roles. All
Mexicans with few exceptions, centralists and federalists, conservatives and liberals, were agreed on preserving Mexico for Mexicans,
ousting foreigners, resisting invaders. A caudillo could win or lose his
reputation in fighting for these goals, but he could not monopolize
them.

In July 1829 a Spanish expedition from Cuba landed at Cabo Rojo
and encountered only weak resistance from local militias. On his own
initiative and without specific orders, Santa Anna prepared a vigorous
counter-attack, commandeering three American ships, imposing a
forced loan on merchants, assembling men, arms, and supplies, and
dispatching a fighting force to the scene of action, 800 infantry by
sea, the cavalry by land. He could not resist a burst of rhetoric: 'The
supreme government should be satisfied that I will either perish in
the fight or finish off this bunch of adventurers, worthy vassals of the
wickedest of kings.'[87] He then led the attack on the Spaniards at

[85] Morier to Canning, 15 Nov. 1825, PRO, FO 50/6.
[86] Romeo Flores Caballero, *La contrarrevolución en la independencia: los españoles en la
vida política, social y económica de México (1804–1838)* (Mexico, 1969), 108–52.
[87] Santa Anna to Minister of War, Tuxpan, 11 Aug. 1829, *Boletín Oficial*, no. 6 (17
Aug. 1829).

Tampico on 11 September amidst a fierce rain-storm and won a resounding victory over a force larger than his own.[88] The victory was important for Santa Anna: he became the 'hero of Tampico', a favourite of the whole nation, a saviour of its independence. The *Boletín Oficial* recorded that 'The brave General Santa Anna, intrepid son of Mars, has given the country a day of permanent glory.'[89] It earned for him the rank of general of division and the title 'defender of the *patria*'; and as well as honours from the legislature of Veracruz it brought him national stature. It was now that he began to refer to himself as 'the Napoleon of the West', a man entering politics from a base of military victory, a victory that he used to make a political point, that it was time for a new government. As he returned to his base to recuperate, he considered himself the equal, and more, of any caudillo in Mexico. 'I returned to my estates at Manga de Clavo for a much needed rest, pleading to heaven that I would not have to answer another call to arms.'[90]

Yet Mexico still lacked national unity. As Lucas Alamán pointed out in his first report to Congress as Minister of Internal and External Relations in February 1830, Yucatán continued entirely separate from the federation; an armed group in Tabasco had declared for Yucatán; struggles over the union or division of Sonora and Sinaloa had subverted order in that region; many states were unsettled by the renewal of their legislatures and governors; and the central states of San Luis Potosí, Guanajuato, and Michoacán had formed a private confederation, in defiance of article 162 of the Constitution, and were threatening to reinstate a deposed governor of Tamaulipas by force. 'So the Republic is threatened by general upheaval which could lead to loss of national unity.'[91] Alamán singled out five reasons for Mexico's troubles: secret societies, disorderly elections, abuse of right of petition, poor organization of the militia, and an irresponsible press. He noted that the militias were not considered as part of the armed forces of the nation, but rather as the armies of the individual

---

[88] For reports from the front, as assembled by British observers, see Pakenham to Aberdeen, Mexico City, 2 Sept. 1829, PRO FO 50/55, fos. 100–2; Pakenham to Aberdeen, 18 Sept. 1829, FO 50/55, fos. 166–8; Pakenham to Aberdeen, 30 Sept. 1829, FO 50/55, fos. 189–91.

[89] *Boletín Oficial*, no. 26 (21 Sept. 1829).

[90] Santa Anna, *Memorias*, 25; Pakenham to Aberdeen, 30 Sept. 1829, PRO, FO 50/55, fos. 203–4.

[91] Alamán, *Memoria de la Secretaría de Estado*, 12 Feb. 1830, encl in Pakenham to Aberdeen, 25 Mar. 1830, PRO, FO 50/60, fos. 221–68.

states. As such they had been used to oppose other states and even
the Federation; and they had sometimes been used to interfere in the
internal affairs of other states without the knowledge of the central
government. He condemned attempts by some states to create coalitions on the margin of the Constitution and to pool their armed
forces, actions which could only lead to civil war.

The restoration of centralism in 1835 by Santa Anna and his
associates did not resolve the problem of national unity. It was now
that the Achilles heel of centralism first appeared, the menace of the
United States. The province of Texas refused to accept the dictates
of a centralist—or any other—regime and prepared to defend itself,
taking advantage of internal instability and lack of national consensus
in Mexico, and of the enduring strength of regionalism.

The people altho' much excited against the Texans and against the Americans to whom they attribute the Rebellion, are by no means hearty in the
cause, and there is good reason to believe that there exists a strong party in
the Northern parts of the Republic in favour of the Constitution of 1824. . . .
The State of Zacatecas still burns with indignation at the destruction of its
sovereignty and the putting down of its Militia last year. The people of
Coahuila and Tamaulipas have been always averse to the central form of
government, and as the Texans pretend to have their boundary line along the
line of the River Bravo down to the port of Matamoros, so in the latter place
there exists a party ready to make the attempt at a division of the Republic
from a point farther to the southward. . . .[92]

Santa Anna's reaction to the Texas revolution was that of a caudillo—
personal leadership, scant reference to the central government, informal recruitment of men and resources, demand for loyalty to the
jefe, and a strong streak of terror and cruelty in his methods. It was
also that of a nationalist, though one who operated by instinct rather
than reason. Yet his defeat and ignominy, and the loss of Texas, did
not permanently damage his reputation in Mexico. He returned to
Veracruz in February 1837, paid his respects to the government,
disclaimed any dishonourable conduct, and expressed his determination to retire to private life.

President Bustamante, who governed Mexico between April 1837
and September 1841 in accordance with the centralist constitution of
1836, had to face two interrelated problems besetting all Mexican
governments, the chronic lack of funds, centred in a flawed fiscal

---

[92] Vice-consul Crawford to Bidwell, Tampico, 30 May 1836, PRO, FO 5/102, fos.
23–6.

structure, and the persistent eruption of local revolts, most of them in favour of federalism. Santa Anna meanwhile retained his personal power base in his own hacienda; this he used as a military and political bunker from which he could emerge to make or break governments. And when a nationalist cause materialized in 1838, it was he rather than the government who exploited it. The French invasion of Veracruz, undertaken to exact compensation for damages to French property, gave the caudillo the opportunity at which he excelled. He marched to Veracruz and was basically defeated. But his actions had a familiar ring. Again, his tactics appeared contradictory. Again, his dispatches gave a different version of events than those of other observers. Again, a disaster was called a victory. Again, his reputation was saved by a dramatic personal gesture. He lost a leg in the fighting, and again became a national hero. 'All Mexicans', he claimed, 'putting aside my political errors, will not deny me the only title I wish to pass to my sons: that of the Good Mexican'.[93] All this bore the unmistakable stamp of Santa Anna.

In the internal process of nation-building Santa Anna had little to offer and something to gain, at least tactically, by resisting it. The leading roles were played by civilians and liberals. The principle behind liberal policy was individualism, a belief that the new state could only make progress if the individual were freed from the prejudice of the past, from corporate constraints and privilege, embodied particularly in the *fueros* of the Church and the army. These institutions were seen as rivals to the state, each a focus of sovereignty which should belong to the nation alone. Liberals represented interests as well as principles; the typical mid-century liberals were young upwardly mobile professionals who considered the traditional corporate bodies as major obstacles not only to nation-building but also to their own economic and social ambitions. Santa Anna was alien to this movement. He was tempted to seek short-term advantage by alliance with the Church or collaboration with the army, and his interventions in government frustrated the programme of the liberals for many years. While he may have been a nationalist, he was not a state-builder. He personally corrupted many of the processes of government, in the interests of his power, if not of his pocket. In return for immediate cash to the treasury he offered two kinds of

---

[93] Santa Anna to Minister of War, 5 Dec. 1838, *Boletín Oficial*, no. 3, encl. in Ashburnham to Palmerston, 10 Dec. 1838, PRO, FO 50/116, fos. 100–15.

deals. The first were profits and commissions on arms imports. The second were sales of customs revenues to two parties simultaneously. One object of all this patronage was to retain a body of financial creatures on his side in all circumstances, and on the whole it worked, enabling him in 1838–9 to keep the French at bay and deal with internal revolts.

But against these services have to be set a heavy catalogue of arbitrary and illegal measures: an example of profligacy and corruption in the management of public finances, such as even Mexico had not yet witnessed: the appointment in numerous instances of persons of the worst character to public employments, to the encouragement of vice and immorality, and to the serious detriment of the public interests: and the addition to the already intolerable burden of the military establishment of several hundred promotions and new appointments.[94]

Texas returned to haunt Santa Anna. Mexico was ready to accept an independent Texas but not a Texas annexed to the United States. United States expansionism, encouraged by Mexican anarchy, brought the two countries to war in April 1846. Within a few months the United States army had defeated the Mexican forces and occupied parts of northern Mexico. In California many welcomed the news, while in New Mexico not a few collaborated with the invaders, weary of Indian attacks and attracted by the commercial advantages which incorporation into the Union would bring.[95] Mexico meanwhile did not even have a war government and much of its fighting spirit was expended in civil conflict rather than against the enemy. Eventually, in September 1846, amidst general approval and great jubilation, Santa Anna was recalled as president with Valentín Gómez Farías his vice-president, the one to lead the army, the other to raise money. The caudillo's leadership was again puzzling, as at Angostura he managed to turn victory into defeat. And Gómez Farías, good liberal that he was, sought to finance the war by confiscating Church property, which provoked a conservative military revolt. Having used the liberals to soften up the Church, Santa Anna then forced the latter to accept a different deal, a forced loan of a million and a half pesos. It was a kind of blackmail, well understood by all parties, including the principal victim, the ousted Gómez Farías.

While Mexico indulged in civil war, the United States forces were

---

[94] Pakenham to Palmerston, 3 June 1839, PRO, FO 50/125, fos. 57–66; Pakenham to Palmerston, 1 Aug. 1839, FO 50/126, fos. 13–26, 43–7.

[95] Bankhead to Palmerston, 6 Oct. 1846, PRO, FO 50/200, fos. 36–56.

allowed to land near Veracruz, to win the battle of Cerro Gordo, to take Puebla, and finally, on 14 September 1847, to occupy the capital. An American forces newspaper claimed that Santa Anna 'may justly and properly be styled "the flying Mexican" for he comes like a flash and is again invisible in less time'.[96] Their victory appeared to be too easy; few nationalist guerrillas barred the way, no mass resistance occurred. Mexicans fought bravely, though they were badly officered and their artillery was inferior to that of the enemy. Santa Anna, while not lacking in courage, was faulty in leadership and failed to make the most of his resources or to capitalize on popular hostility to the invaders. His caudillo rival, Juan Alvarez, was critized by many for his inaction and his failure to commit his cavalry.[97] Amidst scenes of heroism, confusion, and terror the Mexicans were forced to accept defeat. Santa Anna resigned as president, and a new government negotiated the peace treaty of Guadalupe Hidalgo in February 1848. Mexico had no army, no money, only territory to negotiate with. The treaty transferred the vast area of New Mexico, Arizona, and California to the United States, which in turn agreed to give up all claims against Mexico and pay an indemnity of 15 million dollars.

Soon voices were raised denouncing Santa Anna as a traitor who had delivered Mexico to the enemy. More considered judgements, such as that of Guillermo Prieto, pointed out that Santa Anna did not personally avoid action, 'and if he could not rightly be regarded as a good general or a statesman, nor could he be called a traitor'.[98] Lucas Alamán described him as a good planner and a disastrous executor, who had never won a single battle but who had his good qualities as well as his bad.[99] Santa Anna was probably the only Mexican in 1846 who could bring together the men and resources needed to defend the country, and this presumably was why he was recalled by many of the people who in 1845 had been most active in expelling him. He was not a national leader. He was a caudillo who could evoke support in specific interest groups but could not arouse a

[96] *The American Eagle*, Veracruz, 26 May 1847, encl. in Giffard to Palmerston, 31 May 1847, PRO, FO 50/124, fos. 104–7.

[97] Moisés González Navarro, *Anatomía del poder en México 1848–1853* (Mexico, 1977), 15.

[98] Guillermo Prieto, *Memorias de mis tiempos, 1828–1853* (2 vols.; Mexico, 1948), ii. 160.

[99] González Navarro, *Anatomía del poder en México*, 27, points out that in fact Santa Anna had won one battle, at Tampico in 1829.

nation. And in spite of its caudillos, its warriors, and its generals, Mexico could not prevent the loss of Texas, California, and the northern states, or inspire in their inhabitants a lasting loyalty. This failure in nation-building alarmed a British observer:

It may indeed by a matter of opinion whether the present race is precisely the one that is most likely to benefit the country, or to develop its great resources, but it becomes a matter of vast importance whether the introduction of the Anglo Saxon restless activities might not be a dangerous alternative, and become in the end a more serious and lasting evil.[100]

The Santa Anna years saw only a partial achievement of Mexican nationalism. Independence from Spain had been won and defended. But national unity had been seriously impaired and almost half the national territory lost beyond recall. As for nation-building, this was still incomplete, its goals unrealized, its aspirants confined to the élite, to young liberals, and to a few artisans. Santa Anna was adroit in raising sectional support among the military, the *agiotistas*, and the economic interests of Veracruz. But he never enjoyed a mass following.

6. *The Caudillos and Economic Nationalism*

Economic imperialism, foreign penetration, external control, these later accretions to the demonology of Latin American nationalism were almost completely absent from the culture of the caudillos. The caudillos represented the dominant interest groups; they were usually personally involved in export-orientated agriculture, committed to free trade, and, with some exceptions, averse to protectionism. They conformed to the post-colonial economies of Spanish America and to the thinking of their civilian associates. In the absence of domestic accumulation they looked abroad and welcomed foreign capital, entrepreneurs, and immigrants. In particular they were prepared to invite a greater British economic presence in their countries than later generations would find acceptable. There were, of course, manifestations of economic nationalism, and in particular of anti-British sentiment, in parliaments, the press, and public opinion. In Argentina anti-British sentiment was epitomized by Dr Manuel

---

[100] Bankhead to Aberdeen, 29 Nov. 1845, PRO, FO 50/187, fos. 201–13; Bankhead to Palmerston, 28 Sept. 1847, FO 50/211, fos. 158–241.

Irigoyen, deputy and senior official in the Ministry of Foreign Affairs under Rosas:

It is obvious that these European powers, far from regarding the colonial system as ended, are determined to maintain it, helping themselves to territories not only in Asia and Africa but also in America. Not content with the Malvinas, England has tried to buy the Californias, and claims the Mosquito coast on the strength of the will of a savage Indian in favour of Queen Victoria, and also seeks to take possession of the River Orinoco from Venezuela.[101]

In Venezuela there were periodic outcries against the iniquities of Great Britain, denunciations of the British Colonial Bank, the British bondholders, and British mercantile privileges. In 1846 concessions to Britain over port dues aroused the fury of the House of Representatives where 'a scene of violence and of personal scurrility occurred, baffling all description. The President [Soublette] was accused of being a traitor to his country, which as evidenced by his conduct in this matter he has clearly sold to the English.'[102] It took little to mobilize a mob for a demonstration against foreigners. Even allowing for prejudice, the British chargé d'affaires struck a recognizable chord when he reported:

The principles of democracy have struck deeper root in Venezuela than in any other part of Spanish America that I have been in... and as the necessary consequence, the middle and lower classes are rude and offensive in their general bearing and conduct, especially in Caracas, where they are almost exclusively composed of coloured people. No outward observances of respect are ever paid by them to the national authorities, much less to the diplomatic and consular agents, towards whom on the contrary there is a vulgar tendency to exhibit disrespect, being viewed with jealousy and dislike, as foreigners; a feeling which, as in the rest of Spanish America, is rife even amongst the upper classes.[103]

The liberal politician, Antonio Leocadio Guzmán, was accused by conservative nationalists of being a British agent, a retainer of the British Anti-Slavery Society, and paid by them through the British Colonial Bank for his presidential election expenses in 1846.[104]

---

[101] House of Representatives, 15 Dec. 1843, *Archivo Americano y Espiritu de la Prensa del Mundo*, no. 11, 295.
[102] Wilson to Aberdeen, 12 June 1846, PRO, FO 80/39.
[103] Wilson to Aberdeen, 7 Aug. 1846, PRO, FO 80/39.
[104] Wilson to Palmerston, 3 April 1847, PRO, FO 80/45; on anti-British sentiment after Páez see George Edmund Carl, *First among Equals: Great Britain and Venezuela 1810–1910* (Syracuse, NY, 1980), 66–7.

In general presidents and caudillos resisted these pressures, declined to participate in nationalist demagogy, refused to harass foreigners, and stood by treaties and conventions. There is no evidence that Rosas or Páez seriously departed from this behaviour, in spite of provocation. Indeed Páez and his party may be said to have held the line against anti-British mobs in Caracas and La Guaira, giving British merchant houses protection which they did not receive from subsequent governments. In the case of Santa Anna, he had reason enough for expressing nationalist outrage, but the reasons usually concerned the United States and to some extent France, rather than Britain. There were practical arguments in favour of respect towards foreigners. Caudillos sought legitimacy and international respect. Adverse foreign reaction to wrongdoing, if translated into blockade or invasion, could cause intolerable expense and damaging material losses. Foreign markets were needed for exports, and in spite of past experience Spanish American governments rarely lost an opportunity to raise foreign loans or to negotiate favourable terms for servicing previous loans. There is, of course, no evidence that the British loans of the mid-1820s promoted caudillism rather than other forms of government.[105] In Argentina, Colombia, and Mexico the receiving governments were constitutional presidencies, and caudillos such as Rosas, Páez, and Santa Anna subsequently inherited debts to be serviced, not money to be spent. If they were relieved of the obligation of going to their own people for financial support, this was a consequence not of the loans but of the social structures of their countries, which forced them to derive most of their revenue from customs duties on foreign imports. For all these reasons caudillos were not normally economic nationalists.

Rosas did not regard the British as imperialists or the estancieros as a collaborating élite. Not for him the paranoia of the Anchorena. He was ruthless towards his opponents in the confiscation of their estates, and hard even on his supporters in conscripting peons and exacting contributions in horses, cattle, and money for his warring army. The policy turned to the advantage of foreigners, who were exempt from these national penalties and obligations. For Rosas was scrupulously correct in his treatment of foreign nationals residing in

---

[105] John J. Johnson, 'Foreign Factors in Dictatorship in Latin America', *The Pacific Historical Review*, 20 (1951), 127–41, asserts that the British loans of the mid-1820s 'did as much to promote the cause of dictatorship in Latin America as any single factor originating outside the area up to that time'.

the province, and they were virtually the only group who received the unqualified protection of the law. Secure in this knowledge, foreigners invested more confidently in land than the natives. Thus did Rosas, otherwise acclaimed for resisting foreign blockades and intervention in the Río de la Plata, indirectly assist the foreign penetration of the Argentine economy. The process was observed by an English land-owner, Wilfrid Latham:

The protection which their 'treaties' secured to foreigners placed them under these circumstances at an advantage over the natives, inasmuch as the former were absolutely exempt from military service and from forced contribu-tions.... Induced by the low price of land and the greater security which they enjoyed, foreigners, more especially the British purchased largely of the lands offered for sale.[106]

As Lucio V. Mansilla remarked, 'You were lucky if you were English in those days.' And Tomás de Anchorena complained bitterly to Rosas about the favour shown to foreigners: 'Your excessive generosity to gringos makes me very angry.'[107]

In the aftermath of independence in Argentina it was the large estancia which created wealth and conferred status. Estancia ex-pansion was a response to the opportunities offered by international trade and government decisions. But it also reflected the preferences of social interests. The hacendados of Buenos Aires, of whom Rosas was one, did not acquire these great estates as mere status symbols. They bought land in order to export and to profit from the oppor-tunities presented by free trade; and the most successful landowners were men of urban origin with powerful business interests, such as the Anchorena. These were the caudillo's constituency. Rosas favoured cattle-breeders at the expense of small farmers, whom he normally declined to protect against foreign grain imports, aware of the political risks involved. From independence to 1835 a low tariff policy prevailed, in favour of consumers and exporters, and in spite of farmer's complaints.

Farmers were not the only critics of free trade. The littoral and interior provinces demanded protection for native industries such as wines and textiles against more cheaply produced foreign goods. Similar demands came from the urban artisans in Buenos Aires, owners or employees of workshops, makers of manufactured goods

---

[106] Wilfrid Latham, *The States of the River Plate*, 2nd edn. (London, 1868), 316.

[107] Tomás de Anchorena to Rosas, 1 Mar. 1846, Juan José Sebreli, *Apogeo y ocaso de los Anchorena* (Buenos Aires, 1972), 167.

for the local market. Numerous small establishments manufacturing clothing, uniforms, shoes, hats, swords, and silverware were scattered about the capital. Quality of product was usually low, the market limited, and technology primitive, but they survived. The urban artisans were numerous enough, therefore, to carry some political weight and, without constituting a major pressure group, to merit consideration. The free-trade argument maintained that protection would raise prices for the mass of consumers, and divert to industry labourers who would be better employed in the agrarian sector. Nevertheless, concern for the adverse balance of payments, if not for industrial labour, was sufficient to keep the protectionist lobby alive and the government interested. In due course Rosas accepted the case for protection, and in the *ley de aduana* of December 1835 he introduced higher import duties. From a basic duty of 17 per cent the tariff moved upwards, giving greater protection to more vulnerable products, until it reached a point of prohibiting the import of a large number of articles such as textiles, hardware, and, under certain conditions, wheat.

The protectionist law of 1835 seems to have been a personal decision of the caudillo, not a consensus established in the government and legislature. How can we account for it? Did he really believe that Argentina could become self-sufficient in industry, decrease its dependence on imports, and resist foreign competition? Does nationalism provide an explanation? According to this argument, the protective tariff was an attempt to give reality to the Argentine Confederation planned in the interprovincial Pact of 1831: Rosas, until then a man of Buenos Aires, began to act as a national ruler, in favour of the 'popular classes' and against foreign interests.[108] It is true that the law of 1835 was designed to make the federalist policy more credible by giving protection to the provinces as well as to Buenos Aires—prohibiting, for example, the import of foreign ponchos. But a 'national' policy would be expected to include concessions on river navigation and control of customs revenue, and there were no signs that Rosas was thinking of this. As for the 'popular classes', they did not enter his calculations as part of the political nation. He did recognize, however, that many people unable to buy land remained on the margin of the economy. While maintain-

---

[108] José María Rosa, 'Miron Burgin, la señorita Beatriz Bosch y la ley de aduana de Rosas', *RIIHJMR*, no. 22 (1960), 329–34; on the 1835 tariff see Lynch, *Argentine Dictator*, 145–53.

ing the hegemony of the estancia, he took steps to help its victims. Subsequently, after the tariff had been amended upwards, he claimed in his Speech to the House of Representatives in January 1837:

The changes made in the customs law in favour of agriculture and industry have begun to have a good effect. . . . The artisan workshops have employment for young people, who under the vigilance of the police have ceased to disturb the streets and thoroughfares, and one should hope that the prosperity of these classes will increase the import of numerous articles of foreign industry which have not been prohibited or charged with extra duties.[109]

It may be that Rosas genuinely sought something for everyone, above all for estancieros, but also for merchants, artisans, workers, and farmers. For he went on to claim that the restoration of law and order had benefited everyone, including the poor: 'Everyone is rich even in his poverty, since he knows that what he has is his own and whatever he earns he can possess.' A doctrine of social immutability.

In the event the policy of protection for arable agriculture and manufacturing industry was not a success. National production did not respond to protection; the tariff merely caused shortages and high prices, and the principal victims were the consumers and the treasury. Rosas soon lost faith in protection. The bias towards a livestock export economy reflected the social structure as well as economic conditions. There were some things a caudillo could not change.

In Venezuela *comercio libre* and the abolition of the Spanish monopoly did not bring the promised fruits. After independence the trend towards monoculture was inexorable and economic distortions soon appeared. There was nothing approaching true free trade. The Colombian tariff of 1826 imposed duties ranging from 7.5 per cent to 36 per cent on most imports; this was primarily a revenue tariff but it also had a protective content to satisfy national economic interests. State monopolies were further protected by prohibition of the import of foreign tobacco and salt, while the agriculturalists of northern Colombia and coastal Venezuela demanded and received protection for their plantation products. The manufacturing sector, however, was not so protected. The liberal economic policy of the republic left artisan industry to fend for itself, and manufactures such as textiles could not compete with the flood of cheaper foreign goods. Rafael

---

[109] *Mensaje* (1 Jan. 1837), in Archivo Histórico de la Provincia de Buenos Aires, *Mensajes de los gobernadores de la provincia de Buenos Aires 1822–1849* (2 vols.; La Plata, 1976), i. 113.

Revenga, the economist most closely associated with Bolívar, attributed the decadence of industry in Venezuela to excessive import of manufactures, many of which could be produced at home. Revenga appreciated that Venezuela was not in a position to industrialize: 'Our country is predominantly agricultural; it will develop mining before manufacturing; but it must strive to diminish its present dependence on foreign powers.'[110] But the slight tendency towards protectionism during the final dictatorship of Bolívar did not prevail in Venezuela. During the hegemony of Páez and his allies, while agriculture was protected, the claims of artisan industry were ignored and it was left exposed to the competition of imported manufactures. The artisans, most of whom were *pardos*, lacked any voice or influence in Congress and the administration.[111] Yet the fact remains that protection in itself could do little for the national economies without the growth of consumers and the development of labour, capital, and skill. To this extent the caudillo in Venezuela, no less than in Argentina, was in touch with basic realities.

Páez led a coalition of Caracas landowners, merchants, and officials, which he held together on a platform of peace and security, arbitrating between interests and keeping them in balance. This in turn strengthened his own position: they needed him, and he needed them. His bias towards the centre-north detracted from his llanero interests once he was in power. He came to identify with the political, economic, and social interests of the Caracas agrarian and commercial groups in opposition to the development of production and export outlets for the livestock economy of the llanos, which was similar in its potential though not in its political strength to that of Buenos Aires. The fear was that the llanos would challenge the political hegemony of Caracas, whose agricultural economy of coffee and cacao, after a promising start, entered into crisis in the 1840s. Conflict of interest and the power of the landowner–merchant alliance were seen in the abolition of the state tobacco monopoly in 1833 with adverse effects on production and trade in Barinas and Guayana, while the monopoly land was redistributed to the northern oligarchy. The same interest group managed to prevent a free discussion of the role of livestock exports; they persuaded the government to impose restrictions on such exports through the ports of the Orinoco to the

---

[110] Revenga, 7 Aug. 1829, *Hacienda pública de Venezuela*, 203.
[111] Pérez Vila, 'El gobierno deliberativo', 67–9.

British West Indies, overtly in favour of the domestic meat market. Páez also took lessons in political economy from the British consul general, Robert Ker Porter, at whose house he was a frequent visitor, not least during moments of tension and indecision.[112] Ker Porter worked hard to secure British recognition of independent Venezuela and confirmation of the trade treaty of 1825; he secured more for Britain in tariff concessions than Britain granted Venezuela. But Páez was not deterred. From the consul he learnt the benefits of free trade, the advantages of a British connection, the duty to abolish slavery. Although he later claimed to have been an opponent of slavery, Páez was also a landowner and a collaborator of the landed oligarchy, and there was a work force of 180 slaves on his estate La Trinidad.[113] He then became convinced of the need for abolition in order to promote trade with Britain, but he had to compromise his principles for the sake of the Caracas oligarchy. With a commitment to free trade on the other hand Páez could satisfy both Ker Porter and his Venezuelan allies. He began his independent administration with a cut in export duties and a moderation of import duties, decrees which 'have awakened a degree of confidence both in the estate holder and in the merchant'.[114] Between 1830 and 1835 Páez abolished export duties on certain products such as coffee and cotton and reduced them on others such as cattle and hides. The Venezuelan economy underwent some growth and much distortion. A considerable amount of money and precious metals were exported, not to pay for imports or to balance trade but to pay debts contracted since independence, especially with foreign financiers, which implied a diminution of importing capacity.[115]

In the 1840s the liberals attacked the conservative foreign debt policy and the concentration of capital in the National Bank as responsible for tight money and credit and the shortage of specie.

The existence of so large a deposit in the Bank also induces demands for pecuniary aid for the protection of class interests, especially on the part of the agriculturalists; and encourages a disposition to national extravagance; but the evil does not rest here; it is known that the Bank, to secure the favour of

---

[112] *Sir Robert Ker Porter's Caracas Diary, 1825–1842*, ed. Walter Dupouy (Caracas, 1966), 298, 711, 757, 759, 870, 1005, 1020, 1029; on the trade treaties of 1825–35, and their bias towards Britain, see Carl, *First among Equals*, 31–42.

[113] *Ker Porter's Caracas Diary*, 434.

[114] Ker Porter to Bidwell, 31 Oct. 1830, PRO, FO 18/78.

[115] Yoston Ferrigni Varela, *Crecimiento y depresión: La economía venezolano en la época conservadora 1828–1848* (Caracas, 1983), 10, 23, 30, 48.

influential people, has advanced about 400,000 dollars = £64,000 to four
individuals; about 120,000 dollars = £19,200 of which have been lent to
General Paez.[116]

At the same time internal disorder discouraged the entry of new
capital into the country and caused further reductions in existing
stock through the repayments of loans to cover military expenses.
Problems were compounded by the prevailing tax policy. The administration was too weak to impose new taxes or even to collect
existing domestic taxes. Thus more than 75 per cent of the government's revenue came from import tariffs.[117] This percentage increased
with the abolition of the tobacco monopoly and tithes in 1833, when
internal taxation virtually disappeared. Yet even import duties did not
yield their full potential. Already in 1834 the British minister referred
to 'the ruinous increase of the contraband trade pursued from the
banks of the Orinoco, to the Lake of Maracaibo, carried on by natives
in conjunction with native mercantile houses'.[118] In 1843 contraband
was estimated at one-quarter of legal imports and attributed in part to
'low paid customs officials'.[119] Edward Eastwick, financial com-
missioner for the General Credit Company, was told by an Anglo-
Venezuelan colleague that

a finance minister of Venezuela has proved that of the two hundred millon
dollars worth of goods imported into the country during the first sixteen years
of independence, one hundred and twenty-nine and a half millions' worth
were smuggled. . . . At present the annual loss to the government by contraband and fraud of various kinds, is reckoned at six millions. . . . Indeed one
would not be wrong in saying that the incessant revolutions which distract
this unhappy country, all commence at the custom-houses. Owing to the
frauds of the officials, the revenue falls short; to make up the deficiency,
the customs are raised until the necessaries of life are too dear for men of
small means. This discontent is sown broadcast, and discontent leads to
conspiracies.[120]

As imports were encouraged, both formally and informally, it was
difficult for Venezuela's agricultural exports to keep pace with the

---

[116] Wilson to Aberdeen, 13 Mar. 1844, PRO, FO 80/25.
[117] According to British reckoning, 90 per cent of 'national income' and 71 per cent
of 'national municipal revenues' were derived from customs duties: Wilson to Aberdeen, 7 Feb. 1846, PRO, FO 80/38.
[118] Ker Porter to Bidwell, 9 Jan. 1834, PRO, FO 18/106.
[119] O'Leary to Aberdeen, 30 June 1843, PRO, FO 80/22.
[120] Edward B. Eastwick, *Venezuela: Or, Sketches of Life in a South-American Republic;
with the History of the Loan of 1864*, 2nd edn. (London, 1868), 60–1.

influx of foreign goods, particularly as export prices fell in the 1840s. A money shortage was inherent in underdevelopment of this kind. As agriculture expanded, it absorbed large amounts of capital. But agriculture was slow in turning investment into profits and could not rapidly replace money it had withdrawn from circulation. The resulting lag in profits tightened credit further. High transport rates stemming from lack of internal development, and a shortage of foodstuffs due to emphasis on commercial crops, increased dependency on imports; this again worsened the balance of payments, which in turn withdrew more specie from circulation. Venezuelans understood these facts of economic life, but interest groups were strongly entrenched.[121]

Agricultural production was becoming more diversified during the Páez years, and in the highlands of Caracas, Aragua, and Carabobo there was a notable shift from cacao to coffee. Between 1829 and 1842 the value of coffee exports increased 194 per cent, with an average annual rate of increase of 8.6 per cent.[122] In 1830–1 coffee comprised some 40 per cent of the total value of exports, cacao 29 per cent, indigo 18 per cent, the cattle industry 5 per cent, and cotton and tobacco comprised the rest. But coffee, though it matured more quickly than cacao and could be planted more densely, needed both capital and labour. Landowners without capital reserves of their own borrowed on the money market, while lenders were now assisted by the credit law of 10 April 1834 which eliminated the restrictions on interest rates and loan ceilings characteristic of the colonial period and created a more or less free money market. The law was well received by planters and merchants alike. The prospects of coffee expansion at a time when world demand and prices were rising lured landowners into borrowing at very high interest rates from private investors, mainly merchants, who were the only source of credit. The dearth of capital pushed up interest rates to 36 per cent and never under 9 per cent.[123]

When the boom ended in 1842, following a fall in world prices for coffee, planters found themselves over-extended, credit tightened, and lenders began to close in. The law of 10 April 1834 stipulated that in case of inability to pay the property of the debtor would be

---

[121] Fermín Toro, *Reflexiones sobre la ley de 10 de abril de 1834*, in *Fermín Toro (Pensamiento Político Venezolano del Siglo XIX*, i, Caracas, 1960), 211–12.

[122] Ferrigni, *Crecimiento y depresión*, 16, 18, 22.

[123] O'Leary to Aberdeen, 30 June 1843, PRO, FO 80/22.

sold at the going auction prices, which were rarely the original value. Small, medium, and even large haciendas were affected. Fermín Toro cited a number of hard cases, such as that of a merchant who made a mortgage loan of 3,000 pesos to a hacendado at the beginning of 1836; a year later this had grown to 11,300 including capital and interest, fourteen months later to 15,704, and three months later, in December 1838, to 18,635. A hacienda in Tapipa, valley of the Tuy, with 15,000 cacao trees, 4,000 of coffee, four slaves, house and meadows, was auctioned for 318 pesos, its true value 12,385.[124] There followed a conflict between agricultural producers trapped in indebtedness and a financial sector demanding payment or foreclosure, which became one of the ingredients of Venezuelan politics for decades to come. The agricultural associations, to which not all hacendados belonged, demanded in 1845 financial assistance from the state in the form of low-interest and long-term loans, an end to the use of surplus revenue to make foreign debt payments to England, indemnities for slave emancipation, and repeal of existing credit laws.[125] Congress resisted these demands and continued to protect the National Bank against its critics. Official British opinion thought the agricultural lobby was unrepresentative and that 'distress is almost exclusively confined to the Province of Caracas, and to proprietors whose improvidence and want of industry have brought them into their present difficulties'.[126] The agrarian agitation, linked as it was to denunciation of foreign exploiters, came to a head during the presidency of Soublette, behind whom of course stood Páez:

Upon no point of his public policy has the President General Soublette been attacked with so much personal virulence, more especially by the Agricultural Associations, as with reference to an assumption, that he was sacrificing the national interests in favour of the foreigners, squandering, as it was popularly miscalled, the public moneys in the redemption of the foreign debt of Venezuela.[127]

Yet the same lobby demanded the establishment of a state credit scheme, to be financed by yet another English loan, 'for the benefit of a privileged minority of the nation'. The agriculturalists and their friends in Congress could not succeed as long as Páez held firm, but they were closing in on the caudillo.

---

[124] *Fermín Toro*, i. 107, 172–3, 225.
[125] Wilson to Aberdeen, 20 Apr. 1844, PRO, FO 80/25.
[126] Wilson to Aberdeen, 27 Sept. 1844, PRO, FO 80/26.
[127] Wilson to Aberdeen, 7 Mar., 31 May 1845, PRO, FO 80/32.

The Mexican economy presented a different picture. Industry underwent vigorous growth in the period 1837–42, at a time when the external sector was in depression. The political conjuncture was also favourable. Following the extreme liberal and anti-clerical experiment of 1831–4, the conservatives returned to power in 1835 behind Santa Anna, who inaugurated two decades of centralist and protectionist rule. Conservatism became associated in liberal minds with import prohibitions and forced industrialization. The capital invested in industry came from merchants seeking to diversify out of the unstable external sector. Finding few opportunies either in mining or in commercial agriculture, they turned to urban manufacturing, in Mexico City, Puebla, Guadalajara, Querétaro, cities where unemployed but socially conscious artisans expressed a powerful case for protection and threatened to become a focus of political agitation in an unstable alliance with larger industrialists.[128] Textile manufacture required access to cotton. This was grown predominantly in Veracruz, the state of Santa Anna, the state with most political influence outside of the capital, and the state with greatest experience in protecting its interests. The growers successfully preserved their market by ensuring that importation of cotton was prohibited without special licence, more difficult to obtain than those permitting the importation of finished goods. A few favoured speculators with access to Santa Anna received such licences while their competitors did not. Once the goods had been manufactured, factory owners faced two additional problems, competition from cheaper foreign products and difficulties in marketing their goods throughout the country. Protectionism was the policy of the Mexican government in the 1830s, particularly during the presidencies of Bustamante, when Lucas Alamán held some influence. But money could prise open most doors, and even Bustamante allowed a loophole through Tampico. Protest was so powerful that it helped Santa Anna to overthrow Bustamanate in 1841, though he too was willing to grant import permits in return for hard cash.

Textiles were not the only protectionist lobby in Mexico. The tobacco industry contained a triple interest—cultivation, manufac-

---

[128] Guy P. C. Thomson, 'Protectionism and Industrialization in Mexico, 1821–1854: The Case of Puebla', in Christopher Abel and Colin M. Lewis (eds.), *Latin America, Economic Imperialism and the State* (London, 1985), 125–46; Torcuato S. Di Tella, 'The Dangerous Classes in Early Nineteenth-Century Mexico', *JLAS*, 5, 1 (1973), 79–105.

ture, and sale—and the parts were not always in harmony with the whole. Around these parts raged constant political battles for advantage. After a brief, and shattering, experience of free trade (1833–4), the monopoly inherited from the colonial regime was revived under pressure from the *cosecheros*. In 1835 Santa Anna began to adopt more conservative economic policies, and the Veracruz growers looked towards him expectantly. But his influence declined in 1836 and it was the merchants, not the planters, who won the war of prices and controls. In 1837 and 1839 the tobacco company was granted favourable monopoly contracts by the government. Santa Anna returned to power in October 1841 backed by the military, bureaucrats, tobacco planters, and other financial groups, who supplied the money to stage the revolt against Bustamante. In return, the whole tobacco industry, planters, officials, and *empresarios*, were awarded a new deal, cancelling the 1839 contract, returning the monopoly to government administration, and compensating the company with extremely generous terms. Now the planters could rely on the government to purchase more tobacco and to legislate on their behalf. Santa Anna satisfied these when he decreed (20 December 1841) a prohibition on the import of all foreign tobacco. He did not pay the tobacco bondholders everything they wanted, but he compensated them with other public properties, and made some money for himself. Santa Anna's government thus bailed out the tobacco industry and put it into profit, but at great cost to the state. The whole operation was regarded as a necessary piece of patronage, for many incomes were at risk and many jobs at stake.[129] But patronage was an instrument of personalism; it tended to bypass institutions of state and to subvert political accountability. Congress no doubt was involved; and even Santa Anna had to justify himself at the bar of the house, where interests and ideas converged. But politicians too were subject to material influence, personal pressure, and the temptations of patronage. Congress too was a client.

An unstable alliance of merchants, industrialists, and producers of raw materials for industry, such as cotton growers and sheep raisers, urged and obtained tariff protection or full import prohibition. Yet in spite of modest financial and technical progress, manufacturing in Mexico proved incapable of generating its own capital and continued

---

[129] David W. Walker, 'Business as Usual; The Empresa del Tabaco in Mexico', *HAHR* 64, 4 (1984), 675–705.

to depend on import merchants for funding. No new middle class arose, no dynamic entrepreneurs emerged; industry continued to depend on merchants and artisans. It flourished when the external sector declined, and declined when the external sector revived, that is when new opportunities appeared for investment in mining and agriculture about 1850.[130] By this time protectionism was discredited, partly because industry itself did not respond, partly because the winners were the producers of raw materials rather than the manufacturers. Santa Anna too was discredited, irrelevant to government and economy alike. The Santa Anna years saw the politicization of the whole public sector, and would-be monopolists and protectionists—in textiles, armaments, infrastructure projects—all pressured government or *golpistas* to seize their chance and share out the gains. There was no coherent economic policy, and in the event little government revenue.

The richest pickings went to the *agiotistas*, the financiers of the time. Yet their record was not completely negative.[131] Like Argentina and Venezuela, Mexico based its fiscal system on taxes levied on foreign trade. The Mexican government was not incapable of imposing direct taxation on property and wealth; it did so during the French blockade, though for an extraordinary and temporary purpose.[132] But the main source of ordinary income remained customs duties, through which contraband flourished and revenue waned. The function of revenue was not simply to finance public policy but also to reward friends and buy off enemies. If it ceased to flow, revolts followed, as the military and associated interest groups reached directly for resources. At this point, as the wealthy would not pay taxes and foreigners would not make loans, Mexican governments turned to the internal money market to obtain additional funds at the best rates of interest available. These were provided by merchants, some Mexican, some foreign, willing to invest their capital in government, to invest it moreover in all governments, thus providing continuity of a kind. The *agiotistas* lent money, invested in agriculture, mining, and industry, and provided infrastructure services (at a price) to governments which were incapable of doing these things themselves. So they served the state, and eventually by 1850 came to

---

[130] Thomson, 'Protectionism and Industrialization in Mexico', 143.
[131] Barbara A. Tenenbaum, *The Politics of Penury: Debts and Taxes in Mexico, 1821–1856* (Albuquerque, NM, 1986), 82, 142.
[132] Ashburnham to Palmerston, 1 Oct. 1838, PRO, FO 50/115.

demand a better state, capable of providing roads, railroads, and other services to satisfy their growing economic interests, beyond mere money lending.[133] They helped to finance Santa Anna, and their eventual disillusion helped to undo him. The caudillo had led the Mexican economy into a blind alley.

Rosas, Páez, Santa Anna, all in their way were guardians of national resources, none were wedded to economic nationalism. Rosas and Páez each represented distinct interest groups in the agro-exporting sector; neither of them wished to alienate foreigners or prejudice foreign markets; and both subscribed more or less to free trade. The Mexican economy was not so simple. Inheritor of a wealthy past and possessor still of a mining industry, Mexico had agricultural, manu-facturing, and commercial sectors, each demanding privileges and looking for some kind of protection. The social structure was more complex and interest groups competed more skilfully than those of Argentina and Venezuela. As a manipulator, distributor of patronage, arbitrator of conflicts, a caudillo in Mexico was less certain of his identity and more reliant on political manœuvre than his counter-parts elsewhere.

The age of the caudillos was not an age of conspicuous national-ism. The economies of Spanish America did not yet attract sufficient capital, trade, and immigration to arouse nationalist responses, though the seeds of suspicion were there. Foreigners were treated as potential clients, to be normally cultivated, sometimes deceived, but rarely rebuffed. Economic policy reflected further features of the caudillo nation: it was personalist, geared to interest groups, and lacking in permanent structures. Were these also the marks of the social policy of the caudillos?

---

[133] Tenenbaum, *The Politics of Penury*, 134–7.

5
THE NECESSARY GENDARME

1. *The Typology of Caudillism*

Caudillos are known to history as instruments of division, destroyers of order, enemies of society and of each other. Even Páez was moved to complain, 'I cannot understand why some Chiefs who are perfectly well placed are so eager for anarchy'.[1] It is true that many caudillos captained rural hordes and manipulated urban mobs; plunder and land confiscations were features of their rule. Owners of property and estates had reason to fear caudillo power, and caudillos came to be regarded as obstacles to progress, investment, and growth. But this is only part of the record. In the post-colonial societies of Spanish America caudillos fulfilled a vital function on behalf of republican élites as guardians of order and guarantors of the existing social structure. In times of trial and tension no one doubted that their personal power was more effective than the theoretical protection of a constitution.

In the years to 1830, as has been seen, the caudillos established their identity, increased their wealth, and accumulated a variety of functions. The caudillo began as a regional chieftain, deriving his power from control of local resources, especially of haciendas, which provided access to men and supplies. The war of independence raised the value of his assets, and enabled him to become a military chieftain whose services were indispensable to the cause of liberation. Caudillism was then perpetuated by post-war conflicts, between unitarists and federalists in Argentina, between rival caudillos or caudillo groupings in Venezuela, between neighbouring states in various parts of Spanish America. The caudillo's domain began to grow from local to national dimensions. Here, too, supreme power was personal, not institutional; competition for offices and resources was violent and the achievements were rarely permanent. But the caudillo as warrior does not exhaust the typology of caudillism.

---

[1] Páez to Bolívar, 9 Jan. 1828, in O'Leary, *Memorias*, ii. 118.

The caudillo soon adapted to civilian society and came to represent specific interest groups. In some cases he was the representative of an extended family network based on regional haciendas, the creature as well as the leader of his fellows, and possessing little personal power outside the kinship structure. More commonly the caudillo simply represented regional interests, defending local resources against the claims of the capital, demanding a say in economic policy, and asserting local rule against central control. Again, as the centre often employed force, a region would commit its defence to a local strong man who had already proved his worth as a warrior. But defence was not enough. Many caudillos were only local until they became national, federalist until they became unitarist. On a national scale, the fruits of a *golpe* were more spectacular than those of local power. At this stage another image of the caudillo emerged—the caudillo as benefactor, as distributor of patronage. Caudillos could attract a necessary clientage by promising their followers office and other rewards when they reached power. And clients would attach themselves to a promising patron in the expectation of preferment when he reached the top. The reward most prized was land, and a caudillo was nothing if he could not acquire and distribute land.

The caudillo as warrior, regional chieftain, hacendado, and *patrón* are obvious models which have tended to overshadow the caudillo as guardian of social order. How did he acquire the role of prime protector, and fulfil it in the decades after 1830?

2. *War and Social Disorder*

The revolution against Spain was more than a struggle for political independence. It was also the occasion of social protest, as the lower sectors rose not only against Spaniards but against all those who had deprived them of rights and opportunities. The slaves fought for their emancipation, the *pardos* and other mixed groups for equality, and the popular sectors in general for advancement.

In Argentina the political élite was conscious of a new danger from below and anxious to preserve the social distinctions inherited from the colony. The expansion of estancias in the late colonial period pressed hard on the inhabitants of the pampas and landowners were distinctly aware of disorder and disobedience in the vicinity of their estates. The work force on the estancias of Buenos Aires, it is true, was already more stable and employable than is often supposed.[2] But outside the sector of working peons, the gauchos, a specialized type not to be confused with the rural population in general, still lived a marginal and independent existence, resentful of discipline from state or estancia. As for the city of Buenos Aires, it had long been the home of delinquents and vagrants as well as of merchants and officials, and the prevailing class structure had the sanction of the new state as well as the support of the local élite. In 1810 only 'decent' people were admitted to the revolutionary process: 'Negroes, boys and other common people' were excluded from popular elections.[3] Even so, the lower classes were admitted to some political processes; they were used as a mob under their *alcaldes* and led out to defeat counter-revolutionaries and rival factions. New radical leaders outside the traditional élite were tempted to seek a power base among the popular sectors, and to bring them on to the streets to menace their opponents. The lower classes were also militarized. The revolution needed armies to carry its message to distant fronts, in the Littoral, Upper Peru, and beyond the Andes. It was important to motivate as well as to mobilize, to instil patriotic and republican values in a hitherto apolitical mass, and to impart too a sense of egalitarianism. Thus the mass of the people, many in ignorance, were incorporated into the revolution.

In the pampas the situation was different. It was difficult to inculcate political propaganda in the rural and gaucho population, but an estanciero could lead his peons into what were in effect military and political actions on behalf of the revolution. Outside the estancia violence prevailed. The only expression of the state was spasmodic, an expedition to secure a frontier or a military patrol to quell specific disorder. But the gaucho population lived by disorder, and the slightest loss of control by Buenos Aires encouraged insubordination. The rebellion of Buenos Aires against Spain was the trigger for rebelliousness in the pampas against Buenos Aires, which in turn led to a kind of counter-insurgency. The first junta, in 1810, commissioned Colonel Pedro Andrés García to inspect frontier forts and to assess the possibility of assembling the rural population in villages. He reported a state of anarchy in the countryside. His estimate was that about one-third of rural people were idle and nomadic vagrants;

---

[2] Gelman, 'The Gaucho and the Rural History of the Colonial Río de la Plata', 715–31.
[3] Cited by Halperín Donghi, *Politics, Economics and Society in Argentina*, 166.

these were joined by delinquents and outlaws; others went over to the Indians as caudillos to organize raids on whites and attacks on estancias. He found 'crimes unchecked, evil-doers increasing, barbarism, disorder among the settlements, ruin and insecurity in the countryside'.[4] The government itself was provocative. In the wars of independence vagrants were conscripted into the army or the work force by the combined efforts of the *porteño* government, the estancieros, and local officials. So the gaucho was forced into service on behalf of a revolution from which he received no obvious benefit.

The Río de la Plata did not produce a Hidalgo, much less a Piar, but there was one caudillo who spoke for the rural dispossessed, and others who were tempted to exploit popular forces. Artigas had a place in his programme for the victims of agrarian change and also for Indians, whom he expected to benefit from his plans of colonization and development.[5] He wanted to raise the indigenous population of the Littoral from their 'shameful degredation', to be given land, if necessary in his own province: 'I want the Indians in their villages to be governed by themselves, so that they can look after their own interests, as we do ours.'[6] Policy of this kind, together with his agrarian reformism, lost him the support of some landowners and alerted caudillos in other parts of the Littoral. In Salta Martin Güemes, the caudillo of the north-west frontier, recruited support from the popular sectors. According to Colonel La Madrid, Güemes attacked the royalist army 'with his militias, or gauchos, as he called them'; 'the gauchos of Salta were crazy for their general Güemes and fought for him with the greatest enthusiasm'.[7] These popular militias lived off the land and its owners, while Güemes himself requisitioned supplies from estancias, and demanded contributions for the war effort. Populism of this kind was essentially a method of waging war, not of changing the agrarian structure. But it had social implications, for it meant that the caudillo acquired a power base outside the upper class and for the first time militarized and to some extent politicized the popular sectors; all this with the blessing of the central government in defence of the revolution. The lesson was clear: it was the

[4] Pedro Andrés García, 'Informe', and 'Viaje', in Angelis, *Colección*, iii. 203–16, 219–60.

[5] See Chap. 3, sect. 1.

[6] Artigas to José de Silva, governor of Corrientes, 3 May 1815, Artigas to Cabildo Gobernador of Corrientes, 9 Jan. 1816, in Azcuy Ameghino, *Artigas en la historia argentina*, 248, 250, 254–6.

[7] Aráoz de La Madrid, *Memorias*, i. 54, 56.

caudillos who could influence the popular sectors, either to mobilize them or to control them.

In Venezuela the social structure was more complex than in Argentina and the impact of revolution more violent. Bolívar spoke of 'this amazing chaos of *patriots*, godos, self-seekers, blancos, pardos, *Venezuelans*, *Cundinamarquis*, *federalists*, *centralists*, *republicans*, *aristocrats*, the good and the bad, and the swarm of hierarchies which divide each of these groups'.[8] Reformist policies in favour of slaves and Indians affected only minority groups and were unlikely to threaten the existing order of society. The *pardos*, on the other hand, were far from being a minority. The largest single group in Venezuelan society, yet the victims of discrimination by law and convention alike, they emerged from colonial society ready for revolution. War gave them a kind of equality, new opportunities, and new leaders; but war also denied them the richest prizes and showed them the limits of toleration. As a social phenomenon the war of independence can be seen as a competition between republican and royalist creoles for the allegiance of *pardos* and recruitment of slaves. In Bolívar's hands the revolution became a kind of coalition in which the *pardos* were a subordinate partner under creole control. They were not allowed autonomous leaders. This was why Bolívar had to confront and defeat the challenge from the republican caudillo, Manuel Piar.

In creole thinking Piar was a prototype of the racist demagogue, a kind of anti-caudillo. A royalist chronicler reported: 'Piar was one of our most terrible enemies, adventurous, talented, and with great influence among the castes, to whom he belonged. He was thus one of the few Venezuelans who could inspire the greater part of the population.'[9] According to a republican, 'Piar, seeing himself isolated, and belonging to the pardo class, a party respected by us, had no option but to become their leader and try to arm them in order to achieve his ambition. Fortunately he did not succeed and had to flee.'[10] Bolívar had Piar hunted down and executed for attempting to incite race war and encourage anarchy. *Pardo* domination, or *pardocracia* as he called it, was even less justifiable in his eyes when equality was already on offer to the blacks and mixed races and they now had a place in the revolution under white leadership. Even this controlled mobilization carried risks. In the early years of the war, he

---

[8] Bolívar to Nariño, 21 Apr. 1821, in *Selected Writings*, i. 264.
[9] Díaz, *Recuerdos sobre la rebelión de Caracas*, 336.
[10] General Bartolomé Salom, in O'Leary, *Narración*, i. 436.

later recalled, Negroes, *zambos*, *mulatos*, and whites were all welcome, as long as they could kill Spaniards, though there was no money to pay them:

> The only way of maintaining ardour, rewarding exceptional actions, and stimulating valour was by promotion, so that today men of every caste and colour are amongst the generals, leaders, and officers of our forces, though the majority of them have no other merit than brute strength. This was once useful to the Republic but now, in peacetime, is an obstacle to peace and tranquility.[11]

From 1815–16, therefore, growing numbers of *pardos* were incorporated into the army of liberation: they were needed to fill the gaps in the patriot ranks left by creole casualties and desertions; and they themselves were imbued with greater expectations from wartime social mobility. The traditional structure of the republican army was transformed, and while the creoles retained military and political control, the *pardos* had more opportunities to advance to higher ranks and offices. But war acted as a social dissolvent in more than one sense: it divided the *pardos* against each other, incorporating some into the officer corps and the upper sectors, and leaving the rest at the bottom of society, potential recruits for further stages of protest and rebellion.

3. *The Imperatives of Caudillism*

Conditions after independence were not propitious for constitutional government. Social heterogeneity, lack of consensus, and absence of political traditions placed liberal constitutions under severe strain and destabilized the new republics almost as soon as they were formed.

In Argentina the post-war republic inherited a degree of social anarchy which alarmed people of property. The popular classes in Buenos Aires were still capable of producing a mob to stage demonstrations or worse in favour of one party or another and to work on the common soldiery. The overthrow and assassination of Manuel Dorrego in December 1828 brought out an angry crowd in the city: 'The lower classes, who from the first had espoused the cause of Dorrego were loud in their execrations against his murderers, and employed themselves actively and with success in seducing the soldiery; the women especially have taken a great share in these

---

[11] Peru de Lacroix, *Diario de Bucaramanga*, 58–9.

proceedings.' Rivadavia and others were threatened with personal violence.[12]

In the province of Buenos Aires the unitarist *golpe* and execution of Dorrego weakened the hand of the state, undermined social order, and unleashed a wave of unrest among groups already alienated from government and society. The gauchos of the countryside, still unreconciled to the state, marginal groups on the wild southern frontier, barred from land but sought for labour, and nomadic Indians hunting for resources, all had reasons to resent authority and all could strike terror into landowners. The war with Brazil (1825–8) and consequent blockade were felt by all sectors of the rural population, inflating prices, reducing estancia exports and production, and increasing the conscription of peons for the army. War was overtaken by another scourge, the great drought of 1828. For over three years there was no rain; lakes, rivers, and wells dried up, vegetation disappeared, crops and cattle suffered.[13] Adversity aroused anger and the rural poor were ready to rise in 1828–9, not in a coherent or co-ordinated movement but in a series of protests extending across the south and west of the province.[14] Indians attacked white estancias for horses and cattle. Bands of *montoneros* under minor caudillos underwent classic transformation from outlaws, to guerrillas, to freedom fighters, or, as they were sometimes called, *anarquistas*, without ceasing to be bandits.

These were the elements encountered, exploited, and to some extent assembled by Rosas in his successful bid for power in 1829, when he himself became a *jefe de montoneros* and fought a guerrilla war against the regular forces of General Lavalle and the unitarians. First he recruited among his landed supporters and expected client estancieros to come to his service with peons, horses, and cattle; those who held back realized later in 1829 that they had missed a winning venture and hastened to explain.[15] He instructed his supporters to make their base in the south of the province, his home ground, and to wage economic war on Lavalle and his allies. This

[12] Parish to Aberdeen, 12 Jan. 1829, PRO, FO 6/26.

[13] Charles Darwin, *Journal of Researches . . . during the Voyage of H.M.S. 'Beagle' round the World*, 9th ed. (London, 1890), 96.

[14] Pilar González Bernaldo, 'El imaginario social y sus implicaciones políticas en un conflicto rural: El levantamiento de 1829', 4–6, 7–10, 20–1 (unpublished paper kindly supplied by the author).

[15] José Antonio Beja to Rosas, 1 Oct. 1829, AGN, Buenos Aires, Secretaría de Rosas, Sala X, 23-8-4.

was the *guerra de recursos*, designed to achieve its objectives by waste and destruction of the estancias of the unitarians, or as the British consul described it 'a gaucho warfare against the properties in the country of all those who were known to be parties to the revolution'. To wage this war, however, Rosas had to recruit rural hordes from the lower sectors.

In December 1828 there were a number of risings in the north and south of the province, evidence of a subsistence as well as a political crisis, which he contrived to turn in his favour. He already had prestige among the 'friendly' Indians and many supporters among their provincial associates, men on the margin of rural society, near-delinquents with no regular work, clients of the caudillo, to whom they looked as some kind of saviour. Officials in the south of the province reported gangs of 'Indians, deserters and every kind of villain', also 'anarchists', roaming the countryside attacking estancias and defying the representatives of law and order.[16] The ambiguity of the caudillo's position served his purpose. Was he the leader of rural rebels? Or was he the protector of society against their anarchy? It was the recruitment of Indians by Rosas which provoked most comment, and caused the unitarists to regard Rosas's movement as 'the revolt *en masse* of the barbarous Indians and the licentious mob'.[17] In Buenos Aires it was reported that at the battle of Navarro 'more than 200 pampa Indians fought on Dorrego's side, those who had their camps on the estancia of the commander general of the countryside, don Juan Manuel de Rosas'.[18] General La Madrid recorded a 'great gathering of the militia and the pampa Indians on the hacienda of Rosas', under the command of Rosas's overseer Molina, a '*mulato* deserter' who had lived among the frontier Indians and subsequently received employment from Rosas.[19] This incongruous alliance of federalists, gauchos, outlaws, and Indians was held together not by social interest, which lacked cohesion, but by Rosas himself, who was the ultimate leader recognized by all in different degrees. As he advanced on Buenos Aires he clearly demonstrated the existence of popular forces and his ability to control them.

---

[16] Lynch, *Argentine Dictator*, 39.

[17] Ricardo Levene, *El proceso histórico de Lavalle a Rosas* (ANH, *Obras de Ricardo Levene*, 4; Buenos Aires, 1972), 262.

[18] Juan Manuel Beruti, *Memorias curiosas*, in *Biblioteca de Mayo* (17 vols.; Buenos Aires, 1960–3), iv. 4010.

[19] Aráoz de La Madrid, *Memorias*, i. 292–3.

The Montoneros in great numbers, and apparently proceeding with an extraordinary subordination to their leaders, advanced slowly towards the City. Considering the composition of their force, their conduct indeed appears to have been unexpectedly regular. The strictest orders are understood to be given by Rosas to respect all property, and his officers are said to be determined to punish all excesses in the most summary manner.[20]

There were few others who could achieve this degree of social control, a qualification which made Rosas almost indispensable to the élite. When he entered Buenos Aires and restored power to the federal party, he was able to name his own price. The House of Representatives was divided between those who favoured dictatorship and those who feared despotism, but eventually they voted Rosas extraordinary powers and elected him governor on 6 December 1829 at the age of thirty-five. He subsequently told the House that he was uniquely qualified for the task, because 'no one has had my opportunity to establish contact with men of all classes and conditions'; and as for 'the extraordinary powers', 'our normal and ordinary laws have never been sufficient to preserve the country from the political upheavals which have beset it'.[21]

In Venezuela the need for a hard heart and a firm hand was even more imperative. Now the creoles were in power, that is the same families who had denounced the colonial government for opening doors to *pardos* in the university, the Church, and civil and military office. And it was the creoles who determined economic and social policy. Those *pardos* who worked in artisan occupations suffered from independence, when local industry lost ground to foreign competition. Workers in the rural sector learnt that the republic was a harsher taskmaster than the colony. Some were already incorporated into plantation production and trapped in adverse labour relations with the hacienda. Those who had escaped peonage often worked in subsistence agriculture; many more found a life for themselves in the cattle economy of the llanos; and not a few survived on the margin of the agrarian sector, living by plunder and violence. Independence gave a new impetus to land concentration, as the victorious caudillos competed for haciendas in the centre north and powerful ranchers sought to establish yet greater private property rights in the llanos. Landowners observed a mass of free and unemployed rural dwellers

[20] Parish to Aberdeen, 20 Apr. 1829, PRO, FO 6/26.
[21] Rosas to House of Representatives, 1832, encl. in Fox to Palmerston, 31 May 1832, PRO, FO 6/34.

and considered that the time had come to sweep them into plantations and ranches, mobilize them for production, and pay them
minimum wages.

For the popular sectors, therefore, independence was a form of
regression. Political mobilization ended with the war. Social mobility
was thwarted by élite resistance and their own poverty. In default of
legitimate ways of advance some had recourse to banditry, protest,
and rebellion. The llaneros designed their own mechanisms of survival. When the republic imposed deterrents against the export of
cattle in order to restore resources, contrabandists developed an
active trade through the Orinoco to the Caribbean, and when challenged took to the hills. Thus wartime bandit-guerrillas converted
into rustlers and contrabandists. Others regrouped under minor
caudillos to practise traditional forms of plunder. An Indian bandit,
Francisco Javier Perales, terrorized the area of Upper Apure and
Casanare throughout the 1820s. Dionisio Cisneros, a royalist caudillo,
continued his war on creole society long after the republic was
established and acquired an almost patriarchal status in the Valleys
of the Tuy. In September 1827 one of his bands attacked and
plundered a village only five miles outside Caracas. They bound the
men, raped the women, robbed the houses, and made off with horses
and cattle.[22] Throughout the llanos local caudillos and their bandit
followers continued their own war of independence. And outside the
llanos, in Maracaibo in 1838, there was a minor rebellion under
Francisco María Faria, an expression of pure banditry. The popular
sectors were perceived as a distinct danger to the creole government,
ready material for manipulation by caudillos or malcontents or even
post-war royalists. The danger was aggravated by racial tensions,
black resentment, and *pardo* frustration. In the years around 1830
black rebellion was a recurring threat to peace in Venezuela.

In the late 1820s Valencia, Barcelona, and Cumaná were scenes of
pardo disaffection, evidence of a high degree of group consciousness
and a readiness to use violence.[23] In 1827, when Bolívar was in
Venezuela, there was an insurrection of blacks in Cumaná and
Barcelona, where their numbers were increasing through immigration
from Haiti; they received short shrift from the Liberator, though

---

[22] *Ker Porter's Caracas Diary*, 29 Sept. 1827, 288–9; Landaeta Rosales, *Gran
recopilación geográfica, estadística e histórica de Venezuela*, ii. 235; Richard W. Slatta (ed.),
Bandidos: The Varieties of Latin American Banditry (Westport, Conn., 1987), 42.

[23] *Ker Porter's Caracas Diary*, 21 Mar. 1827, 5 Apr. 1827, 229, 233.

many survived to fight another day. There was a further black rebellion in Cumaná in September 1831 when Policarpo Soto, 'a
fearsome caudillo', led Negroes and slaves against the whites.[24] In
Valencia in December 1830 a black was arrested for trying to subvert
troops, saying 'that Valencia ought to become a second Hayti. That
all the whites ought to be murdered, and that he had a strong band of
blacks, who would aid them in the execution of this glorious task.'[25]
Caracas itself was not immune.

In May 1831 a rebel group suddenly went rampant in Caracas,
attacked the gaol, killed the guards, and freed one hundred prisoners.
Were they brigands from the mountains or urban dissidents? Were
they delinquents or guerrillas? According to the British consul, Ker
Porter, they were a *pardo* band who had organized themselves to
massacre the whites, and they included several women and 'some of
the most respectable people of colour'. The government reacted
severely: 'the greatest zeal and activity has been shewn by the authorities and upper classes of citizens, as well as the better disposed of
the people of colour'.[26] When some of the rebels were taken and
executed, there was further defiance, followed by more arrests and
more confessions. 'Every detail that becomes developed of the plan',
recorded Ker Porter, 'is of a most horrid and bloody nature—in fact
nothing less than the extermination of the Whites. The perpetrators
are composed of the people, of slaves, disbanded soldiers, and I
regret to add unemployed and disappointed officers.' There was a
black leader named Severo, a person of intelligence, with some talent
and education, and a plan of government.[27] Even allowing for the
prejudice and alarmism of Ker Porter, there were signs here of deep
discontent among the masses, in which race, delinquency, and political protest were inextricably intermixed and found expression in
recurring outbursts of violence and occasionally a plan of alternative
government. The economic context was one of extreme destitution,
many people condemned to live in an almost permanent subsistence
crisis, as Ker Porter recorded. 'The terror in the City seems abat-

---

[24] Cockburn to Canning, Caracas, 24 Apr. 1827, PRO, FO 18/67; 'Sobre la
revolución que se tramaba en Cumaná contra los blancos', AGN, Caracas, Secretaría
del Interior y Justicia, XXXVII, fos. 169–78.

[25] *Ker Porter's Caracas Diary*, 16 Dec. 1830, 517; Ker Porter to Palmerston, 30
Apr. 1831, PRO, FO 18/87.

[26] Ker Porter to Palmerston, 27 June 1831, PRO, FO 18/87.

[27] *Ker Porter's Caracas Diary*, 16, 17, 18, 24, 27 May 1831, 16 June 1831, 548–9,
550, 551, 556.

ing—but neither poverty nor *actual want*.' And again: 'No one can picture the scenes of actual want, and literal starvation that occur in this city daily'.[28]

Local evidence in these years confirms the reports of Ker Porter. In 1833 officials in La Victoria, Maracay, reported a conspiracy 'to destroy the white class of society'. Posters were stuck on walls advocating 'Death to the whites!' The danger was that 'the small number of whites who live in this canton have no weapons with which to defend themselves.' The government decided to place a unit of troops there. In 1838 a rising of runaway slaves disturbed the peace of Puerto Cabello; armed with machetes and lances, they joined with outlaws and criminals to terrorize nearby villages, 'exploiting the weakness of the authorities'. In Ocumare in 1840 the detention of a slave for punishment sparked off a violent rising of slaves on a hacienda belonging to Martin Tovar, particularly dangerous 'in a place like this where everyone are slaves and there are no security forces'. In Guarenas in 1841 two bandit gangs, one of ten the other of twelve blacks, armed with guns and machetes, launched a series of robbing and killing expeditions, storing their booty in a farmhouse.[29] A minority of whites at the top, and below them a mass of racial malcontents—this was the volcano of which Bolívar spoke.

4. *The Prime Protector*

How was the threat of mass rebellion or race war contained in these post-colonial societies? By what means did the creole élite keep control and preserve order? They had little faith in institutions: they sought a personal and proximate power.

In Buenos Aires, observed a newspaper report, order and security were best assured not by general laws but 'by the character of our worthy governor; that is where we will find all the guarantees which good citizens can desire.'[30] Rosas soon reassured the good citizens.

---

[28] Ibid. 27 May, 1 June 1831, 550, 552.

[29] Governor of Maracay to Minister of Interior, 28 Mar. 1833, AGN, Caracas, Sec. Int. y Just., LXX, fos. 157–8, 164–5; Gobierno Superior Político de Carabobo, Valencia, 19 Dec. 1838, ibid. CLXXXII, fos. 221–2; Santiago Almenar, Justice of the Peace, to Jefe Político, Ocumare, 8 July 1840, ibid. CCXI, fo. 214; B. Manrique, provincial government, Caracas, 12 Mar. 1841, ibid. CCXXIV, fos. 207–8.

[30] *El Lucero*, no. 78 (9 Dec. 1829), encl. in Parish to Aberdeen, 12 Dec. 1829, PRO, FO 6/7. See also Ernesto H. Celesia, *Rosas, aportes para su historia*, 2nd edn. (2 vols.; Buenos Aires, 1968), i. 103–4.

While he may have manipulated popular forces to gain power, he showed that he had little use for them thereafter and that his political base was among the élite. His first administration (1829–32) was a conservative one: it represented property, especially landed property, and it guaranteed internal peace and stability. He strengthened the army, protected the Church, silenced the critics, muzzled the press, and sought to improve the financial credit of the state. Rosas came back to power in 1835 on the record of his first government. He had already impressed the estancieros by his ability to impose order, his bias against personal and property taxation, and his land and frontier policy. He began by expanding the southern frontier and increasing the stock of land. He then proceeded to sell public land cheaply, and ended by giving it away to the officers who fought in his campaigns and the politicians who collaborated with his system. While he dispensed patronage, he also protected it. According to John Henry Mandeville, the British minister closest to Rosas, the governor was a despot who maintained order by shooting people without trial, by virtue of the supreme power which the House of Representatives had voted him. Rosas was a stark caudillo dressed in legal robes. Indians, gauchos, political enemies, all those who infringed social order as he saw it were executed by military firing squad:

Since Rosas's administration there has been little to fear from [the gauchos]. I do not say that their love of plunder, the natural propensity of a savage, is extinct among them but as the Captain General invariably shoots them, or makes them food for powder by making soldiers of them if they indulge in this propensity, a robbery, to my knowledge, by violence, is unknown. When they kill it is through revenge. They never forgive a blow, or an infidelity in their mistresses.[31]

Caudillo terrorism, however, at least in the case of Rosas, was selective and exemplary. Applied expertly, its mere demonstration was sufficient to cow the rest of the population without need to use it every day. Rosas had other techniques in his armoury of persuasion. He proceeded by demagogy as much as by despotism. Impelled by an awe of the mob, he sought in a curious way to identify with it, the better to appease it. The lawlessness of the countryside, vividly remembered from his first years of estancia ownership, left him with an overwhelming sense of living on the edge of chaos; and the insolence experienced from the hordes of vagrants and villains on his own estancia bred in him a determination to conquer anarchy, first in his

---

[31] Mandeville to Strangways, Private, 18 Oct. 1836, PRO, FO 6/53.

own environment, then in the political world beyond. There was a period in the late 1820s when he seems to have genuinely feared an autonomous movement of protest from below, a movement which he sought to capture and curb. He claimed that he deliberately cultivated the people 'of the lower classes', and that he had gaucherized himself in order to impress them: 'I thought it very important to gain a decisive influence over this class in order to control it and direct it.'[32] His claim was confirmed by General La Madrid: 'In spite of the severity with which he forced them to obey, Rosas was the hacendado who had most peons, because he payed them well and joined in their horse-play during breaks from work, and he patronized all the villains and deserters who made for his estancias and no one could touch them.'[33]

Rosas cultivated another sector of the popular classes, the urban blacks and *mulatos*. The blacks looked to Rosas as a protector, and so did the slaves. Some slaves regarded him as an escape route, a means of emancipation, and it was not unknown for runaway slaves from Brazilian vessels to make their way to his headquarters to petition for freedom. Foreign slaveowners in Buenos Aires were especially liable to lose their slaves, and slaves could gain their freedom by the traditional method of enlisting in the army.[34] Rosas had many blacks in his own employment and many more in his political service. He did not raise them socially, but neither did he discriminate against them racially. They gave him useful support in the streets and were part of his 'popular' following. The blacks in turn gave Rosas their blind support and, with the lower classes in general, flocked to the Carnival of Rosas, where they beat their drums, marched, danced, and shouted 'Viva el Restaurador'. These orgies of drinking and fighting were a cynical hint to the upper classes of the danger lurking in the shadows without a strong restraining hand.

The Venezuelan ruling groups addressed the problem of social order by first defining the political nation as narrowly as they could; the Constitution of 1830, as has been seen, virtually disfranchised the lower sectors. But constitutions alone could not ensure order and stability; they could establish the rules of political life but not enforce

---

[32] 'Nota confidencial de Santiago Vázquez', 9 Dec. 1829, in Arturo Enrique Sampay, *Las ideas políticas de Juan Manuel de Rosas* (Buenos Aires, 1972), 131–2.

[33] Aráoz de La Madrid, *Memorias*, i. 199.

[34] Thorndike to Rosas, 11 Dec. 1840, and Manigot y Meslin to Rosas, 24 Feb. 1841, AGN, Buenos Aires, Sala 10, 17-3-2, Gobierno, Solicitudes, Embargos.

them. Granted the constitutional history of Venezuela in the colonial and independence periods, it was not surprising if, as O'Leary said, men were everything, institutions nothing.[35] *Pardo* militancy and insubordination in the masses called for closer control and more immediate power than that provided by laws. This was one of the missions of caudillos.

The Venezuelan ruling class looked to José Antonio Páez, a caudillo by training and temperament, a military leader who had a personal power base in the llanos yet was not a creature of the llaneros, to fulfil the role of strong man. Páez entered public life illiterate in culture and politics. But he was not entirely inarticulate on the state of Venezuela in general and the llanos in particular. 'The greater part of this country', he wrote to Bolívar, 'is nothing more than the remains of a Spanish colony, and thus lacks the essentials for establishing a Republic'; and he thought it 'less likely to respond to government by laws than by bayonets'.[36] But Páez was also conscious of his great personal power, and in 1822 he wrote to Santander: 'I have been one of the high authorities accustomed to act on my own initiative... I commanded a corps of men whose only law was my will, I coined money and did everything an absolute lord can do in his states.'[37] From his power base in Apure he reminded Bolívar of the many sectors who looked to him for personal decisions. These, however, still needed to be legitimized by true 'authority', combining prestige and power in an office of state:

Here I am not sure if I am acknowledged even as Commandant General, and if I am obeyed it is more out of custom and consent than because I am authorized to command. These people consult me simply as a protector of religion, to appoint priests and organize churches; as a lawyer, to decide their lawsuits; as an officer, to grant their pensions, salaries, commissions and promotions; as a leader, to administer justice; as a friend, to help them in their needs; and even slaves who were previously freed and are now unwisely reclaimed by their masters come to me to complain and await my decision for their enslavement or freedom.[38]

The creole élite did not delay in giving Páez the authority he sought, at once ample and independent. Many landowners saw the

---

[35] O'Leary, *Narración*, ii. 557.

[36] Páez to Bolívar, 1 Oct. 1825, in O'Leary, *Memorias*, ii. 58; Páez to Minister of War, 15 Sept. 1822, in *Archivo Páez*, ii. 122.

[37] Quoted by Laureano Valenilla Lanz, *Cesarismo democrático, Obras completas*, i (Caracas, 1983), 88 n. 1.

[38] Páez to Bolívar, Achaguas, 31 Mar. 1827, in O'Leary, *Memorias*, ii. 86–7.

caudillo as the only man who could free Venezuela from corrupt and malign officials who collaborated with local criminals and made life hazardous for law-abiding citizens. A group of hacendados in the western coastal district of Gibraltar complained that 'our properties, and those of many others, are ruined, victims of the ambition, despotism and intrigues of a small group of dangerous men.... There have been assassinations, illegalities, misappropriation of public funds, diversion of fines to the pockets of judges and other frauds, violence against decent citizens, scandalous robberies, housebreakings, the whole situation an affront and insult to the highest civil authority in this Department.'[39] They wanted a purge of minor officials, who should be punished, replaced, and their successors subject to a powerful senior magistrate. Congress promised to do something, but experience taught complainants that an appeal to congress was not enough.

The Venezuelan oligarchy needed Páez, above all, because he was one of the few leaders who had some political credit among the *pardos* and llaneros, and virtually the only leader who could control the popular classes. He was the caudillo 'whose influence in the plains is all powerful and whose very name is an army'.[40] He was their *gendarme necesario*, the law enforcer who could pacify the llaneros, organize the peons, control the slaves, and keep the mob at bay.[41] And if he were not their guardian he might well be their destroyer, re-enacting the role of Piar or imitating the action of Padilla. Level de Goda, a former royalist official, denounced the *pardo* leaders for constituting, in alliance with the white traditionalists, a new élite which ruled independent Venezuela. The leader of this oligarchy, according to Level de Goda, was Páez, 'who is a pardo and, far from possessing any virtues, has been steeped in crimes since he was a youth'.[42] Páez himself, at least in his writings, did not make a great issue of race or worry about the status of his own family. But his son, who was at West Point, wrote home to say that he and his two brothers were known as *mulatos* in the United States, and his father was being called a *mulato* in the Philadelphia newspapers, 'a terrible

---

[39] Hacendados to Venezuelan Congress, Maracaibo, 9 June 1830, AGN, Caracas, Sec. Int. y Just., VI, fos. 289–90.
[40] *Ker Porter's Caracas Diary*, 28 Mar. 1837, 960.
[41] Valenilla Lanz, *Cesarismo democrático*, 79.
[42] Andrés Level de Goda, 'Antapodosis', *Boletín de la Academia Nacional de la Historia*, 16 (1933), 631.

blow for me'.[43] Páez claimed to stand for equality: 'For a man of talent, whatever his origin, colour does not remove claims to merit; colour will always be an accident....'[44] The social structure was another matter.

Páez ruled with and for the élite, and although he himself had come up through the ranks he defined the government of Venezuela as narrowly as the most traditionalist of his associates. He conformed to élite values and supported the prevailing structures, though they were not to the benefit of the popular classes. He was as sensitive as any of the élite to threats to law and order in Venezuela, and he was merciless to slave insubordination. In 1828, urged by Bolívar to revive the Venezuelan economy and rescue the country from depression, Páez assembled a junta in Caracas: 'I brought together for this purpose hacendados, treasury officials, lawyers, and merchants.'[45] This was the political coalition which Páez led; it was also a perfect description of the ruling class of Venezuela. He regarded this class as his natural advisers. He agreed with them to tighten up control of local government and police officials throughout Venezuela by restoring the colonial office of *corregidor* and placing it over the municipalities, again taking advice from 'the most enlightened men in the capital, called together in a junta'.[46] They were evidently seeking an official of an absolutist type, and eventually found him in the justice of the peace.

Páez was not a monster of repression. Many observers compared his relaxed style unfavourably with the ruthlessness of Bolívar, who rarely hesitated to send dangerous caudillos to the firing squad. Páez preferred pacification to persecution, and he frequently used one of the basic resources of the caudillo as an alternative means of persuasion. The patron–client relationship, essential to many of the caudillo's roles, was also an instrument of social control. As such it was not a mere formality. When invoked it had to deliver benefits; otherwise the pact would lose credit and the *patrón* lose face. A client disillusioned could become an enemy, an outlaw, or a rebel. Then force replaced trust and the *abrazo* became a blow. The state in

<hr>

[43] J. A. Polanco Páez to Páez, 8 Jan. 1826, AGN, Caracas, Intendencia de Venezuela, CCLXXXVI. I am obliged for this reference to Sir Edgar Vaughan.

[44] Páez, *Autobiografía*, i. 464.

[45] Páez, *Autobiografía*, i. 416; Páez to Bolívar, 26 Aug. 1828, in O'Leary, *Memorias*, ii. 157.

[46] Páez to Bolívar, 7 Oct. 1828, in O'Leary, *Memorias*, ii. 170.

Venezuela was too poor to be coercive, and the caudillo's prudence reflected penury as well as moderation. But a weak state was an encouragement to civil war in which rival caudillos called on their own clients to come to their aid. Páez began his political life as the supreme caudillo, and the llanos of the south and east were virtually his client territories. But he did not fulfil his wartime promises to the landless llaneros and once he lost their trust he had to struggle to maintain his position in the plains. Then his personal dominance over his immediate clients, on his haciendas and *hatos*, in the bureaucracy and the armed forces, became even more important, and in general remained intact. Outside the boundaries of powerful estates, however, the llanos were a byword for lawlessness. To control minor caudillos and bandit chieftains Páez often relied upon his moral authority as a *patrón* rather than the expensive operations of security forces.

The culmination of the *patrón* was the godfather. *Compadrazgo* acquired a special place in Hispanic culture from its religious significance in the context of a sacrament. When in 1831 Páez wanted to conciliate Dionisio Cisneros, royalist guerrilla turned bandit chief and one of the most bloodthirsty of all the mountain outlaws, he began by capturing a son of Cisneros and having him baptized. Páez became the infant's godfather, and his mistress, Bárbara Nieves, the godmother. The president of Venezuela thus made himself a *compadre* of the bandit and subsequently went to interview him in his lair in the Tuy Valleys surrounded by his wild and fearsome followers, now 'legitimized' by his new status and co-opted into the army as a colonel, but still refusing to come into civilization. Páez assured him, 'I have obligations towards you and you towards me—in view of the spiritual kinship we have acquired since the day I had your son in my arms to receive the baptismal waters.'[47] Cisneros did not undergo a complete conversion, and a year later, perhaps to strengthen the friendship, Páez stood as godfather to another of Cisneros's children. This time the bandit chief came to Caracas, where the cream of society crowded into the president's house to gape at this startling figure, a dark, silent man in a blue jacket and dirty white trousers, with a searching and suspicious look of 'untamed ferocity'. Páez presented him proudly to the British consul and other

---

[47] Páez to Cisneros, 24 Sept. 1831, in *Ker Porter's Caracas Diary*, 575–6, 586; see also Pérez Vila, 'El Gobierno Deliberativo', 61 n. 53.

public figures. And whatever his misgivings, Ker Porter admitted that Páez by his clemency had brought to an end a decade's campaign which had cost tens of thousands of pesos and the lives of countless soldiers with nothing to show for it: 'General Páez by these honourable means, has accomplished what Bolívar with all his transcendent talents and greatness could not effect'.[48]

5. Patricians or Populists?

Did caudillos such as Rosas and Páez have a mass following? Did they bypass élite constitutions to establish direct relations with the popular classes? Were they true populists?

Rosas was not a populist caudillo. Cultural affinity with the gauchos and popular sectors was not the same as social solidarity. Contemporary observers, especially the British, often reported that the lower classes of town and country supported Rosas: 'The Gauchos, or inhabitants of the country districts, are ardently attached to General Rosas, to whom, as their acknowledged chief and benefactor, they have long looked up with an incredible devotion.'[49] Rosas himself explained to Mandeville that 'there is no aristocracy here to support a government, public opinion and the masses govern.'[50] Henry Southern believed that 'It is the secret of his power that he taught the Gaucho of the plains that he was the true master of the towns. It was on the basis of troops of his own cattle-breeders and drivers and horse tamers that he first established his authority which he has maintained to this day by a cunning and dextrous use of the same arm.'[51] Some of the confusion in these impressions arises from an imprecise use of the term gaucho, to mean rural people in general. But the population of the pampas was not homogeneous. Many country dwellers were neither gauchos nor peons; they were independent families living on small ranches or farms, or earning a living in a *pulpería* or a village. Greater precision would distinguish between the sedentary rural dwellers working on the land for themselves or for

[48] *Ker Porter's Caracas Diary*, 17 Oct. 1832, 653–4.
[49] Gore to Palmerston, 21 Oct. 1833, PRO, FO 6/37.
[50] Mandeville to Aberdeen, 7 July 1842, PRO, FO 6/84.
[51] Southern to Palmerston, 22 Nov. 1848, Historical Manuscripts Commission, Palmerston Papers, GC/SO/241.

their *patrón*, and the pure gaucho, who was nomadic and independent, tied to no estate.[52]

The agrarian structure, therefore, did not favour a mass rising. The core of Rosas's forces comprised his own peons and dependants, who had to follow him in war as they laboured for him in peace. When he was governor of Buenos Aires he did not cease to be an estanciero and employer of a large work force. He managed his estates through his *mayordomos*, for whom he was not primarily the governor but 'el *patrón*', and things were done 'por orden del *patrón*'.[53] Beyond his own retainers he could raise 'friendly' Indians, outlaws, and no doubt a number of pure gauchos. Whoever they were, the peons of Rosas were his servants rather than his supporters, his clients rather than his allies. On those occasions when Rosas needed to make a critical political advance, he enlisted the horsemen of the countryside and the mob in the city. But these forces lasted only as long as he needed them. Once Rosas had the apparatus of the state in his possession, once he controlled the bureaucracy, the police, the *mazorca*, and above all the regular army, he did not need or want the popular forces of the countryside, who were promptly sent home. It was the army camped at Santos Lugares which gave him his ultimate power.[54] As for the militias, they were officered and led by the justices of the peace, by regular army commanders, and by estancieros. The fact of belonging to a military organization did not give the peons political power or representation, for the rigid structure of the estancia was also built into the militia, where the estancieros were the commanders, their overseers the officers, and their peons the troops. These troops did not enter into direct relationship with Rosas: they were mobilized by their *patrón*, which meant that Rosas received his support not from free gaucho hordes but from estancieros leading their peon conscripts. Rosas controlled a network of sub-caudillos, 'a set of turbulent and licentious chieftains with their needy dependants, whose very existence is civil commotion', and who were part of his political spearhead in 1834.[55] In this way otherwise socially dangerous classes were brought into the service of the élite, employed but also controlled.

[52] Brown, *A Socioeconomic History of Argentina*, 158–9.
[53] Rosas to Laureano Ramírez, 11 Mar. 1845, AGN, Buenos Aires, Sala 10, 43-2-8.
[54] Lynch, *Argentine Dictator*, 110–12.
[55] Gore to Palmerston, 17 Apr. 1834, PRO, FO 6/40.

Yet this does not resolve the question, was Rosas a populist? The history of populism offers many examples of authoritarian leaders who come from outside the social groups they lead.[56] There is more than one way of allocating benefits. The evidence indicates, however, that Rosas did not provide any real benefits to the popular sectors. No land was granted to the gaucho, no property assigned to the peon. Land concentration prevented the mass of the people from acquiring even small estates, while estancia expansion increased the demand for labour. Gauchos and peons were the victims of a traditionally harsh regime imposed by the estancieros on those whom they regarded as *mozos vagos y mal entretenidos*, rogues and vagabonds, who sat in groups gambling, or singing to a guitar, drinking maté or liquor, but not usually working.[57] The once free gauchos were gradually subjected to more and more constraints to drive them into the estancias and keep them there. Vagrancy was defined as a crime, for which the punishment was beating, imprisonment, hard labour, and conscription. Rosas continued to apply the existing regulations against vagrancy, and he ordered forced recruitment of levies; in his speech at the beginning of the legislative session of 1836 he reported the strong action taken against *vagos y mal entretenidos* and the increased numbers conscripted into the forces.[58]

In Venezuela Páez used land as a medium of mobilization very early in his campaign, and in Apure he made specific promises to his wild llanero followers, *zambos* and *mulatos* most of them, men without land who had been converted from hunters or ranch hands into soldiers and fought with high expectations. In the event they did not receive their reward, as Bolívar acknowledged: 'They are men who have fought long and hard and who, believing that they deserve much, feel thoroughly humiliated and miserable.' He warned that excuses would not work 'with men accustomed to get what they want by force', and warned that peace would be more fearful than war.[59] Páez too gave credit to the special character and contribution of the llaneros, and in words that echoed those of Bolívar warned the central government of the consequences if promises were not ful-

---

[56] This is to use the term 'populist' in a wider sense than that which restricts it to multi-class alliances characteristic of the decades after 1930.

[57] Gastón Gori, *Vagos y mal entretenidos; Aporte al tema hernandiano*, 2nd ed. (Santa Fe, Argentina 1965), 18; Slatta, *Gauchos and the Vanishing Frontier*, 109–11.

[58] Lynch, *Argentine Dictator*, 116.

[59] Bolívar to Gual, 24 May 1821, *Selected Writings*, i. 266; Briceño Méndez to Minister of Finance, 20 July 1821, in O'Leary, *Memorias*, xviii. 399–401.

filled: 'Already they are refusing military service, demanding payment of their due, forming bands to rob on the highways. And if a bold and clever leader placed himself at their head, would not the brave, vengeful, and corruptible llaneros follow him, wage war, and destroy the very thing they helped to create?'[60] But in the same letter he thanked Santander for facilitating the grant of the hacienda La Trinidad, on which he had set his heart. The protestations of Páez were not sincere: he was more interested in his own acquisitions than in those of his men, and after the end of hostilities he spent much of his time speculating in military land vouchers and acquiring the best national properties for himself, taking particular pride in the ranch of San Pablo and the hacienda of Tapa-Tapa. Minor caudillos followed suit, and Venezuelans witnessed a scramble for land at the top in place of an agrarian policy for all. There were bitter complaints over the failure to distribute land to the llaneros and other ex-soldiers. From east to west there were accusations of favouritism, inertia, and inefficiency. A complainant in Cumaná drew attention not only to family influence but also to 'deference to class' in favour of the few against the many.[61]

The programme of land distribution during the Páez years (1830–47) was designed to raise revenue, not to grant social benefits to the rural poor. These had little chance of moving up from *jornaleros* (day labourers) to *colonos* (tenant farmers); 80 per cent of the new titles were for ranch land in Apure and Barinas and represented less than 1 per cent of the private land in the country. Landowners in the centre-north and ranchers in the llanos wanted a dependent labour force not a population of free peasants. Like the gauchos in Argentina, the llaneros were tamed, deprived of customary rights over wild cattle, classified as vagrants, prevented from travelling without a passport, and herded into haciendas, there to find that debt peonage was enforced by the state.[62] The *ley de azotes*, or Lash Law (23 May 1836, in force until 1845), decreed death or hard labour for theft of property, and flogging for lesser crimes. It was a notorious cause of

---

[60] Páez to Santander, 15 Jan. 1822, *Archivo Páez*, ii. 24.
[61] *Alerta* (Cumaná), 10 Feb. 1826, *Materiales para el estudio de la cuestión agraria en Venezuela*, i. 476; see above, pp. 101–4.
[62] *Materiales para el estudio de la cuestión agraria en Venezuela*, vol. i, pp. cii–cxvi; *Materiales . . . enajenación y arrendamiento de tierras baldías* (Caracas, 1971), vol. i, pp. xxxi–xxxv; Robert Paul Matthews, *Rural Violence and Social Unrest in Venezuela, 1840–1858: Origins of the Federalist War* (New York Univ. Ph.D. thesis, 1974), 54–64, 152–3.

resentment, protest, and revolt among the rural population, caught as they were between the repression of the planters and the connivance of the judges. But there were many other irritants. According to the police code of Carabobo in 1843, 'any labourer or servant caught gambling shall be condemned as a vagrant'. And in towns those found 'habitually sleeping in the streets because they do not have a home shall be classified as vagrants and deprived of rights of citizenship'.[63]

The populism of the caudillos, therefore, was simply part of the florid rhetoric and empty promises with which they normally began their rule. The revolution and the post-war settlement stopped short of the popular classes, and the caudillos erected the necessary barriers to limit social change and preserve political privilege. They put together powerful coalitions of land, trade, and office, arbitrated in their disputes, and presided over their interests. But they were not mere creatures of the élite. Their indispensability gave them leverage and enabled them to act with an independent sovereignty. After all, as landowners and patrons in their own right caudillos had their personal bases, whose power was usually greater than that of any single component of the coalition.

6. *The Caudillo System of Power: Conditions and Methods*

The caudillos exercised various systems of control to exclude mass participation and restrain popular pressures. In Buenos Aires, from 1829, Rosas ruled as a straightforward dictator without a constitution. He had institutions, accepted as more or less legitimate, but these served his own plan and had no life outside his will. The electoral law of 14 August 1821, which remained in force throughout the next three decades and beyond, established direct elections and universal male suffrage; all free men from the age of twenty had the right to vote, and all property owners over twenty-five had the right to be candidates for election.[64] This was the law and there were no literacy or property qualifications for voters. But in practice the illiterate gauchos and urban populace could not vote as free men. The govern-

---

[63] Acuerdo de la Corte Suprema, 29 Oct. 1845, AGN, Caracas, Sec. Int. y Just., CCCXIX, fos. 16–17; *Materiales para el estudio de la cuestión agraria en Venezuela: Mano de obra* (Caracas, 1979), i. 277.

[64] Bushnell, *Reform and Reaction in the Platine Provinces*, 22–3.

ment sent a list of official candidates, and it was the task of the justices of the peace to ensure that these were elected. Open and verbal voting, the right of the justices of the peace to exclude voters and candidates whom they considered unqualified, the intimidation of the opposition, these and many other malpractices made elections a mockery. Rosas frankly admitted that they had to be controlled, and he condemned as hypocrisy the demand for free elections. Throughout his rule elections were staged simply as a display of 'popular' support, to call and recall the caudillo 'by acclamation'.[65]

The key agent of control in the countryside was the justice of the peace. The office was established in 1821 and its original judicial and administrative functions were expanded to include those of commander of militia, police chief, and tax collector. Rosas took control of the justices in the campaign of 1829 and from then onwards they were his creatures. The justices administered and policed the legal constraints imposed on the rural population. They pursued criminals, deserters, and vagrants; they applied orders of confiscation against estancias; they recruited for the militia. In general they were either willing accomplices or helpless instruments of a policy expressed in arrest, confiscation, conscription, or worse, directed against anyone who could be branded an opponent of the regime or a social misfit. They were the front line of the *rosista* state, serving an apparatus consisting of the bureaucracy, the police, paramilitary squads, and above all the army. Rosas recruited, equipped, armed, and purged an army of the line, detachments of which were used against the popular sectors of the countryside to round up conscripts. It was the army camped outside Buenos Aires and stationed on the various fronts of the Río de la Plata that was the ultimate sanction of his power. The size of this army is difficult to gauge, but in the 1840s it was probably in the region of 20,000 men with a militia of 14,400, a large army in relation to the level of population. Defence consumed 50 to 60 per cent of the total budget.

In Venezuela the system of caudillo government was different. To organize a new state, develop a reasonably efficient bureaucracy, maintain an army, pay war debts, all needed resources, which a poor treasury of a poor country could not supply. The ruling élite wanted security but refused to pay taxes to support security forces. They did not even contribute much to customs duties. Export duties were

---

[65] Hamilton to Palmerston, 11 Dec. 1834, PRO, FO 6/41.

progressively reduced to make Venezuelan exports more competitive, while rising import taxes were evaded by contraband. The customs revenue of Venezuela, moreover, had to go much further than the corresponding income of Buenos Aires, which was targeted on its own province and employed only secondarily in subsidizing the rest. By the end of the 1840s the Venezuelan treasury was engaged in a desperate search for further sources of income at a time of depression when it feared to impose new taxes and found it impossible to attract loans or finance for the public sector.[66] In these circumstances the caudillo was expected to produce results without resources. Caudillism could almost be defined as a response to the penury of the state; it was thought to be a cheaper form of government. The Venezuelan caudillo could not afford to maintain a military regime or establish a police state, creating instruments of power which might in any case fall into the hands of dissidents and rivals; personalist solutions and informal expedients took their place.

In Venezuela formal power was apparently constitutional and nonmilitary. Daniel F. O'Leary, while British consul in Caracas, concluded somewhat complacently:

Considering the heterogeneous elements of which this community is composed, the extremely democratic character of its institutions, the non-existence of an efficient police, the insignificance of the military establishment (the whole force of the republic does not exceed five hundred men) the actual political state of Venezuela too closely resembles a political phenomenon, to warrant conclusions therefrom favourable to its durability. As it is, Venezuela is the only country of Spanish America that enjoys a government of laws, and wherein persons and property are perfectly secure and respected.[67]

No doubt Páez believed the same. He was constitutional president from 1830 to February 1835, when he was succeeded by Dr José María Vargas, whose candidacy he had not supported. In July 1835 Vargas, a medical doctor who had studied at the University of Edinburgh, was deposed by men of a different type, the discontented military caudillos of independence.

The Revolution of the Reformists began during the night of 7 July. A party of infantry marched to the home of President Vargas and placed him under arrest, while other detachments occupied Government House, the Treasury, and the Arsenal. The rest of the troops formed in the Cathedral Square, where amidst the inertia and ap-

---

[66] Ferrigni, *Crecimiento y depresión*, 76, 127.
[67] O'Leary to Aberdeen, Caracas, 24 Oct. 1842, PRO, FO 80/17.

parent indifference of the inhabitants Generals Diego Ibarra, Justo Briceño, José Silva, and Pedro Briceño Méndez, with assorted colonels and lesser officers denounced civilian dictatorship, extolled the merits of the military, and proclaimed Mariño as superior chief of the province. Vargas and the vice-president were sent to La Guaira to await exile, but when Mariño entered Caracas a few days later only five or six citizens went out to meet him.[68] Meanwhile in the east Monagas, whom Páez described as 'the caudillo of the malcontents', predictably, 'proclaimed' against Vargas, and rebels also took over the naval base of Puerto Cabello, two points where the revolution dug in more deeply.

Páez was on his estate of San Pablo near Calabozo, about three days' march from the capital. As news and supporters reached him, he decided to come out of retirement and defend the constitution, drawing on resources from his own power base. 'I assembled the fifty men who happened to be on my ranch at the time, and we set out for the capital with the intention of collecting people from all the villages on the way. In Ortiz and Parapara I managed to recruit a number of local men.'[69] On the approaches to Caracas he was received with genuine enthusiasm as a hero of liberation, and once in occupation of the capital he made the appropriate political dispositions to restore constitutional government. According to Ker Porter, 'At day break on the morning of the 28th July, His Excellency entered Caracas at the head of about 500 men, composed of lancers from the plains and armed peasantry'. When the counter-revolution was successful, the constitutional forces were for the most part disbanded, 'and the soldier peasants allowed to return to their homes and agricultural duties'.[70] Puerto Cabello and the east held out longer, but by March 1836 'los facciosos' were defeated and pacification was complete.

The Revolution of the Reformists displayed no marks of a social or economic character, much less of popular support. It was a purely political event and treated as such by Páez. The leaders demanded a federal system of government; the restoration of military and ecclesiastical *fueros*; the establishment of Catholicism as the legal religion of

---

[68] Monagas to Ibarra, 27 July 1835, AGN, Caracas, Sec. Int. y Just., CIX, fos. 144–7, 170; Ker Porter to Palmerston, 14 July 1835, PRO FO 80/2; Parra-Pérez, *Mariño y las guerras civiles*, i. 372–412.

[69] Páez, *Autobiografía*, ii. 221–2.

[70] Ker Porter to Palmerston, 8 Aug. 1835, PRO, FO 80/2; Ker Porter to Palmerston, 12 Jan. 1836, FO 80/3; AGN, Caracas, Sec. Int. y Just., CIII, fos. 99, 111, 127, 243, 268.

the republic; and appointments for the patriots of independence. It was a prescription for the further caudillization of Venezuela. It was also a declaration against Páez personally, who was accused of working only for his own good: 'personal interest is the motive of all his actions'.[71] Yet the leaders emerged largely unscathed; some participants were imprisoned, and the exceptional death sentences were commuted to exile.[72] Mariño had his property confiscated, including his well-known coffee hacienda *El Paño*.[73] Some dangerous men were allowed to escape the net, and in April 1837 Colonel José Francisco Farfán, a llanero caudillo, and several other officers from the rebellion of 1835 raised a revolt of 'sambo ruffians', as Ker Porter described them, in the upper plains of Apure. The revolt was touched off by an attempt, under the *ley de azotes*, to administer a flogging to Farfán and his henchmen for rustling; they killed three judges and, promoting themselves from bandits to political rebels, demanded an end to authoritarian government. Again Páez had to take command of the security forces to defeat and scatter the band.[74]

In 1835 Páez returned power to the rightful president, Dr Vargas, who soon tired of office and resigned in 1836, to be replaced by General Carlos Soublette for the remainder of his term of office, that is until 1839. Páez continued to 'serve' the legitimate presidents, emerging from his estates to put down revolts when it was necessary and in general acting as the gendarme of the constitution. He was re-elected president in 1839 with 210 votes from the 221 provincial delegates, and governed until 1843, when Soublette succeeded him for the constitutional term 1843–7. Directly or indirectly Páez dominated Venezuelan government throughout these years. He recognized his limitations and surrounded himself by able ministers such as Santos Michelena, Andrés Narvarte, and Diego Bautista Urbaneja. Within the limits of a caudillo presidency, there was debate in Congress and discussion in the press; hence the description of this regime of 1830–47 as one of 'gobierno deliberativo'.

[71] Ibarra to Governor of Barcelona, 8 July 1835, AGN, Caracas, Sec. Int. y Just., CIX, fo. 450; J. S. Rodríguez to House of Representatives, 20 Feb. 1836, ibid. CXI, fo. 324.

[72] AGN, Caracas, Sec. Int. y Just., CXI, *passim*.

[73] 'Sobre el embargo de los bienes del General Santiago Mariño como Jefe de la revolución de reformas', AGN, Caracas, Sec. Int. y Just., CXI, fos. 176–90.

[74] Ker Porter to Palmerston, 16 June 1837, PRO, FO 80/5; *Ker Porter's Caracas Diary*, 28 Mar. 1837, 960; Valenilla Lanz, *Cesarismo Democrático*, 76–7; Matthews, *Rural Violence and Social Unrest in Venezuela*, 132–3.

In a formal sense, therefore, Venezuela was governed in these years by a constitutional regime which used force when it was necessary in its own defence but otherwise disposed of little military power. From 1830, in an attempt to remove what he regarded as an obstacle to economic growth, Páez sought to reduce the size of the regular army. A decree of the Congress of Valencia, 22 September 1830, fixed the army total at 2,553 men. By 1833 the regular army was reduced to 'three battalions of infantry, a supernumerary company of infantry, six companies of artillery, and one of cavalry'.[75] In January 1837 the armed forces (army and active militia) were less than 1,300; in 1840 the regular army numbered only 1,000.[76] By 1845 the armed forces consisted of a regular army of 371 and a militia of 465. As for law enforcement, reported O'Leary, 'The Police Force of the Republic amounts to 520; and its cost to about £16,500. This force is defective in numbers and organization.'[77] Even so, for some years military expenditure formed a large part of the budget. In 1831–2, out of a total ordinary expenditure of 1,137,000 pesos, 615,000 pesos or 54 per cent was allocated to defence (army and navy); in 1832–3, in a total budget of 1,169,000 pesos, defence received 689,000 or 58 per cent. In the following years defence spending oscillated between 50 and 60 per cent of the total budget. From 1837 it was down to 45 per cent and by 1845–6 to 23 per cent, with the treasury and internal government taking the lion's share.[78] That a caudillo should cut the defence budget precisely at a time when banditry and insurgency were increasing is only an apparent paradox. The principal centres of lawlessness were in the llanos, a cattle region which ceased to be a priority of Páez once he shifted his base of power and interest to the centre-north, where plantation agriculture dominated and the ruling coalition resided. As long as this region was secure, the llanos could look after themselves.

The llanos remained on the margin of the economy, people and property the prey of endemic banditry, with the situation further deteriorating from 1840. There was usually a close correlation between the level of lawlessness and the state of the economy. Hav-

[75] Ley de fuerza permanente para 1833, AGN, Caracas, Sec. Int. y Just., LXX, fos. 193–4.
[76] Presidencia de la República, *Las fuerzas armadas de Venezuela en el siglo XIX; Textos para su estudio* (12 vols., Caracas, 1963–71), vi. 54–6, 61–84, 330–1, 351; vii. 209.
[77] O'Leary to Palmerston, 22 Feb. 1841, PRO, FO 80/12.
[78] Pérez Vila, 'El Gobierno Deliberativo', 62–3.

ing done their best to neglect if not to obstruct the development of a regional cattle industry in the interior, the oligarchy of the centre-north then sought to supplement their plantation agriculture by penetrating the plains in search of livestock resources. The crisis of the plantation economy from about 1840 caused them to press harder on the llanos for alternative exports. This pressure provoked a reaction from the llaneros in defence of their lands and way of life, at the same time as politicians were cultivating them as a new support base.

Insurgency spread across the interior like sparks from a fire. In early 1844 the police chief of Pedroza in Barinas reported the operations of bandits and rustlers; he killed one chief, Eulogio Tapia, and arrested two bandits who confessed to a plan to assemble a larger group of bandits to attack villages in Barinas. The police chief requested reinforcements from the governor, who sent five soldiers and requested further assistance from the central government.[79] On 12 June 1844 the prison in the town of Cura was attacked and prisoners released by a party of about twenty to forty men 'of the lowest class of society'. Their number being thus increased they marauded around the valleys of Tuy and Aragua in the evident expectation of attracting disaffected guerrillas and marching on Caracas. The local authorities eventually reacted and dispersed them, but a further outbreak at Calabozo drew attention to a new dimension of insurgency through the political involvement of the opposition. A rising of more than 300 rebels in Lezama, Chaguaramos, under Colonel Centeno in October 1844 repudiated the government with the cry 'Long live the liberals! Death to the oligarchs!'[80] In the mountains of Tamanaco another band of forty men under Vidal Toro, combining robbery and political rebellion, made a determined effort to subvert the elections.[81] Guerrillas operating under the Rodríguez brothers and Pedro Aquino came to the fore in 1845–6 and spawned a number of sub-groups. In June 1846 in Sombrero a bandit group of thirty to forty men, well mounted and armed with guns as well as machetes, successfully attacked mule trains, travellers, and town houses, before disappearing into the hills. Drawing evidence from victims, officials reported: 'by

---

[79] Pablo González to Arévalo, 30 Jan. 1844, Arévalo to government, 1 Feb. 1844, AGN, Caracas, Sec. Int. y Just., CCXCIV, fos. 332–4.

[80] Chaguaramos, 18 Oct. 1844, AGN, Caracas, Sec. Int. y Just., CCCIX, fo. 164; Wilson to Aberdeen, 2 Aug. 1844, PRO, FO 80/26.

[81] Antonio Belisario, Chaguaramos, 14 Apr. 1846, Mariano Uztariz, 16 May 1846, AGN, Caracas, Sec. Int. y Just., CCCXXXII, fos. 2–3.

their conversation they belong to the so-called liberals, for they asked about that party in Caracas and spoke of Sr. Guzmán, with whom they are connected, and threatened death to a number of leading citizens in Sombrero and Calabozo'. Other bandit offshoots operating in groups of three, four, seven, and ten appeared suddenly at different haciendas on the same day, always demanding to see the proprietors and taking horses. During the 1850s an area of Apure province, Independencia, became a centre of notorious banditry. According to one local official the area had long been a 'fortress for famous bandits, such as Moreno, Virguez, Vargas, Barsos, and another hundred'. Bands of rustlers openly intimidated landowners, who opted for life as absentees, while merchants in the port of Nutrias bought up the illicit proceeds for export and in a sense legitimized the whole operation.[82]

These reports underlined two basic features of rural disorder. The connivance of landowners, merchants, and officials in rustling and contraband was a sign that they had abandoned the struggle for law and order and preferred to share in the profits of crime. Meanwhile the central government lacked the force and the will necesssary to police the vast regions of the eastern, central, and western llanos. Calabozo had a garrison of thirty, which could not be divided for distant pursuit of bandits and was handicapped by the reluctance of local people to give information. When security forces were available, they too lived off the land, often no better than bandits. Thus the lines between bandit and rebel, and between them and proprietors were blurred, and banditry became an accepted way of life, until it was so politicized that it could no longer be ignored. In 1846, as disorder seeped into the province of Caracas, the government took steps to increase the regular army and budgeted for a strength of 2,000. But by then the political and security situation was slipping out of its control. To fill the vacuum leaders like Páez had to call, not on the public sector, but on their own power base. In his long career Páez fulfilled both roles, in alliance and confrontation with the state.

Venezuela was not a military dictatorship, and unlike the *rosista* state in Argentina, the Venezuelan state did not employ terror as an instrument of policy. In these circumstances the informal power structure was all the more important. Real power was monopolized by

[82] Mariano Uztariz, Caracas, 2 July 1846, 6 July 1846, AGN, Caracas, Sec. Int. y Just., CCCXXXII, fos. 56–7, 64–5, 78; Juan G. Illas, 15 Feb. 1858, ibid. DCXV, fos. 103–4, 347–50.

the oligarchy, a term used at the time to describe that élite coalition of landowners, office-holders, and merchants which Páez had brought together in the late 1820s and which retained power from 1830 to 1847. They needed a strong president, or behind the president a caudillo, to represent their interests, keep the mob at bay, and deal with the provinces. While this was 'constitutional' government, it tended to perpetuate itself in power by excluding all its opponents from office and denying them liberty of the press. It controlled the judges, who were political appointments and served their masters, and who in turn denied a fair hearing to anyone with liberal tendencies. Juries for trial of libel were elected by the municipalities, who themselves were chosen by the electoral colleges, and as these were obviously in the hands of the dominant party, the juries appointed for trial of political libels consisted of political enemies of the accused.[83] The president-caudillo controlled the military governors of the provinces through a system of patronage and clientage and, if this did not produce obedience, through armed force assembled for the occasion from his own retainers and the regular army. Thus was Páez the gendarme of the conservative oligarchy.

It was obvious to all that Páez was the sovereign caudillo even when he was not the president. He demonstrated that a caudillo with economic assets and access to resources could raise an army to conquer power, or having abandoned formal power could still act as guardian of the law and return at the head of a movement to prevent the triumph of caudillo pretenders. This was the case in 1835 when he intervened in defence of Vargas, a weak president and not his own candidate. In their manifesto issued at Curaçao, the defeated military rebels asserted: 'Venezuela can never enjoy peace as long as General Páez is there, for if he is in power he converts the country into his own plaything, and if he is out of power he makes the government his instrument and constantly conspires to return to power. The result is that there is no possibility of a stable and secure system.'[84] Páez did in fact maintain stability, but his system eventually overreached itself.

In the 1840s political tension increased as the export economy ran into trouble and created problems for planters and government alike. About three-quarters of government revenue was derived from import duties, whose diminution in 1842–3 was about 10 per cent. This was

[83] Wilson to Aberdeen, 1 Mar. 1844, PRO, FO 80/25.
[84] Presidencia de la República, *Pensamiento político venezolano del siglo XIX*, xii. 200; Miguel Izard, 'Tanto pelear para terminar conversando', 42.

mainly due to the fall of the price of coffee in the European markets, and coffee accounted for almost half the value of Venezuelan exports.[85] As the liberals sought to make political capital out of the crisis, the conservatives began to flush out their opponents. There were four leading candidates for the presidency in 1846, a sign of continuing personalism rather than political pluralism and of a struggle between the two leading candidates, José Tadeo Monagas and Antonio Leocadio Guzmán. Various forms of electoral pressure and chicanery were practised by the government. Some observers believed that the oligarchy deliberately sought to incite its opponents into protest and rebellion, 'so as to afford an opportunity for crushing them under the semblance of upholding the Constitution and the Laws'.[86] They annulled votes, disqualified electors, and accomplished a variety of frauds, and by these means they did in fact provoke outbreaks of protest and rebellion throughout the country. These were again put down by General Páez and other pro-government caudillos, acting on behalf of the oligarchy, some of whom claimed that their estates had been pillaged and their personnel killed by liberal-inspired bandits.

The strategy was perfectly obvious to contemporary observers, who were also aware of the social implications of the campaign. Racial issues were rarely far from the surface. In 1844 the congressional elections alarmed some by the

selection for deputies of men whose personal character, intelligence and social position afford no guarantee of their independence. One of the deputies is a man of colour, by trade a carpenter, and without any personal qualifications to recommend him peculiarly for the trust. His election has been intended to conciliate the democratic spirit of the artisans and coloured population of Caracas. At Maracaibo a man of colour, by trade a silversmith, has for the same purposes on its own behalf been elected by the Liberal Party; and here it may not be out of place to remark that the election as senators and deputies of artisans and men of colour is not infrequent in Venezuela; and that a man of colour, of great personal merits and military services, is actually one of the members of the Council of State.[87]

To prolong its ascendancy the oligarchy, reported the British minister, 'is resorting to measures alike dangerous and immoral, including the propagation of the standard party cries of "a rising of the slaves", and a "War of Castes", for creating alarm and excitement'.[88] But

---

[85] Wilson to Aberdeen, 13 Mar. 1844, PRO, FO 80/25.
[86] Wilson to Palmerston, 19 Sept. 1846, PRO, FO 80/40.
[87] Wilson to Aberdeen, 22 Oct. 1844, PRO, FO 80/26.
[88] Wilson to Palmerston, 19 Sept. 1846, PRO, FO 80/40.

the opposition contributed to the commotion, and the inflammatory social language of the liberal leader Guzmán introduced a pseudo-revolutionary element into the conflict. As Páez himself recorded:

To attract a following they put it around that under the presidency of Sr. Antonio Leocadio Guzmán they would distribute the property and lands of the rich among the poor, that they would free the slaves, distribute the money of the Bank, and end national and municipal taxes. With a better educated people these inducements would have counted for nothing. But nothing was better calculated to win over ignorant people than to present so liberal a programme. Some unwary people heard the promises and imagined that rights of this kind ought to be won without delay, especially when the case was going to be decided by the vote of the majority in an election.[89]

Law and order deteriorated badly in 1846. Electoral fraud exceeded even normal conservative levels. Freedom of the press was denied to the opposition. And conservative caudillos such as Colonel Francisco Guerrero and General León Febres Cordero employed notorious violence against 'malcontents', bandits allegedly inspired by liberal agitators. The government began to increase the military establishment and to budget for higher security costs.

The Páez system worked effectively until the oligarchy itself produced a dissident from within its own ranks. In 1847 General José Tadeo Monagas was elected president, apparently as a creature of the oligarchy and a client of Páez, and a man whose inferior culture and abilities marked him out as a pliant instrument of his superiors. But Monagas was a wealthy rancher in his own right, headed a large network of clients in eastern Venezuela, and had shown opportunist tendencies in the past. Angel Quintero, confidant of Páez, described him as 'a man of the jungle, divorced from society and alien to politics'. The signs should have alerted Páez, whose job it was to identify rival caudillos, but he did not have the measure of Monagas and perhaps he had become complacent. He backed Monagas on his record of law enforcement in the east, as a kind of surrogate gendarme. As he subsequently said, 'It is absolutely certain that General José Tadeo Monagas owed his election as President to the influence of the people of order (*gente de orden*) and that I contributed a little to his election.' A classic understatement. Yet it was unrealistic to expect that the oligarchy could hold power unchallenged for ever:

In Spanish America political parties are rather banded together by ties of personal interests than combined for the establishment and practical working

---

[89] Páez, *Autobiografía*, ii. 384.

out of principles of government;... but the spirit of exclusiveness and persecution and the illegal and desperate measures adopted, especially of late, by the 'Oligarchy' to perpetuate their political ascendancy, have generated such a general sentiment of discontent and disaffection as compelled them in order to stifle public opinion and to crush all legitimate opposition, to have recourse to a large permanent increase of the military force and establishments, and to systematic means of intimidation and corruption, fatal to the interests of the country.[90]

Soon Monagas began to pursue an independent course, rejecting the political conventions of the time. He had a power base, a reputation, and a clientage of his own, and was known to look after his supporters. To escape from the tutelage of Páez he replaced the administration wished upon him by the oligarchy and in its place appointed his own creatures: Colonel José Felix Blanco, Rafael Acevedo, Colonel Francisco Mejia, whose political bias was towards the liberal party but whose primary allegiance was to the personal policy of the new president.

At this point the oligarchy was alerted and urged Páez to overthrow Monagas and if necessary establish a dictatorship. But in the nature of caudillo politics this was not so easy and during the following decades Venezuela was torn between the government of the Monagas family and the various attempts of Páez to destroy it. In the course of these struggles the Monagas did not hesitate to play the socio-racial card, and on more than one occasion threatened to arm the lower sectors and the blacks against the white oligarchy, if Páez persisted. In 1854 the British minister referred to the threats of José Gregorio Monagas to deliver Caracas 'into the hands of the lower classes of the coloured population to be plundered and ransacked', if General Páez or his supporters approached, and he concluded that 'Rosas was a lamb compared to this monster'.[91]

In truth the *rosista* state was more militarized, more violent, and in the final analysis more vulnerable than the caudillo state in Venezuela. But in both cases the danger to the stability of the caudillo system came from struggles within the élite rather than attacks from below. This did not eliminate the possibility of a populist caudillo who might rise to challenge the necessary gendarme. Caudillos could be re-

---

[90] Angel Quintero cited by Castillo Blomquist, *José Tadeo Monagas*, 44, 53–4; Páez to Gonzalo Peoli, New York, 24 June 1867, ANH, Caracas, Páez Correspondencia, XII, 12, fo. 2; Wilson to Palmerston, 3 Apr. 1847, 20 May 1847, PRO, FO 80/45.
[91] Bingham to Clarendon, 5 Aug. 1854, PRO, FO 80/111.

cruited by royalists, liberators, secessionists, and élites. Theoretically they could also be adopted by the popular sectors. Venezuela nominated one candidate.

7. Challenge from Behind

Ezequiel Zamora was born (1 February 1817) to a patriot family of small ranchers in Calabozo, whites who lost lives and property in the republican cause but did not belong to the creole élite. He received an elementary education in Caracas in the years after independence, but was mainly self-taught and acquired most of his knowledge from his own reading. At the age of twenty-one he established himself in Villa de Cura as a dealer in cattle and other agricultural goods, buying and selling the products of haciendas and *hatos*. He began as a small merchant, but did not hesitate to invoke the law of 10 April 1834 to exact repayments from indebted landowners, even as far as liquidation of their assets. By 1846 he had capital of 15,000 pesos.[92] While Zamora was generous to the poor, he was not a friend of criminals; as a loyal lieutenant of militia he acted for the government in pursuing bandits and rebels. During the revolt of 1844, when political dissidents freed prisoners from the gaol of Villa de Cura to augment a group of bandits, vagrants, and peons, and in the name of the liberal party launched a crude and disorderly attack on government establishments, Zamora aligned with the local authorities in defence of law and order.[93] While he did not glory in violence, he could be ruthless when necessary, as the royalist turned bandit Centeno learnt to his cost:

The ringleaders of the popular commotion within the canton of Orituco having refused to lay down their arms and to surrender themselves up for trial, the main body of the rioters to the number of about 500 was on the 8th instance attacked and defeated by General Zamora with some companies of provincial militia; the two ringleaders, Col. Centeno and Captain Alvarado amongst others, being killed in the encounter.[94]

But Zamora was not unaffected by the conditions which bred banditry. Soon this tall, thin, sharp-featured merchant with a black

[92] Adolfo Rodríguez, *Exequiel Zamora* (Caracas, 1977), 38, 51.
[93] Matthews, *Rural Violence and Social Unrest in Venezuela*, 161.
[94] Wilson to Aberdeen, 16 Nov. 1844, PRO, FO 80/26.

moustache and serious expression, was a familiar figure in the Valleys of Aragua and surrounding plains, whose people he came to know and interests to serve.[95] When he joined the *guzmancista* liberals in 1840 he added a new dimension to political protest.

The liberal programme in Venezuela was not one of revolutionary change, but it contained three policies which distinguished it from that of the oligarchy: it promised to abolish the law of 10 April 1834 and free planters from the moneylenders; it was sharply critical of the National Bank for its monopoly and privileges; and it appeared to favour, though obscurely, the interests of domestic industry. Agriculturalists, whom the government had favoured so much, and artisans, whom they had so neglected, united in opposition to Soublette and his mentor Pácz in the decisive years 1845–6. The plight of small and medium planters, caught between the collapse of the market and the demands of their creditors, made them the natural supporters of the liberal opposition to the oligarchy, among whose wealthy merchants and large hacendados the creditors were to be found. The Agricultural Society of Caracas demanded 'immediate and effective aid' to planters not as a privilege but as a reprieve to the whole economy.[96] The liberals, too, were landowners, though they were able to identify with small farmers and even to link with popular insurgency in the llanos. Guzmán was a substantial proprietor, owner of six haciendas of coffee and sugar, three houses, a store, and various slaves, the whole worth some 107,000 pesos.[97] He was by no means a social revolutionary, but a skilful demagogue who could give the masses an illusion of reform without undermining Venezuelan institutions. In the pages of his weekly, *El Venezolano*, he used the most violent language and vituperation, but it was pure propaganda, devoid of social and economic analysis and of specific policies. The liberals proclaimed 'Tierras y hombres libres', but this was a slogan not a programme; the object was not to change society but to recruit a political following and gain power.

While Zamora distanced himself from the rebellion of 1844, possibly seeing it as the mere exploitation of popular forces by élite

[95] Federico Brito Figueroa, *Tiempo de Ezequiel Zamora* (Caracas, 1974), 15–34.

[96] Agricultural Society of Caracas to President of Republic, 20 Nov. 1843, AGN, Caracas, Sec. Int. y Just., CCLXXXVIII, fo. 2; Pérez Vila, 'El Gobierno Deliberativo', 71–88; and see Chap. 4, sect. 6.

[97] Brito Figueroa, *Tiempo de Ezequiel Zamora*, 47 n. 21; Matthews, *Rural Violence and Social Unrest in Venezuela*, 151–3.

dissidents, he had been active on the radical side of the liberal movement since 1840, combining his merchant activities in Villa de Cura with efforts to raise political consciousness among the rural population of the Valleys of Aragua and the Llanos of Guárico, an area of large plantations owned by a wealthy few, among them Páez himself, and worked by peons and slaves who were ready recipients of liberal propaganda. Zamora denounced slavery, land concentration, and the harsh agrarian laws:

God made all men equal in body and soul. So why should a bunch of thieves and scoundrels be able to live off the labour of the poor, especially of those whose skin is black? When God made the world he distributed water in common, and sun and land. So why have the *godos* seized the best lands, woods, and water supplies, which are really the property of the people?[98]

It was crude and simple, but effective enough for the audience he met on his rounds of business and politics. He founded the Liberal Society of Villa de Cura, not an urban or intellectual group but a network of protest linking hundreds of peons. Its ideas could be summarized as land and liberty for the people, popular elections, alternating government, and an end to the oligarchy. It was a vague and inchoate programme, lacking specific proposals, but it sounded more radical than the political liberalism of Caracas, and it frightened conservatives. As it spread from Villa de Cura to the Sierra de Córdoba and zones near the Lago de Valencia, so it attracted outlaws and their caudillos, dissident peasants, and fugitive slaves. Remembering Boves, the oligarchs and moderate liberals distrusted Zamora and his movement as dangerous enemies of existing society and property, especially during the economic crisis of 1840–5 when agriculture experienced conditions of depression which, as Páez said, 'favoured agitations promoted by the rebellious'.[99]

Zamora was a conspicuous candidate for Villa de Cura in the elections for the provincial assembly in 1846, and on a platform of land distribution to peons and tenant farmers he fought a more radical campaign than the liberals in Caracas. His reputation, programme, and associates alarmed local landowners, merchants, and politicians, and the parish assembly of Cura accused him of electoral malpractice, annulled his campaign, and deprived him of voting rights.[100] Zamora reacted angrily and was promptly arrested; and

---

[98] Quoted by Brito Figueroa, *Tiempo de Ezequiel Zamora*, 55–6.
[99] Páez, *Autobiografía*, ii. 381.
[100] Brito Figueroa, *Tiempo de Ezequiel Zamora*, 82–3.

although he was acquitted and freed the experience convinced him that political action was not enough. He demonstrated his new faith in August 1846 when a conciliatory meeting between Páez and Guzmán arranged by moderate mediators was sabotaged by violence. As Guzmán travelled to the conference, gathering some 4,000 followers along the way and an armed 'escort' led by Zamora, liberal insurgents in the llanos sought to force the pace of events. Conditions were already unstable. The Rodríguez band, a mixture of pure bandits and political dissidents, eluded the authorities throughout 1845–6, spreading demands for an end to slavery, land monopoly, and municipal taxes. In April 1846 there was a rising of blacks in the Valleys of Río Chico, said to be preparing 'a revolution' to gain freedom for all blacks and slaves; on 3 May a group of these rebels fired on a patrol and again they appeared to be linked to liberal politics. For some months government officials reported an increasing militancy by armed bands hostile to the government, an unwillingness of the people to provide intelligence or co-operate with the authorities, and a renewed sense of alarm among people of property at the mounting disorder and insecurity. 'It is among the proletarian class, everywhere the most numerous, that the fatal contagion of anarchy has most taken hold; local authorities have no confidence at all in the reserve militia to maintain security'.[101] As Páez and Guzmán rode with their escorts to Maracay, revolution was in the air.

On 1 September the peasant caudillo Francisco José Rangel, known as 'el Indio', assembled some 300 peons, slaves, and ex-slaves, and led them out in revolt; shouting 'Land and free men!', they planned to link up with other insurgents in the llanos, march on Maracay and from there to Caracas, where they would place Guzmán in power. First they occupied nearby haciendas, notably that of Yuma, property of one of Páez's political associates, Angel Quintero; there they killed the manager, freed the slaves, and burned the property titles. This was the model: estates of the oligarchy were attacked, overseers killed, and property looted. Rangel and many of his followers had been expelled from their farms and constituencies, and they wanted insurrection not interviews. Zamora too rejected the idea of conference and compromise, and offered his arms to Guzmán

---

[101] Report of War Ministry, 22 July 1846, AGN, Caracas, Sec. Int. y Just., CCCXXVII, fos. 80–3; see also AGN, Caracas, Sec. Int. y Just., CCCXXXII, fos. 116–27; Wilson to Palmerston, 19 Sept. 1846, PRO, FO 80/40; Matthews, *Rural Violence and Social Unrest in Venezuela*, 50–51.

to defeat the oligarchy and finish with Páez.[102] When Guzmán failed to respond, Zamora took to the hills and, with other rural caudillos, recruited hacienda peons, landless peasants, and fugitive slaves, armed them with shotguns, machetes, lances, and clubs, and began a war of guerrillas across the llanos, determined 'to cast off the yoke of the discredited oligarchy and to gain at last the great conquests which were promised by independence'.[103]

Zamora joined forces with Rangel in the Valley of Manuare in early September. It was a meeting of civilization and barbarism, in which 'the Indian', naked from the waist up, carrying in his huge hands an ancient gun, and wearing his ferocity like a guerrilla's badge, submitted force to reason. Zamora recorded that 'Rangel turned up one afternoon with a few men, seven or eight perhaps, and offered me a larger band which he had assembled; I received from him at that meeting a number of "vivas" recognizing me as a caudillo of the liberal party.'[104] Rangel and his 'muchachos' elected Zamora general, and he in turn made Rangel a colonel. Zamora was the expert in procuring arms and supplies, most of them plundered from estates. Recruits were found among landless peons, *jornaleros*, fugitive slaves, escaped convicts, and a few ruined planters, many of them already enlisted by minor caudillos. He established links with a network of pro-liberal chiefs—Calvareño, Aquino, Aguado, the Echeandía brothers, Medrano, El Agachado—and aimed to direct and co-ordinate all the rebel factions between Guárico and Aragua, to turn bandits into soldiers, and to incorporate them in the Army of the Sovereign People, under a basic policy of war on the oligarchy, popular elections, land, and freedom.[105]

Zamora called his people to arms with a denunciation of the oligarchs and the government of Soublette: 'Friends! Tomorrow morning at 8 o'clock we march with the Liberal Army of Guzmán to take the liberal town of San Francisco, and there I will cry, Long live freedom! Long live the Sovereign People! Long live Guzmán! Down with any Oligarch who opposes us, for he will pay with his miserable life, and have his head cut off.'[106] In the square of San Francisco de

---

[102] Brito Figueroa, *Tiempo de Ezequiel Zamora*, 95–6.
[103] Quoted ibid. 122.
[104] Quoted by Rodríguez, *Zamora*, 95.
[105] Brito Figueroa, *Tiempo de Ezequiel Zamora*, 123–5.
[106] Ezequiel Zamora, Jefe del Pueblo Soberano, Canton de Corralitos, 19 Sept. 1846, AGN, Caracas, Sec. Int. y Just., CCCXXXII, fo. 102; Rodríguez, *Zamora*, 97, 103.

Tiznados he addressed his followers: 'We fight to give a better deal
to the poor . . . the poor have nothing to fear, nothing to lose; let the
oligarchs tremble, for there will be neither rich nor poor, the land is
free and for all.' Again he announced war against the government of
Soublette, and threatened decapitation of their opponents. Thus
within a few months a respectable provincial merchant had thrown in
his lot with the most vicious bandoleros of the llanos, Indians, *mulatos*,
blacks, men to whom liberals and oligarchs all looked the same and
who were more interested in plunder than policy. Zamora's policy in
the event was lacking equally in precision and radicalism: to defend
the Constitution of 1830, 'and to make the situation of the poor
happier'. His military power too was unimpressive. The government
had responded promptly to the insurrection, mobilized the regular
army and militia, increased the military budget, and named Páez
general-in-chief of the army. Rangel's forces were no match for
regular troops under Colonel Francisco Guerrero, veteran of the war
of independence, and they were destroyed in a particularly bloody
battle at Laguna de Piedra, where, as Guerrero reported, 'no prisoners were taken'.[107] Zamora escaped with Rangel and other chiefs
to the mountains of Las Mulas. But he was not content to be a
guerrilla on the run. He wanted to command an army and win a war.

After an underground visit to Caracas to obtain news and support,
Zamora regrouped his forces in November 1846 and with Rangel
reshaped the Army of the Sovereign People into a force which at its
peak totalled some 1,300 men. Páez now sent his protégé, Colonel
Dionisio Cisneros, to seek and destroy the rebel army. But the old
guerrilla turned gendarme was over-estimated and under-motivated,
and the rebels won the battle of Los Bagres (28 November 1846)
near Villa de Cura, and then the battle of La Culebra (24 February
1847). Their confidence restored from these victories in the plains,
the rebels seemed poised to attack coastal towns, and then overreached themselves. Their own tactics were unnecessarily bloody; in
La Culebra Rangel cut out the tongue of an informer and burnt
down the house of a conservative. It became clear that the cry of land
for the landless and the relentless plunder of property were targeted
primarily on government supporters, while liberal haciendas remained immune; and the call for slave freedom was linked to the

---

[107] Wilson to Palmerston, 21 Oct. 1846, PRO, FO 80/40; Brito Figueroa, *Tiempo
de Ezequiel Zamora*, 128.

need for recruits, again from conservative haciendas. The government forces reacted accordingly. An army commander advised that total destruction of the guerrillas could only be achieved by a policy of terror against the rural population, 'burning all the farms and houses and turning out the families', otherwise the guerrillas would have access to recruits and supplies as soon as the security forces left.[108] Cisneros was shot for dereliction of duty, which 'has at least put an end to the career of a sanguinary partisan leader, who for years was the scourge of society under the pretext of upholding the cause of Spain'.[109] Superior numbers and experience eventually told in favour of the government forces, and the rebel army was defeated at the pass of Pagüita in the llanos of Caracas on 1 March 1847, when both sides suffered heavy losses. Rangel was mortally wounded and his head delivered to the capital in brine. Zamora fled to the interior where he was eventually captured. In the wake of the rebellion the government established 'the peace of the gallows'.

March 1847, the month of Zamora's defeat, was also important for other events. On 1 March José Tadeo Monagas became president; fifteen days later he expressed his disgust at the fanaticism of the conservatives when he was sent the head of Indio Rangel, calling the deed *una barbaridad*.[110] At his trial Zamora declared to his interrogators: 'I believed that a government which has broken the law ought to be restrained by force . . . from what I read in the newspapers I concluded that there was more than sufficient reason to persuade me to make the revolution without knowing a caudillo, because I believed that everyone should rise in mass against oppressive rulers'. As for his political objectives: 'I attacked the government for the reasons I have just given. . . . I frequently issued serious warnings to my troops not to commit any criminal act, and I made them realize that such abominable and antisocial conduct was only fit for Cisneros.'[111] These were the words of a radical, not a revolutionary. From the beginning of the rebellion until his capture Zamora's programme contained no hint of social revolution. Rangel, it is true, set out not only to defeat the oligarchs but to confiscate land and property and distribute them to the poor. When Zamora's captors interrogated him

---

[108] Quoted by Brito Figueroa, *Tiempo de Ezequiel Zamora*, 146.
[109] Wilson to Palmerston, 3 Apr. 1847, PRO, FO 80/45.
[110] Rodríguez, *Zamora*, 129; Castillo Blomquist, *José Tadeo Monagas*, 69.
[111] Quoted by Brito Figueroa, *Tiempo de Ezequiel Zamora*, 170, 176; Matthews, *Rural Violence and Social Unrest in Venezuela*, 107–8.

on this point, he specifically denied that this was his intention, admitting that it may have been that of Rangel.[112] Condemned for conspiracy and other crimes, he was sentenced to death on 27 July 1847, confirmed by the Supreme Court on 28 October. Monagas commuted the death sentence to imprisonment, but Zamora escaped and took refuge in a friendly hacienda outside Caracas. From then his political fortunes changed. On 24 January 1848 a mob violently attacked the conservative Congress and triggered off a revolt by Páez, still the gendarme of the oligarchy but no longer that of the government. As Monagas began to summon his clients, he commissioned Zamora in the national army.

Zamora provoked contradictory responses, most of them exaggerated. His demands for social reform, land distribution, abolition of slavery, and free government, together with his formation of a rebel army, earned him a support base even among peasants who stayed at home; the élite branded him a revolutionary. Yet by 1849 Zamora had achieved little on behalf of the oppressed. At the age of thirty-two he had spent three years in political activity, a little less in military action to overthrow the government of Soublette, two in prison charged with assassination, and over a year serving Monagas in the western llanos, a minor caudillo in the service of the president. During the revolution no land was appropriated, and if property was plundered it was for the rebels not for the poor. He joined the resistance to the conservative invasion of 1849, and when Páez was defeated it was Zamora, his escort, who saved his life to hand him over to justice. From 1853 he was governor of Guayana in Ciudad Bolívar, where he received the decree abolishing slavery (25 March 1854) with no more ardour than he received other decrees.[113]

In serving Monagas, Zamora served a president whose rule, behind the façade of the constitution, was as informal and personalist as that of any other caudillo. As an important rancher, Monagas commanded a power base different from that of the coastal oligarchy but no less effective; he had nothing to lose in cancelling the much-maligned credit law in 1848 and in declaring a moratorium on debt repayment for the benefit of indebted planters, and much to gain in extending his constituency. So his was an orthodox caudillism. He established his family, rewarded his supporters, and cultivated his clients. He purged the army and militia of Páez officers and reorganized them in

---

[112] Rodríguez, *Zamora*, 117–18.   [113] Ibid. 199.

his own image. He reinforced his power base by commuting death sentences on liberals and rebels, and by judicious use of land grants. In 1848–57 55 per cent of all public land distributed was concentrated in ten concessions, of a size which no poor farmer could afford. The Monagas family received vast concessions in Barcelona, Cumaná, and Guárico amounting to 11.6 per cent of all land alienated; the friends and cronies of the president also received large land grants in eastern Venezuela.[114]

Páez, therefore, was not the only gendarme. Monagas, demagogue though he was, fulfilled a similar role, serving other political allies, confiscating a different set of properties—including some of Páez—and building up a different base of support, but basically maintaining the system. Meanwhile insecurity in the llanos continued undiminished. In the years around 1850 the nucleus of rural rebels in the llanos of Apure, Barinas, and Portuguesa formed by the so-called Indian faction of Guanarito, consisted of a number of genuine Indians but also of fugitives from economic and social adversity, ex-slaves, landless peons, bankrupt traders, whose war cries were 'We are all equal! Down with the reactionaries! Property in common! A country for the Indians!'[115] They were called *proletarios* by the conservative press, and operated out of highland hideouts under petty caudillos to link up with radical groups in the towns of the plains. The most important of these groups, called the *Club maldito* by its enemies, was active in Puerto Nutrias under the leadership of Padre Ramírez, an unfrocked priest of Guanarito. The government sent out expeditionary forces from Ciudad Bolívar and San Fernando de Apure, and finally established a military post in Villa de Guanarito, whose political chief reported that this was insufficient 'to control the rebellion throughout the llanos supported as it is by inhabitants of different ages with the cry "we are all equal, the lands are common", a programme which attracts all the rebel and hungry proletarians'.[116] Conditions of this kind were common throughout rural Venezuela. Landowners slept uneasily in their beds or preferred to live in Caracas; country roads were dangerous; and travellers often had to pay protection money to bandits or rebels, if they were lucky enough to escape with their lives. The élites still needed a gendarme.

[114] *Materiales. . . Enajenación y arrendamiento de tierras baldías*, vol. i, pp. lxv–lxviii, 571–84, 550–3; Castillo Blomquist, *José Tadeo Monagas*, 94–5, 176–7.
[115] Brito Figueroa, *Tiempo de Ezequiel Zamora*, 268.
[116] Quoted ibid. 269.

Political conflict in Caracas and social turmoil in the llanos were breeding grounds for caudillo warfare, and this erupted with great ferocity in 1858. The dominant idea of Zamora in the Federal War seemed to be political rather than social. His proclamation of 29 March 1859 to people and soldiers called for 'Equality between Venezuelans, the rule of the majority, the true Republic, Federation'. In a speech in the main square of Araure on 6 April 1859 he promised to be in Caracas within the year and, as in 1846, he spoke of the need 'to confiscate lands and distribute them, for the land belongs to no one, it belongs to everyone', but before this could be done it was necessary 'to make the revolution'.[117] He was killed in battle in 1860 before he could fulfil the promise. His words remained the words of a politician, and the leading caudillos remained gendarmes of the élite, not makers of a revolution.

8. *Caudillos and* Campesinos *in Mexico*

In Mexico no less than elsewhere the élites were terrified by social anarchy. The time of insurgency, when major caudillos unleashed violent revolution and minor caudillos exploited it, remained a painful memory for many years to come. Hidalgo's entry into Guadalajara left a vivid impression of revolution in action: he freed slaves, abolished tribute, and redistributed land. He proposed to restore lands belonging to Indian communities, whether these had been rented out to estates or simply usurped by them. Fears and expectations were raised in equal measure. Yet the truth was not so alarming. Most of the Bajío insurgents were estate peons without community land.[118] Before the revolution Hidalgo had purchased the hacienda of Jaripes and some of his fellow rebels were owners of large estates. As proprietors they were not proposing a total redistribution of land. The social policy of Morelos was also basically moderate. He wanted to improve Indian status, protect Indian funds, and restore Indian community land. But he promised no redistribution of property and he said little about hacienda peons; he could hardly do so when his

---

[117] Quoted ibid. 313, 321–2.
[118] Hugh M. Hamill, Jr., *The Hidalgo Revolt: Prelude to Mexican Independence* (Gainesville, Fla., 1966), 136; Tutino, *From Insurrection to Revolution in Mexico*, 134–7 (on Hidalgo), 187–9 (on Morelos).

closest supporters Galeana and Bravo were large landowners. For creole patriots the agrarian problem would be resolved by simple restoration of lands to Indian communities; this would also synchronize with insurgency by placating Indians and castes and hitting *peninsulares*. Even so, the majority of *campesinos* preferred to stay at home; Morelos could not raise a great army and guerrilla warfare in isolated regions was virtually his only option, a type of warfare which directly damaged estates and placed creole lives at risk.

Moderation in policy, violence in action, this was a fatal mixture. In releasing social forces, inflaming feuds, and creating conditions of race war, Hidalgo and Morelos caused a great fear. Minor caudillos like Albino García who aroused pent-up peasant fury without compensatory political aims or social restraint were regarded by creoles of all classes as outright terrorists, against whom they needed strong and prompt protection. In this context Iturbide arrived as a gendarme, stronger than the rest, and capable of providing political leadership and internal security.

Independent Mexico was not entirely empty of social change or of propensity for violence. Hacendados were badly hit by the effects of war and depression, and many had to break up their estates and sell land to survive. Their demand for cheap labour was all the more insistent. Indian communities now faced greater creole aggression for land. As Tadeo Ortiz, associate of Morelos, wrote: 'The Indian population of New Spain has lost rather than gained from the revolution; they have exchanged ancient rights for new privileges, which are less secure'. And José Joaquín Fernández de Lizardi observed that 'there are rich landowners who have ten, twelve and more haciendas, and some which cannot be traversed in four days, while millions of people do not have a few inches of land of their own'. The agrarian system continued to be weighted in favour of great landowners: 'A rich man takes possession of all the land round a village and imposes his own law there, so that the dependent inhabitants are forced by necessity to enter into tenancies and other arrangements under highly unfavourable conditions.'[119] *Campesinos* were held dependent either by semi-servile rentals paid in labour or by debt peonage. Hacienda peons received only one peso a week and a small ration of maize and

[119] Quoted by Jean Meyer, *Problemas campesinos y revueltas agrarias (1821–1910)* (Mexico, 1973), 39, 40; Javier Ocampo, *Las ideas de un día: El pueblo mexicano ante la consumación de su Independencia* (Mexico, 1969), 259; on social relations in rural Mexico after independence see Tutino, *From Insurrection to Revolution in Mexico*, 226–30.

beans. Social relations deteriorated, between communities and estates, tenant farmers and hacendados, peons and their employers.

Law and order were threatened on two fronts, by bandits and by peasant rebels, and the caudillos were expected to react to both. Banditry was part of the infrastructure of Mexico, a preferred way of life by social outcasts, failures, and delinquents, a short cut to wealth, an informal method of trade and transit. Bandits preyed not only or even mainly on remote routes but on the highways between commercial centres. The road from Mexico City to Puebla and Veracruz was a constant scene of ambush and plunder in the 1830s and 1840s. In 1844–5 the American minister was robbed twice in eight months on the road from Puebla to the capital. A number of British officials suffered the same fate near Puebla. 'On Saturday last a party of arrieros, or carriers, with an escort of twenty Dragoons, were attacked within a few leagues of Mexico by a band of fifty men, all well mounted and armed, who took off all the property with which the arrieros were charged, the escort having one and all run away'. The robbers were well known to the authorities and apparently operated with impunity within a mile of the residence of General Inclán, Commandant General of the Puebla district.[120] Banditry was an irritant but not a priority of the government. Peasant rebellion was another matter.

The Mexican ruling élite lost its unity at independence, as land, mining, and commerce disintegrated into separate and sometimes rival social groups. Although not united in their interests, they tended to present a common front to social disorder. As protest tended to be regionally based, so the central government left it to the interest groups in the regions to resolve. In March 1830 Vicente Guerrero and Juan Alvarez led the south in a rebellion centred on the Costa Grande, riding out from their haciendas and calling on their Indian followers to fight for their rights against the *gente de razón*. The overtly populist and racist character of the rebellion masked a basically political objective, to overthrow the government of Bustamante and restore Guerrero to power. And the rebels did not raise the whole of the south. The government forces were placed under the command of another regional caudillo, Nicolás Bravo, whose efforts against his rivals were eventually rewarded when Guerrero was captured, tried

---

[120] Bankhead to Aberdeen, 30 May 1845, PRO, FO 50/185, fos. 149–56. See also Paul J. Vanderwood, 'Nineteenth-Century Mexico's Profiteering Bandits', 11–31.

for crimes against the state, and executed in February 1831.[121] Alamán said that the execution of Guerrero saved Mexico from dissolution. No one spoke too much of race war, but the Mexican élites slept more peacefully after the elimination of Guerrero.

The enforcement of rural security was made easier by divisions within the peasant ranks. Differing in their economic functions, the various rural groups were an amorphous mass consisting of hacienda peons, hired labourers, sharecroppers, squatters, tenant farmers, and owners of small farms. Peasant movements differed from each other socially, economically, and by region, though all showed a common discontent against the agrarian system and in some cases attracted allies from other social groups hoping to direct or manipulate rural agitation for political purposes.[122] The rebellion of Olarte in Papantla, Veracruz, illustrated a number of these features. A conjunction of grievances needed only the hand of a leader to bring them to life. The landowners of the region had invaded Indian community lands for cattle grazing. The Indians themselves had been accused by customs officials of arms smuggling. And the Bishop of Puebla had prohibited Indian celebrations in Holy Week. Leadership arrived in the person of Mariano Olarte, who in 1832 had fought the government of Bustamante and been promoted to lieutenant colonel by Santa Anna. From then on he was undisputed chief of a large part of Veracruz. He used his power to protect Indians from abuses and exactions, and was known as 'padre del pueblo'. Soon he led a large Indian rebellion, at first for essentially peasant objectives, then invoking national politics with a demand for the restoration of 'the representative, popular, and federal regime'. Olarte fought a guerrilla war, and so was difficult to overcome. But his own death at the hands of government troops and the surrender of the sub-chiefs brought the rebellion to an end in 1838.[123] Further sporadic Indian outbreaks in the state of Veracruz continued in 1845-9, with the aim of restoring their status as owners of land instead of as mere tenants.

Santa Anna, caudillo of Veracruz, remained aloof from all these movements. His own *clientela* came from the upper sectors and it was with their interests that he identified. His representations on behalf of the cotton and tobacco growers of Veracruz were made for planters not for peons. His civilian support base was reinforced by a number

[121] Green, *The Mexican Republic*, 205-9.
[122] Reina, *Las rebeliones campesinas en México*, 15-16.
[123] Ibid. 325-33.

of reliable friends in the higher bureaucracy. Support from land-owners, clergy, and *agiotistas*, groups who possessed means and in-fluence of their own, was less secure, depending on what he could do for them at any given time. For military action he could draw on his own hacienda peons, supplemented by *jarochos* from the rural popula-tion of Veracruz, and the local militia. But his principal base of power was rooted in the regular army, and the military in turn looked to him for patronage and promotion, usually not in vain. It was Santa Anna's ability to recruit, assemble, and motivate the military to meet par-ticular crises that preserved his reputation with the politicians and explains their repeated readiness to forget the past and recall him to power. Santa Anna was regarded as the last resort against anarchy, the ultimate caudillo, the necessary gendarme. As such he preserved himself for national enterprises, leaving peasant rebels to the atten-tion of regional caudillos. A test of his attitude and tactics occurred in 1842.

In Guerrero hacienda expansion pressed on the lands of the Indian communities, disputing their rights, expropriating land, and divert-ing water supply. Once expropriated, the Indians were forced into tenancies, and exorbitant rents became another grievance. The Guerrero Indians rose in early 1842, resisted the hacendados, and repudiated government attempts to pacify them. Military action made it worse, and the rebels repaid violence with violence. Santa Anna requested Alvarez, the caudillo of the south, to intervene: 'I am annoyed to see that a number of Indian pueblos on the Pacific coast have revolted on the most ridiculous pretexts, and I am surprised that you, who rightly enjoy so much prestige among them, have not used your influence to make them lay down their arms and restore peace to those valuable regions'.[124] Alvarez, a caudillo of rural origins whose influence among Indians and *campesinos* was derived from his overt sympathy with their interests, was an obvious choice for de-legated power. On this occasion he persuaded the Indians to return home, but once they demobilized they were overwhelmed by govern-ment forces. Alvarez proposed, more positively, that Indian grievances should be the subject of a legal judgment based on property titles. As this would tend to favour the Indians Santa Anna refused, and instead offered an amnesty. This took the impetus out of the re-bellion, and the Indians retired in the mistaken belief that their

[124] Santa Anna to Alvarez, 18 Mar. 1842, ibid. 86–7, 91.

property rights would be investigated. A similar peasant rising took place in 1848–9 in northern Morelos; haciendas were invaded to recover communal lands by force, in this case with the connivance of troops of the National Guard. Again it was repressed without difficulty.[125]

The *indulto* offered by Santa Anna in 1842 meant little to the Indians when they found that legal investigation of titles was not to take place. Thus land grievances, compounded by a capitation tax, provoked a further uprising; numerous districts in Morelos rose in a movement which soon spread from Guerrero into Oaxaca. Alvarez was accused by the authorities of fomenting renewed rebellion by offering the Indians land and suppression of taxes. The position of the southern caudillo, in fact, was ambiguous; he manipulated the rebels in the federalist interest and as a support base for his regional power, exploiting the fact that the rebels cried 'Death to the despot General Santa Anna!' The government, caught between the Indian demand for land restitution and the pressure of the hacendados for protection, opted for a military solution. Troops were sent in, chieftains were killed. This eventually crushed the rebellion of 1842 and another in 1844.[126] The Indians had no real leadership outside their own chieftains, while the hacendados had the government on their side. Alvarez, a landowner himself, offered sympathy but not support, preferring to exploit peasant discontent as a lever in his regional push against Santa Anna. Alvarez told the Indians that their cause was just but not their methods, for there were laws and institutions to which they could appeal; meanwhile they should join the alliance against the tyrant Santa Anna who was the cause of all Mexico's ills. Thus the caudillo of the *campesinos* simultaneously cultivated his constituency and preserved his political legitimacy.

The Mexican caudillos, national and regional, made few concessions to Indian rebels and peasant protesters. They either repressed them, in the case of Santa Anna, or manipulated them, in the case of Alvarez. As landowners themselves they were part of the prevailing structure of power. On basic issues of land concentration, peasant grievances, and Indian rights they stood firmly on the side of the hacendados in defence of property and security. In a period of expanding tenant production the insecurity of hacienda tenants at

[125] Ibid. 157–60.
[126] Ibid. 92–8, 109, 115–16.

the mercy of exploiting landlords became the latest in the long list of peasant grievances. In growing conflict between villagers and hacendados, as in the region of Chalco, the authorities sanctioned force against rural violence. And they were not slow to play the race card. In 1848, when the peasants of San Juan Teotihuacan and Otumba in the state of Mexico rose against the 'whites', the government treated it as a 'war of castes', though in fact it was an attempt by Indian communities under their priests to recover land lost to the haciendas.[127] Repression became a substitute for reform.

The rural crisis worsened as a consequence of the American war of 1847, when peasants suffered from land devastation, harsher demands from their masters, and heavier exactions from the state. The war administered a great shock to Mexico's social order. Civil conflict had opened the gates to the American invaders and then prevented Mexico from resisting the enemy from without. The war in turn encouraged further social disorder and opened the way to what the élite regarded as the enemy within. There were three distinct areas of conflict. In the south a full-scale caste war erupted in July 1847 when thousands of Mayas rose in rebellion in Yucatán demanding land rights and lower taxes; and within a short time they were giving the whites a terrible lesson in terror and retribution. In the north Indian tribes, pushed southwards by the expansion of the United States and the weakness of Mexico, invaded haciendas and mining settlements in an orgy of looting and killing. In Central Mexico there was another focus of rebellion, in which social movements and banditry became inextricably mixed.[128] Deserters from the army, fugitives from justice, vagrants and marginal elements took advantage of Mexico's military defeat and subsequent anarchy to form armed bands which terrorized the countryside, while peasant movements had to struggle to keep their autonomy. Tomás Mejía, a soldier-turned-rebel, linked peasant discontent to groups of dissident military and civilian officials in a rebellion stretching from Querétaro to San Luis Potosí, joined in the course of 1848 by Indian communities in the state of Hidalgo. A more serious threat to the authorities was presented by Eleuterio Quiroz, another army deserter, whose rebellion centred on Guanajuato and had a more exclusively peasant

---

[127] Ibid. 61. On expansion of tenant farming, and violence in Chalco, see Tutino, *From Insurrection to Revolution in Mexico*, 232–41, 255–6.
[128] González Navarro, *Anatomía del poder en México*, 38–48; Reina, *Las rebeliones campesinas en México*, 291–2; Tutino, *From Insurrection to Revolution in Mexico*, 252–6.

constituency.[129] Quiroz and his followers won a number of victories against federal troops, and this attracted further support from peasants in the region of Río Verde, some of them landless peons, others tenant farmers on haciendas. Quiroz raised peasant demands in March 1849, and they now included distribution of uncultivated lands, lowering of rents, and abolition of forced labour on haciendas.[130] The government and hacendados, both threatened by mass unrest and for the moment deprived of the presence of Santa Anna, were saved by the war indemnity which provided the funds to strengthen the army. They joined forces to defeat peasant rebellion, shoot Quiroz (6 December 1849), and offer enough marginal concessions to buy off the rebels. They then planted a number of military colonies in the Sierra Gorda to keep the peace.

Meanwhile in Guerrero rural conditions were unstable long before 1848. The Indian protest of 1843–4 had been brought under control but not resolved. The position of Alvarez was still contradictory, a caudillo who was not quite trusted as a gendarme. His basic aim was political, to keep the south as his personal domain and resist encroachment by the central government. He had a peasant *clientela* and power to influence if not to control it. He encouraged peasants to recover their communal lands and supported not only their appeals to the courts but even invasion of haciendas, denouncing hacendados who appropriated 'both the land of private individuals and those of communities, and then have the affrontery to claim right of property without any legal title, reason enough to explain why the people demand justice, protection, and help'.[131] On the other hand he was the owner of five properties and publicly disapproved of violent protest and direct action. In January 1849 the peasants of Chilapa again rose in rebellion, this time under the Indian Domingo Santiago, repudiating in particular high taxes. The sequence of events was typical: the first reaction of the authorities was repression, which in turn led to further Indian violence and the extension of the rebellion. The Indians could not meet tax demands because their economic situation had deteriorated as they slipped down the agrarian slope from owners of land to tenants paying rent. According to a newspaper report, 'Various pueblos of the district tried to destroy the town and

[129] Meyer, *Problemas campesinos y revueltas agrarias*, 13–14, 64–5.
[130] Reina, *Las rebeliones campesinas en México*, 297, 300–2.
[131] Quoted by Meyer, *Problemas campesinos y revueltas agrarias*, 60; Díaz Díaz, *Caudillos y caciques*, 206–7, 225.

demanded that the rentals cease for ever, and that the property of the rich pass to them, since they are poor in spirit and it has been prophesied. These were their actual words.'[132] Alvarez was again involved. If the Indians regarded him as a protector, the army expected him to pacify rebellious peasants. But there were times when, for various reasons, he was an instigator of these movements. That of 1849 was one of them.

Officially Alvarez moved to calm the rebels and end the rebellion. But in fact he encouraged disobedience to the central government, and the Indians thanked him for his 'paternal protection'. He seems to have taken political advantage of the rebellion in order to obtain the elevation of Guerrero into a full state of the federation; this in fact was achieved in October 1848 when the districts of Acapulco, Chilapa, and Taxco were integrated into a new state and Alvarez was appointed its commandant general. The landed oligarchy of the region also gained, acquiring more influence in national politics. But the peasants of the south received no tangible benefits. The rebel pueblos, armed with nothing more than bows, arrows, and machetes, continued to harass the army in guerrilla operations, difficult to resist and costly to the state. Alvarez had proved to be an unreliable gendarme. Rightly or wrongly many Mexicans believed that the absence of Santa Anna deprived them of their only protector during the anarchy of the years 1847–8. Foreign observers agreed: 'Notwithstanding his faults and errors, I know of no person at this time so capable of being at the head of public affairs as General Santa Anna; for it is he alone, in possession of power, who is able to stay the march of anarchy.'[133] This was reason enough to call him back in 1853.

9. *Caudillo Models in Spanish America*

Argentina, Venezuela, Mexico—each in its way demonstrated the same truth. The caudillos exercised power through an alliance of interest groups, in which the popular sectors played a greater or lesser role according to the balance of society and the exigencies of

---

[132] *El Siglo XIX* (14 Mar. 1849), quoted by Reina, *Las rebeliones campesinas en México*, 117.
[133] Bankhead to Palmerston, 29 Aug. 1847, PRO, FO 50/211, fos. 143–7.

the time. The caudillos were creatures of conditions and agents of élites, but they also had their own scale of values and chose their own modes of social control. The preferred protector, the necessary gendarme, this was the image most coveted by the caudillos. As a framework of reference it accommodates both Rosas and Páez. The logical sequence of wartime anarchy, peacetime expectations, popular unrest, the call for a protector, and the resultant caudillo state, can be followed in some detail in Argentina and Venezuela, less explicitly in Mexico. Rural banditry and rebellion obviously aroused alarm and indignation among the Mexican élite, but internal security was regarded as a task for various agencies: it was often left to hacienda forces led by landowners; and in northern Mexico from 1850 it was even privatized, by means of state contracts with guerrillas for the defence of property.[134] In the last resort it was regarded as a duty of the professional army rather than a personal mission of the caudillo. Regional caudillos were equivocal in their responses, sometimes authors of rebellion, sometimes agents of the state. Nevertheless the basic assumptions in Mexico were the same. Santa Anna stood for law and order and his normal response to social protest was to suppress it. Unlike Rosas and Páez he did not possess a private army of hacienda peons, to be deployed when the regular security forces were unavailable or subverted by rivals. Mexico had a tradition of a professional army and powerful generals, and it was with these that Santa Anna had to negotiate in order to fulfil his role of law enforcer. His clientage network was less simple and less accessible than that of Páez. But no one doubted his social credentials or his ability to assemble a political and military coalition. The instinct of conservatives in crisis was to turn to the strongest caudillo in Mexico: when in doubt they called for Santa Anna. And he turned to them when he looked for clients.

Elsewhere in Spanish America the sequence from anarchy to security did not necessarily conform to this model. There were alternative routes to law and order. The ruling groups could impose an authoritarian constitution and a strong presidency, and if the revenue was sufficient they could maintain an army or security forces capable of fulfilling the role of gendarme. This was the Chilean option. Yet again, a civilian government at the centre could leave the maintainance of order in outlying provinces to local élites, which meant in

---

[134] González Navarro, *Anatomía del poder en México*, 66–7.

effect to local caudillos. This was not so different from the standard model: it was dispersed caudillism, or caudillism in miniature, and reflected a known tendency in Spanish America, to leave well alone on the periphery as long as disorder did not seep into the centre. This was the Colombian option.

In Colombia the llanos of Casanare, like those of Venezuela, were a breeding ground of caudillos, and they left a legacy for post-war politicians. In 1831 Juan Nepomuceno Moreno, a primitive caudillo, led a force of llaneros from Casanare across the Andes into Bogotá, and threatened to bring down the government of Rafael Urdaneta and replace it with his own dictatorship. The llanero troops terrorized the *bogotanos* and gave the impression of barbarians occupying a civilized city and replacing the rule of law by anarchy. Eventually the crisis was resolved and Moreno took his troops back to the llanos. But New Granadans had been given a taste of life under the caudillos and they did not like it.[135] The experience reinforced the determination of the Colombian élite to create a civilian government and to reduce the influence of the military in politics. The Constitution of 1832 limited the standing army to a size 'no larger than is indispensably necessary'. Subsequent civilian governments cut back the defence budget and personnel, and in general subjugated the military.

This did not eliminate the regional *jefes*. Governments had to co-opt caudillos like Moreno because they were the only means of imposing order in the remoter regions, and the only agents capable of controlling the wild llaneros and keeping them where they belonged, in the llanos. So the civilian élite used Moreno to achieve their own ends. He was not the only gendarme. General Tomás Cipriano de Mosquera and General José María Obando were also capable of leading caudillo rebellions against the central government, though on the whole they supported constitutional rule against rebellion and used their power to sustain public order, not unlike Páez in Venezuela. Obando in particular, described by Bolívar as a 'bold and cruel bandit, a vile assassin', was an aggressive military and caudillo figure, who could raise cavalry from his own estates in the valley of Patía and, again like Páez, count on a wider following outside his homeland in the south.[136] A curse or a cure? The Colombian élite were un-

---

[135] Jane M. Rausch, *A Tropical Plains Frontier: The Llanos of Colombia, 1531–1831* (Albuquerque, NM, 1984), 217–22, and 'Juan Nepomuceno Moreno: Caudillo of Casanare', paper kindly provided by the author.
[136] Peru de Lacroix, *Diario de Bucaramanga*, 79.

certain of Obando, a man to be watched, with the capacity both to defend and to subvert the constitution. In the last resort he was useful as a constraint on lesser caudillos scattered around the edges of the state, many of them bandits, Indians, and *mulatos*. Colombia did not lack caudillos but the politicians kept them from centre stage. The political landscape contained a variety of features, the standard caudillo, the Colombian species, and growths of other kinds. Contrast provides clues to interpretation. In the first place, the prototype of the Spanish American caudillo was the co-opted caudillo, the strong man chosen by a coalition of interest groups to deliver appropriate policies and conditions in the years after 1830. Second, political ideas and experience were powerful influences in persuading oligarchs to grant or deny power to a caudillo; a preference for constitutions and a hatred of personal power and military pretensions were just as relevant as economic interests in reaching political decisions. Third, the level of social tension was a basic guide to political behaviour. When the mob howled and rural rebels stirred, people who valued order called for a protector; where agitators were remote and local élites vigilant, then the need for a gendarme at the centre became less urgent. Finally, the personal ability of a regional chief to recruit troops and assemble resources was a vital qualification for success; when such a chief was willing as well as able, then the central oligarchy hastened to co-opt him and to complete a political deal at once mutual, effective, and economical. The respective roles of personal power and élite control in determining the caudillo's ascent and survival were evenly balanced, and can be studied in the careers of individual leaders.

II
Caudillo Careers

6

JUAN MANUEL DE ROSAS:
ARGENTINA 1829–1852

1. *The Making of a Caudillo*

Rosas was too young to be a hero of independence and his career was
built not on his war record but on his role in post-war Argentina.
Nevertheless his curriculum vitae opened appropriately for a caudillo.
He was of pure patrician origins. The Rosas family had been among
the creole élite for generations. His grandparents were an old colonial
family of landowners and officeholders. His father was a landed
proprietor and an officer. Rosas himself was a great landowner and
military commander, while his wife came from the *porteño* upper class
and had been born to wealth. His academic education was basic and
brief, but he was trained for his role and it was on the estancia that
he learnt what he needed to know. He soon left his parents' estate to
work on his own account, first in the meat-salting industry, then in
the accumulation of land. He bought two estancias, Los Cerrillos and
San Martín, in the Guardía del Monte on the Salado up against the
Indian frontier, and these were his most important properties. From
1818 he amassed further land for himself and at the same time acted
as adviser and buyer for his cousins, the Anchorena. He was the
leading expert on land values, investment opportunities, estate management, and he more than anyone appreciated the new economic
and political power of the estancia.

Rosas was at the front of estancia expansion and helped to promote
the transition of Buenos Aires from viceregal capital to export centre.
He was not simply a representative of the new frontier. He and the
Anchorena were at its heart, owners of private fiefdoms in land
among the best in the province. Arriving by night at Los Cerrillos,
Charles Darwin was so impressed by its extent that he thought it was
'a town and fortress'.[1] What was the final size of these great estates?

---

[1] Carlos Ibarguren, *Juan Manuel de Rosas: Su vida, su drama, su tiempo* (Buenos
Aires, 1961), 5, 22–3, 44, 59, 87; Tulio Halperín Donghi, *Argentina: De la revolución*

The Anchorena group were the largest landowners in the whole province, holding in 1830 eight properties totalling 1,312 square miles, in 1852 2,559 square miles.[2] The total holdings of Rosas are less easy to calculate. In his will he specified certain claims which his heirs should make against the government of Buenos Aires for rightful compensation. He referred to '116,000 head of cattle, 40,000 sheep', which he had supplied to the government of Buenos Aires; then '60,000 head of cattle, including cows, bullocks and calves, 1,000 prime steers, 3,000 fine horses, 100,000 sheep, 100,000 brood mares, and the rest of my property, which the government has appropriated since 2 February 1852'. It would require vast estancias to support all this livestock; the official estimate was 136 square leagues (1,414 square miles).[3]

To manage such a domain was a constant challenge, and the line between order and anarchy was very finely drawn. Rosas complained of 'the mob of idlers, vagabonds and delinquents' who consumed cattle wastefully, and of rustlers who robbed by night. And he had no time for the small, struggling rancher: 'The wealthy estancieros have slaves, peons, transport, places to cure the hides, to store the tallow, to make use of the offal. The others might work hard but they do not have the wealth or the power of these estancieros, unless they become their dependants.'[4] Rosas mastered rural life and brought a professional competence to estate management: 'I am a hacendado and from my youth I have worked, applying reason and reflection to our principal sources of wealth.'[5] He organized his rural programme down to the last detail, and imposed his iron will on every subordinate. The key word in his vocabulary was *subordinación*, by which he meant respect for authority, for social order, for private property. His own estancia was a state in miniature; he created a society out of nothing, a disciplined work force, equipped to defend itself against Indians without and anarchy within. He came to dominate the nomadic gauchos, the idle peons, the rebellious Indians, the entire pampa

de independencia a la confederación rosista (Buenos Aires, 1972), 181; Carretero, *La propiedad de la tierra en la época de Rosas*, 14; Darwin, *Journal*, 52–3, 85.

[2] Brown, *A Socioeconomic History of Argentina*, 179–84.

[3] Rosas's will, art. 7, in Antonio Dellepiane, *El testamento de Rosas* (Buenos Aires, 1957), 96. Enrique Arana(h), *Juan Manuel de Rosas en la historia argentina* (3 vols.; Buenos Aires, 1954), ii. 292–3, gives a figure of 80,000 head of cattle in the rodeo of 1846 in Los Cerrillos, San Martín, and 26 other sites.

[4] Alfredo J. Montoya, *Historia de los saladeros argentinos* (Buenos Aires, 1956), 50–3.

[5] Ibid. 54.

environment. An estanciero who could do this had passed a test of leadership and was an asset to his fellows. Any member of the élite isolated in rural Argentina ran a certain risk in the early years of independence before the state had been organized and order imposed. Vagrants proliferated and became part of the social base of *montoneros*, undisciplined and allegedly 'lacking in respect' for their superiors. The unitarian General Paz described being stopped in the interior and 'surrounded by a party of gauchos who did not know who I was, or affected not to know, and they pointed their weapons at me on the pretext that I was an enemy; it was not easy to dissuade them'.[6] In a time of insubordination even his enemies acknowledged the useful implacability of Rosas, and many people followed him because he was a conservative caudillo first and a federalist politician second, a leader who would look after the élite, whatever their allegiance.

In 1820 Rosas had to turn his cowboys into cavalry and divert the power of the estancia to the rescue of Buenos Aires. The defence of capital and province against the petty caudillos and predators of the interior was not an alien cause but one close to his most important interests and values. This was his first direct action against the dreaded anarchy, the first display of that peculiar mixture of protection and menace which became a hallmark of his rule. From action he acquired military power, a political reputation, and more land. Yet he quickly returned to his estancia and stayed there. He was not in sympathy with the Rodríguez administration, much less with that of Rivadavia, who was appointed president of the United Provinces of the Río de la Plata in February 1826, and came to power with a unitary constitution and a modernization programme. Rivadavia projected economic growth through free trade, foreign investment, immigration, and liberal institutions, the whole enclosed in a united Argentina, for the sake of which Buenos Aires would relinquish its monopoly of customs revenue and share it with the nation. The entire model was rejected as a dangerous irrelevancy by Rosas and his associates, who represented a more primitive economy—cattle production for export of hides and salt meat—but one which brought immediate returns, preserved the province's resources for the province itself, and remained true to the country's traditions. The mentality of Rosas at this point was that of a provincial *jefe*, not a national

---

[6] José María Paz, *Memorias póstumas*, 2nd ed. (3 vols.; La Plata, 1892) i. 46 n. 1.

leader. In the latter half of 1826, at the head of a network of friends, relations, and clients, Rosas allied himself to the federalist party which he was eventually to absorb and destroy.[7] He joined this party not for reasons of political ideology, which he did not possess, but because unitary policy threatened to strip Buenos Aires of its assets and thwart its supremacy. The federalist politicians accepted his support without considering the risks involved, and the provincial caudillos were naïve enough to believe that they had found a new champion against the pretensions of the capital. Rivadavia bowed to the combined force of his opponents and resigned from the presidency. In a sense it was true to say that Rivadavia was brought down by Rosas, but Rosas did not yet rule. It was the real federalists who came to power, led by Manuel Dorrego, now at last elected governor of Buenos Aires in August 1827.

The new regime promptly recognized the services and the status of Rosas. On 14 July he was appointed Commandant General of the Rural Militias in the province of Buenos Aires. To his strong economic base he now added the greatest military power in the province. And he used his authority to reassure yet again the estancieros of the south by applying a coherent frontier policy consisting of three things: new settlements grouped around forts, protection by military garrisons, and a buffer of friendly Indians. He also persuaded the ranchers to collaborate with his militia by providing supplies, for which they would be paid by the government and rewarded with peace and security. As militia commander, frontiersman, and rancher, Rosas now had unique qualifications for a move on power, should the occasion arise. Security on the frontier and in the countryside depended upon political stability at the top and on getting the right decisions from the politicians in Buenos Aires. According to the political thinking of Rosas and his associates, this could no longer be assumed: it had to be imposed. The opportunity soon came. In December 1828 Dorrego was overthrown in a coup engineered by General Juan Lavalle leading the military recently returned from the war with Brazil and by a small group of politicians allied to the mercantile and intellectual élite, the whole representing a unitarian reaction against caudillos, *montoneros*, and other manifestations of provincialism. It was a further stage in the conflict between the career politicians and the new economic forces, between the professionals of

[7] Enrique M. Barba, *Como llegó Rosas al poder* (Buenos Aires, 1972), 8.

independence and the landed interest. Dorrego was defeated by the unitarian army and shot on orders of Lavalle, leaving a gap in the federal leadership which was instantly filled by Rosas.

Rosas had no serious rival. As commander of militia he had secured a virtual monopoly of military power in the countryside. His peaceful negotiations on the frontier had gained him Indian friends, allies, and recruits. His achievements had also won him the respect of the estancieros, who basked in unwonted peace and security. And the crisis of subsistence in the pampas in 1828–9 enabled him to recruit popular forces above all in the south.[8] Rosas himself commented on the social character of the movement: 'All the poor classes of town and country are against the rebels and also a great part of the men of means. I believe that the only people with them are the bankrupts and speculators who form the mercantile aristocracy.'[9] In April 1829, when Lavalle marched on Santa Fe, revolts occurred throughout the province of Buenos Aires, and the whole countryside appeared to be under military occupation of units acting in the name of Rosas. In April Rosas defeated the regular army of Lavalle and from then onwards gradually increased his stranglehold on the capital while simultaneously preventing a blood-bath. The caudillo entered Buenos Aires on the night of 3 November 1829, to be received not simply as a military servant of the government but as a victor and leader of the federalist party. He was now ready for power, but not just any power. When, on 6 December, he was elected governor, he was granted *facultades extraordinarias*; this amounted to absolute power, as proposed by Tomás de Anchorena and supported by a virtually unanimous vote of the House of Representatives.[10]

How can we explain the rise of Rosas? What made this particular caudillo? In the first place, he represented the advent to power of a new economic interest, a new social group, the estancieros. New clashed with old. In effect the Buenos Aires landowners overthrew the existing rulers, the politicians, bureaucrats, and military who had been in power since 1810, and took direct possession of the government of the province through their representative Rosas. In 1829 Rosas and his hordes succeeded in dismantling the remnants of the

[8] See Chap. 5, sect. 3.
[9] Rosas to López, 12 Dec. 1828, in Manuel Bilbao, *Historia de Rosas* (Buenos Aires, 1961), 197–8; Irazusta, *Vida política de Juan Manuel de Rosas*, i. 189.
[10] Levene, *El proceso histórico de Lavalle a Rosas*, 256–62; Barba, *Como llegó Rosas al poder*, 124, 147.

army of independence already weakened by the war with Brazil; thus, the defeat of Lavalle was the defeat of a professional army, a rival force, by the rural militia of Rosas and his estanciero allies. Rural activities extended into the capital, where they were indistinguishable from the interests of exporters and importers; indeed estates and warehouses were often in the same hands. British merchants and native entrepreneurs were firm supporters of Rosas and joined the coalition of groups behind the supreme leader. Conditions, then, created the caudillo. He was the living image of the estancia and the militia, the guarantor of unity between province and port, the agent of alliance between urban and rural federalists. This is a simple explanation of the rise of Rosas, but not a complete one. It ignores his specific qualifications, his career, his training, and his power to move events. He was a caudillo by nature before he became governor by election, and he endowed—or distorted—the governorship with his own caudillo qualities.

Rosas himself, therefore, provides the second reason for his rise. He was a caudillo in his own right. His personal experience was unique and did not conform exactly to the model of merchant-turned-landowner which characterized so many of his peers. While he inherited social status, he created his own wealth, founding estancias, recruiting the work force, organizing production and accumulating capital in the rural sector itself. There was truth in his claim, 'I went out to work with no more capital than my own credit and industry.'[11] He was a pioneer of frontier expansion, extending the area of cattle raising, and taking the initiative some years before the big push southwards from 1820. Unlike the Anchorena, who relied on managers or on Rosas himself, he was not an absentee landlord; he was a working estanciero, operating at every stage of production. Even when he was governor, and to the end of his rule, he still guarded his ultimate power base and supervised by correspondence every detail of the administration of his estates, admonishing overseers, checking accountants, punishing peons.[12] To a caudillo whose personal wealth was founded not on the state but on his own estancias the accounts and the wages bill were of particular interest and these were reported

---

[11] Adolfo Saldías, *Historia de la Confederación Argentina: Rosas y su época* (9 vols.; Buenos Aires, 1958), i. 25–6; Rosas to Josefa Gómez, 8 Dec. 1865, in *Cartas del exilio 1853–1875*, 67.

[12] Rosas to Laureano Ramírez, 11 Mar. 1845, AGN, Buenos Aires, Sala 10, 43-2-8.

to him quarterly. From such an account in 1841 it appeared that the overseer of the estancia San Martin was paid 150 pesos a month and various grades of peons between 10 and 50 pesos a month, incomes which were reasonable for the time if not lavish.[13] Overseers of Rosas estates had to earn their salaries. And his work force knew he was watching; if peons were leaving he wanted to know why; and he always insisted on employing captive and friendly Indians.

Thus Rosas became a natural leader of the estancieros by his example and his authority. But he was shrewd enough not to rely on one support base alone. As a rancher he came into direct contact with gauchos, peons, Indians, rogues and vagabonds, and other people of the pampas, all of them potential workers on his estates or recruits for his militia. In the estancia he was an absolute ruler and from his peons he demanded unqualified obedience. His methods impressed by their results: 'This was the way Rosas began to acquire a reputation. In the southern countryside in particular there was more obedience to his orders than to those of the government itself.'[14] Thus he exerted authority not only over his own peons but over the rural masses beyond his private boundaries, up to the Indian frontier and beyond. The reason for his success was simple: he rewarded allegiance. On campaign against the unitarians in 1830, he told the treasury that if funds for his rural and military expenses were not forthcoming, he would defray them from his own estates: 'I will quit rather than lose the credit I have gained among my people at the cost of so many risks and sacrifices. To cover the offers of sheep that I made to the *caciques* and *caciquillos* who accompanied me, 25,000 to 30,000 head in all, I am taking them from my own estancias, for I do not have the funds to buy them, and the offer was made for the spring.' His ascendancy over 'friendly' Indians, manipulated no doubt by his agents, was reflected in the words of the cacique Cachnel at a pro-Rosas demonstration in Tapalqué in June 1835: 'Juan Manuel is my friend, he has never deceived me. I and all my Indians will die for him. If it had not been for Juan Manuel, we would not be living as we do in brotherhood with the Christians. . . . The words of Juan are the same as the words of God'.[15] For the Indians leviathan held no

---

[13] Juan José Becar to Rosas, 31 May 1841, AGN, Buenos Aires, Sala 10, 25-9-2, Correspondencia confidencial, Secretaría de Rosas.

[14] La Madrid, *Memorias*, i. 198–9.

[15] Rosas to García, San José, 13 Oct. 1830, in Nicolau (ed.), *Correspondencia inédita entre Juan Manuel de Rosas y Manuel José Garcia*, 46; *Gaceta Mercantil* (July 1835), in

terror; Rosas was indeed a mortal God. To his dominance of land and labour and his influence among his peers Rosas brought another qualification. He had more military experience than any other estanciero, as he showed in his rescue of Buenos Aires in 1820 and his leadership of the forces of the countryside against Lavalle's veterans in 1829. Meanwhile he had been appointed militia commander of the province, a government commission which added legitimacy to his informal power base.

When Rosas entered Buenos Aires in November 1829 he had prepared himself for leadership. He had established his career not through political or bureaucratic office but through informal authority. He first created his power then offered it to the state. In the previous decade he had fashioned a caudillo's stronghold in the countryside, partly on his own initiative, partly as a delegate of the government. He had served the state and he had used the state, not least as a source of land and a purchaser of products. While he represented the landowners, he also represented himself, the most powerful of all the landowners. Could they have found anyone better qualified than Rosas? Probably not. To this extent, he had a strong bargaining position. He was not their creature, he was their superior.

The Rosas system, therefore, was a product of environment and personality. But there was also a third factor. The caudillo emerged not simply as a product of nature, but in response to specific events. The landed élite and their allies in the federal party were presented with a number of challenges which they perceived as impossible to meet by constitutional means alone. In 1820 the caudillos of the littoral and their *montonero* hordes were deaf to negotiation and were only resisted by comparable caudillo power. In 1825–7 the policy of the unitarians, peaceful though it appeared in the hands of Rivadavia, was hostile to federalist interests and was backed by a ruthless political machine which did not hesitate to kill opponents. When it also received the support of the professional military, seeking a role on their return from Brazil, it seemed to Rosas and his associates that their enemies were about to capture the state. In 1828 the federal governor Dorrego was defeated not at the polls but on the battlefield and he was then executed by the unitarian military. This was the

Antonio Zinny, *La Gaceta Mercantil de Buenos Aires, 1823–1852* (3 vols.; Buenos Aires, 1912), ii. 244.

proof the *rosistas* needed. They had to take possession of the state before their enemies did, to destroy or be destroyed. The caudillism of Rosas, in this rationale, emerged in the cycle of conflict which characterized Argentine politics in the years 1820–9; it developed in response to the progress of his political enemies, grew in power and legitimacy until it brought him within reach of his goal in the war of 1828–9, and carried him into office for twenty years. Each side blamed the other for terrorism, but in the last resort each side practised terrorism. The caudillo was the father and the child of violence.

The *rosista* state was constructed in the image of the estancia. Society itself was built upon the *patrón*-peon relationship. Rosas was the supreme *patrón* who gave security in return for service. He constantly reminded his countrymen of the political turmoil of the years 1810–29 and of the humiliation suffered by Buenos Aires at the hands of subversives within and provincials without. He claimed that the unitarians had brutalized public life by a campaign of assassinations; and personally he did not wish to be another Dorrego. So he demanded total sovereignty. He explained the origins of his regime in Hobbesian terms as a desperate alternative to anarchy among a people living in a state of nature where life was nasty and property at risk:

Society was in a state of utter dissolution: gone was the influence of those men who in every society are destined to take control; the spirit of insubordination had spread and taken widespread roots; everyone knew his own helplessness and that of others; no one was prepared either to order or to obey. In the countryside there was no security for lives or property.... The inevitable time had arrived when it was necessary to exercise personal influence on the masses to re-establish order, security, and laws; and whatever influence on them the present governor had, he was greatly tormented, because he knew the absolute lack of government resources to reorganize society.[16]

An apocalyptic vision of Argentina, but one which dominated the thinking of Rosas. 'Despotism', conceded John Stuart Mill, 'is a legitimate mode of government in dealing with barbarians.'[17] This was the political creed of the untutored caudillo.

[16] Rosas, *Mensaje* (31 Dec. 1835), in *Mensajes de los gobernadores*, i. 83–4.
[17] John Stuart Mill, *On Liberty* (London, 1926), 73.

2. *Conservative Dictator*

Rosas directed his political life according to prejudice rather than
principle. Society he divided into those who commanded and those
who obeyed. Order was the supreme good, subordination the highest
virtue. His view of the past was coloured by these simple ideas. The
colonial regime, he believed, had been a golden age of strong government and stable institutions. The Revolution of May 1810 was necessary but flawed; it gave Argentina independence but it left a vacuum
in which anarchists prevailed and rebels ruled. He himself came
forward to rescue the country from chaos in 1829, and to reimpose
the due distinction between ruler and subject. And out of chaos order
emerged. The estanciero who had harassed his overseers and staked
out his peons in the sun became the governor who goaded his justices
of the peace and filled the gaols to overflowing. In place of a constitution he demanded personal sovereignty, and in 1835 he justified
the possession of 'a power without limits' as vital to dispel anarchy: 'I
have been careful not to make any other use of it than is absolutely
necessary for the order and peace of the country.'[18] Later, in exile,
he claimed that he had taken over an anarchic, divided, disintegrat-
ing, bankrupt, and unstable country, 'a hell in miniature', and made it
a place fit to live in. 'For me the ideal of good government would be
paternal autocracy, intelligent, disinterested and indefatigable.... I
have always admired the autocratic dictators who have been the first
servants of their people.'[19]

The enemy of autocracy was liberalism. This was the real crime of
the unitarians, not that they wanted a united Argentina but that they
were liberals who believed in secular values of individualism and
progress. He identified them with Freemasons and intellectuals, 'men
of enlightenment and principles', subversives who undermined order
and tradition and whom he held ultimately responsible for the assassinations which debased Argentine political life from 1828 to
1835.[20] The constitutional doctrines of unitarians and federalists did
not interest him and he was never a true federalist. In 1829 he

---

[18] Rosas to López, 23 Jan. 1836, in *Correspondencia entre Rosas, Quiroga y López*, ed.
Enrique M. Barba (Buenos Aires, 1958), 310.
[19] Interview of Vicente G. and Ernesto Quesada with Rosas, Southampton, 1873, in
Sampay, *Las ideas políticas de Juan Manuel de Rosas*, 215, 218–19.
[20] Rosas to overseer, 3 Mar. 1835, in Saldías (ed.), *Papeles de Rozas*, i. 134: in
Spanish, 'hombres de luces y de los principios'.

denied belonging to the federal or to any party, and expressed contempt for Dorrego. In an interview with the Uruguayan envoy Santiago Vázquez on the day after he took office he insisted, 'I tell you I am not a federalist, and I have never belonged to that party. Had I belonged to it I would have given it leadership, a thing which it has never had.... All I want is to prevent disaster and restore institutions, but I am sorry they have put me in this post, because I am not made for governing.'[21] This was a ritual disclaimer common among caudillos. Once in office he had no intention of failing for lack of power. He thought and ruled as a centralist and stood for the hegemony of Buenos Aires. He explained political divisions as expressions of social structure, interpreting the conflict of 1828–9 and its aftermath as a war between the poorer sectors and the mercantile aristocracy. 'The question is between an aristocratic minority and a republican majority.'[22] 'The federal masses are composed of the people of the countryside and the lower orders of the city, but these are not the people who direct the policy of the government.'[23] A unitary system, he used to say, was more appropriate to an aristocracy, federalism to a democracy. In the autumn of 1839 he preached to his coterie in the evening under the ombu trees at Palermo: 'He argued that we were democrats or federals, which for him is the same, since the time of the Spaniards.'[24]

But this was mere rhetoric, and convinced only the sycophants. There was no democracy in Argentina and the people did not rule. Rosas made use of the lower sectors but he did not represent, much less enfranchise, them. He had a horror of social revolution, and he cultivated the popular classes, not to give them power or property, but to divert them from protest and defiance. There was a lesson here for other rulers, he believed, not least those in Europe. The Revolution of 1848 in France was his favourite warning, a conflict between those who had no stake in society and reasonable men of property; and the French government was itself to blame for paying insufficient attention to the lower classes.[25] What he advocated, of

[21] For the complete text of this celebrated interview see Sampay, *Las ideas políticas de Juan Manuel de Rosas*, 129–36.

[22] Rosas to López, 17 May 1832, in *Correspondencia entre Rosas, Quiroga y López*, 158.

[23] Rosas to López, 1 Oct. 1835 (ibid. 267).

[24] Enrique Lafuente to Félix Frías, 18 Apr. 1839, in Gregorio F. Rodríguez (ed.), *Contribución histórica y documental* (3 vols.; Buenos Aires, 1921–2), ii. 468–9.

[25] Rosas to San Martín, Mar. 1849, 15 Aug. 1850, in Saldías (ed.), *Papeles de Rozas*,

course, was not social reform but propaganda and control. In this sense he did indeed have a lesson to teach: he anticipated populist dictators of a later age, treating Argentines with that peculiar mixture of concern and contempt which was pure *rosismo*. Rosas had a talent for manipulating popular discontents and turning them against his enemies in such a way that they did not damage the basic structure of society. By a skilful exhibition of demagogy and nationalism he was able to give an illusion of popular participation and create a sense of identity between *patrón* and peon. But his federalism was empty of social content and he was never a nation-builder. Rosas destroyed the traditional division between federalists and unitarians and made these categories virtually meaningless. He reduced politics to *rosismo* and anti-*rosismo*.

What was *rosismo*? Its power base was the estancia, a centre of economic resources and a medium of social control. The estancia gave Rosas an independent income, the support of fellow estancieros, and the means of recruiting an army of peons, gauchos, and vagrants. In 1829 he not only defeated the unitarians, he also demonstrated his ability to control the dangerous classes. He then so exploited men's fear of anarchy that he was able to demand and obtain absolute power. Rosas touched a chord in many Argentines, even his enemies, who saw around them a savage society which still needed taming. The unitarian General Paz was disgusted at the behaviour of the *montoneros* who took him prisoner in May 1831: 'To see the hilarity and jubilation with which those people greeted my downfall, as though it were some great gain for their prosperity and welfare! I would feel ashamed and detest the human race, except that such behaviour can be explained by the total ignorance and savagery of these people of the countryside'.[26] The landed élite responded positively to Rosas. The House of Representatives which voted him into power on 6 December 1829 was dominated, as Saldías observed, by 'men distinguished in society for their position, their wealth, or the role they had long played in public life'.[27] On 13 April 1835 the same class again elected Rosas to office. And in July 1835 from all corners of the province the most prominent of the estancieros travelled to

i. 303, ii. 57. For another interpretation of the 'popular' character of Rosas's policy see Halperín Donghi, *Argentina: De la revolución de independencia a la confederación rosista*, 301–4.

[26] Paz, *Memorias póstumas*, iii. 25.
[27] Saldías, *Historia de la Confederación*, ii. 112.

Buenos Aires to mount guard before the governor's house as a mark of 'respect' and 'deference'.[28] Some estancieros, it is true, opposed Rosas. There were some who had political objections to him, unitarians who disliked his federalism, federalists who abhorred dictatorship. In 1838 there was an element of economic opposition to him, when his policy led to the French blockade, which in turn damaged the export business of the estancias. From this thinking sprang the rebellion of the south in 1839, an exceptional action which Rosas was able to crush through his other source of power, the state itself.

Armed with absolute power in 1829, renewed in 1835, Rosas proceeded to take total possession of the state apparatus—the bureaucracy, the police, the standing army. With the ultimate means of coercion in his hands, he ceased to rely on the irregular forces of the countryside. They could return home, the estancieros to supervise their estates, the peons to earn their wages, the gauchos to become ranch hands or serve in the army. The French observer Martin de Moussy explained: 'The dictatorship, which at first relied upon the gaucho element and the montoneros to preserve its power, quickly broke these instruments of its ascent. It created a compact army, increased the infantry and artillery, and reduced the cavalry to a secondary role'.[29]

Rosas was now sovereign ruler in a state moulded to the interests of the estancieros and the demands of an export economy. Populism gave way to persuasion: police took the place of politicians. Caudillism became a classical despotism, but it was despotism with a singular organization and a style of its own. Total political control was imposed. No rival loyalties were allowed, no alternative parties permitted. From press and pulpit a sole truth was delivered, and every public act conveyed the cult of Rosas. The caudillo was built into a heroic leader, a one-man government, a saviour and protector of his people, while an official political movement took the place of constitutional choice. Party activists in alliance with the police applied systematic terrorism against 'the enemy within'. The detection of dissidents and the elimination of opponents engaged a large part of the resources of the state, as a system of conformity was applied which was almost totalitarian in character. All this bore the personal stamp of Rosas.

[28] *Gaceta Mercantil* (19 July 1835).
[29] Victor Martin de Moussy, *Description géographique et statistique de la Confédération Argentine* (3 vols.; Paris, 1860–4), ii. 645–6.

3. *Personal Government*

Rosas ruled from 1829 to 1832 with absolute sovereignty. After an interregnum, during which his supporters destabilized the government in Buenos Aires and the assassination of Quiroga threatened to renew turmoil in the provinces, he returned to office as a restorer of law and order in March 1835 and governed for the next seventeen years with total and unlimited power. The House of Representatives remained an instrument of the governor, whom it formally 'elected'. It consisted of forty-four deputies, half of whom were annually renewed by election. But only a small minority of the electorate participated, and it was the duty of the justices of the peace to deliver these votes to the government. The assembly, lacking legislative function and financial control, was largely an exercise in public relations for the benefit of foreign and domestic audiences, and it normally responded obsequiously to the initiatives of the governor. It was his custom to send his resignation to the House from time to time, but this was never accepted.

While he controlled the legislature, Rosas also dominated the judicial power. He not only made law, he interpreted it, changed it, and applied it. The machinery of justice no doubt continued to function: the justices of the peace, the judges for civil and criminal cases, the appeal judge, and the supreme court, all gave institutional legitimacy to the regime. But the law did not rule. Arbitrary intervention by the executive undermined the independence of the judiciary. Rosas took many cases to himself, read the evidence (often supplied by his local henchman Vicente González), examined the police reports and, as he sat alone at his desk, gave judgement, writing on the files 'shoot him', 'fine him', 'imprison him', 'to the army'.[30] Rosas also controlled the bureaucracy. One of his first and most uncompromising measures was to purge the old administration; this was the simplest way of removing political enemies and rewarding followers, and it was inherent in the patron–client organization of society. The new administration was not extravagantly large and further economy was imposed by leaving vacancies unfilled. But appointments of all kinds were reserved for political clients and federalists; other qualifications counted for little. Rosas instinctively distrusted reformed unitarians and convert federalists and refused to have them in his

---

[30] AGN, Buenos Aires, Colección Celesia, 22-1-12, fos. 101–14.

administration, arguing that they regarded amnesty as a sign of weakness: 'They will learn to improve and cooperate with us when they see that we are resolute in punishing the wicked and rewarding the good.' In short, Rosas was a dictator, the name employed by exiles such as Sarmiento and Alberdi. 'As he told me himself', remarked the British minister Southern, 'he wields a power more absolute than any monarch on his throne.'[31]

The caudillo's rule reached into every corner of the province through the justices of the peace, his officers at the front, caudillos in miniature, whose powers mirrored those of their master. He scrutinized their appointments and monitored their every action. In his view ignorant justices who were ideologically sound made better officials than *ilustrados* who were a political risk: 'For a justice of the peace in the countryside common sense suffices, together with good motivation and honourable intentions, even if he lacks education.' Qualifications for the office can be seen in a typical nomination for a vacancy in Moron de la Concepción by the outgoing justice:

Don Juan Gil is proposed for Justice of the Peace in the coming year 1842. He is a native of Tucumán, married, aged 46, a substantial hacendado and cattleman, with some 200,000 pesos in capital. Excellent conduct, literate, commendably active and zealous, a local alcalde since 1835, and nominated several times as Justice. He is a lieutenant in the militia and served in the sacred cause of federation in 1829 when the savage unitarians rose in rebellion . . . in 1839 he joined Colonel Ramírez against the rebels in Dolores and Monsalve and when the savage unitarian Lavalle invaded the province in 1840 he served with his troops.[32]

Propaganda was an essential agent of *rosismo*: a few simple and barbarous slogans passed for ideology and these permeated the administration and impressed a nervous public.[33] People were obliged to dress in a kind of uniform and to use the federalist colour, red.

[31] Rosas to García, 10 Apr. 1830, in Nicolau (ed.), *Correspondencia inédita entre Juan Manuel de Rosas y Manuel José García*, 31; Southern to Palmerston, Private, 27 Jan. 1850, HMC, Palmerston Papers, GC/SO/251.

[32] González to Rosas, 18 Nov. 1841, AGN, Buenos Aires, 10, 25-9-2, Correspondencia confidencial, Secretaría de Rosas. For Rosas's views on justices and *ilustración* see Rosas to García, 10 Apr. 1830, in Nicolau (ed.), *Correspondencia inédita entre Juan Manuel de Rosas y Manuel José García*, 31.

[33] Irazusta, *Vida política de Juan Manuel de Rosas*, ii. 25; Celesia, *Rosas, aportes para su historia*, i. 629–30, ii. 207–8, 452–5, 486; Ibarguren, *Juan Manuel de Rosas*, 239. Southern to Palmerston, 16 Jan. 1849, PRO, FO 6/143; Southern to Palmerston, 16 July 1849, FO 6/144.

Women were expected to wear red ribbons in their hair, men to have a fierce and hirsute look and wear red silk badges bearing the inscription 'Long live the Argentine Confederation. Death to the Savage Unitarians'. This was also the heading of official documents. The symbolism was a form of coercion and conformity. To adopt the federal look and the federal language took the place of security checks and oaths of allegiance. Federal uniformity was a measure of totalitarian pressure, by which people were forced to abandon a passive or apolitical role and to accept a specific commitment, to show their true colours. Political ritual of this kind was unique in Spanish America and anticipated the style of later dictatorships. An invention of Rosas himself, it was an object of contempt among his more cultivated followers but adopted with enthusiasm by his coarser retinue.

The Church was a willing ally, except for the Jesuits, who were readmitted to Argentina and proved a disappointment to the caudillo. They actually remained aloof from federal politics and refused to be used as propagandists, until in 1841 the chief of police was instructed by the government 'not to issue passports for the interior or for abroad to any of the Jesuit fathers' and they were soon expelled.[34] The rest of the clergy were not so independent. Portraits of Rosas were carried in triumph through the streets and placed upon the altars of the principal churches.[35] Sermons glorified the dictator and extolled the federal cause. 'If it is right to love God Our Lord', preached Fray Juan González in 1839, 'so it is right to love, obey, and respect our Governor and Restorer of the Laws, D. Juan Manuel de Rosas'.[36] The clergy became enthusiastic auxiliaries of the regime, caudillos of the *barrios*, who preached that to resist Rosas was a sin. Political orthodoxy was also propagated by secular agents, and the printing presses of Buenos Aires were kept fully employed turning out

---

[34] AGN, Buenos Aires, 10, 17-3-2, Gobierno, Solicitudes, Embargos. Héctor José Tanzi, 'Las relaciones de la Iglesia y el Estado en la época de Rosas', *Historia*, 9, 30 (Buenos Aires, 1963), 5–28; Francisco Avella Cháfer, 'Ideas y sentimientos religiosos de don Juan Manuel de Rosas', *Nuestra Historia*, 2, 6 (1969), 339–52; Raúl Héctor Castagnino, *Rosas y los Jesuitas* (Buenos Aires, 1970), 39.

[35] John Anthony King, *Twenty-Four Years in the Argentine Republic* (London, 1846), 353–4; *Gaceta Mercantil* (June–Aug. 1835), in Zinny, *La Gaceta Mercantil*, ii. 244–5; *Gaceta Mercantil* (21 Oct. 1839).

[36] Quoted in *Agresiones de Rosas*, in Andrés Lamas, *Escritos políticos y literarios durante la guerra contra la Tiranía de D. Juan Manuel de Rosas*, ed. Angel J. Carranza (Buenos Aires, 1877), 266.

newspapers in Spanish and other languages containing official news and propaganda, for circulation at home and abroad.[37] The *Gaceta Mercantil* also expressed, however incoherently, the political ideas of Rosas, his 'Americanism' and his efforts to inculcate a sense, if not of Argentine nationalism, at least of independent identity. As Southern observed:

He evidently regrets the absence in these people of a spirit of national independence: with the view of exciting this feeling—a powerful instrument in the hands of an efficient ruler—many of the documents and speeches in the Gazette are expressly written and published. The 'Gazeta Mercantil' which is immediately under his care . . . is read every day in every corner of the country by the district authorities; the judge of peace reads it to the civilians, and the military commandant to the persons connected with the Army. The Gazette is in fact part of a *simulacrum* of government, which is kept up with a perfection of which only a man of the force of character, and of the inflexible and untiring nature of general Rosas is capable.[38]

Rosas came to have his principal residence at Palermo, where a staff of 300 served the caudillo, ranging from officials and secretaries to servants, overseers, and peons. More than one English visitor remarked on his country style, his ruddy countenance and stout figure: 'In appearance Rosas resembles an English gentleman farmer—his manners are courteous without being refined. He is affable and agreeable in conversation, which however nearly always turns on himself, but his tone is pleasant and agreeable enough. His memory is stupendous: and his accuracy in all points of detail never failing'.[39] One of his secretariat reported: 'This tiger is very tame towards his immediate servants'; but he was a hard taskmaster and could suddenly fly into a rage and emit threats of throatcutting like the vilest of his henchmen.[40] Surrounded by his staff, Rosas placed himself at a distance from his ministers; in effect he reduced the system of government to two sectors, his personal secretariat which

---

[37] Félix Weinberg, 'El periodismo en la época de Rosas', *Revista de Historia*, 2 (Buenos Aires, 1957), 81–101; Fermín Chavez, *Iconografía de Rosas y de la Federación*, in Pradere and Chavez, *Juan Manuel de Rosas*, ii. 31–40; Elías Días Molano, *Vida y obra de Pedro de Angelis* (Santa Fe, 1968), 73–7.

[38] Southern to Palmerston, 16 July 1849, PRO, FO 6/144.

[39] Southern to Palmerston, 18 Oct. 1848, PRO, FO 6/139; Southern to Palmerston, Private, 22 Nov. 1848, HMC, Palmerston Papers, GC/SO/241. MacCann, *Two Thousand Miles' Ride*, ii. 5, 9.

[40] Lafuente to Frias, April 1839, in Rodríguez, *Contribución histórica y documental*, ii. 461.

exercised real power, and the ministries whose function was more formal. This was personal government of the crudest kind; all policy decisions and most executive ones were taken by Rosas, often dictated while striding up and down his long office, his secretaries scurrying after him. No attempt was made to organize delegation of administrative powers and functions. The only exception was the work done by his daughter Manuelita, who acted as a kind of filter through whom business of an extra-judicial character, including petitions for clemency, was transmited.

The ultimate sanction was force, controlled by Rosas, applied by the army, and financed from the meagre income enjoyed by the state. The regime was not, strictly speaking, a military dictatorship: it was a civilian government which employed a compliant military. But the military establishment, consisting of the regular army and the militia, existed not only to defend the country but to occupy it, not only to protect the population but to control it. Conscripted from peons, vagrants, and delinquents, officered by professional soldiers, kept alive by booty and exactions from the estancias, the army of Rosas was a heavy burden on the rest of the population. If it was not particularly efficient, it was numerous—perhaps 20,000 strong—and active, constantly engaged in foreign wars, interprovincial conflicts, and internal security.[41] But war and the economic demands of war, while they meant misery for the many, made fortunes for the few. Defence-spending provided a secure market for certain industries and employment for their workers: the fairly constant demand for uniforms, arms, and equipment helped to sustain a number of small workshops and artisan manufactures in an otherwise depressed industrial sector. Above all the military market favoured several large landowners. Proprietors such as the Anchorena had long had valuable contracts for the supply of cattle to frontier forts; now the armies on other fronts became voracious consumers and regular customers. The army and its liabilities, however, increased at a time when revenue was contracting, and something had to give. When the

---

[41] 'Estado que manifiesta la fuerza efectiva con que se halla cada una de las divisiones', 16 Mar. 1842, AGN, Buenos Aires, Sala 10, 26-5-1; AGN, Buenos Aires, Sala 7, 22-2-1, fo. 65; Mandeville to Palmerston, 17 Feb. 1841, PRO, FO 6/78; Gen. J. T. O'Brien to Aberdeen, Jan. 1845, FO 6/110. The strength of a single militia regiment, the Regimiento 6 de Milicias Patricias de Caballería de Campaña, in 1842, was 1,343; see 'Estado General', Chascomús, 1 May 1842, AGN, Buenos Aires, Sala 10, 25-9-2.

French blockade began to bite, from April 1838, not only were people thrown out of work and hit by rapid inflation but the government saw its basic revenue from customs fall dramatically. Faced with heavy budget deficits, and reluctant to tax the income or property of his supporters, Rosas immediately imposed severe expenditure cuts. Most of these fell on education, the social services, and welfare in general. The University of Buenos Aires was virtually closed. When priorities were tested, Rosas did not even make a pretence of governing 'popularly'.

The contrast between military and social spending reflected circumstances as well as values. The enemy within, conflict with other provinces and with foreign powers, and the obligation to succour his allies in the interior, all caused Rosas to maintain a heavy defence budget. Some of these choices were forced upon him, others were preferred policy, yet others reflected a contemporary indifference towards welfare and were not exclusive to caudillism. In any case the consequences were socially retarding. In the 1840s the interior ministry received on average between 6 and 7 per cent of the total budget, and most of this was allocated to police and political expenditure, not to social services. Defence, on the other hand, received absolute priority. The military budget varied from 4 million pesos, or 27 per cent of the total, in 1836, to 23.8 million, 47 per cent, during the French blockade in 1840, to 29.6 million, 71.11 per cent, in 1841. For the rest of the regime it never fell below 15 million, or 49 per cent.[42]

This was the system of total government which sustained Rosas in power for over two decades. The majority of people obeyed, some willingly, others out of habit, many from fear. 'The Tyrant of the River Plate'—was Rosas aptly named? No doubt his government was tyrannical. But it also responded to conditions inherent in Argentine society, where people had lived for too long without a common power to keep them all in awe. Rosas superseded a state of nature, in which life could be brutish and short. He offered an escape from insecurity and a promise of peace, on condition that he was granted total power, the sole antidote to total anarchy. To exercise his sovereignty Rosas used the bureaucracy, the military, and the police. Even so

[42] Sir Woodbine Parish, *Buenos Ayres and the Provinces of the Rio de la Plata*, 2nd ed. (London, 1852), 520; Burgin, *The Economic Aspects of Argentine Federalism*, 49, 167, 198, 202–3.

there was some opposition. Internally there was an ideological opposition, partly from unitarians and partly from younger reformists; this came to a head in an abortive conspiracy in 1839 and continued to operate from its base in Montevideo. A second focus of internal opposition was formed by the landowners of the south of the province. As the justice of the peace of Chascomús reported, 'Commandant Rico was at the head of a considerable armed force in support of the insurrection led by Don Benito Miguens and Don Pedro Castelli. A number of hacendados were accomplices in the rebellion. . . . The whole extent of the country as far as Bahía Blanca was roused to insurrection. . . .'[43] The rebels issued a statement to the French Admiral Leblanc upholding the principles of liberty and the cause of Lavalle and the Argentines against the tyranny of Rosas, and appealing to the French alliance in the common struggle, but not to French conquest and occupation as Rosas alleged.[44] Opposition stemmed not from ideology but from economic interest. Already harassed by demands upon their manpower and resources for the Indian frontier, they were particularly hit by the French blockade, which cut off their export outlets and for which they held Rosas responsible. But the rebellion of October 1839 did not synchronize with the political conspiracy and it too was crushed.

Finally, there was an external opposition to the regime, partly from other provinces and partly from foreign powers. If this could link with internal dissidents, Rosas would be in real danger. To oppose Rosas, of course, was a crime for which there was no reprieve. He lived in personal anticipation of danger and in 1839 fear of assassination was a daily obsession. One of his secretariat reported:

The dictator is not stupid: he knows the people hate him; he goes in constant fear and always has one eye on the chance to rob and abuse them and the other on making a getaway. He has a horse ready saddled at the door of his office day and night; I am not exaggerating, there is an Indian appointed solely as his bodyguard. . . . From rising to retiring Rosas is spurred, whip in hand, with hat and poncho, always ready to mount his horse. He strikes me

---

[43] José Antonio Linera to Rosas, 31 Oct. 1839, AGN, Buenos Aires, Colección Celesia, 22-1-12, fo. 315.

[44] Cuartel General en Dolores, 5 Nov. 1839, AGN, Buenos Aires, Archivo Adolfo Saldías, Sala 7, 3-3-81, fos. 126–9. On the revolution of the south see Emilio Ravignani, *Rosas: Interpretación real y moderno* (Buenos Aires, 1970), 21–34; Angel J. Carranza, *La revolución del 39 en el sur de Buenos Aires* (Buenos Aires, 1919), 128, 175.

as a man who while murdering someone to rob him is constantly looking round at the slightest noise. . . .[45]

Tormented by insecurity, Rosas held in reserve another weapon, terror.

Rosas used terror as an instrument of government, to eliminate enemies, discipline dissidents, warn waverers, and, ultimately, control his own supporters. Terror was not an exceptional or episodic device, though it was regulated according to circumstances. It was an intrinsic part of the Rosas system, the distinctive style of the regime, its final sanction. Rosas himself was the prime author of terror, ordering executions without trial by virtue of the extraordinary powers vested in him. But the special agent of terrorism was the *Sociedad Popular Restaurador*, a political club and a para-military organization. The Society had an armed wing, commonly called the *mazorca*.[46] These were the active terrorists, recruited from the police and militia, from professional cutthroats and criminals, forming armed squads who went out on various missions, killing, looting, and menacing. While the *mazorca* was a creature of Rosas, it was more terrorist than its creator: like many such death squads it acquired in action a semi-autonomy which its author believed he had to allow as a necessary means of government. State terrorism had a timetable. Its incidence varied according to the pressures on the regime, rising to a peak in 1839–42, when French intervention, internal rebellion, and unitarian invasion threatened to destroy the Rosas state and inevitably produced violent reactions. It is impossible to measure the terror. Political executions claimed a large number of victims, more than the 250 acknowledged by the regime, less than the 6,000 alleged by the opposition, and perhaps in the region of 2,000 for the period 1829–52. Rosas was not a mass killer; he did not need to be. Selective assassination was enough to instil terror. And the peak of 1839–42 was not typical of the whole regime but rather an extraordinary manifestation of a general rule, namely, that terrorism existed to enforce submission to government policy in times of national emergency. If ever a government ruled by the principle of intimidation it was this. Rosas acted according to a pure Hobbesian belief that fear

---

[45] Lafuente to Frias, April 1839, in Rodríguez, *Contribución histórica y documental*, ii. 458.

[46] On the terror and the role of its agents see Lynch, *Argentine Dictator*, 209–46.

is the only thing which makes men keep the laws. In political terms his methods worked. Terror helped to keep Rosas in power and the people in order for some twenty years, as one of a number of factors in 1829–32 and 1835–8, as a major instrument of government in 1839–42, and as a latent threat from 1843 to 1852. In this sense terror served its purpose.

Rosas also applied economic terror, hitting his enemies and their families where it really hurt, in their property. The fundamental law of expropriation was the decree of 16 September 1840, issued at a time when the combined pressure of French and unitarian enemies heightened the sense of danger. This made every type of property belonging to unitarians liable for the damage done by General Lavalle and his invading army. The policy was designed to deprive the estancieros opposing the government of their economic base. And federalists whose loyalty was in doubt were equal sufferers, as a few examples show.

Marcelino Galíndez petitioned Rosas to lift the confiscation order placed upon his estancia in Arroyo de las Flores, a property administered and half-owned by his son. Whatever the political opinions of his son, he protested, he himself had always been a true federalist, serving the cause with all his resources since 1820, as Rosas well knew.[47] Another federalist, Pedro Capdevilla, owner of an estancia in Chascomús, explained to Rosas that 'by one of those incidents occurring in every revolution my family and I are victims of a misfortune'. After lengthy and loyal service in the federal cause, he claimed, he was overtaken by the rebellion of 1839 in Chascomús. The rebels under the 'savage' Castelli arrived at his estancia, and while he was looking to the safety of his family 'before preparing to leave', the government forces came. He immediately presented himself to General Prudencio Rosas and was given various tasks before being taken ill. While convalescing in Buenos Aires he heard that his estancia had been confiscated. Worse still, this penalty included 'a hateful and undeserved classification' as a political suspect. Therefore, when Lavalle invaded the province and the events of April 1842 unfolded, in spite of a clear conscience he feared for his life and fled to Montevideo and exile where he learnt firsthand 'the wickedness of the savage unitarians'. Now he had returned to Buenos Aires and on

---

[47] Galíndez to Rosas, 11 Dec. 1840, AGN, Buenos Aires, Sala 10, 27-7-4, 1840 A–C.

behalf of his family he implored Rosas to hear him.[48] But favour once lost was difficult to regain, and petitions of this kind, insecurity and fear in every line, usually met with a chilling silence.

People waited for hours, for days, in the courtyard of the dictator's *quinta* at Palermo to present pleas and petitions in the hope of instant justice. Widows and mothers complained bitterly to Rosas of the hardship inflicted on their families. One widow requested the return of an estancia confiscated by the justice of the peace in the district of Lobos. Her husband, she claimed, had never been a unitarian, yet 'he ended his days on 20 August 1840, with his throat cut and his body mutilated in the vicinity of Cañuelas... he died at the hands of violent men, Federalists in name, but really enemies of you and the Holy Federal System, which my husband sincerely professed.'[49] Numerous other women wrote to Rosas, a wife seeking the return of an estancia on which her family depended for subsistence, a mother claiming that her husband was caught in Montevideo not as an exile but by the blockade, while her son was never a unitarian and the family needed its rightful property. Many petitioners alleged that their property had been confiscated by justices on false accusations of unitarian beliefs, whereas they were 'notoriously federalist'.[50] Confiscations, then, were part of the armoury of a terrorist state. They also gave the government a new source of patronage from which to reward its followers. Years later, in Southampton, Rosas was asked to comment on his reasons for this decree, and replied: 'If I was able to govern that turbulent country for thirty years, taking charge when it was in full anarchy and leaving it in perfect order, it was because I always observed this rule of conduct: to protect my friends at all costs, and to destroy my enemies by any means.'[51]

4. *Crisis and Collapse*

Rosas could not apply terror so easily in the interior of Argentina and there he had to proceed by stealth and diplomacy. In the north and

---

[48] Capdevilla to Rosas, 30 Jan. 1844, AGN, Buenos Aires, Sala 10, 27-7-4.

[49] Antonina Villamayor to Rosas, 12 Jan. 1841, AGN, Buenos Aires, Sala 10, 17-3-2, Gobierno, Solicitudes, Embargos.

[50] AGN, Sala 10, 17-3-2, Gobierno, Solicitudes, Embargos.

[51] Ernesto Quesada, *La época de Rosas: Su verdadero carácter histórico* (Buenos Aires, 1923), 78-9.

west he cultivated friends and fought enemies. In the Littoral he succeeded gradually in imposing allied, dependent, or weak governors. In Uruguay success did not come so easily, for local caudillism was supported by émigré unitarians and foreign enemies. France instituted a naval blockade from 1838 to 1840, which fortunately for Rosas failed to synchronize with the unitarian army of General Lavalle. While the unitarians were defeated in the western provinces, Uruguay proved to be a running sore. Rosas imposed a blockade on Montevideo in 1843, but the subsequent siege lasted nine years. British intervention was now the complicating factor.

In the course of 1843 British naval forces broke the blockade of Montevideo, saved the city, prolonged the war, and pinned down Rosas to a long and costly siege. In addition to defending the independence of Uruguay, Britain also sought to open the rivers to free navigation. Anglo-French naval forces imposed a blockade on Buenos Aires from September 1845, and in November a joint expedition forced its way up the River Paraná, convoying a merchant fleet to inaugurate direct trade to the interior. But the expedition encountered neither welcoming allies nor promising markets, while the blockade hit foreign trade rather than the local enemy. A caudillo like Rosas was protected by the very primitiveness of his country. Argentina's simple export economy made it virtually invulnerable to outside pressure. It could always revert to subsistence and sit it out, waiting for pent-up trade to reopen while its cattle resources accumulated and no one starved. As for the British, they simply blockaded their own trade. Yet Rosas resisted the British without molesting their subjects. In fact the British enjoyed a particular advantage from their treaty status, which gave them exemption from military service, forced loans, and livestock requisitions. Assisted by the low price of land and, in a time of political tension, by the absence of competition from nationals, they bought their way into the rural sector. In the 1840s they advanced rapidly in the sheep industry, acquiring land and flocks, and furthering the improvement of creole sheep by crossing them with merino imports.[52]

Rosas was not alarmed by British penetration of the Argentine economy, seeing it as a natural process and a mutual benefit. He could afford to be magnanimous, as he undoubtedly earned great credit from the naval intervention of 1843–6. His defiance, deter-

[52] Lynch, *Argentine Dictator*, 292–4.

mination, and ultimate survival placed him among the nation's heroes and made him a patriot for posterity. Argentina rallied round Rosas. The House of Representatives lauded him for giving the foreigners a lesson and teaching them to keep to commerce. Lorenzo Torres, a *rosista* nationalist, spoke for patricians and populace alike when he denounced the intervention as 'a war of vandalism in which the principal role has been played by foreign swine'.[53] Rosas also received accolades, if little practical assistance, from other South American nations for his resistance to the imperial giants, and even Andrés Bello was moved to commend him for 'conduct in the great American question which places him in my opinion in the leading ranks of the great men of America'.[54] Americanism of this kind was not an aspect of Argentine nationalism, whose day had yet to come. But it served some of Rosas's propaganda purposes. When the emergency was over and the British returned to seek peace and trade, they found the regime stronger than ever, the economy improving, and a golden age beginning. But appearances were deceptive.

There were flaws at the heart of *rosismo*, even in its prime. How could it perpetuate itself and prolong the stability which was its pride and its apologia? A caudillo was not a monarch, the product of hereditary succession. A caudillo could not even appoint a successor, much less make way for an heir; dictator by nature, the one thing he could not dictate was an orderly transfer of power. A personal regime of this kind was helpless before the future, its policies overshadowed by impermanence. Brought to power by violence, a caudillo could perish in the same way, and the system for which he stood could be destroyed in an instant by the action of an enemy. In addition to his caudillo's power, Rosas possessed a formal legitimacy, and to it he held fast. But this too was a violent grip. Where was the opposition? Who would dare nominate an alternative? What rival candidate would risk raising his head in an election? From 1840 to 1851 the House of Representatives went through the motions of re-electing him, and Rosas equally predictably refused to accept. Diffidence was expected of a caudillo and never diminished his determination to govern. Having come to dominate Buenos Aires, Rosas now wished to confirm his sovereignty in the provinces, but not through a constitutional

---

[53] *Archivo Americano*, n.s. no. 3, 501–31.

[54] Andrés Bello to Baldomero García, 30 Dec. 1846, in Irazusta, *Vida política de Juan Manuel de Rosas*, v. 205.

settlement. He was still convinced that the provinces were not ready for a constitution, and he was not entirely wrong. In some provinces educated people were so scarce that it was impossible to form tribunals of justice, which in earlier debates had led one deputy to exclaim 'these peoples are ruled by no system of government, only by the sword'.[55] The only constitutional provision was the Treaty of the Littoral of 1831, which left the national organization to a congress to be convened by agreement of the provinces.

Rosas preferred other means, a direct appeal to the provinces, where by a skilful compound of force and cajolery he had imposed a kind of *pax rosista*. When in 1849 he refused re-election in Buenos Aires one of the reasons he gave was that 'his reputation in the Province and the Republic has naturally declined'. This view was transmitted across Argentina and the *rosista* militants went into action to prove it wrong, as was intended. In province after province rallies were held and governors and assemblies competed with each other in political sycophancy, acclaiming Rosas, imploring him to continue, and giving him titles of their own invention. Rosas himself had already begun, from at least 1848, to use grander though presumptuous titles of a more national kind, such as *Jefe Supremo de la Nación*. As a result of the campaign of 1849 he now called himself *Jefe Supremo de la Confederación Argentina*. In his Message of 1850 to the House of Representatives he spoke of the governors and peoples of the provinces 'who obey and respect the orders of the supreme head of state', and of 'the Argentine government which speaks to its legislative body', thus claiming a national character for his government. No doubt this reflected his real power and influence, but it did not mean that a national state existed or that Buenos Aires possessed the machinery to govern one. To the very end Rosas set himself against a constitutional organization of Argentina and stood firm for an undefined confederation in which Buenos Aires exercised hegemony over an assortment of satellites.

The political views of Rosas never wavered: 'for me the ideal of happy government would be a paternal autocracy'.[56] In 1850 the autocrat was still secure in his ultimate power base, the city and province of Buenos Aires. Here in his familiar stronghold he kept a

[55] Emilio Ravignani (ed.), *Asambleas constituyentes argentinas* (6 vols., Buenos Aires, 1937–9), iii. 225.

[56] Interview with V. Quesada, Feb. 1873, in Quesada, *La época de Rosas*, 230–1.

tight control, permitted no contradiction, contemplated no change. Rosas seemed as powerful as ever, destined to outrule everyone, and to deliver at the last the benefits he had always promised. As there was no way of removing the caudillo from within, he could only be destroyed from without. Provincial hostility on its own, however, was not enough, for the provinces did not have the military power to tip the balance against Buenos Aires. Any province taking the initiative would need the added weight of external support.

In the course of 1851 there were signs that Justo José de Urquiza, the caudillo of Entre Ríos, was organizing opposition in the Littoral and talking of a constitution. Rosas could not ignore the challenge. His press criticized such views as anarchy: 'to organize the country is to disturb it'.[57] But while Rosas tamed the interior by his diplomacy, military force, and political pressure, he could not apply the same methods to the Littoral, where economic grievances coincided with foreign interests to create an alternative focus of power. These provinces needed trading rights for the river ports of the Paraná and the Uruguay; they wanted a share in customs revenue; and they demanded local autonomy. With outside assistance they could become the Achilles' heel of Rosas. The caudillo of Entre Ríos was too careful to risk his future without the guarantee of powerful land forces. And Brazil was ready to oblige.

Brazil had its own account to settle with Rosas. Determined to prevent satellites of Buenos Aires becoming entrenched in Uruguay and the Littoral, and anxious to secure free navigation of the river complex from Matto Grosso to the sea, Brazil was ready to move in opposition to the 'imperialism' of Rosas, or impelled by an imperialism of its own. An ally was at hand in Entre Ríos. Urquiza, like Rosas, was a rural caudillo, the owner of vast estates, the ruler of a personal fiefdom several hundred square miles in extent, with tens of thousands of cattle and sheep, and four *saladeros*. He made a fortune in the 1840s as a supplier to besieged Montevideo, an importer of manufactured goods and an exporter of gold to Europe. His private ambitions combined easily with provincial interests, and as a politician he was willing to supplant Rosas and initiate a constitutional reorganization of Argentina. He displayed, moreover, greater deference to education, culture, and freedom than his rival, and he had a superior reputation with the émigré intellectuals in Montevideo. In the person

---

[57] Lynch, *Argentine Dictator*, 304–5.

of Urquiza, therefore, the various strands of opposition came together, and he placed himself at the head of provincial interests, liberal exiles, and Uruguayan patriots in an alliance which was backed by sufficient Brazilian money and naval forces to tip the balance against Rosas. The dictator was thus confronted not from within but from without, by the Triple Alliance of Entre Ríos, Brazil, and Montevideo, which went into action from May 1851. But even within, his position was not what it used to be.

The security of Rosas depended not only on repression but also on patronage. He was the centre of a network of interest groups, who looked to the regime for continuing benefits. The key to the system lay in export performance. Good export prices satisfied the landowners and *saladeristas*, who were also virtually immune from taxes. The army also looked to the government for the funding which would enable it to meet its expenses as an instrument of the state and a major buyer in the internal market. Only an abundant and constant customs revenue could sustain such an allocation of resources and at the same time uphold the state. This was one of the reasons why Rosas could never agree to relax the customs monopoly of Buenos Aires or relinquish economic control in favour of the provinces. The whole system thus rested upon three bases, the supremacy of the landowners, the satisfaction of the army, and the subordination of the provinces. And now the supports were less reliable.

The economic structure on which the Rosas system rested was beginning to shift. Cattle-raising was the preferred policy of the Rosas regime. It required relatively low investments in production and technology, and Rosas gave it the land, labour, and security it required. But cattle-raising yielded a limited range of exports, mainly hides and jerked beef, and faced declining markets and competition from other producers, not least in the Littoral. The economy of Buenos Aires had to diversify or stagnate. The answer first appeared in the form of sheep-farming, which soon came to threaten the dominance of the cattle estancia. It was through the export of wool that Argentina first developed its link with the world market, its internal productive capacity, and its capital accumulation.[58] The final outcome of the wool cycle lay in the future but its beginnings were positive enough to make the Rosas economy an anachronism, a legacy

---

[58] Hilda Sabato, 'Wool Trade and Commercial Networks in Buenos Aires, 1840s to 1880s', *JLAS* 15, 1 (1983), 49–81.

from another age. On the pampas between Buenos Aires and the River Salado sheep were beginning to drive cattle from the land as, from the 1840s, estancia after estancia passed into the hands of the sheep farmers. The large purchases of land by foreigners, the multiplication of sheep, the diversification of exports eroded the rural base of *rosismo*, which had always found its strength among ranchers and peons, not among farmers and shepherds. Sheep-farming introduced social as well as agricultural change, attracting new settlers far removed in values and style from the rural *jefes* and their *montoneros* who first rode in support of Rosas. Sheep-farmers, their partners, and shepherds remembered little of the 1820s; they were less ideologically committed to Rosas than the original cattle-ranchers of the province, less militarized, less politicized, less mobile, more domestic and 'civilian' than the *rosista* estancieros of the past. This implied a weakening of the primitive social base of *rosismo*, rooted in the cattle estancia and the rural militia.

Economic shift in the Argentina of Rosas was the context of crisis rather than its cause. To see the caudillo as a casualty of agrarian change would be to anticipate events and to invoke the simple explanation in preference to the complex. Rosas himself was an expert in rural economics and observed—indeed participated in—the trends of the times. His own estancias incorporated every kind of farming, livestock, sheep, and arable, and he was as likely as any proprietor to change his priorities and move to new pastures. Indirectly, however, economic change threatened him for it affected the provinces as well as Buenos Aires. The Littoral too, similarly endowed as Buenos Aires, underwent steady agricultural growth in these years. Livestock produce, locally processed, left the estancias of Entre Ríos and Corrientes for shipment by river to foreign markets; sheep-farming joined the cattle estancia in the export sector and at mid-century Entre Ríos was the home of 2 million sheep as well as 4 million cattle.[59] When the trade of Buenos Aires suffered the bottleneck of blockade these provinces could enter into open if unauthorized competition. This was not yet serious economically, least of all in wool, but it had political implications. Provincial landowners, merchants, and consumers eventually recoiled against the domination of Buenos Aires, its control of customs, monopoly of federal revenues, and restriction of river navigation. It was a unitarian, Florencio Varela, who pre-

[59] Brown, *A Socioeconomic History of Argentina*, 214–15.

dicted that the provinces of the Littoral would be the hidden reefs on which the dictatorship foundered, and that the demand for free navigation would unite them into a league to confront Rosas. 'The littoral provinces of the Paraná, ruined by a continuous series of futile and useless wars, and impoverished by the economic isolation and tutelage to which they are subject, have more interest than any other people in the world in promoting such a league.'[60]

Now more than ever Rosas needed his internal power base. Yet it too failed him. In Buenos Aires itself the outward signs of popular allegiance were undiminished, and the *rosista* political machine, the magistrates and the priests, could still bring people into the streets to demonstrate their fealty in parades, fireworks, and other extravagant gestures. But people were also sickened by years of war: always the threat of another enemy, always the promise of another victory, always the demand for more recruits and resources, with terror the ultimate sanction. Even towards the end Rosas used to say to his senior associates: 'Those who wish me well, will go with Head-quarters; those who remain behind, will have their throats cut.'[61] In the countryside support for Rosas was more spontaneous. As the army of Urquiza marched through the pampas into the province of Buenos Aires it had to contend not only with a parched and burning land stripped of resources but also with a sullen people, scarce and scattered but unco-operative and visibly *rosista*. According to César Díaz, commander of the Uruguayan Division, the allied army saw clear signs that 'the spirit of the inhabitants of the countryside of Buenos Aires was completely favourable to Rosas', though this was attributed to force: 'it was obvious that the terror which this man instilled had become deeply rooted and that up to then no influence had weakened it'. Even Urquiza was shocked to see 'that a country so badly treated by the tyranny of that barbarian had rallied in mass to his support'.[62] What these outsiders failed to realize, or to acknowledge, was that Rosas had applied his terrorism to the propertied not the popular classes.

[60] Florencio Varela, *Comercio del Plata* (23 June 1846), in *Rosas y su gobierno (escritos políticos, económicos y literarios)* (Buenos Aires, 1927), 65.

[61] 'Los que me quieren, acompañarán al ejército, los que quedan, serán degollados', Southern to Palmerston 22 Nov. 1848, HMC, Palmerston Papers, GC/SO/241; Gore to Palmerston, 4 Jan. 1852, 2 Feb. 1852, PRO, FO 6/167.

[62] César Díaz, *Memorias, 1842–1852: Arroyo Grande; sitio de Montevideo; Caseros* (Buenos Aires, 1943), 220, 223, 229.

Rosas, in short, was not abandoned in his bunker; he could still count on the allegiance of his traditional followers. Why then, as the allied army approached the capital in the early days of 1852, was there no popular rising on his behalf, comparable to that of 1829? There were various reasons. In the first place the basic backing for Rosas in 1829 had come from the estancieros, who left nothing to chance but actively mobilized their peons for Rosas and federalism. Twenty years later many estancieros, their peonage reduced by conscription and their prospects blighted by war, preferred to keep their distance, waiting for peace and prosperity to return. Second, rural insurgency in 1829 had a spontaneous character stemming from popular protest during a subsistence crisis. Since then Rosas had depoliticized Buenos Aires, province and capital, by a campaign of persecution and terror, which had taken the spontaneity out of such popular support as existed and reduced everything to his leadership. If the mortal God failed, leviathan collapsed. Finally, there could be no mass rising in the countryside, as the regime's recruiting officers had already stripped it bare, and able-bodied men were either in the army or in hiding. As the ancient magistrate explained to W. H. Hudson's family, 'most of the young men had already been taken, or had disappeared from the neighbourhood in order to avoid service', and to make up his quota he had to take boys of fifteen.[63] A makeshift army, it was the last hope of Rosas.

Rosas was not a great general and he squandered his military assets both before and during the crisis. His defence arrangements were defeatist and badly timed. He had, of course, lost two regular armies—Urquiza's and Oribe's—to the enemy, when their commanders turned traitors and opened a huge gap in his Littoral front. This was the result of a basic error in his strategic planning. He had allowed the security of the regime to become dependent upon the loyalty of provincial caudillos, pouring scarce resources into their armies and concentrating his major defence effort on forces which he could not directly control and which in the event could be lost by the decision of their commanders. A number of regional military chieftains also deserted the *jefe supremo* and made nonsense of the idea of an 'Argentine confederation'. He was forced back to his ultimate power base, the city and province of Buenos Aires. Yet even here the military failed him and he had to admit that his army was in poor

---

[63] W. H. Hudson, *Far Away and Long Ago*, 99.

shape, with insufficient officers, inferior instructors, inexperienced troops. As Rosas prepared to meet the danger he had first sensed in 1839, he appeared to be less prepared than ever: there was disorder in the ranks, confusion and loss of morale among commanders, while the military chiefs on whom he had lavished so much privilege and property proved to be broken reeds.[64] In the end his armed forces, a terrible scourge on his own people, were helpless before external enemies. These, backed by Brazilian naval power in the Río de la Plata, were too powerful for Rosas. On 3 February, at Monte Caseros, he was comprehensively defeated: he rode from the field of battle, took refuge in the house of the British chargé d'affaires, boarded HMS *Conflict*, and sailed for England and exile.

Sarmiento noticed how easy the end had been: 'The defeat of the most feared tyrant of modern times has been accomplished in a single campaign, at the centre of his power, in one pitched battle, which opened the gates of the city, seat of his tyranny, and closed all possibility of prolonged resistance.'[65] But this was not the end of the caudillos. Urquiza conquered terror by terror, and replaced the rule of Rosas by his own brand of dictatorship. According to the diarist Beruti, 'A new tyrant, replacing his master Rosas, has stationed his troops throughout the city, giving the inhabitants a terrible fright. . . . Urquiza entered as liberator and has become conqueror.'[66] It was another decade before national reorganization began. Meanwhile economic life had to go on, ranchers to produce, merchants to trade, the British to sell, and Rosas's former clients soon accommodated themselves to new patrons.

Nearly all the chiefs in whom Rosas placed any confidence are now in the service employed by Urquiza, the same persons whom I have often heard swear devotion to the cause and person of General Rosas; no man was ever so betrayed. The confidential clerk that copied his notes and dispatches never failed in sending a copy to Urquiza of all that was interesting or important for him to know; the chiefs who commanded the vanguard of Rosas' army are now in command of districts. Never was treason more complete.[67]

---

[64] Rosas to Pacheco, 30 Dec. 1851, Academia Nacional de la Historia, *Partes de Batalla de las Guerras Civiles*, iii: *1840–1852* (Buenos Aires, 1977), 497–500; Irazusta, *Vida política de Juan Manuel de Rosas*, viii. 306–9.

[65] Lynch, *Argentine Dictator*, 330–3.

[66] Beruti, *Memorias curiosas*, 24 June 1852, in *Biblioteca de Mayo*, iv. 4107.

[67] Gore to Palmerston, 9 Feb. 1852, HMC, Palmerston Papers, GC/GO/64; see

5. *The Rosas Model*

Rosas was a standard caudillo with singular features. He used to say there was madness in his family, and many believed him.[68] Did this make him a megalomaniac? More likely his political behaviour derived from a combination of group leadership and personal idiosyncracy, following the classic route of caudillism: regional power, élite allies, seizure of the state, personal dictatorship, and survival through violence. He came from the creole élite of land and militia, blending that dual qualification essential for leadership in the Río de la Plata; but he forswore his inheritance and acquired these assets anew for himself, extending the family tradition through his own initiative. His was an active not passive preparation for power. Thereafter he moved up and down the scale of caudillism, high in some achievements, lower in others, but by any standards emerging as an ultra-caudillo. He was not a soldier in the army of independence but acquired military experience in the conflicts of post-war Argentina, where the capacity to recruit forces for service on the frontier, in the pampas, or in the capital was more important than the ability to lead a regular army. He was a regional chieftain before he was a servant of the state and it could almost be said of Rosas that the state needed him more than he needed the state.

While he acquired legitimacy as an elected governor, he dictated high terms for his appointment, exploiting people's horror of chaos and refusing to serve without absolute power. Of all the caudillos of Spanish America Rosas was the most explicit in using the argument from anarchy. Unread in Hobbes, he insisted that the only way his countrymen could emerge from a state of nature and escape from a life of insecurity was by conferring total power on one man. At the same time he repudiated the idea of a contract for the whole of Argentina, reluctant to spell out the rights of the provinces. Instead he acquired an informal hegemony over the interior through a mixture of diplomacy, clientage, and force. He then moved up the scale of caudillism and enhanced its innate absolutism. By virtue of the extraordinary powers vested in him, he bypassed the normal process of law and imposed a personal dictatorship in which he employed

also Gore to Palmerston, 9 Feb. 1852, PRO, FO 6/167, and HMC, Palmerston Papers, GC/GO/65.

[68] Southern to Palmerston, Private, 6 Mar. 1849, HMC, Palmerston Papers, GC/SO/243.

terror as a medium of government and cruelty as a form of persuasion. Through state terrorism he destroyed the opposition and disciplined his own supporters. But he targeted his terrorism, sparing the popular classes and preserving his influence over them, an influence which people of property were happy to acknowledge. Outside the formal world of patron and client, many people in Argentina identified with Rosas, individuals, groups, institutions. Estancieros saw a successful rancher, peons a gaucho chieftain, merchants an able businessman, townspeople a tireless administrator, priests an uncompromising traditionalist. For every Sarmiento there were thousands of *rosistas*, for every Varela hordes of federalists. Rosas had a comprehensive identity; he reconciled the enmities in Argentine society and controlled its aggression. But he himself provoked hatred and opposition and in course of time prepared his own demise.

The economy flagged and land use changed. While the regime reflected a specific stage of development and served a particular social interest, Rosas was not a slave of the livestock economy, a captive of the estancieros, or a man incapable of adjustment. Consequently the shift from cattle estate to sheep farm was the framework rather than the cause of his downfall. Rosas was a casualty of political and military events which he helped to provoke and failed to anticipate. He applied policies which aroused opposition, outside Buenos Aires if not within, and his opponents were strong enough to defeat him. The Brazilians could not have invaded Argentina without an ally inside; and Urquiza could not have rebelled without foreign support. Together they were too powerful for Rosas. The caudillo who had neglected national organization and failed to rally the provinces to a greater Argentina, at the end found himself isolated in a situation where personal sovereignty and individual allegiance were not enough, and where his own client groups, conscious of a new balance of power, did not have the commitment or the will to save him. Rosas proved the limits as well as the strengths of caudillism.

7
JOSÉ ANTONIO PÁEZ: VENEZUELA
1830–1850

1. *Preparations for Power*

José Antonio Páez began life without the normal qualifications for leadership in Spanish America, élite origins and landed wealth. Unlike Rosas he inherited neither social status nor family property, and his only asset in 1810 was his age. Born on 13 June 1790, he was old enough to fight in the war of independence and to profit from it. He seized his chance. War was the making of Páez and promoted him from poverty and obscurity to wealth and power.

Poverty and obscurity, of course, were relative, and the majority of Venezuelans began life with worse prospects than Páez. He was born near Acarigua in a corner of Barinas, far from Caracas and the society of the coast. Son of Antonio Páez and María Violante Herrera, he came from a family which was Canarian in origin and perhaps possessed an element of mixed blood, though the young Páez certainly passed for white among the swarthy inhabitants of the llanos. His father was a minor employee of the Spanish tobacco monopoly in the town of Guanare, and possessed neither the will nor the money to educate his son. Páez emerged from his childhood illiterate, instructed in little beyond Christian doctrine, and more equipped for fighting than reading. At the age of seventeen he was involved in a violent affray in which he killed a man. His action was self-defence but he thought it prudent to abandon Barinas and his brief acquaintance with the frontier of civilization.[1] He took the traditional route of outlaws, flight into the llanos, and there entered easily into the life of a cattle peon on a ranch, learning llanero skills the hard way, receiving brutality from the black overseer and a knowledge of livestock farming from the proprietor. On 1 July 1809 at Canaguá he married Dominga Ortiz, a docile and in the event

[1] Páez, *Autobiografía*, i. 4–6.

long-suffering woman. She bore him ten children, of whom eight died in infancy, leaving only Manuel Antonio and María del Rosario. She also brought him 2,000 head of cattle, horses, and mules, enough to start a small ranch of his own, though without title to land; he managed his windfall successfully until it disappeared in the war of independence.[2]

The line dividing lawful from lawless activities in the llanos was thin and, like many of his contemporaries, Páez crossed and recrossed it at will, as he searched for subsistence and security in a society which marginalized many rural people and forced them into armed bands under leaders who emerged through their natural ability. While driving cattle near Banco Largo in mid-1809 he encountered a group of slaves in revolt at Las Huerfanitas. He took over their leadership, and assembled a force of 350 men, most of them llaneros. Five days later he attacked the town of Calabozo with 600 men and his band was driven off. A group of 200 llaneros followed him into Apure, one of a number of bands operating on the margin of law and society, and ready to move from banditry to guerrilla operations in the course of 1810.[3]

The career of Páez exemplified the relative importance of education and experience in the making of a Venezuelan caudillo. When the war of independence began he was already trained in llanero ways and, though completely uncultured, had risen above his fellows. Of medium height, he possessed great physical strength and agility, with broad shoulders and a muscular frame. According to O'Leary, 'His good health showed in his clear skin, which would have been very white had he not been sunburned. Caution and suspicion were written on his face. Born of humble parents he owed nothing to education.'[4] He resisted royalist inducements and became a cavalry captain in the army of the First Republic. Skilled with the lance and the lasso he immediately extended his fighting experience in a series of guerrilla engagements which gave early proof of his instinct for manœuvre and attack, his powers of survival and endurance. From the beginning he was a true caudillo and the llanero soldiers were his personal followers: 'I had little faith in the patriotism of those men;

---

[2] 'Testamento en extracto del General José Antonio Páez en 1865', ANH, Caracas, Landaeta Rosales, Estudios y Documentos, VI, IX—70, fos. 8–10.

[3] Gilmore, *Caudillism and Militarism in Venezuela*, 71.

[4] O'Leary, *Narración*, i. 451.

they only served because of regard for me.'[5] He was confident of his role.

Páez fought first under various revolutionary caudillos, none of whom measured up to his own proficiency. In one engagement he mortally wounded José María Sánchez, a royalist noted for his strength and valour, and was saying a prayer over him to assist in his last agony when he noticed that Sánchez was drawing out a dagger. 'I confess my charity withered', wrote Páez, and he finished him off with a lance thrust.[6] A brief period in the army of Urdaneta convinced him that military discipline was not for him. He preferred the independent authority of a guerrilla chieftain. So he assembled his own force in distant Casanare and led them back into action in Apure and Barinas, outriding, outswimming, and outfighting the fiercest llaneros, and acquiring a reputation among his own men and among potential recruits in the royalist camp as one of the few guerrillas who did not kill prisoners. He already exercised a primitive patronage, offering to appoint as captain any llanero who brought him forty men. He also acquired a reputation as a guide and protector of the common people, for he had to provide shelter, sustenance, and occupations for thousands of refugees, men, women, and children. This did not prevent him treating his llanero troops with the ruthlessness they required, and if he was *compadre* to some he was feared by many. In September 1816 in Trinidad de Arichuna he displaced Colonel Santander as commander-in-chief of the Army of the West, when he was chosen by a movement of chiefs and officers, seconded by a great many local people, as a leader better able to organize and inspire the defence of the republic against the royalist enemy. 'They told Santander that they considered themselves in imminent danger and surrounded by the greatest adversities. They had therefore resolved to confer on me the supreme command and blindly to obey my will, confident as they were that I was the only one who could save them from the danger threatening on all sides.' Páez described this as 'one of the most remarkable events of my life and perhaps the first of many strokes of fortune that have come my way'.[7] What he meant was that this was the day when he was recognized as a caudillo, that unique type of leader required by the people and the

[5] Páez, *Autobiografía*, i. 27.
[6] Ibid. i. 52.
[7] Ibid. i. 86–7.

conditions of the western llanos. But it raised another question. To whom was he accountable? Reluctant though he always was to accept a higher authority, and after campaigning for over a year as an independent commander, he recognized Bolívar as the Supreme Chief of the republic.

Recognition did not mean agreement. In 1818, in a series of disputes with Bolívar over basic strategy and tactics, Páez showed his strengths and weaknesses, his skill as a guerrilla and his lack of generalship, his knowledge of the llanos and his failure to see beyond the next river, his superb leadership of horsemen and his under-estimation of the Spanish infantry, his acceptance of Bolívar and his temptation to rebel. Tension with Bolívar, whom Páez admired yet resented, continued during the campaign in New Granada and his own disputed role in the Venezuelan sector. He spent almost the whole of 1820 in Achaguas, recruiting troops, organizing supplies, and reinforcing other groups.[8] He continued to see the war as a series of fronts, none more important than his own. But the authority of Bolívar and the imperatives of the war eventually persuaded the regional caudillos to accept a place in the military structure of liberation, and while they never acquired the professionalism of true soldiers like Sucre and Urdaneta they became an effective part of Bolívar's army. Páez too, who subsequently claimed that 'order and subordination were my principles', joined the great army of liberation that converged upon Carabobo in June 1821 and led his llanero cavalry in a decisive contribution to victory.[9] Bolívar singled out Páez for special mention and in the name of Congress promoted him on the battlefield to the rank of general-in-chief: 'The indomitable valour, energy, and daring of General Páez contributed supremely to our final and splendid triumph'.[10] After the battle it was Páez who marched with Bolívar to Caracas and took the city without resistance. The path marked out so decisively by Páez was that followed by many lesser caudillos and their followers in the years between 1810 and 1821: from cattle peon, to outlaw, to guerrilla fighter, to republican hero. And like them, just as he did not take easily to military discipline, so he was loathe to accept political constraints.

[8] Tomás Michelena, *Resumen de la vida militar y política del ciudadano esclarecido General José Antonio Páez* (BANH, FHRV, Caracas, 1973), 28.

[9] Páez, *Autobiografía*, i. 156.

[10] Bolívar to Vice-President of Colombia, 25 June 1821, in O'Leary, *Memorias*, xviii. 338; Bolívar, Proclama, cited in Páez, *Autobiografía*, i. 187.

The caudillos, now released from wartime discipline, had to be brought into political culture and initiated in the ways of civil society. Bolívar assigned them regional commands in the new state of Colombia. In Venezuela the core region went to Páez, who was appointed commandant-general of the department of Venezuela. There his first duties were to mop up pockets of royalist resistance, bring the seige of Puerto Cabello to a successful conclusion, pursue enemy guerrillas, and impose law and order in a country still governed by local institutions inherited from the colony and a society deeply split by social and racial divisions. But he soon acquired a political role. In 1825, in the course of his duties, he was obliged to recruit a militia; his methods brought him into conflict with the intendant in Caracas, General Juan de Escalona, and with the central government in Bogotá, which crassly arraigned him before Congress. He decided to defy the government, and local opinion rallied round him. From the time of the Valencia insurrection in April 1826, the so-called *cosiata*, he became in effect the chosen leader of a secessionist movement. His own interpretation of these events was simple. He believed that soldiers such as he were valued only in wartime, to be cast aside by civilian politicians when danger was past. As for secession, the root cause was that Venezuelans and Colombians did not like each other. Armed with these convictions, and guided no doubt by chosen advisers, he began his political ascent.

His promotion was not won by chance or by the intrigues of associates. He achieved political leadership by virtue of his own assets. The war had given him an ascendancy and influence over the llaneros and, by reputation, a special relation with the popular classes in general. His record as a warrior gave him a strong influence among the Venezuelan military. Judicious use of patronage assured him a support base within the bureaucracy. And he was in the process of consolidating his position among the Venezuelan élite, not least among the hacendados and merchants of the centre-north. Even Bolívar had to recognize the force of Páez's position and from 1827 accepted him as the *de facto* ruler of Venezuela, subject only to his own authority as president of Colombia. But he confided to his associates that he acted by *force majeure*, and that he had serious doubts about Páez, whom he saw as an insincere and authoritarian figure, doing well in his own business deals, incapable of independent judgement or even of writing his own letters:

General Páez is the most ambitious and vain man in the world: he has no desire to obey, only to command; it pains him to see me above him in the political hierarchy of Colombia; he does not even recognize his own incompetence, so blinded is he by pride and ignorance. He will always be an instrument of his advisers and a mere spokesman for orders and decisions that are not his own. I regard him as the man most dangerous for Colombia, for he has means of action, determination, and prestige among the llaneros, who are our cossacks; and whenever he wishes he can secure the support of the people and of the blacks and *zambos*. This is my great fear, which I have confided to few people and now disclose in confidence.[11]

Nevertheless the political interregnum presided over by Páez from 1827 eased the transition to full secession in 1830. To his fame as a Spanish American liberator, therefore, Páez now added the prestige of leading Venezuelan independence. But his position did not rest on military and political experience alone. He had also, as Bolívar implied, been constructing his personal power base.

Páez was determined to make himself a great landowner and he set out systematically to accumulate property. Conditions were propitious for his project. In Venezuela land was concentrated and underutilized, with only a small percentage of the national territory in private hands and currently productive.[12] Páez laid the first foundations of his fortune in the llanos, where conditions were different from those in the more crowded centre-north but where land concentration had also begun to appear in the colonial period, as northern hacendados expanded southwards and newcomers looked for land in the cattle regions. Large tracts of pasture land began to accumulate in private hands, and major ranches were created out of hitherto small properties in the southern and western llanos, their landlords residing in San Fernando de Apure, Calabozo, and often in Caracas.[13]

In spite of the spread of private property, large *hatos* occupied only a fraction of the llanos before 1810. Most of the land was unclaimed, or held by virtue of property in cattle, in small, scattered, and vaguely defined properties of the kind acquired by Páez in 1809 and subsequently lost in the war of independence. Customary usages regarded

---

[11] Peru de Lacroix, *Diario de Bucaramanga*, 71-2.

[12] According to Codazzi, less than 10 per cent of agricultural land was under cultivation, and less than 30 per cent was privately owned: Agustín Codazzi, *Resumen de la geografía de Venezuela* (3 vols.; Caracas, 1940), i. 63, 345.

[13] Federico Brito Figueroa, *La estructura económica de Venezuela colonial* (Caracas, 1963), 212-21.

pastures as common property and fencing was unusual. On the plains cattle rather than land was the symbol of wealth, and for the majority of llaneros possession of cattle did not yet imply a right to land ownership.[14] Independence destroyed this state of rural innocence. The wars damaged the cattle industry, and while they increased the amount of untitled land they also unleashed more claimants. Both sides raided herds for supplies and booty, while traditional rustlers made the most of new opportunities. Livestock decreased from 4.8 million head of cattle in 1812 to 256,000 in 1822, and increased to only 2 million in 1839.[15] In 1811 republican legislation sought to impose severe penalties for cattle-hunting and at the same time to create precisely defined landholdings in the area. But disorder continued during the war, and with peace the llaneros returned home expecting to find traditional usages in place and still regarding cattle as a free resource. The proprietors, of whom Páez was now spokesman, had other ideas. Acting as *jefe superior*, he issued a new law for estates and ranches in the llanos (25 August 1828), demanding respect for private property and its boundaries, forbidding transit without permission of the owner, and giving ranchers ownership of wild cattle on their estates.[16] Meanwhile the llaneros found it difficult to compensate for loss of cattle rights by ownership of land. The policy of paying off republican soldiers with land grants did not work; few had capital or livestock to start a ranch, and many sold their titles to wealthy creoles, including high-ranking military officers. Land concentration was thus reinforced by the entry of a new élite. One of these was Páez.

At San Pablo near Calabozo Páez established an immense *hato*, where he ruled as a sovereign and lived like a llanero, still an expert rider and cowboy, now stouter than the wartime caudillo and dressed in a red striped linen shirt, a pair of white trousers, and a broad brimmed hat: 'his luxuriant curling black hair . . . and his dark brows and mustachios gave a marked character to his face'. He told the British minister, Ker Porter, 'that he had purchased three estates, now forming the whole of what he called San Pablo, embracing an extent of forty leagues in circumference, and for which he had not

[14] Carrera Damas, *Boves*, 195–6.
[15] Codazzi, *Resumen de la geografía de Venezuela*, i. 178–81.
[16] 'Reglamento para hacendados y criadores del Llano', 25 Aug. 1828, *Materiales para el estudio de la cuestión agraria en Venezuela*, i. 511–16.

paid more than about nine thousand dollars—£1,500'.[17] That was for the land only: he had in addition stocked it with cattle. In one rodeo alone Ker Porter saw 12,000 head of cattle herded by 150 peons to undergo branding 'as the Páez property', in addition to hundreds of mules and horses. This was in 1832. In January 1848 the Hato de San Pablo had 20,000 head of cattle, 700 mares, 300 mules, and about 500 horses, 'all of which property was seized by José Tadeo Monagas'.[18] The San Pablo properties, said Páez, were 'very dear to my heart'.[19] But he had others. Nearby he owned a smaller ranch, La Yegera. To the south, in the savannas beyond the River Apure, where the yearly cycle of sun and flood turned parched earth to luxuriant grassland and formed a paradise for wildlife, he owned a great ranch, San Pablo de Paya, 150,000 acres of prime pasture, the site in 1846 of 100,000 head of cattle and 10,000 horses. To the east of this he acquired El Frío and, still in Apure, the truly enormous ranches of Mata Gorda and Mata Totumo, which he was still in the process of developing in the 1840s, not to mention Los Laureles, which he staked out in 1846.[20] To round off his cattle estates, he had a small property near Rincón Hondo which he inherited from General Rafael Ortega. And in the province of Barinas he possessed two *hatos* and various landed properties.

Páez was not satisfied to be a rancher alone and the llanos were not the whole of his world. The centre of the Venezuelan economy and the home of the traditional oligarchy was the plantation sector in the centre-north, and it was this which Páez was determined to conquer in the years after independence. As a victorious general entitled to rewards, and a political figure with influence in the state, he had instant access to government and through it he secured the property on which he had set his heart, the hacienda of La Trinidad near Maracay in the fertile valleys of Aragua. This great cacao, sugar, and coffee estate, with a fine if decayed house, and handsome terraces and gardens, was formerly the property of an *émigré*, the marquis of Casa León, and was sequestered by the republicans during the war.

---

[17] *Ker Porter's Caracas Diary*, 11–12 Nov. 1832, 674–89, 698.

[18] 'Testamento en extracto del General José Antonio Páez en 1865', ANH, Caracas, Landaeta Rosales, Estudios y Documentos, VI, IX—70, fo. 12.

[19] Páez, *Autobiografía*, ii. 219.

[20] Ramón Páez, *Wild Scenes in South America: Or Life in the Llanos of Venezuela* (London, 1863); Spanish transl., *Escenas rusticas en Sur America* (BANH, FHRV 8, Caracas, 1973), 131–2, 169, 193, 235–49.

Páez applied for it soon after Carabobo and against considerable competition and 'in consideration of services rendered' he was adjudicated the property in November 1821, in exchange for the Yagua ranch and the payment of hacienda wages in arrears.[21] In 1828, for a rent of 6,000 pesos a year, Páez leased the estate, with its 180 slaves, to an Englishman, John Alderson, who had to struggle to obtain a return on his investment.[22] Páez himself subsequently invested large sums in an apparently vain attempt to make it profitable. But it was productive enough to have an embargo laid upon two-thirds of its crop by Monagas during the rebellion of 1848, at which time it was being managed by George Gosling, a British subject and Páez's attorney.[23] This was not the caudillo's only hacienda. From General Mariño he bought the hacienda Los Cocos. From the University of Caracas he leased the cacao hacienda Chuao at a rent of 4,000 pesos a year. Starting from a low base—its slaves in rebellion and its plantations too small to be profitable—he invested considerable sums in making it productive; in 1848 it contained 106,000 cacao trees, 400,000 coffee, and 50 beds of indigo, quite apart from extensive buildings and an effective slave force.[24] Labour relations were apparently a problem and Páez stationed there a virtual garrison of troops, allegedly financed by the treasury, to prevent its numerous slaves from robbing the hacienda of its products.[25] In Aragua Páez had a sugar refinery, in the region of Valencia a dairy farm, and in Puerto Cabello he owned the customs. He also had a number of urban properties, houses in Barinas, Valencia, Maracay, and Caracas.

His agricultural enterprises were highly commercialized. As well as exporting from his ranches and plantations, he sold to the internal market and to the state. According to his enemies he had a virtual monopoly of meat sales in the domestic market. By any standards

---

[21] Castillo to Soublette, Bogotá, 21 Nov. 1821, *Materiales para el estudio de la cuestión agraria en Venezuela*, i. 316–17.

[22] *Ker Porter's Caracas Diary*, 16 Feb. 1829, 434; John Hawkshaw, *Reminiscences of South America from Two and a Half Years' Residence in Venezuela* (London, 1838), Spanish transl. *Reminiscencias de Sudamérica* (Caracas, 1975), 105–7.

[23] Wilson to Palmerston, 31 Mar. 1848, PRO, FO 80/55; Rafael Ramón Castellanos, *Páez, peregrino y proscripto (1848–1851)* (Caracas, 1975), 66–9.

[24] 'Testamento en extracto del General José Antonio Páez en 1865', ANH, Caracas, Landaeta Rosales, Estudios y Documentos, VI, IX—70, fo. 12.

[25] Pedro Tomás de Córdoba, *Memorias geográficas, históricas, económicas y estadísticas de la isla de Puerto Rico* v. 310, ANH, Caracas, Landaeta Rosales, Estudios y Documentos, VI, LX—70, fo. 3.

Páez was a leading rancher, hacendado, and businessman. Even his debts were large: at the turning point of his career, in 1848–9, they amounted to 187,852 pesos of which the largest was 116,000 to the National Bank. According to British sources, at that date the Bank had 'lent out for indefinite periods to General Páez and other political partisans fully a half of its paid up capital'.[26] By his own efforts he had hauled himself up into the élite. As ruler of Venezuela his power and policy synchronized with his economic position. In the period 1827–30 his economic ideas looked distinctly promising to agricultural producers, exporters, and foreign merchants. From 1830 he more than fulfilled that promise. Páez now operated from a superior personal power base within the élite. He was at least their equal in economic power; their superior in access to the military; and their protector in defence against the populace. Meanwhile he was also making great efforts to improve his social standing.

Páez began life without pen or book and was left with an enduring sense of inferiority. Officers in the British Legion noted his qualities as a llanero warrior, his generous and affable nature, but one of them also reported:

When I served with him, Páez could neither read nor write, and until the English came to the Llanos, had never used a knife and fork, so rough and uncultured had been his former life; but when he began to meet the officers of the British Legion he copied their way of living and their dress, modelling himself as much as possible upon them, that is, as far as his lack of education allowed.[27]

Páez quoted this passage in his *Autobiografía* as 'fine and true', and if he was embarrassed by his lack of culture he was never ashamed of his origins. O'Leary described him as completely illiterate, a good guerrilla leader but ignorant of military strategy and organization, and he too noticed his sense of inferiority: 'In the presence of those he thought better educated than himself he was silent and even nervous, and refrained from taking part in conversation or expressing opinions. But with his inferiors he was coarse and loquacious, and not averse to practical jokes.'[28] During the war

---

[26] ANH, Caracas, Landaeta Rosales, Estudios y Documentos, VI, IX—70, fos. 14–15; Wilson to Palmerston, 6 Mar. 1848, PRO, FO 80/55.

[27] Quoted by R. B. Cunninghame Graham, *José Antonio Páez* (London, 1929), 108–9, 114–15, 134, and by Páez, *Autobiografía*, i. 130; see also Valenilla Lanz, *Cesarismo democrático*, 92–3.

[28] O'Leary, *Narración*, i. 451.

illiteracy was not a great handicap, though he had other weaknesses, being prone to epileptic fits when excited or crossed, and defective in his judgement of Bolívar and higher policy.

In the post-war political life of Venezuela Páez found illiteracy a handicap and took steps to correct it. As Ker Porter remarked, 'Feeling this inferiority, and anxious to improve, he has, within these very few years, applied himself to writing and reading; which acquirements, until then, he was totally ignorant of. He knows little of the duties of public life, beyond the knowledge he has acquired at the head of his troops.'[29] His cultural level remained low. He was addicted to gambling of every kind, playing for high stakes, and his favourite Sunday amusement was cock-fighting. His personal entourage in Caracas was a group of armed llaneros, part bodyguards, part sporting cronies, who could also double as musicians and singers when required.[30] And his private life—actually quite public—was not exemplary. His wife Dominga seems to have been a good and loyal woman. She accompanied him during the war, but in December 1818 he sent her away and instructed her to stay in Barinas; there she remained for the next thirty years separated from her husband, to emerge on his downfall still loyal enough to support him during his imprisonment in 1850. He had concubines and a permanent mistress, Bárbara Nieves, a lady from Valencia, 'darkish with fine eyes' though reputedly mercenary.[31]

Páez also sought to escape from his political illiteracy. 'I left the life and isolation of the savanna for a public stage completely unknown to me.'[32] Emerging as the strongest of what he called 'caudillos of the military hordes', he took advice from various sources. He called frequently on the British consul 'to talk politics', and in the next fifteen years Páez and Ker Porter became firm friends.[33] His first Venezuelan advisers were a small and much criticized coterie chosen from a spectrum of interest groups: Mariño, a caudillo coarsened by choice rather than upbringing, who as minister of

---

[29] Ker Porter to Canning, 26 July 1826, PRO, FO 18/35; *Ker Porter's Caracas Diary*, 1 Aug. 1826, 119–20.

[30] *Ker Porter's Caracas Diary*, 3 Aug. 1835, 870.

[31] Will of Dominga Ortiz, ANH, Caracas, Landaeta Rosales, Estudios y Documentos, VI, IX—70, fos. 8–10; Córdoba, *Memorias geográficas*, v. 310, ibid. fo. 3; *Ker Porter's Caracas Diary*, 4 Dec. 1832, 693.

[32] Páez, *Autobiografía*, i. 259, 264.

[33] *Ker Porter's Caracas Diary*, 25 May 1828, 385.

war used to sign state papers on the billiard table during a game; Dr Miguel Peña, a clever but unprincipled politician whose career was blighted by financial scandal; Colonel Francisco Caraboño, an opinionated military colleague; and Tomás Lander, representing the commercial interest.[34] These were the people who encouraged Páez in his resentment of legislators and centralists in Bogotá and ultimately in his separatism. In April 1826 he resisted a summons to Bogotá and raised the banner of revolt, first in Valencia, then in the department of Venezuela, appealing to a motley clientage of llaneros, military officers, and extreme federalists, and taking a decisive step in the direction of Venezuelan independence. Páez rarely indulged in political speculation. He did not generalize on Venezuelan identity, simply remarking that factors of distance and communication, and 'the jealousies and rivalries between Venezuelans and New Granadans' made separation inevitable; 'no caudillo could have inspired it', only the people themselves.[35] Bolívar sent O'Leary on a mission of pacification. The Irishman found Páez at Achaguas in Apure, in the house of Colonel Cornelio Muñoz, seated on a stool, playing a violin, his only audience a blind Negro. O'Leary saw him as Nero amidst the ruins of a great state, a spectre which Páez's final words did not dispel: 'I hope the president will not force me to be his enemy and destroy Colombia with civil war.'[36] Páez had learned to play the nationalist card, and in 1830 he promoted a new constitution with a Venezuelan president, though like any good caudillo he went through the motions of declining the office, 'his conscience telling him the mental powers which enabled him to conquer in the field, were not the same he must be called upon to exert in the Cabinet'.[37]

2. *President and Protector*

'He was ambitious for power, but he wanted absolute power, the power to abuse and to get his own way.'[38] O'Leary's judgement on

[34] Ibid. 1 Aug. 1826, 120–1.
[35] Páez, *Autobiografía*, i. 260, ii. 12.
[36] O'Leary, *Narración*, iii. 66; O'Leary, *'Detached Recollections'*, 22; Manuel Pérez Vila, *Vida de Daniel Florencio O'Leary primer edecán del Libertador* (Caracas, 1957), 302–4.
[37] Ker Porter to Aberdeen, 8 July 1830, PRO, FO 18/78.
[38] O'Leary, *Narración*, i. 452.

Páez, echoing that of Bolívar, contained an element of truth and also of prejudice. Equally that of Ker Porter, who asserted that 'General Páez may rank as the purest and most disinterested patriot among his fellow countrymen, and second only in military glory and greatness to Bolivar.'[39] Páez sought independence, personal and national. He resented taking orders from anyone or being subordinate to anything. During the war he wanted an independent command for himself. In peacetime he wanted an individual sovereignty, free from supervision by Bogotá; in the process of exerting his will he helped to make Venezuela a nation state. Páez usually defended his actions, though not with ideas; his speeches to Congress were replete with rhetoric and his proclamations a byword for bombast. He did not even have the crude political discourse of Rosas, and one looks in vain for political speculation.

The career of Páez, like that of Rosas, was a product of élite backing and personal driving force. There the comparison ended. The Venezuelan élite was not so violently divided as that of Argentina, and unitarists and federalists were not yet at each other's throats. Conditions were right for a consensus among the oligarchy, and this corresponded to Páez's own nature. When he became the first president of independent Venezuela in 1830 he did not claim special powers, or insist on particular terms, but accepted the constitution as it was and ruled within its laws. He shed the disreputable advisers of the 1820s and surrounded himself with a group of expert ministers who were among the best political talents in South America, among them Santos Michelena, secretary of the treasury and exponent of economic liberalism; later recruits, such as Angel Quintero, landlord, slave-owner, and ultra-oligarch, were more conservative but hardly less able. Páez was a general who abolished the army's *fuero*, reduced its numbers, and limited its pay.[40] He established an essentially civilian government, excluding the military chiefs, keeping the caudillos at a distance, and regarding the army as a kind of peace corps. In November 1832 Ker Porter found him at his *hato* of San Pablo clearing land for pasture and wielding a machete alongside his peons, anxious to demonstrate that the president who shared their danger during war now joined them in serving peace, and to

[39] Ker Porter to Duke of Wellington, 9 Feb. 1835, PRO, FO 80/2.
[40] Eleonora Gabaldón, *Las elecciones presidenciales de 1835 (la elección del Dr. José María Vargas)* (BANH, FHRV, Caracas, 1986), 54–61.

encourage the Venezuelan military 'from the General in chief to the
simple soldier, to consider the country no longer in want of their aid
as its defenders, but as its cultivators'.[41]

The legislative input of his first presidency reflected the progressive
mood of liberation. He abolished the *alcabala*, established generous
immigration laws, began the first expansion of primary education,
founded a national library, and allowed freedom of religion. He
favoured his interest groups, of course, reducing duties on agricultural exports, raising them on agricultural imports, while giving
artisans no protection against foreign manufactures. But he probably
argued that there was no alternative. It was a kind of enlightened
despotism, which some opinion thought preferable to other political
options of the time. Santos Michelena was scathing about the candidates for president and representatives in the elections of 1835,
writing to Soublette: 'In England none of them would have escaped
the treadmill or Botany Bay, and here they are candidates for
the highest positions'.[42]

Páez was relatively mild in his reaction to revolts, as long as the
revolts were politically inspired, as they usually were, and took place
within the élite, as they usually did. The conservative, militarist,
revolt of Monagas in eastern Venezuela in 1831 was the first trial of
strength between the president and the regional caudillos. It ended
with Páez and Monagas more or less shaking hands, Monagas accepting the constitution in return for total amnesty for his side. It was
an early example of Páez's clemency in dealing with rebels, and
aroused some indignation among politicians.[43] But Páez had to
temper his policy to the realities of power. He knew that movements
of this kind were encouraged by the weakness of government. At the
beginning of the revolt the provincial administration of Cumaná
had to admit that 'the funds of the public treasury are completely
exhausted . . . there are no regular troops to rely on, only the militia'.[44]
A similar revolt broke out in San Lárazo, Trujillo, in April 1831,
when dissidents claimed that the province's liberties had been violated
and its interests damaged by separation from Colombia; again Páez

---

[41] *Ker Porter's Caracas Diary*, 10 Nov. 1832, 679.

[42] Quoted in Gabaldón, *Elecciones presidenciales de 1835*, 127.

[43] Ker Porter to Palmerston, 11 July 1831, PRO, FO 18/87; Páez, *Autobiografía*,
ii. 145; Castillo Blomquist, *José Tadeo Monagas*, 28–9.

[44] Diego Valenilla to Ministry of Interior, 20 Jan. 1831, AGN, Caracas, Sec.
Int. y Just., XXIV, fo. 338.

personally led the army to crush opposition, and avoided turning a routine rebellion into a major dispute.⁴⁵ While revolts of this kind did not have a social cause, they could draw support from the rural dispossessed and feed on rural distress. They could also impoverish the countryside. As Ker Porter pointed out, the revolts themselves caused such interruption and damage to agriculture 'that one half of the population must be driven to exist by open robbery, whilst the other sinks into poverty and actual want'.⁴⁶ Agrarian reform, however, was alien to the mentality of Páez and to most of his contemporaries.

Páez favoured the plantations over the plains, hacendados over ranchers; and demands for lower taxes on livestock and increased security in the llanos were given low priority in the regime's economic programme. Caudillos responded essentially to interest groups, clients, and lobbies, and the cattle lobby was not powerful enough to compete with the political influence of the hacendados. While banditry in the *llanos* was allowed to run its course, it could not be tolerated in hacienda country. The bandit Cisneros operated too close to plantations for the comfort of the oligarchy, and this was why Páez exerted himself to remove the danger and to turn Cisneros from crime to service, first by military operations, then by invoking *compradazgo*, and finally by luring the bandit into civilization. He used to say to his colleagues, 'If I can persuade this Indian to wear shoes, we have won.' For his part, in a display of pure personalism, Cisneros always insisted that he had never submitted to the government or the republic but only to his *compadre*: 'he adhered to the law of his *compadre* and to no other.'⁴⁷

Peon protest against the society of the Páez years contained an element of land hunger and a demand, however incoherent, for redistribution. But the regime was too wedded to the interests of the hacendados, and these wanted a dependent labour force, not a free peasantry. The shift from cacao to coffee changed the hacendado's reliance on slave labour to a search for *jornaleros*. But rural wages were too low to retain plantation workers, who fled from one estate to another, or chose a life of subsistence, or drifted into banditry. One of the functions of the caudillo was to guarantee proprietors the

⁴⁵ Revolución de San Lázaro en Trujillo, 1831, AGN, Caracas, Sec. Int. y Just., XXVII, fos. 271–303.
⁴⁶ Ker Porter to Palmerston, 30 Apr. 1831, PRO, FO 18/87.
⁴⁷ Páez, *Autobiografía*, ii. 161, 167; see Chap. 5, sect. 4.

labour relations they needed. Planters sought the collaboration of the authorities in limiting peon mobility. Provincial laws extended the classification of *jornaleros*; enforced contracts of work; insisted that debts could only be paid off by labour; made possession of a certificate of completed service obligatory for all travel by peons; imposed arrest and punishment for vagrancy; and penalized flight from work by jail sentences. Anti-vagrancy legislation was revised from time to time and under the presidency of Páez's protégé, Soublette, was brought up to date in the law of 1 April 1845 clarifying the 'crime of vagrancy'. In all parts of the republic, in Coro, Cumaná, Guayana, Trujillo, Barinas, Barquisimeto, and Barcelona, *jornaleros*, muleteers, artisans, who were usually described as illiterate, were arrested for vagrancy and sentenced to imprisonment, public works, or more commonly two years' service on a private hacienda.[48]

The Páez years were a paradise for proprietors. Laws and their enforcement were invariably biased in favour of property, and it was virtually impossible for a peon to appeal against his patrón. The political links between magistrates and landowners were too close to permit impartial administration of justice; local judges, usually incompetent as well as partial, whose decisions were often the immediate cause of rebellions, tended to classify all rural poor as *jornaleros* and thereby subject to oppressive police laws and of course disfranchised. The only recourse left to the peon was to take to the hills, where he became prime material for recruitment into a bandit group, the one institution offering him the twin satisfactions of security and defiance. Parts of the llanos were no man's land, where fleeing peons met fugitive slaves, political rebels, and common criminals in a society which moved in and out of banditry almost by nature and often by chance. A report from Morón in 1833 described a state of disorder in the region of Carabobo where, for lack of a police presence, more than thirty 'fugitive slaves and other villains' had established a base.[49] This was an experience repeated across the whole of the Venezuelan interior.

Banditry was an end in itself, a way of life, hostile to authority but not necessarily partial to politicians. To the extent that authority impeded their activities, bandits were willing to oppose the govern-

[48] AGN, Caracas, Sec. Int. y Just., 1845–51, CCCXXIV, fos. 81–9, 92–103, 104–13, 115, 117, 185–200, 264–78, 360–82, 410–20; CCCXXXII, fos. 289–302.

[49] Carabobo, 14 May 1833, AGN, Caracas, Sec. Int. y Just., LXX, fos. 350–3.

ment, declare themselves political rebels and attack local authorities. Thus rebels and bandits were often indistinguishable, feeding off each other. Páez made little effort to suppress bandits, as long as they did not concert their efforts against the regime. A number of factors positively favoured them. First, political divisions—between central government and provincial caudillos, between conservatives and liberals—encouraged bandits to exploit opportunities, and tempted government and opposition alike to use bandits against their enemies. Second, the high export demand for hides encouraged illicit rustling and quick sales to contrabandists or even to open export outlets, everyone—police, judges, merchants, and ranchers—conniving in handling stolen goods. A third factor was the weakness of the Venezuelan state outside Caracas and the centre-north. Páez surrounded himself with good ministers at the centre, but government broke down in the provinces, where judges were often corrupt and *corregidores* of poor quality, and where the government did not have the resources to mount effective action. State poverty precluded an effective police presence. At a local level there was not so much a scramble for jobs as a wave of resignations, 'because funds are not sufficient to defray the costs'. The office of *corregidor* was not particularly popular, nor well paid, and could ruin a person financially if he had to neglect his own affairs; so these officials had the option of continuing their private business at the expense of the administration of justice, or concentrating on official duties with the prospect of 'certain ruin'.[50] Even the prisons were insecure. In April 1831 prisoners from Colonel Castañeda's revolt were placed in the gaol in Carora alongside local criminals and were promptly freed by their fellow *facciosos* who proved to be too numerous for the local militia.[51] In March 1833 the *jefe político* of Orituco reported his concern over the state of law and order in the Canton of Güires, where a combination of delinquency and political violence had converted the region 'into a haven and retreat for dangerous men'.[52] Officials in San Fernando reported in April 1833 that sixteen escaped prisoners remained grouped and armed.[53]

---

[50] AGN, Caracas, Sec. Int. y Just., III, 1830, fos. 62–5, 349–54.

[51] AGN, Caracas, XXVII, 1831, fos. 222–4, 242.

[52] Jefe Político of Orituco, 23 Mar. 1833, AGN, Caracas, Sec. Int. y Just., LXX, fos. 150–4.

[53] Report, San Fernando, 12 Apr. 1833, AGN, Caracas, Sec. Int. y Just., LXX, fo. 347.

Defied by bandits, the government issued more severe laws against crime, the punishment increasing as detection declined. In 1834 Congress promulgated the *ley de hurtos* against fugitive slaves and other rural delinquents, defining virtually all protest as robbery or vagrancy. This was followed by the *ley de azotes* (23 May 1836). In addition to decreeing death, imprisonment, or hard labour for theft, the new law provided floggings for lesser offences (under 100 pesos). The law was designed to speed up the judicial process, but was stigmatized by the floggings. These were not even an effective deterrent; they simply damaged the reputation of the *paecista* governments without increasing their effectiveness. From 1840 the newly formed Liberal party regularly denounced the *ley de azotes* as barbarous and counter-productive. Recorded robbery increased substantially in the years around 1840 at a time when the lash was being administered with corresponding frequency. By the time the law was amended in 1845 to abolish flogging, liberals had earned much political credit among outlaw groups.[54] There was still, of course, a gap between repressive laws and their application, between the attack on bandoleros and the rate of success. The failure to apply repression effectively encouraged the oligarchy to create their own, parallel security forces, which could then also be used for political conflicts, for or against the government, and so introduce a new element of instability.[55]

Yet Páez was not regarded as a failure, even by the security-conscious oligarchy. He kept the peace in the centre-north, and even in the llanos he contained disorder within acceptable limits. Any major insurrection drew a swift response. On completing his term as president in January 1835 Páez retired to his San Pablo ranch, 'my only thought to restore my badly neglected fortune'.[56] But he had other thoughts on his mind. He would have preferred Soublette to Vargas as his successor. The former was a veteran of independence and an experienced administrator; Vargas was a weak if well-meaning civilian who had spent most of the war studying medicine at the University of Edinburgh. Now he was a political lamb thrown to the military lions, and he needed Páez if not as his shepherd at least as his watch-dog. The trial of strength came quickly.

The Revolution of the Reforms in 1835 was led by military

---

[54] Matthews, *Rural Violence and Social Unrest in Venezuela*, 132–3.
[55] Izard, 'Tanto pelear para terminar conversando,' 53.
[56] Páez, *Autobiografía*, ii. 219.

caudillos and discontented officers who struck while the presidency was weak and sought to cover a struggle for power with a veneer of reform. It was a bid by an alternative oligarchy, though for fighting fodder it drew on bandits and malcontents in the regions. The first scene of revolt was Maracaibo, where objectives were confused by local conflicts and where the military could exploit civilian complaints of neglect by central government, especially of defence requirements in a region where the existence of hostile Indians in Sinamaica placed property at risk.[57] In Caracas the rebels were more direct. They denounced the presidency of Dr Vargas, which they claimed had been promoted by 'a faction of reactionaries and financiers and by his own students', and made specific demands that power and appointments be placed in the hands of the traditional military, appealing to what they called their 'imprescriptible right to appropriate the national army in order to reestablish the principles of a popular, representative, alternative, and responsible system'.[58] Reaction to the revolt was mixed. Coro, Calabozo, Apure, Barquisimeto, Guayana all remained loyal to the constitution. The reformists claimed support in Caracas, Aragua, Valencia, Puerto Cabello, and Cumaná. They also had the allegiance of Mariño and Monagas, second and third in the hierarchy of Venezuelan caudillos. But, in spite of their appeals, they did not have the first.

From his ranch at San Pablo Páez issued a proclamation in defence of the constitution and offered his services in its cause. He assembled his own peons and increased his force by personally recruiting supporters on the way to the capital, exploiting his reputation as a liberator, persuading local caudillos to change sides, and in general proceeding by menace rather than battle. He entered the deserted streets of Caracas on 28 July, where he was welcomed as 'the caudillo of the constitution' and where his mere presence was enough to restore constitutional order, as it was in La Guaira. Congress passed a vote of thanks and granted him the title of *Ciudadano Esclarecido*, Illustrious Citizen. Elsewhere towns and provinces in revolt had second thoughts or were persuaded by a show of military force. Vargas was restored, but it was taken for granted that Páez was

[57] Group of Maracaibo citizens to President of Republic, 23 June 1835, AGN, Caracas, Sec. Int. y Just., CIX, fos. 89–95.
[58] Proclamation, 8 July 1835, AGN, Caracas, Sec. Int. y Just., CVIIII, fos. 185–8; see Chap. 5, sect. 6.

in military command and he personally led the counter-insurgency operations. In September he was complaining that lack of horses prevented his proceeding to the Upper Llanos and warning the government he might withdraw in default of resources.[59] But in the course of October, as General in Chief of the Constitutional Army, he restored security to the east. He reported that he had scoured the province of Barcelona 'without persuading the enemy to show his face. . . . I can assure you that General Monagas has no followers. He hides in the woods with thirty men in a state of fright. . . . Amazing that he should have decided to end his career so sadly'.[60] By October the revolutionary factions were defeated in most parts of the country, and a national congress was convoked on 28 October.[61]

The normal law of the Páez regime was that conspirators were sentenced to execution. In 1831, for example, the ministry of the interior recorded the 'execution by sentence of death on Colonel Remigio Fuenmayor, Lieutenant Nicolás Quiroga, Sergeant Justo Nieto, and Pedro Vargas', though it also recorded occasions when the sentence was commuted.[62] Yet his response to rebellions by the senior caudillos was always conciliatory. In 1831 Monagas negotiated a total amnesty for himself and his followers. Now, following a major insurrection, he was allowed to do the same. Páez's method was to use the army to persuade rather than to fight and to wear down the rebels by negotiation. He offered to talk peace with Monagas and then, at Pirital, issued a decree (3 November 1835) ending the war in the east and conceding a pardon to the *facciosos*, a pardon moreover that allowed Monagas and his officers to retain their rank and property.[63] There was some criticism and dissatisfaction in Caracas at the terms of the amnesty and Santos Michelena resigned from the government because the military ranks of those pardoned were recognized. People noted that rebels in the east had now been twice pardoned, and the government lost some standing.[64] Apart from the need to avoid bloodshed, Páez justified his action to the president on

---

[59] Maracay, 9 Sept. 1835, ANH, Caracas, Colección Laureano Villanueva, República, Gobierno de Vargas, Ar. 3, G. 10.

[60] Páez to Vargas, Aragua, 25 Oct. 1835, ANH, Caracas, Ar. G. 20.

[61] AGN, Caracas, Sec. Int. y Just., CIII, fos. 99, 111, 127, 243, 268.

[62] AGN, Caracas, Sec. Int. y Just., XXXVIII, 1831, fos. 140–6; ibid. XCIII, 1834, fos. 151–7.

[63] Páez, *Autobiografía*, ii. 253–55.

[64] Ker Porter to Palmerston, 5 Dec. 1835, PRO, FO 80/1.

the grounds that there was a risk to the army, not of defeat, but of being pinned down and forced to live off the land and to plunder like the rebels, thus alienating the province it had been sent to save, while the rebel forces refused to come to action. Meanwhile, there were no other troops to deal with the rest of the country. Vargas reassured him and advised him not to worry about critics.[65]

Páez had to seek a personal loan from the wife of Monagas to finance the return of his troops to Caracas.[66] He argued that the government did not have the resources or the money to fight a war and that the people did not want war. This was also his policy towards the seige of rebel-held Puerto Cabello. But how could he avoid a prolonged seige and the consequent destruction of town and property?

To secure the surrender of the town without bloodshed and losses it is necessary that the Treasury spends its all and that proprietors in other places be ruined for lack of labour for their agriculture and of the market for their negotiations; and this is why everyone cries for an end to the war. So there are various interests to reconcile and all tend to the same end; and it is necessary in my view to choose the appropriate means to secure it: this is not by way of arms, rather we seek the way that can be promptly applied to avoid the sufferings that delay is causing to individuals, to the nation, and to the government itself.[67]

The way was by *indulto*, which Páez in agreement with Vargas offered to the rebels to secure the surrender of Puerto Cabello on 3 March 1836. Vargas was weak enough to be pressed by Congress into withdrawing the proposal. Páez informed him that this was impossible and advised him, with some irony, to take a tour round the interior of the country for his health, for his peace of mind, for the good of the nation, and for a better understanding of people and opinion outside Caracas.[68] In the event Congress took over and sentenced the leaders to banishment and exile, though not to the death penalty which some were demanding. Shattered by the events of 1835–6, Vargas resigned and left the way open to the presidency of Soublette, a

---

[65] Páez to Vargas, 23 Nov. 1835, ANH, Caracas, Ar. 3, G. 25; Vargas to Páez, 26 Nov. 1835, ibid. G. 26.

[66] Páez, *Autobiografía*, ii. 256; Parra-Pérez, *Mariño y las guerras civiles*, i. 495–6.

[67] Páez to Vargas, San Esteban, 24 Feb. 1836, ANH, Caracas, Ar. 3, G. 30.

[68] Páez to Vargas, Maracay, 1 Apr. 1836, ANH, Caracas, Ar. 3, G. 30.

general more in tune with the thinking of Páez and better able to stand up to Congress.[69]

Páez had won a victory for his mode of government. In a sense he had asserted the power of the supercaudillo over the regional caudillos without engulfing the country in civil war. He had resisted Monagas, a constant thorn in his flesh, while leaving him dominant in his eastern lair. He had destroyed the political power of Mariño, his principal rival, without taking unnecessary revenge. He had proceeded by compromise, though from a power base stronger than that of his rivals. The Revolution of the Reforms and its aftermath illustrated to perfection the political methods of Páez: he preferred to deal rather than destroy. He was never a terrorist; he did not kill opponents, or wipe out dissidents, or depoliticize Caracas. Venezuela was not Argentina, and Páez was not Rosas. Heading a less divided élite than Rosas, he was the nearest Spanish America came to a consensus caudillo.

The following year, in a ritual well known to caudillos, Páez informed the government that after twenty-seven years of uninterrupted public service he had had enough and in particular he wished to resign as General in Chief: 'If I have played any part in securing the internal peace of the Republic, that ought to qualify me to return to the quiet of my home and family and the cultivation of my fields, which I anticipate as the appropriate scene of my old age.'[70] Naturally the government refused his request and Páez continued to fulfil role of prime protector of the constitution and of the interest groups it enshrined. He was only forty-seven and he had just given another example of his indispensability.

Rebellions continued to break the peace of rural Venezuela. In March 1837 Colonel Juan Pablo Farfán and his brother Francisco, well known to Páez as unreliable and insolent guerrilla chiefs during the war of independence and thereafter as leaders of a llanero family who passed easily from ranching to rustling, raised a revolt in the plains of Apure, overtly in favour of 'reforms', in fact following the

---

[69] Ker Porter described Vargas as 'a good *médico* but a wretched President', *Ker Porter's Caracas Diary*, 5 Jan. 1836, 905; see also J. A. de Armas Chitty, *Vida política de Caracas en el siglo XIX* (Caracas, 1976), 20–2.

[70] Páez to Minister of War, 24 July 1837, AGN, Caracas, Sec. Int. y Just., CXI, fo. 361.

murder of local judges who had applied the law of flogging.[71] Páez was specifically appointed by President Soublette to command the counter-insurgency forces, and before he left Caracas his friend Ker Porter advised him not only to crush the rebellion but to use 'the same promptness and severity in punishing the rebels', otherwise clemency would only encourage a repetition.[72] Páez personally led a force of 700 to attack the Farfáns, riding rapidly across the llanos, swimming the Apure by night, and on 26 April at Payara striking suddenly with a group of sixty chosen men against thrice as many. He inflicted a heavy defeat on the rebels in an action in which Juan Pablo Farfán was killed, and which Páez himself acknowledged as one of the fiercest of his career. His victory, the last he won on a battlefield, earned him the title 'the Lion of Payara'. He returned to Caracas in mid-June, the task accomplished for which he was responsible and for which the élite looked to him, to save Venezuela from pillage and slaughter and deliver it from rebels: 'For had such a misfortune befallen the country, at his defeat no obstacle whatever was in the way to impede them—no *army*, no *militia*, no *chief* then.'[73]

For the rest of the decade and during the second presidency of Páez security in the countryside continued to cause concern. To the traditional activities of bandits and rustlers, and the resentment felt by veteran chieftains against the officials of the oligarchy, was added the political campaign of the liberals, which gave a spurious legitimacy to lawlessness. Páez could not deal with every outbreak personally. Most bandits and rebels were left to the local authorities. In the region of Maracaibo a known bandit, Francisco María Faría, invaded across the border from New Granada in 1838, was joined by other groups of outlaws and led his band in attacks on property and people under the pretext of 'reforms' before he was taken and imprisoned.[74] In 1841 nearer to the capital an armed movement, subdivided into two bands, was reported in the vicinity of Guarenas.

---

[71] Páez, *Autobiografía*, ii. 284; Michelena, *Vida militar y política de José Antonio Páez*, 74.

[72] *Ker Porter's Caracas Diary*, 28 Mar. 1837, 960.

[73] Páez, Proclamation, San Fernando, 16 May 1837, encl. in Ker Porter to Palmerston, 16 June 1837, PRO, FO 80/5; *Ker Porter's Caracas Diary*, 17 June 1837, 972.

[74] Juan J. Romero to Ministry of Interior, Maracaibo, 5 Feb. 1838; J. Y. Rojas, High Court of Justice, Valencia, 25 Apr. 1838, AGN, Caracas, Sec. Int. y Just., CLXXXII, fos. 72, 127–8.

The outlaws were fugitive slaves, one 'with a shackle on his left leg', blacks and *pardos*, armed with guns and machetes, and led by one Manuel Torralva 'who has an Indian girl'; they raided haciendas and attacked villages, and kept the proceeds of their plunder in a farmhouse.[75] In the early 1840s the organization and operations of gangs of fugitive slaves increased; parts of the provinces of Coro and Maracaibo, traditionally employers of slave labour, were reported to be in a state of anarchy.[76]

Páez himself was frequently threatened with assassination and was accompanied everywhere by llanero bodyguards. In 1843 the governor of Apure reported that preparations were being made for a revolution led by Colonel Juan Sotillo against General Páez personally, seconded by Juan Vicente Mirabal, who worked for a 'revolution of classes'. But the revolutionaries' prime objective was the assassination of General Páez; with him out of the way, they believed, no one could stop them 'thus demonstrating the conviction of all Venezuelans that Your Excellency is the first and most powerful element of order which the Republic has'.[77] Páez acknowledged that there were always Venezuelans who wished to kill him, but insisted that 'I rely on Providence, on a clear conscience, and on the good sense of my compatriots.'[78] During his second presidency, while the political consensus began to collapse, so too disorder in the interior increased. In 1844 a rising of more than 300 rebels in Lezama, Chaguaramas, under the veteran guerrilla chief Colonel Centeno, while not particularly violent, heralded a new phase of confrontation: 'Up to now they have not committed any crimes other than to repudiate the government and the authorities of Orituco; they protest their refusal to recognize either of these and they cry 'Long live the liberals!' and 'Death to the oligarchs!'[79] As bandits joined a network of political protest, and pressure on the oligarchy grew, so Páez appeared to be the last line of defence against disorder, the only hope for security.

---

[75] B. Manrique, Provincial Government of Caracas, to Ministry of Interior, 5 Mar., 12 Mar. 1841, AGN, Caracas, Sec. Int. y Just., CCXXIV, fos. 204, 207–8.

[76] Francisco de Acosta to Provincial Government, 16 Dec. 1843, to Ministry of Interior, 28 Mar. 1844, AGN, Caracas, CCXCVIII, fos. 339, 352–3.

[77] Governor of Apure to Ministry of Interior, 5 Dec. 1843, Ministry of Interior to Páez, 23 Dec. 1843, AGN, Caracas, Sec. Int. y Just., CCXC, fo. 343, 347.

[78] Páez to Ministry of Interior, 27 Dec. 1843, AGN, Caracas, Sec. Int. y Just., CCXC, fo. 360.

[79] Chaguaramos, 18 Oct. 1844, AGN, Caracas, Sec. Int. y Just., CCCIX, fo. 164.

3. *Caudillo of the Oligarchy*

Páez was elected president for a second time in January 1839, obtaining 212 votes out of the 222 electors qualified to vote.[80] He presided over the Venezuelan state like a patriarch, served only by a primitive bureaucracy, tiny army, non-existent fleet, and an almost empty treasury, and relying on his personal power and prestige to keep order. One of his first steps was to ask Congress to authorize measures for the improvement of coastal defence, providing more forces and artillery, which at the same time could also act against political disturbances and assure 'domestic peace'.[81] Even so, defences were fragile. While Páez was a professional soldier, he was not a military dictator. He subsequently claimed that

The entire military force of the Republic consisted of 800 men, because security rested on public opinion. The money which could have been spent on maintaining a regular army was allocated to improving education, opening roads, improving ports, and constructing public buildings; to encouraging immigrants and civilizing miserable Indians; to paying the state debt and enhancing our internal credit.[82]

This was an idealized view of the regime, distorted no doubt and tending to propaganda. It was Páez's perception and not entirely without basis. But it ignored the significance of his personal power.

While Páez had less power than Rosas and lacked the 'extraordinary faculties' enjoyed by the Argentine ruler, he was more than a constitutional president. He was an oligarchic dictator. He and his political associates in the landed and merchant sectors monopolized power. They manipulated elections in their own interest. They filled the bureaucracy with their own clients. And they appointed the judges from their own party. They could not totally silence Congress, which was the scene of noisy confrontations and a stage for nationalists and demagogues; but the same methods of patronage and influence by which they controlled the rest of the state also enabled them to keep a grip on Congress over vital economic and social policies. So the oligarchy, agreeing on policy, were given an additional argument from patronage. Finally, through use of the law of libel and

---

[80] Secretary of Congress to Páez, 28 Jan. 1839, AGN, Caracas, Sec. Int. y Just., CLXXXIV, fo. 254.

[81] Message to Congress, 30 Mar. 1839, AGN, Caracas, Sec. Int. y Just., CLXXXVI, fos. 226–8.

[82] Páez, *Autobiografía*, ii. 303.

control of compliant juries they also worked to stifle the press, claiming that Páez could not be criticized without danger to the nation, for he was the nation.[83] Yet the primacy of *paecismo* blinded its partisans to the possibility of a reaction. The oligarchy could not entirely freeze politics, evade criticism, or prevent opposition. There were many people who felt excluded by one-party control of government, if only because it could not satisfy everyone. In the countryside there were many tenant farmers and larger planters, especially in coffee production, who were frustrated by the agricultural crisis of the early 1840s: they resented urban financiers who pressed for repayment and criticized the credit laws under which they operated. And in all parts of Venezuela there were claimants to state employment who were disappointed in their expectations.

There was, therefore, a certain inevitability in the formation of a Liberal party in 1840. Liberalism already had a substantial history in other parts of Spanish America, and though the Venezuelan model did not exactly reproduce the features of those elsewhere, its profile was recognizable. The party was essentially a political movement, demanding free elections and an end to one-party government; and its members were themselves ambitious for power. Social change was not one of its objectives, nor was ideology one of its strengths. Issues were taken up as forms of patronage rather than principles. Planters were promised reform of credit laws. Artisans were promised protection. Popular clamour in the countryside was rarely disavowed. There was an egalitarian tone to the message of the liberals which gained them a following among the popular classes, especially in the interior. Páez was denounced as partisan, a manipulator of elections, a defender of the oligarchy. The liberal newspaper *El Republicano*, whose hidden patron was Monagas, attacked him for neglecting the heroes of independence, Mariño, Monagas, and others, and replacing them by his own men such as Angel Quintero. The election of Soublette as president in 1843 was criticized as fraudulent and Páez was branded as the iron fist behind the regime.[84] Thus the scene was set for a confrontation between the oligarchy, who saw themselves

---

[83] Castillo Blomquist, *José Tadeo Monagas*, 37.

[84] Where the liberals had political muscle they too practised electoral fraud: in Maracaibo, 'there was no measure legal or illegal, honest or dishonest which they did not resort to' (Mackay to Wilson, Maracaibo, 4 Oct. 1844, PRO, FO 199/16). On Monagas and *El Republicano* see Castillo Blomquist, *José Tadeo Monagas*, 37.

as the natural rulers of Venezuela, and the liberals, who, however insincerely, managed to fuse political and social protest.

At the conclusion of his second presidency Páez retired to private life on the Hato del Frío, but he continued to be a focus of opinion, hailed by some as the bodyguard of the government, suspect to others as the power behind the president.[85] In September 1844 a revolt broke out in the llanero town of Orituco, provoked by the continuation of government by oligarchs under Soublette and his protector Páez and the belief that the liberals' defeat in the recent elections had been caused by government fraud. Led by Juan Celestino Beomán, known as Centeno, a throwback to royalist guerrillas, it recruited from former rebels, mutinous militia, and common criminals, but also from *jornaleros* and ranch peons who demanded free land and social justice, and received some support from small planters and sharecroppers who denounced the credit laws and excessive rents. The movement grew to about 500 strong and took an anti-Páez and pro-liberal political stance. Officially the liberal party stood back from the rebellion but was not averse to its name being used and acquiring a rural constituency.[86] In the event the Centeno rebellion did not develop beyond a disorderly rampage and posed no real challenge to the government. When dispersed its components formed outlaw groups and reverted to banditry in the central llanos and the agricultural zone. Some of these coalesced into a larger band in the llanos of Calabozo, Tiznados, El Pao, and Orituco, well mounted and armed with firearms, lances, and swords, first under the Rodríguez brothers, then under Pedro Aquino, who led them in robbing cattle and haciendas, taking prisoners, and attacking officials and judges. They were recruited from bandits but proclaimed an 'anarchic' political message: they encouraged the rural masses to disavow local authority and 'the present state of things' and demanded an end to slavery, land monopoly, and municipal taxes. From their conversation and speeches, as reported by local officials, it could be deduced that 'they belonged to the party known as liberals'.[87]

By mid-1846 political and social tensions had reached breaking

---

[85] Wilson to Aberdeen, 22 Oct. 1844, PRO, FO 80/26.

[86] Matthews, *Rural Violence and Social Unrest in Venezuela*, 161.

[87] 'Partidas de facciosos que infestan los llanos de Calabozo', AGN, Caracas, Sec. Int. y Just., CCCXXXII, fos. 1, 5, 65, 102.

point. Planters were pressing the government to reform the credit structure. Peasants were joining bands in the hope of improving their condition. As the oligarchy faced its greatest crisis, liberals made political capital from social discontents. The elections of August 1846 were bitterly fought. The liberals cried fraud and the charge was probably correct, though they themselves were not inexpert in fixing elections. They were provoked when the government suppressed the opposition press. Their outrage was even greater when the conservatives judged their leader, Antonio Leocadio Guzmán, to be implicated in the disturbances, therefore ineligible as an elector, and thereby automatically disqualified as a presidential candidate. In late August conservative and liberal moderates, identifying where true power lay, arranged a meeting between Páez and Guzmán in Maracay in an attempt to reach a reconciliation. This in itself became a political issue and generated further tension. Páez was a caudillo, Guzmán a party leader, the projected meeting outside normal politics. Páez saw himself as an arbitrator. Guzmán regarded him as a partisan. Certainly Páez had no time for liberals:

The discussion on complete social equality had raised the question of castes, and of the better distribution of property and public appointments; and these questions aroused undue hatreds, incited greed, and encouraged ambition, passions which do not respect barriers once they are breached. In these circumstances I found myself situated between two parties, both making demands: one composed of good and enlightened men demanded that I declare open war on the enemy, excluding all negotiation; the other insisted that I join them if I wanted to avoid civil war, which they claimed was imminent.

Páez was also reminded that he had won his reputation as a leader of the 'popular element', 'no longer as manageable as before', but still ready to recognize him as their chief.[88]

The meeting in Maracay, however, was overtaken by the rebellion of the 'Indian' Rangel, a mestizo who had seen both his land and his vote taken away, seconded by Ezequiel Zamora, a radical liberal who recruited a horde of socially motivated peasants.[89] The liberals, whose ranks were dominated by property owners, were not the organizers of the rebellion; but they were politicians whose nature it was to exploit opportunities, just as the party of government used the

[88] Páez, *Autobiografía*, ii. 388–9.
[89] See Chap. 5, sect. 7.

occasion to brand them as revolutionaries and wage all-out war on liberals and rebels alike.

The government of Soublette responded vigorously to the rebellion of 1846 and promptly took the 'extraordinary powers' allowed by the constitution in cases of internal disorder. On 1 September, simultaneously with Rangel's uprising, the executive mobilized the standing army and requested from the Council of State authorization to use regular troops against the bands operating in the interior. The government also obtained the consent of Council and Congress for full mobilization of the militia and the approval of a loan of 300,000 pesos. The governors of Caracas, Carabobo, and Barinas were instructed to send the militia in active pursuit of the rebels; and in the course of October and November over 11,000 men, regular and militia, were under arms at a cost of 500,000 pesos.[90] Páez was appointed general-in-chief of the army, and Monagas second-in-command to pacify the east. Páez was in Maracay when he received the appointment: 'I summoned my peons, always ready to follow me into danger, and at 9 o'clock at night in a heavy downpour I set off'.[91] Soon his peons were joined by units of the regular army and militia and were actively engaged in counter-insurgency. This was a different war, no longer a simple struggle for power between central government and regional chieftains but one between political parties. The rebellion was led by political caudillos rather than traditional military chiefs, and it was directed against a political enemy, not merely the forces of a rival caudillo. The enemy, of course, controlled the regular army. Even so, its victory did not come easily.

Rangel and Zamora united their bands into an army which exploited their knowledge of the terrain and fought an effective guerrilla war. They simultaneously punished the oligarchy and procured resources by raiding haciendas, plundering their contents, and freeing slaves. While the rebels had the sympathy of many small farmers and liberal hacendados, they drew their strength essentially from popular support, mainly that of free labourers, and from the infrastructure supplied by peasant sympathizers. One list of 121 rebel prisoners showed 59 per cent peons, 19 per cent slaves, 19 per cent small farmers, and 3 per cent artisans.[92] But this was not a social

[90] Wilson to Palmerston, 23 Jan., 8 Feb. 1847, PRO, FO 80/44.
[91] Páez, *Autobiografía*, ii. 390.
[92] Matthews, *Rural Violence and Social Unrest in Venezuela*, 184 n. 40.

revolution. The leaders were provoked by the 1846 election results and their prime aim was to win political power; that was specific, while the social message was vague. Linkage to the Liberal party was a weakness as well as a strength. The liberals were divided on social issues but the majority supported the existing agrarian and property structure, indeed belonged to it, and their dominant objective was political power. And militarily the liberals were weaker than the government. Gradually the security forces closed in and at the end of February 1847 a battalion of militia under Major Rodríguez brought the elusive enemy to battle and to bloody defeat at the pass of Pagüita. By May the llanos were pacified.

Páez described the rebellion of Rangel and Zamora not as a social revolution but as a conspiracy between demagogues and liberals to plunge the country into bloodshed and anarchy.[93] It was a crude interpretation and probably disguised his real opinion. His own response was far from cruel. He too knew something of fighting a war in the llanos, and he proceeded in his usual way, threatening the enemy with force yet offering the alternative of surrender. He secured the defection of many rebel caudillos and their followers through guarantees of amnesty without punishment: by means of 'clemency, persuasion, and generosity, employing minimum force and avoiding bloodshed and casualties', he whittled away at enemy numbers, criticized by those who preferred more violent tactics, but confident in his own. The procedure reflected a view of Venezuela which saw order and disorder as easily interchangeable, needing only a caudillo's influence to turn a bandit into a peon. After the defeat of Rangel he completed his personal campaign of counter-insurgency in the valleys of Aragua and the llanos, and was then retired.

In the early months of 1846, before the final collapse of consensus, Páez visited his ranches in Guarico and Apure, to review his property, brand his cattle, and count his peons. He travelled like a potentate, an informal sovereign, accompanied by friends and clients and by his son Ramón, an old boy of Stonyhurst College who was appointed chronicler of the expedition and saw himself as a second Waterton.[94] It was a great display of wealth and power. The party was a hundred strong, cattlemen, muleteers, servants, guards, and

---

[93] Páez, *Autobiografía*, ii. 397.
[94] Ramón Páez, *Escenas rústicas en Sur América*, 21–43; Cunninghame Graham, *José Antonio Páez*, 280–6.

miscellaneous escorts, organized in a column which also comprised scores of pack mules, loaded with provisions, clothes, and arms, and a troop of 200 horses. Leaving Maracay at dawn, the caravan travelled via Villa de Cura to the ranch of San Pablo, where Páez was met by a Negro overseer who, as his master dismounted, knelt on the ground to kiss his hand. The caudillo spent the next months living like a llanero, visiting his various estates in the western llanos, organizing his livestock, inspecting his boundaries, entertaining his friends, dictating his correspondence, while his men brought in a dead bandit and Ramón recorded his father's refusal to stand a third time for the presidency. Páez, it seemed, preferred the candidature of Monagas.

4. *Caudillo in Defeat*

The career of Páez, like that of Rosas, illustrated an obvious truth: caudillism was totally lacking in development. The caudillo did not exist to promote change. He set institutions in a rigid mould and preserved policy in immutable form. This did not necessarily make for stability. The departure of one caudillo and the entry of another caused widespread upheaval in patronage networks, punishment for some, prizes for others.

Monagas was elected president of Venezuela in January 1847 on the strength of his élite credentials and recent success against the rebels in the east; he was backed by the personal influence of Páez and the support of Soublette. Independent of the former administration and, apparently, of the liberals, it was thought he would ease political tensions, while remaining a tool of the *paecistas*, represented in the government by Angel Quintero, minister of the interior.[95] When Páez visited Caracas for the inauguration of Monagas, he was received as though he were the new president, and his shadow hovered over the first months of the new government. Then Monagas came into the sun. He began to create an independent political base, surrounding himself with liberals and showing great leniency towards Guzmán, Zamora, and other rebels. He refused to select governors nominated by the oligarchy and appointed instead men loyal to him, some of whom were veterans of the anti-Páez revolts of 1831 and

---

[95] Castillo Blomquist, *José Tadeo Monagas*, 64–5.

1835. He also sought to undermine the military position of Páez, whose appointment as general-in-chief came to an end with the end of the rebellion. In May 1847 the regular army, expanded during the previous year's conflict, was reduced to 2,500 men and filled with Monagas loyalists. He dismissed the active militia, one of the pillars of government support in combating the rebels of 1846–7, and in its place reorganized the reserve militia, customarily employed only to supplement regular troops in time of domestic crisis. By January 1848 reserve units numbered over 22,000 men. Officers were carefully selected from Monagas's supporters and included recent rebels. Conservatives accused the government of creating this force from many 'questionable elements of society' and using it as a means of arming the masses sympathetic to the new regime.

Meanwhile Monagas was expanding his political constituency and purchasing the support of liberals and landowners. The land law of 10 April 1848, designed overtly to distribute public land in order to raise revenue, promote agriculture, and enable individuals to acquire land, made little difference to the treasury and even less to the agrarian structure. But it enabled the government to reward some powerful supporters. In 1848–57 of all the land affected—in the event only a small part of national territory—55 per cent was distributed in ten concessions, mainly in the ranching lands of Barcelona and Apure. The new regime favoured its own family, friends, and political supporters. The Monagas family acquired 11.6 per cent of the total sold; other individuals among the provincial military and political élites gained even more.[96] Monagas repealed the onerous credit law of 1834. A new law of 28 April 1848 provided that defaulted debtor's property could not be sold for less than 50 per cent of its value, and placed a ceiling of 9 per cent on interest rates. The National Bank, another focus of liberal criticism, began to fail in the late 1840s, owing largely to the new credit legislation, and was legislated out of existence on 23 March 1850. The *ley de espera y quita* of 1841 was reformed on 9 April 1849, to grant payment extensions of six to nine years, while requiring the consent of only half the creditors. Amidst the ensuing outcry from foreign financiers and their governments the Venezuelan treasury in effect agreed to compensate creditors and so abandoned the path of relative fiscal stringency associated with Páez for the mismanagement characteristic of the

---

[96] *Materiales . . . Enajenación y arrendamiento de tierras baldías*, vol. i, pp. xxxiii–xl.

Monagas regime. Monagas also gained favour with liberal politicians by the law of 3 April 1849, which abolished the death penalty for political crimes, and by the new credit law which eliminated the rule that debt could occasion loss of political rights. But it was only a marriage of convenience. Monagas was not a liberal; nor were the liberals *monaguistas*.[97]

The oligarchs, dismayed by the change of policy and loss of valuable offices, looked to their caudillo to deliver them from Monagas and his associates. A meeting between Monagas and Páez was projected in December 1847 at a half-way point between Caracas and Maracay, where it was hoped a deal could be struck. But the arrangement broke down, neither caudillo willing to move too far from his base or to risk losing face. A group of oligarchs wrote to Páez to dissuade him from leaving the country on his private affairs, as planned, but to remain and boldly to proclaim his sentiments concerning the political state of the country and 'to point out to his fellow countrymen the way to their salvation'.[98] The oligarchs were not powerless: they still monopolized the judicial department, still controlled Congress, and were talking of impeaching Monagas. But they needed to escape from the militia and the mob of Caracas. On 23 January 1848, behind closed doors, a resolution to transfer Congress to Puerto Cabello and to provide it with an armed guard was passed by both houses. This was not unconstitutional but it caused excitement among the populace. Among liberals it was regarded as an affront to the executive and a preliminary to impeaching the president and opening the way to a return of Páez and his partisans. On 24, when it was feared that Congress would issue a formal declaration against Monagas, a mob of some 2,000, reinforced by reserve militia, broke into the legislative chamber. Amidst much pushing and shoving and scenes of violent confusion eight men were fatally wounded, including four representatives, one of them Santos Michelena, deputy for Caracas and former minister of Páez. The Monagas regime was not averse to unleashing popular paramilitaries, although the role of Monagas himself in the riot was obscure. He ordered the militia and mob to stop firing, but by then the damage

---

[97] Parra-Pérez, *Mariño y las guerras civiles*, iii. 221.

[98] Quoted in Wilson to Palmerston, 3 Jan. 1848, PRO, FO 80/54. Wilson knew of the letter because a number of British subjects, against his advice, subscribed to it; 'political partisans' he called them.

had been done. He would have been the target of Congress and he obviously profited from Congress's discomfort. He now asked Congress for special powers and armed with these he called up 10,000 militia and proclaimed an act of amnesty for all political offences committed since 1830. The Monagas version of these dramatic events naturally blamed Congress, whose foolish and illegal action in calling in troops to guard members sparked off a counter-riot by the people and was responsible for the resulting casualties. He wrote to Páez: 'I have a right to count on you, as you on me. At all costs we must save the *patria* and its institutions, for which I expect your most effective cooperation and the support of your advice. Let me know your opinion with the frankness of a friend and comrade.'[99]

Páez was not impressed. He felt a personal responsibility for the conduct of Monagas, having promoted his election as president, so he could not remain aloof. He was in Calabozo with Soublette and Quintero when news of 24 January arrived two days later. He informed the president that his acts were unconstitutional; he should take the troops out of Caracas and allow Congress to move to a calmer place. Otherwise, 'who can avoid the war which you have already instigated by murdering the representatives of the people?'[100] On 4 February Páez denounced the attack on Congress and exhorted all patriotic Venezuelans to join him in armed opposition to the government. He argued that the fundamental pact was dissolved and the nation had resumed its rights. In the exercise of those rights some of the Cantons 'have clothed me with sufficient authority to raise an army for the purpose of avenging the outrages inflicted upon the Republic and to mete out punishment to the perfidious Magistrate'.[101] According to the British minister, Belford Hinton Wilson, whose hostility to Páez often warped his judgement, 'It is said that General Páez has assumed the title of "Restorer of the Laws and True Liberty", a name of significant import in Spanish America from its being associated with that of General Rosas.'[102] A more apt comparison was the loss of rural support by both caudillos when it was most needed.

---

[99] Monagas to Páez, Caracas, 24 Jan. 1848, ANH, Caracas, Correspondencia privada, J. A. Páez, XII, 12, fo. 7.
[100] Páez to Monagas, 31 Jan. 1848, in Parra-Pérez, *Mariño y las guerras civiles*, iii. 83–6; Páez, *Autobiografía*, ii. 426.
[101] Páez, Proclama, 4 Feb. 1848, in *Autobiografía*, ii. 430–3.
[102] Wilson to Palmerston, 14 Feb. 1848, PRO, FO 80/54.

Páez moved to the plains of Apure where he anticipated a rising of his faithful llaneros. But the firmest support came from those places in the interior, especially in the west, where the former political networks were still in place. The municipal councils of Chaguaramas and Calabozo, as well as the governors of Maracaibo, Trujillo, and Mérida, all proclaimed allegiance to Páez. From Maracaibo came, by 'popular acclaim', the view that 'the assassinations in Congress have raised suffering to a new level, and made it clear that General José Tadeo Monagas aspires to military dictatorship, at the head of the revolutionaries of 1846 and of known enemies of public liberties.'[103] But translated into troops, the numbers of supporters were few. Inducements of money and rank seemed to have little effect, and Páez was able to assemble only 800 recruits, many of whom were forced to join by local *jefes*. Páez had spent too long away from the llanos, in Caracas and Maracay; in the process of becoming a northern oligarch, he had lost his original power base. Each side 'levied exactions', which often simply meant they plundered the property of the other. But the government had more success and was soon able to muster an army of over 6,000 men, including more recruits from the labouring sectors than Páez. As his other fronts crumbled, Páez faced the government forces under his old comrade in arms, Cornelio Muñoz, who had refused to join the rebels. Páez, with only 500 raw recruits, some of them liberated convicts, was badly defeated at Los Araguatos in the plains of Apure. It was more than a military defeat:

This defeat has deprived General Paez of that prestige which has hitherto been the main source of his political power in Venezuela; namely, the belief that the 'Llaneros' or inhabitants of the plains of Apure could alone be kept in restraint by his influence while they were ever ready at his back to overturn any Government whose existence might be disagreeable to him; for General Muñoz and the men who have fought with him are inhabitants of these plains, who have come forward voluntarily on the present occasion to resist the power and frustrate the ambitious projects of General Paez.[104]

Muñoz reported that his own troops charged into battle with the cry 'Long live the Constitution!' which was answered by the troops of Páez with 'Long live the King José Antonio Páez!' After the battle

---

[103] José A. Serrano, 7 Feb. 1848, AGN, Caracas, Sec. Int. y Just., CCCLXIII, fo. 148.
[104] Wilson to Palmerston, 21 March 1848, PRO, FO 80/55.

Páez fled to Casanare, crossing the Arauco with only twelve men, and from there to Jamaica, St Thomas, and Curaçao. Soon the rebellion lost what popular and peasant support it had in Mérida and Trujillo, and even in Maracaibo all opposition ceased by the end of the year.

Venezuelan caudillos rarely retired. In contrast to Rosas after Caseros, Páez did not abandon his quest for power. Resistance was in his nature and he was reluctant to accept the verdict of the constitution. At the beginning, in 1826, he had staked his political career on rebellion, a rebellion legitimized by its cause and its success. Now, in 1848–9, the mark of the caudillo showed again as he turned to armed rebellion, the last resort of personalism. In Curaçao Páez was the centre of an *émigré* opposition; he had agents in the Caribbean and the United States to mobilize support. On 1 August 1848 he issued a manifesto promising to overthrow Monagas or die in the attempt. Encouraged by growing criticism of the regime as sectarian, militarist, and corrupt, rebels raised their heads again on 21 June 1849. Political disturbances broke out in the provinces of Caracas, Guarico, and Aragua, while in the capital a group of *paecistas* headed by the Belisario brothers attacked the presidential palace and attempted to assassinate Monagas, were repulsed, and fled to the llanos. After a number of encounters notable for cruelty and carnage on both sides, the llanos factions were destroyed in battles which ended on 22 July.[105]

Páez sailed from Curaçao on 2 July with some seventy followers, arms, and supplies in eight Dutch schooners, and landed at Coro, historic graveyard of many exiles' hopes. After only limited success in attracting support on the coast, he pushed inland on 20 July with a force of no more than 750, top-heavy with senior officers and hopeful of reinforcements from the llaneros. But the destruction of the rebel factions and the unsympathetic attitude of the people sealed Páez's fate: 'No longer could I victual my forces, munitions were scarce, troops and officials were shoeless and desertions frequent, and above all, as so frequently occurs in the defence of good causes, the towns did not offer the cooperation they had promised.'[106] Surrounded by government forces exceeding 4,000, Páez surrendered with some 650

---

[105] Riddel to Palmerston, 5 July 1849, PRO, FO 80/63 B; Castillo Blomquist, *José Tadeo Monagas*, 231–2.

[106] Páez, *Autobiografía*, ii. 378.

men on 15 August at Macapo Abajo in the province of Carabobo. He
was imprisoned for months in a small and stifling cell in the Castle of
San Antonio in Cumaná, where he had to lie on the floor to breathe
in fresh air under the bottom of the door, and where the sound of
a distant guitar from the barracks encouraged him to dance for
exercise, a movement 'in marked contrast to the state of my spirits'.[107]
Monagas was not so clement as Páez had been in 1831 and 1835.
There were no executions, but Páez was exiled for life and those
who surrendered with him lost their ranks, employments, titles, and
decorations.[108] He went first to St Thomas and finally reached New
York on 26 July 1850. There he met Garibaldi and with him was
welcomed as a republican hero. He was then sixty, destined to
spend some twenty years in exile.

Macapo was the end of the road for Páez. A caudillo of forty years'
standing asked for a cease-fire knowing that the balance of power
had shifted. Páez had already lost the initiative to Monagas. The time
to have destroyed his rival was in 1847, before he began his regime or
at the first signs of danger; once established, power gained its own
momentum. By 1849 Monagas had given his power base in the east
a national dimension, bringing in his own people, rewarding his
comrades of 1831 and 1835, buying the support of military and
political leaders, and exploiting his credit with regional caudillos to
keep the provinces in line, more or less as Páez had done twenty-five
years previously. As for the popular sectors, a number of *pardo*
generals identified with the regime and acted as a kind of conduit to
the castes. Monagas had a special favourite, the *zambo* general Juan
Sotillo, whom he employed in part as a *capataz* to keep blacks and
pardos in order, in part as a watch-dog to savage his enemies; when
Sotillo caught the Belisario brothers he buried them alive up to their
necks and at a gallop cut off their heads.[109]

Deserted in the power struggle at the top, Páez then found that his
famous llanero base had crumbled, eroded by his long association
with the oligarchs. In the two rebellions of 1848–9 there was no
mass movement for Páez in any part of Venezuela, while Monagas
and his liberal allies, landlords and whites though they were,

[107] Ibid. ii. 443.
[108] Riddel to Palmerston, 4 Sept. 1849, PRO, FO 80/64; Parra-Pérez, *Mariño y las guerras civiles*, iii. 394–5.
[109] Armas Chitty, *Vida política de Caracas*, 54.

succeeded in persuading peasants, blacks, and *pardos* that the government cause was a popular cause. This was not true, but it was the perception of the times, times which had changed since Páez had been the popular hero of the llanos in the years of independence. When Congress debated pardon for all the *paecista* rebels on 17 April 1849, a mob composed of blacks and *pardos* gathered outside shouting 'Long live the sovereign people and death to traitors!'[110] The rebellion was perceived as an élite movement, directed by military and civilian office-holders from the previous regime. These were now minority groups, bound by ties of personal allegiance to their caudillo. Outside his immediate network Páez was losing influence in the bureacracy, as Monagas gave spoils to his clients, and in effect created his own 'party' from consenting liberals and collaborating conservatives. Páez's other base, what he called 'the friendly relations I maintained with many military chiefs, partial by habit and character to revolt and rebellion', was also slipping as Monagas regrouped the army and purged its officers.[111]

The government of Monagas was not basically different from that of Páez, only worse. Caudillos moved within certain limits set by the prevailing trends in the economy and the dominant groups in society. Significant change from one regime to another could only be expected in the incidence of patronage, the level of corruption, the severity of repression, and perhaps the standard of efficiency. By these tests Monagas was inferior to Páez. His government's partiality for 'extraordinary powers', growing militarization, and financial indulgence, soon convinced many Venezuelans that they had a monster over them.[112] In the opinion of the British minister any Venezuelan regime would avail itself 'of the abundant means of corruption inherent in the Executive Power of a despotic democracy'.[113] But this regime was extraordinarily corrupt. Worse, it looked irremovable. The president's military muscle, political monopoly, and personal influence were enough to ensure that his brother, José Gregorio Monagas, became his successor. When the second Monagas was re-elected for a second term in 1855, and then in 1857 for a third, this

---

[110] Parra-Pérez, *Mariño y las guerras civiles*, iii. 141–4.
[111] Páez, *Autobiografía*, ii. 403.
[112] For a different intepretation, which argues that Monagas was more tolerant and constitutional, and no more personalist, than Páez, see Castillo Blomquist, *José Tadeo Monagas*, 263–4.
[113] Wilson to Palmerston, 25 Oct. 1850, PRO, FO 80/74.

time under a new constitution specifically designed to strengthen the executive power of the president, many saw a dynasty in the making and a government monopolized by a family notorious for its longevity and numbers. The conversion of the presidency into a military dictatorship, kept in power by pure personalism, clientage, and corruption, striking terror through racial incitement and threatening death to those who supported Páez, provoked a number of revolts, in 1853, 1854, and 1856.[114] These invoked the name of Páez, who from exile maintained a voluminous though ineffective correspondence with the opposition. In 1858 hostility to the Monagas monopoly coalesced into a great rebellion led by civilian and military élites and recruiting manpower from rural peons. Contact was resumed with Páez in New York. But the liberals and the most powerful conservative faction rejected the old caudillo, preferring General Julián Castro. As the regions rallied around the rebels, Monagas resigned on 15 March 1858, casualty of the first revolt to topple a president since independence. A political revolt in its objectives, it nevertheless recruited support from *colonos* and peons in the countryside, while traditional bandits and outlaws grasped the opportunity to bestir themselves. Thus the post-Monagas regime was left with a violent agrarian movement on its hands, an unresolved problem of the age of caudillism.[115]

In exile Páez settled in the United States and divided his time between *émigré* politics and travel in Europe and the Americas. The downfall of the Monagas opened the way to a reconciliation. An official decree reinstated him in his military rank, his titles, and also his honours, and he was invited home. He landed at Cumaná in December 1858 to receive a hero's welcome and a saviour's status, his mere presence a reassurance. But not for long. He left precipitately in July 1859 to avoid accusations by a paranoid president that he was meddling in politics. The real lesson, however, was that Páez was out of place in the political life of Venezuela at mid-century and scarcely appreciated the new pretensions of hacendados and ranchers, the resentments of tenant farmers and rural labourers, the racial tensions after abolition of slavery, and the resurgence of banditry and criminality in the llanos. All the discontents of urban and rural Venezuela came together to make the Federal War of

---

[114] Guillermo Smith to Bingham, 29 July 1854, encl. in Bingham to Clarendon, 5 Aug. 1854, PRO, FO 80/111.
[115] Matthews, *Rural Violence and Social Unrest in Venezuela*, 275–83.

1858–63, a war beyond the control of Páez but not beyond his interest. In December 1860 a group of 206 leading ranchers in the province of Guarico, seeing no end to the anarchy and violence of contemporary Venezuela and to the guerrilla war raging around them, petitioned the president, Manuel Felipe Tovar, to authorize the return of Páez to be commander-in-chief of the army.[116] The government agreed and Páez returned from the United States on 12 March 1861, this time entering Caracas unostentatiously at midnight. In the course of conversation with Páez, the British minister found him painfully aware of the difficulties of the task ahead 'and of the almost hopelessness of successfully governing this country in its present demoralised and distracted state'. Páez blamed the feeble constitution, which allowed provincial governors, elected by the provinces, to be too independent of central control, nullifying in fact the action of the executive.[117] There spoke the old caudillo.

After futile efforts at pacific negotiations with the federalist chieftains, Páez watched helplessly as Venezuela re-enacted the cycle of civil war, ministerial crisis, and, in September, yet another military coup against the presidency. This time, on 7 September 1861, and following demonstrations in his favour, Páez was offered and accepted the Supreme Civil and Military Command. Like Bolívar, he enjoyed a last dictatorship. It was a curious government. While he strengthened central control he diluted his personal power by appointing a 'Secretary General', Pedro José Rojas, a survival politician, and a 'Council' of seven from the great and the good. He made conciliatory efforts and opened negotiations with the federalists. But some of the military actions he had to undertake against them were of a violence which shocked even his sensibilities, hardened in the war of independence. While this was an absolutist government, enlightened in many ways though resented by federalists, the absolutism was that of Rojas, not Páez, who more and more became a figurehead to be paraded when military action was required but otherwise kept in silence. He did not have the financial resources to be a real dictator, and in the end his most useful function was one of negotiation, a job he understood from the past. He was forced to come to terms with Generals Falcón and Guzmán Blanco, and to agree to abdicate power to a National Convention.

---

[116] Orme to Lord John Russell, 21 Dec. 1860, PRO, FO 80/146.
[117] Orme to Russell, 21 Mar. 1861, PRO, FO 80/150.

Páez left Venezuela for the last time in June 1863 and returned to New York, once more stripped of his property, again uncertain of his future. His correspondence revealed a nostalgia for *la tierra*, disillusion with public life, and a definite decision against further participation in politics. In 1864 he was in a poor state financially and sought in vain to secure money and property which he claimed as his own in Venezuela.[118] His business instincts were still alive, and he tried unsuccessfully to set up an export outlet in the United States for Venezuelan sugar products.[119] By 1867 he was becoming restless for a sight of his native land, its flowers, fruits, and trees. He wrote to his daughters: 'Every day I more admire the bountiful land of Venezuela and long to be there, to be with you and also to have something to do, for life without occupation is the most detestable in the world'. He no longer aspired to great haciendas or ranches; a simple smallholding would be enough 'to keep me in good health'.[120] Writing, or perhaps dictating, his *Autobiografía* gave him an interest but no financial reward: 'I know that the young Cuban, Luis J. Montilla, who has helped me in the writing of the book wrote to a member of the Aldama family with a view to promoting a subscription on my behalf, but as Montilla has said nothing to me I assume that nothing has come of it.'[121] He often complained that after more than thirty years' service to the republic he now lived in poverty. Guzmán Blanco sent him a year's pension, but eventually he was forced to seek work. At the age of seventy-eight he set out for Buenos Aires as commission agent of a cattle company. He arrived in June 1868 and was soon relieved of the need to work by a pension from President Sarmiento. He made new friends and visited Urquiza on his estancia in Entre Ríos, before an outbreak of yellow fever forced him to abandon Buenos Aires and return to the United States.[122] In his eightieth year he still had time for a journey to Peru. He died on 18 June 1873.

---

[118] Páez to Hellmund (Vice-Consul of Holland in Caracas), New York, 15 Sept. 1864, ANH, Caracas, Correspondencia privada, J. A. Páez, XII, 12, fo. 19.

[119] Páez to Hellmund, New York, 24 July 1865, ANH, Caracas, Corresp. priv., J. A. Páez, XII, 12, fo. 1.

[120] Páez to daughters Ursula and Juana de Dios, New York, 19 Nov. 1867, ANH, Caracas, Corresp. priv., J. A. Páez, XII, 12, fo. 1.

[121] Páez to Gonzalo Peoli, New York, 31 Aug. 1867, ANH, Caracas, Corresp. priv., J. A. Páez, XII, 12, fo. 2.

[122] Páez to Hellmund, New York, 21 June 1871, ANH, Caracas, Corresp. priv., J. A. Páez, XII, 12, fo. 26.

8

ANTONIO LÓPEZ DE SANTA ANNA: MEXICO 1821–1855

1. *Mexican Hero*

Antonio López de Santa Anna began life as a professional soldier in the royal army, unlikely qualifications for a republican caudillo. He lacked the élite heritage of Rosas and the war record of Páez, and had to build his reputation on different foundations. Starting as a middle-class creole, he gradually acquired the necessary assets to justify his political ambition.

He was born in Jalapa, Veracruz, on 21 February 1794. His Spanish parents were relatively recent immigrants to Mexico, upwardly mobile as befitted their generation and linked to the commercial and bureaucratic sector of port and province. He emerged from his limited schooling with little knowledge and few options; resisting parental pressure towards a commercial career, he enlisted in June 1810 as a cadet in the Fijo de Vera Cruz infantry regiment. His military prospects survived a minor financial irregularity and he won promotion through vigorous action against insurgency. In 1821 he changed sides, supported the Plan of Iguala, and campaigned against the surviving royalists. The Spaniards never forgave him. They were willing to surrender Veracruz but not to a traitor; Iturbide promptly replaced him by a commander more acceptable to the royalists and Veracruz surrendered. Santa Anna did not appreciate these niceties, but when Iturbide became emperor he worked to ingratiate himself once more. To his troops he cried, 'I cannot contain my delight. . . . Let us hasten to proclaim the immortal Iturbide as emperor and offer ourselves as his most faithful defenders'; while to Iturbide himself he wrote, 'May Your Majesty live for our glory and allow the sweet name of Agustín I to be honoured by our grandchildren'.[1] Within eighteen months he abandoned Iturbide.

Why did he perform another volte-face? He said he abhorred

---

[1] Fuentes Mares, *Santa Anna*, 24–5.

absolutism.[2] But there were other reasons. Santa Anna valued his position in Veracruz and, like many regional caudillos, expected to be left alone in his own power base; so he reacted strongly when Iturbide tried to prise him from the province. Moreover, in supporting Congress against Iturbide, he had his ear to public opinion. He took advantage of the beleaguered emperor's political difficulties and seized the leadership of the movement against him. In the culture of the time a leader had to win a battle and proclaim a plan. Santa Anna owed his victory at Veracruz to the efforts of other republican leaders as well as his own. But the Plan of Vera Cruz (2 December 1822) and the Plan of Casa Mata (1 February 1823) confirmed his constitutional credentials and enabled him to pose as one of the founders of the republic.

The problem for Santa Anna in the new state was to project himself over other contenders for power. At the outset he did not have the economic base of a Rosas or the republican credentials of a Páez. True, he had captured the attention of the Mexican public, but he was not a politician with a party constituency and an organization designed to win elections. He was a professional soldier, the centre no doubt of a network of friends and colleagues, but only one of a number of military leaders with claims and ambitions. How could Santa Anna outrank Bustamante, Barragán, Herrera, Paredes, and Arista, generals with similar backgrounds to his own? He had to create for himself a curriculum vitae, and one so outstanding that when the occasion arose there was no alternative to his bid for power. The occasion was important, to be awaited or fabricated when the moment was right. In the 1820s he was not yet confident that he could achieve the success he required, for he wanted absolute power or nothing. The period 1821–32, therefore, was a time of preparation, each gesture a new qualification, each push a higher step on the ladder. He was building himself a support base, adding new groups to his clientage, extending his power from the region to the nation. The process was similar in object to the caudillo preparations of Rosas and Páez, but it differed in detail. Mexico had more interest groups and more politics than Argentina and Venezuela; the task of Santa Anna was correspondingly greater, his methods more devious than those of contemporary caudillos in South America.

[2] Antonio López de Santa Anna, *Mi historia militar y política, 1810–1874* (Mexico, 1905); English transl., *The Eagle: The Autobiography of Santa Anna*, ed. Ann Fears Crawford (Austin, Tex., 1967), 16.

In 1823, posing as the prime mover in the defeat of Iturbide and not content with a minor appointment in San Luis Potosí, he issued on 5 July a demand for a federal constitution, and declared his *jarochos* 'The Protecting Army of Mexican Liberty'. This was another gesture; he knew the government was already dominated by federalists and was about to prepare a constitution, so he sought to pre-empt the prevailing tendency and claim its leadership.[3] The government was not amused and summoned him to the capital to account for his insubordination. In 1824 they sent him to Yucatán as military commandant; unable to resolve the dilemma between supporting regional interests and obeying government policy, he took what was to become a familiar escape route: he resigned and returned to Jalapa, where his estate provided a base to recuperate and prepare his next move. In August 1825, at the age of thirty-one, he married María Inés de la Paz García, Mexican-born daughter of a Spanish merchant. She was still only fourteen but she brought him a useful dowry and in time came to manage his property affairs during his absence. They began their married life on the hacienda Manga de Clavo.

It was 1828 before Santa Anna ventured forth again, in what might seem a false move except that it was calculated to serve his longer aims. He supported the revolt of Vicente Guerrero and Lorenzo de Zavala against the legally elected president, Manuel Gómez Pedraza, though at first without any military success, either at Perote or Oaxaca.[4] In Oaxaca he was besieged for a month by the forces of the government and was saved only by the victorious coup of Guerrero and Zavala in Mexico City. He expected to be rewarded with the ministry of war, but he returned empty-handed to Jalapa, content at least that he had kept his name before the public as an independent caudillo with demagogic instincts and had further established his identity among the swarm of competing generals. His next adventure was more fortunate. The Spanish invasion at Cabo Rojo in July 1829 gave Santa Anna the opportunity to organize a regional response, assemble and supply a fighting army, and at Tampico on 11 September to lead it victoriously against a larger enemy force. He was promoted General of Division by President

---

[3] Fuentes Mares, *Santa Anna*, 48–9.
[4] Wilfrid Hardy Callcott, *Santa Anna: The Story of an Enigma Who Once Was Mexico* (Norman, Okla., 1936), 65–72. See Chap. 3, sect. 3.

Guerrero and honoured by numerous provinces. This was the victory which gave Santa Anna his national status and decisively advanced his caudillo prestige. For the moment he was content to bury his treasure for future use: 'I returned to my estates at Manga de Clavo for much needed rest, pleading to heaven that I would not have to assume another call to arms'.[5] He remained aloof from the *golpe* of 4 December 1829 which replaced the 'Indian' Guerrero by a conservative Anastasio Bustamante and from the subsequent revolt of Guerrero and Alvarez in the south, resigning from his political and military commands in Veracruz. The days of consensus were over: Bustamante and Alamán inaugurated an ideological conflict between conservatives and liberals which was outside, perhaps above, the political thinking of Santa Anna. For the caudillo of Manga de Clavo it was the presidency or nothing.

Santa Anna profited from two years' retirement to plan his tactics and exploit the opportunities presented. Bustamante led an uncompromising government and his commitment to federalism was questioned by his enemies, unjustifiably according to others.[6] But this was far from being the worst government in Mexican history, and the movement against it appeared to be engineered in support of little more than a rival bid for power. Santa Anna judged he could not gain the presidency by election, for he had no party and others controlled the electoral machine; the way of the *golpe* was the only way.[7] Therefore, in caudillo style, he began to call in his credits and mobilize his military clients, first the officers of the local garrison. In January 1832 he seized his chance; he also seized Veracruz customs receipts totalling 279,000 pesos, intercepted further monies carried in government convoys, and declared himself in revolt, allegedly pressed by 'the entreaties of my *paisanos*'.[8] He presented himself as a mediator between the government and its enemies, a familiar tactic designed to enlarge his following. This was pure rebellion. He called on the *municipios* to lend their support, and gathered together a variety of Veracruz interests, the militia, the rural popular sectors, local delinquents; and a number of foreign merchants advanced money against the promise of future customs

---

[5] Santa Anna, *Autobiography*, 25.
[6] Pakenham to Palmerston, 23 Jan. 1832, PRO, FO 50/71, fos. 73–6.
[7] Costeloe, *La Primera República Federal*, 327–30.
[8] Santa Anna, *Autobiography*, 27.

cuts on imports.[9] As he advanced to military opposition he first secured his home base:

General Santa Anna entered this city yesterday at $6\frac{1}{2}$ p.m. in a chaise and six accompanied by the colonels of the 2nd and 9th Regiments and escorted by a captain's guard of dragoons amid the universal acclamations of the people. He drove to the palace where he was received by a detachment of the 2nd Regiment, military and civil authorities with bands of music. . . . Privately he has informed me that so soon as the agitation experienced by the states is quieted and a confidential ministry installed to the satisfaction of his countrymen he shall lose no time in returning to his farm.[10]

According to the British consul he had 1,000 soldiers and 1,000 irregulars, mostly *jarochos*.

Many other states followed suit, and the revolt gathered a momentum of its own. A revolt of this kind, lasting the best part of a year, could itself ruin a government's administrative and financial performance and prove to be self-fulfilling. As Bustamante pointed out, the rebellion on the coast, though of little consequence in itself, was serious in its destructive effects, taking from the government the customs houses of Veracruz and Tampico, depriving it of revenue, forcing it into debt, and preventing investment in development.[11] The cry of the rebels was for Gómez Pedraza. The fact that he had come out in rebellion in 1828 to exclude Gómez Pedraza from the presidency did not trouble Santa Anna. Consistency was never a priority, or as Bustamante put it, 'there is hardly a Mexican of the smallest penetration who is ignorant of the dissembling and perfidious character of the chief of the insurgents'.[12] Santa Anna now called Gómez Pedraza back from the United States to act in effect as a stepping stone for himself. He passed the idea off as his own, but it was more likely that of Valentín Gómez Farías, whom Santa Anna needed as a political ally. The two made a pact on behalf of the legitimacy of Gómez Pedraza, whose presidency still had a few months to run, to 1 April 1833. The opportunity for Santa Anna was obvious; and the advantage for the conservative interests backing him equally so. The manœuvre proceeded smoothly. Bustamante

[9] Callcott, *Santa Anna*, 88–91; Díaz Díaz, *Caudillos y caciques*, 116.

[10] Welsh to Pakenham, Veracruz, 4 Jan. 1832, PRO, FO 50/77, fos. 18–20.

[11] Bustamante, Speech to Congress, 23 May 1832, in Pakenham to Palmerston, 9 June 1832, PRO, FO 50/72, fos. 97–108.

[12] Bustamante, Speech to Congress, 3 Aug. 1832, in Pakenham to Palmerston, 6 Aug. 1832, PRO, FO 50/72, fos. 331–8.

tried reconciliation and failed; he then tried fighting and was defeated. On 24 December 1832 Gómez Pedraza took possession of the presidency and Santa Anna piously stood back and waited for the elections, now, in the company of politicians, confident of the results. In March Congress elected Santa Anna president and Gómez Farías vice-president as from 1 April.[13] Gómez Farías obtained the power to carry out liberal reforms, Santa Anna the presidency of the republic. But they were both partisans of their own causes, incompatible in aims and in character. Santa Anna escaped from the dilemma by his usual route: he retired to his hacienda, leaving the vice-president to fill the empty treasury and pay the 11,244,567 pesos debt left by the Bustamante government.

General Santa Anna has written to the Government excusing himself for a few months from undertaking the duties of his office. The reason he assigns is the enfeebled state of his health; but it appears to be generally understood that his real motive is to avoid being a party to certain violent measures said to be contemplated by the Chambers, and also to escape from the importunities of the host of adventurers who fought under his colours during the late Revolution.[14]

The rebellion of 1832 took Santa Anna to the top, but not yet on his own terms. He had operated successfully out of his power base. He had demonstrated his ability to attract the generals and put together a military alliance based on several states. He had shown his talent for overthrowing a government with minimum force, employing a small army not in a set battle but to probe and negotiate. Finally he had continued to exercise patience in pursuing his objectives, one at a time; these were not stages in the development of policy but tactical steps to total control. Santa Anna did not have a policy or a political party to express it. So he allowed the politicians their space and waited for the next step, aware that he still had some gaps to fill in his preparations for power.

Santa Anna watched from a distance as events unfolded in the capital. Gómez Farías governed in accordance with the liberal principles of his mentor José María Luis Mora to create a secular society free of privilege and inequality. He realized he could not save federalism and promote liberalism by cutting expenditure, for

[13] Alamán, *Historia de Méjico*, v. 856; Callcott, *Santa Anna*, 96–9; Costeloe, *La Primera República Federal*, 367–9.
[14] Pakenham to Palmerston, 30 Mar. 1833, PRO, FO 50/79, fos. 104–6.

liberals too had to live in a patronage state, to distribute benefits and buy support. He was also aware that it would be dangerous to attack the army head-on and scale down its budget. So it was tactics as well as principles which caused him to tackle the Church, its privilege, wealth, and property. At first Santa Anna allowed the vice-president to have his head, interested no doubt to discover how far a government could go against interests which he himself might one day have to confront. Success would enable Santa Anna to accept the praise; failure would give him the opportunity to come to the rescue of threatened interests. Santa Anne had two reservations about the programme. Liberal reformism was a minority creed, and Santa Anna was more interested in obtaining majority support for his ambition. Second, he judged that the government's anti-clericalism was not a popular cause and might be rejected by the mass of the people. And how would an attack on military privilege be received by the army? These were purely pragmatic and political positions, for Santa Anna did not believe in majority rights or the privileges of the Church as a matter of principle. For him everything was an interest group, to be judged according to its power and success rating. He took his cue from the army reaction.

He came out of Manga de Clavo and assumed his powers as president on 16 May 1833. Ten days later a number of army officers in Morelia under Colonel Ignacio Escalada revolted on behalf of 'religion and the *fueros*'. This was followed by the rebellions of Generals Durán and Arista. The war-cry spread, 'For religion and the *fueros* of the army and the Church', and for Santa Anna as the 'protector of the nation' with dictatorial powers. While publicly repudiating the military rebels—'they only invoke my name to degrade it; I deplore any attempt to destroy the Constitution'—Santa Anna found these outbreaks suitable for manipulation.[15] On the one hand they embarrassed Gómez Farías; on the other they projected Santa Anna, whose military action against the rebels and temporary 'imprisonment' by them earned him some popularity, mixed however with incredulity and doubts as to his real intentions. He was presumably waiting to see which side was strongest before espousing the cause of reform or reaction.[16] While Santa Anna confronted rebels in the Bajío, and a great cholera epidemic ravaged Mexico, Gómez

---

[15] Fuentes Mares, *Santa Anna*, 83.
[16] Pakenham to Palmerston, 11 June 1833, PRO, FO 50/79, fos. 241–7.

Farías was busy secularizing the California missions, suppressing the Pontifical University, removing government sanction for tithes and the force of civil law for monastic vows, and claiming for the state the right to provide to benefices. He was also seeking to transform land owned by the Church into cash for the treasury. After a month in the capital actually occupying the presidency, Santa Anna received permission from Congress to return to his hacienda on 4 December 1833, leaving Gómez Farías to his liberalism and his detractors.

Defenders of privilege worked themselves into paroxysms of rage over the anticlerical programme of Gómez Farías. Alamán saw it as a parody of the French Revolution, in which Santa Anna left to Congress the role of the Convention, assigning to Gómez Farías that of Robespierre. The liberals too lost touch with reality: they overestimated the Church's wealth, calculated wrongly that it could cover the government's debts, and simply drove the clergy into the arms of centralists and conservatives, in the cause not only of liberal ideas but of 'the furtherance of private views and the gratification of party animosity'.[17] The Church authorities reacted strongly and protests poured into Manga de Clavo urging Santa Anna to intervene as president. According to Mora, 'From the month of January letters from the disaffected of all classes and colours began to arrive at Manga de Clavo, some asking the president to place himself at the head of the privileged classes, others to change the composition of the government, and all to return to occupy the presidency.'[18] The clergy had little idea of Santa Anna's religious opinions, though they would find in due course that he too was interested in controlling benefices and tapping church wealth. But he knew how to keep people waiting and allow a head of steam to build up in his favour. The hour for action arrived in April 1834, and this time he judged correctly: power was ripe for his picking. When he arrived in Mexico City on 24 April both the clergy and the party of Gómez Farías were waiting to welcome him. On 29 April he opted for the Church, proclaiming to Mexicans that 'the most fatal tyranny is that which shelters under constitutional forms': 'Neither your religion, nor your liberty, nor your security, nor any of the benefits guaranteed and consecrated by the Constitution shall be violated with impunity.

---

[17] Pakenham to Palmerston, 5 Oct. 1833, PRO, FO 50/80 A, fos. 99–102; Alamán, *Historia de Méjico*, v. 863–4; Tenenbaum, *The Politics of Penury*, 39.
[18] José María Luis Mora, *Obras sueltas*, 2nd edn. (Mexico, 1963), 153.

I am ready to sacrifice myself if necessary in their defence, distancing myself equally from the rigours of tyranny as from the destructive excesses of an ill understood liberty.'[19] There were only a limited number of political groupings in Mexico. Therefore, in deposing those who had helped him to power in 1833, Santa Anna promoted those he had then dismissed, and all within a year. He was never fastidious.

Santa Anna activated his presidency and began to govern. Determined to overcome what he, or his speech writer, described as 'the empire of anarchy', he told Congress that he 'again took up the reins of government at the critical and precise moment in which society was approaching its dissolution'.[20] His policies were more prosaic than his speeches. He negotiated a loan from the clergy; and most of the anticlerical measures were suspended, as were laws concerning the appointment of parish priests. Gómez Farías was forced to leave the country, and while the University was reopened the doors of Congress were locked to shut out the federal party. Once more, wrote Alamán, 'the fate of the country was entirely in his hands.'[21] And also in those of the military. He needed the army, duly rewarded and retuned, to reduce opposition in the states and impose the new order throughout the country. Santa Anna had an enduring affinity with the military, recognizing them as a strong interest group and an important support. Patronage took precedence over politics. Reform was a risky business, while powerful élites like the clergy, army, and landowners could keep him in power. Santa Anna did not act from religious or political convictions, simply from calculation of the balance of power and its effect on his personal objectives. He was a Catholic, of course, and he helped the Church; but he remained independent of it. He was careful to state to Congress that he 'only yielded what was absolutely required by the urgent necessities of the Mexican Church'. He refused to repeal or suspend the laws abolishing civil enforcement of tithes and monastic vows. And he too inherited the attitudes of regalism in the exercise of ecclesiastical patronage.[22]

---

[19] Proclamation of Santa Anna, 29 Apr. 1834, quoted in Pakenham to Palmerston, 12 May 1834, PRO, FO 50/84; see also Fuentes Mares, *Santa Anna*, 90.

[20] Santa Anna, Speech to Congress, 4 Jan. 1835, in Pakenham to Wellington, 14 Feb. 1835, PRO, FO 50/91, fos. 1–25.

[21] Alamán, *Historia de Méjico*, v. 798.

[22] Michael P. Costeloe, *Church and State in Independent Mexico: A Study of the Patronage Debate 1821–1857* (London, 1978), 137–8.

Santa Anna in 1834 conducted a *coup d'état* against his own government. The counter-revolution was successful, and throughout the country it proclaimed 'Religion and General Santa Anna'. But more than religion was involved. The new order was not the invention of Santa Anna alone. The coalition of Church, army, and conservatives reached an understanding with the president, now 'the only authority', that the federalist system be dismantled and replaced by centralism. On 25 May 1834 they agreed on a formula known as the Plan of Cuernavaca which called upon Santa Anna to dismiss Congress and repeal all its anticlerical measures as a prelude to constitutional change. 'Religion, the *fueros* and General Santa Anna are the things proclaimed in this famous Plan', said Mora.[23] As for the constitution, on 3 October the government officially declared itself to be centralist. But the Church recognized that centralism could only survive if it generated enough revenue to support a government. Therefore, on 3 June 1834, nine days after the Plan of Cuernavaca was proclaimed, the Church promised 30,000 – 40,000 pesos to Santa Anna each month for the next six months and accepted the abolition of the tithe. In exchange the government pledged that it would not allow even the suggestion that Church property be expropriated. The bargain between centralists, clerics, generals, and Santa Anna was sealed when the central government announced on 8 December 1834 its right to 'confiscate the treasuries of the states in order to make sure the contribution was paid'.[24]

But federalism was not dead. On 23 March the caudillo of the south, Juan Alvarez, announced a revolt to remove Santa Anna and restore the federal system, and there was a revolt too in Zacatecas, where the governor, Francisco García, pronounced against what he saw as a centralized dictatorship. But Santa Anna was able to call upon his military allies to overcome both. On 11 May 1835 in a single battle he won one of his most crucial military successes when he decisively defeated the militia forces of García in Zacatecas. The road was now open to dismantle the federal system. In October 1835 the bases of a new constitution were published, excluding the word federal. A compliant Congress, now dominated by the coalition, decreed on 3 October 1835 that Mexico should be divided

---

[23] Mora, *Obras sueltas*, 154–5; Costeloe, *La Primera República Federal*, 428–9.
[24] Cited by Tenenbaum, *The Politics of Penury*, 40.

into departments, not states, and that departmental governors should hold office only at the will of the central government, while all state legislatures should cease to function. Centralism was finally enshrined in the constitution of December 1836, which established a strong eight-year presidential system and a Congress with high property qualifications, the powers of both constrained somewhat by the creation of a Supreme Conservative Power 'responsible only to God and public opinion', but also legitimized by the inclusion of a statement of the 'rights of Mexicans'.[25]

Santa Anna spent fifteen years giving himself a unique identity: he was a Mexican hero. Not for him a policy or a party; he cultivated leadership itself. On this basis he established his power and his primacy. He was president and supreme chief, his federalism discarded, his adventures a thing of the past. Opportunism was rewarded: central control was his real ambition. The end justified all the means adopted between 1821 and 1834. Now, in January 1835, having placated the Church, satisfied a number of interest groups, and added to his own qualifications, Santa Anna asked leave of Congress to return to his hacienda, pleading reasons of health. He wanted to possess power rather than administer it. He preferred to retire to his hacienda with his power intact while his agents occupied the government. He was the sovereign, others had the duties. This was not the normal behaviour of a constitutional president. It was personalist, a variation of caudillism. Meanwhile, Santa Anna had been taking other steps to strengthen his caudillo status.

2. *Patron and Proprietor*

Santa Anna recognized early that he needed a personal base for his political career. At the time of his marriage in 1825 to Inés de la Paz García, Mexican-born daughter of a Spanish merchant, he had just acquired a substantial hacienda and she brought him a dowry of money and further property. Manga de Clavo, where he settled his young bride and brought up his family, was situated on the road from Jalapa to Veracruz. It was a large estate, valued at 10,000 pesos,

---

[25] Moisés González Navarro, 'La Era de Santa Anna', *Historia documental de México*, 2nd edn. (Mexico, 1974), ii. 206–10.

endowed at first with only 100 head of cattle but eventually the home of hundreds of peons and thousands of livestock.[26] When, in 1845, he sought to sell the property prior to exile, he set a price of 100,000 pesos and described it as having 12,000 breeding cows on almost 220,000 acres with an income of 20,000 pesos annually.[27] His second hacienda, El Encero, he described as having a house, chapel, and tenant dwellings on a property of about 88,000 acres. The tenants paid rentals of about 1,000 pesos annually and other income amounted to 2,500 pesos. He claimed he had 2,000 calves, 2,000 breeding cows, 300 horses, the whole estate representing an investment of 140,000 pesos. El Encero, too, was situated near Jalapa and with Manga de Clavo covered almost the entire region between Jalapa and Veracruz. A third hacienda, Paso de las Varas, comprised about 175,000 acres, which he valued at 150,000 pesos. In his last will he mentioned a fourth property, Boca del Monte, which he valued at 25,000 pesos.

Inés, a self-effacing but supporting young wife, died in Puebla on 23 August 1844 at the age of thirty-one. He had four children by her, but he also recognized a further four by other women. Some six weeks after her death he married María Dolores de Tosta, fifteen years old compared to his fifty; he took her to El Encero but there were no children by this marriage. In 1844 the property of the couple comprised three haciendas, three houses in the city of Veracruz, another in Jalapa, and mortgages of 79,000 pesos on haciendas belonging to others in the state of Veracruz, with a total value of 1,300,000 pesos.[28] In exile in Colombia in the years around 1850 he rebuilt a ruined house and small estate which he bought cheaply at Turbaco near Cartagena as a possible place of retirement.[29] He claimed in later years, 'My fortune in Mexico consisted of property and my salary. However, as my political enemies have robbed me of both of these, I have nothing. The fabulous fortune which rumor says I have is merely the invention of my enemies, who are attempting to discredit me.'[30] For once he was telling the truth.

The haciendas of Santa Anna were more than houses and estates.

---

[26] Robert A. Potash, 'Testamentos de Santa Anna', *Historia Mexicana*, 13, 3 (1964), 428–40.
[27] Callcott, *Santa Anna*, 84–5, 204–5, 217–8.
[28] Potash, 'Testamentos de Santa Anna', 437–40.
[29] Santa Anna, *Autobiography*, 119.
[30] Ibid. 157.

Manga de Clavo in particular was a political retreat, fortress, and headquarters, the scene of an unvarying routine, the focus of the nation's attention. When crisis occurred, when it was necessary to withdraw from the fray, disconcert his enemies, raise his terms, assume an olympian position, or perhaps, as he always claimed, simply recuperate, he took the road to Manga de Clavo. Once there he lived a simple rural life and followed a kind of health regime. After Tampico, for example, he retired to Manga de Clavo:

The rest and the quantities of milk which I drink have enabled me to recover my lost strength. If I continue with this regime I am confident I will soon enjoy the best of health. I have a good appetite, I sleep well, and I am filled with an extraordinary tranquility of mind. I am more sure every day that this kind of life is the best for men exhausted in body and soul. I would not change mine for any title in the world.[31]

So he cultivated his estate, enjoyed his leisure, drank milk, took a ride in the evening, and shed ambition. This was a legend of his own making. Manga de Clavo was also the centre of his power base, the launching pad for his ambitions, the place where he contemplated titles and planned their acquisition. While other generals made *pronunciamientos*, Santa Anna rode out of Manga de Clavo.

Frances Calderón de la Barca, Scottish wife of the Spanish ambassador, visited Santa Anna at Manga de Clavo in 1839, when he carried some of the scars of battle:

In a little while entered General Santa Anna himself, a gentlemanly, good-looking, quietly-dressed, rather melancholy-looking person, with one leg, apparently somewhat of an invalid. . . . He has a sallow complexion, fine dark eyes, soft and penetrating, and an interesting expression of face. Knowing nothing of his past history, one would have said a philosopher, living in dignified retirement. . . . To judge from the past he will not long remain in his present state of inaction, besides having within him, according to Zavala, 'a principle of action for ever impelling him forward.'[32]

Santa Anna was an emotional man who wept readily in public. He liked women but he liked the *gallos* even more. In this he conformed to caudillo culture, another Páez. While occupying the presidency he might leave the capital for a week at a time to attend lengthy cock-fighting meetings at Cuernavaca.[33] Nearer to Mexico City he had

[31] Quoted by Fuentes Mares, *Santa Anna*, 78.
[32] Frances E. Calderón de la Barca, *Life in Mexico* (New York, 1931), 32–3.
[33] Pakenham to Palmerston, 30 Dec. 1834, PRO, FO 50/86, fos. 218–19.

other diversions. During Whitsuntide at Tlalpan the fair of San Agustín de las Cuevas was a highlight of the social season, when the ladies showed off their French fashions and artisans their good manners, and all classes 'from the peasant down to the beggar' mingled under the trees, drank, danced, socialized, and gambled on the tables and on the cock-fights. Santa Anna joined in enthusiastically in the years 1842–4. Always an avid gambler, he exploited his rank as president to play the populist:

Santa Anna was the life and soul of this emporium of disorder and licentiousness. You could see him in the gaming room surrounded by the leading financiers, playing for high stakes, scooping up other people's money, mixing with petty officials and even with low ranking officers; demanding money without repaying, and cheating for thanks; and when the gambling flagged, the ladies would smile and accompany him to Birján for the bullfighting.[34]

The financiers were only one sector of Santa Anna's *clientela*. Like any upwardly mobile caudillo he attracted support from interest groups and in turn sought to increase his following. His regional base began with a group of followers whom he placed in bureaucratic positions in the principal towns of the state of Veracruz, especially Jalapa and the port itself, and above all in the customs office, the key to government revenue; many of these were mutually linked by bonds of *parentesco*, and were known locally as appointees of Santa Anna. So he had an entry to the provincial bureaucracy.[35] Secondly he received the support of the so-called *jarochos*, or popular sectors of rural Veracruz, who were simply impressed by his military activities in the region before 1829 and obtained a vicarious pleasure in the honours and triumphs of their general. These were an important asset at crucial moments of his career when he needed political and especially military backing. The mobilization of the *jarochos* for his various actions and *golpes* in 1821, 1822, 1828, 1831, and 1838, recalls the similar need of Rosas for gaucho support at critical moments of his ascent to power. Again, in 1841 the *jarochada* joined Santa Anna's troops in his push against Bustamante; and six years later during his campaign against the Americans he mobilized his peons and others among the work force of his estates. So Santa Anna had a military power base in the rural zone of Veracruz, in part drawn

---

[34] Prieto, *Memorias de mis tiempos*, ii. 105; see also Calderón de la Barca, *Life in Mexico*, 203–5, 376–82.

[35] Díaz Díaz, *Caudillos y caciques*, 149–50.

from his own hacienda, in part from the *jarochada*. This was not enough in itself and could not relieve him of the task of cultivating the regular army, but no caudillo could be without a personal base of this kind. He himself preserved his regional roots, identified with the popular culture of rural Veracruz, joined in the addiction of the *jarochos* to fiestas and fighting cocks, and gave at least the impression of listening and helping.[36]

At a national level the most important *clientela* of Santa Anna were the military, or most of them. His own career and identity gave him a community of interest with the Mexican military and made them a primary base of support, strengthened by his practice of rewarding them once he was in power. He had his own reward in 1822, 1829, 1832, and 1834 when his prestige among the military won him national renown. In 1841 his influence with the army enabled him to make a political comeback, and was confirmed again during his dictatorship of 1842–4, when Mexico resembled, according to Miguel Lerdo de Tejada, 'a vast military camp'.[37] On more than one occasion the army refused to move politically one way or the other without the return of Santa Anna, and for all his failure against the United States no one else was more successful or more capable of inspiring the military. As army officers had no other source of income than the army, they depended utterly on the patronage of the president, which often meant Santa Anna. This gave him different problems from those of Rosas, who was able to purge and reform the army and reward his generals with land which was abundantly available, and from Páez, who was never confronted by a large military establishment. Santa Anna had to negotiate with a professional army, as well as with civilian interest groups. But many senior officers were old personal friends of his and he knew the soldiers' language. He had a military mentality and a military ruthlessness. Less terrorist than Rosas, he was more cruel than Páez, and thought nothing of executing prisoners during and after the Texas war.

His civilian supporters were led by a group of friends and paisanos, politicians who helped and collaborated, bureaucrats who aspired to high office. Around 1837, according to Mora, the majority of the *santanistas* were 'aspirants from the privileged and military sectors

[36] Ibid. 150–1.
[37] Ibid. 334.

whose only project was to advance their personal fortune and whose most obvious leaders were Don José Tornel, Don Francisco Lombardo, Licenciado Bonilla, and General Valencia'.[38] Santa Anna operated through patronage, giving clients such as these good jobs in his administration. On the eleven occasions when he was formally president, he targeted his patronage deliberately to reward and encourage, and in the process consolidated a group of identifiable *santanistas*. José María Tornel led the list, with frequent appointments as minister of war, followed by José María Bocanegra, Francisco María Lombardo, Manuel Baranda, Ignacio Trigueros, and in his last administration Ignacio Sierra y Rosso and Luis Parres. Of these only Tornel, Trigueras, and Sierra y Rosso came from the state of Veracruz.[39] Santa Anna conferred the principal ministries, war and treasury, on his most faithful followers, for these posts were the key to maintaining his domination. José María Tornel was his special agent, for it was through the war ministry that the president could manage his relations with the military.

Santa Anna was a favourite of the *agiotistas*, the financial speculators of the time, many of whom played an important role in his return to power on various occasions. He was known to repay those who backed him and his army, and also to expect profits for himself from any financial transactions that he authorized. In 1841, to remunerate those who put up money to finance an army and promote his own presidential bid, he granted, among other favours, cotton import licences, contracts for war supplies, and agreements for the construction of docks, warehouses, and railways at Veracruz.[40] Outside the *agiotistas*, Santa Anna also received the occasional support of other élite groups, landowners, clergy, and entrepreneurs such as Manuel Escandón. But these were not professional *santanistas*. They already had incomes and resources of their own, and were not dependent on the handouts of the caudillo. For them *santanismo* was simply an occasional form of favour, a policy advantage at a particular time, or the protection of interests already gained.

There was no sign of social awareness or populist preferences in the policy of Santa Anna. To gain or return to power he normally relied on the upper classes, the *hombres de bien* and the *gente de orden*,

[38] Mora, *Obras sueltas*, 159.
[39] Díaz Díaz, *Caudillos y caciques*, 152.
[40] Tenenbaum, *The Politics of Penury*, 82, 142.

as in 1834, 1843, 1847, and 1853. And when he sought popular support it was usually by appealing to past 'patriotic' triumphs or promising to gain others. He never offered social benefits, only defence of the *patria*. This contrasted sharply with the policy of Juan Alvarez, the caudillo of the south, who lost no opportunity of projecting a populist image, exploiting the social conditions of his region and treading an expert path between proprietors and peons. Rising from modest beginnings to wealthy hacendado, proprietor of La Providencia and other estates on the Pacific coast, it was easier for Alvarez to play the populist card, isolated as he was from the political problems of the centre and surrounded by Indian communities in need of a defender. Santa Anna never reconciled himself to Alvarez:

Alvarez was a member of the lowest class of Mexicans—direct descendant through his mother of the African race. When he was young he had been a stable boy to General Vicente Guerrero. To Guerrero he owed all the power which he had gained in the mountains of the South. He had practiced cruelties of a savage nature, and the government tolerated him as the lesser of many evils. I myself even went so far as to promote him to the rank of general.[41]

If Santa Anna was critical of Alvarez, he was contemptuous of Juárez. He accused Juárez of ordering him and his family out of Oaxaca when they were fleeing into exile in 1848 and of bearing a permanent grudge against him: 'Once in December, 1828, at the home of Manuel Embides in Oaxaca, he served me a meal when he was dressed in crude cotton trousers and barefooted. I was rather surpised that such a low class Indian would have figured in the history of Mexico.'[42]

Santa Anna's tariff policy owed little to any concern for the artisan classes and even less to economic ideas. As usual he manœuvred between interest groups. He did not automatically accept the arguments of protectionists for high tariffs and a national manufacturing sector. When he did, it was to help entrepreneurs rather than artisans. The Bustamante government, while nominally protectionist, tended to give powerful or influential people permits to import prohibited goods, such as cotton fabrics. In the course of 1841 the manufacturing interest pressed Congress to make it a penal offence to deal in

---

[41] Santa Anna, *Autobiography*, 138–9.
[42] Ibid. 117–18.

prohibited goods and also for more restrictions on imports. Because of his animosity towards the Mexican manufacturing interest, the British minister Pakenham reported the bankruptcy of Lucas Alamán with some satisfaction, commenting that his failure should 'serve to check in some degree the mischievous delusion which has existed in this country respecting the establishment of national manufactures'.[43] In February 1841, when he had been out of politics for some two years, Santa Anna made representation to President Bustamante against the authorization of the import of raw cotton, yarn, and common textiles, speaking on behalf of 'the cotton growers of this Department'.[44]

Santa Anna did not always speak on behalf of the cotton growers, for a few favoured speculators with access to his government received licences to import cotton, concessions denied to their competitors.[45] In the course of 1841 he was approached by merchants in Veracruz for support in their campaign against the additional duty on foreign goods imposed in November 1839 and criticized as excessive in itself and a depressant on trade and customs income; he took up the issue and wrote 'in strong terms' to the government and to leading congressmen recommending the repeal of the additional duty.[46] Santa Anna was not xenophobic. He removed obstacles to prevent foreigners holding landed property; and he was normally opposed to high tariffs on foreign imports. But he was inconsistent. In 1842, during leave of absence at Manga de Clavo, he was pressed by the British minister to prevent a higher tariff on cotton imports, but in spite of all his efforts he could not move the interim president, Nicolás Bravo, to act against manufacturers. Yet he did not repeal the higher duty once he returned to office and he was willing to increase tariffs to satisfy, if only momentarily, importunate interests.[47] His government of 1842–4 raised duties, partly to help a few manufactures, partly to raise revenue, and partly to finance the construction of a railway. The question remains, was his tariff policy a defence of the textile

[43] Pakenham to Palmerston, 26 Mar. 1841, PRO, FO 50/144, fos. 193–202; 8 July 1841, FO 50/145, fos. 285–90.
[44] Santa Anna to Bustamante, 6 Feb. 1841, quoted by Díaz Díaz, *Caudillos y caciques*, 156.
[45] Robert A. Potash, *Mexican Government and Industrial Development in the Early Republic: The Banco de Avío* (Amherst, Mass., 1983), 132–4; Walker, 'Business as Usual: The Empresa del Tabaco in Mexico', 675–705.
[46] Pakenham to Palmerston, 1 May 1841, PRO, FO 50/144, fos. 276–83.
[47] Pakenham to Aberdeen, 21 July 1842, PRO, FO 50/154, fos. 187–9.

manufacturers, or simply of raw cotton producers? Santa Anna was also a spokesman for tobacco growers against the monoply and in April 1841 against the 15 per cent tax on tobacco. But there was little in his policy specifically favourable to artisans.

3. *Absentee Caudillo*

Santa Anna changed sides for Iturbide and then rose against him. He joined a civil war for federalism and then another against it. He supported the accession of a liberal, then favoured the conservatives. Early in his career he was notorious for his opportunism. He did not have a party or a policy; he did not subscribe to any ideology, conservative, liberal, federal, or radical, at least until 1853. He moved with the times and according to circumstances, to obtain the advantages which this gave him. But these inconsistencies and apparent changes of opinion were one of his strengths and were often the key to his predominance. Believing himself superior to all, he came to be 'the temptation of all the parties', and he could appeal to each or rebuff them all, as he frequently did. At the same time his political *personalismo* found support in a numerous group of followers outside the conventional groupings and loyal to his leadership alone.

Santa Anna saw himself as a leader made for Mexico. He had before him various examples of Mexican leaders in the 1820s, Iturbide, Victoria, Guerrero, royalists and liberators, centralists and regionalists, authoritarians and liberals, and he drew inspiration from all in general and none in particular. His personalism was not so extreme that he discounted institutions, constitutions, or even parties; they had to be there to govern Mexico. Santa Anna's particular contribution to the cult of leader was to project him not as a man who governed but as one who intervened when necessary to safeguard the liberty of the people from the disorders of invasion or domestic conflict. In this sense caudillism was a type of leadership, and the caudillo was above government. Santa Anna saw the leader as a protector of the people against misgovernment, and the art of politics consisted in identifying the appropriate protector at the right time. Most of the other candidates failed, and his search culminated in himself. The only ally he really trusted amidst the political turmoil was the army; ideally Santa Anna wanted Mexico ruled by a leader and an army. Unfortunately the army was not homogeneous, and the leader not above faction.

Santa Anna was a man of action, not a political thinker. During his federalist phase he claimed that his political object was to guarantee Mexicans their constitutional rights and 'to break the triple yoke of ignorance, tyranny and vice'.[48] In the same period he declared: 'I have desired no other glory but that of a good citizen.... To proclaim that the Mexicans cannot be governed but by a tyrant is to tell the world that they are out of the pale of civilization'.[49] But privately, on more than one occasion, he expressed other views. He admitted that he abandoned liberty for despotism, though he saw it as an enlightened despotism: 'A hundred years to come my people will not be fit for liberty. They do not know what it is, unenlightened as they are, and under the influence of the Catholic clergy, a despotism is the proper government for them, but there is no reason why it should not be a wise and virtuous one.'[50] His speeches were an amalgam of self-applause, political platitudes, and patriotic rhetoric. He did not have enough ideas to be a liberal or a conservative, creeds which were of no consequence to his ideal of leadership. Santa Anna's personalism lasted until the end of his life. His *Memorias*, although empty of historical evidence and objective value, reflect Santa Anna's perceptions and priorities. The political and military narrative shows not the slightest interest in institutions of government or organization of the army. The author speaks only of his personal role, in the true style of the caudillo.

Santa Anna was a puzzle to his contemporaries. Foreign observers, particularly the diplomats, automatically regarded him as an unprincipled opportunist; or as one British minister remarked after his first meeting, 'I need hardly tell your Lordship that Santa Anna is as little remarkable for the sincerity of his professions, as he is for the the steadiness of his political views'.[51] Mexicans made a greater effort to understand him. According to Lorenzo de Zavala, the absence of 'fixed principles' in Santa Anna was due to his 'lack of knowledge', and this was the reason why he always went to extremes

---

[48] Santa Anna, Speech on installation as President, 16 May 1833, encl. in Pakenham to Palmerston, 30 May 1833, PRO, FO 50/79, fos. 128–33.

[49] Santa Anna, Manifesto, *El Telégrafo* (21 June 1833), encl. in O'Gorman to Bidwell, 28 June 1833, PRO, FO 50/80 B, fos. 152–7.

[50] Santa Anna to Poinsett, 1836, quoted by Callcott, *Santa Anna*, 109.

[51] Bankhead to Aberdeen, 31 Mar. 1844, PRO, FO 50/173, fos. 1–8.

and contradicted himself. 'He does not ponder his actions or calculate their results, and therefore he throws himself into the most
reckless undertakings without any chance of a successful outcome.'[52]
Mora bitterly resented Santa Anna's leadership of the reaction
against the reforms of Gómez Farías in 1833. He called him the
'Attila of Mexican civilization', and presented him as an ignorant
man who was incapable of leading society, whose promises were
worthless, who sought 'absolute power' but used it for trivialities,
and who only survived through daring and obstinacy.[53] Alamán
reflected all the doubts of his contemporaries:

A combination of good and bad features, an obvious natural talent, but
lacking in moral and intellectual qualities; an enterprising spirit, but without
fixed purpose or specific objective; energy and aptitude for government
flawed by grave defects; successful in making general plans for a revolution
or a campaign, but hopeless in the direction of a particular battle, of which
he has won only one.[54]

The charge of inconsistency Santa Anna denied. The fault lay
with the political parties, which divided Mexico and created a need
for reconciliation; therefore he came as an arbitrator, who of necessity had to compromise.[55] One of the few principles which Santa
Anna adhered to, after an early and vociferous commitment to
federalism, was that Mexico needed a strong central government,
and the centralist regime of 1834–46 was an essentially *santanista*
model. Mexico had a national government in the capital, and governors in the departments. But this did not work according to design.
In the first place the central government was too weak to exercise its
powers in the departments, which were left to their own devices
under governors and local interest groups. Second, military expenses
were defrayed at a departmental level and took precedence over civil
salaries. This decentralized the army into regional units living on
regional resources; the generals were thus allowed to cultivate local
power bases from which to pressure the government. Several states
staged revolts against the national government, and although these
were suppressed, it was not so easy to overcome the revolt of Texas,

---

[52] Lorenzo de Zavala, *Ensayo histórico de las revoluciones de México desde 1808 hasta 1830*, in *Obras* (Mexico, 1969), 113.
[53] Mora, *Obras sueltas*, 129, 159.
[54] Alamán, *Historia de Méjico*, v. 688.
[55] González Navarro, *Anatomía del poder en México*, 389.

and Texas in turn further destabilized relations between the centre and the regions.

Santa Anna made Texas his personal campaign, 'preferring the uncertainties of war to ... the life of the palace'.[56] He aimed to crush the revolt as he would that of any other Mexican state, yet he was ignorant of the real situation. The campaign brought out the worst in his character and paraded before the world all his illusions of grandeur. The so-called Army of Operations was little more than a horde driven by hunger to look for better things in Texas. To pay for it he mortgaged Manga de Clavo for 10,000 pesos and raised an advance from Juan M. Erraza guaranteed by forced loans on the northern departments. Amidst great chaos and confusion he was seen to be doing everything and playing every role, from general to corporal, unable to organize, instruct, or delegate. On the expedition itself he behaved like an ignorant caudillo rather than a professional commander, indulging in overkill at the Alamo, authorizing the execution of prisoners, taking an inopportune siesta, and receiving his retribution at San Jacinto, a defeat from which he sought to escape disguised as a peasant and for which he then blamed everyone else. When Santa Anna was taken prisoner on 22 April 1836 he was not only commander-in-chief of the Mexican forces but also president of Mexico. Even worse, he allowed his army to evacuate Texas without a fight and without negotiating, and on 14 May signed a treaty with the president of Texas, preliminary to Mexican recognition of Texan independence. He returned to Veracruz in February 1837 after imprisonment and humiliation in the United States, to be received with the honours due to his rank but without enthusiasm. He retired to Manga de Clavo, ignoring the presidency which nominally he still possessed, and justifying his campaign in a pompous and boastful manifesto, blaming everything on circumstances beyond his control. Officially he resigned the presidency. 'I was grateful for the solitude and peacefulness of Manga de Clavo. I busied myself with domestic life, which seemed, in my melancholy state, as welcome as a desert oasis to the weary traveller.'[57]

The conservative regime set up by Santa Anna in 1834 continued to rule the country without him, and he put aside his old *golpista* habits from 1837 to 1841. On 17 April 1837 Anastasio Bustamante

---

[56] Santa Anna, *Autobiography*, 50.
[57] Ibid. 58.

was elected president by Congress to govern a country still destabilized by conflict between the centre and the provinces, between the government and rebel generals. At Manga de Clavo Santa Anna waited and watched, until people cried 'Save Mexico!', first from the French, then from economic chaos. These proved the opportunities he needed. The French blockade and invasion of Veracruz in 1837 in exercise of gunboat diplomacy enabled Santa Anna to play a hero's role, though again there were various versions of events and numerous ambiguities in his behaviour. He eventually faced the enemy sword in hand as the French artillery fired; he was wounded in the left leg, which had to be amputated, and he retired to his hacienda to recuperate, taking his leg with him. The limb was later transferred to Mexico City where it was placed in a ceremonial resting place. Bustamente was prepared to support the fiction that the Mexicans had won a great victory at Veracruz, perhaps because he needed Santa Anna's support. By late February 1839 the victor was fit enough to return to the capital as interim president during Bustamante's absence against rebel generals, and he was received with acclaim by the crowds. Having established his grip on government he then went to Puebla and took credit for the defeat of General Antonio Mejía by government forces. Returning to Mexico he was again received with enthusiasm: 'He reached the apogee of his glory, his house appeared the home of a prince as the top people flocked to congratulate him on his triumph'.[58] The interim presidency, from March to July 1839, was a resounding success, and the hero bowed out modestly. The defeats of Texas were forgotten, or cancelled out, while Bustamante had to cope with economic difficulties, food shortages, and fiscal deficits. Santa Anna in Manga de Clavo waited his opportunity. But in Mexico City Gómez Farías did likewise.

As Bustamante's government ran out of steam, it came under attack from both radical federalists and extreme conservatives. The regime had failed to deliver stability, development, and security, the hallmarks of conservatism, and become instead a willing victim of speculators, a source of disappointment to its friends and hatred to

---

[58] Carlos María de Bustamante, *El Gabinete Mexicano durante el segundo período de la administración del Exmo. Señor Presidente D. Anastasio Bustamante hasta la entrega del mando al Exmo. Señor Presidente interino D. Antonio López de Santa-Anna* (2 vols.; Mexico, 1842), i. 185.

its enemies. Regional dissidence was accompanied by protests in Mexico City over high taxes, excessive tariffs, and rising prices. In July 1840 a revolt in the capital initiated by disgruntled military, joined by Gómez Farías, and supported by the mob, caused considerable bloodshed and destruction before it was crushed by Bustamante and before Santa Anna had a chance to arrive and show his hand.[59] The caudillo had different targets in his sights. He did not like the constitution of 1836, which had introduced a Supreme Conservative Power as a restraint on the president. Some of his military colleagues had similar views. On 8 August 1841 General Mariano Paredes, commander of Guadalajara, went into rebellion and called for the removal of Bustamante and the assembly of a constituent congress. On 31 August General Gabriel Valencia 'pronounced' in Mexico City. Santa Anna waited a few days to assess the situation and on 9 September led an army of *jarochos* towards Puebla and on to Mexico City, where he arrived on 26 September to join Paredes and Valencia.[60] The rebel generals, or 'three allied sovereigns' as Frances Calderón called them, did not trust each other, but it seems to have been grudgingly accepted by his colleagues that Santa Anna had superior personal qualifications, was popular in the army, and had struck a deal with the necessary financiers. An agreement was reached, the *Bases de Tacubaya*, stating that the Supreme Powers established by the constitution of 1836 ceased to function 'by the will of the nation'; to supply the will of the nation a junta would be chosen by the general-in-chief of the Mexican army, namely Santa Anna, to decide 'with complete freedom' who would provisionally exercise executive power.[61]

Bustamante handed over power to Santa Anna on 9 October 1841 and Congress was dissolved. In the following months Santa Anna exercised almost absolute power. The British minister was impressed by the speed of the coup:

This is the third time since I have been in this country that General Santa Anna has overthrown the Government by military violence: but on the two

---

[59] Pakenham to Palmerston, 29 July 1840, PRO, FO 50/136, fos. 171–80; Michael P. Costeloe, 'A Pronunciamiento in Nineteenth Century Mexico: "15 de julio de 1840"', *Mexican Studies*, 4, 2 (1988), 245–64.

[60] Michael P. Costeloe, 'The Triangular Revolt in Mexico and the Fall of Anastasio Bustamante, August–October 1841', *JLAS* 20 (1988), 337–60.

[61] Pakenham to Palmerston, 9 Oct. 1841, PRO, FO 50/147, fos. 97–107; Fuentes Mares, *Santa Anna*, 169–79.

former occasions, the first in 1828, the second in 1832, he met with considerable opposition, and did not accomplish his purpose until after a great deal of fighting and some serious reverses. On the present occasion his success has been most rapid, I might say unopposed . . . the troops in every part of the country declared in his favour . . . what is more remarkable, persons of every party and of the most opposite political opinions have supported his undertaking, apparently from the impression that any change from the order of things previously existing should be for the better.[62]

Pakenham reported that Mexicans turned to Santa Anna in despair, convinced there was no one else: 'I do not believe that history affords an example of the fate of a country being so completely dependent upon the will of one man.'[63] But there was still some defiance of that will.

In June 1842, following elections which were genuinely popular and which Santa Anna failed to control and preferred not to annul, a constituent Congress dominated by liberals and federalists reacted strongly to the previous centralism and produced a liberal and federal constitution.[64] The whole exercise lacked credibility, for the coup had been made by soldiers looking for personal power and led by the caudillo who was now president and hated federalism. The generals told the assembly in no uncertain terms that a strong executive was required; and Santa Anna informed them that 'the creation of a number of independent and sovereign states is the infallible precursor of ruin'.[65] The assembly stood its ground.

In circumstances of political incompatibility Santa Anna had a standard procedure and this he now followed: he left the presidency to General Bravo and, invoking reasons of health, retired to Manga de Clavo. Such a move by the leader 'more feared than loved' was usually the prelude to a coup, a coup which he preferred to launch from his hacienda rather than his presidential office. On 18 December 1842 the army dissolved Congress; in its place a *junta de notables* was formed consisting of leading conservative landowners, clerics, army officers, and lawyers. The junta produced the Organic Bases (13 June 1843), a constitution acceptable to Santa Anna,

[62] Pakenham to Palmerston, 9 Oct. 1841, PRO, FO 50/147, fos. 97–107.

[63] Pakenham to Palmerston, 8 Nov. 1841, PRO, FO 50/147, fos. 185–8.

[64] Michael P. Costeloe, 'Generals versus Politicians; Santa Anna and the 1842 Congressional Elections in Mexico', *BLAR* 8, 2 (1989), 257–74.

[65] Santa Anna, Speech to Constituent Assembly, 10 June 1842, encl. in Pakenham to Aberdeen, 21 June 1842, PRO, FO 50/154, fos. 148–65.

centralist, conservative, and with no mention of civil rights. The presidential powers were enhanced; the electoral system had income requirements for deputies and senators of 1,200 and 2,000 pesos respectively. The constitution specifically reaffirmed Catholicism as the official religion of Mexico and promised to maintain the *fueros* of the clergy, the army, and mining corporations. Thus the caudillo at last came to power on his own terms through an understanding between the traditional interest groups, and more particularly the military, the bureaucrats, and the businessmen, manipulated by Santa Anna and for him. His success in the presidential elections of late 1843 was almost an afterthought.

While the constitution legitimized Santa Anna, it was the military who maintained him and he them. He authorized the purchase of military supplies in Europe. He increased the infantry and cavalry forces throughout the provinces, adding 18,000 to the existing 12,000; he rewarded officers with promotion to colonels and generals; and he distributed money to the troops, who were the first and sometimes the only group in the public sector to be paid. In effect this administration was a military dictatorship, in which Santa Anna personally imposed an iron rule, muzzled the press, imprisoned critics, and diverted public attention by demagogy. In the process the political parties were ignored and Santa Anna ruled through the army, though he claimed that he ruled responsibly, in the interests of order and peace, and denied that supreme power naturally led to abuse of power:

Many believe that a multitude of mandarins correspondingly restricts the freedom of the people; but experience demonstrates the opposite.... Our people, because of its education, still needs to be led by the hand like a child, though the leader has to be well intentioned, a true patriot and republican, to qualify as the depository of supreme power, whose misuse can occasion many ills.[66]

To glorify enlightened dictatorship and give the republic a ritual to rival that of monarchy the regime promoted the heroic image of Santa Anna. The anniversary of the defence of Veracruz against the French was celebrated with great extravagance. A new theatre was begun in 1842, a statue was erected, and medals were struck describing Santa Anna as 'Benemérito de la Patria', 'Caudillo de la Independencia', and 'Fundador de la República'. The anniversary

[66] Santa Anna to Juan Alvarez, 16 Apr. 1842, in Díaz Díaz, *Caudillos y caciques*, 166.

of the victory of Tampico was celebrated in the streets, the palace, and the cathedral, while Santa Anna played the part of a superior statesman. The cult of the caudillo was carried to extraordinary lengths. On 26 September 1842 his left leg was solemnly buried in a small mausoleum in the cemetery of Santa Paula in a ceremony attended by the top and bottom of society, everyone determined to witness this ultimate curiosity. On all these occasions he was attended by a group of followers, his 'court', who were the centre of a cycle of balls, banquets, and pompous receptions, while his generals in their scarlet and gold uniforms surrounded him 'like peacocks' and the *nouveaux riches* jostled for a place in the social life of *santanismo*.[67]

Yet even now Santa Anna did not personally exercise his presidential power. He was normally to be found at Manga de Clavo, while his ministers performed the work of government. In the first months of 1843 the Bravo administration remained in office. Santa Anna formally occupied the presidency only between March and October 1843 when, pleading ill health, he consigned his presidential duties to General Valentín Canalizo, one of his own creatures. On this occasion, perhaps because of earlier difficulties with Bravo, he specifically retained the right to appoint and dismiss ministers, who were to be left to run their own departments with Canalizo simply *primus inter pares*.[68] In November 1843 Santa Anna was formally elected to the presidency again but did not take up his official duties until June 1844. Santa Anna's aloofness did not mean that the caudillo intended to make himself king, as many suspected; he was simply devising a new type of leadership, a sovereign without a crown, and his model was General Espartero, the coarse and radical caudillo in Spain.[69] The visits to Manga de Clavo became longer, while his favourites in Mexico City made the most of the opportunities he allowed them. On 3 June 1844 he returned to the capital to take the oath and initiate a new period of government. There was a magnificent reception and overwhelming adulation, but the chores of office were not for him and he returned to his hacienda on the death of his wife.

---

[67] Prieto, *Memorias de mis tiempos*, ii. 159–74; Calderón de la Barca, *Life in Mexico*, 443–4.

[68] Doyle to Aberdeen, 30 Oct. 1843, PRO, FO 50/165, fos. 22–3.

[69] Fuentes Mares, *Santa Anna*, 177.

Sovereignty of this kind needed two basic supports, the army and the financiers. The *agiotistas*, many of whom had started out as merchants in the import–export trade, were the characteristic types of the dictatorship, and indeed had played a key role in its creation. The tobacco consortium provided Santa Anna with one hundred troops as he made his bid for power against rival generals. Subsequently Manuel Escandón, an entrepreneur with a finger in many financial deals, helped to make the financial arrangements for the dictatorship. It was an expensive government. War with Yucatán, conflict with Texas, problems with frontier Indians, peasant risings in the south, all served as reasons, or pretexts, to justify constant demands for money. Most of these, it is true, were for the state. But funds also went to enrich Santa Anna and his friends, and it was during this regime that he managed to expand his properties in the state of Veracruz, where he had 5,000 men on his payroll.[70]

The finance of dictatorship relied on short-term, high-interest loans from Santa Anna's favoured group of speculators.[71] The formula for success was to reward each of his support groups in turn—the army, the bureaucracy, the Veracruz planters, the import merchants, and the regional interests—but to help his financiers most of all, as the others were soon to discover. Santa Anna was nobody's fool; he was always cunning enough to punish as well as reward. On 11 October 1841 he stopped payment on all existing funds, including the 'seventeen per cent fund' of 1840 which had been created in repayment of a 2-million-pesos loan, and included some important financiers. Three days later he resumed payments but at half rates. He suspended payments again on 19 February 1842. Some of the *agiotistas* appealed for diplomatic support, others made private deals with the government agreeing to take less than the others. The British minister, Pakenham, helped to obtain a settlement for some in 1842–3, though at lower rates. Santa Anna thus favoured some creditors and penalized others. This was a regime of risks as well as rewards.

Santa Anna also had the support of the Church, who feared him and favoured him and was ready to buy his good will by paying taxes and forced loans. The government, in the absence of a formal agreement with Rome, still exercised considerable powers of pat-

---

[70] Díaz Díaz, *Caudillos y caciques*, 169.
[71] Tenenbaum, *The Politics of Penury*, 57, 61, 65–6, 66–9.

ronage, and Santa Anna made it clear that the alternative to him was anticlericalism. In fact he gave and took from the Church, allowing the Jesuits to return to Mexico, but quickly making demands for funds. Throughout 1842 and 1843 the government issued many decrees affecting church wealth, including a 15 per cent tax on all newly acquired property and capital, and prohibitions against the sale of church ornaments. Santa Anna did not confiscate church wealth; he preserved it in order to tax it. The most significant demand on the Church was the forced sale of the properties of the Pious Fund of the Californias at prices determined by capitalizing the annual rate of return at 6 per cent.[72]

A regime based exclusively on interest groups inevitably found its support base contracting when the money ran out. The Church yielded to the bureaucracy, which lost to the army, which saw the financiers as the only winners. But even the financiers diminished. He progressively alienated his *agiotista* friends by favouring Manuel Escandón and his clique over the rest, and there were rumours that generous commissions were paid to those—including Santa Anna— who awarded military contracts and profits to those who received them.[73] On 11 May 1843 the government stopped payment on debts owed to many speculators and created a special 'twenty-five per cent fund' to handle all of them in exchange for yet another 6 per cent premium. Included in the new fund were 5 million pesos in tobacco bonds (held by Escandón and his associates) for the tobacco monopoly. Eventually Santa Anna's excessive spending and venality proved too much; in any case the *agiotistas* were not an alternative to Congress.[74]

As funds diminished problems mounted. Even military dictatorship could not wipe Mexico's slate clean. Sonora was in the midst of civil war; Puebla and Oaxaca continued in federalist revolt; Yucatán was in a state of virtual independence. For all the rewards Santa Anna had distributed to the military, they solved nothing and won nothing. And for all the alleged power of a centralist regime, the regions continued unstable, while in the south the caudillo Alvarez had

---

[72] Jan Bazant, *Alienation of Church Wealth in Mexico: Social and Economic Aspects of the Liberal Revolution 1856–1875* (Cambridge, 1971), 25–8.

[73] Bankhead to Aberdeen, 30 Oct. 1844, PRO, FO 50/176, fos. 152–4.

[74] The appearance of a pamphlet *Mientras que hay Congreso, no habrá Progreso* was part of a government-inspired campaign against a recalcitrant Congress. Bankhead to Aberdeen, 29 Aug. 1844, PRO, FO 50/175, fos. 247–50.

created a rival base of power. To defend the dictatorship Santa Anna wanted to enlarge the army, then at 30,000. But where was the money? At the moment of crisis the regime faltered because the dictator's allies in the interest groups would not pay direct taxes, and because most of his expenditure went in paying past and present debts. He asked Congress for 4 million pesos for a campaign against Texas to be raised by a property and land tax, and received a hostile reception. He increased his demands to 10 million, and Congress refused; Santa Anna therefore raised money by decree and closed Congress. But it was not simply a question of Congress. Proposals to raise taxes on rural property and on mining and industry were regarded as a betrayal of the very interest groups who had helped him to power; these now persuaded the military to rebel against the dictatorship.[75]

There were two particular fronts of opposition. An Indian rebellion in Chilapa posed a political and financial problem. Santa Anna suspected that the rebellion was instigated by Juan Alvarez, but he had to leave the caudillo of the south to deal with it, reluctant though he was to increase the latter's authority at the expense of the central government. In Guadalajara General Paredes revolted on 1 November 1844, and on 29 November while the president was absent in search of the rebels there was a revolt jointly of Congress and the military garrison in Mexico City. Caught between the two outbreaks, Santa Anna should have been able to extricate himself. He had 11,000 troops, sufficient to defeat Paredes and return to crush his enemies in the capital. At this critical point he showed a failure of nerve and a strange irresolution, a side of his character not normally on view. Perhaps he was demoralized by the news that people of the *barrios* had been rampaging and shouting 'Death to the cripple!' and that a mob had destroyed two statues of him and stripped his name from the Santa Anna Theatre; but the final blow was the news that a gang of hooligans had disinterred his leg and paraded it insultingly through the streets before it was rescued by an officer. He renounced the presidency and resolved to leave the country. Congress formally deposed him on 16 December 1844 on the grounds that he had attempted to subvert the constitution. This was apparently a more 'popular' revolution than usual:

[75] Tenenbaum, *The Politics of Penury*, 46–53.

In no former outbreak of this kind has the people shewn any active part—former Revolutions have been exclusively produced by the Military—but here it is not to be denied that a general expression of dislike and disgust has been manifested against Santa Anna, proceeding not from acts of cruelty or bloodshed, but from a total disregard of publick opinion or interests—and a systematic determination to feed on the resources of the country for his own benefit, and that of persons surrounding him to a degree that even Mexican laxity of principle could no longer endure.[76]

This was a great fall, from absolute president to a common fugitive.

Santa Anna paraded his troops and addressed them from horseback: 'I bore with pride the loss of an important member of my body, lost with glory in the service of our country, and witnessed by some of you on that occasion, but that pride has turned to pain, grief, and despair'.[77] He dismissed his escort and prepared to go. But his defeats were no less sensational than his victories. The courts refused his request for an exit passport, and as he tried to make his escape he was captured by a party of armed peasants and placed under arrest by the military commandant of Jalapa. He survived an assassination attempt and was imprisoned in the fortress of Perote. There he denied Congress's right to put him on trial and blamed others for everything. Among his possessions was found a letter addressed to Manning, Mackintosh and Co. asking them to place under the protection of the British flag the money he had deposited with them, while the rest should go to friends in Jalapa. When he complained of his treatment to the minister of war he was told, 'The letters confiscated from you on your arrest prove that Your Excellency has in cash deposits more money than any other Mexican'.[78] In practice this was not true. Eventually, in May 1845, Santa Anna was amnestied, put on a British steamer, and exiled for life.

'Life' proved to be less than two years. In that time Mexico had four different governments and even more finance ministers, none of whom had enough credibility to reassure prospective taxpayers. Federalists and *santanistas* continued to confront each other; the army still paraded in the wings; and officers still occasionally 'pronounced' for Santa Anna. As generals and politicians destabilized

---

[76] Bankhead to Aberdeen, 31 Dec. 1844, PRO, FO 50/177, fos. 147–58.
[77] Santa Anna, *Autobiography*, 68–70; Fuentes Mares, *Santa Anna*, 179.
[78] Quoted by Fuentes Mares, *Santa Anna*, 181. Bankhead to Aberdeen, 29 Jan., 1 Mar. 1845, PRO, FO 50/184, fos. 1–7, 177–9.

Mexico from within, invaders from the United States attacked her from without.[79] The nation needed a saviour and looked again to Santa Anna, then enjoying a life of banquets and cock-fighting in Cuba, but always happy to return. He had already been in touch with another exile, Gómez Farías, suggesting they should work together to save Mexico. The alliance found some response. Gómez Farías recruited his political friends; Santa Anna encouraged the military; and *pronunciamientos* called for 'Santa Anna and Federation', joining the improbable with the irreconcilable. The former enemies returned; after a pause in El Encero to assess the dominant trends, Santa Anna emerged a reconverted federalist. On 16 September 1846 he and Farías rode together through the capital in an open carriage. The basis of the accord was the constitution of 1824, federalism, an end to the war, and a boundary treaty satisfactory to the United States. Santa Anna looked to federalists because he needed them against the enemies who had ejected him in 1844; and to the Americans because he needed them to maintain him in power by a financial deal. By his own lights it was compromise, not opportunism. The accord was formalized in December when, in a replay of 1833, Congress appointed Santa Anna president and Gómez Farías vice-president. It was a brief reunion.

While Santa Anna left to lead the army, if that was the correct word for tactics designed to protect his ramshackle forces from any encounter with the enemy, Gómez Farías was left to face a power struggle in the capital. His primary task was to find money for the war effort. On 11 January 1847 he decreed the nationalization of ecclesiastical properties to the value of 15 million pesos, about one-tenth of the Church's total wealth; as there was no time for their valuation, he then ordered the immediate confiscation and sale of Church assets estimated at 10 million pesos.[80] The Church protested, looked to its allies and persuaded the military in Mexico City to stage a revolt on 22 February 1847; this was the so-called revolt of the Polkos, which the government sought to counter by recruiting support from vagrants and popular sectors.[81] Santa Anna left the military front and returned as president on 21 March to

---

[79] On the war with the United States see Chap. 4, sect. 5.

[80] Bankhead to Palmerston, 29 Jan. 1847, PRO, FO 50/208, fos. 146–54; Bazant, *Alienation of Church Wealth in Mexico*, 30–1.

[81] Michael P. Costeloe, 'The Mexican Church and the Rebellion of the Polkos', *HAHR* 46, 2 (1966), 170–8.

repeal both decrees, but first received a promise from the Church that it would guarantee a loan of 1.5 million pesos. As the Church had little cash, this meant it authorized the government to raise loans and use Church property as collateral. As for the vice-president, his office was abolished in April. Santa Anna had agreed with Gómez Farías's policies and he condemned in principle the revolt of the Polkos; following his familiar tactics, however, he used the crisis simultaneously to reassure and to exploit the Church. In the process he eroded mortmain and manœuvred the Church into selling much urban property to satisfy repayment to the *agiotistas*.[82]

While the Mexican military and politicians thus fought their own civil war, the real war approached nearer; Santa Anna struggled for supplies, troops, a victory, but achieved none. He mortgaged his own property, scraped together his own resources, recruited his own peons, but to no avail.[83] A caudillo could lead but he could not work miracles. No single person could have inspired the mass of the people in solidarity with the war effort; the majority of Mexicans remained indifferent as to who won, indifferent to the fate of Santa Anna. There was no nationalism, little patriotism. The war, and the deals to end the war, were not really between nation and nation. Various political groups, including Santa Anna, struggled not to defend the country but to strike a bargain with the Americans which would favour their own party. In these conditions there was nothing to stop the United States forces taking Veracruz in March, Puebla in May, and the capital on 15 September. After the defeat at Cerro Gordo the only resistance offered by Santa Anna was to slow up the United States by negotiation. He knew he could not win and he did not want the responsibility of making an inglorious peace. So on 16 September he resigned as president and eventually left the country. He had some money, enough to keep him in voluntary exile. During his period of eclipse he acquired another property, buying and restoring a substantial house in New Granada, the so-called Palacio de Turbaco near Cartagena, around which he assembled a small estate. There he lived with his family like a rich potentate, 'very lame', according to O'Leary, but 'alert and expert on American affairs'.[84] British opinion thought he was finished politically: 'He is

---

[82] Díaz Díaz, *Caudillos y caciques*, 201–2; Tenenbaum, *The Politics of Penury*, 78–85.
[83] Santa Anna, *Autobiography*, 91, 96.
[84] Díaz Díaz, *Caudillos y caciques*, 217.

now rich and old, has married a young wife, has only one leg, and is therefore not very likely to expose himself much'.[85] They were soon proved wrong, and Doyle had to admit: 'knowing as I do the chief men of all parties, I am at a loss myself, nor can I find anyone else who can point out, a single man, hitherto unknown, who offers even a fair hope of extricating this country from its present lamentable condition. Indeed the only party with a known chief is that of General Santa Anna'.[86] Mexico needed its caudillo. Santa Anna had only to sit back and wait.

4. *El Hombre Necesario*

The caudillo was restored in response to conditions; Santa Anna again prospered on the failure of his rivals. Federalism had a second chance in the years 1846–52 and wasted it. Post-war economic depression, it is true, quickened social unrest. The caste war in Yucatán entered a new stage; peasant demands for land and subsistence exploded into violence; grievances of Indian villages against fiscal and hacienda oppression sparked off insurrection in the centre and the north; and in the towns hungry *léperos* provided an unruly mob ripe for social protest or political action. Social anarchy was feared and exploited by politicians, even by *santanistas*, ever alert to government weakness.[87] The federalists, by supporting greater autonomy for the states, hoped to make revolt unnecessary and promote union through co-operation. Like all previous governments they experienced taxpayer resistance and budget deficits, leading to unpaid armies, disaffection, and occasional rebellion. Finance ministers came and went, some lasting only a few days, others stepping out of the ranks of the *agiotistas* to spend a short time in the treasury, before deciding there was more money to be made outside the government than within. In the three years following the peace treaty of February 1848 fourteen finance ministers were appointed; as for the American indemnity, by March 1851 it was almost spent.

[85] Doyle to Palmerston, 4 June 1851, PRO, FO 50/244, fos. 223–8.

[86] Doyle to Malmesbury, 2 Sept. 1852, PRO, FO 50/253, fos. 195–201.

[87] Doyle to Palmerston, 14 May 1848, PRO, FO 50/220, fos. 217–21; Doyle to Palmerston, 14 June 1849, 13 Aug. 1849, FO 50/229, fos. 49–58, 243–85. On post-war social protest see González Navarro, *Anatomía del poder en México*, 28–48, 160–8.

The states were shielded by their representatives in Congress who stubbornly resisted taxes on the resources of their constituencies, reduced in any case by war and insurrection. Members of Congress played the federal system for all it was worth, and to them it was worth a great deal; they recognized that patronage came from the states, not from the central government, and that it was the states who kept them in a job:

To be a Senator or Deputy is become in this country on account of the salary a career much sought for. . . . The conduct of the Deputies may be summed up in the answer given to a friend of mine by one of them, a person of influence, and who was asked why he had voted against a government measure of great importance, and admitted to be of great necessity. 'The General Government has nothing to give, the State Government has, and I don't choose to lose my re-election'.[88]

The reaction in favour of centralism and dictatorship had a certain inevitability. Mexico preferred a caudillo to a congress, and the reason was not far to seek. Federalism had not impressed by its results. None of the five presidents who held office during the absence of the caudillo achieved success or popularity; most had the flaws of Santa Anna without his qualities. State governors were seen to be no less oppressive than national governments. Federal Congressmen could be just as venal as centralists. Federalism prepared its own demise, with no assistance from Santa Anna. Already some ministers were pointing out that the only solution, though not necessarily one advocated by the government, would be a dictatorship or a president with extraordinary powers.[89] The political crisis mounted during 1852 and was the subject of intense debate among liberals, conservatives, and *santanistas*. By the middle of the year the opposition, now composed of both conservatives and moderates, began to formulate a strategy aimed at the overthrow of the latest government, that of General Mariano Arista, and the return of centralism. They needed the promise of financial support and received it from the *agiotistas* who wanted a strong government to collect taxes and create a new infrastructure.[90] They were indispensable to the movement, for only they could assemble the funds to finance a dictatorship. But they could not do it on their own; they too needed allies.

[88] Doyle to Malmesbury, 4 June 1852, PRO, FO 50/252, fos. 153–66.
[89] González Navarro, *Anatomía del poder en México*, 287–8.
[90] Tenenbaum, *The Politics of Penury*, 116–17.

Colonel José María Blancarte, a well known *santanista* officer, 'a man with hairs on his chest, tall and strong', rebelled in Guadalajara against the presidency of Arista and for reform of the constitution. The Plan of Jalisco (26 July 1852) was pure *santanismo*, without yet naming the caudillo, and almost immediately it grew from a local to a national movement. Conservative leaders in Mexico City took up the cry, and José López Uraga, an officer turned politician, spoke openly of their objective, the return to power of Santa Anna as 'the man necessary in the present circumstances'.[91] During the rest of the year the movement gathered momentum, as state after state 'pronounced'. Thus the conservatives, under the direction of Lucas Alamán, exploited the impetus of the *santanistas* and the power of the military and pre-empted the movement. The object was now specific, to invite Santa Anna to become president and establish social order; he should possess dictatorial powers until the promulgation of a new constitution, for which a congress should be called in not later than a year.[92] Arista was denied by Congress the resources to confront the revolt, and resigned on 5 January 1853. On 17 March Santa Anna was elected president by the votes of the states. He had already begun his journey back from Turbaco on 3 March.

Various political interests took credit for the restoration and claimed Santa Anna as their own. But the conservatives and the *agiotistas* were the prime movers, the first through their political machine, the second through their money. Both were willing to support a dictatorship, though not a permanent one. Both wanted stability and strong central government, Alamán in the belief that this was essential for the preservation of a hierarchical social order, the survival of the Catholic Church, and the promotion of economic development; the *agiotistas* in order to guarantee enough revenue to keep them in business and finance national improvement of the infrastructure. Both needed the military in order to win power, and thus it became a triple alliance of the army, the *agiotistas*, and the conservatives. By the beginning of February 1853 they agreed on Santa Anna for president. Why not a politician or a general? Were not the policies more important than the person? Not in Mexico in 1853. They needed something extra, the magic of the caudillo, the

---

[91] González Navarro, *Anatomía del poder en México*, 347.
[92] Carmen Vázquez Mantecón, *Santa Anna y la encrucijada del estado: La dictadura (1853–1855)* (Mexico, 1986), 16–21.

reputation that only accumulated caudillism could earn. Aware of his strengths and weaknesses, conservatives and *agiotistas* planned their approaches to the caudillo.

Lucas Alamán, the self-styled 'representative of all the propertied people, the clergy, and those who want good for their country', wrote a letter to the future president outlining how conservatives and *toda la gente de bien* thought he should behave once in office. After reminding him that he needed conservative support, Alamán advised Santa Anna not to surround himself with sycophants, and not to entrust the government to others and retire to his estates. He should support the Church, 'the only bond uniting all Mexicans'; keep a strong army; repel savage Indians and keep the roads safe; abolish federalism; and avoid congresses and anything to do with so-called 'popular elections'. He further advised the dictator to avoid asking the Church for funds and to procure them instead by selling territory to the United States. Thus he would remain free from deals 'advantageous to the speculators but dishonourable to you'. The conservatives made it clear, therefore, that Santa Anna was returning at their invitation and on their conditions. The letter was a warning as well as a welcome: 'we believe you will share these ideas; but if you do not, we fear that it will be very bad for the nation and for you'.[93] Meanwhile the speculators were writing a letter of their own. When Santa Anna landed at Veracruz in April 1853, two men greeted him at the dockside: Antonio Haro y Tamariz gave him Alamán's letter, while his old friend Manuel Escandón, 'king of the *agiotistas*', presented a different idea, that a company of financiers purchase the rights to collect and retain all taxes for 9 million pesos, 6 million of which would pay government expenses and 3 million outstanding debts.[94] Thus from the outset Santa Anna faced two sets of demands which were mutually exclusive. He himself also had a third interest in mind, that of the military, whom he saw as an indispensable part of the coalition and whose demands he knew did not go much beyond appointments and promotions. In his manifesto at Veracruz (10 April 1853) he stated: 'We will restore to our noble profession the glory which others have sought to take away'.[95] The glory he

---

[93] Alamán to Santa Anna, 23 March 1853, in Francisco de Paula Arrangoiz y Barzábal, *México desde 1808 hasta 1867*, 2nd edn. (Mexico, 1968), 420–3; Fuentes Mares, *Santa Anna*, 247–8.

[94] Bazant, *Alienation of Church Wealth in Mexico*, 31–2.

[95] Quoted by Díaz Díaz, *Caudillos y caciques*, 237.

had in mind would be won not in armed conflict but in the battle of the budget.

Santa Anna re-entered Mexico City after an absence of five years and took office on 20 April 1853; he was fifty-nine and this was his eleventh presidency. His first government was a mixture of conservatives and *santanistas*, almost one of consensus. Alamán became minister of foreign affairs; Manuel Diez de Bonilla minister of the interior; Teodosio Lares minister of justice; Joaquín Velázquez de León minister of development, assisted by Miguel Lerdo de Tejada as chief official, a liberal who advised that the army, the Church, and the bureaucracy were the three interest groups standing in the way of reform. Santa Anna reserved the key ministries of war and finance for longtime *santanistas*, José María Tornel y Mendivil and Antonio Haro y Tamariz.[96] But this was not a reactionary team. The coalition was headed by Alamán, not only because he was the best qualified politician but also because he represented the clergy, the hacendados, and the industrialists; second came Tornel, head of the military; finally the *agiotistas*, who after the death of Alamán came into their own. This was a dictatorship but one which took pride in its ideals of modernization, an early model of 'order and progress', hallmarks of Alamán's conservatism. It was also a personal dictatorship.

Two days after he took office Santa Anna decreed (22 April 1853) the abolition of federalism. The 1824 constitution was suspended; the centralist constitution of 1843 was not seen as an alternative for it placed restraints on the president's power, including his ability to alienate national territory. Santa Anna, therefore, governed without a constitution and took no steps to call a constituent congress. His ministers were encouraged to rule their own departments but were also conscious of the dictator's ultimate sovereignty. The Council of State of twenty-one persons, all appointed by the executive, was also dependent on the dictator and Santa Anna insisted, 'they know that they cannot publish anything without the approval of the government'.[97] It was a rigidly centralist government, which dissolved local legislatures, abolished minor town councils, replaced states by departments, and centralized the revenues of the regions. Direct

---

[96] González Navarro, *Anatomía del poder en México*, 372–3; Vázquez Mantecón, *Santa Anna*, 70–8.
[97] Quoted by Vázquez Mantecón, *Santa Anna*, 69.

taxes on property and incomes characteristic of Santa Anna's previous dictatorship were reimposed, and the dreaded *alcabala* was
restored together with other taxes on consumption. Santa Anna did
not pretend to be a populist.[98]

Santa Anna was quick to promote *santanistas*, clients from Veracruz,
and followers past and present, to the council of state, the bureaucracy, and other tangible rewards. The dictatorship became the centre
of a web of patronage bypassing normal processes of law and administration, and the resources of the state were used to establish
colluding links binding the major interest groups. The conservatives,
still hopeful of modernization, collaborated in spite of the caudillo's
personalism, the greater cause excusing the lesser crime. But the
regime soon lost its two best ministers. Alamán died on 2 June. This
eased the pressure of the conservatives on Santa Anna, without
entirely releasing him from their influence. But the army held more
power than the politicians and Santa Anna would have to fulfil its
expectations; this meant obtaining resources from the financiers.
The army and the *agiotistas* now remained the key to the regime,
with the clergy providing moral support. Army costs soon showed
the incompatibility of the interest groups. Haro proposed to cover
the budget deficit of 17 million pesos with an issue of bonds guaranteed by Church property. The clergy immediately protested. The
only alternative was the *agiotistas*, whose price Haro considered too
high. He therefore resigned on 5 August and for the moment Santa
Anna found other means of producing the money. He began with
the usual recourse of suspending debt fund payments. Then in
December 1853 he concluded a deal with the United States, selling
the Mesilla Valley in southern Arizona, the so-called Gadsden
purchase, for 15 million pesos. This enabled him to maintain political
stability and leave the Church immune.

These ministerial losses opened the way to even greater exercise
of personal power, to the advance of clients and creatures of the
president, and to the persecution of those out of favour. Haro was
replaced by Ignacio Sierra y Rosso, a longstanding friend of Santa
Anna described by the British minister as a mere cypher: 'by profession a soldier, and a remarkably bad one, a worse poet, and a still
worse minister of finance', but useful to Santa Anna because he was

---

[98] Tenenbaum, *The Politics of Penury*, 122–3.

ready to sign any and every order.[99] From August 1853 to August 1855 Santa Anna governed Mexico unrestrained by political reason, living in a country house at Tacubaya outside the capital, remote from the difficulties of ordinary Mexicans, and surrounded by the very sycophants and *agiotistas* against whom Alamán had warned him. He still believed in the old formula, government by the stick. In discussion with the *santanista* Juan Suárez Navarro on the formation of the new ministry, Santa Anna remarked: 'Suárez, my friend, I have a lot of experience and I know that this country needs government by a single person, and blows right and left'.[100] But Suárez too fell from grace. On the sudden death of Tornel on 11 September 1853 he made importunate demands for the war ministry, which angered Santa Anna; he had him arrested and sent to Acapulco to be put on the first boat going to South America.[101] While he undermined dissent, Santa Anna also rebuilt his personal image, encouraged by collaborators in capital and provinces, but catering too for a receptive if partial audience. In December 1853 he was granted the right to continue in office indefinitely and to name his successor. He was not so stupid as to become a monarch or an emperor like Iturbide, but opted for the title 'His Most Serene Highness', as he explained 'not for my own person, but solely for the dignity it confers on all presidents of the Republic'. He re-established the Order of Guadalupe, its membership headed and nominated by himself, as a way of creating a pseudo-aristocracy. While he liked dignity, he did not like criticism. One of his first laws (25 April 1853) gave the president the power to suppress by decree any periodical, a measure which brought to an end a hithero vigorous press.[102] He was served by a secret police who relentlessly pursued so-called *desafectos*. People were arrested late at night on the slightest suspicion of being hostile to the government; and liberal politicians such as Benito Juárez and Melchor Ocampo were sent into exile.

Santa Anna believed that his government of 1853–5 was reformist, a kind of enlightened dictatorship, which improved the administration, restored law and order, established a new infrastructure, and

[99] Doyle to Clarendon, 2 Nov. 1853, PRO, FO 50/261, fos. 179–90.
[100] Juan Suárez y Navarro, *El general Santa-Anna burlándose de la nación en su despedida hecha en Perote* (Mexico, 1856), 280.
[101] Doyle to Clarendon, 3 Oct. 1853, PRO, FO 50/261, fos. 72–5.
[102] Vázquez Mantecón, *Santa Anna*, 201–18.

expanded education, more or less the same achievements that Páez had claimed for his presidencies in Venezuela. His inaugural speech even spoke of 'granting to the labouring class means of subsistence through lucrative employment'.[103] And in his memoirs he claimed that 'In every one of the decrees and orders issued by the government during my administration, everything that affected the safety of our country—its material advancements, its good, and its glory— was provided for.'[104] But the regime had a mania for decrees, as though decrees alone would cure Mexico's ills. In fact the whole impetus of the dictatorship was to satisfy interest groups. Priority went to the army. Santa Anna openly favoured what he called 'the distinguished but depressed military class', and took early steps to increase the size of the army, as he had done in 1842, planning first for an establishment of 90,000, a figure soon reduced to 46,000, unobtainable even by conscription. The rank and file were poor peasants and illiterates who had no interest in fighting for the dictatorship and were excellent material only for desertion. Privileges were for officers. Appointments and promotions were awarded lavishly, especially to those who had helped to depose Arista and restore the caudillo. Military missions were despatched at great expense to Europe and South America. Lucrative contracts for uniforms and equipment were renewed.[105] All this was an enormous burden on the treasury; undertaken without the money to pay wages and bills, it only invited trouble when these had to be settled. The government had the greatest difficulty in paying the garrison of Mexico City; payments to military units got progressively worse the greater the distance from the capital and the less the risk from disaffection. As costs soared, the president justified military expenditure by pointing to the danger of an invasion from the United States. Santa Anna was never stopped for want of a pretext.

The clergy were also favoured. The archbishop and a number of bishops were made honorary members of the Council of State, and the bishop of Michoacán, Clemente de Jesús Mungía, was appointed its president. In the first months of the new regime the Jesuits were re-established and their property, or such as had not been alienated, was restored. The law of 1833 which had removed the civil en-

---

[103] Quoted by González Navarro, *Anatomía del poder en México*, 395.
[104] Santa Anna, *Autobiography*, 143; on the modernizing influence of the conservatives see Vázquez Mantecón, *Santa Anna*, 154–60.
[105] Ibid. 248–63.

forcement of monastic vows was repealed. The clergy in turn gave the regime their support, though they resisted requests for loans. Santa Anna believed he needed the army and the Church to maintain social order. In May 1853 the national guard in the port of Veracruz supported by urban artisans and angry mobs staged a bloody uprising, which was severely repressed and punished on the personal orders of the president. Violence in his own territory was accompanied by another caste war, this time in Oaxaca, both signs of popular unrest which a dictator was not supposed to tolerate. He was, however, aware of his obligations to property owners. He took steps to deal with banditry, often practised with the connivance of local authorities and the collusion of hacendados who were tempted to receive stolen goods. Santa Anna issued a decree by which *alcaldes* of towns and villages and owners of haciendas were made answerable for the robberies committed in their vicinity, a useful measure which had some effect.[106]

One of the strengths of Santa Anna in the past had been his eclectic approach to politics; he appealed to many because he gave himself to none. His very lack of principles was an advantage, for it encouraged the various political groups to believe that he might incline to theirs. And as no one was sure what he stood for nor were they agreed what their target should be. Thus his very faults were a purpose, and they helped to restore him to power in 1853. But the conservative dictatorship which followed ended these illusions. It also ended his own political career. Santa Anna suffered from a permanent inability to see things as they were. The Mexico to which he returned in 1853 was a Mexico poised for political, social, and economic change beyond anything that a traditional caudillo could provide. He seems not to have identified the character of mid-century liberals, their pressure for political reform and social opportunity, and their search for allies. Santa Anna was probably incapable of analysing the possible linkages between the forces of dissent. But he should have learnt by now that any central government in Mexico was vulnerable to two dangers, provincial rebellion and military dissent. Of all the power groups in Mexico the military were the least homogeneous and the least stable; when allied to provincial interests, they posed a formidable threat.

Santa Anna's dream of a permanent dictatorship was frustrated by

---

[106] Doyle to Clarendon, 26 Nov. 1853, PRO, FO 50/261, fos. 207–14.

one obstacle, the regional power of Juan Alvarez, caudillo of the south, a hard, cold, unyielding character whom the dictator did not trust but could not ignore. The power base of Alvarez was formed from a combination of circumstances, the remoteness of his lair from central government, the tradition of informal autonomy inherited from previous caudillos, the growth of large haciendas which gave southern caudillos personal fiefdoms of manpower and resources, and the existence of Indians in almost permanent protest against the loss of their lands to powerful proprietors and their consequent conversion into tenant farmers or dependent labourers. Alvarez, therefore, could cultivate an amorphous clientage of hacendados, Indians, mestizos and blacks of the Costa Grande, and anxious merchants of Acapulco, and could extend his zone of influence beyond his own haciendas, resisting centralism, supporting federalism, and seeking autonomy for a united south as a state in federal Mexico under his domination. Santa Anna, operating out of Veracruz, and Alvarez out of Acapulco and Tecpan, lived in guarded coexistence from 1828 to 1842. During his first dictatorship Santa Anna had to rely on his rival's interest and power in the south to bring the Indian rebellion of Chilapa under control in 1842–3, a rebellion which he believed to be fomented by Alvarez himself.[107] While the influence of Alvarez among Indian communities and popular sectors and his control over the port of Acapulco consolidated his personal base in the south, so the restoration of federalism after 1846 aided his political project. On 27 October 1849 the state of Guerrero was legislated into existence and Alvarez was appointed commandant-in-chief of the new creation. Now, in the midst of his own dictatorship, Santa Anna could not ignore Alvarez, the caudillo whom he implied was more tyrannical than Rosas, who was exacting forced loans from the merchants of Acapulco, and who at the beginning of 1854 was ordering arms from California.[108]

Santa Anna launched his offensive by announcing his intention to improve the road from Mexico City to Acapulco, the financial centre of Alvarez's stronghold, an obvious prelude to sending an army in. He also broke an unwritten rule by intervening in the south to change a number of military personnel and officials on the Pacific

[107] Díaz Díaz, *Caudillos y caciques*, 171–5.
[108] Wilthew to Clarendon, Acapulco, 23 Feb. 1854, PRO, FO 50/271, fos. 103–6; Santa Anna, *Autobiography*, 141.

coast. He removed Alvarez's protégé Ignacio Comonfort from the head of the Acapulco customs and named his own military commander of the port. All this was done without consulting Alvarez, who finally 'pronounced' on 24 February 1854, condemning Santa Anna for illegally selling Mexican territory to the United States and for establishing a despotism. The Plan of Ayutla (11 March 1854) thus united the southern caudillo and the military behind a constitutional programme which would convoke a congress and seek 'liberal institutions'. Politically Santa Anna had no reply to the revolution of Ayutla and simply appealed to past triumphs.[109] Militarily the war dragged on from March 1854 to August 1855 as the national army was fighting in climatically alien territory and desertions were high, while the rebels could not transform their struggle into a national movement. Santa Anna personally led an army of 4,500 and gesticulated outside Acapulco in April 1854 but eventually withdrew and returned to Mexico City on 15 May. On his return, it was reported, 'A triumphal Te Deum was sung by the Archbishop in the Cathedral, triumphal hymns were sung by actors at the theatres, a triumphal dinner was eaten at the Palace, triumphal bulls were killed at the Plaza de Toros ... in fact everything was triumphal except the campaign which was being celebrated'.[110]

The rebellion in the south produced copy-cat effects in various parts of the country in the second half of 1854, in Michoacán, Veracruz, and Tamaulipas, and anarchy spilled over into the countryside as bandits changed their names to *pronunciados*, and robberies became exactions. Government forces hit back and killed the alleged collaborators of rebels; terror was added to terror by army commanders who 'make no hesitation of sacrificing the lives of unfortunate Indians and peasantry who in their reports they proclaim 'Pronunciados' to gain fame and promotion'.[111] To stem the tide the government held a national and 'popular' referendum on 1 December 1854; every Mexican was invited to say (in open voting) whether the president should continue with the full powers he now enjoyed, or if not to whom he should make over the government. There was much pressure and chicanery to yield a good result; but the only people who bothered to come forward were public

[109] Díaz Díaz, *Caudillos y caciques*, 277–8; Vázquez Mantecón, *Santa Anna*, 282–3.
[110] Doyle to Clarendon, 2 June 1854, PRO, FO 50/257, fos. 317–20.
[111] Doyle to Clarendon, 4 Mar. 1855, PRO, FO 50/276, fos. 309–13.

employees who knew they had to vote for Santa Anna or lose their jobs.[112] By early 1855 a stalemate had been reached: neither the government of Santa Anna nor the revolution of Ayutla were capable of overcoming the other. But the confrontation exposed the Achilles heel of the dictatorship which had been there from the beginning.

The campaign in the south had financial implications for Santa Anna. Taxation was high enough to be unpopular yet its yield was too low for government needs. The customs were subject to numerous private contracts and arbitrary levels, harmful to merchants and consumers and hardly advantageous to the treasury. When the British chargé d'affaires protested, the minister of finance replied that he legislated 'for the wants of the Government, not for the good of the people'.[113] Santa Anna, therefore, financed his regime from the Gadsden money, in the event reduced to 10 million pesos and further reduced by selling it in advance at a heavy discount to speculators, and from deals with the *agiotistas*, who propped up the last two years of the dictatorship in the hope of promoting infrastructure development.[114] By October 1854 only 60,000 pesos were left of the Gadsden money, and Santa Anna was living on the *agiotistas*, with some clerical loans. By the end of 1854 the Church still supported Santa Anna, but of the two the *agiotistas* gave him greater financial help. Of course they received many privileges and concessions in return: tobacco monopoly, sugar monopoly, customs farm, the Mexico City–Veracruz railway, permission to import prohibited cotton, and rates of interest sometimes surpassing 100 per cent. By the end of 1854 government expenses amounted to 26 million pesos, against receipts of 16 million.[115] Eventually, in 1855, even the *agiotistas* had to consider their position. By May, after squandering income extravagantly and as scandalous cases of corruption were brought to light, Santa Anna had no money to pay government officials. In June he did not have enough to feed the army, and the rebels were approaching the capital. He described them as 'robbers and assassins', but to defeat them he had to pay the army. At a meeting of the Council of State in early July, when a

---

[112] Doyle to Clarendon, 2 Nov. 1854, 3 Dec. 1854, PRO, FO 50/269, fos. 228–34, 315–19.

[113] Doyle to Clarendon, 2 June 1854, PRO, FO 50/267, fos. 280–312.

[114] Tenenbaum, *The Politics of Penury*, 134.

[115] Doyle to Clarendon, 2 Nov. 1854, PRO, FO 50/269, fos. 228–34.

sub-committee advised the granting of a constitution and others advised the 'stick', Santa Anna replied:

Aye! the stick! the stick! but can I lay it on if I am unsupported? As long as I thought I could rely on the support of the majority of right thinking people I could have recourse to severe measures, but now that I see that what is called the reflective public is against me, the case is changed. These Councillors of State, with all their cringing, vote for a Constitution. What can I do, unsupported, against this cry?[116]

The decision of the *agiotistas* to switch from Santa Anna to Ayutla was fatal. By their reckoning the dictatorship failed on every count: order, authority, peace, development, none were forthcoming. They themselves were entrepreneurs as well as moneylenders; they wanted new public services, roads and railways, access to church land and property. To all these the caudillo appeared an obstacle; he was no longer a good investment.[117] So Santa Anna's authority dissolved as his money supply ran out. The flagrant corruption of the regime deterred new *agiotistas* from replacing the old. The United States held back from further purchases. Even the Church failed him, refusing to give, lend, or mortgage its wealth. Santa Anna was now finished, a political eyesore in an age of reform. He remained true to his reputation to the end. In the *Diario Oficial* of 3 August the minister of war warned that those who spread malicious rumours that the president was about to leave the country would be punished as disturbers of the peace. 'As soon as this Circular appeared there was but one opinion as to the intention of His Serene Highness, namely that as he declared he was not about to leave, he was making preparations to go.'[118] He left Mexico City in the early hours of 9 August 1855 and formally abdicated on 12 August, blaming the malice of some Mexicans and the ingratitude of most. After twenty years of exile and two attempts to make a political comeback, he was allowed to return to Mexico in 1874 but not to recover his confiscated estates. He died in modest circumstances in the capital on 21 June 1876 at the age of eighty-two.

---

[116] Lettsom to Clarendon, 9 July 1855, PRO, FO 50/279, fos. 50–4.

[117] Tenenbaum, *The Politics of Penury*, 136–7.

[118] Lettsom to Clarendon, 16 Aug. 1855, PRO, FO 50/279, fos. 263–71; Vázquez Mantecón, *Santa Anna*, 61.

5. *Variations of Leadership*

The motivation of Santa Anna was as elusive to his contemporaries as it became to later historians. His achievements were no less obscure. What was his career? An epic or a farce? As a president he was a flamboyant failure. As a general he lost his most important battles. As a caudillo he was always there when he was called, yet often absent when he was needed. He shared some of the characteristics of his colleagues in Argentina and Venezuela. Like them he started from a local power base and at the beginning of his political career he advocated the cause of regionalism. As Rosas repudiated a greater Argentina in favour of a powerful Buenos Aires, and Páez defied Gran Colombia in creating an independent Venezuela, so the young Santa Anna rejected centralism for a federal Mexico. The circumstances, of course, were different in each case, but throughout Spanish America the years before 1830 were hostile to the creation of superstates, and in Mexico Santa Anna identified the currents of the time. He subsequently recognized the failure of federalism and disillusion with liberalism, becoming after 1833 as centralist as Rosas and as conservative as Páez; and like Rosas, he was not sensitive to constitutions, ignoring them when it suited him.

He could not ignore the interest groups. This was what he meant when he declared that his mission was 'to promote the conservative principles of society'.[119] Like Rosas and Páez, Santa Anna was the scourge of anarchy and the protector of élites. But Mexico was a more disordered society than either Argentina or Venezuela, and the task to which Santa Anna was called in 1853 was beyond the experience of Rosas and Páez. To expect him to repel Indian invaders, suppress rural rebels, exterminate bandits, and subdue Mayan warriors was to ask him to do the impossible. His élites too were difficult. Politically Mexico was more complex than Argentina and Venezuela, and its caudillo had a more exacting role than Rosas and Páez. Whereas the clergy counted for little in Argentina and Venezuela, the Mexican Church was a powerful and wealthy institution, an obstacle and a temptation to any caudillo. Argentina and Venezuela each had an army, but in neither case did it possess political significance or independent strength. Santa Anna was forced

---

[119] Santa Anna, Manifesto, *El Telégrafo* (21 June 1833), encl. in O'Gorman to Bidwell, 28 June 1833, PRO, FO 50/80 B, fos. 152–7.

to negotiate the seizure of government and the terms of power with a professional military, who had to be cultivated and satisfied. This meant deferring to another interest group, the *agiotistas*, who alone could supply the currency of patronage, whose importance was a reflection of the greater wealth and the relative economic development of Mexico, and whose activities were an opportunity and a constraint for any caudillo.

Santa Anna held power with less continuity than Rosas and Páez. Rosas had absolute power for twenty years and virtually destroyed the opposition. Páez held two presidencies and was the power behind two others, enjoying a period of sixteen years in which the *paecistas* monopolized government at the expense of all rivals. Santa Anna never experienced conditions like these. Even in the years 1834–46, when the centralists were in and the federalists out, Santa Anna did not have security of tenure. In office he had less power than Rosas, out of office less influence than Páez. The Mexican president, moreover, was forced to pay more attention to Congress than did his South American counterparts. In Buenos Aires the House of Representatives was a cipher, a mere platform for the caudillo's propaganda. The Venezuelan Congress usually contained a number of agitators but the majority of its members could be influenced in the regime's favour. Mexico was more politicized and normally Congress contained either too many liberals or too many conservatives for a president's liking. The independence of Congress, of course, can be exaggerated. As one British minister ironically observed, elections in Mexico were usually 'decidedly in favour of the party in possession of the government'.[120] Congress too was an interest: 'to become a senator or deputy is a means of gaining a livelihood from the allowance made to them, and which they take especial care shall be paid to them with great regularity.'[121] Yet Santa Anna still had to expend large sums on influencing representatives or, when this was not possible, he would station soldiers at the door of Congress and dissolve it for the duration.

Santa Anna was never a simple president or a mere general, and the terms are not adequate to describe his position. To secure power and impose his will Santa Anna—and his supporters—found the conventional institutions too restrictive. He was a professional

---

[120] Pakenham to Palmerston, 2 Oct. 1834, PRO, FO 50/86, fos. 80–2.
[121] Doyle to Palmerston, 5 May 1851, PRO, FO 50/244, fos. 118–31.

soldier, it is true, but even in his younger years he was never restrained by discipline or reconciled to subordination. While he normally came to power by *golpes*, these were not simple military *pronunciamientos* of the kind made by an Herrera, a Paredes, or an Arista, but rather the result of cultivating interests and constructing coalitions. As a president in the making or in power, he did not take kindly to the constraints of constitutions, either the federal constitution of 1824 or the centralist constitution of 1834. He required room for manœuvre and preferred to rule by decree. Once in power his instinct was to suspend the constitution, dissolve Congress, and exercise a personal dictatorship. Even this was not the limit of his personalism. It seems to have better satisfied his vanity or his cunning to exercise power at a distance. His practice was to become an absentee president, withdrawing to Manga de Clavo, leaving the work of government to his ministers, allowing interest groups to reveal their hand, overreach themselves, or lose their nerve, and then return to office as a restorer of law and order, an arbitrator of conflicts, a protector of élites, with greater leverage than before. These are not the actions of a constitutional president or even an authoritarian one. But they conform to his ideal of leadership.

Eccentric and original, never a mere reproduction of a Rosas or a Páez, Santa Anna was nevertheless a similar type. In his regional power base, reliance on patron and client networks, cultivation of interest groups, recourse to the *golpe*, aversion to constitutions, and preference for personal dictatorship, Santa Anna was a classic caudillo.

9
RAFAEL CARRERA: GUATEMALA
1837–1865

1. *People's Leader*

Rafael Carrera followed a different route to the top from that of most national caudillos and learnt the art of leadership in more primitive conditions. He was born on 24 October 1814 in Candelaria, a depressed *barrio* of Guatemala City, to Simeón Carrera and Juana Turcios, parents even more obscure than those of Páez, poor artisans who played little part in the formation of the future caudillo. Later known as *El Indio*, in fact he was a mestizo with strong Indian features, a product of indigenous, Negro, and Spanish ancestry.[1] When such types moved upwards they were often called 'Indian' by whites out of prejudice and resentment; but the designation could turn in the caudillo's favour, giving him an Indian image when he needed one, and an alternative appeal to other groups. He was a typical mestizo, or ladino as they came to be called in Guatemala, lacking the community roots of the Indians and the family protection of the whites; he left home at an early age without a formal education, a peon drifting from one estate to another, and eventually enlisted on the conservative side in the federal army during the civil war of 1826–9.

The young Carrera was by all accounts an aggressive character, with an instinctive courage and a native wit, and a determination to become more than a village hero. By 1832 he had left the army and become first an agricultural worker then a pig-dealer in the hill country of Mita. He also became a protégé of Father Francisco Aqueche, the parish priest of Mataquescuintla, for whom he tended

---

[1] John Lloyd Stephens, *Incidents of Travel in Central America, Chiapas and Yucatan*, ed. Richard L. Predmore (2 vols.; New Brunswick, NJ, 1949), i. 177, 195–6; Robert Glasgow Dunlop, *Travels in Central America, being a Journal of Nearly Three Years' Residence in the Country* (London, 1847), 86; Luis Beltranena Sinibaldi, *Fundación de la República de Guatemala* (Guatemala, 1971), 86–7.

the church, rang the bell, and assisted at services. There he married, apparently to his advantage, acquiring land as well as respectability; his bride, Petrona Alvarez, was a pretty mestiza who came, he recorded, from 'one of the principal families', and who subsequently accompanied him on all his campaigns.[2] And there he stayed, a local character, ex-soldier, peasant farmer, son of the Church, illiterate but enterprising, in a sense a caudillo waiting for an insurrection. He was about five feet six inches in height, with straight black hair, and an Indian complexion and expression; he had an imposing personality and an ambition for power. The opportunity arrived in 1837 when a great Indian rising suddenly made him a guerrilla leader and brought him to the attention of the politicians.

While Carrera was in Mita making his modest preparations for power, a national crisis was developing of a kind understood by caudillos everywhere. The background was the liberal project of Mariano Gálvez to liquidate the colonial regime, forcibly to assimilate the Indians, and to impose a programme of modernization on Guatemala. The liberals stood for reform and federalism within the Central American Republic; their victory over the conservatives in the civil war of 1826–9 gave them the opportunity to apply their policies at state level, which Gálvez, governor of Guatemala from 1831, proceeded to do. His policy was acceptable to many of the creole élite, but these were a small minority in a population of 450,000 Indians, 100,000 whites, and 150,000 ladinos. Whereas in Buenos Aires it was the landed interest who reacted to the modernization programme of Rivadavia, in Guatemala it was the popular sectors who were most affected by Gálvez's policy of improving the infrastructure, judicial system, bureaucracy, and education, reforms which were of no immediate interest to the mass of the people, and some of which were positively harmful.[3] At the time the economy was not operating in favour of liberal reforms. Indigo was in depression; cochineal production and export were far from buoyant; and textiles were hit by British imports in spite of illiberal tariff protection. Economic policy, therefore, was disputed even by the élite. But the prime victims of liberal policy were the traditional

---

[2] Rafael Carrera, *Memorias 1837 á 1840* (Guatemala, 1979), 15; Stephens, *Incidents of Travel in Central America*, ii. 113.

[3] Ralph Lee Woodward, Jr., *Social Revolution in Guatemala: The Carrera Revolt*, in *Applied Enlightenment: 19th Century Liberalism* (Tulane University, Middle American Research Institute, pub. 23; New Orleans, 1972), 49–53.

rural sectors, Indian communities working family and communal lands, and peons seasonally employed on plantations. They found ready allies in the Church.

Liberal policy towards the Church could be explained as a desire to create a secular state rather than attack religion, but they tended to ignore explanations while they hastened to restrict privileges and exert closer control. In the years 1829–31 the Guatemalan government expelled Archbishop Ramón Casáus and his fellow friars, censored ecclesiastical correspondence, seized Church funds, and confiscated monastic property. Gálvez went further. The government suppressed the collection of the tithe in 1832, and confiscated more Church property. In 1834 it abolished many religious feast days 'which have the added inconvenience of rendering workless the days immediately following, because of misbehaviour on the feast day itself'.[4] In 1837 the legislature strayed into the area of morals if not of faith, authorizing civil marriage and legalizing divorce. Guatemala was not a secular society and legislation could not make it so. The rural clergy were an integral part of peasant communities. A perceptive American observer noted:

Besides officiating in all the services of the church, visiting the sick, and burying the dead, my worthy host was looked up to by every Indian in the village as a counselor, friend and father. The door of the convent was always open, and Indians were constantly resorting to him.... And, besides this he was principal director of all the public business of the town, the right hand of the alcalde.[5]

The rural clergy joined the cause of the Church to that of the peasant and from pulpit and confessional denounced the liberal government.

The land policy of Gálvez encouraged the private acquisition of public land and even the purchase of Indian community land; this led to further land concentration, which was compounded by encouragement of foreign colonization. Concessions to mahogany cutters and projects to colonize nothern and eastern parts of Guatemala with English settlers caused resentment among the inhabitants of those regions. Between March and August 1834 the Guatemalan government ceded virtually all its public lands to

---

[4] Decree of 20 Feb. 1834, in Lorenzo Montúfar y Rivera Maestre, *Reseña histórica de Centro América* (7 vols.; Guatemala, 1878–88), ii. 76.

[5] Stephens, *Incidents of Travel in Central America*, i. 134.

foreign colonization companies, an area equal to almost three quarters of the total area of the state; it was an attempt to impose a model of development and a new work ethic, but it lent itself to sensational interpretation and was not even a success.[6] When a revolt in Chiquimula in 1835 voiced resentment of foreign penetration, government troops suppressed the rising and fined rebellious towns to pay for the army's expenses. But perhaps the strongest reaction to government policy was caused by tax changes. The Indian tribute had been abolished in 1811, then restored, and suppressed again with independence. Gálvez restored it in 1831. Mestizo peasants and artisans had to pay the *contribución directa*, and the tithe was replaced in 1832 by a land tax of 4 *reales* for each *caballería* of land. Worse was to come. A decree of 1836 designed to rationalize the system imposed a direct poll tax of 2 pesos per capita, a charge which genuinely hurt the peasant, caused great popular disaffection and helped to create an air of crisis in rural Guatemala. Liberals seemed blind to the susceptibilities of the Indian sector, and those in Guatemala learnt no lessons from anti-tax rebellions in Honduras, Nicaragua, and especially El Salvador, where the imposition of a poll tax caused a serious Indian rebellion in 1832–3. In Guatemala Indian resentments were heightened by increasing demands for personal service in road construction and other public works, and liberals were impervious to the irony of infrastructure improvement by forced labour.

The liberals set great store by reform of the Spanish legal system and abolition of the corporate *fueros*. The means chosen were the Livingston Codes, adopted on 1 January 1837, and trial by jury. But these devices were unrealistic in a country where the majority of people were illiterate and class divisions endemic.[7] As the British consul, Frederick Chatfield, reported:

The elections of the State are entirely under the control of the chief, who rules the minor communities through the agency of departmental chiefs, who are predominant in their respective districts, and it is easy to discern that these functionaries either by promises or by intimidation can order the verdicts of juries more or less chosen by themselves.[8]

[6] William J. Griffith, *Empires in the Wilderness: Foreign Colonization and Development in Guatemala, 1834–1844* (Chapel Hill, NC, 1965), 32–52, 151–3.

[7] Montúfar, *Reseña histórica*, ii. 289–5, 333–7. Among other things, the Livingston Codes abolished the death penalty.

[8] Chatfield to Palmerston, San Salvador, 20 Sept. 1837, PRO, FO 15/19, fos. 143–9.

And while the decisions of Indian juries were ridiculed, forced Indian labour had to build the new gaols. The whole experiment was seen as a further case of foreign influence and another example of anticlericalism. 'Death to Trial by Jury' became a popular cry of protest.[9]

In the event the liberals delivered less than they promised. Economic prosperity turned out to be an illusion. The policy of protection was applied too late to restore the fortunes of the domestic textile industry, hit by British competition. The shortage of coinage and high interest rates added to the foreign debt. There were few obvious benefits from liberal anticlerical policy. The government never managed to administer the civil register, and the schools and hospitals which it took over functioned with great difficulty. Liberalism, moreover, resented in itself, was also resented for the ruthless way in which it was enforced and for the power it gave to military *comandantes* in the regions. Enemies of the government were punished by exile and confiscation of property. Government troops terrorized the rural population. Indian villages were burnt and their lands confiscated for resisting the local authority; and those inhabitants who survived the summary proceedings of a military tribunal were transported to a distant place. The officers and troops employed in these operations robbed and plundered a number of estates, and when investigated demanded the restoration of the *fuero militar*; to this the government meekly agreed and extended the privilege to the whole militia, thus effectively subverting the Livingston Code and trial by jury by placing almost every man in the state able to bear arms beyond their application. When Gálvez was accused by his enemies of conferring on himself absolute power and creating a liberal dictatorship, he replied that circumstances compelled him to rule severely, an argument familiar among conservatives and not unknown among reformers. How do you force people to be free? By appealing to reason and authority, replied Gálvez. He was deluding himself. As Carrera put it, 'When attempts are made suddenly to attack and change the customs of the people, it provokes in them such emotion that, no matter how sound the intention of those who seek to change their traditional ways and institutions, they rise in protest.'[10]

[9] Mario Rodríguez, *The Livingston Codes in the Guatemalan Crisis of 1837–1838*, in *Applied Enlightenment*, 1–32.
[10] Carrera, *Memorias*, 12.

Finally, a new scourge appeared and a new grievance. An epidemic
of cholera struck Guatemala in February 1837 and was reported
by foreign observers as a major calamity. Many of the opinions of
Frederick Chatfield were distorted by prejudice and by his conviction
that Central America was basically an 'uncivilized, impoverished and
convulsed' place where an enlightened diplomat 'must be content to
serve as pioneer to those who shall follow him'.[11] But he had direct
experience of the epidemic in neighbouring San Salvador: 'the
Cholera has pressed with much severity upon my house, which
is one of the largest, most airy, and best regulated in the town; it
carried off *all* my servants in the space of a few days, and after the
virulence of the epidemic was supposed to have greatly subsided.' In
Guatemala City almost 3,000 people were stricken, with over 900
dead. But the epidemic attacked especially the Indian masses in
the highland zones of Guatemala where it inflicted great mortality,
mainly among adults, and left many children orphans.[12] The government took reasonable preventive measures, attempted to establish
an effective quarantine, and sent doctors into the villages to treat
the victims.[13] But the local priests declared that this was a divine
punishment on Guatemala, and spread the rumour that government
officials were poisoning the common people as part of a policy of
exterminating the native inhabitants in preparation for repopulating
the country with foreign heretics. The Indian response was dramatic.
Driven into fear and panic by the heavy mortalilty, and believing that
the disease originated in the pollution of the rivers and the deliberate
infection of medicines, they and the mestizos of the high plateau
took to arms, murdering whites, plundering their houses, and preparing to confront the government. Chatfield himself was roughly
seized by enraged Indians at Zugapango on suspicion of poisoning
the river and he felt lucky to talk his way out of a violent end.[14]

Thus the Indians integrated into one mass movement all their
grievances against whites, liberals, and officials. They went on the

[11] Chatfield to Palmerston, San Salvador, 25 June 1837, PRO, FO 15/19,
fos. 95–99ᵛ.
[12] Miles L. Wortman, *Government and Society in Central America, 1680–1840*
(New York, 1982), 262–3.
[13] Jorge Luis Arriola, *Gálvez en la encrucijada* (Mexico, 1961), 130–40.
[14] Chatfield to Palmerston, San Salvador, 26 June 1837, PRO, FO 15/19,
fos. 101–4; Mario Rodríguez, *A Palmerstonian Diplomat in Central America: Frederick
Chatfield, Esq.* (Tucson, Ariz., 1964), 122–4.

rampage singing the *Salve Regina* and crying 'Religion forever', and 'Death to foreigners and heretics'. Gálvez regarded the epidemic as a pretext: their real motivation was 'the destruction of the whites, the return of the archbishop and the friars, the murder and pillage of foreigners, and the ruin of the capital and its inhabitants'.[15] He was not so wide of the mark, but in his anxiety he over-reacted. He sent in troops to the villages of Samaz and Santa Rosa; there they burnt the houses, sold the produce of the lands, and amidst scenes of the utmost brutality executed the supposed ringleaders and expelled the inhabitants. As the liberal dissident José Francisco Barrundia remarked, 'the injustice of these violent and unlawful measures simply aggravated the rebellion they had already started'.[16] Reaction turned into revolution.

2. *The Revolution of Mita*

Peasant rebels were reported to be active in various parts of the highlands from March 1837. The greatest outbreak was in the eastern *montaña*, more mestizo than Indian, and strongly influenced by parish priests. At San Juan Ostuncalco natives rose against officials charged with applying the Livingston Codes. As the cholera panic spread, other uprisings followed in early May, and in June Santa Rosa erupted. From the village of Mataquescuintla there emerged a natural leader whom the rebels, some 1,800 at this point, wanted as their caudillo. 'Thereupon Carrera went to the church to consult the parish priest, who told him: Do not delay, accept their request, because this movement can grow and only you have the ability to control a people in rebellion'.[17] He had other reasons, too, affinity with peasant grievances, many of which were his own, and, in his twenty-third year, a passion to command.

The rebellion of 1837 was not simply a blind response of angry peasants to innovation and infection. In the first place, leadership was decisive. The Indians had a caudillo, Rafael Carrera, who

---

[15] Quoted by David Vela, *Barrundia ante el espejo de su tiempo* (2 vols.; Guatemala, 1956), i. 215.
[16] Quoted ibid. i. 212.
[17] Carrera, *Memorias*, 19.

combined traditional values and popular qualities in a way which appealed to the grass roots of the movement. Everything he did, recruiting, organizing, fighting, was done on his personal authority alone. No doubt the rural clergy supported him with advice, intelligence, and supplies, but they did not dominate much less manipulate him. And Carrera was able not only to lead but also to control these violent and undisciplined troops, some of them pure Indians, others mestizos and *mulatos*. When, on 6 May, about 2,000 terrified peasants rioted against the district governor of Mita, who was trying to quarantine the region, they would have killed him but for the intervention of Carrera and the parish priest. Carrera deployed his men decisively to defeat the first government forces sent against the rebels and from then on was in command, his peasant followers calling him 'Angel', 'Son of God', and the 'Lord'. 'His name was so respected in all the villages, valleys, and hamlets, that everyone hastened to where he was to expound their complaints, and he, in spite of his lack of knowledge and frequent mistakes, listened and judged and left them all well satisfied.'[18] The fame of Carrera spread, and his role was quickly appreciated by observers: 'a man named Carrera, who it seems held a small property at Santa Rosa, after seeing his wife abused, his home and property destroyed, fled into the woods, with several others, to whom no alternative remained but to resist or die, and there raised a standard of revolt, around which the continued severities of the government officers caused numbers to flock'.[19] And he had no difficulty in recruiting. The government's policy of summary execution and the behaviour of its troops saw to that. As Barrundia remarked, 'He became known as a visionary and a saint, and increasing his forces through plunder, terror, and promises to distribute to his troops all the wealth of the country, he came to challenge the supreme authority of the state.'[20]

In the second place, as Gálvez appreciated, the rebellion was not simply an irrational response to cholera and its prevention. Deeper and wider reasons were at work, pre-dating the epidemic and still prevalent long after it had been extinguished: judicial innovation, poll tax, land policy, these were the real objects of peasant hatred. Carrera

---

[18] Ibid. 38.
[19] Chatfield to Palmerston, San Salvador, 5 Feb. 1838, PRO, FO 15/20, fos. 62–69ᵛ.
[20] Quoted by Vela, *Barrundia*, i. 247.

was thus able to exploit the argument that a corrupt and unpatriotic government was giving Guatemalan resources to foreigners, leaving poor Indians and mestizos without land and livelihood and encumbered with tax burdens. It was also hinted that the Catholic religion was marked for extinction by a conspiracy between Gálvez and Protestants. Thus Catholicism, group interest, and national feelings were invoked in a remarkable display of popular traditionalism, enabling conservative caudillos to assemble a populist-type coalition against federalists and liberals, and place themselves under a super-caudillo. According to William Hall, English merchant and consul, 'He persuades all to join him, in order, as it is pretended, to bring about the restoration of the Archbishop and the friars, to destroy the foreigners, and to subvert the government, he being as he asserts supported and countenanced by Barrundia, the leader of the opposition party.'[21]

Third, as Hall suggested, the movement profited from political divisions at the centre, in particular from the split of the ruling Liberal party into two wings, government and opposition, Gálvez and Barrundia. While the government sent troops to deal violently with the rebels and called Carrera a *bandido*, it also made approaches to the *caudillo* and offered him terms, in order to co-opt his force against the political opposition. The more radical liberals, led by Barrundia, also sought to negotiate a deal with Carrera, offering to drop the Livingston Codes and anticlericalism and to recognize the *caudillo* as commander of all the rebel forces in return for his military support for an attack on the government in Guatemala City. These political manœuvres gave Carrera a national status. In late June 1837 he announced a six-point programme for the revolution: abolition of the Livingston Codes; protection for persons and property; return of the archbishop and re-establishment of religious orders; abolition of the poll tax; amnesty for all those exiled from 1829; and respect for Carrera's orders as law under pain of death.[22] A further proclamation in October added the abolition of the law on marriage and divorce, and the cancellation of the English colonization contracts. No doubt these decrees were influenced by

[21] Hall to Chatfield, Guatemala, 29 Dec. 1837, PRO, FO 252/18; Griffith, *Empires in the Wilderness*, 163–5.

[22] Carrera, *Memorias*, 19–20; Woodward, *Social Revolution in Guatemala*, 56; Keith L. Miceli, 'Rafael Carrera: Defender and Promoter of Peasant Interests in Guatemala', *The Americas*, 31, 1 (1974), 72–95.

Carrera's clerical advisers, but he made them his own and they acquired credibility from his endorsement.

Thus the insurrection in the *montaña*, beginning as a local uprising in the eastern part of Guatemala, developed into a general rebellion against the Liberal government. Gálvez replied by taking dictatorial powers and applying repression, reorganizing the militia forces, and imposing trials by military courts. As the troops killed and destroyed, the rebels were forced into the hills, from where they waged irregular war on the security forces and expanded their numbers. Carrera replied to violence with violence, and showed that he had a distinct talent for guerrilla warfare. His bands attacked judges, officials, and government installations; they cut communications, disrupted commerce, and created insecurity; they invaded haciendas and when it suited them assassinated whites.[23] Gálvez had to divert funds from his reform programme to spend on counter-insurgency. So the caudillo simultaneously subverted the government's policy and tied down its forces. With too few troops to occupy the entire country, Gálvez sought to crush and capture the leader. But Carrera learnt how to escape after defeat, evade his hunters, and take refuge among friendly peasants. Raiding, looting, and killing continued and the war, which began as a peasant rebellion, acquired the aspect of a race conflict, as Indians sunk their differences with mestizos, *mulatos*, and *zambos*, and all joined in attacking whites. The rebellion also assumed the style of a religious crusade, and chaplains mixed with the troops, evangelizing, exhorting, even fighting. The caudillo himself explained: 'To encourage the rebel masses, Carrera inspired them with religion; he constantly had church services celebrated in as many villages as he could, he greatly respected the priests, and he ordered that all the troops under his command sing the Salve every night and morning, which became an established custom, performed with the utmost enthusiasm.'[24] As the military situation slipped out of control and his political opponents increased their pressure, Gálvez had to consider resignation. To hasten the day, Carrera released his hordes against the seat of government on 31 January 1838.

[23] Hazel M. B. Ingersoll, *The War of the Mountain: A Study of Reactionary Peasant Insurgency in Guatemala, 1837–1873* (George Washington University, Ph.D. thesis, 1972), 133–9.

[24] Carrera, *Memorias*, 47–8.

In his attack on Guatemala City Carrera deliberately used his Indian troops as an instrument of anti-liberal terror, unleashing some 4,000 drunken and excited guerrillas armed with machetes, staves, and rusty muskets, draped in crucifixes and rosary beads, with sacks on their backs to carry away the plunder, and shouting 'Long live religion, death to foreigners', as they occupied the principal parts of the city and eventually the main square. Carrera himself was dressed in a Spanish General's uniform, looted from the house of General Prem, the government commander, over which he wore a large scapular and crowned the effect with a lady's hat and a green veil, the property of Prem's wife.[25] As he rode through the centre of the city, anxious foreigners were shocked to see that he was accompanied by Barrundia and other members of the opposition. While Carrera negotiated, his Indians rampaged and looted, until, after four days, having extracted money and a political deal from the opposition, the caudillo led them out.[26]

The attack on Guatemala City left a vivid impression on observers. An English eye witness wrote to Chatfield:

A while after came the hordes of barbarians headed by Carrera, only think what a sight—you would have thought there was a return to the age of Alaric when he invaded Rome—the sight was awful and horrible—to witness 4,000 barbarians rude, half naked, drunk and elated, vociferating with all their might—'*que viva la religion y mueran los estranjeros*'.... At the hour of '*Oracion*' they all knelt down in the square and sang the '*Sanctus Deus*' and '*Ave Maria*'.[27]

John Lloyd Stephens, the United States special envoy to Central America, though not personally present, consulted those who were and represented the entry of Carrera and his guerrillas as a confrontation between order and anarchy:

On Wednesday Carrera joined the rebels. He had sent his emissaries to the villages to rouse the Indians, promising them the plunder of Guatemala; and on Thursday, with a tumultuous mass of half naked savages, men, women, and children, estimated at ten or twelve thousand, he presented himself at the gate of the city.... He himself was on horseback, with a green bush in his hat, which was hung round with pieces of dirty cotton cloth covered with

[25] Montúfar, *Reseña histórica*, ii. 574.
[26] Carrera, *Memorias*, 49–52.
[27] Chatfield to Palmerston, San Salvador, 16 Feb. 1838, PRO, FO 15/20, fos. 76–83.

pictures of saints. . . . Many, who had never left their villages before, looked wild at the sight of the houses and churches, and the magnificence of the city.[28]

Carrera taught an unforgettable lesson. The politicians had to buy off the caudillo with 1,000 pesos for himself, 10,000 for his followers, the office of Comandante General de Mita with the rank of lieutenant-colonel, and a supply of arms and ammunition. The threat to Guatemala City and resignation of Gálvez in favour of Pedro Valenzuela, tool of Barrundia and his faction, brought a new phase to the rebellion, during which the presence and power of Carrera exercised an indirect pressure on the new Liberal government and forced it to restrain its liberalism, at the same time enabling the Conservative party to make a comeback. The Church was restored to some of its positions, military governors were removed, and the Livingston Codes were repealed in a decree which gave as the principal reason 'the opinion of the people, unprepared for so important an enterprise'.[29] Thus the decrees reflected the popular will, as voiced by the caudillo. The liberals were now on the defensive, for Carrera had the power and could raise the stakes. Dissatisfied with the government's progress towards his demands, convinced that he was being manipulated by the liberals, and encouraged by the priests, Carrera renewed the guerrilla war and drew further government repression. Fearing an incipient alliance between the Conservative party and the popular sectors, Barrundia called on his liberal ally Francisco Morazán; the entry into Guatemala of the federal president with 1,000 Salvadorean troops in mid March 1838 presented a new challenge to the caudillo.

Morazán came in to control the Guatemalan government and crush the rebellion, and he immediately increased repression. Carrera's father-in-law was captured and shot. The liberals were encouraged to reinstate their programme. Faced with extinction, the guerrillas replied with renewed ferocity, harrassing government forces and officials over an area extending from the Caribbean to the Pacific. Carrera continued to exert great influence among the Indian and mestizo classes and his forces to attack communications between the regions of Guatemala and El Salvador, as Chatfield reported:

---

[28] Stephens, *Incidents of Travel in Central America*, i. 182–3.
[29] Quoted by Woodward, *Social Revolution in Guatemala*, 60.

The Rebellion of Carrera, which is a war of Barbarism against Civilization, has since the departure of the President Morazán from the state of Guatemala assumed fresh vigour; had not Carrera been favoured by the Priests, and did he not continue to receive their cordial cooperation, he would not have been so successful, nor would he last another week, but as matters actually are, it is impossible to predict where his rebellion will stop.[30]

They received support from much of the rural population, the Indians recruited with the help of the clergy, for otherwise they had little liking for mestizos and *mulatos*, and the rest from a range of rural rebels. In March 1838 Carrera survived an assassination attempt by a notorious bandit chief, Andrés Monreal, who was interested only in looting and had been reluctant to leave the capital without a greater reward 'for the hard work they had undertaken in sacking it', and who was himself killed in the attempt on Carrera.[31] But the delinquent element in the guerrillas did not predominate. Carrera had obvious conditions on his side, for guerrillas were cheaper to maintain than regular troops, who had to be forcibly recruited from vagrants and other marginals, armed and paid, and led by officers who were expensive as well as ineffective. Carrera's volunteers were satisfied with little more than a maize cake, a few black beans, and a bunch of plantains, and a peasant could lead two lives, a legal existence tilling his fields combined with a part-time occupation as a guerrilla:

A man who has a patch of maize corn growing, and which does not require his care for 2 or 3 weeks, instead of remaining at home decides upon joining Carrera, on the chance of picking up some sort of booty, he therefore starts off for 15 days, when if he likes his company and the service, he prolongs his visit, merely absenting himself for a day to go and see how his affairs are progressing at home.[32]

In Guatemala City the *carreristas* received ambiguous support from conservatives. These now gained control of the government under the leadership of Mariano Rivera Paz and dismantled the entire liberal programme; but it was a tenuous control and their enemies held the military power. The conservatives sought to preempt Carrera's position politically, while Morazán and the army

---

[30] Chatfield to Palmerston, San Salvador, 16 Aug. 1838, PRO, FO 15/20 fo. 301.
[31] Montúfar, *Reseña histórica*, iii. 99–101.
[32] Chatfield to Palmerston, San Salvador, 16 Aug. 1838, PRO, FO 15/20, fos. 301ᵛ–303ᵛ.

pressed him militarily. At this point, when the caudillo was short of allies, the clergy redoubled their efforts on his behalf in order to sustain the rebellion. In September 1838 Carrera established his headquarters at Villa Nueva, a village about four leagues from Guatemala. On 10 September a printed proclamation by Friar Francisco Lobo, part chaplain, part adviser, and part guerrilla, was circulated in Guatemala City, in which the author styling himself Chief of Staff of 'The Liberating Army for the Protection of Order and Religion of General Rafael Carrera', in the name of religion and justice called on the people to support the caudillo. But government troops suddenly attacked Villa Nueva and inflicted severe defeat and casualties on the rebels. Father Mariano Durán, one of the most active and loyal of the caudillo's partisans, was made prisoner and Carrera himself received a bullet in the thigh.[33] As the army kept up its pressure, summarily executing Father Durán and another priest, Carrera had to buy time to regroup and on 23 December 1838 he agreed to recognize the government and suspend hostilities, in exchange for amnesty and appointment as Chief of the district of Mita in an area comprising about thirteen villages and towns.[34]

The caudillo did not retire and his cause did not collapse. As Morazán and the liberals deposed Rivera Paz and sought to recover their position, Carrera became convinced that there would be no peace, no respite from liberalism, and no place for himself until Morazán was crushed once and for all. He reactivated the revolution, took up arms again, and on 24 March 1839 issued a *pronunciamiento* justifying his action as a response to Morazán's cruelty towards the clergy, destruction of commerce, and confiscation of private property. On 13 April 1839, in the early hours of the morning, Carrera rode into Guatemala City for the second time, now at the head of a large and orderly army, knocked on the door of Rivera Paz with his riding whip, and announced, 'We do not come to kill people but to restore the authorities.'[35] He restored Rivera Paz and a Conservative government and spent the remainder of the year

[33] Chatfield to Palmerston, San Salvador, 4 Oct. 1838, PRO, FO 15/20, fos. 351–6; Ingersoll, *The War of the Mountain*, 186–7.
[34] Chatfield to Palmerston, San Salvador, 6 Feb. 1839, PRO, FO 15/22, fos. 59–60.
[35] Chatfield to Palmerston, San Salvador, 13 May 1839, PRO, FO 15/22; Federico Hernández de León, *El libro de la efemérides: Capitulos de la historia de la América Central* (8 vols.; Guatemala, 1925–66), ii. 79.

mopping up liberal resistance in the rest of the country. He was obviously in charge, and was now called 'the caudillo adored by the people'. His brother Sotero and the guerrilla leaders who accompanied him were appointed high-ranking army officers and district military chiefs.[36] In January 1840 he moved into Los Altos and crushed the independent liberal stronghold in Quezaltenango, leaving tangible benefits for the Indians, freedom from the poll tax, and a promise to settle their land problems. He had still to settle his account with Morazán.

The fate of the federation ran parallel to events in Guatemala. Morazán had transferred the federal capital to San Salvador in 1834 and in the same year won another term of office as president. He presided over a dying institution. In 1838 Congress tried to restore some life to the patient and resolved to transfer to the federal government control of the customs revenues, which was the only way of securing federal finances. The states objected and used the opportunity to leave the union, led by Nicaragua, Costa Rica, and Honduras. The Federal Republic was now in its death throes, brought down by the separatism of the states and the conservative reaction in Honduras, Nicaragua, and Guatemala. In February 1839, on completion of the constitutional term of office by Morazán, Congress dissolved and there was no legal body to nominate his successor. During the rest of the year the various forces lined up for a decisive confrontation between two classic enemies, the liberal general of the federation and the Indian caudillo of Guatemala. This took place on 19 March 1840, when the forces of Carrera, after a bloody campaign, brought Morazán to battle at Guatemala City. It was a battle which became notorious for its savagery and revealed the ruthless side of the caudillo, whose Indians sang *Salve Regina*, shouted 'Long live religion! Long live Carrera! Death to General Morazán!', and attacked without mercy. Carrera defeated the liberal army, killed prisoners, drove Morazán into exile, and persecuted his supporters. According to Chatfield, the victorious force of Carrera consisted of 'an undisciplined peasantry who fought almost without officers, and by a sort of instinctive obedience to the will of their chief'.[37] The bloodbath at Guatemala City was followed

---

[36] Ingersoll, *The War of the Mountain*, 207.

[37] Chatfield to Palmerston, Guatemala, 3 Apr. 1840, PRO, FO 15/23, fo. 153; Stephens, *Incidents of Travel in Central America*, ii. 92–3 and, on the massacre of

by another at Quezaltenango, where the liberals had staged an un-
timely coup for Morazán. The news of yet another liberal strike, after
pacification seemed complete, maddened the caudillo. He assembled
his Indian troops and rushed in a towering rage to Quezaltenango,
pushed back the priests who tried to intervene, ignored the pleas of
frantic wives, and shot the entire government of eighteen liberals in
front of the horrified citizens. These acts of cruelty in Guatemala
City and Quezaltenango gave the *coup de grâce* to liberalism and in
effect brought the revolution of Mita to an end.

Carrera thus came to power with a personal display of terrorism
and a demonstration of savagery by his Indian troops; having per-
petrated two massacres, these were now on the streets of Guatemala
City, a protection against his enemies and a warning to his allies.
Victory in the rebellion and power in the capital owed much to
Carrera's leadership. It also depended on the active support of
Indians and mestizos, who had fought a war which was part peasant
rebellion, part race conflict, and part defence of tradition. And both
Carrera and his followers had the indispensable blessing of the
Church, which helped to assemble this network of interest groups.
But the cause itself was eminently viable.

The collapse of the Central American Federation and of the first
liberal experiment demonstrated an obvious political truth: it was
impossible to change deeply rooted structures of government,
economy, society, and religion by mere legislation. The liberals
sought to replace absolutism in government by representation and
devolution. They sought to replace the influence of the Church by
a secular state. They sought to take the Indians out of special status
and integrate them into a *laissez-faire* society. They sought to replace
mercantilism and protection by free trade. This formula for reform
was a political artifice, unrealistic in the conditions and mentalities
prevailing in Central America. In any case liberal programmes did
not normally produce immediate benefits but promised gradual
progress and long-term change, objectives for which the interest
groups were not prepared to wait. The triumph of Carrera and the
conservative restoration of 1840–70 may have perpetuated traditional
structures but they also conformed to basic social interests, popular
as well as oligarchic. And freedom from politics gave Guatemala

Quezaltenango, 110, 172–5; on the role of Carrera and Chatfield in the battle of 19
March see Rodríguez, *A Palmerstonian Diplomat in Central America*, 230–1.

the stability in which practical reforms could emerge. As the conservative historian, José Milla, wrote, 'Let us seek improvement and progress, let us have *schools and roads* and the rest will follow later.'[38] But this was a conflict of values as well as of interests. Against the utopia of progress, freedom, and equality promised by the liberals, the conservatives preserved a world which was known and understood, in which the priests were in the villages, the Indians in their communities, the landlords on their estates. This was the world of Carrera. This, rather than European models of development, was the immediate destiny of Guatemala. Those who did not belong to the traditional sectors still awaited representation. To these the liberals would make a new appeal in the 1870s.

3. *King of the Indians*

Carrera was now the dominant leader in Guatemala. Through his role in the insurrection of Mita he had accumulated enough military power to impose his will on government without holding high political office, a standard test of caudillism. Theoretically he was simply a brigadier-general in command of the army and subject to the orders of the government, on which he made only modest financial demands for himself and his troops. But in practice he had a caudillo's power and a constituency of his own. He was called 'Son of God' and 'Our Lord' by his followers and he saw himself as a saviour of the Guatemalan people, a protector to whom Indians and peasants brought their petitions and grievances. The position of Carrera was well perceived in 1840 by John Lloyd Stephens:

Heretofore, in all the wars and revolutions the whites had had the controlling influence, but at this time the Indians were the dominant power. Roused from the sloth of ages, and with muskets in their hands, their gentleness was changed into ferocity . . . Carrera was the pivot on which this turned. He was talked of as *El rey de los Indios*, the King of the Indians. He had relieved them from all taxes, and, as they said, supported his army by levying contributions

---

[38] Quoted by Walter A. Payne, *A Central American Historian: José Milla (1822–1882)* (Gainesville, Fla., 1957), 8; on the validity of *carrerismo* see E. Bradford Burns, *The Poverty of Progress: Latin America in the Nineteenth Century* (Berkeley and Los Angeles, 1980), 96–103.

upon the whites. His power by a word to cause the massacre of every white inhabitant no one doubted.[39]

The conservatives could not control Carrera, much less subdue him; they had to cultivate and conciliate the caudillo, to humour and pacify him, for he was the only barrier between order and disorder, between white society and the Indian hordes, between élite dominance and belated retribution. Stephens witnessed in Guatemala City a religious procession in honour of the Virgin, led by a group of masked 'devils', followed by altar boys, priests, floats, the statue of the Immaculate Conception, and the Host.

The whole concluded with a worse set of devils than those which led the procession: five hundred of Carrera's soldiers, dirty and ragged, and carrying their muskets without any order, with fanaticism added to their usual expression of ferocity. The officers were dressed in any costume they could command. A few, with black hat and silver or gold band, like footmen, carried their head very high; many were lame from gunshot wounds badly cured. . . . The city was at their mercy, and Carrera was the only man living who had any control over them.[40]

Stephens, who met Carrera in 1840, was impressed by his combination of extreme youth and sovereign power, and described him as 'more absolute master of Guatemala than any king in Europe of his dominions, and by the fanatic Indians called *el hijo de Dios . . .* and *nuestro Señor*'. At this stage of his career he was still a leader by nature, untamed by responsibility, untouched by compromise. 'So young, so humble in his origin, so destitute of early advantages, with honest impulses, perhaps, but ignorant, fanatic, sanguinary, and the slave of violent passions, he wielded absolutely the physical force of the country, and that force entertained a natural hatred of the whites.'[41]

Carrera was a prime example of the necessary protector; he demanded a price of the conservative élite, and they paid it in 1840–4, years of political adjustment to caudillism. At the same time he was acute enough to realize that his power base would be more secure supported by the clergy and the élite than by the Indians alone. He began to learn the balance of interest groups. He also looked beyond his immediate boundaries and became the major

[39] Stephens, *Incidents of Travel in Central America*, ii. 111–12.
[40] Ibid. i. 171–2.
[41] Ibid. i. 195, 197.

influence in the consolidation of conservative rule not only in Guatemala but also in its neighbours. If the federation had collapsed, so had the state governments, and power was effectively held by regional families and their caudillo chieftains. Carrera began as such a caudillo, exercising military power but challenged for legitimacy by surviving liberals and hopeful conservatives. He took care to install in the governments of Honduras and El Salvador two kindred caudillos, Francisco Ferrera, a lower-class ladino like Carrera himself, and Francisco Malespin, a conservative military officer whose subsequent revolt against Guatemala in 1844 Carrera had to crush. These were intended to guard his back against a liberal reaction; their presence also gave him breathing space to secure his total control in Guatemala itself.

In June 1839 Carrera addressed the new legislative assembly and made it clear who held power; he reminded them of his opposition to the Gálvez reforms and his dedication to tradition and religion. The assembly went ahead quickly to restore colonial structures and Hispanic tradition.[42] They learnt too that this was a particular brand of conservatism, unlike that of earlier élite governments: Carrera's will was law, and he was not amenable to manipulation by conservatives or liberals, refusing to ally himself with any political party, even when he was chief executive. Conservatives had to accept that the creole élites, while socially dominant, could not monopolize political power. They found that if Carrera became irritated with a government, as he did with that of Rivera Paz in December 1841, he would replace it. On this occasion he brought out his Indian troops and trained a cannon on the assembly; Rivera Paz and his colleagues were arrested, and the rest fled over the rooftops.[43] Indians and ladinos now had a part to play, and Carrera insisted from time to time on the priority of peasant interests. When, in August 1840, he sought to retire from the office of commander-in-chief and the assembly refused to accept his decision, a familiar enough ritual among caudillos, he declared that 'I have not obtained [my office] from this assembly; I have been invested with wide powers by the general vote of the people'. And when told that his enemies were calling him a 'cannibal', he issued an indignant proclamation: 'the people are my priority, and I seek as far as I can a

[42] Montúfar, *Reseña histórica*, iii. 370–85 521–5.
[43] Ingersoll, *The War of the Mountain*, 263–4.

remedy for their needs', impeded only by the legislative and judicial powers.[44] Thus Carrera was different things to different men, the saviour, the protector, and the barbarian of Guatemala.

The caudillo cultivated his constituents and interest groups. His people's army was vital to him; it was composed primarily of Indians and mestizos, and contained an élite corps of men from Mataquescuintla, Santa Rosa, and other towns in the highlands of Mita.[45] His old comrades in arms such as Jerónimo Pais, Vicente Cruz, and Mariano Paredes, became generals, officials, and even ministers. His brother Sotero became the *corregidor* of Sacatepéquez, and his other brother Santos served as his personal aide. This was a favoured army and a protected one; a law of 15 October 1840 restored the *fuero militar*.

The Church was an integral part of Carrera's plan. He enabled it to recover some, though not all, of the land lost during the liberal regime. The clergy were restored to their protected status, and the village *curas* continued their role as friends, ministers, and advisers of the Indians, becoming in effect not only spokesmen of the Church but also informal representatives of the state. In 1839 the assembly restored religious orders and invited the exiled archbishop Ramón Casáus to return to his diocese. This was a particular wish of Carrera, as the archbishop acknowledged: 'It appears that God has destined you to redeem the Guatemalan people from their oppression'.[46] In fact the aged archbishop was content to live out his days in Havana and did not wish to return, but Carrera took a close interest in the appointment of his successor, and also in the return of secular priests to their parishes. Education was re-established under Church auspices; and the University of San Carlos was restored, with Father Juan José Aycinena as rector. The Church regained its *fuero*, and the tithe was restored, enforced by the state. The conservatives were more clerical than the caudillo. Carrera objected to the reinstatement of the tithe and took a personal interest in reducing the peasant quota on subsistence products. He refused to tolerate any reduction of religious feast days, even those sanctioned by the papacy. And he objected to the clergy holding political office. He was a friend of religion rather than of clerical power.

---

[44] 13 Aug. 1840, 9 Oct. 1840, quoted by Montúfar, *Reseña histórica*, iii. 506, 513.
[45] Ingersoll, *The War of the Mountain*, 273.
[46] Miceli, 'Rafael Carrera', 80.

Political institutions familiar to the colony were restored: the office of *corregidor* was revived, signifying central control of local government; the merchant guild was re-established and given supervision of road and port development; and the old Spanish *residencia* of public officials was brought back. In response to popular opinion the poll tax was abolished and taxes on foodstuffs were reduced. In 1840 the government restored the tobacco monopoly. But the greatest political change was the incorporation of Indians and ladinos into the government, where they now held offices such as the vice-presidency, ministries, governorships, and high military positions, thus breaking the white monopoly characteristic of the first liberal regime.

Carrera condemned liberal economic and political philosophy as prejudicial to the interests of the people. But he went further than this. He also identified with the popular sectors and sought to promote their well-being, providing a kind of alternative government with its own press and publicity. He denounced free trade and demanded protection for peasants and artisans.[47] Measures were pushed through at his insistence which by charity and paternalism provided better conditions for the masses than had the liberalism of Gálvez. Steps were taken to provide an appropriate administration of justice. In the course of 1839 the assembly restored the legal system prevailing before the Livingston Codes, with a Supreme Court presiding over departmental courts, which in turn supervised local judges. The Indians were accommodated in this system but not as ordinary citizens. The liberals had aimed at integrating the Indians into political and economic life, and making them republican citizens. The conservatives claimed that this meant exploitation of the Indians, loss of respect for authority, and danger of violence and rebellion. The conservatives offered instead paternalism and protection, though this was largely theoretical and it was left to Carrera to continue the struggle for justice.

On 16 August 1839 the Guatemalan legislature, recognizing that Indians were a majority of the population, and that it was 'an object of public interest, not only to protect this numerous class of society, but also to develop and improve its customs and civilization', decreed a code for Indian administration. The committee reporting on the bill preferred colonial paternalism to liberal egalitarianism. The

[47] Montúfar, *Reseña histórica*, iii. 511–12.

colonial regime 'compelled them to work, to provide public services on certain projects and to pay taxes; but it also gave them protection against the influential and the powerful in their land claims'.[48] On 5 December 1839 the constituent assembly passed the Law of Guarantees, written by Juan José Aycinena, which in effect made the Indians wards of the state, the objects of special treatment on the supposition that they were culturally inferior. It followed, therefore, that 'the laws must protect them, in order to improve their education and to prevent their being defrauded of what belongs to them in common or as individuals, and that they should not be molested in their old customs and ways'.[49] And to do this the assembly established a Permanent Commission for the Protection and Development of Indians, headed by the *fiscal* of the Supreme Court, who was to act as protector of the Indians and deal with their appeals and petitions.[50] At the same time the office of *corregidor* was restored, as were the *alcaldes* and governors of Indian villages.

Carrera was aware of the land problem latent in the Mita rebellion and the need to protect village lands from usurpers, whether adjacent villages or private hacendados, who often took land allegedly unclaimed. The many complaints he received from Indians led him to denounce the deficiencies of the system and the ineptitude and abusive behaviour of the departmental judges, who administered inferior justice to peasants yet charged exorbitant fees and fines, and he warned of trouble if things did not improve. He saw himself as a protector of the people against injustice, and stated in 1841, 'The people placed me at the head of the army in order to sustain their rights and remove those obstacles which are opposed to their happiness'.[51] In fact the Indians preferred to take their petitions, individually and collectively, not to the Protector of Indians but directly to Carrera, the one person whom they knew from experience, was able to secure redress of grievances. In the case of land disputes Carrera usually sent such petitions to the Protector and then scrutinized subsequent measurements. But land continued to exercise rural communities. Carrera's overthrow of the government in March

---

[48] Quoted by Woodward, *Social Revolution in Guatemala*, 67.

[49] *Ley de Garantías* (3 Dec. 1839), in Beltranena, *Fundación de la República de Guatemala*, 129–51; Manuel Coronado Aguilar, *Apuntes Histórico-Guatemalenses* (Guatemala, 1975), 486, 528.

[50] Ingersoll, *The War of the Mountain*, 273–4; Miceli, 'Rafael Carrera', 84–7.

[51] Quoted by Miceli, 'Rafael Carrera', 86–7.

1844 resulted in the acceptance of the Guadalupe Agreement, which he helped to draft. The agreement criticized the administration of justice and demanded that changes be undertaken to stop corruption and to ensure fair judgments of land disputes.[52] The evidence suggests that Carrera took an active interest in the restoration of community land to Indian villages and mediated in land disputes as often as practicable, but waged an unavailing campaign against court corruption and powerful usurpers, some of whom were themselves conservatives and *carreristas*. Conservative philosophy did not protect the Indians; without the caudillo's personal intervention they would have gained nothing. And in October 1851 he was still announcing that 'the Indians are not to be dispossessed of their communal lands on the pretext of selling them'.[53]

Carrera had made it clear during the rebellion that excessive taxes were a basic grievance of the poor against the Gálvez regime and that he expected a remedy. In 1839–40 the government responded by abolishing the poll tax, lowering taxes on basic foodstuffs, and financing extraordinary expenditure by forced loans from which the poor were exempt. But no conservative government in Spanish America ever persuaded its followers to pay an income tax or a land tax, and Guatemala was no exception. In subsequent years the government was involved in a number of disputes with Carrera over income and expenditure, the caudillo favouring a policy of economic austerity rather than further taxation and forced loans which might hit the peasantry.

Carrera's record as protector of Indians and peasants in the period 1840–4 was a mixed one, and neither in land litigation nor taxation did he achieve a fundamental shift of power in Guatemalan society. Nevertheless he remained the Indian's caudillo. He was careful to cultivate his constituency, keeping in touch with its problems through trusted officials and his own family. In March 1843 he sent his brother Colonel Santos Carrera on a visitation of Chiquimula and Mita, to report on social and economic conditions and to give encouragement and support. In March 1844, during the absence of Carrera in pursuit of banditry in the west of the country, the capital received news of a great assembly of Indians from Mita apparently

---

[52] Ibid. 88.
[53] Ingersoll, *The War of the Mountain*, 277–9; Coronado Aguilar, *Apuntes Histórico-Guatemalenses*, 486.

intent on rebellion. President Rivera Paz urgently recalled Carrera, who confronted the rebels and signed with them the Treaty of Guadalupe, an instrument to protect the rights of the peasant, peon, and artisan.[54] The Treaty stipulated the election of a constituent assembly to write a new constitution, and insisted on better provisions for land litigation, native industry, and the militia. While the government went through the motions of complying, Carrera made it clear that he stood between them and further popular rebellion not only in the highlands but also among the troops. On 11 December 1844 a frightened assembly, which had already nominated him *Benemérito Caudillo y General en Jefe*, elected him president, anxious that he should fulfil his role not only as protector of the Indians but also as protector of the élites against the Indians. He was then aged thirty and held office, except for a brief interregnum in 1848–9, until his death in 1865.

By now Carrera had acquired some of the personal, as well as the public, instruments of power. He launched his leadership bid in 1837 without a hacienda base or a hacendado coalition. Then, beginning with his wife's property, his landholdings increased with his military fortunes, through his influence with the government, and in return for policy support. And by the time he became president in 1844 he and his relations had amassed a respectable income. In 1841 the assembly voted an annual pension to Carrera's family. The caudillo himself owned a number of properties. In addition to his rich estate at Palencia, he held a grant of land in the Santo Tomás area and another, El Potrero de Barbales, at Chinautla in the Los Altos region, the whole amounting according to one estimate to 100,000 dollars in cash, land, and houses.[55] In 1848, at a time when he needed clerical support against a further rising in the Mita, he agreed to return the estate at Palencia to the Dominican Order, from whom it had been seized by the liberals in 1829 and who now reportedly paid Carrera 15,000 dollars for it.[56] On his death in 1865 his will listed the Hacienda de Batres near Guatemala City; the Hacienda de Buena Vista near Chiquimulilla;

---

[54] Hall to Chatfield, Guatemala, 14 Mar. 1844, PRO, FO 252/18; Chatfield to Aberdeen, Guatemala, 20 Mar. 1844, PRO, FO 15/37; Ingersoll, *The War of the Mountain*, 280–1.

[55] Dunlop, *Travels in Central America*, 88, 248; Woodward, *Social Revolution in Guatemala*, 63–4.

[56] Montúfar, *Reseña histórica*, v. 354.

the Haciendas de Puniom, San Jorge, and Zarza de Pareja in Escuintla; the Haciendas of Las Animas, Panam, and El Rancho in Mazatenango; El Potrero de los Llanos de Culebra near the capital; land in the port of San José; and a small lead and silver mine in Chiantla.[57]

As he made progress and acquired wealth, so he improved his public image and underwent a transformation from guerrilla to statesman. He impressed visitors by his quiet dignity and easy freedom of manners.[58] Already before he became president in 1844 he had moved into a larger house in the capital, and surrounded himself with a more regular and formal guard. He acquired enough literacy to read and write letters and to sign documents, and he did not disguise his sense of innate superiority over government ministers.[59] With his growing wealth and authority, he seemed to be more committed to law and order than to social reform. Did he now distance himself from the Indians and identify with the white élite? Some observers thought he did: 'By allying himself with the whites and mestizoes, he has in great measure lost his influence among the Indians, who say that he has betrayed them'.[60] Did he really lose the revolutionary ardour of his youth? It was a peasant uprising in Mita that gave him the opportunity of leadership in 1837. And it was another peasant uprising in Mita that began the revolt leading to his resignation in 1848. Did he abandon his popular priorities between these two events? The economic and social structures of Guatemala were deeply embedded. Carrera did not achieve a fundamental reversal of power and redistribution of resources. No one demanded, or even conceived, a social revolution of this kind, and for the age in which he lived it would be pointless to debate whether the caudillo was a revolutionary or a reformer. But he imposed significant change. He destroyed the first liberal experiment, he remedied agrarian and fiscal injustices against peasants, he rescued the Indians from abuse and neglect, and he brought the mestizos into power sharing. The white élite never succeeded in regaining full control of the country. Carrera introduced non-whites, principally mestizos, into offices of state. The military ceased to be a force of the élite: Indians made up a considerable portion of the army and were able to gain

[57] Ingersoll, *The War of the Mountain*, 334 n. 10.
[58] Dunlop, *Travels in Central America*, 89.
[59] Stephens, *Incidents of Travel in Central America*, ii. 113–4.
[60] Dunlop, *Travels in Central America*, 90.

minor government offices too. Carrera's relatives and associates, all mestizos, occupied important positions in the military and the bureaucracy. Thus while the legislature still remained largely a preserve of the whites, their monopoly over government was broken, never to be regained. The same was true of landholding, as new proprietors profited from their association with the regime. Carrera was as conscious of his clients as any caudillo, but these were policy changes, not simply the exercise of patronage. In this sense Carrera was a popular caudillo.[61]

4. *Caudillo and President*

Carrera became president of a nation-state, one which separated from the Central American Federation when, on 21 March 1847, he declared Guatemala to be free, sovereign, and independent. According to Chatfield Guatemala possessed the pre-conditions of a nation state:

The advancement of Guatemala in material prosperity, by the gradual development of its agricultural and commercial capabilities, is steady, while a population estimated at one million, an extensive territory, and the possession of several establishments of learning in its Capital, which is likewise the seat of an Archbishopric, may be deemed as constituting powerful elements of independence.[62]

Chatfield believed that the country had the necessary infrastructure for independent development, which Britain should help and support. It had made efforts to improve its roads and bridges; its finances were sufficient to cover the cost of government, to provide for a large portion of the domestic debt, and to begin an attack on the foreign debt. Guatemala's president, moreover, rated comparison with those elsewhere in the Americas:

The President, General Rafael Carrera, who has risen from obscurity to the highest power in the state, has, by his natural capacity, been enabled to restore order in public, and to give a certain degree of effect to the law, and, by means of moderation and firmness, to acquire an influence little inferior

---

[61] See Woodward, *Social Revolution in Guatemala*, 68, for a different interpretation, arguing for a form of social revolution.

[62] Chatfield to Palmerston, Guatemala, 28 Jan. 1847, PRO, FO 15/45, fo. 44.

to that possessed, on a much wider field, it is true, by General Paez in Venezuela and Rosas in Buenos Ayres.[63]

Carrera, however, did not as yet have the absolute power possessed by national caudillos such as Rosas and Páez. True, he was not restrained by a constitution, and the attempts to produce one failed. He was a strong president, and he could frighten people, but his sovereignty did not go unchallenged. The Treaty of Guadalupe and the fall of the conservative government had left behind a number of disgruntled politicians of both parties, operating still in council or constituent assembly, and reluctant to give Carrera a free hand. On 25 January 1845 Carrera 'who has not neglected his private interests since he came into power', obtained leave of absence to visit some of his estates, and malcontents took advantage of his absence to make a bid for power.[64] Conservative politicians quickly liaised with dissident army officers to stage a revolt in the capital on 2 February 1845.[65] Carrera survived through the prompt reaction of his brother Sotero, and with the support of his Indian troops, and assessed a fine of 20,000 pesos on the capital to reimburse them. There were further cries of protest from time to time, allegations that his illiteracy impeded good government, and criticisms of his extravagance, including the building of a useless fort in the capital, 'regardless of the impossibility of supplying it with water and provisions during a contest', according to Chatfield, and designed 'to overawe Guatemala, not to defend it from an enemy', according to Dunlop.[66]

One of the features of Carrera's government and bureaucracy, as has been seen, was the introduction of ladinos into unaccustomed positions of power. Some of his appointments, however, were frankly inferior and even allowing for prejudice Chatfield's reports were revealing. The British consul-general, as dean of the diplomatic corps, was chosen by his colleagues to represent them at an important interview with the president on 23 May 1846. The prospects were not good; Chatfield was the bane of the Guatemalan government, and Carrera had vowed to kill him for having affronted

---

[63] Chatfield to Palmerston, Guatemala, 28 June 1847, PRO, FO 15/46, fos. 145^v–146^v.

[64] Chatfield to Aberdeen, Guatemala, 11 Feb. 1845, PRO, FO 15/40, fos. 60–2.

[65] Hall to Chatfield, Guatemala, 12 Feb. 1845, PRO, FO 252/18; Dunlop, *Travels in Central America*, 109–11, 244–7.

[66] Chatfield to Aberdeen, Guatemala, 4 July 1845, PRO, FO 15/40, fo. 252; Dunlop, *Travels in Central America*, 83.

Guatemala's nationality in a series of claims and naval threats; relations worsened when Lord Aberdeen refused to grant the Guatemalan request for the consul's recall.[67] The purpose of the interview was to affirm the rights of the foreign consuls and to undermine the position of two of Carrera's cabinet ministers, General Jerónimo Pais, minister of finance and war, and José Antonio Azmitia, minister of foreign affairs. Pais was a coarse brute, a close friend and comrade-in-arms of Carrera from the days of rebellion, whose appointment was designed to retain the loyalty and restrain the rapacity of the military forces. Azmitia was an experienced and moderate politician; his appointment was a sign of Carrera's political awareness, and his function seems to have been to soften the impact of Pais, divert from the president the unpopularity of his financial measures, and keep the liberals satisfied. But Pais was in the ascendant, and at least an able administator, while Azmitia was ineffective.[68] Chatfield's account of Pais depicts a character hardly in accord with the supposed values of the regime: he was 'an avowed atheist, a drunkard, and an assassin, ignorant and self willed, with a great idea of his own capacity', apart from having a great hatred of foreign consuls. Chatfield had a higher opinion of Carrera 'who has more natural sense and tact than most of the people about him, but is unfortunately prevented by his inability to read from going into administrative details'.

Chatfield lectured Carrera on the fundamentals of foreign policy: Guatemala needed good relations with foreign powers, whose capital and immigrants were indispensable to the development of the state. Pais, however, had damaged relations with European nations by his hostile attitude, his policy of high duties, and his personal vendetta against the consuls and infringement of their customary rights, actions which would certainly bring retribution, and which seemed to be motivated by a desire to discredit the president himself. After the interview Chatfield stepped outside to have a few words with Pais, who behaved like 'a savage', dismissed Europe as finished, asserted that the future lay with the Americas, twice declared himself to be 'an utter atheist', and alleged that Guatemala had no need of consuls.[69] In July Pais lost his position, a partial victory for Chatfield

---

[67] Rodríguez, *A Palmerstonian Diplomat in Central America*, 270–1.
[68] Dunlop, *Travels in Central America*, 247.
[69] Chatfield to Aberdeen, Guatemala, 1 July 1846, PRO, FO 15/42, fos. 238–49.

and a lesson that caudillos could frighten Guatemalans but not the British. But the influence of Azmitia, whose liberalism was inimical to conservatives and Indians alike, survived and endured.[70] Ultimately this influence weakened and destabilized the government, being out of harmony with the president, preventing the adoption of a fixed policy, and becoming a means by which liberals gradually returned to positions of significance in capital and provinces.[71]

More alarming, however, was the discontent smouldering among the Indians of the highlands over land losses, village elections, and taxes, and a suspicion that their caudillo was neglecting them in preference for whites and ladinos. And gradually many of the traditional controls over the rural population began to reappear—labour quotas for public works, certificates of employment, and levies for the army.[72] Carrera created an *aguardiente* monopoly and in various departments granted it to his friends, family, and even himself. Local government seemed to return not only to its old institutions but to its old ways. Stories of the wicked and corrupt *corregidor* began to circulate again, not least against the caudillo's brother, Sotero Carrera, *corregidor* of Sacatepéquez, denounced by his enemies as a thief and a drunk.

Frustrated by his family and friends and misled by his own judgement, Carrera was also subverted by nature, as floods and famine raised prices, worsened rural conditions, and revived banditry. From the Oriente there were reports that a pretender had emerged, José Lucío López, a caudillo who appealed to the people, claimed supremacy, and challenged Carrera. Lucío was promptly tracked down, killed, and decapitated. But new leaders took his place, and on 16 October 1847 the *Lucíos* attacked Carrera's estate at Palencia, overcame his guards, and seized all the money and arms.[73] Guatemala City was in panic, fearing another invasion. The government branded the insurgents as bandits, but Carrera knew that he had on his hands a revolt of the mountain caudillos and their guerrilla forces. The position of the Indians of Mita and Chiquimula was ambiguous: they assured Carrera that he was still their *jefe*, but they were in rebel

[70] Chatfield to Palmerston, Guatemala, 12 Oct. 1846, PRO, FO 15/42, fo. 398.
[71] Chatfield to Palmerston, Guatemala, 8 Feb. 1848, PRO, FO 15/51, fos. 52–5.
[72] Dunlop, *Travels in Central America*, 90.
[73] Montúfar, *Reseña histórica*, v. 326–8; on the origins of the rebellion of the *Lucíos*, see Pedro Tobar Cruz, *Los montañeses* (Guatemala, 1971), 123–33, and Ingersoll, *The War of the Mountain*, 285–331.

territory and during his absence were persuaded or terrorized into supporting his enemies. Carrera appealed to the Church which responded positively to his call; priests worked on the Indians and went into rebel territory to preach peace. But this time the war of the mountains went badly for Carrera.

As the rebels engaged and disengaged in effective guerrilla tactics, the politicians seized the opportunity to manipulate the president or to manœuvre against him and El Salvador to intervene and exploit his weakness. In February 1848 he was on the point of resigning but the military and conservatives persuaded him to stay and to announce, 'today I become your caudillo again'.[74] But his troubles were only beginning. Liberal propagandists, throwing back the charges of 1837, depicted him to the highland peasants as ready to sell Guatemala to England, to reduce his compatriots to slaves, to subvert their religion, and to capture their children to sell to the English 'who eat them fried'.[75] His brother Sotero was killed in action, while former colleagues defected to the enemy. Counter-insurgency failed to defeat the rebels yet alienated another sector, who claimed to be its victims. The creoles of the Oriente joined those of Los Altos in opposition to Carrera and in August 1848 signed a treaty with the guerrilla leader Francisco Carrillo. This was the last straw and Carrera decided the moment had come to resign. His speech before the assembly on 15 August, ghost written apparently by the historian Alejandro Marure, reviewed his life and work. He exhorted the assembly to protect the Indians 'for they are the hands that work the land', to respect the customs and religion of the peasants, and to see that there were sufficient parish priests to serve the villages.[76] He then left for Mexico.

Chatfield had once doubted the intentions and capacity of Carrera. Now he was sorry to see him go, a statesman replaced by demagogues, a president who failed not through authoritarianism but through indecision and a readiness to heed too much advice, a victim of collusion between the rebels in the hills and his liberal enemies in the capital.

---

[74] Proclamation, 4 Feb. 1848, in Tobar Cruz, *Los montañeses*, 147–8; Chatfield to Palmerston, Guatemala, 8 Feb. 1848, PRO, FO 15/51, fos. 52–7.

[75] Chatfield to Palmerston, Guatemala, 9 Sept. 1848, PRO, FO 15/53, fos. 43–8.

[76] Hernández de León, *El libro de las efemérides*, vii. 349–69.

He has no doubt made mistakes, but it is remarkable that a man ignorant of the commonest rudiments of learning should have had the sagacity to direct his course as he has done, in the midst of the conflicting counsels and ideas of extreme men on all sides. If he has contributed in a degree to the destruction of his own government, his fault has arisen from not appearing to know the danger of acting on the advice of pretended friends, who persuaded him that it was safer for him to remain stationary and resist all change, than to risk the loss of his position by a movement in the onward path which nations must pursue.[77]

The new government, a weak consensus, soon found that it had taken a tiger by the tail. The rebellion in the highlands was now beyond control, a compound of guerrilla aggression, caudillo ambitions, creole manœuvres, and a separatist movement in Los Altos that had a sanctuary in El Salvador, a coalition of interests in which the voice of the Indian was hardly heard. The so-called Army of the People demanded money and military appointments, and funds to purchase the goodwill of villages. As the guerrillas came down from the highlands and pressed on the capital, the government feared a repetition of 1838.[78] Meanwhile Carrera watched events from the Mexican border as the *Lucío* revolt degenerated into banditry, and civil war declined into anarchy; and when he judged the moment right, he moved back into his power base. In the early months of 1849 he entered Los Altos and the Indians rose against the regional creole government.[79] Deputies of Indians approached the caudillo to pledge their loyalty to their old *jefe*. By a combination of guerrilla successes and political gestures Carrera convinced political opinion in Los Altos and Guatemala, especially the conservative leaders, that he was the only saviour the country had, the only hope for peace and order.

In August 1849, as the liberals packed their bags, Carrera was welcomed triumphantly into Guatemala as Commander-in-Chief of the Army with a mission to pacify the rebellious areas. He accepted the task, not only as protector of the Indians but as guardian of law and order and restorer of prosperity for all sectors, for hacendados

---

[77] Chatfield to Palmerston, Guatemala, 18 Aug. 1848, PRO, FO 15/52, fos. 389–91.
[78] Chatfield to Palmerston, Guatemala, 15 Dec. 1848, PRO, FO 15/53, fos. 299–303.
[79] Tobar Cruz, *Los montañeses*, 323–49.

and merchants as well as for poorer victims of insurgency.[80] For the next two years the caudillo pursued pacification ruthlessly, hunting rebels in the highlands, hitting their Salvadoran allies, and crushing not only the *Lucíos* but also the last vestiges of Central Americanism. In the process he re-established his position as prime caudillo, protector of the Indians, gendarme of the conservatives. In caudillo politics such responsibilities usually carried equivalent rights. And this time he made no mistake: he demanded and received absolute power. On 19 October 1851 Carrera again became president of Guatemala, with a conservative constitution and a traditional constituency, and he took office formally on 1 January 1852. On 23 May 1854 he became *presidente vitalicio*, one of the few Spanish Americans to achieve the Bolivarian ideal of a life presidency, an office he held until his death at the age of fifty on 14 April 1865. He had already named his successor.

5. *Popular Caudillism, Conservative Caudillism*

During his life presidency Carrera exercised absolute but not tyrannical power, and if his government was conservative it was also popular. A revolt in Quezaltenango, an old bugbear, sought to depose him in 1856, but once this was crushed he ruled without challenge. He brought to an end the civil wars endemic since independence, and although the Guatemalan army was in action in 1851, 1853, and 1863, these were wars against El Salvador and Honduras, in resistance to border pressures or movements for Central American union. And in 1856–7 he took the lead against the American filibuster, William Walker, sending Guatemala's army to join Central American resistance. Carrera's generals performed a military, not a political function, and while they were an essential prop of the regime, they were not its masters.

Carrera had intellectual as well as military support. The conservative historian José Milla, editor of the government newspaper, the *Gaceta de Guatemala*, was one of those who provided a rationale of the regime.[81] His editorials spelt out the imperatives of conservative

---

[80] Ibid. 349–51.
[81] Payne, *A Central American Historian*, 14–19.

caudillism: military control for political stability; dissemination of religious principles among the people to create a 'new society'; education of the élite for moral leadership through religious control of the University of San Carlos; and the continuation of an aristocratic structure as the only way of social control in a society with a large Indian mass at the bottom.[82] The conservative doctrine was the sole truth in this regime; opposition was not tolerated, liberal authors were discouraged and their writings treated as subversive. So Guatemala reached its political paradise, a landscape without features, a society without change. It was a stark doctrine: authoritarian rule for the common good exercised by an absolute dictator. But it was mitigated in practice by the benevolence of Carrera and the informality of many of the constraints.

Carrera had learnt enough from his first presidency to design a workable and enduring structure of power. He linked his government to those families which had been traditionally powerful in Guatemala and had a stake in maintaining the status quo, especially the Aycinena family, members of which held key posts in the government, the Church, the merchant guild, and the University. An Aycinena was appointed to the office of *corregidor* of the valley of Guatemala, controlling labour for the city and the cochineal plantations.[83] Another was a long-serving rector of the University. But the caudillo was in control, legitimized through the adoption of a constitution of a highly centralized kind (19 October 1851), which remained intact until replaced by a liberal alternative in 1879.

In reaching absolute power Carrera probably diminished his Indian identity, acquiring some of the trappings of creole culture and some of the sources of white wealth. His regime had the support of a kind of aristocracy, one which was a stage removed from the colonial aristocracy but contained many familiar names. Who are the aristocracy? asked Milla in an editorial. Who are the holders of privilege? 'The aristocrats in Central America are all those who, without exception, are distinguished for their richness, their talents, their good conduct, and their social position.... Here are the ones who have an option on offices, the ones who are and have been filling them without anyone ever asking who their grandparents were.'[84]

[82] Ibid. 18–19, 65 n. 50.

[83] Wortman, *Government and Society in Central America*, 269.

[84] *Gaceta de Guatemala* (18 Oct. 1849), quoted by Payne, *A Central American Historian*, 19.

High birth and family history alone were no longer the only criteria; wealth and talent also counted. This was a journalist's perception. In fact the old élite were still in place, qualified by wealth as well as by birth. Yet Carrera never forgot or neglected his original power base, and he continued to reward Indians and ladinos, no doubt according to their rank. For their part the Indians still regarded him as their saviour and protector, and came as individuals, as delegations, as communities to lay their petitions before him and seek direct justice; he listened and he acted. He was not sentimental about Indians. He remained a simple man of action, undisturbed by anguish or nostalgia. If the years 1854–65 did not have the dramatic quality of those of 1839–44, this was because many of the goals had been achieved, Indian claims had been vindicated, opportunities for mestizos had been improved. Moreover, Carrera had learnt from the revolt of the *Lucíos*, that no matter what he did for Indians and mestizos, once he dropped his guard a rival for popular leadership and a contender for caudillo power could emerge. He was under no illusions. Popularity alone was not enough; he had to rule as well as reward.

How can we interpret this political model? How can we explain popular caudillism? It was not simply a war between two ideologies, conservative and liberal, good or bad according to preference. Conditions made one or the other appropriate and possible. In the first place the Indians of Guatemala were not a weak minority. In a total population of 750,000 in 1840 growing to 950,000 in 1860, the Indians constituted two-thirds of the inhabitants, and by their numbers alone were an important power base. In the second place, the popular sectors of Guatemala were not threatened by economic growth and export agriculture. In this sense conservative caudillism responded to prevailing economic conditions and constituted a kind of autarky. To protect the Indians, their lands and their pro- duction, was also to support a semi-subsistence agricultural economy. *Corregidores* controlled labour, and local economies produced com- modities such as corn, wheat, and cotton, which only marginally affected the national and international markets. This made sense in mid-century Guatemala, for commercial conditions were not favourable to growth.

The cash crop which came to characterize the Carrera regime was cochineal (*grana*), a staple article of export, still in demand as a dye in the European textile industry, but generating in the 1850s no more than a moderate prosperity for Guatemala. Unlike indigo, which was primarily a plantation product, cochineal was a crop for small holdings mainly in the hands of ladinos, who cultivated the cactus plants on farms or plots rented from haciendas or village lands. The Indians themselves seldom grew the cochineal itself, but they made the sacks, transported the product to markets, and grew the crops which fed the producers. Economic conditions of this kind were not likely to alienate the peasants from the regime. Of course Carrera had to include élite hacendados, producers, and merchants in his policy, for he did not rule an entirely Indian country, and in any case he needed a revenue from customs duties to pay for the state, the army, and foreign loans. So he had to compromise with a creole merchant society. The élite were allowed to produce cochineal or lease their land for production in the central valley of Guatemala, with a salaried labour force and debt peonage, but they were not allowed to extend their holdings.[85] Although compulsory Indian labour was not abolished under Carrera, the labour demands of cochineal production were not excessive and did not disturb the Indian communities or hinder their practice of subsistence agriculture. The Guatemalan merchant community was allowed to trade in the cochineal dye, but commerce was otherwise restricted and foreign merchants were actively discouraged from establishing a strong presence in Guatemala. This did not prevent Carrera reaching an amicable settlement with Britain in 1859, recognizing its sovereignty over Belize in exchange for a promise to construct a road between Guatemala City and the Atlantic coast, a legal and moral obligation which Britain did not in fact fulfil.[86] Guatemala continued to import British textiles and hardware and Britain continued to dominate the market. But while Guatemala could not ignore the world market, it preserved its autonomy and its culture.

In an age of primitive caudillism Carrera was one of the most primitive of caudillos. His world was totally different from that of Santa Anna, even from that of Rosas and Páez; its structures were more simple, its problems less acute. While Carrera's preparations for leadership were rudimentary, they were appropriate to conditions in Guatemala and yielded quicker results than those of his fellow

[85] Wortman, *Government and Society in Central America*, 258, 268–9.

[86] R. A. Humphreys, *The Diplomatic History of British Honduras 1638–1901* (London, 1961), 83.

caudillos. True, his personal position was initially less powerful than that of Rosas; but the factor of opportunity was more urgent and the demands upon him from conservative forces for a lead against liberalism more pressing. The demographic balance in favour of Indians and mestizos made these a powerful constituency for a caudillo, if he could capture, control, and lead them. This Carrera was able to do, deriving his early strength from a mixture of leadership, preparation, and opportunity, as in the case of other caudillos, but above all from an identity with his power base far closer and more direct than that of Rosas, Páez, and Santa Anna. In the process he became a popular caudillo; but while he identified with Indian society and objectives, he did not remain a regional caudillo, as did Alvarez in Mexico, but won power at a national level and took Indian and peasant interests to centre stage. In this he differed from Rosas, whose relation with the gauchos of the countryside was opportunist and impermanent and exercised to some extent through the medium of the estancieros. He also differed from Páez, who gradually abandoned his early affinity with the llaneros and joined the Venezuelan oligarchy. And he differed totally from Santa Anna, who had little interest in Indian or popular sectors at any stage of his career and dealt only with élites. Carrera, in contrast to these, began and continued as a popular caudillo, and even as life-president did not abandon his original power base.

This power was incorporated into the army, which became an instrument not of the élite but of the caudillo himself and his indigenous supporters. Carrera never had a personal strike force drawn from his own haciendas. He recruited as a leader not a proprietor. The Guatemalan army was an Indian army, officered by *carrerista* commanders who had begun their service in the rebel hordes led by Carrera in 1837–9; it was totally different from the meagre forces of Páez and the professional military with whom Santa Anna had to deal. The army was a personal creation of the caudillo, as was that of Rosas, but unlike the army of Rosas it was never allowed to slip out of the control of the president and become the possession of regional caudillos. In the use of military force against political enemies Carrera responded to spontaneous emotions rather than careful calculations; he was more cruel than Páez and Santa Anna, less terrorist than Rosas.

The power of the Church in Guatemala was more akin to that of the Mexican Church than to the Churches of Argentina and

Venezuela. The Church was not a significant interest group for or against Rosas and Páez. Santa Anna used the Mexican Church occasionally for money and support, but he found that there was a limit to both. Among all these caudillos Carrera was the only true son of the Church, a religionist rather than a secularist, a leader who embraced Catholicism as a conviction as well as a cause and an interest, and one who without ever becoming a clericalist profited from the friendship of the Church at decisive stages of his career. The Indian identity of Carrera was inseparable from his Catholic identity.

Secure in his popular base, military power, and clerical support, Carrera enjoyed firmer foundations for his rule than Rosas, Páez, and Santa Anna, and as a dictator had the edge over his caudillo peers. All the caudillos needed the élites, Rosas the estancieros, Páez the oligarchy, Santa Anna the *gente de bien*. Carrera needed the aristocracy, as they were called in Guatemala, to help him to govern and administer, and to defend conservative values against liberals. But the Guatemalan aristocracy had more need of their gendarme than did the other élites of Spanish America, for Carrera was not simply a strong protector but a universal protector. He was protector of the Indians and therefore their mentor and controller, their natural leader who never lost their allegiance. This gave him great leverage over all the non-Indian interest groups in Guatemala, and ultimately gave him more power and longer power than any other caudillo in Spanish America.

The economy, society, and political balance which combined to make Guatemala propitious for popular caudillism could not be reproduced in all countries of the subcontinent. Few societies had popular classes with concentrated demographic superiority, militarized Indians, and a natural leader, all combining to tip the balance of power in their favour. But when such conditions occurred, they yielded greater stability and more powerful government than any other models of caudillism. The popular caudillo was a rare specimen but one natural to the time and the place.

THE CAUDILLO TRADITION IN SPANISH AMERICA

1. *Origins and Growth*

The caudillo excited the curiosity of contemporaries and the attention of later observers, fascinated by this creature of violence but
hard pressed to find his creator. Explanations invoked the environment, national character, the superficial, and the picturesque, often
taking refuge in 'Iberian values' or 'Hispanic tradition'. The novels
of dictatorship naturally appealed to the imagination and enhanced
the drama and the squalor of the caudillo's world. Sociologists
analysed structures and typologies, and tried to measure the marks
of the caudillo in statistical form. Historians dug ever deeper into
the past, convinced that longevity held the clue. But inquiry has to
proceed with an awareness of time and place. The search for origins
needs a sense of proportion. Mentalities characteristic of the conquest and ideas prevailing in the sixteenth century do not make
realistic explanations of events three hundred years later. As for
Spanish values, these were capable of producing various political
responses and were to be found in monarchy, bureaucracy, and
corporate bodies as well as in less formal concentrations of power.

So how can we explain the caudillo, without seeking escape in
spurious terms which simply postpone the task of analysis? Charisma
means little to the historian and becomes a substitute for an explanation, a word masquerading as an argument. As for *machismo*, it is
a subjective term, so universal in its application that it tells us little
of the Hispanic world. When every man is macho, what is left to
distinguish the caudillo? Even if these elusive concepts are useful to
the social scientist or the builder of models, they are of no service
to anyone trying to reconstruct the past in specific events, circumstances, and persons. Yet it is events that unlock the secrets of the
caudillo. Before 1810 the caudillo was unknown. He emerged not
from tradition, values, or the distant past, but from immediate cir-

cumstances in the decades after 1810, from war, reconstruction, nation-building, and anarchy, each stage producing a need and a response.

The caudillo entered history as a local hero whom larger events promoted to military chieftain. He derived his power from access to nearby resources, especially haciendas, which provided him with men and supplies and enabled him to become a leader of armed bands. But when was he born? The colonial heritage has been blamed for many of the adversities of modern Latin America, and caudillism is one of them. But the Spanish monarchy had no place for autonomous leaders. The imperial state was established on a foundation of institutions, officials, tribunals, and laws, tangible evidence of the high quality of Spanish administration. The quantity too was impressive. Between crown and subject there were some twenty major institutions, while colonial officials were numbered in their thousands. The *Recopilación de leyes de los reinos de las Indias* (1681) was compiled from 400,000 royal *cédulas*, reduced for the sake of convenience to a mere 6,400 laws. The Spanish empire had numerous flaws, but informality was not one of them. Spanish America was part of perhaps the most bureaucratic empire in world history; lawyers not soldiers were its administrators, precedents not personalism its ideal. Between king and viceroy, viceroy and *audiencia*, *audiencia* and intendant, intendant and local officials, there was no space where personal forms of power could grow, and in this multiplicity of laws and usages no functions were left to chance or to chieftains. Before 1810 Spanish America was not propitious for caudillism.

Yet on the margin of colonial society the precursor of the caudillo had already raised his head. Premonitions of change appeared at the end of the colonial period, if not in institutions at least in the social and economic conditions in which caudillism had its roots. Again, this was not the product of traditional structures or established conditions, nor did it happen by chance. It was the direct result of changes in land ownership and land use in various parts of Spanish America in the late eighteenth century. In Venezuela concentration of land ownership through competition within the llanos or from the incursion of northern hacendados resulted in the formation of great ranches whose owners introduced the concept of private property. Communal usages and traditional access to wild cattle disappeared with the establishment of new estates dedicated to livestock production and sale. The llaneros were marginalized and forced to take measures in self-defence. Many grouped themselves in bands under the leadership of local chiefs to live by violence and plunder. In the Río de la Plata the formation of estancias and appropriation of resources in the last decades of the viceroyalty diminished the horizons of the gauchos and criminalized many of their traditional activities. Both in Venezuela and Argentina the frontiers of rural life fell under the influence of armed bands, whose activities reduced some regions to a state of permanent rebellion. Nevertheless, while they rejected the king's law and outraged the king's officials, the bandit chiefs were no more than shadowy prototypes of caudillos. They did not operate far from their hideouts, or make political speeches, or constitute an alternative government.

The precursors of the caudillos, therefore, were nature's leaders, men who reacted aggressively to changing conditions in the late colonial period. They had to earn their reputations. Edmund Burke, who distrusted popular leaders, believed that 'the road to eminence and power, from obscure condition, ought not to be made too easy', for virtue is tried by difficulty and struggle.[1] The first caudillos underwent trial by battle. They were the products of specific conflicts in the years after 1810. The first of these was the war of independence, when the colonial state was destroyed, its institutions were discarded, and political gaps waited to be filled. These were the opportunities for local heroes to begin their public careers, though they did so without clear political convictions. There was an imperceptible progression from llanero or gaucho to vagrant, to bandit, to guerrilla, as armed landowners or new chieftains recruited followers. While the bands might be recruited in the service of various political causes, the underlying motivation responded still to rural conditions, now aggravated by war, and personal leadership, now tested in battle. As the countryside became a kind of armed camp, a target for conscripts and resources, a haven for deserters and delinquents, and a source of diminishing food supplies, so its beleaguered inhabitants sought protection in bands under strong men who would lead them to booty and subsistence. Thus banditry was a product of rural impoverishment and very soon a cause of it.

In the early years of the war the instinct for survival was stronger than ideology. But gradually the caudillo was transformed into a

---

[1] Edmund Burke, *Reflections on the Revolution in France*, 139–40.

war leader, normally a guerrilla leader, sometimes an army chief, recruiting his followers from personal dependants and a wider mix of peons, vagrants, and fugitives from justice or slavery. He needed and gained absolute power, as does any leader in time of war, and he established his relative power in the caudillo hierarchy by the criteria of natural leadership, namely success, popularity, and cruelty. These are universal values not incompatible with a return to civil government in time of peace. But this was a slow and lengthy war, often fought at great distance from the seat of government and military command, conditions which enabled the caudillos to strike roots, to augment and perpetuate their authority. Caudillism, created by war, was then prolonged by post-war conflicts, between unitarians and federalists in Argentina, between rival caudillos or groups of caudillos in Venezuela, between liberals and conservatives in Mexico, and between groups of regional interests in Central America. Caudillism thus emerged when central government was incapable of imposing its will on the whole nation, either because sovereignty was disputed between royalists and republicans, or because the triumphant republicans disagreed among themselves or with their neighbours, or because powerful interest groups competed to control the new executive; in this way local centres of power and decision came into existence and caudillos stepped forward to fill the empty political spaces and establish social order.

The caudillo was legitimized by war and acquired his first functions as a warrior. He soon gained others. The caudillo responded to different kinds of civilian pressure groups. Again, this was a specific stage of historical development, characteristic of the war and its aftermath. In some cases he was the representative of a powerful family controlling and allocating local resources and delivering them for the revolutionary state, such as Facundo Quiroga in La Rioja before he struck out on his own; or he was a leader of local élites united by ties of kinship, such as Martín Güemes, agent of a powerful group of estancieros in Salta, controlled and directed by them without a personal base outside the family network, and recognized by the state as a guardian of the frontier. More commonly, however, the caudillo represented regional interests beyond the mere personal or family base. In the cases of New Granada, Argentina, and Central America, the caudillo defended regional élites and their economic interests against the policies imposed by the centre. In so far as the centre or the capital employed force, the regions would commit their defence to a local strong man, often someone who had proved himself by imposing social order at home. Some caudillos regarded attack as the best form of defence and sought power at the centre. A national caudillo would take possession of the resources of the state, and his family, friends, and region would look towards him with yet greater expectations.

At this point the caudillo exercised a further function, one of his most characteristic: he became a benefactor, a source of patronage. The caudillos would attract a clientage by promising their followers offices and other rewards when they gained power, satisfying friends and buying off enemies. Clients were eager to join the ranks of a patron with good prospects, hoping to benefit from his favour and attention once the enterprise was concluded. A spoils system of this kind depended essentially on personal links: a caudillo's promise was preferred to the offer of a bureaucrat or legislator. Thus the mutual needs of patron and client became one of the fundamental pillars of caudillism in the new republics. The reward most appreciated was land, and the driving ambition of a caudillo was to acquire land for himself and a surplus for his followers. The growth of patronage and its application to political, military, and social advance, acquired a new urgency in the post-war years, when appointments were no longer a gift of the imperial power and, in default of any other system, became another weapon in a caudillo's armoury.

The relation of patron and client mainly benefited the élites, but it was also a link between the caudillos and the popular classes. The process began on the hacienda. The landowner wanted labour, loyalty, and service in peace and war. The peon sought subsistence and security. Thus the hacendado was a protector, possessing sufficient power to defend his dependants against outside intruders, recruiting officers, and rival bands. He was also a provider, who developed and defended local resources, and could give employment, food, and shelter. By providing what his dependants needed and using what they offered, a hacendado recruited a *peonada*. This primitive political structure, born of personal loyalties, built upon the authority of the patrón and the dependency of the peon, was finally incorporated into the state and became the model of caudillism. Individual alliances were enlarged into a kind of social pyramid, where patrons in turn became clients of more powerful men, until the highest point of power was reached and all became clients of a superpatron, who was the culmination of the caudillo hierarchy and the national embodiment of individual power bases.[2] Thus a local caudillo from his rural lair, helped by his client hacendados and their dependants, could conquer the state, for himself, his family, his region. There he would reproduce the personalism and paternalism in which he had been reared. The network was secured by no formal links, only the adhesion of extended interest groups, brought together by loyalty, convenience, and fear.

The caudillo as warrior and patriot, regional chief and patrón, are types of leadership accumulated almost in successive stages in the decades after 1810. His position reached its peak in the role of prime protector, an indispensable service for the republican élites, and once again a response to specific circumstances at a particular time. The wars of independence had undermined traditional social controls, allowed peons, *pardos*, and slaves to claim their share of freedom and equality, and given various caudillos the opportunity to ride to power on the back of these turbulent forces. The popular caudillos taught a lesson in militarizing and politicizing the new insurgents: the caudillos demonstrated that it was they who could mobilize and control the popular classes, that it was they who could lead them to serve or threaten the élites. In the event the masses were deceived: for them independence turned out to be a trick not a triumph. Political expectations ended with the end of the war. Social mobility was frozen by the prejudices of the élites and the poverty of the populace. Mobilization, therefore, was not accompanied by extended participation, and in most cases it was limited to comparatively reduced urban and rural sectors. In the absence of legitimate means to advance, many had recourse to protest and rebellion. In Argentina and Venezuela, in Mexico and Guatemala the activism of the ethnic groups and the insubordination of the masses created problems of public order and demanded the presence of a power which institutions did not provide. This was one of the essential functions of the caudillo.

The ruling élites of Argentina, Venezuela, and other countries saw their caudillos—military leaders who had power bases in the pampas, the llanos, and the highlands but who were not mere instruments of the rural masses—as the most appropriate leaders to

---

[2] Diego Urbaneja, 'Caudillismo y pluralismo en el siglo XIX venezolano', *Politeia*, 4 (1975), 133–51; see the same author's *La idea política en Venezuela 1830–1870* (Caracas, 1988).

fulfil the role of the strong man, the necessary gendarme, the rare embodiment of both authority and popularity. The élites needed Rosas, Páez, Carrera, because they were among the few chiefs who enjoyed a certain influence among the gauchos, the llaneros, and the Indians, and virtually the only leaders in their respective countries who could control the popular classes. In this context the caudillos were an influence not for anarchy, as is sometimes supposed, but for order and stability. Nor were they transients, the authors or victims of daily coups; most of them had great powers of survival and avoided, as Bolívar would have put it, the inconvenience of frequent elections. In the process they exploited their original power base and gave the popular classes a brief illusion of participation, while providing little or nothing in return. The exception, Rafael Carrera, also enjoyed exceptional conditions, namely support from a large Indian mass with whom he could reassure and threaten the élite, and for whom he continued to provide benefits as a guarantee against reaction.

Popular influence of this kind was based in part on ownership of land, which gave a caudillo the twin essentials of respect and resources and enabled him to employ numerous peons. But the linkage was not absolute. All caudillos ended up as landowners, but not all of them started as such. Some of them came from landed families and, like Rosas, added to their patrimony. Others rose to leadership without the benefit of land but acquired it later. A caudillo could recruit his first followers through his personal qualifications for leadership and through the cause itself. Páez, Zamora, and Carrera were all examples of such leaders. So land was an eventual power base but not necessarily the first; there was a greater tendency for caudillos to become landowners than for landowners to become caudillos. Just as landholding was not automatic, nor was access to peons and clients a mere routine. A caudillo might recruit a guerrilla force from his own estates but not normally an army. He had to appeal to a wider group of popular forces, not directly, but via family or client caudillos in the kinship chain. Without this client network he could only rely on his personal influence in recruiting followers, an influence which might vanish with time, as Páez learnt to his cost.

As prime protectors and guardians of order the caudillos relied not only on personal persuasion and moral influence but also employed, in varying degrees, methods of repression. Cruelty was not inherent in caudillism and in some cases the system was less oppressive than presidential regimes. Rosas, of course, had no doubt about the demands of authority and the duty of subordination. Carlyle's view of leadership, that 'there is no act more moral between men than that of rule and obedience', was one which Rosas applied in practice.[3] But Rosas also took precautions. Once he reached power and assumed possession of the state, he sent home the popular forces of the countryside and ruled through the bureaucracy, the police, the *mazorca*, and the army. Rosas was a terrorist caudillo; the knife and the lance were his sanctions, not ultimate but immediate. Páez disposed of less force and was personally less ruthless than his caudillo peers elsewhere; he was more of a consensus caudillo, the right man for Venezuela, where political divisions were less acute than in Argentina and Mexico, where the most persistent peril came from endemic banditry manipulated by dissident politicians and rebel military, and where the state was too poor to react tyrannically. Santa Anna found his main client base in the army; it was an unreliable base but being poorly endowed with alternative leaders it allowed Santa Anna to succeed in a sense by default. Rafael Carrera, product of the most popular power base in Spanish America, joined his Indian troops and mestizo officers into a powerful sanction of government and effective instrument of protection.

Caudillism, therefore, developed in response to specific historical events: the war of independence, the emergence of the nation-state, the post-war tendency to social anarchy, each stage invoking and legitimizing a particular function, and lasting so long that by the time people looked up it was too late. The caudillos were there to stay. But the political conjuncture too was significant in the creation of caudillos and the permanence of their rule. Independence gave an impulse to liberalism and made it a first choice for new governments. The cause of liberation, the ideas of the liberators, the collapse of traditional institutions, all combined to give liberals a natural advantage in the work of state-building; they, not conservatives, had the policies, the people, and the organization to seize the initiative and provide the programmes required in the years after 1820. At the same time the opening of the Atlantic economy to free trade offered new opportunities to producers and exporters which required a political framework and an appropriate policy. Again, the

---

[3] Thomas Carlyle, *On Heroes, Hero-Worship, and the Heroic in History* (London, 1901), 228.

liberals appeared to have the answer—a constitutional state and a market-orientated policy. The decade 1820–30, therefore, was an early spring of liberalism, when leaders sought to reform and modernize their countries, to design constitutions which they could operate, and to devise electoral systems which would enable them to assemble the votes of their creole supporters, perpetuate themselves in power, and impose an economic policy favourable to proprietors and exporters. The political framework was not necessarily more democratic than alternatives: the liberals as much as anyone needed a strong executive; in a sense they were a collective dictatorship whose ideal was strong presidential government. But they pre-empted the terms of progress, and claimed legitimacy through representation.

The conservatives were bemused. Rejects of the times, they found it difficult to make headway, to promote ideas associated with the past, to organize party machines and win elections. Yet they knew that they too were representative: they had constituencies in the corporate bodies deeply rooted in Spanish American society and now alienated by liberal policies—the army, the Church, and in some countries Indian communities—and among traditional artisans. How could they appeal to these constituencies directly, bypassing the electoral process, which they could not guarantee, and mobilizing their supporters, to whom they did not have immediate access? How could they organize their allies and concentrate their power? The answer lay with the caudillos. The call to caudillos, therefore, tended to be a conservative call and the caudillos conformed to conservative policies. In the years around 1830 the conservative reaction in Buenos Aires and Venezuela was in full flow and in each case brought to power an appropriate caudillo. In Mexico the process can be observed in 1834, in Guatemala in 1839. The caudillos were thus a means of tapping conservative support latent in the traditional sectors, support which could not be reflected in liberal-designed electoral systems with restricted suffrage.

In parallel to liberal programmes the 1820s also saw the establishment of great states into which smaller units were incorporated as federalized provinces. This was the Achilles heel of liberalism. The innate weakness of federalism as a system of government, its inability to overcome regional loyalties, and its tendency to ignore local economies, gave conservatives and their caudillo spearheads the opportunity either to secede from liberal superstates, Buenos

Aires from Rivadavia's Argentina, Venezuela from Santander's Colombia, Guatemala from the Central American Federation, or as in the case of Mexico, substitute a centralized and authoritarian alternative to the federal model. The caudillos were agents of the nation-state, and the nation-state was the stage of caudillo ambitions where personalism could flourish and clientage prevail: as the nationalists declared to Páez in 1830, 'General! You are the Patria.'[4]

In taking power the caudillo usually followed a dual process: first he exercised informal authority and then actually took office as supreme executive, whether president or governor. But office did not replace a caudillo's power or become a substitute for his authority: it simply confirmed his position and reinforced his original capacity to take decisions and impose order, a capacity which he had won by his personal qualifications, his response to war, and his reaction to politics.

2. *The Caudillo in Political Theory*

Caudillism soon became a theory as well as a fact. It was rationalized, criticized, and justified. It acquired a literature and a mythology, apologists and critics. As in many theories of authority, caudillo theory came to be expressed as a transition from a state of nature to a civil society, or as a great antithesis between anarchy and order, the greater the anarchy the more absolute the order.

The first great political theorist of Latin America, Simón Bolívar, was not preoccupied with caudillism, concerned perhaps with wider problems and convinced that the new republics suffered from lack of authority rather than lack of freedom. The failure of the First Republic in Venezuela he attributed to federalism and weak government. The collapse of the Second Republic he blamed on disunity and inexperience. He then had to work with the caudillos to revive the revolution. After 1819 he denounced lawyers, legislators, and liberals. In 1826 he identified 'two monstrous enemies' in the speech presenting his draft constitution to the Bolivian Congress. 'Tyranny and anarchy constitute an immense sea of oppression encircling a

---

[4] Vallenilla Lanz, *Cesarismo democrático*, 94.

tiny island of freedom.'[5] The tyrants were not necessarily caudillos. Colombians, he lamented, were 'seduced by freedom', each person wanting absolute power for himself and refusing any subordination. This led to civilian factions, military risings, and provincial rebellion. To counter anarchy he advocated a strong executive power and a life-term president. Yet the paradox of the Bolivian Constitution was that the life-term president was not an absolute ruler but one shorn of patronage and of many other powers which a caudillo would take for granted. For Bolívar caudillos were good or bad according to whether they were instruments of government or anarchy. 'Who is more terrible or cruel', he asked, 'than a soldier turned demagogue?' In describing the political world around him, Bolívar did not isolate caudillism as a particular phenomenon. This was left to subsequent historians.

Domingo Faustino Sarmiento, exiled by a caudillo who was in-toxicated with power, sought to explain the prevalence of caudillism in the land of his birth. Why had primitive caudillos like Rosas and Quiroga come to dominate the political life of Argentina? This was the theme of his greatest work, *Facundo*. He himself had little direct experience of caudillos or their desert terrain, and he relied for his information on reading and on briefings by fellow exiles in Chile. But this was not a disqualification: he had a vision and a thesis. The regime of Rosas, he wrote, was not unnatural to Argentina; on the contrary, it embodied only too well the history and character of its people. The process began with the environment, the pampas. These were Argentina's steppes or deserts, inhabited by horsemen, nomadic hunters, ranch hands, and an occasional outlaw, a 'white savage, divorced from society', all these making up a people called the gauchos, whose vocation was a profession, not to be confused with vagrancy or banditry.[6] The gauchos required an iron discipline from powerful caudillos, who often emerged from the ranks of feudal-style estancieros, and ruled by knife and gun to establish 'the rule of brute force, the supremacy of the strongest', and to save rural society from crime and chaos.[7] Amidst a society already poised uneasily between authority and anarchy, the revolution of

---

[5] Bolívar, Message to the Congress of Bolivia, 25 May 1826, *Obras completas*, iii. 763.

[6] Sarmiento, *Facundo*, 59.

[7] Ibid. 35.

1810 and the reforms of Rivadavia arrived to tip the balance towards disorder and to provoke a corresponding reaction. This gave the gaucho chieftains the chance to seize power, and to unleash a backlash against liberalism. The Argentine Revolution, argued Sarmiento, was a dual movement: 'The cities triumphed over the Spaniards, and the countryside over the cities'. In the process the rural chieftains and their hordes deprived the cities of all marks of civilization, schools, churches, charitable institutions, lawyers' offices, and freedom from terror. 'The barbarism of the interior has come to penetrate even the streets of Buenos Aires'.[8] Among the most vicious of the barbarians was Facundo Quiroga.

Sarmiento endowed Quiroga with the classic physiognomy of the caudillo. His description, confirmed in contemporary portraits, made him a monster even in appearance, a small, stout man with broad shoulders and a short neck, supporting a head covered with dark and closely curling hair, his face further hidden by a black beard and heavy sideburns, a face usually bent downwards so that he looked at people from under dark eyebrows. His early life was a series of outrages, a story of gambling, violence, assaults on women, killings, and rebellions, all indicating a man totally resistant to discipline or orders, a man—in that society—born to rule. 'He considered himself called to command, to rise in one bound, to create for himself, in defiance of civilized society and at war with it, a career combining courage and crime, authority and disorder.'[9] Sarmiento was told that Quiroga had no religion, never went to confession, prayed, or heard Mass: 'He said of himself that he believed in nothing.'

The public career of Quiroga confirmed the traits of his youth and was marked by a cycle of horror and atrocity which personified the struggle in Argentina between civilization and barbarism, liberty and despotism, the cities and the desert, Europe and America. For Quiroga was the natural Argentine, the perfect specimen of the *gaucho malo*: 'Facundo is a type of primitive barbarism; he recognized no form of subjection; his rage was that of a wild beast.'[10] Compared to the professional soldier, José María Paz, a representative of European civilization, an educated officer who was a true republican

---

[8] Ibid. 78, 86.
[9] Ibid. 96.
[10] Ibid. 99, 100.

hero, Quiroga embodied all that was backward and hopeless in Argentina. Atrocities piled on atrocities, victims multiplied, as creoles, peasants, soldiers, and civilians fell to his henchmen, and cruelty culminated in the order to all the inhabitants of the city of Rioja to migrate to the llanos under pain of death. What was the meaning of this relentless horror? His object was to inspire terror, which was the surest way to establish power. 'With him terror took the place of administrative activity, of enthusiasm, of strategy, of everything. Let us not deceive ourselves: terror is a means of government which produces greater results than patriotism and fervour.'[11] This variant of the Hobbesian fear principle came too near the truth for some of Sarmiento's readers, who considered that it was not for liberals to prove the case for terrorism.

Sarmiento, however, believed that the same point had been proved by Rosas. He too exemplified Argentina's nature, rising to power through the barbarism of the people. He too used terrorism as an instrument of government, though he applied it methodically, not indiscriminately, and based it on 'observation and calculation', not on impulse. In the process he treated Buenos Aires as an extension of the desert, and 'destroyed in six years all knowledge of the just and the good'. And Sarmiento repeated that a caudillo using terror got quicker results than any other: 'terror produces greater results than patriotism'.[12]

Sarmiento was making a factual, not a moral, statement. Yet he had to establish an escape route from caudillism and admit the possibility of progress. In 1844 he had already written a frank assessment of Rosas, seeking to understand, the better to condemn. He traced the roots of Rosas's caudillism to the social structure of Argentina and Rosas's skill in exploiting it:

No one knows more shrewdly than General Rosas the social situation of the peoples who surround him. His long tenure of government, and the sharp and penetrating intelligence with which nature has, unfortunately, endowed him and which only mean party prejudice could deny, are sufficient to make him well informed of these things . . . .

Raised to command of his country by a general insurrection of the masses; sustained in office by the power provided by this insurrection; master of this sector and connoisseur of its strength and instincts; conqueror, if not in

[11] Ibid. 179.
[12] Ibid. 211, 220.

battle at least by politics and achievements, of the educated and European-
ized part of the Argentine people; he has come to have a complete understanding of the state of society in South America and always knows exactly
how to touch the right social chords and to produce the sounds which he
wants.[13]

A year later, in 1845, Sarmiento introduced in the final part of
Facundo a programme of national reconstruction which stood in
contrast to the intransigence of the earlier chapters. He suggested
that Rosas was not responsible for his origins, coming from a family
of *godos* who reared him as a creole conservative, and at least he
enforced severe discipline on his own estancias. Moreover, according
to Sarmiento, Rosas had eliminated Quiroga, thus preventing the
establishment of a rival fiefdom, further outbreaks of civil war, and
the proliferation of caudillos. Conditions for internal peace and
economic prosperity were now possible, as could be seen from
the increasing numbers of European immigrants. So Rosas was
presented as a channel to the future, 'a great and powerful instrument of Providence', through whom the country was slowly entering
the path of unity, peace, and progress.[14] People were not naturally
criminals and murderers, he argued; it depended upon the circumstances presented to them. A future Argentina, therefore, would
have a place for honourable supporters of Rosas; even *mazorqueros*
would not be excluded, for among them there were hidden virtues.[15]

Sarmiento himself, however, was not a medium of reconciliation.
When he came to office as governor of San Juan he pursued the last
caudillos mercilessly, regarding his mission as that of a pro-consul
authorized to wage war to the death against robbers and killers and
establish republican peace in the interior. His most notorious victim
was Angel V. Peñaloza, El Chacho, caudillo of La Rioja. In 1863
Sarmiento's forces triumphed, killed their prisoners, and displayed
the head of El Chacho on a pole. In a letter to President Mitre he
defended the treatment of the caudillo, executed without trial and
with unnecessary savagery, as a triumph of civilization over barbarism, and described decapitation as 'another Argentine trait':

[13] Sarmiento, *El Progreso* (8 Oct. 1844), in *Obras de D. F. Sarmiento* (53 vols.;
Santiago and Buenos Aires, 1887–1903), vi. 118–19; *Obras selectas*, ed. Enrique
de Gandia, vol. iii: *Juan Manuel de Rosas: Su política, su caida, su herencia* (Buenos
Aires, 1944), 103–6.
[14] Sarmiento, *Facundo*, 261–2, 264–8, 292–3.
[15] Ibid. 303.

'If we had not cut off the head of that inveterate scoundrel and placed it on display, the mob would not have quietened down in six months'.[16] So, with pen and sword, Sarmiento pursued his prey, and presided over the last hours of the caudillos, convinced that to defeat barbarism it was necessary to become more barbarous than the barbarians.[17] Enemy of the *gaucho malo*, he was nevertheless one of the few Argentines of his time who saw that to redeem the gaucho it was necessary to give him land and schools.

As a writer, Sarmiento had to elevate what he destroyed and give it a publicity beyond its merits. In bringing the world of the caudillo into the glare of history *Facundo* enhanced its flaws, like sunlight on a shanty town. Even so, his analysis of the caudillos drew a mixed response. Some were disturbed by his realism, others by his supposed equivocation. Juan Bautista Alberdi criticized the thesis that civilization was located in the cities and barbarism in the country as 'an error of history and observation'. In fact the contrast was not completely unfounded. As a result of independence there was a shift of power from the urban and civilian centres characteristic of colonial rule towards rural bases of wealth and decisions, a shift which modern historians have identified as a militarization and ruralization of power. Through this change, moreover, creole provincial families like the Sarmientos came to be excluded from office and prospects by the emergence of rural caudillos and the dominance of their *montoneros*. Nevertheless, Alberdi had a point. It is a matter of history that the May Revolution in Buenos Aires inspired a two-way conflict, in which Buenos Aires provoked the provinces by imposing the revolution without negotiating with the local élites, and the interior reacted in a way which threatened the political and commercial interests of Buenos Aires. Moreover, the antithesis of city and wilderness was not exact. Alberdi argued that it was precisely in the country that the productive classes resided, working in silence for wealth and prosperity, while the cities were full of vagrants, muggers, and idlers. The criticism could be taken further. Buenos Aires was an extension of the countryside, where cattle products were processed, warehoused, and exported, where the greatest estancieros preferred to live and, through their caudillo, to rule the

---

[16] Quoted in José S. Campobassi, *Sarmiento y su época* (2 vols.; Buenos Aires, 1975), i. 548.
[17] Ibid. ii. 8.

province. In turn profits earned in Buenos Aires were invested in rural production; in many cases entrepreneur and estanciero were one and the same. So if Buenos Aires was the indispensable port, the pampas were the source of wealth and exports.

Alberdi too attempted to understand Rosas and the reasons for his political durability. His cool appraisal of Argentina thirty-seven years after the May Revolution, published as a pamphlet on 25 May 1847, while hostile to Rosas, shocked many exiles by its complacent view of the dictatorship. He saw the regime as a natural product of time and place. 'Wherever there are Spanish republics, created from former colonies, there you will have dictators.' This did not mean that Rosas was a mere tyrant. If he wielded a rod of iron, he also possessed political talent and he had won such a reputation that he was better known in the world than Bolívar and Washington. He represented the typical qualities of Argentina. 'As all outstanding men, the extraordinary development of his character reflects that of the society to which he belongs. Rosas and the Argentine Republic are mutually dependent things; he is what he is because he is Argentine; his rise supposes that of his country.' He had many achievements to his credit: he had repelled Britain and France, created a powerful and in effect a unified state, and established peace. Rosas moreover had promoted the lower classes to power and had helped to educate them in government and politics. Nevertheless, concluded Alberdi, the dictator had wasted his opportunities; in the final analysis he failed, because he had not given Argentina a constitution:

There is no written constitution in the Argentine Republic, nor are there individual laws of a fundamental character. The operation of those which used to exist in Buenos Aires is suspended, while General Rosas retains indefinitely the *suma del poder público*. . . . He is a dictator, a leader invested with despotic and arbitrary powers, in the exercise of which there is no counterweight. . . . To live in Buenos Aires is to live under the regime of a military dictatorship. Extol the moderation of that power if you wish, in which case it will be a worthy dictatorship. But in our time ideas have reached a point where mixed constitutions have more appeal than benevolent dictatorships.[18]

[18] Juan Bautista Alberdi, *La República Argentina, treinta y siete años después de su Revolución*, Valparaiso, 25 May 1847, in *Obras completas* (8 vols., Buenos Aires; 1886–7), iii. 223, 225, 241.

If Alberdi was lenient towards the dictatorship, it was perhaps a reflection of the exile's search for a national identity and an Argentine consensus and his anxiety not to exclude even the *rosistas*; and he did not care to denigrate his country before a foreign audience.[19] In his *Bases* for the political organization of Argentina, published in 1852, he was less constrained and described dictatorship as a 'perpetual provocation to conflict . . . Dictatorship is institutionalized anarchy'.[20] Nevertheless, while rejecting crude dictatorship, Alberdi seems to have been seeking a strong presidential government which would preserve elements of monarchy and aristocracy, a kind of progressive authoritarianism capable of influencing elections, dominating public opinion, imposing modernization, and encouraging economic progress.[21] Such a government required allegiance from the whole people, and it was a useful by-product of a Rosas-style despotism that it encouraged 'the habit of obedience' which could subsequently be put to better use. John Stuart Mill would make a similar point when he argued that a people who have still to learn 'the first lesson of civilisation, that of obedience', are likely to learn it not from a representative assembly, which would simply reflect their own insubordination, but only from a military despot, who thus carries them through a necessary stage of progress towards representative government.[22] Alberdi argued along similar lines. He maintained that Argentina had not been disqualified from constitutional government by its addiction to caudillism. Unlike Sarmiento, he believed that even the caudillos were redeemable:

Those uncouth and wild chiefs have improved their persons and characters in the school of authority, where men of inferior condition frequently enhance and raise their qualifications. To govern for ten years is to take a course in politics and administration. Those men are now yet further means of establishing in the interior a stable and useful settlement.[23]

Argentina led the way in theorists as well as caudillos, and few other Spanish American societies produced a Sarmiento or Alberdi. Mexican liberals, like those of Argentina, were naturally hostile to dictatorship, though they were sometimes tempted to tolerate it

[19] Jorge M. Mayer, *Alberdi y su tiempo* (Buenos Aires, 1963), 342–7.

[20] *Las 'Bases' de Alberdi*, ed. Jorge M. Mayer (Buenos Aires, 1969), 353.

[21] Tulio Halperín Donghi, *El espejo de la historia: Problemas argentinas y perspectivas hispanoamericanas* (Buenos Aires, 1987), 29–30.

[22] Mill, *Representative Government*, 220–1.

[23] *Las 'Bases' de Alberdi*, 389, 392.

while focusing their attention more on the forces of conservatism in society favourable to dictators. But Mexican conservatives, too, were cool towards caudillos, regarding them as a risky means of restoring traditional values and a form of government inferior to that which could be provided by the conservative party. Carlos María Bustamante, the chronicler of Mexican insurgency and post-independence politics, and the source of much of the specific evidence of the deeds of Mexico's military and political heroes, provides few clues to the secret of Santa Anna's success, regarding him as a monster, a demon, and a traitor, unworthy to rank among Mexican heroes and unworthy apparently of extended interpretation. Even his *Apuntes para la historia del gobierno del General D. Antonio López de Santa-Anna* is stronger in description and denunciation than in critical analysis. Lucas Alamán provided in his *Historia de México* a more basic framework for a conservative interpretation of Mexican history. Like Sarmiento, he had a horror of rural barbarism and its leading exponents, the caudillos and bandits; he despaired of national unity and was appalled when politicians broke ranks to make deals with dissidents. Unlike Sarmiento, however, he respected Hispanic values; for him the last example of civilization in Mexico had been the peace and prosperity provided by the Bourbon state, whose golden years contrasted cruelly with the disorder and impoverishment of the country at mid-century.[24]

The antithesis of civilization and barbarism was not, of course, invented by Sarmiento or exclusive to Argentina. It was used about the same time in Central America by Frederick Chatfield, the British consul, who described the rebellion of Carrera as 'a war of Barbarism against Civilization'.[25] A similar antithesis, between culture and anarchy, was applied to mid-Victorian England by Matthew Arnold, though his culture was knowledge, his anarchy worship of wealth, and his barbarians the aristocracy. The antithesis also underlies Thomas Carlyle's discourse on heroes and its application to South America. According to Carlyle, great men are the prime subject of history. Given the political instability of the times and the vain search for solutions, hero-worship is a natural and reassuring tendency. Heroes, he argues, rise in various forms, but

[24] D. A. Brading, *The First America: The Spanish Monarchy, Creole Patriots, and the Liberal State 1492–1867* (Cambridge, 1991), 634–46.

[25] Chatfield to Palmerston, San Salvador, 16 Aug. 1838, PRO, FO 16/20, fo. 301.

the ultimate hero embodies virtually the whole typology: prophet, priest, poet, teacher, and ruler of men, 'he to whose wills our wills are to be subordinated'.[26] The rule of the hero is preferable to any other form of government. 'Find in any country the Ablest Man that exists there; raise him to the supreme place, and loyally reverence him; you have a perfect government for that country; no ballot-box, parliamentary eloquence, voting, constitution-building, or other machinery whatsoever can improve it a whit. It is the perfect state; an ideal country.'[27] Carlyle's heroes have special personalities as well as functions. They do not need to adopt a declamatory style, show ambition, claim greatness. The true heroes are the strong silent men of history, silently thinking, silently working, inhabiting 'the great Empire of silence', which seems to have been Carlyle's political paradise.[28]

In his essay on Dr Francia, in many ways a flippant, condescending, and heavily ironic work, redeemed only by the author's originality in studying Paraguayan history in 1843, he shows a rare sympathy for the strange dictator, condemned to govern such a country, such a people, who needed to be whipped and tamed and rid of their idle, lawless, and brutish ways. He argues that the people of Paraguay, or the 'guachos' as he calls them, were 'not yet fit for constitutional liberty'. The 'liberty' provided by the politicians' government was only 'peculation, malversation', and 'various forms of embecility'. To free Paraguay of this disorder a new revolution was indispensable, one which Francia provided: 'The eyes of all Paraguay . . . turn to the one man of talent they have, the one man of veracity they have'.[29] Francia gave them order and peace and they could say: 'All South America raging and ravening like one huge dog-kennel gone rabid, we here in Paraguay have peace, and cultivate our tea-trees.'[30] So Francia ruled his Paraguay as an enlightened dictator, and imposed not a reign of terror but 'a reign of rigour'.[31] He was for Carlyle a 'lonesome Dictator' surrounded by half-wits and illiterates, with no

[26] Carlyle, *On Heroes*, 225, 232.
[27] Ibid. 226.
[28] Ibid. 257–8.
[29] Thomas Carlyle, 'Dr. Francia', in *Critical and Miscellaneous Essays* (4 vols.; London, 1888), iv. 269, 277.
[30] Ibid. 278.
[31] Ibid. 280.

one to talk to, no one to understand him. 'O Francia, though thou had to execute forty persons, I am not without some pity for thee!'[32] Carlyle came to be known in Spanish America, and in Venezuela José Gil Fortoul was familiar with his works.[33] But his essay on Dr Francia, which also discussed Bolívar and other liberators, produced little response and in general he remained without influence or following. Positivist historians, on the other hand, had a specific if delayed impact which endured into the late nineteenth century and beyond. The philosophy of Auguste Comte was designed not only to provide a new theory of knowledge but also one of social structure and change from which a system of social planning could be developed. The political framework of this was a dictator based on popular consent, ruling for life with the aid of a technocratic élite, and promoting economic progress in an ordered society. The French positivist historian Hippolyte Taine wrote that the human condition required over and above established institutions 'an elective or hereditary gendarme ever on the alert and with an iron hand, who through his actions inspires fear and through fear maintains peace'.[34] This caught the eye of the Venezuelan scholar and journalist, Laureano Vallenilla Lanz, who fashioned it into a thesis of Venezuelan history, *Cesarismo democrático*, first published in 1919.

Vallenilla Lanz was not a mere mouthpiece of dictatorship or a spokesman for a particular caudillo. His book was designed and written before Juan Vicente Gómez came to power, and seems to have arisen from his own research and ideas.[35] He subsequently served the Gómez regime, as Director of the National Archives, editor of the government newspaper *Nuevo Diario*, and Venezuelan minister in Paris. But his history and politics were part of the same conviction that dictatorship was natural and necessary to Venezuela, an expression rather than a denial of true democracy. On the basis of his research into the late colonial, independence, and post-independence periods of Venezuelan history, he concluded that Venezuela was a turbulent society in which semibarbarous *montoneros*

---

[32] Ibid. 293.
[33] Germán Carrera Damas, *Historia de la historiografía venezolana (Textos para su estudio)*, 2nd edn., vol. i (Caracas, 1985), 489.
[34] Quoted by Vallenilla, *Cesarismo democrático*, 79.
[35] Nikita Harwich Vallenilla, 'Estudio preliminar', in Vallenilla Lanz, *Cesarismo democrático*, p. xxxviii.

could erupt at any time into aggression, murder, and robbery, unless controlled by a stronger force; experience taught that this control must be committed not to the law but to the most prestigious and feared caudillos. Thus in Venezuela 'the Caudillo has constituted the only force of social order'.[36]

Vallenilla traced the social origins of the caudillos to the lowest sectors of society: 'as almost all the caudillos active in the struggle for independence came from the same social group, most of them [royalists and republicans] were equally ignorant and fanatical.'[37] But for him the individual and personal characteristics of caudillos were less important than the permanent structural factors explaining robbery, plunder, violence, assassination, and the brutal instincts of the popular masses. The incorporation of the llaneros into the army of liberation was not due primarily to the leadership of Páez but to the material desires of the nomad peoples. Vallenilla tended to interpret caudillism in a determinist way, conditioned by structures and circumstances. He explained the rising of 1846 not as a response to political leadership or as a stage in liberal policy or even as an aspect of caudillo politics: 'This was the sole and essential criterion, the social conscience of a semi-barbarous and militarized people among whom the nomad, the *llanero*, the bedouin, were preponderant in numbers and through the powerful force of their might'.[38] Not all of these interpretations are valid. Many of the caudillos came from the colonial élite; caudillo leadership and decisions were essential to the recruitment of a band no less than the social conditions in the llanos; and the rebellion of 1846 was a conjunction of various factors. Elsewhere, he himself emphasizes the significance of personalism. The politicians, he argued, both conservatives and liberals, sought to eliminate personalism by ending the presidential pretensions of Páez and submitting him to 'the rule of the constitution'.

They did not realise that the personal power of the Caudillo was the true and effective constitution of the country, and that to try and establish order by strange laws without counting on the direct and effective action of the gendarme could only increase anarchy, systematize disorder, and open the way to agitators who would also invoke abstract principles and demand the

---

[36] Vallenilla Lanz, *Cesarismo democrático*, 79.
[37] Ibid. 64.
[38] Ibid. 122.

application of the Constitution to satisfy their personal grievances and ambitions for power.[39]

At the heart of Vallenilla's rationale of the caudillo was the concept of the necessary gendarme, the leader called upon to control the masses, establish order, and keep the peace. He was the protector of society, against insurrections of troops, plundering by llaneros, attacks by urban *mulatos*, agitation of ex-slaves, and imminence of race war. After independence Páez and other caudillos had to fulfil their supreme duty 'to protect with their authority the renascent social order against those bands that laid waste the fields, sacked and burnt the villages, threatened the authorities, and killed the whites'.[40] Yet there is a fatal ambiguity in the concept of the necessary gendarme. Was he the representative of the masses? Or was he the protector of the élites against the masses?

Vallenilla argues that Venezuela, like all pastoral societies, had an egalitarian character derived not from equality of rights but from 'equality of conditions' in the llanos and from the 'levelling instincts' of the Venezuelan people, which prevented the dominance of any one caste, class, or oligarchy.[41] The revolution for independence had been quickly followed by a social revolution, in which, backed by the masses, 'the Caudillos, through their great achievements, came to occupy the highest positions in the nascent Republic and were in reality the true exponents of the revolution'. The example of Páez, rising from a ranch peon to supreme chief of the republic, rich, flattered, and feared beyond all others, was bound to encourage the popular classes and to motivate them to bestir themselves, to pull themselves up, to conquer all the heights, and to breach the barriers erected by the colonial regime against democratic progress. 'Páez, Supreme Chief of the Nation, has signified a thousand times more for Venezuelan democracy than all the sermons of the Jacobins and all the sacred principles enshrined in Constitutions.'[42] So the caudillo derives his authority from the 'unconscious suggestion of the majority'; 'the democratic Ceasar ... is always the representative and the regulator of popular sovereignty'.[43] It is a peculiar definition

[39] Ibid. 123–4.
[40] Ibid. 81.
[41] Ibid. 128–9, 132.
[42] Ibid. 130–1.
[43] Ibid. 122–132.

of democracy, but an essential component of the artifice constructed
by Vallenilla.

Vallenilla Lanz was not the only caesarist in Latin America. The
Peruvian writer Francisco García Calderón also argued for the
need of caudillos in times of crisis, when the instability of Spanish
America's heterogeneous societies called for the firm hand of a
strong leader. But *Cesarismo democrático* occupies a leading place in
the political literature of Latin America. Perhaps it tells us more
about its own time than about the revolution for independence and
its aftermath; but even as a work of historical reference it still lives,
a source of specific data, telling phrases, and original insight. Like
most political theorists, Vallenilla provides a partial, though in-
structive, explanation of the origin and nature of power. His thesis
enshrines the purest version of progressive authoritarianism, producing, from a state of Hobbesian anarchy, the necessary gendarme,
not as a transitional creature on the way to better things but as the
supreme form of government. Yet the book has its flaws. Its purely
theoretical constructs do not accord with history, with the emergence
of a class structure in Venezuela, the incorporation of the caudillos
into the creole oligarchy, the absence of any kind of equality or
democracy in Venezuela in the nineteenth century. They do not
even clarify completely the concept of the necessary gendarme. Is
he a protector of the oligarchy? A protector of the masses? Or is
he the protector of the whole of society against disorder from its
violent and anarchic elements?

The problem remains unresolved, and to this extent Vallenilla is
less lucid than Hobbes. 'During the time men live without a common
power to keep them all in awe, they are in that condition which is
called war; and such a war, as is of every man against every man'.
The only way to defend themselves from the injuries of one another
and the invasion of outsiders is to give up their rights of government
and to confer all their power upon one man. 'For by this authority,
given him by every particular man in the Commonwealth, he has the
use of so much power and strength conferred on him, that by terror
thereof, he is enabled to form the wills of them all, to peace at home,
and mutual aid against their enemies abroad.'[44] The argument serves
the nineteenth-century caudillo as well as the seventeenth-century
absolutist.

---

[44] Thomas Hobbes, *Leviathan* (London, 1976), 64, 89–90.

3. *The Three Ages of Dictatorship*

Rosas, Páez, Santa Anna, and Carrera belonged to an age of primitive caudillism, a phenomenon characteristic of the first half of the nineteenth century, when the economies of Spanish America languished in prolonged stagnation, societies were still dominated by hacendados and military, and the caudillos could rule their countries with little more knowledge of administration than that learnt on their estates or in the army. The defeat of conservatives and the rise of liberals did not necessarily eliminate caudillism and replace it by constitutional forms. It is true that in the decades after 1850 Argentina began to destroy its caudillos and to substitute constitutional government and national organization, but the same interest groups who had supported the caudillos now supported another form of authoritarianism, the republican president. In Mexico politicians sought to break the cycle of coup and counter-coup, and to create a presidential regime based on political and social reform, but in Mexico too the liberals eventually found that they needed a strong executive if only to impose liberalism.

In Venezuela caudillism secured a new lease of life in the second half of the nineteenth century. In the years 1848–63 personalism, clientelism, and reluctance to retire, still characterized the exercise of power, only now it was in the hands of federalists, not conservatives. During this period a new generation of caudillos emerged, men who replaced the heroes of independence and who were nurtured not on patriot or conservative doctrines but on the ideologies of liberalism and federalism. In 1858, with the overthrow of José Gregorio Monagas, the struggle for federalism became the inspiration of major caudillos such as Ezequiel Zamora and Antonio Guzmán Blanco, as well as of the minor caudillos in the provinces. The end of the Federal War in 1863 and the accession of Guzmán Blanco to the presidency in 1870 inaugurated a new phase but not a new structure of caudillism. Guzmán was a caudillo and a modernizer, a dictator and a liberal. He did not have a regional power base, a chain of haciendas or a force of peons. He made his way to the top as a soldier, a politician, and a power broker who could reconcile the interests of regional caudillos, hacendados, and merchants, and allow to each their appropriate quota of power and influence.[45] As

[45] Quintero, *El ocaso de una estirpe*, 21–2.

a caudillo he was his own man, but also a child of his age. He was a caudillo who became a magnate rather than the reverse. Personalism was a key to his actions, violence and cunning his methods; his economic links were to the commercial oligarchy; and he gave the impression, if nothing more, of governing in the name of the liberal cause and of the people. As economies and their political framework were changing, so caudillism was becoming more complex.

In the years after 1870 Latin America entered a period of strong export growth. As foreign capital was invested in agriculture and mining, so resource patterns changed: land use and subsoil wealth were expanded, capital was subject to greater accumulation, and modest progress in technology was recorded. Many economies modernized production, commercialized distribution, and improved their infrastructures—port installations, maritime communications, telegraphs, railways, and roads—to speed the export of products and raw materials. Export-led growth and the incorporation of Latin America into the world market were accompanied and stimulated by new waves of European immigration, above all to Argentina and Brazil, which simultaneously increased—and improved—the work force and multiplied consumers. These developments also promoted social change, whose visible expression was rapid urbanization and increased social mobility. While material prosperity was not shared by all sectors of the population, it gave birth to new groups, who were neither landowners nor peasants, but people who, directly or indirectly, depended on commerce, production, and technology. The middle classes of government and business were beginning to emerge.

Primitive caudillism could not survive in the new economic and social environment. In the first place the caudillos were obstacles to development. Foreign investment, on which the new model of growth depended, needed a minimum of political stability and continuity to guarantee its profits and remittances. Caudillos were not necessarily ephemeral, as has been seen, but their reputation was against them, and it was perceptions that counted. Second, economic development and diversification gave birth to new pressure groups, much more powerful and wealthy than those known to the caudillos and often allied to foreign interests. Rulers had to learn new forms of patronage and clientage. Third, immigration was not indiscriminate. The immigrants, in many cases refugees from political as well as economic adversity, sought by preference regimes which were more or less constitutional, free from secret police and the call in the night. Finally, the new states, products of economic growth and possessors of improved financial resources derived from tax revenues and foreign loans, could not tolerate the existence of political rivals of the caudillo type. The state now had a professional army, modern arms beyond the capacity of a caudillo, and railways capable of extending its authority to the farthest corners of the republic. The state also had a new ideology, positivism, which gave its leaders a theory of social structure and change and introduced the possibility of social planning by a technocratic élite operating under dictatorial government. Positivism had ready reception among those who sought to explain the political and economic backwardness of Latin America and who welcomed the promise of renovation and modernization. To government élites and planners it provided legitimacy for the prevailing economic model and its authoritarian framework. For the middle classes it was a mixture of reformism and conservatism, promising material progress without threatening the social structure.

The pressure of changing conditions and the influence of imported ideology were the framework from which emerged the model of the new dictator, variously called the modernizing dictator or, borrowing the Comtian nomenclature, the dictator of order and progress.[46] Not all of these post-primitive dictators achieved progress or modernization, and perhaps a more appropriate title would be the oligarchic dictator, thus emphasizing the common denominator to be found in his relationship with the dominant élites. The new dictator could be a caudillo in origin, as Guzmán Blanco in Venezuela, and like the caudillo he could be called president and coexist with a legal constitution. But his government was no longer caudillist in structure. While the new dictators might display various caudillo characteristics—personalism, reliance on patronage, propensity to violence—they were also marked by two novel features. First, the dictator worked within a system of government increasingly centralized; larger bureaucracies, more powerful armed forces, and greater revenue enabled him to extend his rule beyond the capital and its province through the length and breadth of the country and to pounce quickly on local dissidents. Second, he had to manage a balance of social forces very different from those manipulated by

[46] Wolf and Hansen, '*Caudillo* Politics: A Structural Analysis', 178.

the primitive caudillo. The new dictator operated as the agent of a political alliance far more complex than the previous alliance of hacendados and military. He was the representative of various interest groups linked to the export economy: landowners, merchants, bankers, foreign businessmen, and client bureaucrats. His rewards no longer derived from simple plunder of the economy, but from deals with the alliance or its components. While a landed estate was still highly valued, a foreign bank account was now an indispensable adjunct to any dictatorship. In turn the dictator acted as the gendarme of the alliance, the chief of the army and of the police, the protector who eliminated all threats to the coalition. The sanction behind the modern dictatorships, it is true, was still violence and state terror, but the political process was no longer as crude as that of their predecessors. Primitive caudillism had never resolved the problem of political succession. The normal method of replacing a caudillo was by a *golpe*, with all its disadvantages. The oligarchic dictators discovered an alternative to the *golpe*, electoral fraud. Thus many of the new dictators survived politically by frequent re-election.

The archetype of this school of dictators was Porfirio Díaz, who ruled Mexico from 1876 to 1911. In his case the label 'order and progress' had some meaning. Peace, stability, centralization, these were the essential conditions for foreign investment and economic growth, which in turn provided the resources to augment the state, extend its agencies, and enforce its decisions. Order encouraged growth, growth generated order. As the export economy grew, as ports were improved and railways built, as industry expanded and trade increased, so the regime appeared to be vindicated and interest groups satisfied. True, villages lost land to haciendas, Indians and peasants were dispossessed and reduced to peons, and the gaols were full to overflowing. But at the centre of the dominant coalition the dictator held firm, co-opting regional oligarchs, incorporating local caciques, managing his clients, and crushing opposition. Yet the power base of order and progress was less secure than it seemed. The collapse of the Porfirian state and the dissolution of central authority in the years after 1910 enabled popular caudillos to seize power and fill the political space, and Mexico reverted to an earlier form of caudillism, in which armed bands dominated the regions and threatened the centre. The new caudillos, however, were not mere reproductions of the old; they were forced to recruit followers from wider peasant and labour sectors, and to offer more radical social reforms than their predecessors. There was thus a transition from traditional to revolutionary caudillos.[47] At the same time another familiar figure reappeared in a new guise, the cacique, or local boss, who through methods of coercion and paternalism assembled a following and acted as a middleman between the rural community and outside government.[48] The revolution institutionalized the relations between the centre and the corporate organizations linked to the official party, the PRI; the caciques were thus marginalized and became more and more dependent on offices and resources derived from above.[49] Between them, the *porfiriato* and the revolutionary state transformed and then eliminated traditional caudillism in Mexico.

Few other Latin American dictatorships reached the status of the *porfiriato*, though some approximated to the model. The peoples of Central America learnt by bitter experience how oligarchic dictators ruled. The governments of Manuel Estrada Cabrera and Jorge Ubico in Guatemala, as well as those of José Santos Zelaya and Anastasio Somoza in Nicaragua were examples of dictatorships of this kind, though with priority towards order rather than progress, a tendency towards corruption rather than modernization, and a survival date well beyond the classic age of the model. Central America remained fixed in the mould of oligarchic dictatorship until the revolution of the 1970s. There were various reasons for this. The Central American oligarchy, a powerful class of landowners, controlled the whole economy of the region and exercised a political despotism through the agency of the dictators. It is true that they faced serious threats in the course of the twentieth century, above all the Sandino rebellion in Nicaragua and the peasant revolt of 1932 in El Salvador. Up to the 1930s the armies of Central America were inferior institutions, badly trained and armed. Then, with the help of the United States and the approval of the oligarchy, new armies were created which crushed the slightest attempt at

---

[47] Alan Knight, 'Peasant and Caudillo in Revolutionary Mexico 1910–17', in D. A. Brading (ed.), *Caudillo and Peasant in the Mexican Revolution* (Cambridge, 1980), 37–40; Heather Fowler Salamini, 'Revolutionary Caudillos in the 1920s: Francisco Múgica and Adalberto Tejeda', ibid., 170.

[48] Gilbert M. Joseph, 'Caciquismo and the Revolution: Carrillo Puerto in Yucatán', ibid. 197.

[49] Luis Roniger, 'Caciquismo and Coronelismo: Contextual Discussions of Patron Brokerage in Mexico and Brazil', *Latin American Research Review*, 22, 2 (1987), 73–4.

popular rebellion and shared political power with the civilian oligarchy. The combination of oligarchic power and military dictatorship ended by closing the doors of political systems which were already highly exclusivist.[50] Some changes the oligarchy could not avoid. The production of coffee encouraged a minimum of modernization and the emergence of a small middle class, while the growth of industry increased the importance of labour. But these new groups were too weak to constitute a populist power base. At the same time, in resisting pressures towards modernization, above all the demands for political participation, the dictators became despots. In Nicaragua the *somocista* regime established a dynastic despotism and so monopolized power that all classes were excluded, workers, middle sectors, even the oligarchy, and in the end only the Somoza family remained within its political fortress. The hereditary dictatorship—this was the exhibit of the Somozas in the museum of politics. It was the culmination of the process, a solution originally sought by some of the primitive caudillos, and one containing a certain logic.

Primitive caudillism and oligarchic dictatorship were two types and stages of personalist rule. There was a third example, the populist dictatorship. This too had its roots in economic change. The World Depression of 1930 dealt a shattering blow to Latin America: it caused a dramatic drop in production and exports, led to mass unemployment, and provoked a nationalist reaction which was as much political as economic in inspiration. There was a shift towards alternative regimes and political extremism. The new politics did not conform to a single mould but included great variety of experimentation. In most of Latin America the reaction favoured the right rather than the left, and the instinct was to revive the traditional export-led economies rather than replace them by new models. In some countries radical or reformist regimes were ousted by movements of the right which offered to replace weakness and uncertainty by a firm government with a strong sense of direction. In Uruguay in 1933 the president, Dr Gabriel Terra, abolished the collegiate executive power, dissolved Congress, and made himself dictator. In Venezuela the dictatorship of Juan Vicente Gómez yielded nothing to the Depression and gave no perceptible sign that

[50] John Weeks, 'An Interpretation of the Central American Crisis', *Latin American Research Review*, 21, 3 (1986), 31–53.

it would change its methods of government or reduce the primacy of petroleum. In Argentina the revolution of 1930 which overthrew Hipólito Yrigoyen, although it received some support from those sectors suffering from high inflation and unemployment, was essentially a military coup led by conservative forces who established a dictatorship in alliance with the landowning class.

Nevertheless, oligarchic dictatorship and the authoritarian state were not the only examples of Latin America's response to the World Depression. The case of Brazil was more typical. In Brazil the Depression produced a populist dictatorship, and the masses rallied in favour of the strong man, Getulio Vargas, hoping he could bring them immediate relief from their privations, while he in turn sought a political base among the urban workers and middle classes. In the process of applying new economic and social policies, Vargas strengthened the state. Activities and services traditionally handled by the *coronéis*, Brazil's equivalent of the caciques, who supplied the gap left by weak municipalities and delivered the votes of the rural electorate, were gradually taken over by agents of national institutions, though the domains of many rural strong men remained untouched.[51]

What does populism mean in this context? The populist state, product of economic depression, was an interventionist state which sought to defend the national economy against foreign pressure and protect the more vulnerable groups against the social effects of shortages, inflation, and unemployment. Thus, populism favoured a protectionist economic policy, and a transfer of resources from agriculture to industry; it expanded labour's share of income, and established the first systems of social security in Latin America. At the same time it was a consensus state seeking electoral representation: its political base was a multi-class alliance, and characteristically the political framework of populism was a coalition of the middle class, bureaucrats, and industrial workers.[52] Some of the primitive caudillos, Rosas for example, evoke vague premonitions of populism: dynamic leadership, economic protection, the appeal to the populace as well as to proprietors. But populism obviously

---

[51] Roniger, 'Caciquismo and Coronelismo', 74–5.
[52] Michael L. Conniff (ed.), *Latin American Populism in Comparative Perspective* (Albuquerque, NM, 1982), 13–23; Torcuato S. Di Tella, *Latin American Politics: A Theoretical Framework* (Austin, Tex., 1990), 97–116.

represented a further stage of political development than caudillism. The caudillo operated from a rural base in an agrarian society, and centred his power in a combination of direct personal relations. The populist leader extended his area of operation to the cities, and his instrument of power was the party. The caudillo was sustained by a series of regional economies and income from customs duties, the populist by appropriating in one way or another the revenue of a centralized state. The populist state was not necessarily a dictatorship. In Mexico the regime of President Lázaro Cárdenas (1934–40) can be seen not only as an extension of the Mexican Revolution but also as a product of the Depression. The political change towards social reformism and economic nationalism, under a strong president not very dissimilar to a dictator, was the populist reaction in Mexico to the tensions caused by the Depression.

Populist dictatorship probably reached its peak in the rule of Juan Domingo Perón in Argentina. In his case the populist model was almost perfect. A strong leader, an interventionist state, a nationalist policy, and a multi-class alliance. These classic components of the populist dictatorship were there from the beginning, when Perón assembled a power base consisting of a mass following combined with key sectors of the upper classes, the military, and the industrialists. In 1945 he led into power a coalition of labour, conservative, and nationalist groups; he then dissolved the parties and replaced them by the Peronist party: 'I'm your leader now. I give the orders and you follow them'.[53] Personal leadership resting on a populist base brought tangible benefits to urban workers and to the military, and it appealed to a wider range of interest groups than did traditional Argentine government. But there was a price to pay. Peronism did not allow for alternatives. It became impossible to obtain any job in the bureaucracy without the endorsement of a Peronist and without an identity card of the Peronist party.[54] And while the political base of government was apparently democratized by the extension of participation to new social groups, the tensions thereby unleashed encouraged the leader to take dictatorial powers, to make everything depend upon himself, to subordinate Congress and the judiciary to his will, to have recourse to the methods of the police

---

[53] Quoted by Joseph A. Page, *Perón: A Biography* (New York, 1983), 139, 161; see also Di Tella, *Latin American Politics*, 116, 138–41.
[54] Félix Luna, *Perón y su tiempo* (3 vols.; Buenos Aires, 1984–6), ii. 17.

state, and finally to urge his working-class supporters to violence. Perón justified his dictatorship in terms of his populism. In July 1955 he declared to Peronist legislators: 'We come from a revolution, not from politics or political action. Revolutionary movements convey rights not available to political action. We are the interpreters of the revolutionary will of the Argentine people.'[55] But populist dictatorships could not escape their military origins, and by 1955 the army and other elements of the populist coalition had ceased to believe in Perón's revolutionary rights, and did not trust his capacity to protect their interests or even to provide good government.

4. *The Shadow of Caudillism*

The history of dictatorships is not the whole history of Latin America. There is another history, one of constitutional progress: presidential government in Chile, the conservative republic in Argentina, the single-party state in Mexico, social democracy in Costa Rica. Cycles of dictatorship and democracy have succeeded each other in response to internal turmoil or external shock. As crisis could spawn caudillos, so crisis can revive constitutions. Nevertheless, even in constitutional regimes traces of the past seem to survive. From primitive caudillism, through oligarchic dictatorship, to populist leaders, the caudillo tradition has left an imprint on the political process. Or so it is perceived.

Perhaps the strongest caudillo quality to survive the hazards of history and the attentions of historians, and to remain an essential component of Latin American political culture is *personalismo*, described by one historian as 'the substitution of ideologies by the personal prestige of the chief'.[56] Personalism means in practice that people tend to give loyalty and obedience to the person who rules rather than to the office he holds.[57] The belief that government and bureaucracy should apply general policies impartially through impersonal institutions is totally alien to this habit of thought. Personalized loyalties and individual allegiance are things which

[55] Quoted ibid. iii. 293.
[56] Germán Carrera Damas, *El culto a Bolívar* (Caracas, 1969), 228.
[57] Luis Britto García, *La máscara del poder* (Caracas, 1988), 93–101.

make the democratic as well as the caudillo system function. People have more confidence in accepting a personal promise from a political chief than a statement in a party manifesto or a guarantee by a government official. Personalism is thus something learnt from experience, a legacy from the age of caudillism, when it was first practised as a form of government. It has been bequeathed not only to governments but also to trade unions. In Argentina Peronist trade-union leaders, operating as typical caudillos, derived their authority less from bureaucratic office than from personal struggles and individual renown.[58]

The bond between patron and client, expressed in the time of the caudillos in its primitive form of *patrón*–peon, is an essential element of social relations in Spanish America. Patronage is a passport to politics. There is no other way to achieve success. It is true that patronage politics does not completely remove the need for a programme; parties, like caudillos, crave a cause, but this is less important than access to power and privilege. Government is seen not as an instrument of policy but as a source of office, promotion, contract, licence, permission to break the law, and other forms of patronage. Political decisions and obedience are motivated by giving and receiving rewards, and politics are seen as a defence of the nearest interest groups—immediate family, extended family, friends, and clients—rather than a service for the common good. Relations between members of these groups are characterized by confidence and mutual aid, towards outsiders by fear and distrust. Again, these habits have been learnt by experience. The first caudillos could only trust their friends and supporters, subsequent generations of dictators their immediate interest groups. For the popular classes it is an obvious preference; now as then they live in a world where policy is a delusion and the only security lies in solidarity with their group and its leader.

In Argentina the word caudillo endured in the post-caudillo age to describe not a chieftain on horseback but a political cacique, or boss: now the caudillo was a man who could assemble votes in a *barrio*, a city, or a province, and deliver them to the party. The new political caudillos expressed the same values and employed the same methods as the primitive *jefes*, that is personalism and patronage. Without the personal link between patron and client the political

[58] Di Tella, *Latin American Politics*, 113, 136–7.

parties could not function. The political chief needs a *clientela*, and he obtains votes not by general declarations to the electorate but by specific promises to clients. The cause, or the programme in action, becomes the gift or sweetener.[59] In some cases these clients are individuals—friends, extended families, political collaborators, party workers—and the system is open to corruption. In other cases the client is an economic interest—a business enterprise, a social sector, a particular region—and political patronage is a form of negotiation with the corporate groups in a society. The system of patronage is inherent in political parties such as the Peronists in Argentina, Acción Democrática in Venezuela, and the PRI in Mexico—though by no means exclusive to these—and means that the parties normally gain power not on the basis of a clear ideology or a firm policy, but through the distribution of rewards in the style of the caudillos. In the days of primitive caudillism the characteristic reward was land or booty, though not on a scale that would change the agrarian structure, for that would be classified as policy. The rewards were given by the caudillo as personal gestures, for a special occasion, on impulse, at a request, and basically the intention was always to secure a following. The resource utilized was usually one in which the state had a surplus. In the nineteenth century this was land; from 1920 Venezuelan caudillos could reward from a new resource, petroleum income. In contemporary politics rewards are no longer treated as booty but as promises made by political parties, but these promises are made to people as clients with expectations, not citizens with rights. And rewards, especially offices, jobs, and perquisites, are promoted as gifts of the party rather than donations of the state.

The succession was always a problem for the caudillos. Some tried to remain in power for life; others to create a dynasty; most to nominate their successors. A caudillo would nominate either a weak successor, whom he could dominate, or a similar successor, whom he could support, or an unacceptable successor, whom he would have to depose. Few were as successful as Rafael Carrera, who opted for life presidency and nominated his successor, a pure Bolivarian formula. Even Alberdi was convinced that strong presidential government must be able to influence elections, to avoid dependence on public opinion and excessive discontinuity in office. Modern political parties do not work in exactly the same way as those of

[59] Britto García, *La máscara del poder*, 225.

the liberal oligarchies, but political manipulation rather than pure democracy operates in the choice of presidential candidates. The political parties try to control the succession by nominating candidates who will not upset the status quo and will be acceptable to the political interest groups. In Mexico presidential and other candidates emerge from the arcane selection procedures of the PRI, where deals, rather than democracy, prevail. In Venezuela powerful political figures, usually ex-presidents with long survival records, dominate the selection procedure.[60] In Argentina Peronist leadership was monopolized for so long by Perón that succession problems were postponed to rise with greater force when Peronism had to survive without Perón.

The caudillos are dead, but caudillo values endure. Or do they? Precision in tracing ideological influences, intellectual causation, and political lineage is notoriously elusive, not least in a phenomenon like dictatorship, recurring, long-lived, and clothed in many forms. The temptation inherent in seeking origins and survivals is to exaggerate those values and practices in which the influence of the past is shown, and by linking later developments too closely with their predecessors to obscure change and innovation. Traces of the primitive caudillo can be found in Perón, signs not necessarily inherited in unbroken sequence from Juan Manuel de Rosas, but exhibited by all dictatorships when subject to pressures from above and below. Absolutism, exclusivism, abuse of patronage, recourse to violence, these practices are common to both dictators, but who is to say that Perón received them from primitive caudillism rather than authoritarian liberalism, or the world of the twentieth century? Many of the features of contemporary politics in Latin America, for example authoritarianism, demagogy, and violence, might appear to be survivals of caudillism, but on closer inspection are seen to be so common and universal that they could belong to almost any political tradition; others, such as nepotism, patriarchism, and corruption, are attributable not so much to caudillos as to social behaviour under the caudillos for which they themselves were not specifically responsible.

History is often used to justify as well as to explain, to trace modern ills to former injustices as well as to seek the truth of things; so contemporary problems and responses are imputed to the colonial

---

[60] Ibid. 154–69.

legacy, the caudillo influence, the dependency experience, inducing a political fatalism which sees the hand of history in every crisis. The caudillo casts his shadow still over Spanish America, a presence from the past which cannot be effaced.

BIBLIOGRAPHY

I
Primary Sources

1. *Archives*

Archivo General de la Nación, Buenos Aires
Sala 7. Documentación Donada y Adquirida
Archivo Adolfo Saldías–Juan Farini
Colección Celesia
Sala 10. División Nacional, Sección Gobierno
Correspondencia Confidencial, Secretaría de Rosas
Gobierno, Solicitudes, Embargos

Archivo General de la Nación, Caracas
Gobernacion y Capitanía General, vols. xxii–lxviii, 1779–98
Secretaría del Interior y Justicia, vols. iii–ccclxxvi, 1830–48

Archivo de la Academia Nacional de la Historia, Caracas
General José Antonio Páez, Correspondencia Privada
Oficios del General Páez
Landaeta Rosales: Documentos de los Archivos, Escritos y Documentos

Archivo General de Indias, Seville
Audiencia de Buenos Aires: Legajos 140–3
Audiencia de Caracas: Legajos 167, 201

Biblioteca Nacional, Madrid
MSS. 3073

British Library, London
Additional MSS. 17,592, 32,604
Additional MSS. 43,124, 43,126, 43,127 (Aberdeen Papers)
Egerton MS. 1815

Historical Manuscripts Commission, London
Palmerston Papers
  General Correspondence

Public Record Office, London
Foreign Office, General Correspondence
  FO 6, Argentina, 1823–52
  FO 15, Central America and Guatemala, 1837–55
  FO 18, Colombia, 1826–34
  FO 80, Venezuela, 1835–63

FO 50, Mexico, 1824–55, 1864, 1867
Embassy and Consular Archives
FO 199, 1844–59, Venezuela

2. *Published Documents and Contemporary Works*

ALAMÁN, LUCAS, *Historia de Méjico* (5 vols.; Mexico, 1849–52).
ALBERDI, JUAN BAUTISTA, *Escritos póstumos* (16 vols.; Buenos Aires, 1895– 1901).
—— *Obras completas* (8 vols.; Buenos Aires, 1886–7).
—— *Las 'Bases' de Alberdi*, ed. Jorge M. Mayer (Buenos Aires, 1969).
ANGELIS, PEDRO DE, *Colección de obras y documentos relativos a la historia antigua y moderna de las provincias del Río de la Plata*, 2nd edn. (5 vols.; Buenos Aires, 1910).
ARÁOZ DE LA MADRID, GREGORIO, *Memorias del general Gregorio Aráoz de La Madrid* (2 vols.; Buenos Aires, 1860).
Archivo de Sucre (Caracas, 1973–).
Archivo Histórico de la Provincia de Buenos Aires, *Mensajes de los gobernadores de la provincia de Buenos Aires 1822–1849* (2 vols.; La Plata, 1976).
ARELLANO MORENO, ANTONIO (ed.), *Mensajes Presidenciales*, i: *1830– 1875* (Caracas, 1970).
ARRANGOIZ Y BARZÁBAL, FRANCISCO DE PAULA, *México desde 1808 hasta 1867*, 2nd edn. (Mexico, 1968).
AUSTRIA, JOSÉ DE, *Bosquejo de la historia militar de Venezuela* (2 vols.; Madrid, 1960).
AZARA, FÉLIX DE, *Memoria sobre el estado rural del Río de la Plata y otros informes* (Buenos Aires, 1943).
BERUTI, JUAN MANUEL, *Memorias curiosas*, Biblioteca de Mayo (17 vols.; Buenos Aires, 1960).
BOLÍVAR, SIMÓN, *Cartas del Libertador*, ed. Vicente Lecuna (12 vols.; Caracas, 1929–59).
—— *Escritos del Libertador* (Caracas, 1964–).
—— *Obras completas*, 2nd edn., ed. Vicente Lecuna and Esther Barret de Nazarís (3 vols.; Havana, 1950).
—— *Proclamas y discursos del Libertador*, ed. Vicente Lecuna (Caracas, 1939).
—— *Selected Writings of Bolívar*, ed. Vicente Lecuna and Harold A. Bierck, Jr., (2 vols.; New York, 1951).
BUSTAMANTE, CARLOS MARÍA DE, *Apuntes para la historia del gobierno del General D. Antonio López de Santa-Anna* (Mexico, 1845).
—— *Cuadro histórico de la revolución mexicana* (3 vols.; Mexico, 1961).
—— *Continuación del cuadro histórico de la revolución mexicana* (4 vols.; Mexico, 1953–63).

—— *El Gabinete Mexicano durante el segundo período de la administración del Exmo. Señor Presidente D. Anastasio Bustamante hasta la entrega del mando al Exmo. Señor Presidente interino D. Antonio López de Santa-Anna* (2 vols.; Mexico, 1842).

CALDERÓN DE LA BARCA, FRANCES E., *Life in Mexico* (New York, 1931).

CARRERA, RAFAEL, *Memorias 1837 á 1840* (Guatemala, 1979).

CODAZZI, AGUSTÍN, *Obras escogidas* (2 vols.; Caracas, 1960).

—— *Resumen de la geografía de Venezuela* (3 vols.; Caracas, 1940).

CORTÁZAR, ROBERTO (ed.), *Cartas y mensajes del General Francisco de Paula Santander, 1812–1840* (10 vols.; Bogotá, 1953–6).

DARWIN, CHARLES, *Journal of Researches into the Natural History and Geology of the Countries Visited during the Voyage of H.M.S. 'Beagle' round the World*, 9th ed. (London, 1890).

DELLEPIANE, ANTONIO, *El testamento de Rosas* (Buenos Aires, 1957).

DÍAZ, CÉSAR, *Memorias, 1842–1952: Arroyo Grande; sitio de Montevideo; Caseros* (Buenos Aires, 1943).

DÍAZ, JOSÉ DOMINGO, *Recuerdos sobre la rebelión de Caracas* (Madrid, 1961).

DUNBAR TEMPLE, ELLA (ed.), *La accion patriótica del pueblo en la emancipación: Guerrillas y montoneras* (CDIP 5; 6 vols.; Lima, 1971–5).

DUNLOP, ROBERT GLASGOW, *Travels in Central America, being a Journal of Nearly Three Years' Residence in the Country* (London, 1847).

EASTWICK, EDWARD B., *Venezuela: or, Sketches of Life in a South-American Republic; with the History of the Loan of 1864*, 2nd edn. (London, 1868).

ESPOZ Y MINA, FRANCISCO, *Memorias*, ed. M. Artola (BAE 146–7; Madrid, 1961–2).

GRAHAM, GERALD S., and HUMPHREYS, R. A. (eds.), *The Navy and South America 1807–1823: Correspondence of the Commanders-in-Chief on the South American Station* (London, 1962).

HAWKSHAW, JOHN, *Reminiscences of South America from Two and a Half Years' Residence in Venezuela* (London, 1838).

—— *Reminiscencias de Sudamérica: dos años y medio de residencia en Venezuela* (Caracas, 1975).

HEREDIA, JOSÉ FRANCISCO, *Memorias del Regente Heredia* (Madrid, n.d.).

HUMBOLDT, ALEXANDER VON, *Ensayo político sobre el reino de la Nueva España*, 6th Sp. edn. (4 vols.; Mexico, 1941).

—— *Personal Narrative of Travels to the Equinoctial Region of the New Continent during the Years 1799–1804* (6 vols.; London, 1814–29).

Instituto de Historia Argentina y Americana 'Doctor Emilio Ravignani', *Archivo del brigadier general Juan Facundo Quiroga* (4 vols.; Buenos Aires, 1957–88).

KING, JOHN ANTHONY, *Twenty-Four Years in the Argentine Republic* (London, 1846).

LAMAS, ANDRÉS, *Escritos políticos y literarios durante la guerra contra la tiranía de D. Juan Manuel de Rosas*, ed. Angel J. Carranza (Buenos Aires, 1877).

LATHAM, WILFRID, *The States of the River Plate*, 2nd edn. (London, 1868).
LEMOINE VILLICAÑA, ERNESTO, *Morelos, su vida revolucionaria a través de sus escritos y de otros testimonios de la época* (Mexico, 1965).
LÓPEZ DE SANTA ANNA, ANTONIO, *Mi historia militar y política, 1810–1874* (Mexico, 1905).
—— *The Eagle: The Autobiography of Santa Anna*, ed. Ann Fears Crawford (Austin, Tex., 1967).
MACCANN, WILLIAM, *Two Thousand Miles' Ride through the Argentine Provinces* (2 vols.; London, 1853).
MARTIN DE MOUSSY, VICTOR, *Description géographique et statistique de la Conféderation Argentine* (3 vols.; Paris, 1860–4).
MICHELENA, TOMÁS, *Resumen de la vida militar y política del ciudadano esclarecido General José Antonio Páez* (BANH, FHRV 6; Caracas, 1973).
MILLER, JOHN (ed.), *Memoirs of General Miller in the Service of the Republic of Peru*, 2nd edn. (2 vols.; London, 1829).
MORA, JOSÉ MARÍA LUIS, *Obras sueltas*, 2nd edn. (Mexico, 1963).
NICOLAU, JUAN CARLOS (ed.), *Correspondencia inédita entre Juan Manuel de Rosas y Manuel José García* (Instituto de Estudios Histórico-Sociales; Tandil, 1989).
ODRIOZOLA, MANUEL DE (ed.), *Documentos históricos del Perú* (10 vols.; Lima, 1863–79).
O'LEARY, DANIEL FLORENCIO, *Memorias del General O'Leary* (34 vols.; Caracas, 1981).
—— *Memorias del General Daniel Florencio O'Leary: Narración* (3 vols.; Caracas, 1952).
—— *The 'Detached Recollections' of General D. F. O'Leary*, ed. R. A. Humphreys (London, 1969).
PÁEZ, JOSÉ ANTONIO, *Archivo del General José Antonio Páez* (BANH, FHRV 3–4; 2 vols.; Caracas, 1973).
—— *Autobiografía del General José Antonio Páez* (BANH, FHRV 1–2; 2 vols.; Caracas, 1973).
—— 'Correspondencia del General Páez (1826–27)', *BAGN* 129, 33 (1945), 301–62.
—— 'Correspondencia del General Páez (1827)', *BAGN* 133, 34 (1946), 29–43.
PÁEZ, RAMÓN, *Wild Scenes in South America: Or Life in the Llanos of Venezuela* (London, 1863).
—— *Escenas rústicas en Sur América: O la vida en los llanos de Venezuela* (BANH, FHRV 8; Caracas, 1973).
PARISH, SIR WOODBINE, *Buenos Ayres and the Provinces of the Rio de la Plata*, 2nd edn. (London, 1852).
PAZ, JOSÉ MARÍA, *Memorias póstumas*, 2nd edn. (3 vols.; La Plata, 1892).
—— *Memorias póstumas*, ed. Armando Braun Menéndez (Buenos Aires, 1945).

PERÚ DE LACROIX, L., *Diario de Bucaramanga* (Caracas, 1976).
PORTER, Sir Robert Ker *Porter's Caracas Diary, 1825–1842*, ed. Walter Dupouy (Caracas, 1966).
POSADA GUTIÉRREZ, JOAQUÍN, *Memorias histórico-políticas* (*BHN* 41–4, 4 vols.; Bogotá, 1929).
Presidencia de la República, *Las fuerzas armadas de Venezuela en el siglo XIX: Textos para su estudio*, 12 vols.; Caracas, 1963–71).
—— *Pensamiento político venezolano del siglo XIX: Textos para su estudio* (15 vols.; Caracas, 1960–2).
PRIETO, GUILLERMO, *Memorias de mis tiempos, 1828 a 1853* (2 vols.; Mexico, 1948).
RADAELLI, SIGFRIDO A. (ed.), *Memorias de los virreyes del Río de la Plata* (Buenos Aires, 1945).
RAVIGNANI, EMILIO (ed.), *Asambleas constituyentes argentinas* (6 vols.; Buenos Aires, 1937–9).
REVENGA, JOSÉ RAFAEL, *La hacienda pública de Venezuela en 1828–1830*, ed. Pedro Grases and Manuel Pérez Vila (Caracas, 1953).
RODRÍGUEZ, GREGORIO F. (ed.), *Contribución histórica y documental* (3 vols.; Buenos Aires, 1921–2).
ROSAS, JUAN MANUEL DE, *Cartas del exilio, 1853–1875*, ed. José Raed (Buenos Aires, 1974).
—— *Correspondencia entre Rosas, Quiroga y López*, ed. Enrique M. Barba (Buenos Aires, 1958).
—— *El pensamiento político de Juan Manuel de Rosas*, ed. Andrés M. Carretero (Buenos Aires, 1970).
SALDÍAS, ADOLFO (ed.), *Papeles de Rozas* (2 vols.; La Plata, 1904–7).
—— *Papeles de Rosas*, i: *1829–1834* (Buenos Aires, 1948).
SANTA ANNA. See López de Santa Anna.
SARMIENTO, DOMINGO FAUSTINO, *Campaña en el ejército grande aliado de Sud América*, ed. Tulio Halperín Donghi (Mexico, Buenos Aires, 1958).
—— *Facundo*, edición crítica y documentada, Prólogo de Alberto Palcos (La Plata, 1938).
—— *Obras de D. F. Sarmiento* (53 vols.; Santiago and Buenos Aires, 1887–1903).
—— *Obras selectas*, ed. Enrique de Gandia, iii: *Juan Manuel de Rosas: su política, su caída, su herencia* (Buenos Aires, 1944).
STEPHENS, JOHN LLOYD, *Incidents of Travel in Central America, Chiapas, and Yucatan*, ed. Richard L. Predmore (2 vols.; New Brunswick, 1949).
SUÁREZ Y NAVARRO, JUAN, *El general Santa-Anna burlándose de la nación en su despedida hecha en Perote* (Mexico, 1856).
Universidad Central de Venezuela, *Materiales para el estudio de la cuestión agraria en Venezuela (1829–1830)*, i (Caracas, 1964).
—— *Materiales para el estudio de la cuestión agraria en Venezuela (1829–1860): Enajenación y arrendamiento de tierras baldías*, i (Caracas, 1971).

—— *Materiales para el estudio de la cuestión agraria en Venezuela (1810–1865).*
Mano de obra: Legislación y administración, i (Caracas, 1979).

VARGAS, JOSÉ SANTOS, *Diario de un comandante de la independencia americana 1814–1825*, ed. Gunnar Mendoza L. (Mexico, 1982).

ZAVALA, LORENZO DE, *Ensayo histórico de las revoluciones de México desde 1808 hasta 1830*, in *Obras* (Mexico, 1969).

ZINNY, ANTONIO, *La Gaceta Mercantil de Buenos Aires, 1823–1852* (3 vols.; Buenos Aires, 1912).

II
Secondary Works

AGUIRRE, CARLOS, and WALKER, CHARLES, (eds.), *Bandoleros, abigeos y montoneros: Criminalidad y violencia en el Perú, siglos XVIII–XX* (Lima, 1990).

AMARAL, SAMUEL, 'Rural Production and Labour in Late Colonial Buenos Aires', *JLAS* 19, 2 (1987), 235–78.

ARANA(H), ENRIQUE, *Juan Manuel de Rosas en la historia argentina* (3 vols.; Buenos Aires, 1954).

ARCHER, CHRISTON I., *The Army in Bourbon Mexico, 1760–1810* (Albuquerque, NM, 1977).

—— 'Banditry and Revolution in New Spain, 1790–1821', in Paul J. Vanderwood (ed.), 'Social Banditry and Spanish American Independence', *Biblioteca Americana*, 1, 2 (1982), 59–90.

ARMAS CHITTY, J. A. DE, *Vida política de Caracas en el siglo XIX* (Caracas, 1976).

ARNADE, CHARLES W., *The Emergence of the Republic of Bolivia* (Gainesville, Fla., 1957).

ARRIOLA, JORGE LUIS, *Gálvez en la encrucijada* (Mexico, 1961).

ARZE AGUIRRE, RENÉ DANILO, *Participación popular en la independencia de Bolivia* (La Paz, 1979).

AZCUY AMEGHINO, EDUARDO, *Artigas en la historia argentina* (Buenos Aires, 1986).

BARBA, ENRIQUE M., *Como llegó Rosas al poder* (Buenos Aires, 1972).

—— *Quiroga y Rosas*, 2nd edn. (Buenos Aires, 1974).

BAZANT, JAN, *Alienation of Church Wealth in Mexico: Social and Economic Aspects of the Liberal Revolution 1856–1875* (Cambridge, 1971).

—— *Cinco haciendas mexicanas: Tres siglos de vida rural en San Luis Potosí 1600–1910* (Mexico, 1975).

BELTRÁN GALLARDO, EZEQUIEL, *Las guerrillas de Yauyos en la emancipación del Perú 1820–1824* (Lima, 1977).

BELTRANENA SINIBALDI, LUIS, *Fundación de la República de Guatemala* (Guatemala, 1971).

BERNALDO DE QUIRÓS, CONSTANCIO, and ARDILA, LUIS, *El bandolerismo andaluz* (Madrid, 1973).

BETHELL, LESLIE (ed.), *The Cambridge History of Latin America*, iii (Cambridge, 1985).

BONILLA, HERACLIO, 'Bolívar y las guerrillas indígenas en el Perú', *Cultura, Revista del Banco Central del Ecuador*, 6, 16 (1983), 81–95.

—— et al., *La independencia en el Perú*, 2nd edn. (Lima, 1981).

BRADING, D. A., *The First America: The Spanish Monarchy, Creole Patriots, and the Liberal State 1492–1867* (Cambridge, 1991).

—— *Haciendas and Ranchos in the Mexican Bajío: León 1700–1860* (Cambridge, 1978).

—— *The Origins of Mexican Nationalism* (Cambridge, 1985).

—— (ed.), *Caudillo and Peasant in the Mexican Revolution* (Cambridge, 1980).

BRITO FIGUEROA, FEDERICO, *Historia económica y social de Venezuela* (2 vols.; Caracas, 1966).

—— *Tiempo de Ezequiel Zamora* (Caracas, 1974).

BRITTO GARCÍA, LUIS, *La máscara del poder* (Caracas, 1988).

BROWN, JONATHAN C., *A Socioeconomic History of Argentina, 1776–1860* (Cambridge, 1979).

BURGIN, MIRON, *The Economic Aspects of Argentine Federalism 1820–1852* (Cambridge, Mass., 1946).

BURKE, EDMUND, *Reflections on the Revolution in France* (London, 1986).

BURNS, E. BRADFORD, *The Poverty of Progress: Latin America in the Nineteenth Century* (Berkeley and Los Angeles, 1980).

BUSHNELL, DAVID, 'The Last Dictatorship: Betrayal or Consummation?', *HAHR* 63, 1 (1983), 65–105.

—— *Reform and Reaction in the Platine Provinces 1810–1852* (Gainesville, Fla., 1983).

—— *The Santander Regime in Gran Colombia* (Newark, Del., 1954).

BUVE, RAYMOND T. J., 'Peasant Movements, Caudillos and Land Reform during the Revolution (1910–1917) in Tlaxcala, Mexico', *Boletín de Estudios Latinoamericanos y del Caribe*, 18 (1975), 112–52.

CALLCOTT, WILFRID HARDY, *Santa Anna: the Story of an Enigma Who Once Was Mexico* (Norman, Okla., 1936).

CAMPBELL, LEON G., *The Military and Society in Colonial Peru 1750–1810* (Philadelphia, 1978).

CAMPOBASSI, JOSÉ S., *Sarmiento y su época* (2 vols.; Buenos Aires, 1975).

CARDOSO, CIRO (ed.), *México en el siglo XIX (1821–1910): historia económica y de la estructura social* (Mexico, 1980).

CARL, GEORGE EDMUND, *First among Equals: Great Britain and Venezuela 1810–1910* (Syracuse University/UMI, Ann Arbor, Mich., 1980).

CARLYLE, THOMAS, 'Dr. Francia', in *Critical and Miscellaneous Essays* (4 vols. in 2; London, 1888), iv. 249–94.

—— *On Heroes, Hero-Worship, and the Heroic in History* (London, 1901).

CARRANZA, ANGEL J., *La revolución del 39 en el sur de Buenos Aires* (Buenos Aires, 1919).

CARRERA DAMAS, GERMÁN, *Boves: Aspectos socio-economicos de su acción histórica* (Caracas, 1968).

—— *El culto a Bolívar* (Caracas, 1969).

—— *Historia de la historiografía venezolana (Textos para su estudio)*, 2nd edn., vol. i (Caracas, 1985).

—— 'El nacionalismo latinoamericano en perspectiva histórica', *Revista Mexicana de Sociología*, 38, 4 (1976), 783–91.

—— *Venezuela: Proyecto nacional y poder social* (Barcelona, 1986).

CARRETERO, ANDRÉS M., 'Contribución al conocimiento de la propiedad rural en la provincia de Buenos Aires para 1830', *Boletín del Instituto de Historia Argentina 'Doctor Emilio Ravignani'*, 2nd ser. 13, 22–3 (1970), 246–92.

—— *La propiedad de la tierra en la época de Rosas* (Buenos Aires, 1972).

CASTAGNINO, RAÚL HÉCTOR, *Rosas y los Jesuítas* (Buenos Aires, 1970).

CASTELLANOS, RAFAEL RAMÓN, *Páez, peregrino y proscripto (1848–1851)* (Caracas, 1975).

CASTILLO BLOMQUIST, RAFAEL E., *José Tadeo Monagas: Auge y consolidación de un caudillo* (Caracas, 1984).

CELESIA, ERNESTO H., *Rosas, aportes para su historia*, 2nd edn. (2 vols.; Buenos Aires, 1968).

CHEVALIER, FRANÇOIS, *Land and Society in Colonial Mexico: The Great Hacienda* (Berkeley, Calif., 1963).

CHIARAMONTE, JOSÉ CARLOS, 'Finanzas públicas de las provincias del Litoral, 1821–1841', *Anuario del IEHS*, 1 (Tandil, 1986), 159–98.

—— 'Legalidad constitucional o caudillismo: el problema del orden social en el surgimiento de los estados autónomos del Litoral argentino en la primera mitad del siglo XIX', *Desarrollo Económico*, 26, 102 (1986), 175–96.

COLLIER, SIMON, 'Nationality, Nationalism and Supranationalism in the Writings of Simón Bolívar', *HAHR* 63, 1 (1983), 37–64.

CONNIFF, MICHAEL L. (ed.), *Latin American Populism in Comparative Perspective* (Albuquerque, NM, 1982).

CORONADO AGUILAR, MANUEL, *Apuntes Histórico-Guatemalenses* (Guatemala, 1975).

COSTELOE, MICHAEL P., *Church and State in Independent Mexico: A Study of the Patronage Debate 1821–1857* (London, 1978).

—— 'Generals versus Politicians: Santa Anna and the 1842 Congressional Elections in Mexico', *BLAR* 8, 2 (1989), 257–74.

—— 'The Mexican Church and the Rebellion of the Polkos', *HAHR* 46, 2 (1966), 170–8.

—— *La Primera República Federal de México (1824–1835)* (Mexico, 1975).

—— 'A Pronunciamiento in Nineteenth Century Mexico: "15 de julio de 1840"', *Mexican Studies*, 4, 2, (1988), 245–64.

—— 'The Triangular Revolt in Mexico and the Fall of Anastasio Bustamante, August–October 1841', *JLAS* 20 (1988), 337–60.

CUNNINGHAME GRAHAM, R. B., *José Antonio Páez* (London, 1929).

DÍAZ, BENITO, *Juzgados de paz de campaña de la provincia de Buenos Aires (1821–1854)* (La Plata, 1959).

DÍAZ DÍAZ, FERNANDO, *Caudillos y caciques: Antonio López de Santa Anna y Juan Álvarez* (Mexico, 1972).

DÍAZ DÍAZ, OSWALDO, *Los Almeydas* (BHN, 99, Bogotá, 1962).

DI TELLA, TORCUATO S., 'The Dangerous Classes in Early Nineteenth-Century Mexico', *JLAS* 5, 1 (1973), 79–105.

—— *Latin American Politics: A Theoretical Framework* (Austin, Tex., 1990).

DOMÍNGUEZ, JORGE I., *Insurrection or Loyalty: The Breakdown of the Spanish American Empire* (Cambridge, Mass., 1980).

ECHEVERRÍA, ESTEBAN, *Dogma socialista* (La Plata, 1940).

EISENSTADT, S. N., and RONIGER, LUIS, 'The Study of Patron–Client Relations and Recent Developments in Sociological Theory', in S. N. Eisenstadt and Rene Lemarchand (eds.), *Political Clientelism, Patronage and Development* (London, 1981), 271–95.

ESDAILE, CHARLES J., *The Spanish Army in the Peninsular War* (Manchester, 1988).

FERRIGNI VARELA, YOSTON, *Crecimiento y depresión: La economía venezolana en la época conservadora 1828–1848* (Caracas, 1983).

FISHER, JOHN, *Government and Society in Colonial Peru: The Intendant System 1784–1814* (London, 1970).

FLORES GALINDO, ALBERTO, *Aristocracia y plebe: Lima 1760–1830* (Lima, 1984).

—— *Buscando un Inca: Identidad y utopia en los Andes* (Lima, 1987).

FUENTES MARES, JOSÉ, *Santa Anna, el hombre*, 5th edn. (Mexico, 1984).

FUNDACIÓN, JOHN BOULTON, *Política y economía en Venezuela 1810–1976* (Caracas, 1976).

GABALDÓN, ELEANORA, *Las elecciones presidenciales de 1835 (la elección del Dr. José María Vargas)* (BANH, FHRV, Caracas, 1986).

GARAVAGLIA, JUAN CARLOS, 'Economic Growth and Regional Differentiations: The River Plate Region at the End of the Eighteenth Century', *HAHR* 65, 1 (1985), 51–89.

—— and GELMAN, JORGE, *El mundo rural rioplatense a fines de la época colonial: estudios sobre producción y mano de obra* (Buenos Aires, 1989).

GELLNER, ERNEST, *Nations and Nationalism* (Oxford, 1983).

GELMAN, JORGE, 'New Perspectives on an Old Problem and the Same Source: The Gaucho and the Rural History of the Colonial Río de la Plata', *HAHR* 69, 4 (1989), 715–31.

GIANELLO, LEONCIO, *Estanislao López* (Santa Fe, Argentina, 1955).

GIL FORTOUL, JOSÉ, *Historia constitucional de Venezuela*, 2nd edn. (3 vols.; Caracas, 1930).

GILMORE, ROBERT L., *Caudillism and Militarism in Venezuela, 1810–1910* (Athens, Oh., 1964).

GIMÉNEZ, MANUEL MARÍA, *Memorias del coronel Manuel María Giménez, ayudante de campo del General Santa-Anna, 1798–1878* (Mexico, 1911).

GONZÁLEZ BERNALDO, PILAR, 'El imaginario social y sus implicaciones políticas en un conflicto rural: El levantamiento de 1829' (unpublished paper).

GONZÁLEZ GUINÁN, FRANCISCO, *Historia contemporánea de Venezuela*, 2nd edn. (15 vols.; Caracas, 1954).

GONZÁLEZ NAVARRO, MOISÉS, *Anatomía del poder en México 1848–1853* (Mexico, 1977).

—— 'La era de Santa Anna', *Historia documental de México*, 2nd edn., ii, (Mexico, 1974), 155–254.

—— *Raza y Tierra: La guerra de castas y el henequén* (Mexico, 1970).

GORI, GASTÓN, *Vagos y mal entretenidos: Aporte al tema hernandiano*, 2nd edn. (Santa Fe, Argentina, 1965).

GREEN, STANLEY C., *The Mexican Republic: The First Decade 1823–1832* (Pittsburgh, 1987).

GRIFFITH, WILLIAM J., *Empires in the Wilderness: Foreign Colonization and Development in Guatemala, 1834–1844* (Chapel Hill, NC, 1965).

GUARDINO, PETER, 'Las guerrillas y la independencia peruana: Un ensayo de interpretación', *Pasado y Presente*, 2, 3 (1989), 101–17.

HAIGH, ROGER M., *Martín Güemes: Tyrant or Tool? A Study of the Sources of Power of an Argentine Caudillo* (Fort Worth, Tex., 1968).

HALPERÍN DONGHI, TULIO, *Argentina: De la revolución de independencia a la confederación rosista* (Buenos Aires, 1972).

—— *El espejo de la historia: Problemas argentinas y perspectivas hispano-americanas* (Buenos Aires, 1987).

—— 'La expansión ganadera en la campaña de Buenos Aires (1810–1852)', *Desarrollo Económico*, 3 (1963), 57–110.

—— *Guerra y finanzas en los orígenes del estado argentino (1791–1850)* (Buenos Aires, 1982).

—— *Hispanoamérica después de la independencia: Consecuencias sociales y económicos de la emancipación* (Buenos Aires, 1972).

—— *Politics, Economics and Society in Argentina in the Revolutionary Period* (Cambridge, 1975).

—— 'La revolución y la crisis de la estructura mercantil colonial en el Río de la Plata', *Estudios de Historia Social*, 2 (1966), 78–125.

—— 'El surgimiento de los caudillos en el marco de la sociedad rioplatense postrevolucionaria', *Estudios de Historia Social*, 1 (1965), 121–49.

HAMILL, HUGH M., JR. (ed.), *Dictatorship in Spanish America* (New York, 1965).

—— *The Hidalgo Revolt: Prelude to Mexican Independence* (Gainesville, Fla. 1966).

HAMNETT, BRIAN R., *Roots of Insurgency: Mexican Regions, 1750–1824* (Cambridge, 1986).

HARWICH VALLENILLA, NIKITA, 'Venezuelan Positivism and Modernity', *HAHR* 70, 2 (1991), 327–44.

HERNÁNDEZ DE LEÓN, FEDERICO, *El libro de las efemérides: Capítulos de la historia de la América Central* (8 vols.; Guatemala, 1925–66).

HOBBES, THOMAS, *Leviathan* (Everyman's Library; London, 1976).

HOBSBAWM, ERIC J., *Bandits* (New York, 1981).

—— *Primitive Rebels: Studies in Archaic Forms of Social Movement in the Nineteenth and Twentieth Centuries* (Manchester, 1959).

HUDSON, W. H., *Far Away and Long Ago* (Everyman's Library; London, 1967).

—— *Tales of the Pampa* (London, 1916).

HUMPHREYS, R. A., *Tradition and Revolt in Latin America* (London, 1969).

HÜNEFELDT, CHRISTINE, 'Cimarrones, bandoleros y milicianos: 1821', *Histórica*, 3, 2 (1979), 71–89.

IBARGUREN, CARLOS, *Juan Manuel de Rosas: Su vida, su drama, su tiempo* (Buenos Aires, 1961).

INGERSOLL, HAZEL M. B., *The War of the Mountain: A Study of Reactionary Peasant Insurgency in Guatemala, 1837–1873* (George Washington Univ. Ph.D., thesis, 1972; University Microfilms, Ann Arbor, Mich., 1972).

IRAZUSTA, JULIO, *Vida política de Juan Manuel de Rosas, a través de su correspondencia* (8 vols.; Buenos Aires, 1970).

IRIBÁRREN, JOSÉ MARÍA, *Espoz y Mina, el guerrillero* (Madrid, 1965).

IZARD, MIGUEL, *El miedo a la revolución: La lucha por la libertad en Venezuela (1777–1830)* (Madrid, 1979).

—— *Orejanos, cimarrones y arrochelados* (Barcelona, 1988).

—— 'Ni cuatreros ni montoneros: Llaneros', *Boletín Americanista*, 31 (1981), 83–142.

—— *Series estadísticas para la historia de Venezuela* (Mérida, 1970).

—— 'Sin domicilio fijo, senda segura, ni destino conocido: Los llaneros del Apure a finales del período colonial', *Boletín Americanista*, 33 (1983), 13–83.

—— 'Sin el menor arraigo ni responsabilidad: Llaneros y ganadería a principios del siglo XIX', *Boletín Americanista*, 37 (1987), 109–42.

—— 'Tanto pelear para terminar conversando: El caudillismo en Venezuela', *Nova Americana*, 2 (1979), 37–82.

—— 'Venezuela: Tráfico mercantil, secesionismo político e insurgencias populares', in Reinhard Liehr (ed.), *América Latina en la época de Simón Bolívar* (Berlin, 1989), 207–25.

JACOBSEN, NILS, and PUHLE, HANS-JÜRGEN (eds.), *The Economies of Mexico and Peru during the Late Colonial Period, 1760–1810* (Berlin, 1986).

JOHNSON, JOHN J., 'Foreign Factors in Dictatorship in Latin America', *The Pacific Historical Review*, 20 (1951), 127–41.

JONES, OAKAH L., *Santa Anna* (New York, 1968).

JOSEPH, GILBERT M., 'Caciquismo and the Revolution: Carrillo Puerto in Yucatán', in D. A. Brading (ed.), *Caudillo and Peasant in the Mexican Revolution* (Cambridge, 1980), 193–221.

KATZ, FRIEDRICH (ed.), *Riot, Rebellion, and Revolution: Rural Social Conflict in Mexico* (Princeton, NJ, 1988).

KEDOURIE, ELIE, *Nationalism*, 2nd edn. (London, 1961).

KNIGHT, ALAN, 'Peasant and Caudillo in Revolutionary Mexico 1910–17', in D. A. Brading (ed.), *Caudillo and Peasant in the Mexican Revolution* (Cambridge, 1980), 17–58.

KUETHE, ALLAN J., *Military Reform and Society in New Granada, 1773–1808* (Gainesville, Fla., 1978).

LANDAETA ROSALES, MANUEL, *Biografía del valiente ciudadano general Ezequiel Zamora* (2 vols.; Caracas, 1961).

—— *Gran recopilación geográfica, estadística, e histórica de Venezuela* (2 vols.; Caracas, 1889).

LEVENE, RICARDO, *La anarquía de 1820 y la iniciación de la vida pública de Rosas* (Academia Nacional de la Historia, *Obras de Ricardo Levene*, 4; Buenos Aires, 1972).

—— *El proceso histórico de Lavalle a Rosas* (ANH, *Obras de Ricardo Levene*, 4; Buenos Aires, 1972).

LIEHR, REINHARD (ed.), *América Latina en la época de Simón Bolívar* (Berlin, 1989).

LOMBARDI, JOHN V., CARRERA DAMAS, GERMÁN, and ADAMS, ROBERTA E., *Venezuelan History: A Comprehensive Working Bibliography* (Boston, Mass., 1977).

LOY, JANE M., 'Horsemen of the Tropics: A Comparative View of the Llaneros in the History of Venezuela and Colombia', *Boletín Americanista*, 31 (1981), 159–71. *See also* Rausch, Jane M.

LUNA, FÉLIX, *Perón y su tiempo* (3 vols.; Buenos Aires, 1984–6).

LYNCH, JOHN, *Argentine Dictator: Juan Manuel de Rosas 1829–1852* (Oxford, 1981).

—— 'Bolívar and the Caudillos', *HAHR* 63, 1 (1983), 3–35.

—— 'Los caudillos como agentes del orden social: Venezuela y Argentina, 1820–1850', in Antonio Annino et al. (eds.), *America Latina: dallo stato coloniale allo stato nazione* (2 vols.; Milan, 1987).

—— 'Los caudillos de la independencia: Enemigos y agentes del estado-nación', in Inge Buisson et al. (eds.), *Problemas de la formación del estado y de la nación en Hispanoamérica* (Bonn, 1984), 197–218.

—— *The Spanish American Revolutions 1808–1826*, 2nd edn. (New York, 1986).

—— *Spanish Colonial Administration, 1782–1810: The Intendant System in the Viceroyalty of the Río de la Plata* (London, 1958).

MCFARLANE, ANTHONY, 'Civil Disorders and Popular Protests in Late Colonial New Granada', *HAHR* 64, 1 (1984), 17–54.

—— 'The "Rebellion of the Barrios": Urban Insurrection in Bourbon Quito', *HAHR* 69, 2 (1989), 283–330.

MANSILLA, LUCIO V., *Rozas: Ensayo histórico-psicológico* (Paris, 1913).

MASUR, GERHARD, *Simon Bolivar* (Albuquerque, NM, 1948).

MATTHEWS, ROBERT PAUL, *Rural Violence and Social Unrest in Venezuela, 1840–1858: Origins of the Federalist War* (New York Univ. Ph.D. thesis, 1974; University Microfilms, Ann Arbor, Mich., 1979).

MAYER, JORGE, *Alberdi y su tiempo* (Buenos Aires, 1963).

MAYER, JEAN, *Problemas campesinos y revueltas agrarias (1821–1910)* (Mexico, 1973).

MICELI, KEITH L., 'Rafael Carrera: Defender and Promoter of Peasant Interests in Guatemala', *The Americas*, 31, 1 (1974), 72–95.

MILL, JOHN STUART, *On Liberty* (Everyman's Library; London, 1926).

—— *Representative Government* (Everyman's Library; London, 1926).

MILLER, GARY M., 'Status and Loyalty of Regular Army Officers in Late Colonial Venezuela', *HAHR* 66, 4 (1986), 667–96.

MITRE, BARTOLOMÉ, *Historia de Belgrano y de la independencia argentina*, 6th edn. (4 vols.; Buenos Aires, 1927).

MONTOYA, ALFREDO J., *La ganadería y la industria de salazón de carnes en el período 1810–1862* (Buenos Aires, 1971).

—— *Historia de los saladeros argentinos* (Buenos Aires, 1956).

MONTÚFAR Y RIVERA MAESTRE, LORENZO, *Reseña histórica de Centro América* (7 vols.; Guatemala, 1878–8).

NICOLAU, JUAN CARLOS, *Rosas y García: La economía bonaerense (1829–35)* (Buenos Aires, 1980).

OCAMPO, JAVIER, *Las ideas de un día: El pueblo mexicano ante la consumación de su Independencia* (Mexico, 1969).

O'PHELAN GODOY, SCARLETT, *Rebellions and Revolts in Eighteenth Century Peru and Upper Peru* (Cologne, 1985).

OLVEDA LEGASPI, JAIME, *Gordiano Guzmán: Un cacique del siglo XIX* (Mexico, 1980).

OSORNO CASTRO, FERNANDO, *El insurgente Albino García* (Mexico, 1982).

PAGE, JOSEPH A., *Perón: A Biography* (New York, 1983).

PARRA-PÉREZ, CARACCIOLO, *Mariño y la independencia de Venezuela* (5 vols.; Madrid, 1954–7).

—— *Mariño y las guerras civiles* (3 vols.; Madrid, 1958–60).

PAYNE, WALTER A., *A Central American Historian: José Milla (1822–1882)* (Gainesville, Fla., 1957).

PEÑA, DAVID, *Juan Facundo Quiroga*, 2nd edn. (Buenos Aires, 1971).

PÉREZ VILA, MANUEL., *Aportes a la historia documental y crítica* (BANH, 73; Caracas, 1986).

—— 'El gobierno deliberativo: Hacendados, comerciantes y artesanos frente a la crisis, 1830–1848', in Fundación John Boulton, *Política y economía en Venezuela 1810–1976* (Caracas, 1976), 33–89.

—— *Vida de Daniel Florencio O'Leary primer edecán del Libertador* (Caracas, 1957).

PETIT MUÑOZ, EUGENIO, *Artigas: federalismo y soberanía* (Montevideo, 1988).

POTASH, ROBERT A., *Mexican Government and Industrial Development in the Early Republic: The Banco de Avío* (Amherst, Mass., 1983).

—— 'Testamentos de Santa Anna', *Historia Mexicana*, 13, 3 (1964), 428–40.

PRADERE, JUAN A, and CHÁVEZ, FERMÍN, *Juan Manuel de Rosas* (2 vols.; Buenos Aires, 1970).

QUESADA, ERNESTO, *La época de Rosas: su verdadero carácter histórico* (Buenos Aires, 1923).

QUINTERO, INÉS, *El ocaso de una estirpe* (Caracas, 1989).

RAMÍREZ, SUSAN E., *Provincial Patriarchs: Land Tenure and the Economics of Power in Colonial Peru* (Albuquerque, NM, 1986).

RAUSCH, JANE M., *A Tropical Plains Frontier: The Llanos of Colombia, 1531–1831* (Albuquerque, NM, 1984). See also Loy, Jane M.

—— 'Juan Nepomuceno Moreno: Caudillo of Casanare' (unpublished paper).

RAVIGNANI, EMILIO, *Rosas: Interpretación real y moderna* (Buenos Aires, 1970).

REINA, LETICIA, *Las rebeliones campesinas en México, 1819–1906* (Mexico, 1980).

RIVAS VICUÑA, FERNANDO, *Las guerras de Bolívar* (7 vols.; Bogotá, 1934–8, Santiago, 1940).

RIVERA SERNA, RAÚL, *Los guerrilleros del Centro en la emancipación peruana* (Lima, 1958).

RODRÍGUEZ, ADOLFO, *Exequiel Zamora* (Caracas, 1977).

RODRÍGUEZ, MARIO, *The Livingston Codes in the Guatemalan Crisis of 1837–1838*, in *Applied Enlightenment: 19th Century Liberalism* (Tulane University, Middle American Research Institute, pub. 23; New Orleans, 1972), 1–32.

—— *A Palmerstonian Diplomat in Central America: Frederick Chatfield, Esq.* (Tucson, Ariz., 1964).

RODRÍGUEZ MIRABAL, ADELINA C., *La formación del latifundio ganadero en los llanos de Apure, 1750–1800* (Caracas, 1987).

RODRÍGUEZ MOLAS, RICARDO E., *Historia social del gaucho*, 2nd edn. (Buenos Aires, 1982).

RODRÍGUEZ O., JAIME E., *The Emergence of Spanish America: Vicente Rocafuerte and Spanish Americanism 1808–1832* (Berkeley, Calif., 1975).

RONIGER, LUIS, 'Caciquismo and Coronelismo: Contextual Discussions of Patron Brokerage in Mexico and Brazil', *LARR* 22, 2 (1987), 71–99.

ROSA, JOSÉ MARÍA, *La caída de Rosas*, 2nd edn. (Buenos Aires, 1968).

—— 'Miron Burgin, la señorita Beatriz Bosch y la ley de aduana de Rosas', *RIIHJMR* no. 22 (1960), 329–34.

SABATO, HILDA, 'Wool Trade and Commercial Networks in Buenos Aires, 1840s to 1880s', *JLAS* 15, 1 (1983), 49–81.

SALA DE TOURON, LUCÍA, DE LA TORRE, NELSON, and RODRÍGUEZ, JULIO C., *Artigas y su revolución agraria 1811–1820* (Mexico, 1878).

SALDÍAS, ADOLFO, *Historia de la Confederación Argentina: Rosas y su época* (9 vols.; Buenos Aires, 1958).

SALAMINI, HEATHER FOWLER, 'Revolutionary Caudillos in the 1920s: Francisco Múgica and Adalberto Tejeda', in D. A. Brading (ed.), *Caudillo and Peasant in the Mexican Revolution* (Cambridge, 1980), 169–92.

SAMPAY, ARTURO ENRIQUE, *Las ideas políticas de Juan Manuel de Rosas* (Buenos Aires, 1972).

SCHMIDT, S. W. *et al.*, *Friends, Followers and Factions* (Berkeley, Calif., 1976).

SETON-WATSON, HUGH, *Nations and States* (London, 1977).

SLATTA, RICHARD W., *Gauchos and the Vanishing Frontier* (Lincoln, Nebr., 1983).

—— (ed.), *Bandidos: The Varieties of Latin American Banditry* (Westport, Conn., 1987).

STREET, JOHN, *Artigas and the Emancipation of Uruguay* (Cambridge, 1959).

STRICKEN, A., and GREENFIELD, S. (eds.), *Structure and Process in Latin America: Patronage, Clientage and Power Systems* (Albuquerque, NM, 1972).

SZUCHMAN, MARK D., *Order, Family, and Community in Buenos Aires 1810–1860* (Stanford, Calif., 1988).

TALMON, J. L., *The Origins of Totalitarian Democracy* (London, 1970).

TAYLOR, WILLIAM B., 'Bandit Gangs in Late Colonial Times: Rural Jalisco Mexico, 1794–1821', in Paul J. Vanderwood (ed.), *Biblioteca Americana*, 1, 2 (1982), 37–56.

—— *Drinking, Homicide and Rebellion in Colonial Mexican Villages* (Stanford, Calif., 1979).

—— *Landlord and Peasant in Colonial Oaxaca* (Stanford, Calif., 1972).

TENENBAUM, BARBARA A., *The Politics of Penury: Debts and Taxes in Mexico, 1821–1856* (Albuquerque, NM, 1986).

THOMSON, GUY P. C., 'Protectionism and Industrialization in Mexico, 1821–1854: The Case of Puebla', in Christopher Abel and Colin M. Lewis (eds.), *Latin America, Economic Imperialism and the State* (London, 1985).

TOBAR CRUZ, PEDRO, *Los montañeses* (Guatemala, 1971).

TORRE REVELLO, JOSÉ, *El marqués de Sobre Monte* (Buenos Aires, 1946).

TRUEBA, ALFONSO, *Santa Anna*, 3rd edn. (Mexico, 1958).

TUTINO, JOHN, *From Insurrection to Revolution in Mexico: Social Bases of Agrarian Violence 1750–1940* (Princeton, NJ, 1986).

URBANEJA, DIEGO, 'Caudillismo y pluralismo en el siglo XIX venezolano', *Politeia*, 4 (1975), 133–51.

—— *La idea política en Venezuela 1830–1870* (Caracas, 1988).

VALLENILLA LANZ, LAUREANO, *Obras completas*, i. *Cesarismo democrático* (Caracas, 1983).

VANDERWOOD, PAUL J., *Disorder and Progress: Bandits, Police and Mexican Development* (Lincoln, Nebr., 1981).

—— 'Nineteenth-Century Mexico's Profiteering Bandits', in Richard W. Slatta (ed.), *Bandidos: The Varieties of Latin American Banditry* (Westport, Conn., 1987), 11–31.

—— (ed.), 'Social Banditry and Spanish American Independence', *Biblioteca Americana*, 1, 2 (1982).

VAN YOUNG, ERIC, *Hacienda and Market in Eighteenth-Century Mexico: The Rural Economy of the Guadalajara Region, 1675–1820* (Berkeley, Calif., 1981).

—— 'Mexican Rural History since Chevalier: The Historiography of the Colonial Hacienda', *LARR* 18, 3 (1983), 5–61.

VÁZQUEZ, JOSEFINA ZORAIDA, 'Los primeros tropiezos', in El Colegio de México, *Historia general de México* (4 vols.; Mexico, 1976), iii. 9–34.

VÁZQUEZ MANTECÓN, CARMEN, *Santa Anna y la encrucijada del estado: la dictadura (1853–1855)* (Mexico, 1986).

VELA, DAVID, *Barrundia ante el espejo de su tiempo* (2 vols.; Guatemala, 1956).

WALKER, CHARLES, 'Montoneros, bandoleros, malhechores: Criminalidad y política en las primeras décadas republicanas', *Pasado y Presente*, 2, 2–3 (1989), 119–37.

WALKER, DAVID W., 'Business as Usual: The Empresa del Tabaco in Mexico', *HAHR* 64, 4 (1984), 675–705.

WEEKS, JOHN, 'An Interpretation of the Central American Crisis', *LARR* 21, 3 (1986), 31–53.

WEINBERG, FÉLIX, 'El periodismo en la época de Rosas', *Revista de Historia*, 2 (Buenos Aires, 1957).

WOLF, ERIC R., 'Kinship, Friendship, and Patron–Client Relationships in Complex Societies', in M. Banton (ed.), *The Social Anthropology of Complex Societies* (London, 1966), 1–22.

—— and HANSEN, EDWARD C., '*Caudillo* Politics: A Structural Analysis', *Comparative Studies in Society and History*, 9 (1966–7), 168–79.

WOODWARD, RALPH LEE, JR., *Social Revolution in Guatemala; The Carrera Revolt*, in *Applied Enlightenment: 19th Century Liberalism* (Tulane University, Middle American Research Institute, pub. 23; New Orleans, 1972), 43–70.

WORTMAN, MILES L., *Government and Society in Central America, 1680–1840* (New York, 1982).

YÁÑEZ, AGUSTÍN, *Santa Anna, espectro de una sociedad* (Mexico, 1982).

ZORRILLA, RUBÉN H., 'Estructura social y caudillismo en la Argentina, 1810–70', *Nova Americana*, 2 (1979), 135–67.

—— *Extracción social de los caudillos 1810–1870* (Buenos Aires, 1972).

GLOSSARY

abigeo	rustler
aduana	customs, customs house
alcabala	sales tax
alcalde mayor	district officer, comparable to a *corregidor*
arrochelados	fugitives in the llanos, often Indians, who gather in a particular haunt
artiguismo	doctrine or movement of Artigas
audiencia	high court of justice with administrative functions
Banda Oriental	'the east shore', i.e. of the River Uruguay and the Río de la Plata, equivalent to modern Uruguay
bandido, bandolero	bandit
blancos de orilla	poor whites
cabildo	town council
cacique	Indian chieftain, chief, boss
campesino	peasant
castas	persons of mixed or black descent
caudillo	leader, whose rule is based on personal power rather than constitutional form
clientela	a group of clients, a following
compadrazgo	status of godfather
corregidor	district officer
creole	American-born Spaniard
cuatrero	rustler
estancia	large cattle ranch (estanciero: owner of an estancia)
fiscal	attorney
fuero	right, privilege, immunity, conferred by membership of profession or community
gaucho	mounted nomad, free cowboy, inhabitant of the pampas of Argentina
hacienda	large landed estate, plantation (hacendado: owner of a hacienda)
hato	ranch (Venezuelan) (*hatero*: owner of a *hato*)
jarocho	native of Veracruz; peasant of coastal Veracruz
jefe	chief, chieftain
jornalero	rural day-labourer
ladino	meztizo, non-Indian

llanos	plains (llaneros: plainsmen)
mayordomo	overseer
mazorca	semi-official terrorist squad
mestizo	of mixed white and Indian descent
montonero	guerrilla fighter
mulato	of mixed white and negro descent
municipio	town council, township
paecismo	policy or movement of Páez (*paecista*: follower of Páez)
pardo	mulatto, of mixed white and black descent
parentesco	kinship
partida	band, party, group
patria	native land, fatherland
patrón	patron, master, boss
peon	rural labourer, employee of hacienda or estancia
peninsular	Spaniard born in the Peninsula
porteño	of Buenos Aires, inhabitant of Buenos Aires
pueblo	people, village
pulpería	general store and bar
rancho	small farm
republiqueta	mini-republic, guerrilla enclave
rochela	a group of fugitive Indians, or vagrants, and the place where they gather
rosismo	policy or movement of Rosas (*rosista*: follower of Rosas)
santanismo	policy or movement of Santa Anna (*santanista*: follower of Santa Anna)
suma del poder	absolute or dictatorial power
vago	vagrant
vagos y mal entretenidos	rogues and vagabonds
zambo	of mixed black and Indian descent

INDEX